Macroeconomics and the Japanese Economy

MACROECONOMICS AND THE JAPANESE ECONOMY

Hiroshi Yoshikawa

OXFORD UNIVERSITY PRESS
1995

Oxford University Press, Walton Street, Oxford OX2 6DP
Oxford New York
Athens Auckland Bangkok Bombay
Calcutta Cape Town Dar es Salaam Delhi
Florence Hong Kong Istanbul Karachi
Kuala Lumpur Madras Madrid Melbourne
Mexico City Nairobi Paris Singapore
Taipei Tokyo Toronto
and associated companies in
Berlin Ibadan

Oxford is a trade mark of Oxford University Press

Published in the United States by
Oxford University Press Inc., New York

British Library Cataloguing in Publication Data
Data available
ISBN 0-19-823326-4

Library of Congress Cataloging in Publication Data
Data available
ISBN 0-19-823326-4

1 3 5 7 9 10 8 6 4 2

Typeset by Pure Tech (India) Ltd, Pondicherry
Printed in Great Britain
on acid-free paper by
Bookcraft (Bath) Ltd.,
Midsomer Norton, Avon

To Setsuko and Momoko

- econ prop – book
- ID Readings
- ID report + interview
- POLS 4750 topic

PREFACE

Does science retrogress? Looking at the state of macroeconomics in the past two decades, I cannot help but feel that it sometimes does. Some economists believe confidently in the march of progress; macroeconomics has become more 'dynamic', 'endogenous', built on proper 'optimization' or whatever. I do not share this view.

The research of the past two decades (culminating in the real business cycle theory) has simply made macroeconomics akin to Walrasian microeconomics. Dr Pangloss in Voltaire's *Candide or Optimism* (a caricature of Leibniz, the progenitor of the neoclassical theory), once believed to be dead in the realm of macroeconomics has returned to life. In the midst of calamity, the great earthquake in Lisbon, he consoles people with the assurance that 'things cannot be otherwise for it is impossible for things not to be where they are, because everything is for the best'. For all misfortunes, he teaches Candide that 'the pre-established harmony is the most beautiful thing in the world'. The term 'optimum', the key concept for neoclassical theory, incidentally originates in Leibniz's philosophy. Macroeconomics today evidently has many admirers of Dr Pangloss. But like a sailor in *Candide*, I am very sceptical of his doctrine.

Instead of following Dr Pangloss, I have searched for a 'new' approach to macroeconomics, which draws upon the experience of the Japanese economy. This book is the outcome. It is Keynesian in spirit, but departs from the 'New Keynesian' economics.

The neoclassical theory grants well-known market failure; and it is natural for economists who wish to avoid the restrictive neoclassical conclusions to turn to those market failures. But for the purpose of macroeconomics, they seem of secondary importance. Discussing the possibility of market failures is one thing, and building macroeconomics is another. To me, imperfect competition seems much more relevant. A step forward, and we reach real demand constraint. The role of money and price flexibility in the economy is also an issue which has intrigued economists for a long time. For the reasons explained in Chapters 1 and 9, on this issue, too, this book departs from the 'New Keynesian' economics.

The ousted prince in mainstream macroeconomics is real demand constraint. Many economists seem to believe that taking as exogenous a part of real aggregate demand is ad hoc, and is intrinsically wrong. On the other hand, they believe that taking factor endowments as exogenous, as in the neoclassical theory, is legitimate, presumably because it appears to be an undeniable fact that production factors are physically given in each period. However, if it is indeed a fact that production factors are physically given, it does not necessarily follow that we can best model our economy in such a way that production factors are fully employed to be the ultimate determinants. We cannot make everything endogenous, and it is a matter of judgement which variables we can most productively take as exogenous when we consider growth and fluctuations of the macroeconomy. In Chapter 1 I argue that the assumption that real demand constraint is ad hoc and inconsistent with rational behaviour is a premature verdict.

In addition to preferences and technology, the neoclassical theory takes factor endowment as a fundamental determinant of the economy. It implies, among other things, that the marginal products of labour in all the sectors are equated. I contend that this is a poor characterization of the economy in the long run as well as the short run. I imagine that the most advanced economy consists of many 'jungles' *à la* W. Arthur Lewis, with stepwise marginal products; some sectors even enjoy increasing marginal products, but all the sectors are constrained by demand. Demand determines the utilization of factors.

In Chapter 10 I argue that real demand constraint matters even for growth because investment is strongly conditioned by prospective demand. In this respect, perhaps, this book departs from the 'Old Keynesian' economics as well. In relation to this point, I maintain that technical progress has two functions. We would certainly say that technical progress has occurred when we obtain more output with the same input; this is indeed the conventional definition of technical progress. Granted this function of technical progress on the supply side, I maintain that it has another, hitherto neglected, function; by way of the introduction of new products, the improvement of quality, and/or lowering the prices of existing products, technical progress creates demand which would be absent otherwise. Neoclassical models can accommodate new products, quality changes, and lower prices, but, of course, in the neoclassical way. I propose that demand-creating technical progress is something which bridges the gulf between the principle of effective demand and economic growth: and with it propose to consider supply-side factors with demand in a different way from that ordinarily adopted in neoclassical theory. My study of the Japanese economy has convinced me that a new approach is called for.

Methodology and research are also in great dispute in macroeconomics. Under the banner of rational expectations, some economists have argued very strongly that the ultimate goal of macroeconomics is to recover the so-called 'deep parameters' characterizing preferences and technology; and once that has been done, economic policy becomes or should become a simple exercise of quasi-engineering. According to this view, 'economic policy', properly defined, should mean a reasonably stable 'policy reaction function'.

Again I do not share this view. To me, the trouble with this sort of approach lies in its disregard of the fact that, unlike microeconomic phenomena such as substitution of goods and services in response to price change, macroeconomic phenomena such as growth and fluctuations are not things that really repeat themselves. It is fashionable to emphasize that business cycles are the recurrent phenomena, and to talk about 'shocks'. But those 'shocks' are all different in nature and, therefore, not strictly stochastic; it is most important for us to identify what those macroeconomic 'shocks' are each time they occur, and decide what to do with them. I rather follow D. H. Robertson who, in his 'New Introduction' (1948) to *A Study of Industrial Fluctuation,* confessed to 'an abiding sense of the difficulty of providing neat little models of the trade cycle and (*a fortiori*) neat little packets of therapeutic pills'.

Indeed it would not be an exaggeration to say that there are very few theories or principles in macroeconomics which can command universal application even as a crude approximation. This is not to deny the role of theory or of mathematical and econometric methods in macroeconomics, however. Among the very few, one promising candidate deserving the name of theory is the principle of effective demand which mainstream macroeconomics has discarded. Still, any useful theory or model in macroeconomics is bound to be a snapshot of the economy, not a grand model. I am convinced therefore, that macroeconomics must always be supplemented by history. In this respect, I believe that a country study is particularly useful in macroeconomics. I present the Japanese material to those economists who pursue an approach to macroeconomics that is not based on neoclassical logic, and hope that someone will paint on a larger canvas in due time.

I had the privilege of being a student of Professors Hirofumi Uzawa at Tokyo, and James Tobin at Yale. I have been given their encouragement throughout the course of writing this book. Professor Tobin very kindly read parts of the book in draft form and offered many valuable comments and criticisms. The book in its present form would still not meet his standards, but I believe that, thanks to his comments, it has been substantially improved.

I also owe a great deal to many other people. Professor Kazuo Ueda, an old friend, generously allowed me to use some of our joint works. So did Professors Fumio Ohtake, Tetsuji Okazaki, and Yoshiyuki Takeuchi. At various places, I have been fortunate enough to have the company of Professors Ken-ichi Inada, Yoichi Shinkai, Chikashi Moriguchi, Masanao Aoki, Koichi Hamada, Yoshiyasu Ono, Keizo Nagatani, Kazumi Asako, Michio Morishima, Takashi Negishi, Akiyoshi Horiuchi, Kazuo Koike, Katsuhito Iwai, Tsuneo Ishikawa, and Masahiro OkunoFujiwara from whom I have learned a lot.

In 1991, I was able to spend five months with my family as the Nissan fellow at Oxford where I seriously started writing this book. I should like to express my special gratitude to Professor Arthur Stockwin and Ms Jenny Corbett at the Nissan Institute for their hospitality while we were there, and also for having given us an opportunity to glimpse British life. During my stay at Oxford, Mr Eric Maisel, then an American graduate student, kindly took the trouble to correct my English.

At OUP, Mr Andrew Schuller as my editor and also a friend, has helped me throughout. I also thank Mr Jason Pearce. At Tokyo, I owe Ms Tsukasa Atsuya a special gratitude for her excellent typing. At the final stage, a group of graduate students, Ms Masako Oyama and Messrs. Taizo Motonishi, Satoshi Kawanishi, and Tsunao Okumura helped me in proofreading.

Finally it is my pleasant duty to acknowledge financial support from the Japanese Ministry of Education (Grant-in-Aid for Scientific Research), and the Suntory Foundation. I also acknowledge that some chapters of this book draw heavily on my articles originally published in *American Economic Review, Economic Studies Quarterly, Economica, European Economic Review, Journal of Japanese and International Economies,* as well as those which originally appeared in books published by Macmillan and University of Chicago Press.

H. Y.

Tokyo
11 April 1995

CONTENTS

List of Figures

List of Tables

1

Introduction

Exogeneity is an attribute of the chosen framework of thought, not an attribute of the events themselves.

Matthews *et al.* (1982)

This book puts forward a 'new' approach to macroeconomics which draws upon the experience of the Japanese economy. The approach is akin to what Tobin (1993) calls the 'Old Keynesian View', and therefore is not really new. But, by maintaining that *real* demand constraints are important not only in the short run, but also in the long run, it goes beyond what is normally understood as the Keynesian approach. In this respect, and in others to be explained shortly, this book departs from the 'New Keynesian economics'. (See Mankiw and Romer (1991) for a collection of works under this heading.) My study of the Japanese economy has convinced me that a new approach is called for.

Macroeconomics was once synonymous with Keynesian economics, but that day is gone. Over the last twenty years, increased emphasis has been put on optimization by economic agents in a Walrasian environment. Not surprisingly, this emphasis has made macroeconomics look more like traditional microeconomics. The gospel of Pareto optimality, with some modest cautions against possible market failures, now flourishes in the macroeconomics literature. This approach has been seen as a welcome progression of the discipline by many economists, particularly those who subscribe to the Walrasian general equilibrium theory. For example, in the 1985 Yrjö Jahnsson Lectures, Lucas made the following observation:

> The most interesting recent developments in macroeconomic theory seem to me describable as the reincorporation of aggregative problems such as inflation and the business cycle within the general framework of 'microeconomic' theory. If these developments succeed, the term 'macroeconomic' will simply disappear from use and the modifier 'micro' will become superfluous. We will simply speak, as did Smith, Ricardo, Marshall and Walras, of *economic* theory. If we are honest, we will have to face the fact

that at any given time there will be phenomena that are well-understood from the point of view of the economic theory we have, and other phenomena that are not. We will be tempted, I am sure, to relieve the discomfort induced by discrepancies between theory and facts by saying that ill-understood facts are the province of some other, different, kind of economic theory. Keynesian 'macroeconomics' was, I think, a surrender (under great duress) to this temptation. (Lucas 1987: 107–8)

Unfortunately, general equilibrium theory is in fact not nearly as solid as some economists wish to believe. One needs only recall the fact that in the real world the major activity of the firm is to change its production possibility set through innovation. And most innovations are embodied in investment and are therefore strongly conditioned by the prospect of demand. The assumption of a given production possibility set upon which intertemporal general equilibrium models are built dispenses with a whole range of relevant questions and conceals such vital issues as changes in the competitiveness of nations.

The more sophisticated economic analyses are, the less relevant they tend to become. What is now simply forgotten in macroeconomics is the crucial role of real demand in economic growth and fluctuations. Drawing on the Japanese experience, this book maintains that real demand in fact constrains the microeconomic behaviour of individual agents, as well as growth and fluctuations of the macroeconomy. I surmise that the major thesis of the book would apply to other well developed economies as well as Japan's.

The first part of this introductory chapter discusses the current state of macroeconomics and sets out the motivation of the book. The second part briefly surveys post-war developments of the Japanese economy in order to provide a background for the analyses in the subsequent chapters.

1.1 ANOTHER WAY OF APPROACHING MACROECONOMICS

In the last twenty years, the macroeconomic main stream has followed neoclassical theory: the Lucas–Sargent rational expectations approach in the 1970s, and the Kydland–Prescott real business cycle theory and endogenous growth theory in the 1980s. This body of work is well known and so needs no general introduction (see e.g.

Lucas 1987; Kydland and Prescott 1982; Plosser 1989; P. Romer 1986; and Grossman and Helpman 1991).

Recently, however, the pendulum seems to have swung back somewhat. Some economists even argue that, 'after two decades of ferment, macroeconomics may be in the process of returning to a state similar to that of the 1960's' (Mankiw and Romer 1991: 15). In any case, the heading 'New Keynesian Economics' has been coined to underline the existence of a group of alternatives to the neoclassical approach. Since this book revolves around a kind of Keynesian economics that differs from 'New Keynesian Economics' in some important respects, it is useful to explain how they differ.

Money, Price, and Real Aggregate Demand

New Keynesian Economics endorses an old cliché: 'According to the Keynesian view, fluctuations in output arise largely from fluctuations in nominal aggregate demand. These fluctuations have real effects because nominal wages and prices are rigid' (Ball *et al.* 1988: 1). Taylor (1989), for example, comparing economic fluctuations in Japan and the United States during the period 1972–86, finds that 'real GNP fluctuations in Japan are so small compared to those in the United States, especially in the last twelve years, that *actual* GNP in Japan behaves much like the smooth *potential* GNP trend for the United States'. He attributes these observed differences in the amplitude of the fluctuations of real GNP between Japan and the United States to differences in nominal wage/price flexibility, which in turn were generated, according to him, by the synchronized wage-setting, or *Shunto*, in Japan. This is the standard New Keynesian view.

Taylor's finding, however, is not quite robust. The fluctuations of real GNP are much smaller in Japan than in the United States for the 1972–86 period, as Taylor found, but they are *greater* in Japan for the earlier period of 1960–72: standard deviations of the growth rate of real GNP are 2.5% for Japan and 1.7% for the United States. Synchronized wage-setting, or *Shunto*, was in effect throughout the whole period. The explanation for output stability must therefore be sought somewhere other than with nominal price–wage flexibility. Chapter 2 explains why the variability of real GNP in Japan had begun to lessen in the early 1970s. It shows that the causes for the change are real.

In any case, New Keynesian Economics takes nominal or monetary shocks as the major disturbances, and argues that they have real effects because nominal wages and prices are rigid or sticky. Given this view, the main research agenda is to show how these rigidities arise from the microeconomics of wage- and price-setting. Accordingly, an array of explanations have been produced, including costly price adjustment, the staggering of wages and prices, efficiency wages, and so on. These contributions illuminate why nominal rigidities may arise in the economy, but they miss the essential point of Keynesian macroeconomics, namely the principle of effective demand, because they take fluctuations in *nominal* aggregate demand as the major shock causing fluctuations in output. This point is essential.

> The central Keynesian proposition is not nominal price rigidity but the principle of effective demand (Keynes 1936, ch. 3). In the absence of instantaneous and complete market clearing, output and employment are frequently constrained by aggregate demand. In these excess-supply regimes, agents' demands are limited by their inability to sell as much as they would like at prevailing prices. Any failure of price adjustments to keep markets cleared opens the door for quantities to determine quantities, for example real national income to determine consumption demand, as described in Keynes' multiplier calculus. . . .
>
> In Keynesian business cycle theory, the shocks generating fluctuations are generally shifts in *real* aggregate demand for goods and services, notably in capital investment. Keynes would be appalled to see his cycle model described as one in which 'fluctuations in output arise largely from fluctuations in nominal aggregate demand' (Ball, Mankiw, and Romer, 1988, p. 2). The difference is important. The impact on real purchases of a one-time one percent shock to aggregate nominal spending will be eroded if and as nominal prices increase in response, and eliminated once prices have risen by the same one percent as nominal spending did. But suppose it is real demand that initially rises one percent. At the prevailing prices nominal spending will rise one percent too. But if and as prices rise in response, the one percent real demand shock becomes an ever larger amount of nominal spending. Its impact is not mechanically eroded by the price response; if it is absorbed, the process is subtle and indirect. (Tobin 1993: 46–7)

In Keynesian macroeconomics, *real* aggregate demand is the variable that determines the course of output. Money supply, government expenditure, interest rates, investment, exports, exchange rates, whatever—all affect output only to the extent that they affect real aggregate demand. During any period, a part of real demand is, of course, endogenously generated, but there is always an exogenous part as well; and this exogenous component is not necessarily confined to the public expenditure and demand affected by money supply. Thus, in Keynesian theory, real aggregate demand plays the role of ultimate causal factor in explaining the macroeconomy that factor endowment plays in neoclassical theory.

Instead of real demand, New Keynesian Economics focuses on nominal aggregate demand. Moreover, fluctuations in nominal aggregate demand are very often, if not always, identified with changes in the nominal money supply. In both theoretical and empirical literature, demand shocks often mean changes in nominal money supply (see e.g. Blanchard and Kiyotaki 1987 and Blanchard and Quah 1989). If nominal price P changes proportionally with fluctuations in the money supply M, then real quantity of money M/P remains unchanged, leaving real variables such as output and employment intact. It is plain, therefore, that changes in M will affect real variables if prices are for some reason sticky. The classical neutrality of money appears inevitable so long as prices are flexible. However, this standard exercise of taking the exogenous change in money supply as a starting-point does not adequately capture what happens in the real economy except perhaps in the case of hyperinflation.

In 'normal' times, simultaneous increases in both money supply and output are observed when, in response to an increase in output, the central bank seeks to smooth the nominal interest rate by increasing the supply of money. In the *IS–LM* framework, monetary policy is customarily considered as an exogeneous increase in nominal money supply M. If price P changes proportionally, then M/P remains unchanged; but, so long as P is rigid, M/P increases and the *LM* curve shifts downward, making output Y increase. This is the standard interpretation. The outcome in the real economy, however, is often different. Output increases in response to a *real* demand shock: the *IS* curve shifts, say, from IS_0 to IS_1 in Fig. 1.1. If money supply were kept constant, the interest rate i would have to change. To smooth the interest rate, the central bank frequently allows M to change, hence the *LM* curve shifts from LM_0 to LM_1. We observe simultaneous increases in M and Y in the case illustrated in Fig. 1.1. What makes output change is essentially a *real* demand shock, rather than an increase in money supply.

Chapter 9 demonstrates that the Bank of Japan has indeed very often smoothed the interest rate, and that observed fluctuations in money supply were often merely a mirror-image of changes in output. When the central bank actively changed the interest rate, output would change in response, depending on the interest elasticity of expenditure. Money supply is again endogenously determined to

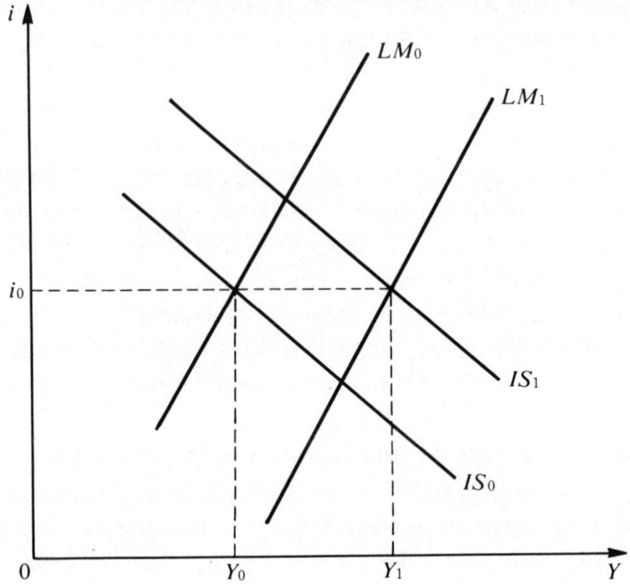

Fig. 1.1. Money supply and output in the *IS–LM* model

be consistent with the new level of interest rate. In short, the Bank of Japan has full power to control the nominal interest rate, and monetary policy in Japan is essentially an interest rate policy: see Chapter 9, and papers in Singleton (1993).

In neoclassical theory, real interest rates are the equilibrators of goods markets. Their adjustment is crucial to the equilibrium theory; market interest rates must keep investment equal to saving at their full-employment levels. Keynesian theory and casual observations cast a serious doubt on this possibility. As Tobin puts it,

> Can interest rates do the job? The Keynesian insight is that the institutionally fixed nominal interest rate on currency, generally zero, limits the adjustment of nominal interest rates on non-money assets and imparts to them some stickiness even when they are above zero. As a result, after an aggregate demand shock they may not fall automatically to levels low enough to induce sufficient investment to absorb full employment saving. (Tobin 1993: 53)

For this reason, real interest rates become essentially monetary phenomena. The Bank of Japan determines the nominal interest rate, and at the same time also the real interest rate. As far as the determination of output is concerned, quantities determine quantities. Flexibility of prices plays a secondary role.

Market Failures and Imperfections

It is only natural that microeconomically oriented theorists seeking foundations for Keynesian economics turn to market failures and imperfections: externalities, increasing returns, and imperfect competition. These approaches rely on market failures and lead to the conclusions that justify Keynesian-flavoured government policies.

Diamond (1982, 1984), for example, demonstrates the possibility of Pareto-inferior equilibria in a search model. In his model, because of externalities, the probability of success, p, in selling a firm's products, y, depends on the amount of output in the market as a whole, Y: $p'(Y) > 0$. Given the cost of production $c(y)$ ($c' > 0$, $c'' > 0$), the firm maximizes its expected profit:

$$p(Y)y - c(y). \tag{1}$$

In the symmetric equilibrium, each firm produces the same amount, and therefore, with a trivial change in notation, the following equality holds:

$$p(y) = c'(y). \tag{2}$$

In contrast, the Pareto optimality is obtained when

$$p(y) + yp'(y) = c'(y). \tag{3}$$

Free competition leads to the Pareto-inefficient equilibrium, and so a government policy such as a subsidy for production is justified. Diamond offers an example in which the aggregate level of economic activities does indeed generate this sort of externality in search.

Another source of market failure is increasing returns to scale. Kiyotaki (1988) offers an example. His model has two periods, the present and the future. Investment made in the present period determines capital stock K in the future. Since I is an increasing function of the level of anticipated output Y in the future, the relation between Y and K is as line A drawn in Fig. 1.2. The model, however, assumes the following production function:

$$Y = F(L, K) = K^{\theta - \delta} L^{\delta} \quad (\theta > 1, \theta - \delta < 1). \tag{4}$$

Labour service L is endogenously determined by the household's optimization, but it has an upper bound, N $L < N$. The above production function exhibits increasing returns to scale in so far as L and K increase proportionately. When L reaches N, however, it shifts to decreasing returns. One thus obtains the other relation between Y and K, drawn as line B. As is clear in Fig. 1.2, multiple equilibria are possible, the bearish equilibrium (E_1) being Pareto-inferior.

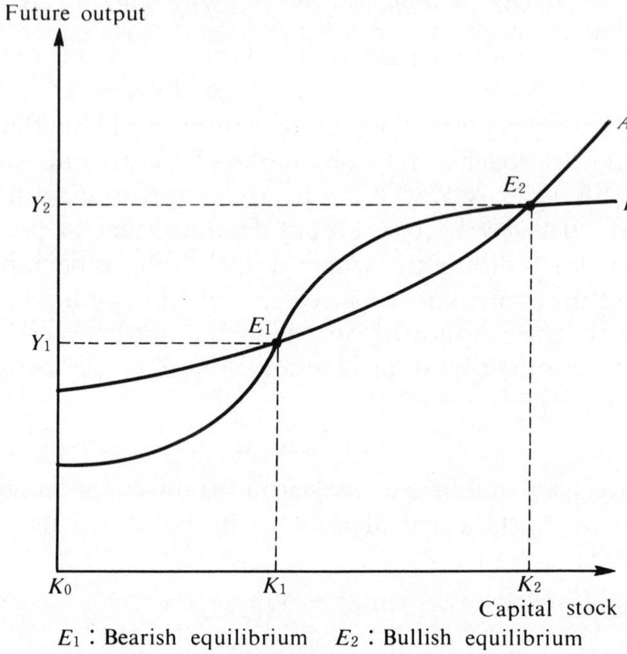

Fig. 1.2. Increasing returns and multiple equilibria

The model intends to open the door for Keynesian-flavoured government policy, but it is, in fact, a classical model. There is no involuntary unemployment. An increase in investment is made possible only at the expense of consumption. Moreover, the goods market equilibrium is attained by adjustment in the real interest rate. There have been many endeavours to draw Keynesian-like conclusions from essentially classical models. However, to generate market failures is one thing, but to give microeconomics foundations for Keynesian macroeconomics is another.

It is, on the other hand, plain that Keynesian economics diverts itself from the Walrasian equilibrium based on perfect competition. Weitzman, for example, argues that

> the ultimate source of unemployment equilibrium is increasing returns. . . . With sufficient divisibility in production, each unemployed factor unit has an incentive to produce itself out of unemployment and market the product directly. In effect, the unemployed are induced to create on their own scale an exact replica of the full employment economy from which they have been excluded. . . . Increasing returns to scale, understood in a broad sense, is the primary obstacle blocking unemployed factor units from producing on their

own. When Say's Law is thus stymied, the easy road to automatic full employment is closed. (Weitzman 1982: 788, 792, 801)

The mere fact that production takes non-negligible time, coupled with imperfect capital markets, would also entail involuntary unemployment of production factors.

Increasing returns to scale at individual firm level induces us to leave the realm of perfect competition. This is not a problem, since in any case the natural habitat of effective demand macroeconomics is a monopolistically competitive microeconomy. In fact, New Keynesian Economics emphasizes the crucial role of imperfect competition in understanding Keynesian macroeconomics. The only trouble with some of those models is that fluctuations of aggregate demand, which shift individual demand curves facing monopolistically competitive firms, are assumed to be caused primarily by changes in real money supply (see e.g. Blanchard and Kiyotaki 1987). One might suppose that this assumption is made merely as a convenient example, even a metaphor. But the practice is prone to lead us to the rather futile exercise of trying to generate non-neutrality of money, and to misleading interpretations of the observed relationship between money and income. So long as imperfect competition is meant to be a central feature of models trying to provide a theoretical underpinning for Keynesian economics, the factors that shift individual demand curves facing firms must be taken as real. Such a model of imperfect competition is not actually so different from the fixed-price approach of Clower (1965), Barro and Grossman (1971), and Malinvaud (1977) as it appears at first sight.

Price and Quantity

The fixed-price approach has been criticized for its lack of a theory of how prices are determined. In particular, it does not explain why a rationed seller does not attempt to reduce its price in order to increase sales. In other words, the fixed-price approach does not explain how a non-Walrasian equilibrium can be sustained once one allows firms to change prices. This is the basic motivation for a model of imperfect competition (see e.g. Hart 1982). Under certain assumptions, however, a model of imperfect competition leads to a conclusion very similar to the fixed-price approach.

Suppose that the firm maximizes the following profits by choosing the appropriate levels of output, y and price, p:

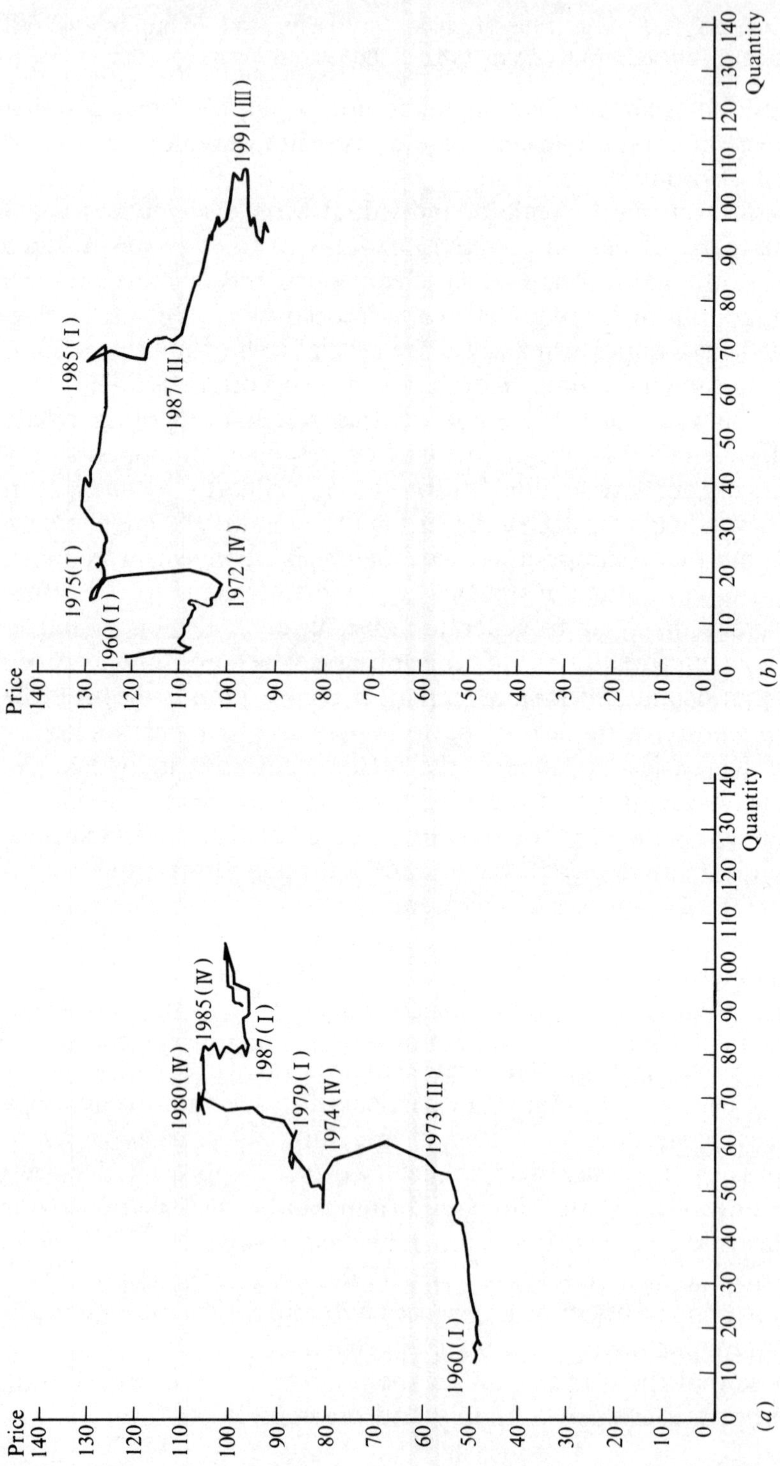

Fig. 1.3. Price and quantity, 1960(I)–1993(IV) (*a*) Manufacturing industry (b) Electric machinery
Source: Price is wholesale price index (WPI) (1990 = 100); quantity is the index of industrial production (IIP) (1990 = 100).

$$py - cy, \quad y = (p/P)^{-\eta} Y \tag{5}$$

where Y is the aggregate demand, P is the aggregate price level, and c is the unit cost. Given the price elasticity of demand,

$$\eta = -\frac{d\left(\frac{y}{Y}\right) \Big/ \frac{y}{Y}}{d\left(\frac{p}{P}\right) \Big/ \frac{p}{P}},$$

the profit-maximizing price becomes

$$p = \frac{c\eta}{\eta - 1}, \tag{6}$$

and, in the symmetric equilibrium with a continuum of firms on [0, 1], output is

$$y = Y. \tag{7}$$

When aggregate demand fluctuates, price remains constant while output changes proportionately. This outcome is, of course, precisely the assumption made in the fixed-price approach.

The price remains constant when output changes because the marginal cost is almost constant. Indeed, the analysis of the seasonal cycle in Chapter 9 demonstrates that the seasonals in production match almost exactly the seasonals in shipments.[1] This seasonal evidence against production-smoothing, together with the non-existence of seasonality in price, suggests the insignificance of increasing marginal costs. We also observe that, for most manufactured products, the correlation at industry level between growth of output and a change in price is overwhelmingly *negative* (see Houthakker 1979). This implies that, in explaining changes in price, shifts of the supply curve are more important than movements along an upward-sloping supply curve.

There are certainly some empirical studies that show that supply curves are in fact upward-sloping (see e.g. Shea 1993). However, the issue is not really whether the slope of supply curve is significantly different from zero, but rather, the relative contribution of cost shocks on the one hand, and demand shocks on the other, in the fluctuations of price.

Fig. 1.3 shows raw data on quarterly price (Wholesale Price Index, WPI) and quantity (Index of Industrial Production, IIP) indices for the Japanese manufacturing and electric machinery industries. A

[1] For the USA, Barsky and Miron (1989) report a similar result.

glance at the data reveals that price significantly changed within a relatively short period of time owing mainly to occasional cost shocks, while in most other periods quantity changed from quarter to quarter largely unaccompanied by corresponding price changes. For the manufacturing industry as a whole, the three major cost shocks were the two oil shocks in the 1970s and the sharp appreciation for the yen during 1985–6. For the electric machinery industry, the effect of the second oil shock on price was relatively minor, and, thanks to a stream of innovations in the industry, prices declined continuously throughout the 1960s and also in the 1980s. This figure, of course, does not necessarily deny upward-sloping supply curves, but it does suggest that price changes arising from demand shocks are relatively minor. We would not be grossly misled if we assumed almost flat marginal cost curves; that is, quantity changes in response to real demand while price changes in response to costs.

To say that price is sticky is an exaggeration, however. The price of even a manufactured product, let alone raw materials, is often very flexible. Fig. 1.4, for example, plots price against traders' inventory stock of beam. At the beginning of 1992 the price of beam was ¥60,000 per ton, but by June 1993 it had fallen to ¥40,000, a decline in price of more than 30 percentage points within a year and a half. Beam is, of course, a manufactured product, but its stock of inventory is traded on the commodity market, and the price is

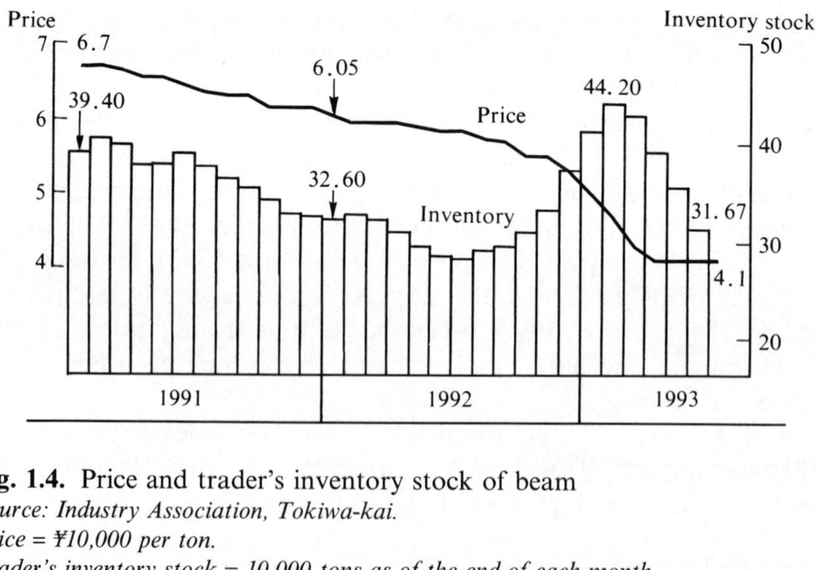

Fig. 1.4. Price and trader's inventory stock of beam
Source: Industry Association, Tokiwa-kai.
Price = ¥10,000 per ton.
Trader's inventory stock = 10,000 tons as of the end of each month.

determined in a manner similar to that observed in most asset markets.

In summary, I follow Kalecki (1954) and Okun (1981) in proposing that there are two kinds of price determination in the economy. One relates to what Kalecki calls 'demand-determined' prices, applicable mainly to raw materials, while the other refers to 'cost-determined' prices, mainly of finished goods. Okun uses the terms 'auction markets' and 'customer markets'. Auction markets apply not only to raw materials and agricultural commodities, but also to some manufactured products such as beam. However, Fig. 1.3 suggests that, when manufactured products are taken as a whole, costs that reflect changes in factor prices, such as wages and oil prices on the one hand and technical progress on the other, are the major determinant of price, and that, given the existing capacity and technology, the marginal cost is fairly constant. As a consequence, changes in real demand are mostly absorbed by changes in output. Investment occasionally brings about a reduction of price through the introduction of innovations or the enlargement of capacity when economies of scale can be enjoyed; in such a case, output also increases, depending on the price elasticity. Apart from transitory fluctuations, then, price is determined basically by supply factors. Chapter 8 demonstrates that even exchange rates, while determined in asset markets in the short run, follow the path determined by supply factors in the long run. Given this observation, for the sake of simplicity, this book mainly uses the fixed-price approach. Adoption of the framework of imperfect competition suggested above would result in only trivial differences. For my purposes in this book, I ignore the complexity of industrial organization,[2] and simply adopt quantity constraints under the fixed price.

The important question to be resolved is how microeconomic behaviour and macroeconomic outcomes will change in the quantity-constrained economy compared with those in the Walrasian equilibrium. Chapters 5, 6, and 7 study the labour market, household

[2] Most macroeconomic models legitimately assume one commodity though they emphasize product differentiation under monopolistic competition. As a result, they are prone to model the behaviour of firms as if they were *within one industry*. That is why we see industrial organization having so much influence on macroeconomics these days. I believe, however, that it adds little insight while introducing unnecessary complexity for the purpose of macroeconomics. In macroeconomics, the input/output type industrial structure within an economy as a whole is much more important than industrial organization within an industry; the important issue is the interaction of industries rather than the interaction of firms.

savings, and corporate investment, respectively. Households and firms are always (nearly) rational, of course, when faced with a choice among possible alternatives; the real issue is what alternatives are available. Chapters 5, 6, and 7 suggest that households and firms do indeed face quantity constraints, and are not Walrasian price-takers.

The Japanese labour market offers a particularly interesting opportunity for the study of macroeconomics. The unemployment rate in Japan is, by comparison with other industrialized countries, extremely low. At the same time, thanks to the synchronized wage negotiations and good labour–management relations, real wages in Japan are considered flexible by international standards. However, the role of flexible real wages differs depending on whether the economy is in the Keynesian or Walrasian state. Chapter 5 discusses various aspects of the Japanese labour market, using a model that incorporates quantity constraints facing both the household and the firm.

The Business Cycle

The business cycle is one of the most conspicuous of macroeconomic phenomena, and yet ample experience has produced few firm conclusions about the 'whys' or 'hows'. It elicits probably the widest range of macroeconomic theories and policy prescriptions in the field of economics.

Chapter 2 analyses the post-war business cycle in Japan. It starts by rejecting monetarism, which had largely faded by the early 1980s, and maintaining that real factors are important in explaining the business cycle. It then goes on to demonstrate that, as far as the Japanese business cycle is concerned, the important factors are real demand shocks rather than productivity shocks. The business cycle during the 1950s and 1960s was caused basically by fluctuations in domestic demand; accompanying the cycle was double-digit economic growth. Population flow from rural agricultural areas to urban cities, leading to the setting up of many additional households, fundamentally conditioned both the economic growth and the business cycle fluctuations. Beginning in the early 1970s, however, the amplitude of business cycles in Japan became significantly smaller than those in the earlier period. An explanation of this structural change serves to demonstrate the importance of historical perspectives in interpreting macroeconomic phenomena.

Devoid of historical perspectives, standard models based on the optimization of a representative household often produce absurd assertions about the business cycle. Lucas (1987), for example, postulates a particular multi-period utility function for a representative household, and then, given parameter values, estimates the costs of consumption fluctuations over time. He finds that, if aggregate consumption fluctuations of the magnitude experienced since the Second World War were eliminated entirely, this would be 'the equivalent in utility terms of an increase in average consumption of something less than one tenth of a percentage point'. With total US consumption in 1983 of $2,000 billion and a population of 234 million, this amounts to mere $8.50 per person. He concludes that 'economic instability at the level we have experienced since the Second World War is a minor problem'.

The costs of consumption fluctuations that Lucas considers are intertemporal allocation costs. This is a natural definition in the standard neoclassical framework.[3] As Fair (1989) points out, however, a quite different picture emerges when one considers the quantity-constrained economy. In such an economy some households would like to work at the current set of wages and prices but cannot find jobs. Fair argues that, if the US economy had succeeded in eliminating the 1979–82 recession and had followed the 3% growth path, then about $560 billion morc in output would have been produced in three years. This amounts to annual $800 per person, compared with $8.50 in the Lucas case. Beyond that, the Lucas-type argument misses the point of the business cycle as a major economic problem on at least one account. The business cycle is *not* a transitory phenomenon, as is often thought: it always has long-run consequences.

Long-Run Consequences of Demand Constraints

The standard view, ranging from Keynesian theory to the Friedman–Lucas monetarism, holds that business cycles are nothing but transitory deviations from supply-determined levels of potential output. Demand failures are therefore short-run problems. There are, however, many channels through which apparently transitory fluctuations exert permanent effects on the economy. Some of those effects are now well appreciated under the heading of *hysteresis.* Motivated by persistently high unemployment in Europe, Blanchard and

[3] The analysis of the business cycle based on a representative agent's optimization naturally leads one to a misleading analogy between the seasonal and business cycles: see e.g. Hall (1991).

Summers (1986), for example, argue that the presence of labour-management bargaining can cause temporary deviations of actual unemployment from equilibrium to affect equilibrium unemployment. Equilibrium unemployment, in this case, depends on the history of actual unemployment.

Among factors causing hysteresis, the most important is perhaps investment. It is well known that, empirically, investment responds more significantly to real factors, such as capacity utilization or sales, than to financial factors. Chapter 7 provides a theoretical explanation for this stylized fact. In any case, investment is plainly the most cyclically sensitive demand component. Aside from the obvious effect on future capital stock, there are some other channels through which seemingly temporary effects of changes in investment are translated into permanent effects. For example, even R&D investment is known to be affected by cyclical fluctuations. The business cycle therefore affects future productivity. One might suppose that a deceleration in capital accumulation or the slowing pace of product and process innovations would be compensated for by a subsequent recovery of investment so long as the recession is temporary. This might be the case in an imaginary closed economy, but in reality, international competition often prevents this from occurring. Thus arises hysteresis.

The point can perhaps be best illustrated by the story of the integrated circuit (IC) industry. The Japanese IC producers are large electric companies such as NEC, Toshiba, and Hitachi, whereas the US counterparts, except for Texas Instruments (TI), consist mainly of small venture capital business in Silicon Valley, California. As a result, because of capital market imperfection, investment in the United States is said to be more susceptible to economic downturns than is the case in Japan. Severe four-year cycles, named 'silicon cycles', have steadily shifted international competitiveness from the United States to Japan. In the late 1970s, the United States controlled 85% of the world market for the 4K DRAM integrated circuit, while in 1988, with the development of the 1M integrated circuit, the world market share had shifted to Japan, which held 90% of the market *v.* 5% for the United States.

The story does not actually end there. When the IC industry grows, the industry that produces IC-making machines also grows. Thus, in tandem with the growth of the Japanese IC industry, the Japanese IC-making machine industry has become the leading supplier in the world market (see Table 2.23 below). The reason for this parallel growth of the two industries is that close communication between them is essential for generating innovations and technical progress, and for such close communication, geographical location matters. And all this, like Adam Smith's famous theorem, depends upon the size of the market. The size of the market in turn is strongly conditioned by the business cycle. In this way, apparently temporary effects of demand failures can leave potentially permanent scars on the economy.

The inter-industry relation described above which augments long-run growth may be called a kind of Marshallian externality. The importance of Marshallian externality is well appreciated. P. Romer (1986) went so far as to argue that it is *the* key factor underlying modern economic growth. The crucial point is that, as Young (1928) so eloquently argued, increasing returns, whether internal to firms or based on Marshallian externalities, depend on demand constraints; and these demand constraints are *not* necessarily the outcome of individual economic agents' optimization.

Demand is not, of course, monopolized by Keynesian economics. Neoclassical theory, including the Real Business Cycle model, pays careful attention to setting out the household's choice problem over consumption, saving, labour, and leisure. Analysis of this choicc problem determines the household's and the firm's demand for goods. The essence of Keynesian economics, however, is that *exogenous* economy-wide demand constraints make all the economic agents quantity-constrained, and thus quantities are determined by quantities. Some economists might think that the assumption of exogenous demand constraints is plainly inferior to the analysis that endogenously determines demand. Not quite. Exogeneity is an attribute of the chosen framework of thought, not an attribute of the events themselves. Neoclassical theory endogenously explains prices and quantities, given exogenous factor endowments. The new 'endogenous growth theory' such as that in Grossman and Helpman (1990), for example, explains economic growth in terms of exogenously given *inputs*, which are used intensively in ordinary production and in R&D activities. Keynesian theory, in contrast, explains quantities, including utilization levels of production factors, by exogenously given *demand constraints*, which are not necessarily derived from households' optimization.

The best examples in the Japanese experience would be the First World War and the Korean War. It was the wars, rather than the outcomes of households' optimization, that brought about the boom by way of raising aggregate demand, despite the fact that they were adverse supply shocks. Most Japanese economists agree that they exerted permanent effects on the Japanese economy through the kind of channels discussed previously. Demand constraints, therefore, strongly condition economic growth as well as the business cycle.

In the famous controversy on the decline in the British manufacturing industry in the late nineteenth century, Habakkuk (1962) argues that investment, and therefore the pace of technological progress, slowed down in Britain *because the growth rate of demand sharply fell*:[4]

> Thus for the first six or seven decades of the nineteenth century market prospects in England were favourable to the creation of new capacity; there were vigorous sources of demand for U.K. goods. This increased demand was not, of course, independent of the technical efficiency of English industry, but given the initial English superiority it proceeded even in the absence of technical progress, and it warranted an increase in capacity which gave English manufacturers excellent opportunities of adopting new methods and gaining experience.
>
> After the 1870's the market prospects for British goods were less favourable to the creation of new capacity. In the first place, once England had become an industrial state, the possibilities of an increase in income from intersectoral shifts, within the English economy were much more limited. In the second place, so far as foreign markets were concerned, though the increase in their real income was considerable, particularly in the U.S.A. and Germany, there was a decline in their marginal propensity to import from the U.K. The propensity would in any case have declined as these countries developed their own manufacturing industry, but the speed of the decline was accelerated by the tariffs which these countries imposed, and also by the fortuitous incidence of technical discovery in the key industry of the period—steel. . . .
>
> The net effect of these changes was to make new investment in iron and steel less profitable in Britain than in Germany and America during a period when many new technical methods were available to be incorporated. . . . While it may be true that the larger economy can more easily avail itself of the advantages to be derived from specialisation and mass production, there is no reason to believe that the differences between Britain and the U.S.A. at the end of the nineteenth century were significant from this point of view. The important difference was not in the size of the market but in its rate of growth. (Habakkuk 1962: 205–6, 208)

Investment, the engine of economic growth, is constrained by prospective growth of demand. Chapter 10 presents a new model of

[4] Landes (1969), on the other hand, minimizing the role of demand constraints, emphasizes a lack of entrepreneurship in Britain in the late nineteenth century.

economic growth based on an explicit investment function where demand constraints play a crucial role. The model echoes the Habakkuk thesis. Stressing the role of demand constraints not only in the short run but also in the long run, Chapter 10 goes beyond New Keynesian Economics as well as Old Keynesian Economics.

Whatever one's view, one always needs historical perspectives for the healthy development of macroeconomics. This book draws upon the Japanese experience. The next section briefly surveys post-war developments of the Japanese economy in order to provide a background for the analyses in the subsequent chapters.

1.2 THE JAPANESE ECONOMY

Rebuilt from ashes after the Second World War, the Japanese economy has emerged as a major economic nation, sharing 16% of the world GNP in 1988. This section surveys the post-war Japanese economy in order to provide background for the analyses in the following chapters.[5]

The post-war period (1945–92) can be conveniently divided into four sub-periods: (1) the post-war reconstruction, 1945–55; (2) the high-growth period, 1955–70, (3) the stagnated 1970s; and (4) the present, 1980–93.

The Reconstruction: 1945–1955

The first decade after the Second World War, particularly 1945–50, was devoted mainly to the reconstruction. The story of the Japanese economy is today likely to be told as a simple success story. In retrospect, Japan certainly succeeded in the reconstruction. However, during the period of 1945–50 the Japanese economy was in turmoil, a situation akin to that of present-day Russia. Chapter 3 explains the problems Japan faced and describes how those problems were overcome.

In 1946, Japan's real GNP fell to half of its pre-war peak. Famine was not fatal, but consumption did fall close to the minimum subsistance level (see e.g. Table 3.2, which charts the deteriorating

[5] This book deals with the post-war Japanese economy. Readers interested in the century-long developments of the Japanese economy since the 1867 Meiji Restoration are referred to Ohkawa and Rosovsky (1973), Minami (1986), and Inada *et al.* (1992).

body size of schoolchildren). The fall of output was caused not so much by a shortage of capital as by a lack of raw materials, which was, in turn, brought about by an interruption of imports. At the same time, the Japanese economy suffered from hyperinflation. Although not as severe as the historically notorious hyperinflation experienced by Germany after the First World War, it was still as high as 30 per cent *per month*. The wholesale price index rose 70 times between 1945 and 1950.

The turmoil of the economy drastically changed income and wealth distribution. The pre-war affluent disappeared. On the whole, the self-employed, including farmers and traders, were gainers, while both workers and corporations were big losers. As we would expect, the household saving rate was very low, even negative, for workers' households. For the post-1955 period, the Japanese personal saving rate has been extremely high by international standards (Chapter 6), and some suggest that a national characteristic such as Confucianism has something to do with this high rate. It is instructive, therefore, to recall the period when the Japanese saving rate was very low. When the economic environment forced it upon them, the Japanese, undoubtedly much more traditional than at present, had to cope with a negative saving rate!

Facing a fall of output, the government naturally sought to ensure an equal distribution of basic commodities such as food among households and firms by means of various subsidies. This brought about a sizeable government deficit, which was, either directly or indirectly, monetized by the Bank of Japan. The result was hyperinflation. There is no denying that the rapid growth of money generated this way was at the root of the inflation problem, but Chapter 3 shows that an increase in velocity was also an important factor. The subsidies and transfers, by making wage increases easy, also discouraged producers from pursuing efficiency.

When the Cold War started in 1948, the US occupation policy shifted from the demilitarization and democratization of Japan towards the reconstruction and recovery of the economy in order to turn Japan into a stronghold against communism. In 1949 the so-called Dodge Plan urged the Japanese government to cut its deficit drastically. The government carried out this plan, and was actually able to achieve a budgetary surplus by 1950. Inflation subsided. Very instrumental in this disinflation was the adoption of a single exchange rate: 360 yen to the dollar. As expected, however, the Dodge Plan's recommendations caused the Japanese economy to lapse into a deep recession.

Through this incessant turbulance, the so-called 'Japanese firm' emerged during this period. The Japanese firm today is commonly celebrated for its distinctive labour relations, encompassing lifetime employment, seniority wages, and enterprise unions. However, in the post-war chaos, there was no such thing as lifetime employment, seniority wages, or co-operative enterprise unions in Japan: massive discharges, militant labour unions, and long strikes prevailed. Chapter 3 explains how the Japanese firm as we understand it today emerged through painful trial and error during this turbulent period.

The fragile Japanese economy was suddenly salvaged by the Korean War, which broke out in June, 1950. As a result of the war, Japan's exports increased by 65% in 1951. This export boom brought the Japanese economy an immediate recovery from the 'Dodge recession'. Most importantly, the boom contributed to a growth of long-overdue investment. The most important factor behind the high investment of the early 1950s was the abundant opportunities for introducing new technology. During the Dodge recession, firms had not been able to commit themselves to massive investment. The Korean War encouraged them to make such investment by providing the prospect of strong demand. In this way, the early 1950s saw the introduction of a wide range of innovations, both home-made and borrowed from abroad. For example, innovations in the steel industry, particularly in rolling technology, succeeded in reducing the cost of steel products by 40% between 1951 and 1954. Substantial external economies thus created rapid expansion of machinery industries in the late 1950s and the 1960s.

Attempts to foster innovation in coal mining, however, failed in the end. Table 1.1 shows the sources of energy for the Japanese economy. In 1958, coal lost its price advantage over oil; and the importation of oil, moreover, was liberalized in 1962. By the end of the 1960s, the primary energy source had changed from coal to oil. Coal miners numbered 322,000 in 1957 but only 135,000 in 1963. This structural change in energy, coupled with the growing rate of innovations being introduced in the manufacturing industries, naturally heightened social tensions, culminating in the 283-day-long strike at the Miike coal mine in 1960. The outcome of this strike was an end to the deplorable labour–management relations that existed in Japan after the Second World War.

The year 1955 marked the end of the reconstruction period. In that year, 40% of workers were engaged in agriculture, and the Japanese

Table 1.1. Sources of energy, 1935–1984 (%)

	Coal	Oil	Water power	Natural gas	Nuclear power
1935	73.0	12.4	13.3	0	0
1945	70.2	1.2	26.3	0	0
1950	58.4	7.1	23.0	11.5	0
1955	50.2	20.2	21.2	8.4	0
1960	42.1	37.7	15.3	4.9	0
1965	27.5	58.4	11.3	2.8	0
1970	20.7	70.8	6.3	1.8	0.4
1975	16.5	73.3	5.8	2.6	1.7
1980	17.0	65.8	5.7	6.4	5.1
1984	19.2	58.3	4.7	9.6	8.2

Source: MITI, *Statistics of Energy*.

economy was still characterized by its traditional pre-war structure. And yet, foreign trade had returned to 'normal' by liberalization, and Japan had joined GATT. The famous *Shunto*, or synchronized wage negotiation, also started in 1955; the Liberal Democratic Party, which was to be a ruling party for 38 years until 1993, was formed in 1955; above all, per capita real GNP finally surpassed the pre-war peak level in that year. The White Paper of the government declared that 'postwar reconstruction is over'.

High Economic Growth: 1955–1970

The Japanese economy enjoyed rapid economic growth during the 15-year period of 1955–70 with the average growth rate of real GNP above 10%. It is no exaggeration that this was one of the most notable periods in the history of Japan. The traditional agricultural society had been completely transformed into a modern industrial society by the end of the 1960s.

Economists still find it difficult to understand how and why the Japanese economy enjoyed such high growth. The growth was led basically by the manufacturing industry (Table 1.2). Chapter 2 explains the mechanism that generated high growth during this period. It begins by observing that in 1955 the Japanese economy was still a labour-abundant economy, with almost a half of its work-force in agriculture. In this respect, I follow the tradition of Japanese economists who have applied variants of the model developed by Lewis (1954) to the century-long development of the Japanese

Table 1.2. Growth in real GDP by sectors, 1955–1970 (¥ billion)[a]

	Agriculture	Manufacturing and construction	Tertiary
1955	7,907	8,152	14,819
	(100)	(100)	(100)
1970	9,086	56,517	68,341
	(115)	(693)	(461)

[a] Index (1955 = 100) in parentheses.

economy[6] (see e.g. Ohkawa and Rosovsky 1973; Minami 1986; and Inada *et al.* 1992). In the Lewisian model, however, population flow in the dual economy is taken to be solely a *result* of the growth of the modern manufacturing sector. And the key factor behind this industrial growth is low real wages, made possible by the existence of disguised unemployment in the agricultural sector. Demand for products of the manufacturing industry is assumed to emerge automatically as production grows. In reality, however, demand does not automatically emerge. That is why the Lewisian model applies only to Japan and a few newly industrialized economies (NIEs), but not necessarily to the majority of developing countries.

Chapter 2 describes how, in Japan, the large-scale population flows led to a dramatic increase in the number of households during the 1950s and 1960s. When three generations of family members had kept a traditional single household in rural villages, such households would have needed only one of each consumer durable such as refrigerators, television sets, washing machines, and cars. When the young agricultural workers left their rural villages for urban industrial areas, they formed new households on their own. This additional household formation necessarily generated additional demand for houses, consumer durables, and electricity. In this way, the population flow ultimately sustained high domestic demand-led growth during 1955–70; the population flow was a *cause* of the high growth as well as a result. This virtuous circle for high economic growth was lost around 1970, a few years before the first oil embargo in 1973. Chapter 10 presents a model of demand-led growth which describes the Japanese experience during this period.

[6] Most economists apply the Lewis model to the pre-war Japanese economy. Minami (1970) argues that the turning-point of the Japanese economy from the 'dual' economy to the 'modern' economy was around 1960. In this book, I argue that the Lewis mechanism works in the post-war period as well. Chapter 2 and 10 explain this in great detail.

On the supply side, a particularly important factor was the low price of oil, pegged at the level of $2 a barrel throughout the period. Moreover, post-war breakthroughs in maritime transport, such as the invention of the mammoth tanker, significantly reduced transportation costs. There is no doubt that these developments worked to the advantage of the poorly resource-endowed Japanese economy. To the extent that increasing returns were enjoyed in the energy-resource-intensive industries, they contributed to economic growth. Wright (1990) suggests that the origins of US industrial success during the period 1879–1940 lie in the US abundance of natural resources. In an era of high transport costs, the uniquely resource-rich United States enjoyed a tremendous advantage. This advantage has been eroded in the post-war period as substantial reductions in transport costs have made natural resources 'commodities' rather than part of the 'factor endowment' of individual countries. Japan was, of course, the counterpart of the United States in this process, so, as the US advantage was eroded, Japan's ability to import more of its needed resources increased.

Throughout this period, labour continued to flow from agriculture to the manufacturing industry. The majority of the work-force, most of it young, had a good elementary education, but was unskilled. Young female workers at transistor plants were symbolic of the period. What made possible the replacement of skilled labour by cheap and available unskilled labour was, of course, the innovations brought about as a result of vigorous investment.

Take the steel industry once again as an example. The industry had depended heavily upon skilled labour. The new Linz–Donawitz (LD) revolving furnace, the key innovation of the period, which made some skills obsolete, substantially shortened the production period of steel. This new type of furnace was first introduced in Japan in 1957, whereas the US steel industry introduced it only in 1963. In 1960 the production of steel in Japan was 20 million tons as against 100 million tons in the United States; by 1970 the figures were 100 million versus 120 million tons. By the end of the 1960s, steel had become one of Japan's most important exports, accounting for 15% of total exports.

The Japanese petrochemical industry provides another example. Its growth since 1956, shown in Table 1.3, symbolizes the Japanese economy during this period. Massive investment made possible economies of scale, with the price of ethylene falling from ¥75 per kilogram in 1960 to ¥30 in 1970. This drop in price led in turn to reductions in the prices of many consumer durables and investment goods. The table shows that the peak year for the level of investment in the petrochemical industry was 1970.

While there is no doubt that the petroleum industry was strongly affected by the oil shock, it had already faced 'structural change' during the years preceding the first oil shock in 1973. Watanabe and Saeki (1984), experts on the petrochemical industry, point out that 'the turning point for the petrochemical industry in Japan was not brought about by the oil price hike in 1973'. The development of the

Table 1.3. Investment in the petrochemical industry, 1956–1980

	Capacity for ethylene production ('000 tons)	Investment (¥ million)	Real investment[a] (1970 = 100)
1956	0	8,349	3.3
1957	0	24,017	9.5
1958	43	23,396	9.9
1959	115	27,555	11.5
1960	115	38,494	15.9
1961	160	66,435	27.2
1962	316	55,904	23.3
1963	378	62,017	25.4
1964	633	91,229	37.3
1965	1,080	110,921	45.0
1966	1,190	77,202	30.6
1967	1,565	109,215	42.5
1968	1,970	202,837	78.3
1969	2,480	216,547	81.8
1970	4,010	274,299	100.0
1971	4,330	251,762	92.5
1972	4,980	152,467	55.6
1973	4,980	140,195	44.1
1974	5,065	240,818	57.7
1975	5,145	280,650	65.3
1976	5,185	226,853	50.0
1977	5,215	192,680	41.9
1978	5,235	110,643	24.7
1979	6,079	117,016	24.3
1980	6,257	200,614	35.4

[a] Real Investment is Investment deflated by WPI.

Source: Watanabe and Saeki (1984: 99, table V-1).

petrochemical industry is typical, not exceptional. This is a crucial point when considering the high economic growth of the Japanese economy and its end in the early 1970s. The next chapter discusses this problem in greater detail.

The Stagnated 1970s

Whatever the causes, the high growth period for Japan ended in the early 1970s. The average growth rate of real GNP during the 1970s fell to 4.7% from the 11% rate for the preceding period.

The 'turbulent decade' opened with a crisis of the international financial system. Following the European currency crisis in May 1971, on 15 August US President Nixon abruptly suspended the convertibility of the dollar. This ended the era of the gold–dollar standard with fixed exchange rates, which had lasted for a quarter of a century since the end of the Second World War. With the December implementation of the Smithsonian Agreement, the yen appreciated from ¥360 to ¥308 per dollar. Then, in February 1973, the yen was finally freed to float.

Some economists blame floating exchange rates for the rather poor performance of the Japanese economy during the following decade. But, as discussed in Chapter 2, the relative contribution of exports to growth *rose* during the 1970s compared with the 1960s. The assertion above is, therefore, unwarranted. Fixed exchange rates exert discipline against worldwide inflation, particularly for non-key currency countries, through the balance of payments; however, they cannot be said to encourage the harmonious growth of productivity across countries. Fixed exchange rates are impossible when growth rates of productivity across countries differ significantly. Chapter 8, in fact, demonstrates that a movement of the yen–dollar rate since 1973 has broadly reflected a differential in productivity growth between Japan and the United States.

Appreciation of yen in 1971–2 was, furthermore, nothing but a movement towards equilibrium from a highly undervalued level. And yet the Japanese government, inexperienced in the intricacies of floating exchange rates, overestimated the deflationary effects of the appreciation of the yen. In 1972 high-powered money was allowed to grow by 34% and M_2 by 25%. As could be expected, such a lax monetary policy, at a time when real GNP was at its potential or 'natural' level, generated very high inflation. The WPI rose by 21.3% for the portion of 1973 preceding the oil shock.

When the first oil embargo hit the world economy, the price of oil rose from $2.6 per barrel in January 1973 to $11.7 a year later. This aggravated indigenous inflation in Japan at a time when tight monetary policy to combat high inflation was bringing about a deep recession to the economy. The growth rate of real GNP fell to –0.4% in 1974, the lowest ever in the post-war period.

The standard analysis of stagflation in the 1970s, such as that by Bruno and Sachs (1985), focuses basically on the supply side. It is reasonable, however, to hold that the demand side also played an important role in stagflation. As pointed out above, high inflation in Japan was triggered by excess demand. Demand was responsible for the 1974–5 recession as well. The theoretical challenge is to integrate the demand and supply sides within a framework. Chapter 4 offers a solution to this problem and shows that demand constraints were in fact important in explaining the recession during this period. This case is strengthened when we compare the 'poor' performance of the Japanese economy after the first oil shock in 1973–4 with its 'good' performance after the second oil shock in 1979–80. Chapter 4 shows that investment is in fact the key to understanding the Japanese economy during the two oil shock periods.

In any case, at the time of the first oil crisis, the macroeconomic performance of the Japanese economy, in terms of both growth rate and inflation, was the worst among OECD countries. Investment, which had led high growth in the 1950s and 1960s, sharply decelerated. In parallel with this development, net savings by sector also changed significantly during the 1970s (Fig. 1.5). The government budget, which on average had been balanced up to the mid-1970s, was in deficit. Government expenditure sustained the stagnated Japanese economy during this period. The personal saving rate, which had risen during the high growth period, did not significantly decline, even though the growth rate fell sharply in the 1970s. Chapter 6 analyses the household saving rate in Japan, focusing on its relation to housing/land prices.

In many respects, the early 1970s marked a sharp turning-point for the post-war Japanese economy. And yet there was, of course, some continuity from the preceding period. Above all, there was the continued high productivity growth in the broadly defined machinery industries. High levels of investment in the 1960s brought about high productivity growth in the manufacturing industries as a whole (Table 1.4); productivity growth in the machinery industries is

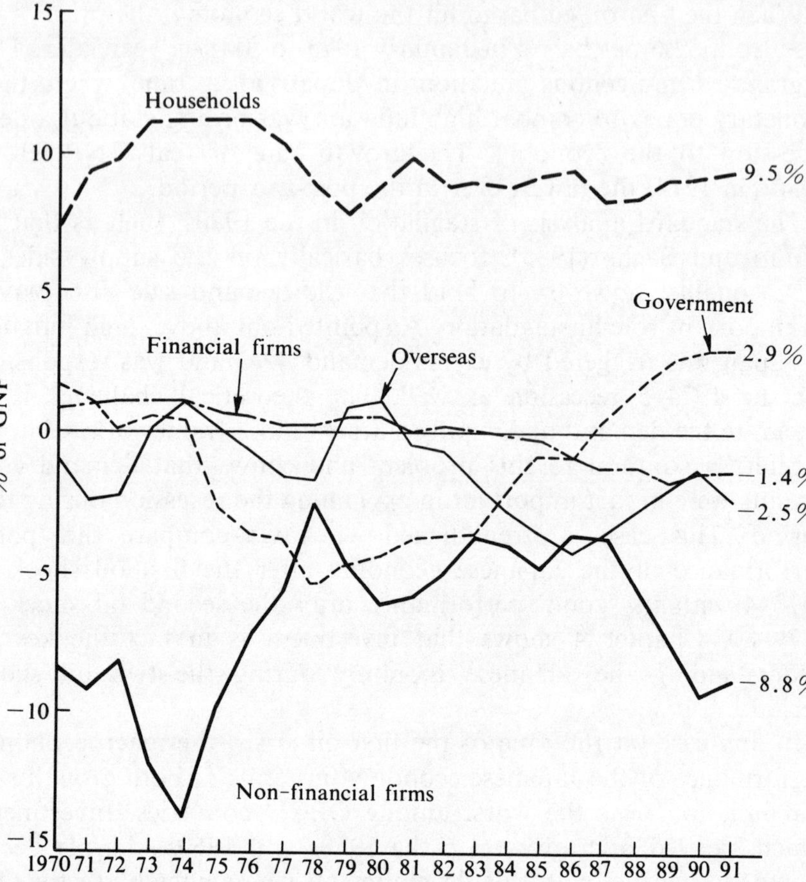

Fig. 1.5. Net saving (saving minus investment) by sector, 1970–1991, as a percentage of GNP

conspicuous by international comparison, particularly in the second half of the 1960s. This trend continued through the 1980s.

The first oil shock, although it was an adverse supply shock to the Japanese economy as a whole, in fact had some favourable effects on the machinery industries. In the first place, the increase in costs arising from the oil embargo was very slight in these industries compared with others such as chemical, paper, and metal. Therefore, when a sharp increase in the real price of oil, equivalent to a terms-of-trade deterioration in Japan, brought about the 10% depreciation of yen, the machinery industries benefited by gaining in international competitiveness. In addition, when the newly created oil money was eventually loaned to developing countries through inter-

Table. 1.4. Productivity growth by industry[a] in Japan, the United States, Germany, and the United Kingdom, 1960–5 and 1965–70 (%)

Japan		USA		West Germany		UK	
1960–4							
Manufacturing average	30.1	Manufacturing average	23.7	Manufacturing average	17.4	Manufacturing average	17.3
1 Petroleum and Coal	89.0	1 Chemical	34.8	1 Ceramics	41.8	1 Chemical	35.6
2 Transportation machinery	73.2	2 Petroleum and coal	34.1	2 Shipbuilding	35.3	2 Transportation machinery	24.3
3 Chemical	45.1	3 Metal	29.3	3 Fabric	31.2	3 Ceramics	22.4
4 Iron and steel	37.8	4 Fabric	28.2	4 Wood products	29.6	4 Fabric	18.9
5 Precision machinery	37.1	5 General and electric machinery	25.8	5 Chemical	29.0	5 Wood products	17.3
6 Electric machinery	33.6			6 Food	15.0	6 Refined fabrics	17.0
7 Rubber	31.0	6 Rubber and plastic	24.7	7 Refined fabrics	14.9	7 Food	14.8
8 Paper and pulp	29.6	7 Transportation machinery	24.3	8 Nonferrous metal	10.0	8 Paper and printing	14.5
9 Fabric	28.4	8 Paper	23.6	9 Iron and steel	7.0	9 General and electric machinery	13.7
10 General machinery	27.0	9 Metal products	22.5	10 Transportation machinery	5.5	10 Leather	13.0
		10 Wood products	20.7				
1965–70							
Manufacturing average	89.0	Manufacturing average	7.9	Manufacturing average	25.6	Manufacturing average	14.6
1 General machinery	168.4	1 Chemical	21.6	1 Chemical	58.7	1 Chemical	46.7
2 Iron and steel	123.3	2 Food	17.5	2 Electric machinery	39.2	2 Fabrics	31.9
3 Electric machinery	119.7	3 Petroleum and coal	15.2	3 Iron and steel	37.5	3 General and electric machinery	25.5
4 Metal products	108.7	4 Paper	10.2	4 Wood and paper	33.5	4 Ceramics	12.5
5 Chemical	91.7	5 Metal products	9.4	5 Fabrics	29.2	5 Food	8.8
6 Nonferrous metal	88.9	6 Ceramics	8.7	6 Nonferrous metals	25.3	6 Refined fabrics	7.3
7 Paper and pulp	86.3	7 Rubber and plastic	7.4	7 Food	24.1	7 Paper and printing	5.6
8 Transportation machinery	85.4	8 Fabrics	7.2	8 Transportation machinery	23.7	8 Transportation machinery	5.2
9 Precision machinery	80.6	9 Wood products	6.5	9 Ceramics	22.0	9 Metal	3.6
10 Fabrics	76.2	10 General and electric machinery	0.0	10 General machinery	20.3	10 Leather	0.8

[a] Cumulative growth rate over the five-year period.

Source: EPA, *The White Paper of the Japanese Government*, 1973.

national financial intermediaries, these growth-oriented developing countries needed to import machinery. In this way, machinery became the product that enjoyed exceptionally high demand in the generally depressed 1970s. Growth led by demand makes productivity growth possible (see Chapter 10 for an explicit model). Through this virtuous circle, the Japanese machinery industries had established unparalleled international competitiveness by the end of the 1970s. The share of broadly defined types of machinery in Japan's exports rose from 35% in 1965 to 63% in 1980.

Behind the vigorous technological progress in the Japanese machinery industries, there was, of course, a pool of engineers of high quality. Fig. 1.6 shows the cumulative number of graduate students in Japan by discipline. Since the early 1960s, Japan has deliberately concentrated its investment in human capital on science and engineering. The number of undergraduate students at the University of Tokyo, for example, was 2,500 each year in 1958, but it had increased to 3,000 by 1964. This increase reflects almost entirely the increase in the number of students in engineering, from 400 to 800. The same applies to many other colleges and universities. There is no denying that this pattern of higher education has contributed to productivity growth in the manufacturing industry.

In passing, I note that investment in human capital on a scale such as shown in Fig. 1.6 is not necessarily the outcome of profit maximization by private organizations. This fact reminds us of the difficulty of modelling the economic growth within a well defined and yet narrow scope of economics. In any case, equipped with extremely high international competitiveness in machinery industries, Japan entered the 1980s.

The 1980s and the Early 1990s

In terms of the growth rate of real GNP, the 1980s did not differ significantly from the 1970s for the Japanese economy: 4.2% for the 1980s versus 4.7% for the 1970s. And yet, the 1980s saw some new events and problems which were non-existent, or only in the process of developing, during the previous decade. First, the size of the Japanese economy, measured by GNP or assets, had become conspicuously large in the world economy. Second, the trade surplus had also become extremely large, creating 'the Japan Problem'. Third, beginning in 1987, the Japanese economy experienced a rather severe business cycle: prolonged boom and subsequent bust. During this

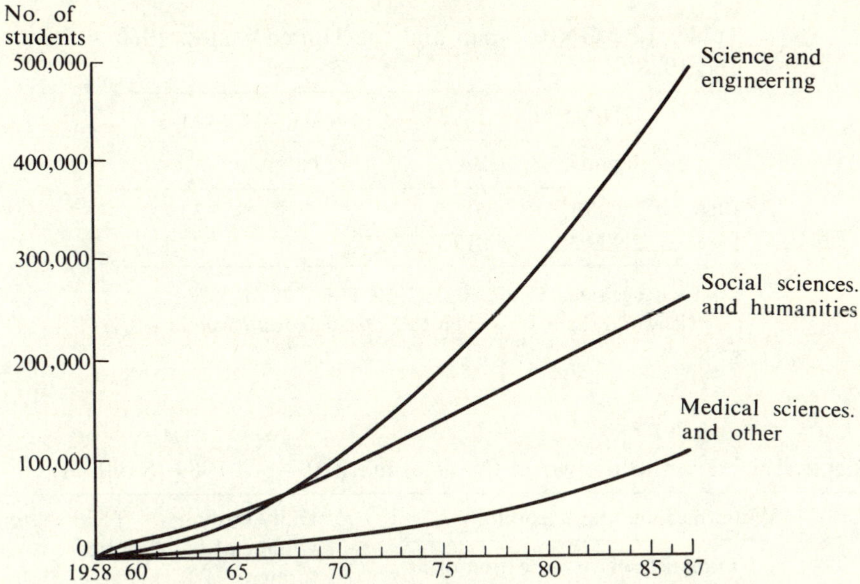

Fig. 1.6. The cumulative number of graduate students, 1958–1987
Source: Ministry of Education.

boom, investment, which had stagnated for a decade, rose to an unprecedentedly high level. In 1988 the absolute amount of fixed investment in Japan finally exceeded that in the United States. At the same time, stock and land prices mushroomed in the late 1980s, only to fall in the early 1990s.

Table 1.5 compares Japan's GNP with that of the United States. One might interpret the change over three decades as a 'normal convergence'. Yet in reality, this convergence seems an important factor underlying any Japan problem. The Japanese economy has grown conspicuously large, measured not only by GNP but also by assets. Continuing current account surpluses in the 1980s necessarily increased Japan's net foreign assets to $290 billion, the world's largest, holding by the end of 1988. In contrast, the United States, whose $100 billion in 1980 constituted the world's largest level of net foreign assets, became the world's largest debtor, with $370 billion of net foreign debt. With this shift, Tokyo has naturally emerged as one of the world financial centres (Table 1.6).

The direct Japan Problem is, of course, trade imbalance. Japan's current account, which on average had been balanced to the end of the 1960s, shifted into surplus for the first time during the 1968–72 period. This created trade frictions with the US textile and steel

Table. 1.5. GNP, Japan and the United States, 1960 and 1988[a]

	GNP ($ billion)		World share (%)[b]	
	Japan	USA	Japan	USA
1960	36.1	515.3	2.8	33.4
1988	2,909.3	4,819.1	16.0	27.1

[a] Exchange rates: $1 = ¥360 for 1960; $1 = ¥126 for 1988.
[b] The world share is based on IMF, *International Financial Statistics*.

Table. 1.6. Japan in the world financial market: April 1989 ($ billion)

	International bank lending[a]		Daily trading volume of foreign exchanges[b]	Total share price[c]
	Nationality of bank	Location of financial centre		
Japan	1,562 (38)	998 (20)	115	3,800
USA	620 (15)	508 (10)	129	2,500
UK	241 (6)	1,090 (21)	187	740

[a] June 1988 (BIS). Proportions of worldwide lending in parentheses.
[b] April 1989 (BOJ).
[c] End 1988.

industries. The two oil shocks in the 1970s, however, turned Japan's trade balance from a surplus into a deficit. But in the early 1980s, triggered by the US fiscal and monetary policy mix under the Reagan administration, Japan's current account surplus again rose sharply, from $7 billion in 1982 to $90 billion in 1987. Seen as a ratio relative to GNP, it peaked at 4% in 1986; it then gradually declined to 1.1% in 1990, before recession once again raised it above 3% in 1992. At the July 1993 Tokyo summit meeting, leading nations once again identified Japan's trade surplus as one of the most significant and disturbing factors in the world economy. Some even suggested that the trade surplus be taken as indicative of the 'closedness' of the Japanese economy. Chapter 8 maintains that this kind of argument is basically wrong.

The 1980s also saw a sharp appreciation of the yen. Starting from ¥240 per dollar after the Plaza Agreement in the autumn of 1985, the yen had steadily appreciated: to ¥168 in 1986, ¥128 in 1988, ¥105 in the summer of 1993, and finally to ¥99 on 21 June 1994. Chapter 8 analyses trade imbalances and the exchange rate, the focal point of policy discussion in the 1980s. It maintains that the standard Mundell–Flemming model does a good job of explaining trade imbalances in the 1980s, but that it cannot adequately explain the sharp appreciation of the yen. By proposing a new definition of the equilibrium exchange rate, it shows that the trend in the actual exchange rate beginning in the early 1970s broadly followed a movement of this equilibrium exchange rate, which in turn reflected a differential in productivity growth across countries.

On the other hand, it is also true that the exchange rate often deviated from its equilibrium rate to a considerable extent for fairly long periods. The prolonged overvaluation of the dollar in the early 1980s is an obvious example; during the four-year period 1981–5, the equilibrium yen continued to appreciate but the actual yen depreciated. This divergence can be explained only by fiscal and monetary policies, in particular a sudden increase in the US fiscal deficit. For a more recent period, my analysis in Chapter 8 suggests that in 1992 the equilibrium exchange rate was about ¥107 per dollar, while most surveys of Japanese firms indicate about ¥110–¥115 for the equilibrium rate in 1993. If we take ¥110 for the equilibrium rate in 1993, the actual exchange rate during the period was about ¥100–¥105. The yen therefore seemed overvalued by about five to ten percentage points.

This overvaluation of the yen in the very midst of one of the worst recessions (1991–4) threw cold water on the Japanese economy. More important from the long-run perspective, the overvalued yen in the early 1990s led many Japanese firms in manufacturing industries to start shifting their factories overseas, particularly to Asian countries. Some fear that the Japanese manufacturing industry may become hollow in future; the fear rests on the alleged fact of life that innovations cannot develop separately from factory production.

In fact, in all the present discussions of the Japanese economy, optimism and pessimism are mingled. On the bright side, Japan is the most important supplier of investment goods to fast-growing east Asia; the level of investment is still high by international standards; and the vigour of innovations has not yet faded. On the dark side, although evidently overshadowed by the present recession, some key industries such as cars and integrated circuits appear to have started to lose their international competitiveness; financial institutions are still paralysed by bad loans made in the late 1980s; the population keeps steady at close to zero growth rate and will be ageing rapidly over the next twenty years.

Whatever one's position in the field of economics worldwide, one needs to have a good understanding of the Japanese economy, and it is to this that I wish to contribute.

2

Growth and Business Cycles: A Quest for the Right Explanation

Very rapid economic growth is perhaps the most important characteristic of the post-war Japanese economy. Although its growth rate in the pre-war period was already among the highest of the developed countries, this accelerated in the post-war era; 3.2% for 1889–1938 as against 6.7% for 1955–88. Fig. 2.1 shows the growth rate of real GNP for Japan in comparison with the United States. For the period spanning nearly three decades, the growth rate of the Japanese economy almost always exceeded that of the US economy. Table 2.1, showing both means and standard deviations of growth rates of real GNP for Japan and the United States, substantiates this fact. Leaving theoretical explanation of the determinants of growth rate for Chapter 10, this chapter explores post-war economic growth and business cycles in Japan.

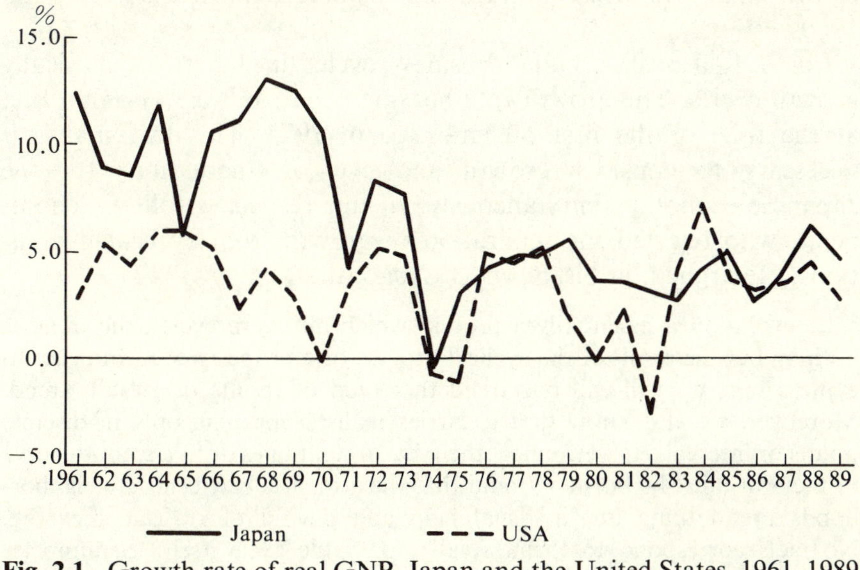

Fig. 2.1. Growth rate of real GNP, Japan and the United States, 1961–1989

Table. 2.1. The growth rate of real GNP, Japan and United States, 1961–1989

	Japan (%)		USA (%)		Correlation (Japan–USA)
	Mean	s.d.	Mean	s.d.	
1961–89	6.4	3.6	3.3	2.3	0.38
1961–72	9.8	2.7	3.9	1.8	−0.18
1973–89	4.1	1.8	2.8	2.6	0.48

Table 2.1 highlights a very significant fact: that the growth rate of the Japanese economy fell from about 10% to 4% in the early 1970s. This sharp decline in the growth rate is actually the most conspicuous phenomenon concerning the post-war Japanese economy. At the same time, measured by standard deviation, fluctuations of the growth rate became much less volatile. For the United States, on the other hand, the average growth rate fell only slightly, and, unlike Japan, its standard deviation became larger in the early 1970s. Horie *et al.* (1987), using deviations, from trend estimated by a Bayesian approach, demonstrate that in addition, for both the United States and the United Kingdom, there was no such significant 'structural change' in the growth rate of real GNP around the early 1970s as there was for Japan. This chapter explains why the growth rate of the Japanese economy declined so sharply around the early 1970s, and at the same time became much more stable than in the 1950s and 1960s.

Fig. 2.1 also shows that business cycles in Japan are basically growth cycles. The growth rate became negative (–0.8%) only once, at the time of the first oil embargo in 1974. This fact makes it necessary to consider growth and cyclical fluctuations for the Japanese economy simultaneously. In this respect, I follow Schumpeter, who rejected the separation of growth from cyclical fluctuations. He argued, in his *Business Cycles*, that,

> since evolution is essentially a process which moves in cycles, the trend is nothing but the result of the cyclical process or a property of it. In order to express this, we will call our trend the trend of results or Result Trend. Moreover, we also know that it carries realistic meaning only in discrete points or intervals. If we connect them by straight lines or fit a smooth curve to them, it must be borne in mind that the stretches between the neighborhoods are nothing but a visual help and devoid of realistic meaning. No facts correspond to them. Real is only the cycle itself. (Schumpeter 1939: 206)

In contrast, a widely accepted view is that growth and business cycles can be separated. And many believe (although I do not) that growth is determined basically by supply factors. As briefly observed above, however, at least in the case of the Japanese economy, a significant change in the nature of business cycles accompanied a sharp decline in the growth rate around 1970. Schumpeter argued that growth and business cycles are integrated if only the cycle is real. For the business cycle, there is no consensus among academic economists on why the business cycle happens at all.

This chapter begins by analysing the nature of post-war business cycles in Japan. Using industry data, I first derive a measure of the relative contribution of macro shocks to changes in output for each industry. The subsequent analysis depends heavily on this measure, which I call the 'macro ratio'. Based on the macro ratio, Section 2.1 first rejects monetarism, and demonstrates that real shocks were important. I then find that macro fluctuations were caused mainly by fixed investment, particularly construction, in the 1950s and 1960s. Given this finding, I ask myself whether fluctuations of construction were in turn caused by innovations (increases in total factor productivity) in construction-related industries or construction demand. Comparing the data on total factor productivity at the industry level with the macro ratios, I conclude that construction *demand* rather than total factor productivity was responsible for the output fluctuations in the 1950s and 1960s.

Section 2.2 considers the mechanism of rapid economic growth during the period 1955–70, and its end. It singles out population flow from rural agricultural areas to urban industrial cities, and accompanying high household formation, as the ultimate factor that sustained such high growth of domestic demand in the 1950s and 1960s. I maintain that this mechanism of high growth had faded before the first oil embargo in 1973.

Section 2.3 deals with the post-high-growth period, 1970–90. It begins by explaining why the Japanese economy became more stable than in the previous period. To a large extent, the stability can be attributed to the stability of investment. This section explains, by referring to three *real* factors, why investment became more stable in the 1970s. It also comments on the role of investment in equipment and construction. Finally, it can be seen that, for the subsequent decade (1975–85), export—again a demand factor—played the major role in the Japanese business cycle.

As we shall see shortly, a major change in the nature of business cycles in fact accompanies a sharp decline in the growth rate around the early 1970s. By analysing changes in the nature of business cycles, this chapter seeks to determine the ultimate causal factor lying behind the 'structural change' of the Japanese economy. In so doing, it attempts to explore what really determines a nation's economic growth.

2.1 POST-WAR BUSINESS CYCLES IN JAPAN

Business cycles are a conspicuous phenomenon and have attracted economists' attention for more than a century. As a result of this attention, an extraordinary number of theories purporting to explain the causes of business cycles have emerged: one need only recall the thickness of Haberler's 1939 work to gauge their total (see Haberler 1964). These theories have shown no sign of converging over time; in fact, as I shall explain in a moment, recent controversy in this area has once again underscored the depths of the divisions among academic macroeconomists. Naturally, this controversy has very important implications for stabilization policies.

With this in mind, it is clear that any work that clarifies the underlying theory is significant, and I suggest that analyses of business cycles in various countries will prove especially useful in this regard. Of course, we could not hope that a particular theory would apply uniformly to all countries; nor would we expect it to hold over all time periods. I believe, therefore, that close studies of business cycles in a historical context are essential. This section takes the first step towards achieving that goal by carefully examining post-war Japanese business cycles.[1] For reference, Table 2.2 shows the chronology of post-war business cycles in Japan.

Contending Theories

Before proceeding with our analysis, it will be useful to summarize the ongoing debate on business cycle theories, since there is no current consensus in the economics profession about the major causes of aggregate fluctuations of the economy. The existing theories can be divided broadly into two schools: one Keynesian and the other neoclassical.

[1] For pre-war and early post-war business cycles in Japan, see Shinohara (1961), Fujino (1968), and Minami (1986).

Table. 2.2. Chronology of post-war business cycles in Japan

Cycle no.	Expansion	Recession
		1949(2)–1950(5) (16 months, Dodge Deflation)
1	1950(6)–1951(6) (13 months, Korean War)	1951(6)–1951(10) (4 months, post-Korean War)
2	1951(10)–1954(1) (27 months, consumption boom)	1954(1)–1954(11) (10 months)
3	1954(11)–1957(6) (31 months, *Jimmu* boom)	1957(6)–1958(6) (12 months)
4	1958(6)–1961(12) (42 months, *Iwato* boom)	1961(12)–1962(10) (10 months)
5	1962(10)–1964(10) (24 months, Tokyo Olympic boom)	1964(10)–1965(10) (12 months, structural change)
6	1965(10)–1970(7) (57 months, *Izanagi* boom)	1970(7)–1971(12) (17 months, Nixon shock)
7	1971(12)–1973(11) (23 months, development boom)	1973(11)–1975(3) (16 months, first oil shock)
8	1975(3)–1977(1) (22 months)	1977(1)–1977(10) (9 months)
9	1977(10)–1980(2) (28 months)	1980(2)–1983(2) (36 months, second oil shock)
10	1983(2)–1985(6) (28 months)	1985(6)–1986(11) (17 months, yen appreciation)
11	1986(12)–1991(4) (53 months, *Heisei* boom)	1991(5)–1993(10) (30 months, *Heisei* recession)

Source: Economic Planning Agency.

The Keynesian position is that both real and monetary factors are important in business cycles; for real factors advocates emphasize the role of *demand shocks* rather than supply shocks, with the notable exceptions of the two oil shocks in the 1970s. Among real demand shocks, Keynes himself put a particular emphasis on investment:

> If we examine the details of any actual instance of the trade cycle, we shall find that it is highly complex and that every element in our analysis will be required for its complete explanation. In particular we shall find that fluctuations in the propensity to consume, in the state of liquidity-preference, and in the marginal efficiency of capital have all played a part. But I suggest that the essential character of the trade cycle, and, especially, the regularity of time-sequence and of duration which justifies us in calling it a *cycle*, is mainly due to the way in which the marginal efficiency of capital fluctuates. The trade cycle is best regarded, I think, as being occasioned by a cyclical change in the marginal efficiency of capital, though complicated and often aggravated by associated changes in the other significant short-period variables of the economic system. (Keynes 1936: 313)

In principle, of course, any real demand can play the same role as investment in business cycles.

The neoclassical school, in turn, can be divided into two main streams of thought: Friedman–Lucas monetarism, and real business cycle theory. The basic tenet of monetarism is well known: that unanticipated money supply is the major cause of business cycles. Business cycles are an 'economic problem' which can be remedied by stabilizing the money supply.

Real business cycle theory, on the other hand, argues that the economy is best modelled as a floating Walrasian equilibrium. According to this view, the aggregate economy, even though it fluctuates, is in fact always at a Pareto optimum, and therefore stabilization policies are uncalled for. In real business cycle theory, money plays little or no role in causing fluctuations; rather, attention is focused on productivity shocks.

Given the theoretical background, the following agenda for empirical analysis is important:

1. One can test the expectational error theory of monetarism. To my knowledge, in the existing literature this test has been performed using only aggregate data. The theory emphasizes microeconomic behaviour, in particular expectations formation, and therefore it is important to construct a test using cross-sectional data. Such a test can also determine whether real factors are important in business cycles.

2. If real factors have been important in business cycles, the next step is to see what kind of real shocks were important in a particular case.

By investigating industry data, I attempt to answer the above questions in the context of post-war Japanese business cycles. I first obtain a measure of aggregate macroeconomic shocks by estimating my basic aggregate and industry output equations. During a given cycle, the production of each industry is affected by both aggregate macroeconomic shocks and industry-specific microeconomic shocks. Here, we are particularly interested in measuring the relative importance of these two kinds of shock in each industry. Behind the conspicuous economy-wide movement of aggregate production, we also observe a diversity in production changes across industries. By investigating this diversity, we can shed light on the nature of business cycles in post-war Japan.

Next, I test a version of monetarism using the results obtained in the way described above. The test rejects this theory, and as a result I shift my attention to an analysis of the importance of real shocks. The natural question then is, what kind of real shocks were important in the post-war business cycles in Japan? I find that investment in the 1960s and the early 1970s, and exports thereafter, are the major impulses generating business cycles. As is well known, both Keynesian and real business cycle theories emphasize the importance of real shocks, but the former assigns the leading role to the demand side whereas the latter stresses the role of direct technological shocks to production functions. I explore which view is more acceptable, and conclude that the Keynesian view is more consistent with the post-war Japanese experiences.

Estimates of Industry Production Equations

Business cycles are, by definition, a macroeconomic phenomenon, meaning that the economic activities of various industries and regions move in tandem. However, the consistency of parallel movements in production across sectors of the economy should not be exaggerated. In fact, many economists have noted a diversity in production changes across industries. To illustrate this diversity, Table 2.3 shows the correlations of production across manufacturing industries in Japan. This relationship should yield fruitful information on the nature of business cycles, and is the basic motivation of my present analysis.

Table. 2.3. Correlations of production across manufacturing industries, 1958–1984

	Iron	Nonf.	Fab.	Ind.	Elec.	Trans.	Prec.	Cer.	Chem.	Med.	Pet.	Pulp	Text	Wood	Food	Rub.
Correlations of production across industries: 1958(I)–1984(III)																
Iron and steel	1.00															
Nonferrous metals	0.83	1.00														
Fabricated metals	0.82	0.88	1.00													
Industrial machinery	0.85	0.75	0.71	1.00												
Electrical machinery	0.81	0.75	0.64	0.88	1.00											
Transportation equipment	0.59	0.35	0.45	0.54	0.43	1.00										
Precision instruments	0.16	0.27	0.04	0.42	0.36	−0.09	1.00									
Ceramics, stone, and clay products	0.86	0.88	0.83	0.89	0.83	0.50	0.41	1.00								
Chemicals (excl. med., drugs)	0.75	0.75	0.82	0.69	0.69	0.52	−0.01	0.79	1.00							
Medicine and drugs	0.08	0.11	0.29	0.15	−0.11	−0.08	0.03	0.13	−0.02	1.00						
Petroleum and coal products	0.66	0.60	0.80	0.48	0.38	0.46	−0.32	0.55	0.74	0.36	1.00					
Pulp, paper, and paper products	0.75	0.81	0.66	0.79	0.88	0.28	0.48	0.88	0.73	−0.08	0.35	1.00				
Textiles	0.72	0.77	0.73	0.69	0.79	0.53	0.15	0.81	0.84	−0.15	0.54	0.81	1.00			
Wood and wood products	0.66	0.81	0.84	0.59	0.52	0.31	0.17	0.78	0.83	0.14	0.60	0.67	0.74	1.00		
Food and tobacco	0.02	0.01	0.00	0.03	0.03	0.20	0.13	0.09	0.26	−0.48	−0.09	0.14	0.24	0.22	1.00	
Rubber products	0.74	0.77	0.61	0.85	0.86	0.28	0.56	0.83	0.55	0.06	0.34	0.82	0.63	0.53	−0.04	1.00
Correlations of production across industries: 1958(I)–1974(IV)																
Iron and steel	1.00															
Nonferrous metals	0.87	1.00														
Fabricated metals	0.86	0.87	1.00													
Industrial machinery	0.83	0.78	0.73	1.00												
Electrical machinery	0.80	0.80	0.66	0.89	1.00											
Transportation equipment	0.57	0.44	0.58	0.42	0.25	1.00										
Precision instruments	0.02	0.07	−0.24	0.31	0.40	−0.41	1.00									
Ceramics, stone, and clay products	0.87	0.89	0.88	0.89	0.85	0.52	0.18	1.00								
Chemicals (excl. med., drugs)	0.72	0.73	0.88	0.64	0.60	0.64	−0.30	0.74	1.00							
Medicine and drugs	0.27	0.18	0.40	0.41	0.16	0.19	−0.03	0.35	0.21	1.00						
Petroleum and coal products	0.70	0.64	0.89	0.54	0.40	0.62	−0.46	0.65	0.84	0.51	1.00					
Pulp, paper, and paper products	0.71	0.81	0.63	0.78	0.89	0.17	0.49	0.85	0.55	0.12	0.35	1.00				

Textiles	0.69	0.78	0.75	0.62	0.69	0.53	0.00	0.80	0.83	0.07	0.62	0.72	1.00			
Wood and wood products	0.71	0.79	0.86	0.60	0.57	0.59	−0.19	0.74	0.88	0.18	0.74	0.57	0.86	1.00		
Food and tobacco	−0.19	−0.17	−0.17	−0.25	−0.25	0.11	−0.01	−0.20	0.04	−0.48	−0.16	−0.16	0.06	0.06	1.00	
Rubber products	0.69	0.77	0.59	0.85	0.92	0.10	0.51	0.82	0.45	0.20	0.33	0.85	0.58	0.48	−0.27	1.00
Correlations of production across industries: 1975(I)–1984(III)																
Iron and steel	1.00															
Nonferrous metals	0.70	1.00														
Fabricated metals	0.70	0.92	1.00													
Industrial machinery	0.90	0.67	0.70	1.00												
Electrical machinery	0.84	0.65	0.63	0.88	1.00											
Transportation equipment	0.65	0.19	0.19	0.75	0.70	1.00										
Precision instruments	0.43	0.66	0.62	0.60	0.31	0.30	1.00									
Ceramics, stone, and clay products	0.86	0.89	0.87	0.91	0.80	0.48	0.71	1.00								
Chemicals (excl. med., drugs)	0.84	0.83	0.81	0.78	0.81	0.37	0.34	0.86	1.00							
Medicine and drugs	−0.49	−0.12	−0.10	−0.53	−0.75	−0.65	0.15	−0.32	−0.49	1.00						
Petroleum and coal products	0.56	0.45	0.40	0.30	0.40	0.11	−0.02	0.39	0.65	−0.28	1.00					
Pulp, paper, and paper products	0.84	0.87	0.83	0.83	0.86	0.42	0.46	0.93	0.95	−0.49	0.46	1.00				
Textiles	0.78	0.77	0.73	0.81	0.94	0.54	0.35	0.82	0.86	−0.65	0.39	0.92	1.00			
Wood and wood products	0.60	0.88	0.88	0.57	0.46	−0.05	0.60	0.82	0.76	0.07	0.36	0.79	0.59	1.00		
Food and tobacco	0.68	0.59	0.64	0.78	0.72	0.42	0.43	0.78	0.75	−0.49	0.26	0.78	0.70	0.59	1.00	
Rubber products	0.86	0.77	0.66	0.87	0.75	0.63	0.69	0.90	0.75	−0.37	0.38	0.82	0.74	0.64	0.69	1.00

The method of estimation used is similar to that of Altonji and Ham (1986).[2] We first take the movement of real GNP as exogenous and define its innovations as 'macro' shocks. Most studies of specific industries treat aggregate output such as GNP as exogenous and ignore the feedbacks from a specific industry to aggregate output. This common practice would not be overly misleading if the size of each sector were small relative to the aggregate output considered. In this context, I point out that aggregate output in my analysis is real GNP, not the total output of manufactured goods produced by industries belonging to the manufacturing sector.

Next, I postulate that the sources of changes in each industry's output consist of two types of shock: the macro shock and the micro shock. Industry-specific shocks are by construction independent of macro shocks. It may appear somewhat arbitrary to draw a strict line between macro and micro shocks. After all, even if a certain shock hit only one industry, it will generally lead to changes in output in other industries too, since the industries are interrelated as input–output analysis indicates. However, if these kinds of inter-industry effects are really significant, they will be expressed through changes in aggregate variables such as real GNP and therefore, according to my definition, will be classified as macro shocks. In other words, I define the part of the change in an industry's output that is correlated with real GNP as that caused by macro shocks. And this is irrespective of whether those shocks were originally economy-wide and hit all industries simultaneously or initially hit one industry but, through the input–output relationship, produced aggregate fluctuations. For my purposes, I feel that this definition of macro shocks is reasonable.

The equations to be estimated are:

$$Q_t^i = M^i(L)\,Y_t + u_t^i, \tag{1}$$

where the dependent variable Q_t^i in (1) is a detrended *natural logarithm* of the quarterly index of industrial production in industry i at time t; Y_t is the similarly detrended natural logarithm of quarterly real GNP;[3] and $M^i(L)$ is a polynomial function of the lag operator L, defined as

$$L^n x_t = x_{t-n} \quad (n = 0, 1, 2, \ldots).$$

[2] For other possible methods of estimation and their practical difficulties in the present context, see Altonji and Ham (1986).

[3] The quarterly variable Q_t^i was constructed as a simple average of seasonally adjusted monthly data compiled by MITI. In the equation $\ln\hat{Q}_t^i = a + bt + ct^2 + Q_t^i$, $\ln\hat{Q}_t$ is the log of the original index; Q_t^i is the residual; a, b, and c are estimated coefficients; and t is time.
Y_t was also derived in the same manner as Q_t^i:

It is necessary to make a brief comment on my assumption of *deterministic trend* or the *trend-stationary* process generating real GNP and industrial production. The unit roots literature, following a seminal work by Nelson and Plosser (1982), once gave the impression that most economic time series have a unit root, and that it is intrinsically inappropriate to detrend such time series in a deterministic way. This impression is simply wrong, however.

The essential difference between the trend-stationary specification and the integrated specification lies in the nature of the data-generating process. And in fact, it is extremely difficult, in practice, to discriminate between the two models, almost impossible for finite samples: see Christiano and Eichenbaum (1989), Campbell and Perron (1991), and Je Jong *et al.* (1992). Besides, unit-root tests are known to be not robust, depending on whether or not the presence of a break point is allowed in trend; Perron (1989) shows how standard tests of the unit root hypothesis against trend-stationary alternatives cannot reject the unit root hypothesis, even asymptotically, if the true data-generating process is that of stationary fluctuations around a trend that contains a break point; he then demonstrates that, for 11 out of the 14 US series analysed by Nelson and Plosser, the unit root hypothesis is rejected.

The presence of a break point is extremely important for the Japanese data because there is a good consensus that most Japanese time series, let alone real GNP, exhibit a 'structural change' around 1970, a much greater change than for other countries such as the United Kingdom and the United States. Using the quarterly data for 1955–94, Soejima (1994) in fact shows that, when a break point is allowed around 1971–2, the unit root hypothesis is rejected against the trend stationary hypothesis for both real GNP and industrial production.[4] Meanwhile, McCallum (1993) points out that there is a

$$\ln \hat{Y}_t = 10.34 + 0.032t - 0.129 \times 10^{-3}t^2 + Y_t,$$
$$(1029.7) \quad (71.9) \quad (-31.8)$$

where $\ln Y_t$ is the log of the original series and Y_t is the residual of the equation. The sample period was 1959(I)–1983(IV). The figures in parentheses are t-values.

[4] The unit root test for real GNP is a popular topic: see Campbell and Mankiw (1987), Cochrane (1988), and Perron (1989) for the USA. For Japan, see Takeuchi (1991), Iwamoto and Kobayashi (1992), and Soejima (1994); they all use the quarterly data. Takeuchi *et al.* divide the whole sample into two sub-sample periods around 1971, and then apply the unit root test for each sub-sample separately; they do not reject the unit root hypothesis for real GNP. On the other hand, Soejima (1994) allows a break point in trend, and applies the unit root test for the whole period, 1955–94; he rejects the unit root hypothesis.

tendency for similar results to be obtained from the differencing and deterministic detrending methods, provided that serial correlation corrections are applied to the residuals of the relationship being studied. This suggests that it is not so crucial to difference the data or remove deterministic trends as some economists once maintained. Here, I assume the trend stationarity for real GNP and industrial production.

I assume that Y_t follows an autoregressive (AR) process:

$$Y_t = a(L)Y_{t-1} + \varepsilon_t, \tag{2}$$

where ε_t is a white noise error. The industry-specific micro shocks, u_t^i, are in turn generated by the autoregressive equations,

$$u_t^i = a^i(L)u_{t-1}^i + v_t^i. \tag{3}$$

Here v_t^i is a white noise error and $a^i(L)$ is a polynomial function of L.

At this stage, the economic interpretations of the estimated equations (1) and (2) are flexible. As discussed previously, there are two reasons why we observe parallel movements in production across industries: first, the economy is subject to common, economy-wide shocks; and second, industry-specific shocks induce correlations in output across sectors because of significant input–output feedback effects. The dominant role of the economy-wide shock is emphasized by monetarists. In this case, the important macro shock is, of course, unanticipated movements of the money supply. Idiosyncratic shocks are often assumed to cancel out in the aggregate.

On the other hand, in some of the recent models of real business cycles, such as that of Long and Plosser (1983), initial real shocks are assumed to affect a particular sector directly. Inter-industry dependence of production propagates this idiosyncratic shock to the economy at large. In the present analysis, I do not attempt to disentangle these two sources of parallel movements in production across industries. The more important the common economy-wide shock, and/or the more tightly the production of various industries is interrelated, the greater is the role of what we call 'macro' shocks. In other words, the industry-specific micro shock u_t^i is that part of an industry's production that is, for whatever reasons, not significantly correlated with real GNP.

From (1) and (3), we obtain

$$Q_t^i - M^i(L)Y_t = a^i(L)[Q_{t-1}^i - M^i(L)Y_{t-1}] + v_t^i. \tag{4}$$

I first estimated equation (2). For the macro variable Y_t, I used quarterly real GNP, and obtained the following equation for Y_t in my sample period 1959 (I)–1983 (IV):

$$Y_t = \underset{(21.9)}{0.91}Y_{t-1} + \tilde{\varepsilon}_t, \text{ s.e.} = 0.014, \tilde{\varepsilon}_t, \text{ estimated residual,} \tag{5}$$

(t-ratio in parentheses).

Given the difficulty mentioned above, I did not attempt to make the unit roots test. It is interesting to note that Japanese real GNP is often well described by a first-order autoregressive model, whereas US real GNP is typically found to have a second-order AR representation (see e.g. Blanchard 1981, and Rose 1986). Examining Table 2.4, we see that Japanese real GNP is well explained by an AR(1) representation during the rapid growth period of the 1960s, while changes in real GNP during the 1970s and 1980s more closely approximate those in the United States.

Table 2.4. Real GNP, Japan and the United States, 1959/1960–1983[a]

Japan: 1959(I)–1983(IV)	
$Y_t = 0.91\, Y_{t-1} + \tilde{\varepsilon}_t$	SE = 0.014
(21.9)	
Japan: 1959(I)–1970(IV)	
$Y_t = 0.91\, Y_{t-1} + \tilde{\varepsilon}_t$	SE = 0.016
(12.7)	
Japan: 1971(I)–1983(IV)	
$Y_t = 1.16\, Y_{t-1} - 0.24\, Y_{t-2} + \tilde{\varepsilon}_t$	SE = 0.011
(8.49) (– 1.80)	
USA: 1960(I)–1983(IV)	
$Y_t = 1.30\, Y_{t-1} - 0.45\, Y_{t-2} + \tilde{\varepsilon}_t$	SE = 0.010
(13.6) (– 4.67)	

[a] Figures in parentheses are t values; $\tilde{\varepsilon}_t$ is the estimated residual.

I next estimated equation (4) for 16 Japanese manufacturing industries using the method of nonlinear least squares.[5] The orders of $M(L)$ and $a(L)$ of (4) are selected as Table 2.5. In fact, although I estimated (4) for larger orders of lags, most of them do not affect the estimation results. I also tested the sub-sample stability of the model using a likelihood ratio test. Since there is a strong consensus among

[5] It is more asymptotically efficient to estimate equation (4) jointly for the 16 industries than to estimate each industry equation independently, since the error terms may be correlated across equations. However, I chose the second approach because the date of structural change varied across industries, and because of the computational difficulty of joint estimation of such a large number of nonlinear equations.

Table 2.5. Estimated industry equations, 1959–1984

	M_0	M_1	M_2	a_1	a_2	SEE	Q	Macro ratio	s.d. of Q^i
Iron and steel									
1959(I)–1984(III)	0.892	0.710	0.324	1.30	−0.540	0.0253	6.5	0.475	0.091
	(0.173)	(0.162)	(0.172)	(0.0857)	(0.0824)				
Nonferrous metals and products									
1959(I)–1975(I)	0.730	0.454	0.209	1.50	−0.695	0.0278	2.6	0.238	0.101
	(0.209)	(0.236)	(0.207)	(0.105)	(0.105)				
1975(II)–1984(III)	0.832	−0.272	0.00776	1.12	−0.354	0.0181	4.47	0.054	0.059
Fabricated metals									
1959(I)–1975(I)	0.896	1.32	0.736	1.11	−0.382	0.0351	8.16	0.811	0.116
	(0.260)	(0.245)	(0.265)	(0.129)	(0.128)				
1975(II)–1984(III)	0.595	−0.0976	−0.0237	0.975	−0.192	0.0245	10.26	0.035	0.060
	(0.639)	(0.581)	(0.621)	(0.132)	(0.126)				
Industrial machinery									
1959(I)–1971(I)	1.07	1.26	0.331	0.843	0.0354	0.0415	9.06	0.356	0.149
	(0.406)	(0.356)	(0.397)	(0.157)	(0.147)				
1971(II)–1984(III)	1.16	0.586	0.840	1.48	−0.620	0.0241	5.45	0.465	0.126
	(0.300)	(0.308)	(0.302)	(0.111)	(0.111)				
Electrical machinery									
1959(I)–1974(II)	0.847	0.996	0.505	1.43	−0.530	0.0275	4.38	0.460	0.124
	(0.225)	(0.262)	(0.231)	(0.102)	(0.0891)				
1974(III)–1984(III)	3.23	1.85	0.530	1.13	−0.414	0.0298	1.66	0.772	0.134
	(0.609)	(0.540)	(0.497)	(0.160)	(0.162)				
Transportation equipment									
1959(I)–1984(III)	0.594	0.701	0.405	1.03	−0.220	0.0281	7.34	0.455	0.081
	(0.209)	(0.198)	(0.208)	(0.0953)	(0.0955)				
Precision instrument									
1959(I)–1974(II)	−0.331	0.334	0.192	1.22	−0.327	0.0300	11.91	0.012	0.091
	(0.264)	(0.258)	(0.250)	(0.125)	(0.121)				
1974(III)–1984(III)	2.88	0.00786	0.0320	1.53	−0.578	0.0293	14.09	0.236	0.132
	(0.703)	(0.662)	(0.551)	(0.139)	(0.140)				
Ceramics, stone, and clay products									
1959(I)–1974(II)	0.500	0.753	0.309	0.974	−0.166	0.0179	3.44	0.813	0.062
	(0.143)	(0.136)	(0.148)	(0.132)	(0.123)				
1974(III)–1984(III)	1.33	0.303	−0.393	1.50	−0.649	0.0164	1.94	0.192	0.067
	(0.345)	(0.321)	(0.272)	(0.111)	(0.103)				

Chemicals (excl. med. and drugs)									
1959(I)–1973(II)	0.801	0.675	0.507	1.05	−0.418	0.0194	0.834	0.833	0.077
	(0.160)	(0.133)	(0.161)	(0.124)	(0.108)				
1973(III)–1984(III)	1.12	1.57	−0.0838	1.13	−0.412	0.0325	4.16	0.528	0.088
	(0.500)	(0.481)	(0.446)	(0.144)	(0.143)				
Medicine and drugs									
1959(I)–1973(IV)	−0.353	0.454	0.919	1.11	−0.345	0.0463	0.164	0.181	0.093
	(0.376)	(0.356)	(0.373)	(0.126)	(0.126)				
1974(I)–1984(III)	−0.589	−0.629	−0.953	1.00	−0.254	0.0283	13.5	0.371	0.073
	(0.479)	(0.457)	(0.475)	(0.141)	(0.128)				
Petroleum and coal products									
1959(I)–1984(III)	0.513	0.501	0.275	0.859	0.0106	0.0229	14.0	0.370	0.069
	(0.175)	(0.167)	(0.173)	(0.0960)	(0.0943)				
Pulp, paper, and paper products									
1959(I)–1973(III)	0.331	0.316	0.350	1.23	−0.402	0.0147	8.70	0.662	0.044
	(0.121)	(0.122)	(0.119)	(0.120)	(0.0987)				
1973(IV)–1984(III)	1.08	1.09	−0.139	1.36	−0.671	0.0242	4.77	0.307	0.082
	(0.341)	(0.322)	(0.341)	(0.119)	(0.116)				
Textiles									
1959(I)–1975(I)	0.361	0.354	0.330	1.44	−0.581	0.0169	2.95	0.422	0.057
	(0.133)	(0.153)	(0.133)	(0.111)	(0.118)				
1975(II)–1984(III)	0.700	0.564	0.433	1.08	−0.462	0.00757	4.15	0.616	0.046
	(0.176)	(0.156)	(0.176)	(0.0908)	(0.0759)				
Wood and wood products									
1959(I)–1974(II)	0.457	0.432	0.147	0.662	−0.177	0.0165	3.24	0.762	0.042
	(0.146)	(0.119)	(0.140)	(0.140)	(0.138)				
1974(III)–1984(III)	0.551	−0.133	−0.132	1.39	−0.521	0.0187	7.80	0.024	0.053
	(0.398)	(0.375)	(0.316)	(0.131)	(0.131)				
Food and tobacco									
1959(I)–1979(I)	0.267	0.177	0.106	0.491	−0.0201	0.0551	11.3	0.129	0.068
	(0.525)	(0.488)	(0.553)	(0.158)	(0.158)				
1970(II)–1984(III)	0.705	0.343	0.509	0.622	−0.0388	0.0239	7.11	0.375	0.037
	(0.323)	(0.345)	(0.305)	(0.137)	(0.141)				
Rubber products									
1959(I)–1984(III)	0.699	0.529	0.128	1.17	−0.345	0.0247	5.36	0.373	0.072
	(0.179)	(0.178)	(0.180)	(0.0939)	(0.0873)				

Note: Figures in parentheses are standard errors.

economists that the Japanese economy experienced a significant 'structural change' sometime in the early 1970s, I checked the stability of the model for every quarter from 1970(I) to 1975(IV). Where the assumption of stability was not rejected, the model was estimated using data for the whole sample period. Where this was not the case, I report separate estimation results for the two sub-sample periods in Table 2.5. In most industries, industry-specific micro shocks $a^i(L)$ follow a second-order autoregressive model and their coefficients show humped-shaped patterns. The coefficients of $M^i(L)$ in (4), which reflect the effect of macro shocks on the level of industry production, differ across industries and across time.

Measuring the Relative Contribution of Macro Shocks

Coming to the crux of our argument, I next attempt to measure the relative contributions of macro and micro shocks in explaining the movement of output in each industry. This can be easily done if both macro and micro innovations ε_t and v_t are in fact orthogonal. Such is the case, since the current value of GNP is included in the equation for industrial production, and therefore the residual for the equation must be uncorrelated with GNP and hence with the innovation in GNP. I tested the serial correlation of v_t by calculating the sixth-order Q-statistic reported in Table 2.5. (The critical χ^2 value is 16.8 at the 1% level of significance and 12.6 at the 5% level of significance.) In almost all cases, we cannot reject the hypothesis that v_t is white noise. Since ε_t and v_t are both white noise and orthogonal to each other, the percentage of changes in Q generated by macro shocks can be calculated as

$$\frac{(M_0^2 + M_1^2 + M_2^2)\sigma_y^2 + 2(M_0M_1 + M_1M_2)\sigma_{yy-1} + 2M_0M_2\sigma_{yy-2}}{\sigma_Q^2}, \qquad (6)$$

where σ_Q^2 and σ_y^2 are the variances of Q and Y, respectively, and σ_{yy-1} and σ_{yy-2} are the autocovariances of Y_t and Y_{t-1} and Y_t and Y_{t-2}, respectively. I refer to this measure as the 'macro ratio' and report these ratios for each industry in Table 2.5.

For convenience, I will refer to the two sub-sample periods as the 'rapid growth period' and the 'post-oil shock period'; but in fact, the division of sample periods differs slightly across each industry as reported in Table 2.5. I emphasize that my selection of names for the sub-sample periods is not meant to suggest that the 'structural change' that occurred in the Japanese economy was solely attributable to the first oil shock in 1973; indeed, I will later argue that *domestic* factors dating from about 1970 were most instrumental in causing structural change.

The macro ratios in Table 2.5 reveal the different economic behavioural patterns of manufacturing industries which are often concealed by the conspicuous movements of aggregative economic activity, i.e. by business cycles. At this stage, I have not yet given any specific interpretations to the macro ratios, but I will use these ratios extensively in my subsequent analyses.

A Test of Monetary Theory of Business Cycles

One important theory of the business cycles is monetarism, although this has lessened in significance since the mid-1980s. As is well known, monetarists argue for the dominant role of monetary shocks, and, in particular, stress the role of unanticipated changes in the money supply. As we will see below, the modern monetarist theory with rational expectations has specific implications for the macro ratios of industries. Taking advantage of this fact, I test a version of the rational expectations monetary theory of business cycles.

The theoretical model is similar to one considered by Lucas (1973) and is as follows. Production in industry i at time t, Q_t^i, is generated by

$$Q_t^i = \alpha_i[P_t^i - E(P_t|\Omega_t^i)] + \lambda_i Q_{t-1}^i \quad (0 < \alpha_i,\ 0 < \lambda_i < 1). \tag{7}$$

Changes in Q_t^i are caused basically by *perceived relative prices* $P_t^i - E(P_t|\Omega_t^i)$. Here P_t^i is the log of the price level in the ith industry at time t, and $E(P_t|\Omega_t^i)$ is the expected value of the log of the *general* price level, P_t, conditional on information available in industry i at time t, Ω_t^i. I follow Lucas by assuming that Q_{t-1}^i appears in (7), but a more general lag pattern would not affect the results we are most interested in. To be specific, the macro ratio ((14) below) is kept intact.

The economics behind this model is well known. The information available to suppliers in the ith industry at t comes from two sources, one macro, the other micro. First, firms enter period t with a knowledge of the past course of observable macro variables such as Y_{t-j}, $P_{t-j}(j = 1, 2,\ldots)$. While this information does not permit exact inferences of the log of the current general price level, P_t, it does determine a prior distribution on P_t, common to firms in all markets. I assume that this distribution is known to be normal, with mean $\bar{P}_t$ and a constant conditional variance σ_p^2.

Second, I suppose that the actual price in the ith industry deviates from the economy-wide average by an amount that is distributed independently of P_t. Specifically, let the percentage deviation of the price in the ith industry from the average P_t be denoted by Z_t^i, where Z_t^i is normally distributed with mean zero and variance τ_i^2, and Z_t^i is distributed independently of P_t. Note that this τ_i^2 summarizes the firm's past observation on the sizes of *relative price variation*. Then the observed price in industry i, P_t^i (in logs), is the sum of two independent, normal variables:

$$P_t^i = P_t + Z_t^i. \tag{8}$$

The information set Ω_t^i relevant for estimation of the unobserved (by suppliers in industry i at time t) P_t then consists of the observed price P_t^i and the price history summarized in $\bar{P}_t$.

To utilize this information, suppliers use (8) to calculate the distribution of P_t, conditional on P_t^i and $\bar{P}_t$. This distribution is normal with mean θ_i and variance σ_p^2. Here we have

$$E(P_t \mid \Omega_t^i) = E(P_t \mid P_t^i, \bar{P}_t) = (1 - \theta_i)P_t^i + \theta_i \bar{P}_t, \tag{9}$$

$$\theta_i = \frac{\tau_i^2}{\sigma_p^2 + \tau_i^2}. \tag{10}$$

From (7) and (9), we then obtain

$$Q_t^i = \alpha_i \theta_i (P_t^i - \bar{P}_t) + \lambda_i Q_{t-1}^i. \tag{11}$$

Using (8), we can rewrite (11) as

$$Q_t^i = \alpha_i \theta_i (Z_t^i + P_t - \bar{P}_t) + \lambda_i Q_{t-1}^i. \tag{12}$$

In a similar fashion, we can obtain the corresponding macro equation,

$$Y_t = \alpha\theta(P_t - \bar{P}_t) + \lambda Y_{t-1}. \tag{13}$$

Here, α, θ and λ are the average values of α_i, θ_i and λ_i respectively. α, θ and λ may actually be values that are averaged over much broader sectors than the ones explicitly considered in the present analysis.

Now, (12) and (13), which were derived from a specification of rational expectations monetary theory, correspond to the equations estimated in the previous section. Z_t^i and $P_t - \bar{P}_t$ in (12) are what I called the industry-specific micro shock and macro shock, respectively.

As Lucas (1973) argued, a proper test of the theory embodied in (12) cannot be performed using time-series data alone, since the parameter θ_i is not really a constant, but varies systematically (recall (10)). Here we need cross-sectional information. Lucas himself used aggregate cross-country data, an approach that is somewhat problematic. Despite all the institutional differences, he directly compares hyperinflationary economies such as Argentina with those of Japan and the United States. In contrast, the present analysis uses inter-industry information within one country to test the theory. I believe that this is more consistent with the theory than the cross-country test.

From (12) and (13), it is easy to calculate the macro ratio in the previous section. The macro ratio in (12) is given by

$$\frac{\sigma_p^2}{\tau_i^2 + \sigma_p^2} = 1 - \theta_i . \tag{14}$$

Note that this ratio is independent of α_i and λ_i, which differ among industries. Since we have already obtained an estimate of the macro ratio, to test the theory in question we can compare this with (14). In (14), τ_i^2 is the *unconditional* variance of the relative price in industry i, and σ_p^2 is the variance of the general price *conditional only on the macro variables*. I perform two different tests.

In the first test, I directly calculate (14). τ_i^2 can be easily obtained as the variance of $(P_t^i - P_t)$. Here P_t^i is the wholesale price index (WPI) for the products of the ith industry, and P_t is the GNP deflator (both in logs). Since σ_p^2 is the variance of the general price level conditional only on aggregate information, I estimate the macro price equation,

$$P_t = \sum_{i=1}^{8} b_i P_{t-i} + \sum_{i=1}^{8} c_i M_{t-i} + \sum_{i=1}^{8} d_i Y_{t-i} + \eta_t, \tag{15}$$

and then use the variance of the residuals of this estimated equation as a proxy for σ_p^2 in (14). Here M_t is M2 + CD and Y_t is real GNP (both in logs). The estimates of (15), and the macro ratios (14) obtained in this way, are shown in Tables 2.6 and 2.7, respectively.

Table 2.6. Regression estimates for equation (15)

Sample	Constant	b_i	c_i	d_i	$\bar{R}^2$	$Q(d.f.)$	Conditional variance
1962(II)–	-0.364×10^{-4}	0.711	0.405	0.244	0.969	9.7(21)	0.0000806
1974(IV)	(−0.0141)	(19.4)	(4.59)	(1.93)			
1975(I)–	−0.0203	0.979	0.175	−0.227	0.991	8.88(18)	0.0000489
1984(III)	(−3.289)	(8.16)	(8.40)	(0.77)			

Note: Figures in square brackets are *F*-values.

Table 2.7. The macro ratio (equation (14) in the text)

Industry	Sample period	
	1962(II)–1974(IV)	1975(I)–1984(III)
Iron and steel	0.0086	0.0045
Nonferrous metals	0.0045	0.0039
Fabricated metals	0.0085	0.0052
Industrial machinery	0.0143	0.0074
Electrical machinery	0.0327	0.0164
Transportation equipment	0.0328	0.0147
Ceramics	0.0103	0.0048
Chemicals	0.0072	0.0028
Petroleum	0.0104	0.0049
Paper and pulp	0.0052	0.0033
Textiles	0.0111	0.0136
Wood	0.0059	0.0044
Food	0.0190	0.0051

Theoretically, these ratios must be equal to the macro ratio obtained previously (Table 2.5). I tested this equality by running the regression

$$MR_1^i = e + fMR_2^i + \varepsilon_i. \tag{16}$$

Here MR_1^i is the macro ratio of the ith industry obtained previously (shown in Table 2.5) and MR_2^i is the ratio derived here (shown in Table 2.7). The estimation results for (16) are listed in Table 2.8. The theoretical model requires that the coefficient of MR_2^i, f, be one and that the constant be zero. Table 2.8 shows that MR_2 bears no relation to MR_1 and that the restrictions of the coefficient are rejected.

Table 2.8. Regression estimates for equation (16)

Sample	Constant	f	$\bar{R}^2$	*F*-values for restriction of two coefficients	
1962(II)–1984(III)	0.401	3.66	– 0.03	$F(2,24)$	40.78[a]
	(5.19)	(0.61)			
1962(II)–1974(IV)	0.624	−7.79	0.02	$F(2,11)$	32.68[a]
	(5.61)	(−1.12)			
1975(I)–1984(III)	0.147	29.64	0.33	$F(2,11)$	26.60[a]
	(1.56)	(2.61)			

Note: Figures in parentheses are *t*-values.

[a] The restrictions are rejected at 1% significance level.

Above I used equation (15) to obtain the variance of the general price level conditional only on the macro variables. One problem associated with this test, however, is that the macro price equation (15) may not be structural; in other words, it may not be invariant under different policy regimes. Taking this possibility into account, I performed another test, which is much more in accord with the spirit of rational expectations. For this purpose, I needed an equation to describe aggregate demand in the economy. Here, following Lucas (1973), I assume

$$Y_t + P_t = M_t. \tag{17}$$

where M_t is taken as the log of either *nominal* GNP or the money supply, which is in any case determined by government policies. The private sector's knowledge about government policies is summarized in the subjective distribution of $(M_t - M_{t-1})$, which under the rational expectations hypothesis is identical to the objective distribution of the variable. To be more precise, again in line with Lucas (1973), assume that $(M_t - M_{t-1})$ is a sequence of independent, normal variables with mean m and variance σ_m^2. Then, in the Appendix to this chapter, I show that σ_p^2 in (14) is, for small σ_m^2, an increasing function of σ_m^2:

$$\sigma_p^2 = h(\sigma_m^2), \; h(0) = 0, \; h' > 0. \tag{18}$$

We approximate the h function in (18) by the linear function

$$\sigma_p^2 = a\sigma_m^2, \quad a = h'(0) = \frac{1}{(1+\alpha)^2}, \quad 0 < a < 1. \tag{19}$$

This linear approximation is possible when both σ_p^2 and σ_m^2 take on small values, which is indeed the case. Then the macro ratio in each industry in (14) becomes

$$\frac{\sigma_p^2}{\tau_i^2 + \sigma_p^2} = \frac{ar_i}{1 + (a-1)r_i}. \tag{20}$$

where

$$r_i = \frac{\sigma_m^2}{\sigma_m^2 + \tau_i^2} \tag{21}$$

Since σ_m^2 is the *unconditional* variance of the rate of change in either nominal GNP or the money supply, we can easily calculate r_i (Table 2.9). Equation (20) implies that the macro ratios shown in Table 2.5 are nonlinear functions of r_i. Note that the parameter a in (20) must be strictly less than one; if a is one, α becomes zero, and this means that the aggregate supply function, the most important

Table 2.9. Estimates of r_i

Industry	Sample	
	1962(II)–1974(IV)	1975(I)–1984(III)
Iron and steel	0.283	0.267
Nonferrous metals	0.166	0.243
Fabricated metals	0.280	0.296
Industrial machinery	0.396	0.374
Electrical machinery	0.605	0.573
Transportation equipment	0.606	0.545
Ceramics	0.321	0.281
Chemicals	0.248	0.185
Petroleum	0.321	0.281
Paper and pulp	0.193	0.208
Textiles	0.337	0.526
Wood	0.212	0.263
Food	0.468	0.290

building block of the theory, is non-existent. I estimated a in (20) by a nonlinear regression, and then tested whether it actually lies between zero and one. The results are shown in Table 2.10. For the pre-first-oil-shock period, the estimated coefficient is significantly different from one. Since the estimated coefficient of a does not take on a value strictly less than one in either period, the test once again rejects the rational-expectations-based monetary theory of business cycles.

The Nature of Real Shocks: The Importance of Construction Demand

We found above that the monetary theory of business cycles is inconsistent with the post-war Japanese experience. From a different

Table 2.10. Estimation of equation (20)[a]

$$MR_1^i = \frac{ar_i}{1 + (a - 1)r_i} + \hat{\varepsilon}_i$$

Sample	a	SE
1962(II)–1974(IV)	2.492 (2.62)	0.315
1975(I)–1984(III)	1.086 (4.22)	0.182

[a] Figures in parentheses are t-values; $\hat{\varepsilon}_i$ is the estimated residual.

angle, Chapter 9 also shows that monetarism does not make sense in the case of the Japanese economy. This suggests that real shocks have been very important forces in generating business cycles in Japan. The next problem is to explore what kind of real shocks were important. To answer this question, I again refer to the macro ratios derived previously.

Since business cycles are a phenomenon of changes in the aggregate economy, clearly we need to focus on industries with high macro ratios. For convenience, I have summarized the previously obtained macro ratios (Table 2.5) in Table 2.11. As the table indicates, in the period of rapid economic growth during the 1960s, the industries with high macro ratios were (1) chemicals, (2) fabricated metals, (3) ceramics, stone, and clay products, (4) pulp, paper, and paper products, and (5) wood and wood products. Remarkably, all of these industries, with the exception of chemicals, are very closely linked to the construction industry and construction projects. For example, according to the 1980 Japanese Input–Output table, the ¥18 trillion worth of manufacturing production generated by construction projects (both private and public) was allotted among industries as

Table 2.11. A comparison of macro ratios: changes in the relative contribution of macroeconomic shocks to output fluctuations, 1959–73 and 1974–

	Rapid growth period (1959–73)	Post-first-oil-shock period (1974–present)
Iron and steel	0.48	0.48
Nonferrous metals and products	0.24	0.05
Fabricated metals	0.81	0.04
Industrial machinery	0.36	0.47
Electrical machinery	0.46	0.72
Transportation equipment	0.46	0.46
Precision instruments	0.01	0.24
Ceramics, stone, and clay products	0.81	0.19
Chemicals (excl. medicine, drugs)	0.83	0.53
Medicine and drugs	0.18	0.37
Petroleum and coal products	0.37	0.37
Pulp, paper, and paper products	0.66	0.31
Textiles	0.42	0.62
Wood and wood products	0.76	0.02
Food and tobacco	0.13	0.38
Rubber products	0.37	0.37

follows: fabricated metals, ¥5 trillion; ceramics, stone, and clay products, ¥5 trillion; paper and wood products, ¥4 trillion; others, ¥4 trillion. Conversely, production in the four industries singled out above is generated mostly by construction. Therefore, there is a strong one-to-one correspondence between production in industries with high macro ratios and in construction activity in general. This suggests that aggregate fluctuations in the 1960s are construction-related.

Given this finding, I next carried out a Granger causality test for Japanese real GNP and investment.[6] Table 2.12 shows that investment causes real GNP in the sense of Granger during the pre-first-oil-shock period of rapid growth, but not during the post-first-oil-shock period. These findings infer that Japanese business cycles in the 1960s are construction-induced. In the next section, I will discuss this point in greater detail.

If in fact business cycles in Japan in the 1960s *were* related to construction activity, there still remains the important question: is the variability of construction largely demand-induced, or is it supply-related? As I noted earlier, Keynes (1936) and Keynesians

Table 2.12. Causality test between investment and GNP, 1953–1983[a]

From	To	F
1953(II)–1983(IV)		
Investment	GNP	3.51[b]
GNP	Investment	0.89
1953(II)–1973(IV)		
Investment	GNP	2.84[b]
GNP	Investment	0.73
1974(I)–1983(IV)		
Investment	GNP	1.71
GNP	Investment	1.04

[a] 8-period lags.
[b] Significance at the 5% level.

[6] The variables are the time-detrended natural logarithms of the original variables. I note that construction is, of course, not exactly equal to investment but is its most important component. In 1980, the ¥49 trillion of private investment consisted of ¥32 trillion of construction and ¥17 trillion of investment in machinery and other investment. Public investment (¥23 trillion) consisted of construction (¥19 trillion) and other investments (¥4 trillion).

emphasize the importance of the demand side, whereas recent real business cycle theorists such as Kydland and Prescott (1982) and Long and Plosser (1983) stress the role of direct technological shocks to production functions.[7] It is of course very difficult to conduct a formal econometric test to determine which view is more acceptable. As I explain below, however, the data seem to favour the Keynesian position.

Kuroda *et al.* (1986) estimated, for manufacturing industries, the growth rates of total factor productivity (TFP) for two sample periods. Their estimates of TFP growth take into account inter-industry propagation effects through the input–output matrix (a point emphasized by Long and Plosser 1983), and therefore are particularly useful for our analysis. The figures in Table 2.13 are the ratios of each industry's growth rate of TFP to overall average: they are measures of the *relative* importance of an industry's growth rate of TFP after taking into account inter-industry repercussion effects. If direct productivity shocks to production functions are in fact the most important generating force to business cycles, then we should expect a positive correlation between the macro ratios in Table 2.11 and the TFP data in Table 2.13.[8] A comparison of the two tables, however, immediately shows that the TFP figures for the four construction-related industries with high macro ratios are quite low.

More formally, we can test whether there is a positive correlation between the two measures. This test statistic is shown as 'rho' in the last row of Table 2.13: it is not significantly different from zero for either sample period. I therefore conclude that *movements in construction were demand-induced rather than supply-induced.* In other words, fluctuations in construction in the 1960s did not occur because of technological innovations in such industries as fabricated metals, ceramics, paper products, and wood, but rather because of investment *demand.*

[7] It is very doubtful that these direct technological shocks to production functions are significant enough to generate aggregate fluctuations, because most new technologies are embodied in investment, leaving unchanged the productivity of the existing stock. Because of the time-to-build delay, only future capital's productivity is affected, and hence technological changes correspond to investment *demand* shocks rather than to supply shocks, as in real business cycle theories. Greenwood *et al.* (1988) take this issue into their analysis. For other criticisms of real business cycle theories, see Summers (1986).

[8] As Long and Plosser (1983) and Kuroda *et al.* (1986) show, the largest response is usually in the sector where the shock originates.

Table 2.13. Measures of total factor productivity, 1960–9 and 1973–1979

	1960–9	1973–9
Iron and steel	3.57	2.97
Nonferrous metals and products	0.99	0.88
Fabricated metals	0.50	0.65
Industrial machinery	0.93	1.03
Electrical machinery	0.95	0.99
Motor vehicles	1.09	1.02
Transportation equipment	0.33	0.49
Precision instruments	0.22	0.57
Ceramics, stone, and clay products	0.66	0.76
Chemicals (excl. med. and drugs)	2.30	1.85
Petroleum and coal products	1.01	1.31
Pulp, paper, and paper products	1.51	1.30
Textiles	2.24	1.54
Wood and wood products	0.80	0.77
Food and tobacco	0.51	0.79
Rubber products	0.59	0.57
Rho[a]	0.23	0.41
	(0.40)	(0.13)

[a] See text for the correlation. The figures in parentheses are the probabilities of obtaining the estimated values under the hypothesis that the correlations are zero.

Source: Data are from Kuroda *et al.* (1986).

2.2 THE PERIOD OF RAPID ECONOMIC GROWTH AND ITS END

The conclusion that fluctuations in the 1960s was generated by investment demand, particularly in construction investment, leads us to seek the factors lying behind the high and volatile investment that brought about an unprecedentedly rapid economic growth.

The Mechanism Generating Rapid Economic Growth

Table 2.14 shows the correlation of investment across industries for two periods. We observe strong parallels in investment across various sectors during the high-growth period. This means that economy-wide rather than industry-specific factors spurred investment demand in the 1960s.

Several factors are believed to have contributed to rapid economic growth of the Japanese economy during the 1950s and 1960s. The

Table 2.14. Correlations of investment across industries, 1966–1972 and 1973–1985

	Food	Text	Pulp	Chem.	Iron	Nonfer.	Fab.	Gen.	E. Mach.	Trans.	Elec.	Serv.
1966(I)–1972(IV)												
Food	1.00											
Textiles	−0.14	1.00										
Pulp and paper	0.06	0.50	1.00									
Chemicals	0.47	0.49	0.48	1.00								
Iron and steel	−0.14	0.15	0.10	0.22	1.00							
Nonferrous metals	0.46	−0.15	0.27	0.46	0.30	1.00						
Fabricated metals	0.32	0.40	0.22	0.39	0.29	0.15	1.00					
General machinery	0.31	0.51	0.37	0.66	0.46	0.30	0.75	1.00				
Electrical machinery	0.23	0.51	0.31	0.59	0.61	0.37	0.67	0.84	1.00			
Transportation equipment	0.45	0.46	0.53	0.46	0.40	0.30	0.56	0.60	0.66	1.00		
Electricity	0.16	0.40	0.33	0.42	0.02	0.12	0.02	0.12	0.38	0.27	1.00	
Services	−0.30	0.24	0.06	0.10	−0.07	−0.20	−0.28	−0.09	0.19	−0.30	0.45	1.00
1973(I)–1985(I)												
Food	1.00											
Textiles	0.12	1.00										
Pulp and paper	0.21	0.13	1.00									
Chemicals	0.03	−0.11	0.33	1.00								
Iron and steel	−0.12	0.08	−0.29	−0.04	1.00							
Nonferrous metals	0.06	0.05	0.15	0.20	−0.14	1.00						
Fabricated metals	0.06	0.13	0.18	0.02	−0.28	0.18	1.00					
General machinery	0.20	0.28	0.10	0.12	−0.31	0.07	0.32	1.00				
Electrical machinery	0.16	0.30	−0.04	−0.16	−0.25	0.03	0.56	0.52	1.00			
Transportation equipment	0.20	−0.17	−0.01	−0.03	−0.21	0.20	0.24	0.36	0.51	1.00		
Electricity	−0.12	−0.05	0.02	−0.37	−0.05	−0.50	0.14	0.04	0.16	0.01	1.00	
Services	0.18	0.38	0.02	−0.10	−0.06	−0.31	0.26	0.34	0.53	0.22	−0.03	1.00

abundance of importable foreign technology is often mentioned as one such factor. A sharp decline in marine transport costs is another. Total factor productivity in marine transportation grew at the annual rate of 10% in the post-war era compared with 2%–3% in the pre-war period. This naturally gave a leverage to resource-poor Japanese economy. In fact, Wright (1990) argues that the origins of US industrial success lie in that country's uniquely rich endowment of natural resources in an era of high transport costs, and that this advantage has been eroded as a sharp decline in marine transport costs has made natural resources commodities, rather than part of the 'factor endowment' of individual countries, in the post-war era. Granted that these factors are very important, I shall suggest that demographic trends played a particularly important role in the process of rapid economic growth.[9]

Recall that the Japanese economy in the 1950s and 1960s was a two-sector economy consisting of a rural agricultural sector and an urban manufacturing sector. In 1950, nearly half of the total labour force was still engaged in agriculture (see Table 5.1 below). However, in the process of economic growth, population began to flow from the countryside into the towns. The dual structure of the economy enabled the manufacturing sector to hire labour at a level of real wages which, given a degree of 'disguised' unemployment in the agricultural sector, was lower than the marginal product in the industrial sector. Growth of the manufacturing sector, therefore, could lead to high profits in that sector rather than to an increase in real wages. The high profits in turn were supposed to induce a high rate of investment. All this is, of course, what Lewis (1954) describes as a typical process of growth of the underdeveloped dual economy.

The Lewis model has been successfully applied to the century-long development of the Japanese economy by a number of economists (see e.g. Ohkawa and Rosovsky 1973; Minami 1968, 1970; and Inada *et al.* 1992). In the Lewis model, however, population flow between two sectors is taken to be solely the *result* of the growth of the modern manufacturing sector. Umemura (1961), Minami (1970), and Ono (1972) demonstrate that internal migration was in fact quite sensitive to the growth of the manufacturing sector; more people left rural agricultural areas for urban industrial cities in booms, and vice

[9] Economists such as Keynes (1937*a*) and A. Hansen (1939) have, in fact, noted the significant effects that demographic factors exert on the macroeconomy.

versa. Yearly fluctuations of population flow were therefore a result of industrial growth. In the Lewis model, the key factor behind this industrial growth is the low real wages made possible by the existence of disguised unemployment in the agricultural sector. However, in contrast to the Lewis model, in what follows I argue that, in the case of the post-war Japanese economic growth (1955–70), population flows between two sectors comprised the major factor generating high demand for products of the industrial sector; that is, in my view, population flow was a *cause* as well as a result of economic growth.

According to Lewis's theory, population is supposed to flow continuously from the rural agricultural sector to the urban industrial sector, as actually happened in Japan. Among Asian developing countries, however, this population flow occurred substantially in only a few countries. For example, the rate of population outflow from the agricultural sector is about 4% on average for Korea and Taiwan, whereas it is merely 1% for Phillippines and Indonesia. Besides, the major absorbing sector in Korea and Taiwan is the manufacturing industry, while in Phillippines and Indonesia it is actually service sector. One might argue that service sector would qualify as a 'modern' sector. In fact, Watanabe and Adachi (1992) estimate the percentage of 'modern' services in the service sector as a whole as mere 12%–14% for the Phillippines and Indonesia; the rest centres on the urban 'informal' sector, which includes all sorts of odd jobs on the street from selling peanuts to drawing a *becha*.

Thus, Lewis's theory does not actually hold for many developing countries. The basic problem of the theory is that growth of the modern industrial sector is sustained by high profits guaranteed by repressed real wages, while demand for products in such modern industrial sector is assumed to emerge automatically as production grows; in reality, however, demand does not automatically emerge.

The post-war Japanese growth during the period 1955–70 was basically led by domestic demand, and in this process, population flow and household formation played a crucial role. Because of the large-scale population flows (see Fig. 2.2), the number of households dramatically increased during the period of high economic growth, as explained above (Fig. 2.3). I emphasize the fact that in this period the growth rate of households formed a hump shape at a high level, while the growth rate of population was quite stable at a much lower level of about 1%. As a result, for two decades beginning in 1955,

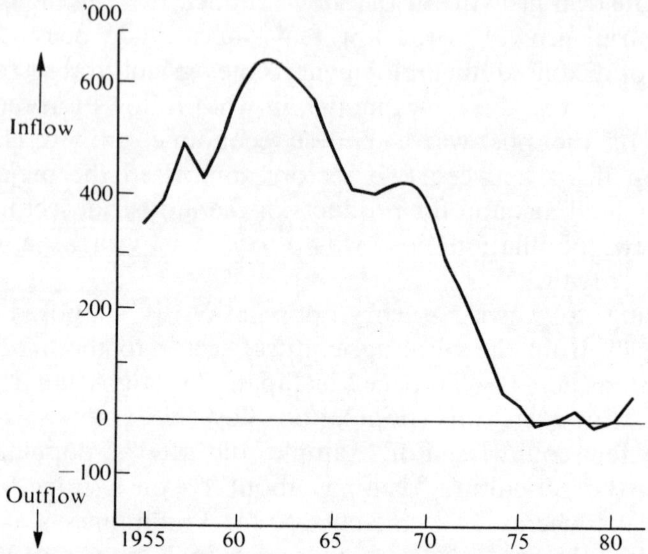

Fig. 2.2. Population flow, 1955–1980
Inflow into and outflow out of the Tokyo, Osaka, and Nagoya metropolitan areas.
Source: Statistical Bureau, Management and Co-ordination Agency, *Annual Report on Internal Migration.*

population in Japan increased from 90 million to 110 million, i.e. by 20%, while the number of households increased by 80%.

Table 2.15 records household formation during this period by types of household. Traditional, three-generation merged households hardly increased. Instead, 'core' or 'nuclear' households, consisting of a married couple, possibly with unmarried children, and unmarried single households dramatically increased, particularly in urban

Table 2.15. Growth of households by type, 1955–1975 ('000)

	1955	1975
'Core' households, consisting of a married couple possibly with unmarried children	10,366	19,980
Three-generation-merged households	6,353	6,988
Unmarried single households	596	4,236

Source: Statistical Bureau, Management and Co-ordination Agency, *Annual Report on Households.*

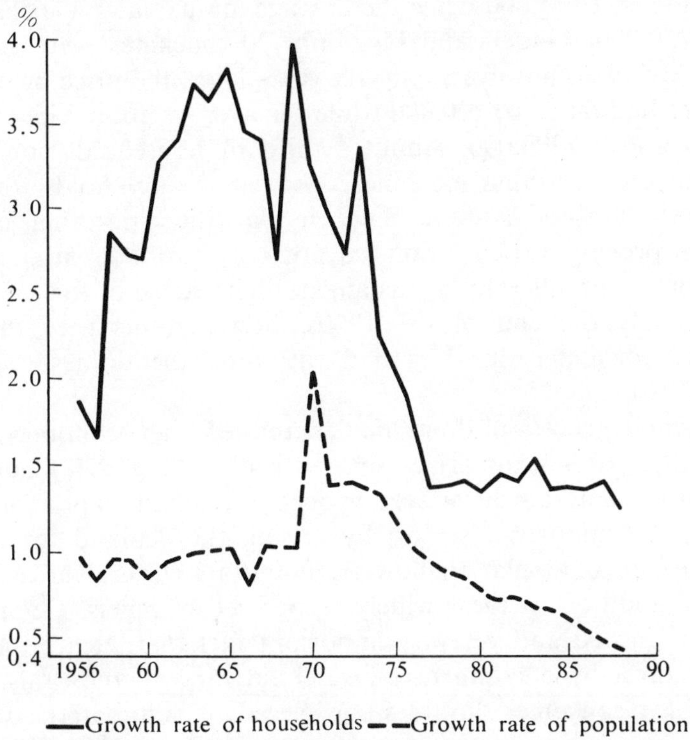

Fig. 2.3. Growth rates of household and population
The figure 1970 is an outlier; Okinawa prefecture (Ryukyu Island) was returned to Japan by the United States in 1970.

industrial areas. As previously mentioned, when three generations of family members kept a traditional single household in rural villages, each such household would have needed only one refrigerator, television set, washing machine, and car. When young people left their rural villages for urban industrial areas, they formed new households. Each of these new households necessarily generated additional demand for houses, consumer durables, and electricity. In this way, the rural–urban population flow sustained high domestic demand in the period of high economic growth, 1955–70.

Along with the creation of a larger number of households, the high growth period saw the diffusion of newly available consumer durables. This diffusion was facilitated by the steady decline in prices of those products over time on the one hand, and an increase in incomes on the other. Electric washing machines, for example, first appeared in the Japanese market in 1949; at the time, a machine cost ¥54,000 while the average annual labour income was about ¥50,000. Understandably, only 20 machines were sold per month! By 1955, however, only six years later, the price of washing machines had fallen to ¥20,000 while the average annual income had risen to above ¥200,000. About a third of households could then afford to own washing machines. The same story holds for other consumer durables as well. Since it was the cities that led this diffusion process, urbanization led not only to the creation of new households but also to a sustained high demand for consumer durables. By the end of the 1960s, however, most of the then available consumer durables had saturated the domestic market (Table 2.16).

This whole process of domestic demand-led high economic growth during 1955–70 is summarized schematically in Fig. 2.4. Channels 1 and 2 in the diagram have been widely recognized: capital accumulation in the industrial sector, by raising the demand for labour, brings about a population flow from the agricultural areas to the cities. In addition to these widely recognized channels, I emphasize the oft-neglected and yet very important fact that such population flow, in turn, by creating new households and thereby raising the demand for consumer durables and electricity, ultimately sustained

Table 2.16. Diffusion of consumer durables, 1959–1974 (%)

	Urban industrial areas	Rural agricultural areas
Refrigerators		
1959	11.1	3.4
1964	77.6	57.7
1969	97.5	91.2
1974	107.2	108.2
Washing machines		
1959	44.2	24.4
1964	85.9	76.5
1969	99.9	97.0
1974	101.8	102.9
Black and white TV sets[a]		
1959	42.9	23.5
1964	110.5	101.4
1969	118.1 (27.0)	110.3 (22.7)
1974	— (107.2)	— (106.0)

[a] Figures for colour TV sets are given in parentheses for 1969 and 1974.

Source: Economic Planning Agency, *Survey of Household Consumption*.

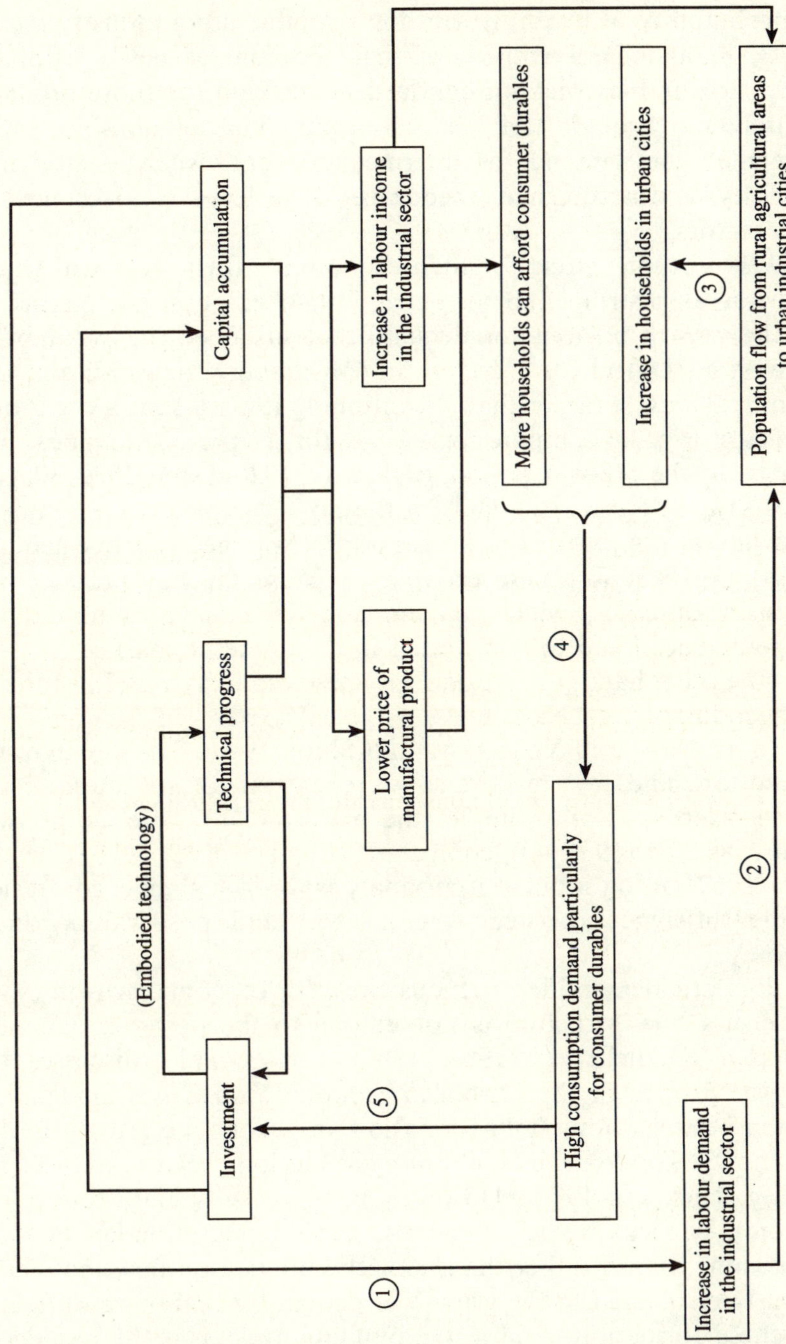

Fig. 2.4. Domestic-demand-led high economic growth of the Japanese economy, 1955–1970

the profitability of investment in the manufacturing industry (channels 3, 4, and 5). I emphasize that the role of newly available consumer durables was not confined to demand for those products themselves: through the input–output interrelationship, they augmented the demand for intermediate goods such as steel and electricity, and accordingly encouraged high levels of investment in those sectors.

In this virtuous circle for high economic growth, low real wages were not as instrumental as Lewis (1954) emphasized. Rather, it was the growth of domestic demand that sustained the profitability of investment. And for a growth in consumption demand, a steady rise in real wages, rather than a continuing low wage, is a contributing factor. Fig. 2.5 compares real wages for the pre-war and post-war periods. In the pre-war period, except for 1920–1 and 1929–30, real wages saw little increase, while in the post-war period they enjoyed steady growth. A steady rise in real wages sustained effective demand for the post-war Japanese economy because the key product was consumer durables, which, having not yet achieved international competitiveness, had to find outlets in the domestic market.

On the other hand, the pre-war Japanese economy was, like today's newly industrialized economies, a typical export-led economy (see Shinohara 1961, and Yoshikawa and Shioji 1990). The key industry was cotton, and low real wages were critical for its international competitiveness. For example, the export–GNP ratio in pre-war Japan was 20% (1931–40), compared with 10% in 1955–70. Chenery *et al.* (1962), using input–output analysis, drew a similar conclusion on the differences between the pre-war and post-war Japanese economy.

A domestic-demand-led virtuous circle for economic growth based on Lewis's dual structure is not unique to the post-war Japanese economy. Kindleberger (1967, 1989), for example, discusses the post-war growth of the European economy in a Lewis model. The relation between household formation and economic growth is also well known. The so-called building cycle has long been acknowledged (see e.g. Hickman 1974). However, in the case of the pre-war US economy, particularly before the restrictive immigration law of 1924, it was immigration rather than domestic population flow that endogenously responded to the growth of demand for labour and fuelled household formation. And in the building cycle, it is the residential construction industry that creates the link between household formation and economic growth.

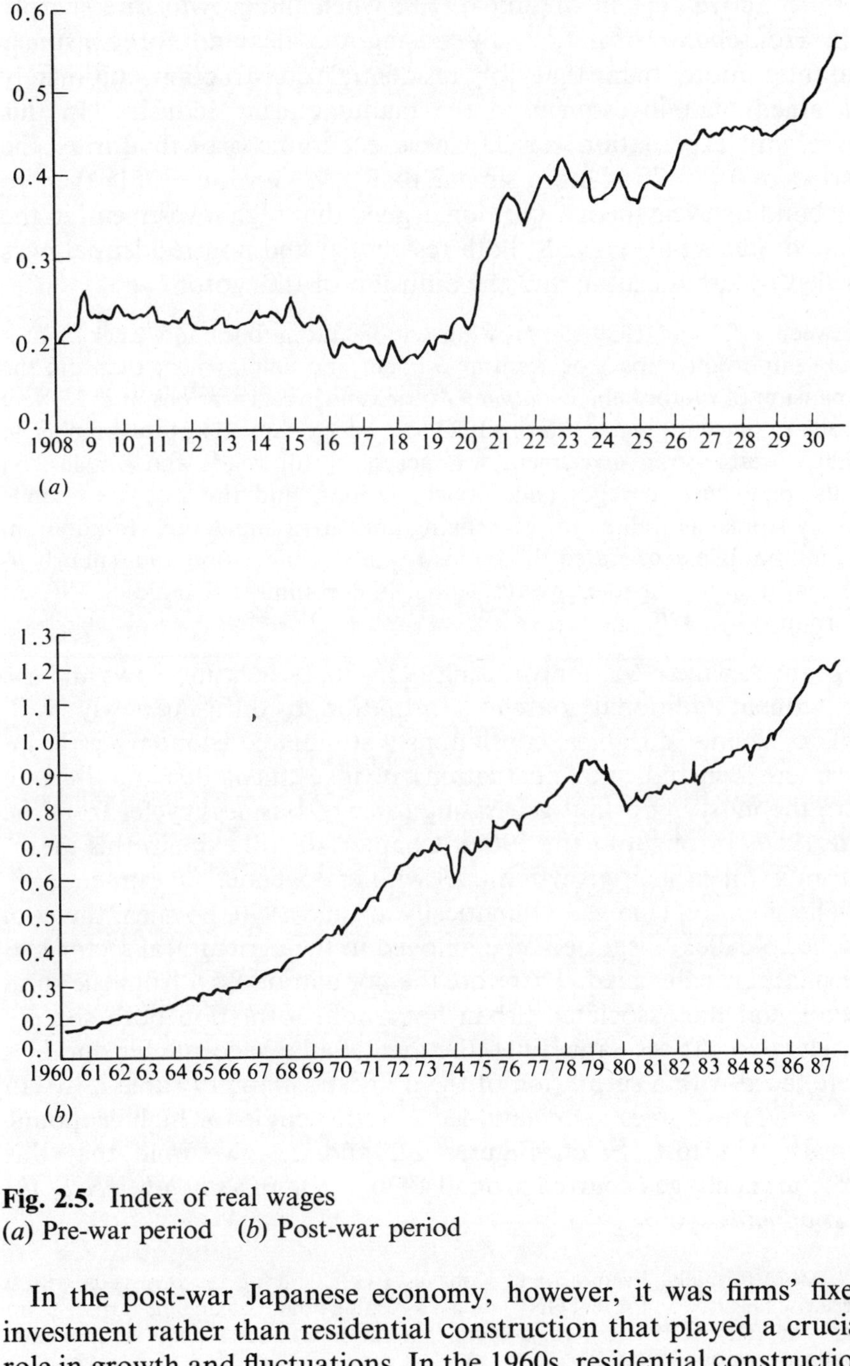

Fig. 2.5. Index of real wages
(*a*) Pre-war period (*b*) Post-war period

In the post-war Japanese economy, however, it was firms' fixed investment rather than residential construction that played a crucial role in growth and fluctuations. In the 1960s, residential construction accounted for less than half of total private construction. Its share rose to above 70% in the mid-1970s, when the growth rate sharply fell. Household formation, by raising the demand for consumer durables more than that for residential construction, ultimately sustained high investment in the manufacturing industry. In this sense, my explanation for Japanese economic growth during the period of 1955–70 is more similar to R. A. Gordon (1951) than to the building cycle theory. Gordon argued that high investment, in the United States in the 1920s, both residential and non-residential, was fuelled by urbanization and the diffusion of the motor car:

> Between 1923 and 1929 the growing *use* of automobiles and trucks had a more important impact on total investment and employment than did the expansion of motor vehicle *output*. Motor vehicle registrations in 1929 were about 75 percent greater than in 1923 and nearly three times the number in 1920. . . . large-scale investment was necessary for roads and bridges, oil wells, pipe lines, garages and service stations, and tire and automobile supply stores, as well as for oil refining and tire manufacture. In addition, the automobile accelerated the trends toward urbanization and 'suburbanization,' stimulating thereby residential and commercial building. (R. A. Gordon, 1951: 130)

In the Japanese economy during 1955–70, population flows and the consequent additional household formation, by diffusing newly available consumer durables, continuously stimulated economy-wide investment demand, and fluctuations in investment demand were in turn the most important generating force of business cycles from the late 1950s throughout the 1960s. Chapter 10 will explain this mechanism in an explicit growth model with endogenous investment.

The situation changed dramatically around 1970. By then, the pool of the so-called 'disguised' unemployed in the agricultural sector had been largely exhausted. Therefore the population flow from the rural sector and the associated urban household formation both sharply decelerated. At the same time, the then available consumer durables were faced with a saturation of the domestic market (Table 2.16). In this way, the domestic-demand-led virtuous circle for high economic growth was lost. From Figures 2.2 and 2.3, we note that this structural change occurred around 1970, *a few years in advance of the first oil embargo in 1973*.[10]

[10] More formally, Iwamoto and Kobayashi (1992), using the regression with a piecewise linear trend for real GNP, sought a turning point. Rolling the turning point from 1969(III) to 1974(II), they found that the point that attains the minimum standard error is 1971(IV).

The structural change is clearly seen for individual industries as well as for the macroeconomy. We can refer to Table 1.3, which shows the time series of capacity and investment in the petrochemical industry. By the end of 1960s, the industry had faced the major turning-point (Watanabe and Saeki 1984). The situation of the industry was typical rather than exceptional. Then the first oil shock hit the Japanese economy, which had already undergone structural change caused by domestic factors explained above.

Before we turn to the post-high-growth period beginning the 1970s, I will review other explanations for the end of Japan's high economic growth.

Other Explanations for the End of Rapid Economic Growth

I explained the end of rapid growth during the period 1955–70 by the domestic structural change of the Japanese economy which had occurred by the end of the 1960s, before the first oil embargo in 1973–4; Chapter 10 provides an explicit model. A popular view, on the other hand, attributes the end of high growth to the first oil shock. There are two slightly different explanations.

Bruno and Sachs (1985) explicitly introduce raw materials and energy into a gross production function. In this analysis, the firm is assumed to maximize the present value of the following net cash flow:

$$\int_0^{\infty} [Q_t - w_t L_t - \pi_t R_t - \phi(\alpha_t) K_t] e^{-rt} dt, \tag{22}$$

where w and r are real wages and the real interest rate, respectively. The gross output, including raw materials, Q, is produced according to the well-behaved production function,

$$Q = F(K, L, R), \tag{23}$$

where K, L, and R are capital, labour, and raw materials/energy, respectively. The value added in the economy as a whole or GNP, Y, is given by

$$Y = Q - \pi R, \tag{24}$$

where π is the real price of raw materials/energy.

Finally, the rate of capital accumulation, $\alpha = \dot{K}/K$, is subject to the convex adjustment cost $\phi(\alpha)$:

$$\phi(0) = 0, \ \phi'(0) = 1, \ \phi' > 0, \ \phi'' > 0. \tag{25}$$

Given the initial stock of capital K_0 and real factor prices, w, π, and r, the firm chooses the optimal time path of capital accumulation, and variable inputs L and R, so as to maximize (22). The necessary conditions for optimality are

$$\partial F/\partial L = w, \tag{26}$$

$$\partial F/\partial R = \pi, \tag{27}$$

and

$$\phi'(\alpha_t) = q_t, \tag{28}$$

$$q_t = \int_0^\infty \Delta_s \left[\frac{\partial F}{\partial K} - \phi(\alpha_s) \right] \mathrm{d}s, \tag{29}$$

where $\Delta_s = \exp[-\int_s^t (r - \alpha_u)\mathrm{d}u]$. Equations (28) and (29) imply Tobin's q theory of investment. Chapter 7 explains the problems of the q theory and demonstrates that the q theory does *not* actually hold under the plausible assumptions. For the moment, however, I will follow Bruno and Sachs in this regard.

In this framework, the oil shock can be identified with an unanticipated permanent increase in π at time 0. Our major concern is to see the effect of an increase in π on the growth rate, α. Equation (28) shows that α depends on q, while (29) shows that q in turn depends on the marginal product of capital, $\partial F/\partial K$. The effect of an increase in π on $\partial F/\partial K$ can be analysed by the factor price frontier shown in Fig. 2.6. A curve in the diagram corresponds to a particular π. Point A is the equilibrium where both capital and labour are fully employed at the real raw material/energy price π_0. On the assumption that production function (23) is weakly separable with respect to value added and raw materials/energy,

$$Q = F(V(K, L), R), \tag{30}$$

the factor price frontier homothetically shifts inwards when π is increased.[11]

The oil shock is therefore equivalent to a Hicks-neutral technical regress. For K and L to be fully employed, both real wages and the marginal product of capital must decrease. A decrease in the marginal product of capital becomes larger if, for any reason, a decline in real wages is not realized to an extent indicated by point C in the diagram. In any case, a decline in the marginal product of capital caused by an increase in the real raw material/energy price entails a

[11] Wago (1983) estimates the translog cost function dual to the production function, and finds a major structural change for 1974. Specifically, energy, R in the text, is a substitute for other inputs before the first oil shock, but it is a complement after the oil shock.

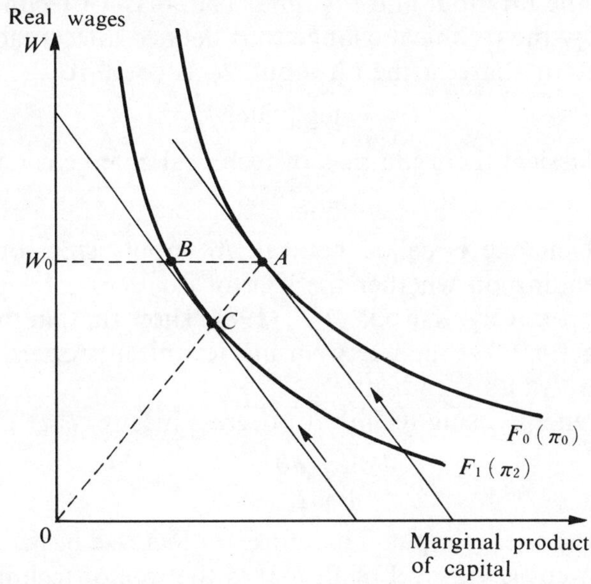

Fig. 2.6. Factor price frontier

decline in q, and accordingly a decline in the growth rate, α, *as long as the real interest rate does not proportionately decline*. This is the Bruno–Sachs explanation for deceleration of growth in terms of the oil shock.

Note that in this explanation the basic reason for growth deceleration lies in an inflexibility of the real interest rate. If the real interest rate declined proportionately with the marginal product of capital, then an increase in the real material/energy price would leave the growth rate intact. Bruno and Sachs (1985) emphasize the role of demand factors in their empirical analysis of worldwide stagflation in the 1970s, but analytically, demand and supply sides are not fully integrated. As explained above, their analytical framework focuses on the supply side. Chapter 4 introduces a way to integrate both demand and supply constraints within a unified framework, and also demonstrates that the demand constraints were indeed very important in the case of the Japanese economy in the 1970s.

Another approach, which focuses on the supply side of the economy to explain deceleration of growth, is Jorgenson (1988). Jorgenson emphasizes the bias of technical change. A technical change is expressed as $\partial F/\partial t$ in the following production function:

$$Q = F(X_1, \ldots, X_n, t), \tag{31}$$

where X_i is the ith input and t is time. The 'bias' of technical change indicates how the technical change thus defined affects factor shares. Since the factor share of the ith input, σ_i, is equal to

$$\sigma_i = \partial \log Q / \partial \log X_i \tag{32}$$

in the neoclassical theory, a bias of technical change is defined as

$$\partial \sigma_i / \partial t \gtreqless 0. \tag{33}$$

A technical change is called neutral, ith-input-using, or ith-input-saving depending on whether the sign of $\partial\sigma_i/\partial t$ is zero, positive, or negative, respectively. Kuroda *et al.* (1984) show that, in the Japanese economy of 1969–79, the energy-using technical progress was dominant in almost all the industries.

Now the energy-using technical progress means that

$$\frac{\partial(\partial \log Q/\partial t)}{\partial \log E} > 0, \tag{34}$$

where E is the energy input. Therefore, an increase in the real energy price, by lowering the level of E, makes the rate of technical change decelerate. This is the essence of the Jorgenson argument. The conclusion of his analysis is as follows:

> I have emphasized that there are important sources of the slowdown in Japan associated with the falloff in upgrading of the labor force. However, the most important single factor in the Japanese slowdown is the sharp decline in the rate of technical change. I have now succeeded in linking that decline directly to energy prices through the energy using bias of technical change in Japan. (Jorgenson 1988: 221)

Jorgenson's analysis rests entirely on traditional growth accounting. His result (Table 2.17) actually attributes nearly half of the fall in the rate of economic growth in the 1970s to capital input. And yet, noting that, 'after the energy crisis as well as before, the growth rate of capital input was higher than that of output', he argues that, 'rather than causing the slowdown, the growth of capital after the energy crisis contributed to the continued growth of output at unsustainable levels'. Thus, he concludes that 'the decline in the growth rate of capital is not the cause of the slowdown in Japanese economic growth'.

Capital accumulation is certainly not exogenous. But then, what brought about a fall in the rate of economic growth and thereby caused the decline in the growth rate of capital in the first place? Jorgenson's answer is, of course, a fall in the rate of technical change caused by the oil shock. In growth accounting, technical progress is

Table 2.17. Sources of economic growth (%)

	1960–79	1973–9
Average growth rate of:		
Net output	8.3	3.8
Capital input	9.6	6.0
Labour input	3.1	1.5
Rate of contribution to growth of:		
Capital input	5.0	2.9
(Quality)	(1.8)	(0.5)
(Quantity)	(3.2)	(2.4)
Labour input	1.5	0.8
(Quality)	(1.0)	(0.5)
(Hours worked)	(0.5)	(0.4)
Technical change	2.0	0.1

Source: Jorgenson (1988).

identified as that part of economic growth that cannot be explained by contributions of production factors, the so-called 'residual'. I argue, however, that whether or not the residual measured by the growth accounting method really captures technical progress is an open issue. Chapter 10 proposes an alternative interpretation.

These two approaches—Bruno and Sachs (1985) and Jorgenson (1988)—both attribute a fall in the rate of economic growth in the 1970s ultimately to the oil shock in 1973. Neither can explain, however, why the second oil shock which occurred in 1979 did not bring about a similar fall in the rate of economic growth; the average growth rates of real GNP for 1973–80 and 1981–90 are 4.1% and 4.2%, respectively. During the first oil crisis (1973–4) the oil price quadrupled, while in the second oil crisis (1979–80) it only doubled; so it might be argued that the first oil crisis hit the Japanese economy harder than the second one. But transfer payments to OPEC necessitated by an increase in the oil price, when seen as relative to GNP, were actually comparable during two oil crises: 3.8% and 4.1%, respectively. The supply-side analyses, such as Bruno and Sachs (1985) and Jorgenson (1988), which attribute a fall in the rate of economic growth to the first oil crisis, are therefore inconsistent with the fact that the second oil crisis did not entail a similar fall in the growth rate. Nor can they explain why the growth rate of the oil-importing South Korean economy fell so sharply during the second oil crisis while the effect of the first oil crisis was relatively small, just the opposite of the Japanese case. Chapter 4 will take up this problem again, maintaining that demand is an indispensable part of any reasonable explanation of what happened in the 1970s.

I do not mean to argue that the oil crisis did not affect the supply side of the Japanese economy at all, but I do argue that a permanent fall in the rate of economic growth beginning in the early 1970s was caused by a *domestic* structural change, as explained in this section, rather than by the first oil crisis. In this respect, I concur with Maddison (1987). By his careful growth accounting, Maddison finds that the growth rate of real GDP in Japan would have been 3.8% during 1973–84, compared with its actual value 3.6%, 'if it had been possible to maintain the relation between energy growth and GDP growth in the previous period' (his table 15*b*). In his view, the effect of the oil shocks on growth rate is plainly minor.

2.3 THE POST-HIGH-GROWTH PERIOD: 1970–90

In any case, the Japanese economy saw a major structural change around 1970. Table 2.1 shows that the rate of growth of real GNP was halved from 10% to 4%, but at the same time, in the early 1970s the Japanese economy became much more stable than in the preceding high-growth period. As explained in the previous section, the fundamental factors to cause this structural change were the exhaustion of the disguised unemployment in the rural agricultural sector and the saturation of the domestic market for the then available consumer durables by the end of the 1960s. The structural change is reflected in virtually all the variables, but most importantly in investment.

Investment and the Stability of the Japanese Economy

In the 1970s and 1980s, the Japanese economy became much more stable than in the preceding high-growth period. Taylor (1989), for example, comparing Japanese and US business cycles, notes that 'real GNP fluctuations in Japan are so small compared to those in the United States, especially in the last 12 years, that *actual* GNP in Japan behaves much like the smooth *potential* GNP trend for the United States'. In the high-growth period, however, real GNP fluctuations in Japan were actually greater than those in the United States. What brought about the stability of real GNP in Japan beginning in the 1970s?

West (1992), based on a simple macro model of the Japanese economy, breaks down movements of the real GNP during 1975–87 into cost shocks and demand shocks. His conclusion is that demand shocks are estimated to account for nearly nine-tenths of the movement of GNP. This result, and my own analysis in the previous section, naturally lead us to analyse the behaviour of demand components. Table 2.18 shows the means and standard deviations of the growth rates of real GNP and demand components. The stability of consumption measured by the standard deviation of the growth rate remains the same for two periods. Exports and residential construction are actually more unstable in 1974–89 than in 1956–73. The stability of real GNP in 1974–89 was clearly brought about by the behaviour of fixed and inventory investment. Here I focus on fixed investment.

Table 2.18. Growth rates of real GNP and demand components, 1956–1989 (%)

	1956–73		1974–89	
	Mean	s.d.	Mean	s.d.
Real GNP	9.2	2.4	3.9	1.6
Consumption	8.7	1.7	3.6	1.7
Private fixed investment	17.3	14.0	5.4	6.7
Residential construction	15.3	6.3	1.7	8.4
Inventory investment	93.6	271.5	46.9	131.0
Government expenditure	7.1	4.0	2.5	3.7
Exports	13.2	6.7	8.6	7.6
Imports	15.0	10.5	5.2	9.1

Source: EPA, *National Income and Product Accounts*.

Three closely related factors can explain why investment became much more stable in the early 1970s than in the high-growth period. First is the effect of aggregation. Investment in the economy as a whole, I, is, of course, the sum of investment in the ith sector, I_i:

$$I = \sum_{i=1}^{n} I_i . \tag{35}$$

Therefore the variance of the growth rate of I, Var $(\dot{I}/I)$, can be written as

$$\mathrm{Var}(\dot{I}/I) = \sum_{i=1}^{n} v_i^2 \, \mathrm{Var}(\dot{I}_i/I_i)$$

$$+ \sum_{i \neq j} v_i v_j \operatorname{Cov}\left(\frac{\dot{I}_i}{I_i}, \frac{\dot{I}_j}{I_j}\right) \tag{36}$$

$$= \sum_{i=1}^{n} v_i^2 \sigma_i^2 + \sum_{i \neq j} v_i v_j \rho_{ij} \sigma_i \sigma_j,$$

where

$$v_i = I_i / I$$

$$\sigma_i^2 = \operatorname{Var}(\dot{I}_i / I_i)$$

$$\rho_{ij} = \operatorname{Cov}\left(\frac{\dot{I}_i}{I_i}, \frac{\dot{I}_j}{I_j}\right) \Big/ \sigma_i \sigma_j.$$

For $\operatorname{Var}(\dot{I}_i/I_i)$ to become small, σ_i and/or ρ_{ij} must become small. We first focus on changes in ρ_{ij}.

In the high-growth period, economy-wide factors spurred investment, and as a result, strong parallels in investment across various industries are observed. This situation changed dramatically around 1970: see the low and negative correlations for the second period in Table 2.14. This suggests that a change in ρ_{ij} contributed significantly to the stability of investment.

To substantiate this proposition, I calculated the hypothetical Var $(\dot{I}_i/I_i)$ under two assumptions: that first σ_i and then ρ_{ij} remained the same in the second period (1974–89) as in the high-growth period (1956–73) (see Table 2.19). This shows that, even if the variances of investment in individual industries had not declined, the variance of investment in the economy as a whole would have declined from 15.6 to 10.5. Beginning in the 1970s, investment seems to have been governed by micro-specific rather than economy-wide factors. By making the timing of investment among industries more

Table 2.19. Changes in the stability of investment, 1956–1989 (%)

	Standard deviation of the growth rate of private fixed investment[a]	
	1956(I)–1973(IV)	1974(I)–1989(I)
Actual	15.6	7.2
σ_i fixed at the 1956–73 level	15.6	10.5
ρ_{ij} fixed at the 1956–73 level	15.6	9.7

[a] Real investment by industry; 19 industries (see text for details)

Source: EPA, *National Income and Product Accounts*.

de-synchronized, the stability of investment in the economy as a whole was enhanced. The calculation above suggests that this effect alone explains more than half of the decline in the variance of the growth rate of investment in the second period.

Apart from the effect of a decline in ρ_{ij}, two other factors have caused a decline in Var $(\dot{I}_i/I_i)$. One is an increase in the share of the non-manufacturing sector. Investment in the non-manufacturing sector, compared with that in the manufacturing sector, is stable: standard deviations are 14.1 and 8.8 (1968(II)–1990(IV)), respectively. An increase in the share of the non-manufacturing sector from 54.1% (1968–72) to 63.8% (1973–90), therefore, necessarily contributed to the stability of total investment beginning in the 1970s.

The motives for investment also underwent a major change. The Development Bank of Japan has surveyed the investment activities of large corporations according to motive. This survey reveals that in 1969 67.4% of investment was for the purpose of augmenting capacity, but the proportion declined to 28.7% in 1980. Now measured by standard deviation of the growth rate, the volatility of investment motivated by capacity augmentation is much greater than that of other kinds of investment such as labour/energy-saving and R&D (research and development), which were 24.8% and 14.0%, respectively, in 1977–90. A change in the motives for investment, therefore, also contributed to the stability of total investment.

I emphasize that the three factors mentioned above are all *real* rather than monetary. Some economists argue that stability of monetary growth is responsible for the stability of real GNP. Suzuki, for example, referring to Fig. 2.7, argues that

> As you can see, since 1975 the money growth rate in Japan has become more stable and the uncertainty associated with it has also decreased due to the announcements of targets. And since 1976 there has been an accompanying decrease in the variability of the inflation and real growth rates. (Suzuki 1988: 83)

However, the major player that brought about the stability of real GNP beginning in the 1970s was investment, and the stability of investment in turn was caused by three *real* factors. As will be explained in great detail in Chapter 9, the stability of monetary growth is basically nothing but a mirror image of the stable real economy. Chapter 9 will also explain why the causality often runs from the real economy to money.

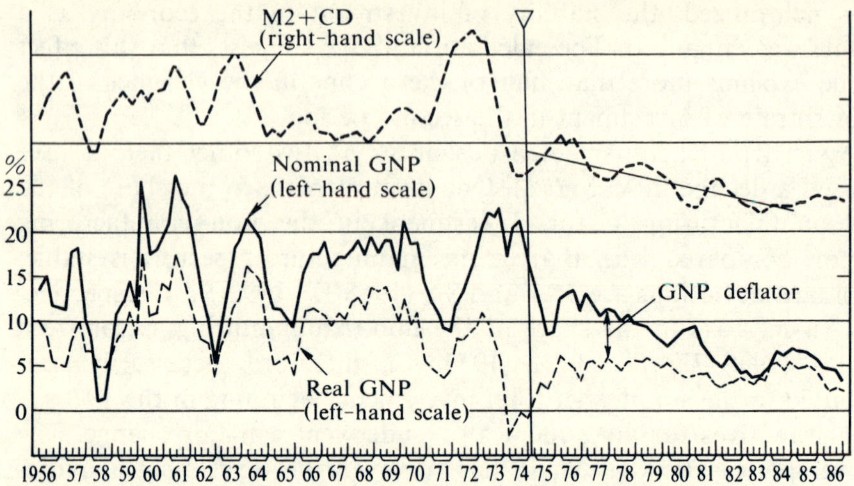

Fig. 2.7. Growth rate of money and real GNP, 1956–1986
Growth rates of money stock and GNP are calculated not against the previous quarter, but against the same quarter the previous year.
'M2 + CD' data (before 1979(I), 'M2' data) are averages of end-of-month observations; for example, the first quarter is an average of the data at the end of January, February, and March.
Source: Suzuki et al. (1988).

Equipment and Construction

Before leaving the subject of investment, it is worth pointing out another interesting fact. Fig. 2.8 shows the respective proportions of investment in equipment and investment in construction. In Japan, during the high-growth period the share of construction investment was higher than that of equipment investment. After the average growth rate fell from 10% to 4%, these proportions were reversed, and by the mid-1980s, the share of equipment investment had risen to about two-thirds of the total.

De Long and Summers (1991), on the other hand, using UN and Penn World cross-country data, document a strong correlation between the growth rate of real GDP per worker and the equipment investment/GDP ratio. According to their estimates, over 1960–85, a one-percentage-point increase in the equipment investment/GDP ratio is associated with an increase of about 0.3 percentage point in the growth rate of per capita GDP. They interpret this correlation as causal, and argue that it is not just investment, but *equipment*

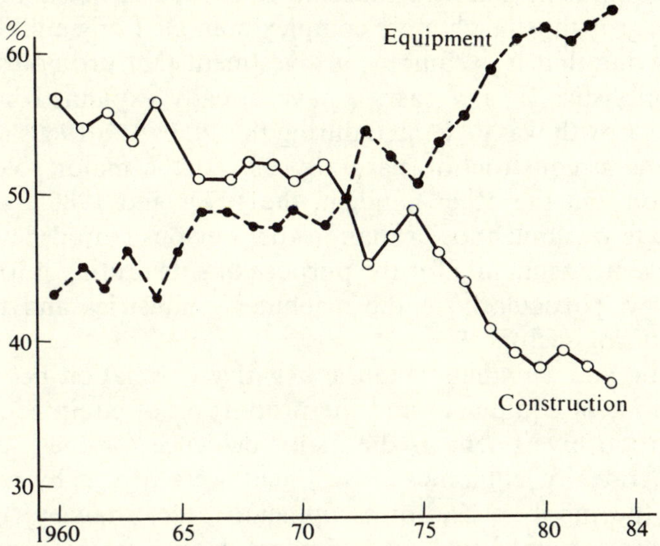

Fig. 2.8. Equipment investment and investment in plant, 1960–1984

investment that promotes economic growth. As will be explained in Chapter 7, the average investment/GDP ratio in Japan is about the same in real terms for both the high-growth period (1955–70) and the subsequent low-growth period (1970–90). Fig. 2.8, therefore, shows that the post-war Japanese experience contradicts the De Long–Summers thesis that investment in equipment promotes economic growth more than investment in construction.

De Long and Summers seem to hold that most new technologies are embodied in equipment rather than in buildings. However, equipment that embodies new technology may be introduced simply as a substitute for other inputs, such as labour and energy, for a *given output*; the introduction of new equipment, therefore, is not straightforwardly linked to growth. On the other hand, high economic growth sooner or later necessitates the augmentation of capacity, and thereby investment in construction. Besides, within a reasonable range, new technology often, if not necessarily, enlarges the optimal size of plant. For Japan, this was indeed the case during the 1950s and 1960s. Gigantic steel mills and chemical plants in coastal industrial regions were surely the symbol of the high-growth era. They all involved high investment in construction.

All this, of course, is not to say that it is investment in buildings that promotes economic growth. Rather, the role played by investment in equipment and investment in construction in the process of economic growth is much more complex than De Long and Summers assert. Saying that it is equipment investment that promotes growth is too simplistic. In any case, I have already explained how high economic growth was generated during the 1950s and 1960s in Japan. Investment in construction naturally played the major role during that period. On the other hand, in the 1970s and 1980s, when the growth rate was much lower than in the previous period, investment in equipment was mainly for the purpose of substituting it for labour and energy, particularly in the machinery industries and the non-manufacturing sector.

De Long and Summers take the negative correlation between the *relative* price of equipment and the proportion of equipment investment in total investment as the major evidence for their argument that high rates of equipment investment were driven by rightward shifts of the supply curve for equipment, rather than by rightward shifts of the demand curve for equipment. However, this argument is not convincing. Since most equipment is tradable, equipment prices are equalized across countries. When high productivity growth occurs mainly in the tradable sector or the manufacturing industry, the relative price of tradables necessarily declines in those countries where productivity has grown (Balassa 1964). Chapter 8 will demonstrate that this was indeed the case for Japan. The negative correlation between the relative price of equipment and quantities of equipment invested in, therefore, does not establish the supply-side causation.

The Dominant Role of Exports

Japan's high growth in the 1950s and 1960s was led by domestic demand. In contrast, in the early 1970s up to the mid-1980s, the growth and business cycles of the Japanese economy were dominated by exports. The high rate of investment in the 1960s had gradually endowed Japanese manufactured goods with the international competitiveness they needed. At the same time, high growth itself contributed to this competitiveness by allowing firms to take advantage of increasing returns and learning by doing; Chapter 10 provides an explicit analysis on this point. Given this background, the structural change that occurred around 1970 made exports the engine of growth of the Japanese economy, in place of domestic demand. This change is clearly visible for the car industry, the most important export industry (Fig. 2.9); the growth of the Japanese car industry was led by domestic demand in the 1960s and by exports thereafter.

Meanwhile, the two oil shocks in the 1970s save a strong stimulus to innovation in the Japanese manufacturing industry, particularly in the machinery industries: by the end of the 1970s the machinery sector came to dominate the growth and business cycles of the Japanese economy. This is reflected in the macro ratios presented in Section 2.1. Table 2.11 shows that the macro ratios of all four of the construction-related industries singled out earlier dramatically declined in the 1970s, whereas the macro ratios for the machinery sector increased, with the surge in the electrical machinery macro ratio being particularly conspicuous.

The first oil shock, although it was an adverse supply shock to the economy as a whole, in fact had some favourable effects on the machinery industries. In the first place, the increase in costs arising from the oil embargo was very slight in the machinery industries compared with industries such as chemical, paper, and metal; the energy coefficients in the 1973 input–output table were 9.9 (chemical), 7.2 (iron and steel), 4.7 (paper and pulp), and 1.4 (machinery), respectively. Therefore, when a sharp increase in the real price of oil,

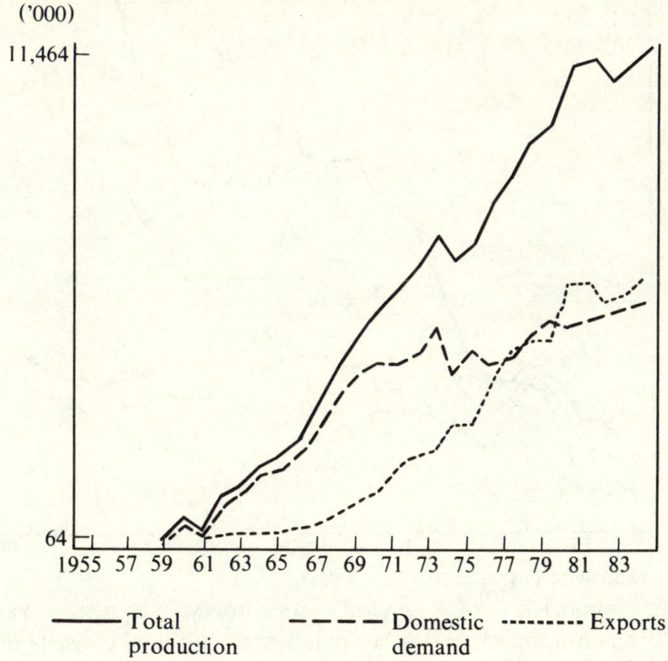

Fig. 2.9. Growth of the motor vehicle industry in Japan, 1955–1983

equivalent to a terms-of-trade deterioration in Japan, brought about the 10% depreciation of the yen, the machinery industries benefited by gaining in international competitiveness. During the period 1973–6, the WPI in machinery industries increased by only 25.2% in Japan compared with a 40.3% increase in the United States. And yet, during the same period the yen depreciated against the dollar by nearly 10%. This meant that the price competitiveness of the Japanese machinery industries improved by 25%.

Beyond that, the oil embargo created a huge transfer of money from the oil-importing countries to OPEC; about $16 billion in the case of Japan. This newly created oil money was then eventually loaned to developing countries through international financial intermediaries. To sustain domestic investment, the growth-oriented de-

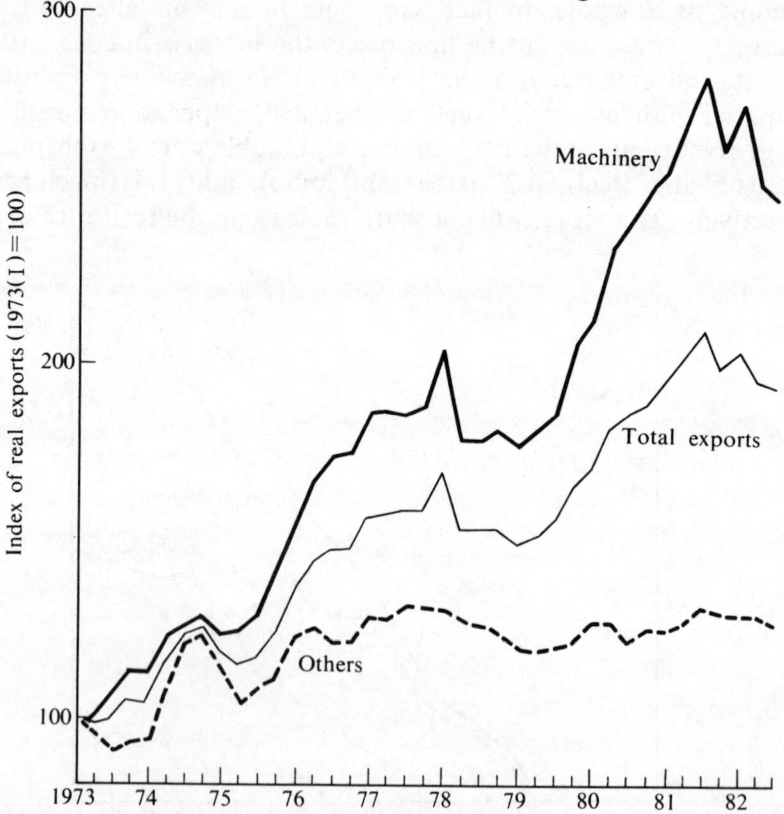

Fig. 2.10. Japanese exports in the 1970s
'Machinery' consists of general machinery, electric machinery, transportation equipment, and other machinery. 'Others' consists of fabrics, chemicals, non-metal materials, and metal products.
Source: Ministry of Finance, *Statistics on Foreign Trade.*

veloping countries needed to import machinery. In this way, machinery became the product that enjoyed exceptionally high demand, particularly by developing countries, in the generally depressed post-first-oil-shock world economy. Helped by price competitiveness, the Japanese machinery industry emerged as a chief supplier to meet this worldwide demand. Fig. 2.10 describes the situation diagrammatically.

After the second oil shock in 1979, debt crises forced many developing countries to curtail their imports. But in place of them, the United States, backed by the overvalued dollar, became the major importer of machinery. In 1970, the share of machinery in Japan's total exports was still less than 50%, but by the mid-1980s it had risen to 71% (Table 2.20).

Table 2.20. Japanese exports by industry, 1960–1985 (%)

	Food	Fabrics	Chemicals	Materials	Metal products	Machinery
1960	6.3	30.2	4.5	4.2	14.1	23.5
1965	4.1	18.7	6.5	3.1	20.3	35.2
1970	3.4	12.5	6.4	1.9	19.7	46.3
1975	1.4	6.7	7.0	1.3	22.5	53.8
1980	1.2	4.8	5.2	1.4	16.4	62.8
1985	0.7	3.6	4.4	1.2	10.5	71.8

Source: Ministry of Finance, *Statistics on Foreign Trade*.

The emergence of the machinery sector was brought about by high rates of investment in this sector (Table 2.21). In Table 2.14 we observed that the strong positive correlations in investment across various industries that was so prevalent in the 1960s vanished in the 1970s. The machinery bloc, consisting of general machinery, electric machinery, and transportation equipment, is an exception, however. These industries share a common catalyst, the integrated circuit (IC). Integrated circuits enormously enlarged the potential areas of innovation. Innovation in the machinery industry is very often initiated by the users of the machines. Innovations made possible by close communication between users and producers lead naturally to the emergence of a closely linked machinery bloc consisting of several sub-industries. The IC industry provides an illustrative example of this.

In the 1980s, Japan overtook the United States as world leader in IC production (Table 2.22). Along with IC producers, the Japanese

Table 2.21. Average growth rates of real investment by industry, 1975–1985

	%
Economy-wide average	4.5
Construction	2.4
Ferrous	−2.1
General machinery	6.4
Electric machinery	18.0
Cars	8.3
Precision instruments	15.7
Retail	1.9
Finance	0.3
Service	14.8
Real estate	6.0

Source: 'Real Investment by Industry', in EPA, *National Income and Product Accounts*.

Table 2.22. IC production, by country, 1980–1990 (%)

	1980	1990
USA	60	37
Japan	25	50
Europe	13	11

Source: VLSI Research.

IC equipment manufactures also grew during the same period (Table 2.23). Given the nature of innovations, which makes frequent face-to-face communication invaluable, it is often not satisfactory for users of machines and equipment to import them from geographically distant foreign producers.

Innovations generated by interactions between users and manufacturers of machines make a virtuous (vicious) circle in the growth (decline) of the machinery industries quite probable. As explained above, exports played a vital role in the virtuous circle in Japan. We already observed with respect to Fig. 2.9 that the growth of the Japanese car industry was led by exports in the 1970s and 1980s. From Fig. 2.11, which shows the ratio of exports to total production in electric machinery industry, we can see the overwhelming importance of exports for this industry.

Exports consisting mainly of machinery did indeed become a major force generating growth and business cycles of the economy as a

Table 2.23. The top ten semiconductor equipment manufacturers, 1980 and 1990

Name of firm	Country	1980 sales (US$m)	Name of firm	Country	1990 sales (US$m)
Perkin-Elmer	USA	150.7	Tokyo Electron	Japan	706
GCA	USA	116.0	Nikon	Japan	692
Applied Materials	USA	115.2	Applied Materials	USA	572
Fairchild Test Systems	USA	105.2	Advantest	Japan	423
Varian	USA	89.9	Canon	Japan	421
Teradyne	USA	82.5	Hitachi	Japan	304
Eaton	USA	78.9	General Signal	USA	286
General Signal	USA	57.0	Varian	USA	285
Kulicke & Soffa	USA	46.8	Teradyne	USA	215
Takeda Riken	Japan	46.0	Silicon Valley Group	USA	204

Source: VLSI Research.

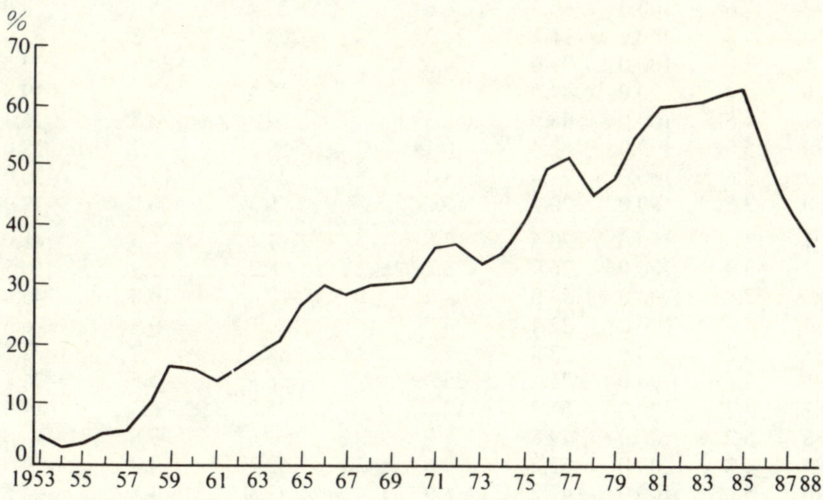

Fig. 2.11. The ratio of exports to total production in the electric machinery industry

Table 2.24. The growth rate of real GNP and the relative contribution of demand components, 1953–1990 (%)

	Growth rate	GNP	Con-sumption	Public expenditure	Private fixed investment	Inventory investment	Net exports
1953	7.7	100.0	134.3	4.4	46.1	– 53.3	– 31.5
1954	2.8	100.0	51.3	6.3	24.0	15.7	2.7
1955	10.8	100.0	54.6	– 0.8	3.4	32.2	10.6
1956	6.3	100.0	61.2	– 0.7	49.2	– 2.4	– 7.3
1957	8.9	100.0	49.1	– 1.0	47.3	16.6	– 12.2
1958	6.9	100.0	83.0	10.3	17.3	– 47.9	37.1
1959	11.2	100.0	53.2	6.8	34.7	11.6	– 6.4
1960	12.5	100.0	44.3	3.7	51.5	4.8	– 4.3
1961	11.8	100.0	33.0	4.2	48.1	26.0	– 11.3
1962	7.7	100.0	83.3	12.8	49.4	– 67.0	21.4
1963	10.1	100.0	53.6	8.2	28.8	18.6	– 9.2
1964	9.9	100.0	47.6	4.4	38.9	5.8	3.3
1965	6.4	100.0	66.1	12.4	15.8	– 26.7	32.4
1966	11.6	100.0	58.6	6.9	34.3	3.2	– 3.0
1967	10.9	100.0	57.2	5.5	47.0	13.3	– 22.9
1968	13.5	100.0	41.3	5.2	46.7	5.7	1.0
1969	12.2	100.0	50.0	4.5	48.1	– 1.4	– 1.2
1970	8.8	100.0	42.9	6.0	59.1	6.7	– 14.8
1971	4.3	100.0	74.8	12.3	34.1	– 35.5	14.4
1972	8.4	100.0	63.7	6.4	41.5	– 0.7	– 10.9
1973	7.6	100.0	68.3	6.6	57.4	5.8	– 38.0
1974	– 0.8	– 100.0	– 11.7	20.2	– 250.4	59.3	32.6
1975	2.9	100.0	99.0	24.5	– 15.7	– 80.3	72.5
1976	4.2	100.0	44.5	9.9	18.4	7.4	19.8
1977	4.8	100.0	48.0	8.3	24.1	3.3	16.3
1978	5.0	100.0	62.4	10.1	52.6	– 7.2	– 18.0
1979	5.6	100.0	73.4	8.3	32.9	11.8	– 26.0
1980	3.5	100.0	20.2	6.6	0.3	– 6.9	79.9
1981	3.4	100.0	20.6	12.8	27.1	– 1.5	41.0
1982	3.4	100.0	76.9	6.2	8.2	– 1.9	10.5
1983	2.8	100.0	57.9	8.9	– 2.4	– 10.8	46.4
1984	4.3	100.0	32.4	4.7	26.7	9.9	26.3
1985	5.2	100.0	33.4	5.2	36.6	2.7	22.1
1986	2.6	100.0	75.1	25.3	26.6	– 4.5	– 36.1
1987	4.3	100.0	57.7	12.5	25.2	– 6.3	– 14.0
1988	6.2	100.0	49.5	9.0	39.6	9.8	– 18.6
1989	4.8	100.0	52.2	0.6	62.2	4.0	– 19.5
1990	5.2	100.0	47.2	8.9	47.8	– 4.5	– 4.5

Source: EPA, *National Income and Product Accounts*: for 1953–5, 1970 constant prices (1978); for 1955–70, re-estimated values based on SNA, 1965 constant prices (1988); for 1971–90, 1985 constant prices (1991). For 1974, when the growth rate was negative, the negative figures in relative contribution mean that those components declined. The sum for 1974 is, therefore, – 100 rather than 100.

whole in the 1970s and the 1980s. For example, the percentage contribution of exports to the growth rate of real GNP was –8.3% for the period 1963–73, but since then it climbed to an astonishing 40.2% for the period 1980–4 (Table 2.24). Similarly, the simple correlation between industrial output and exports is –0.41 for the period 1960 (III)–1971 (IV), but it is 0.56 for 1972 (I)–1985 (IV). The change in the sign of correlation is consistent with the view that in the 1960s changes in output were *not* export-led; rather, exports were a 'vent for surplus production'. In contrast, in the 1970s and the early 1980s, exports became a major force generating business cycles in Japan.

I also estimated a vector autoregression (VAR) model containing quarterly investment, exports, and gross domestic demand to obtain the variance decomposition of each variable. Since the variance decompositions stabilize after 10 quarters, the results in Table 2.25 are for 10 quarters ahead. They suggest that investment was very autonomous in the period 1966(IV)–1973(I), while exports were very autonomous in the period 1973(II)–1984(IV).

Table 2.25. Variance decompositions of investment, export, and gross domestic demand

	SE	Investment	Exports	GDD
1966(IV)–1973(I)		(10 quarters ahead)		
Investment	0.0679	72.93	14.48	12.58
Export	0.0603	29.35	39.91	30.74
GDD	0.0339	51.96	20.18	27.86
1973(II)–1984(IV)		(10 quarters ahead)		
Investment	0.0494	43.28	51.53	5.18
Export	0.0907	25.92	71.51	2.57
GDD	0.0112	32.50	27.80	39.70

Note: Based on VAR with 4-period lags.

In passing, these results imply, first, that the assertion that the flexible exchange rate regime is responsible for a fall in the rate of economic growth, presumably because it makes the exchange rate more unpredictable, is simply inconsistent with facts, at least in the case of the Japanese economy, since the relative contribution of exports to growth *increased* in the 1970s and 1980s. On the other hand, they are consistent with the fact that the correlation between the Japanese and US business cycles is higher in the period of the

1970s and the 1980s than it was in the previous period (Table 2.1; see also Bank of Japan 1985*b* and Suda 1987). Export-led growth created a surge of current account surplus and trade frictions among Japan, the United States, and Europe in the 1980s. At the same time, the high rate of innovation in the machinery industries brought about a sharp appreciation of yen in the 1980s. These problems are discussed in Chapter 8.

2.4 CONCLUDING REMARKS

Several important conclusions can be drawn from the analyses of growth and business cycles in post-war Japan. First, *real demand* is the key factor determining business cycles; demand for investment, particularly in construction, and for exports played the dominant role for both the 1955–70 and the 1975–85 periods. (See also Section 4.4 below for a comparison of the two oil shock periods.)

This is not to say that money plays no role in the business cycle. Chapter 9 will show that monetary policy does indeed affect the real economy. Complementing the analysis of this chapter, however, it will also show how money supply very often responds to changes in output, and will thereby explain why monetarism is misleading.

Second, this chapter explained, though only informally, how productivity is linked to economic growth. It rejected the real business cycle theory, in which productivity shocks affect growth directly, through the production function. Rather, I maintain that the extent to which technical change bears the fruit of economic growth depends crucially on how it affects the growth of demand. For example, by lowering the prices of consumer durables, technical change certainly contributed to high growth of domestic demand in Japan in the 1950s and 1960s. It also made the Japanese a major world exporter of machinery in the 1970s and 1980s. In both cases, technical change raised the growth rate in a *roundabout* way through its subsequent effects on demand, not through a direct shift of the production function. The causality could also run the other way round. There is a significant effect of demand on technical progress. The effect of the emergence of the Japanese IC industry on Japanese IC equipment manufacture is a good example (Table 2.23).

All these points, together with the well-known fact that investment is significantly affected by demand, lead us to the conclusion that *real* demand is important not only in business cycles but also in economic growth. Japan's experience strongly suggests that this thesis is worth a serious consideration. Chapter 10 will present a model in which demand plays a crucial role in economic growth.

APPENDIX

In this appendix, I show that the variance of the general price level conditional on the macro variables, σ_p^2, is an increasing function of σ_m^2, as is seen in equations (18).

The macroeconomic model in the text consists of the following equations:

$$Y_t = \alpha\theta(P_t - \bar{P}) + \lambda Y_{t-1}, \tag{A1}$$

$$Y_t + P_t = M_t, \tag{A2}$$

$$M_t - M_{t-1} = m_t \sim N(m, \sigma_m^2). \tag{A3}$$

Equations (A1) and (A2) lead to

$$M_t - P_t = \alpha\theta(P_t - \bar{P}) + \lambda Y_{t-1}. \tag{A4}$$

Then, from (A3) and (A4), we obtain $\bar{P}_t = E(P_t \mid M_{t-j}, P_{t-j}, Y_{t-j};\ j \geqslant 1)$ as follows:

$$\bar{P} = M_{t-1} + m - \lambda Y_{t-1}. \tag{A5}$$

From (A4) and (A5), therefore, we have

$$P_t = \frac{M_t}{1+\alpha\theta} + \frac{\alpha\theta M_{t-1}}{1+\alpha\theta} + \frac{\alpha\theta m}{1+\alpha\theta} - \lambda Y_{t-1}. \tag{A6}$$

The conditional variance, σ_p^2, is

$$\sigma_p^2 = \frac{\sigma_m^2}{(1+\alpha\theta)^2}. \tag{A7}$$

Note that (A7) is *not* a final expression for σ_p^2, since under rational expectations θ is dependent on σ_p^2,

$$\theta = \frac{\tau^2}{\sigma_p^2 + \tau^2}, \tag{A8}$$

where τ^2 is a weighted average of τ_i^2. Substituting (A8) into (A7), we obtain

$$\sigma_p^2 = \frac{\sigma_m^2(\sigma_p^2 + \tau^2)^2}{[\sigma_p^2 + (1+\alpha)\tau^2]^2}. \tag{A9}$$

σ_p^2 is a real solution of (A9) and must also be positive. Denoting σ_p^2 by x, we can rewrite (A9) as

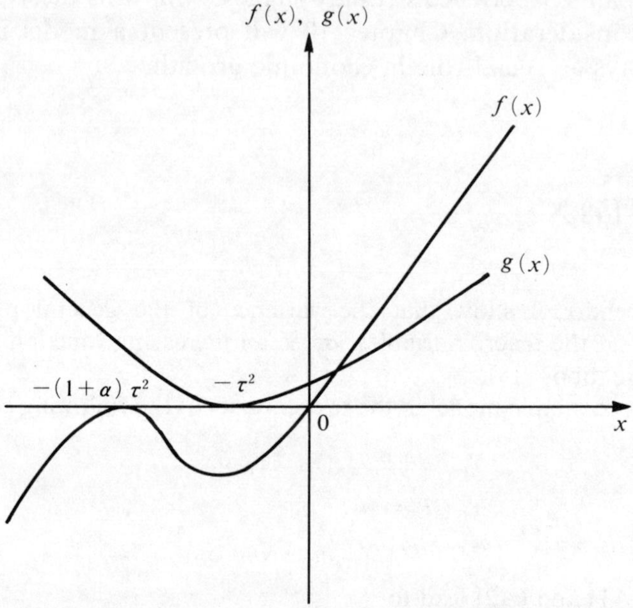

Fig. 2.12. The relation between σ_p and σ_m

$$x\,[x + (1 + \alpha)\,\tau^2]^2 = \sigma_m^2(x + \tau^2)^2. \tag{A10}$$

Let us call the left-hand side of (A10), $f(x)$ and the right-hand side, $g(x)$. Then the graphs of $f(x)$ and $g(x)$ look like the ones in Fig. 2.12. It is clear from the diagram that, if a real solution for (A10) exists, it is unique, positive, and also in an increasing function of σ_m^2. For $\sigma_m^2 = 0, x = 0$ is in fact a solution. Therefore, by continuity, such a solution exists for small σ_m^2. The result can be summarized as

$$\sigma_p^2 = h(\sigma_m^2)\ ,\ h(0) = 0,\ h'(0) = \frac{1}{(1+\alpha)^2} > 0 \text{ for small } \sigma_m^2. \tag{A11}$$

This is equation (18) in the text.

3

Post-War Turmoil, 1945–1954: The Japanese Economy in Disorder

This book is concerned in large part with the Japanese economy after the mid-1950s, when the rapid economic growth started. The performance of the Japanese economy since then has on the whole been so good that one is apt to forget the period of turbulence that immediately followed the war. This chapter describes the difficulties the Japanese economy faced in the first decade after the war (1945–54), and explains how it overcame those difficulties. We hope that the Japanese experience in this period may provide useful guidance for economies in disorder today, including Russia, East European and other developing countries.

After the war, real output inevitably fell because of the destruction of capital stock and the interruption of imports of raw materials from abroad. Section 3.1 reveals that the lack of raw materials was, in fact, much more damaging than the shortage of capital stock. There was absolutely no way of avoiding this economy-wide decline in real output. The question then was, how was this burden to be shared among the people? Obviously, the preferred solution, in order to minimize social instability in a turbulent economy where per capita consumption has fallen to a bare subsistence level, was to burden the wealthy more than the poor. The Japanese government attempted to achieve this goal through the implementation of various economic policies (Section 3.2). In particular, the government took control of the distribution of rice, the basic foodstuff, and subsidized it at a low price. This subsidy for rice, in addition to other numerous subsidies, resulted in a huge government budget deficit. The deficit was subsequently financed by the Bank of Japan, and thus led to high inflation. High inflation wiped out the debts of tenant farmers and also the nominally denominated assets of the wealthy such as bank deposits or government bonds. In this way, inflation substantially equalized asset–debt distribution. The pre-war affluent disappeared.

On the other hand, in the course of high inflation, the official and black market prices substantially diverged, and this divergence was taken advantage of by farmers and other self-employed merchants and entrepreneurs. Employed workers' share of total income significantly declined, while that of the self-employed dramatically increased in this period. Workers, both blue-collar and white-collar, and corporate firms were all big losers.

The subsidies and transfers that were the major cause of the government budget deficit, and therefore ultimately of inflation, made wage hikes easy and discouraged producers from pursuing efficiency. By abolishing many subsidies and transfers, the Dodge Plan in 1949 restrained wage increases and inflation on the one hand, and encouraged producers to strive to improve the efficiency of their businesses on the other. The adoption of a single exchange rate was instrumental. I argue, however, that real factors, notably a recovery of real output, also contributed to disinflation in 1949–50, together with a severe budget cut which resulted in a sharp decline in money supply; the contribution of decelerated velocity to disinflation was quite substantial (Section 3.3).

The first post-war decade also saw very turbulent labour–management relations. Firms often attempted massive dismissals. Bitter strikes lasted a long time. And in the early years, the militant labour movement even campaigned for firms to be labour-managed. Plainly, in the first decade after the war, there was nothing like what we understand today as the high-performing Japanese firm. From this chaos, however, by painful trial and error, seniority wages, co-operative enterprise unions, and long-term employment emerged. Section 3.4 describes this process.

Section 3.5 outlines the Japanese economy in the early 1950s. Helped by the Korean War (1950–1), the Japanese economy soon recovered from the Dodge recession, and firms started making large-scale investment, above all, to introduce new technologies. Thanks to this massive investment, some industries such as steel were able to achieve internationally competitive productivity during this period. By 1955, the Japanese economy had completed its preparation for high growth. The chapter concludes by arguing that equitable income distribution in the post-war Japanese economy significantly contributed to high economic growth.

3.1 THE DIFFICULTIES FACED BY THE JAPANESE ECONOMY, 1945–1949

The Japanese economy suffered from an unprecedented fall of economic activity after the war coupled with hyperinflation. This section focuses on the source of the economic difficulties and the consequences of the hyperinflation.

The Real Economy

The real sector of the Japanese economy faced two major difficulties immediately after the war: the destruction of the capital stock, and the continued interruption of imports of raw materials from abroad.

It is estimated that, overall, capital stock decreased by 25% in 1945 from its wartime peak, falling to roughly the 1935 level. However, the destruction of the capital stock necessary for domestic production was actually relatively small. For example, 24.6% of buildings (including 3 million houses), 7.5% of ports, 3.5% of bridges, 7.0% of railways, and 80.6% of civilian ships were destroyed. With the exception of the damages suffered by marine transport, damage to the transportation system as a whole was relatively small. Production capacity in the iron and steel industry was almost intact, and in the textile industry fell only by 10%. However, in the machinery and chemical industries, capacity decreased by 25% and 30–50%, respectively. Production equipment in the consumer goods industries was severely damaged, not only by the strategic bombing, but also by the Japanese government itself, which had scrapped and used such equipment for steel-making during the war.[1] One consequence of the severe damage in the chemical industry was a shortage of fertilizer for agricultural use, and this aggravated the food problem after the war.

Many Japanese economists believe that the interruption in the import of raw materials from abroad was much more damaging to the Japanese economy than the destruction of capital stock. In fact, the first *Economic White Paper* of the Japanese government, published in 1947, clearly states that 'the cause of low production lies not in shortages of capital or labour, but in shortages of raw materials, coal, and electricity'. The production of steel, for example, was 320,000 tons in 1946, which amounted only to 7.1% of the 1935 level, and 4.3% of the 1946 capacity; with regard to cement, the 1946 production was only 18% of the 1935 level and 23% of the 1946 capacity.

Evidently, the bottleneck was not capital, but raw materials and energy, most of which Japan had to import. The war and the subsequent occupation, cutting Japan off from the world market,

[1] Miyazaki and Ito (1989: 174–9).

Table 3.1. Gross national expenditure at constant prices (1934–6 calendar year base), 1935–1951 (¥ million)

	Year[a]	Total	Private consumption	Government consumption	Gross domestic capital formation	Surplus of current account	Exports etc.	Imports etc.
CY	1935	16,631	10,726	2,611	3,140	154	4,205	4,051
	1936	17,157	11,003	2,618	3,405	131	4,471	4,340
	1937	21,220	11,540	4,247	4,572	861	5,407	4,546
	1938	21,935	11,382	5,491	4,745	317	4,978	4,661
	1939	22,117	10,839	4,688	6,007	583	5,255	4,672
	1940	20,796	9,723	4,896	5,967	210	5,684	5,474
	1941	21,130	9,410	6,134	6,415	–559	4,433	4,992
	1942	21,405	8,956	6,460	6,557	–568	3,246	3,814
	1943	21,351	8,469	7,445	5,857	–420	2,910	3,330
	1944	20,634	7,006	7,301	6,462	–135	2,310	2,445
FY	1946	11,594	6,826	1,123	4,077	–432	102	534
	1947	12,573	7,410	828	4,845	–510	247	757
	1948	14,211	8,391	1,360	4,987	–527	362	889
	1949	14,524	9,297	1,619	4,041	–433	753	1,186
	1950	16,115	10,077	1,838	3,893	307	1,614	1,307
	1951	18,207	11,040	2,022	4,715	430	2,187	1,757

[a] CY denotes calendar year; FY denotes fiscal year.

Source: Somu-cho (Management and Co-ordination Agency) (1987).

turned the country back into a virtually closed economy. Table 3.1 shows that the amount of imports in 1946 was one-eighth of the 1935 level in real terms. Moreover, the recovery of imports was very slow: it took a decade for them to return to the pre-war peak level.

In addition to the decrease in imports, the domestic production of coal also fell substantially because the Korean and Chinese coal miners, most of whom were called up during the war, had left the mines. As a consequence, the number of coal miners suddenly dropped, from 460,000 in 1944 to 270,000 in 1945, or 40%. This process also created chaotic situations such as frequent strikes and even riots at many coal mines.

Since capital stock substantially decreased and availability of raw materials/energy was interrupted, it is no wonder that production fell dramatically. Table 3.1 shows that real GNP in 1946 decreased by 50% relative to 1939. Food consumption fell close to the minimum subsistence level. The 1947 *White Paper* illustrated the seriousness of the problem by citing the diminishing body weight and height of school-children (Table 3.2). As will be explained later, the trouble was most seriously felt by urban employee families. In line with the slow recovery of imports, it also took a decade for real GNP to return to the pre-war peak level.

Table 3.2. The body size of Japanese schoolchildren, 1937–1946

	School year or Grade					
	1	2	3	4	5	6
Height (cm)						
1937	110.3	116.4	120.3	125.5	130.5	134.7
1946	107.0	111.9	116.9	121.0	125.6	129.9
Weight (kg)						
1937	18.4	20.4	22.5	24.7	27.2	29.8
1946	17.6	19.6	21.3	23.3	25.2	27.5

Source: *Economic White Paper of the Japanese Government*, 1947.

Unemployment was another serious problem. Between the end of the war and May 1947, more than 5 million war veterans who were demobilized abroad, and other Japanese having lived in ex-colonies, returned to Japan. Most of these were of working age, and they amounted to roughly 7% of the total population and 16% of the work-force. On the other hand, real GNP fell to half of the pre-war peak, and industrial production to a third. Not surprisingly, mass unemployment had been foreseen by the government. However, it turned out that the officially unemployed numbered only 667,000 in 1947, less than 2% of the work-force. These figures mask, of course, the prevalence of disguised unemployment, both in rural agriculture and in urban manufacturing. Discouraged workers, discounted as part of the work-force, were estimated to have reached 6% of the work-force in 1947. In whatever way this disguised unemployment was absorbed in the economy, it necessarily lowered labour productivity. The monthly coal production per worker, for example, dropped from 17.5 tons in 1936 to 5.4 tons in 1946. Similarly, the monthly cement production per worker was only 14 tons in 1946 compared with 25 tons in 1944. On the whole, the labour productivity fell to a third of the pre-war peak.

All in all, the basic problems the Japanese economy faced in those days were supply-side issues and not the aggregate demand deficiency. For example, high unemployment, whether official or disguised, was caused by shortages of raw materials and energy rather than by a lack of demand. Output fell for the same reason. There was also a misallocation of resources among sectors, most notably caused by a radical shift of demand from military to civilian use. *Minjutenkan*, the conversion of products into civilian uses, was an important task for the government and the firms.

Despite the serious difficulties confronting the economy, during the first five years after the war real GNP increased by 40%. Most of this increase was absorbed by consumption. In contrast, investment increased very little (Table 3.1). It was only natural that per capita consumption should recover after having fallen to the minimum subsistence level during and immediately after the war. At the same time, we must note that output increased by 40% without a corresponding increase in capital stock. This in turn suggests a sharp increase in capacity utilization during this period. Indeed, it sharply increased in key industries between December 1946 and December 1949: from 4% to 48%, 45% to 73%, 16% to 56%, and 23% to 82% in the steel, nonferrous metal, chemical, and ceramic industries, respectively. The drop in capacity utilization caused by shortages in raw materials and/or intersectoral misallocations of resources was much more serious than the war-time destruction of capital stock.

Inflation

The Japanese economy suffered from hyperinflation accompanied by the sharp decline in real output (Table 3.3). This inflation was

Table 3.3. Post-war inflation in Japan, 1945–1950

	WPI	Ratio of black-market to official prices
1945	100	n.a.
1946	464	7.2
1947	1375	5.3
1948	3651	2.9
1949	5961	1.7
1950	7045	1.2

Source: Okura-sho (Ministry of Finance) (1978).

certainly not as bad as the historically notorious hyperinflation experienced by Germany after the First World War. Still, at one point it was as high as 30% *per month*, and even the official wholesale price index rose 70 times between 1945 and 1950.

What were the major effects of this hyperinflation? As is well known, if all nominal values, including wages, assets, and debts, change in exactly the same proportion, it is conceivable that inflation will leave all the real variables intact no matter how high it rises.[2] In reality, of course, most inflation does affect the real economy.

There are two main problems associated with hyperinflation. First, severe hyperinflation makes money essentially useless as a medium of exchange, and results in a return to a barter economy. This undoubtedly entails a substantial loss in efficiency in the real economy. Second, inflation, if it does not destroy the monetary system altogether, is almost certainly not neutral to the real economy. Nominal prices and wages vary at different rates, and as a result relative prices change. Also, not all assets and liabilities are perfectly indexed against inflation. Therefore, in the course of inflation incomes and assets are redistributed among groups of people and/or factors of production. This second effect of inflation on the real economy tends to affect distribution rather than macroeconomic efficiency, although it is certainly possible that the redistribution of income and wealth in turn has a macroeconomic impact on the real economy.[3]

In the case of post-war Japanese hyperinflation, the monetary system did not collapse. Some barter exchanges did take place, but

[2] The Tobin effect of inflation on the real interest rate may not make money 'super-neutral', but it is ignored in the present discussion.

[3] In the post-First World War German inflation, the collapse of the middle class living on nominally fixed incomes contributed to the rise of the Nazis; inflation certainly had a real effect.

only marginally. During the course of inflation, however, official and black market prices diverged significantly (Table 3.3); in 1946, the black market prices of investment and consumer goods were, respectively, more than seven and eight times the official prices. The black market indeed prevailed. For example, in 1947 the percentage of rice purchased by households on the black market was about 30% in terms of quantity and 80% in terms of expenditure. Such black market transactions, including barters, certainly affected macroeconomic efficiency. However, the monetary system operated with little macroeconomic inefficiency; the major real effect of inflation was therefore distributional.

High inflation redistributed both income and wealth. On the asset/liability side, there were three major effects. First, the value of national government bonds in real terms dropped to nearly zero. As a result of a large-scale issue of war bonds, the government had become the largest net debtor by the end of the war (see Table 3.4); inflation wiped out this debt.

Table 3.4. Financial assets and liabilities, by sector, end Dec. 1946 (¥ million)

	(1) Assets	(2) Liabilities	(3) (1)–(2)
Financial institutions	342 469	374 949	– 32 480
Government[a]	74 114	249 543	– 175 429
Private	380 574	179 064	201 510

[a] Local governments are included; public companies are excluded.

Source: Okura-sho (Ministry of Finance) (1978).

Second, and in a similar fashion, the real value of deposits was reduced significantly. In February 1946 the government implemented the Emergency Financial Measures (Kin-yu Kinkyu Sochi) in an attempt to force citizens to deposit all circulating cash into banks and (in principle) to forbid withdrawals of such deposits except for the minimum amount necessary to survive. As of 2 March, the old currency in circulation was invalidated. Firms' deposits were also frozen, and all the inter-firm transactions were settled by means of transfers of these frozen deposits. Such transactions, and firms' wage payments by cash to their employees, all had to be authorized beforehand.[4] During 1946, over 70% of total deposits were frozen, and in the interim inflation reduced the real value of the deposits to less than one-quarter.[5] As a result of these measures, financial institutions, seriously damaged by the reduction in real terms of their national and corporate bonds, were able to recover.

Lastly, the real value of debts held by tenant farmers also declined, to almost nil. In the 1946 Land Reform (Nochi Chosei-ho), landowners were forced to sell a certain portion of their tenant lands (80% of the total acreage of tenant land) to the government, which subsequently sold this land to the tenant farmers. Thus, the tenant farmers were in debt to the government for the purchase price of such land. However, because the purchase price was determined on the basis of prices in November 1945, these debts were reduced to nearly zero as a result of the subsequent inflation. There had already been a gradual weakening in the power of landlords since the 1930s, and particularly during the war, through such measures as rent controls, the protection of tenancy rights, and the rationing of rice. And yet, beyond doubt, the effect of the 1946 Land Reform was quite substantial. Ownership of farmland was indeed drastically changed (Table 3.5). Not only did the reform bring about a more equal distribution of assets and income among the rural inhabitants, but also it contributed ultimately to the democratization and social/political stability of post-war Japan. High inflation, in effect, served to implement a massive transfer of tenant acreage without compensation.[6]

In addition to the substantial redistribution of assets and liabilities, incomes were also significantly redistributed. Table 3.6 shows the distribution of national income. We can observe that income distribution drastically changed from the pre-war period (1934–6) to 1946. First of all, employees' income share fell, from 39.3% to 31.8%, a drop of 7.5%. Rent and corporate income also fell, by 9.2% and 7.3% respectively. In contrast, the proportion of income accruing to the self-employed increased by an astonishing 31.6%. This increase is in part a reflection of the land reform of 1946. That is not, however, the whole story. The effect of the land reform should be roughly

[4] For firms, authorized settlement by means of frozen deposit transfers did not work well because it was based on official prices. Firms had to actually acquire necessary raw materials with cash on the black market. The Ministry of Finance soon allowed banks to make loans to firms, and firms to withdraw cash, which was ultimately supplied by the Bank of Japan.

[5] Ministry of Finance (1976*b*: 116–18). See also Bank of Japan (1985*a*).

[6] See Kawagoe (1993) on the Land Reform in post-war Japan.

Table. 3.5. The 1946–1947 land reform

	1941	1949	1955
Farmland area ('000 ha)[a]			
Owner-cultivated	3,099 (54)	4,274 (87)	4,678 (91)
Tenant-cultivated	2,660 (46)	643 (13)	462 (9)
Total	5,759 (100)	4,917 (100)	5,140 (100)
No. of farm households ('000)[a]			
Owner[b]	1,656 (31)	3,564 (57)	4,200 (70)
Owner-cum-tenant[b]	1,123 (21)	1,735 (28)	1,308 (22)
Tenant-cum-owner[b]	1,093 (20)	458 (7)	285 (5)
Tenant[b]	1,516 (28)	489 (8)	239 (4)
Total	5,412 (100)	6,247 (100)	6,043 (100)

[a] Percentage distributions of farmland area and farm households are shown in parentheses.

[b] Owner: farmer who owns more than 90% of his cultivated land; owner-cum-tenant and tenant-cum-owner: farmers who own 50%–90% and 10%–50% of their cultivating land, respectively; tenant: farmer who owns less than 10% of his cultivating land.

Source: Kawagoe (1993: 196, table 8.6).

Table 3.6. Distribution of national income, 1934–1950 (%)

	1934–6 (CY)	1946 (FY)	1947	1948	1949	1950
Total	100.0	100.0	100.0	100.0	100.0	100.0
Compensation of employees	39.3	31.8	33.2	29.2	43.5	42.6
Incomes of owners of unincorporated enterprises	32.4	64.0	65.1	54.5	47.4	45.9
Agriculture	14.5	28.6	26.8	23.1	20.8	19.1
Manufacturing	3.8	8.8	11.8	10.2	9.5	12.2
Commerce	8.3	9.3	12.9	11.4	9.1	4.8
Rent	10.3	1.1	0.8	0.7	0.7	0.8
Farm rent	4.4	0.3	0.2	0.1	0.1	0.1
Interest	6.9	2.0	0.9	0.8	1.1	1.4
Corporate reserve	8.3	1.0	1.0	2.4	5.1	9.1

Source: Keizai Shingi-cho (Economic Deliberation Agency), *Sengo Nihon no Kokumin Shotoku* (National Income of Postwar Japan).

equal to the decline in the share of the agricultural rent, which was only 4.1%. Therefore the rest of the increase in the share of the self-employed incomes from agriculture, namely 11%, must be accounted for by other factors, such as changes in the relative prices in favour of agricultural products. It is also interesting to note that in 1947 the proportion of the self-employed incomes from agriculture fell slightly, while the share of the self-employed incomes from manufacturing and trade (retail and wholesale) kept rising, to 11.8% and 12.9% from their pre-war levels of 3.8% and 8.3%, respectively.

In short, the effect of the land reform on income distribution was substantial, but it is clear that, quite apart from the land reform, economic conditions very strongly favoured the self-employed. Specifically, the divergence between the official and black market prices was used to advantage by the self-employed. The data on the self-employed in those days are, not surprisingly, very meagre. However, a detailed study of retail and wholesale shops conducted by the city of Niigata, a large city facing the Japan Sea, provides a very interesting result. For example, the annual sales of wholesalers totaled ¥6,001 million for 1948, while the corresponding operating costs, including wages, rent, utility, advertisement, and so on, were a mere ¥22 million or 0.36%. A similar study conducted in 1951, on the other hand, reports the operating costs as about 8% of the total states. A comparison of two studies leads us to conclude that in the late 1940s the operating costs for distribution were extremely low. This in turn suggests that during that time the income of the self-employed in trade essentially came from the monopoly rent arising from their underground access to commodities rather than from the normal value added in trading. Perhaps this is the general characteristic of an economy in turmoil where the supply of commodities is inelastic. The same was observed in Russia in the early 1990s, for example.

Exploited by the self-employed, employed workers, (both white-collar and blue-collar) and corporate firms suffered in 1946–8, the period of high inflation. Table 3.7 shows incomes, expenditure, and the saving rate of employee households living in Tokyo. The saving rate never reached 2% during this period, and even net dissavings occurred in 1948. Nowadays, some attribute the high household saving rate in Japan to a national characteristic. However, when economic circumstances are sufficiently adverse, even the Japanese will dissave! As Chapter 6 explains in detail, the household saving rate reached high levels only after the Japanese economy returned to its growth path beginning in the mid-1950s.

Table 3.7. The saving rate of employee households in Tokyo, 1947–1950

	1947	1948	1949	1950
Income (¥)	54,517	151,072	186,037	149,401
Expenditure (¥)	53,507	154,414	183,049	140,372
Saving (¥)	1,010	− 3,342	2,988	2,220
Saving rate (%)	1.9	− 2.2	1.6	1.5

Source: City of Tokyo, *Annual Survey of Households*.

Corporate firms also suffered. For example, in 1947 the four largest steel companies reported ¥1,258 million as total revenues and ¥1,860 million as total costs, incurring a loss of ¥602 million, almost half of total revenue. The situation was similar in most other corporate firms.

3.2 ECONOMIC POLICIES, 1945–1949

Japan was under the Allied occupation from August 1945 until the ratification of the Japan–US peace treaty in 1951. During that period, the Supreme Command for the Allied Powers (SCAP), consisting mainly of US military forces, played an overwhelming role in determining the course of reform and economic policies in Japan.

The power of SCAP can best be illustrated by relating the following episode. Two American officers in SCAP were in charge of the reform of the Japanese elementary school. One favoured coeducation and the other, segregated classes. Failing to reach a decision they finally opened up a map of Japan and drew a dividing line down the centre of the country. As a result, since then, the eastern part of Japan has had segregated classes while the western part has had coeducational classes in all state-run schools! For the most important and drastic reforms, including land reform, the *Zaibatsu* dissolution, and the labour reform, the Japanese government was given little opportunity to voice its options. Economic policy measures as well, were decided under the strong guidance of SCAP.

Broadly speaking, in the early stage of occupation, the aim of SCAP and US government policy was the demilitarization and democratization of Japan. Policies were often punitive. For example, in December 1945 SCAP planned to remove all the existing capacity in Japan to produce more than 2.5 million tons of iron and steel and to ship the excess-capacity plant to the Philippines as a part of reparation. The plan was eventually given up, but such a policy stance of SCAP naturally deterred firms from making any serious investment in the early years under occupation. The Cold War, which started in 1948, brought important changes in occupation policy. Emphasis was then significantly shifted towards the reconstruction and recovery of the Japanese economy in order to make Japan a stronghold against communism.

Imports

As explained in the previous section, after the war real output fell to such a low level that per capita consumption dropped to a bare subsistence level. It was therefore most urgent for the government to secure enough food in order to avoid famine. In this respect, food imports were absolutely imperative: roughly a quarter of food consumption in those days depended upon imports. The US government had ruled that exports and imports be permitted only under the approval and supervision of SCAP, and that only essential goods be imported ('The United States Initial Post Defeat Policy Relating to Japan': SWNCC-150/3). Accordingly, food imports were given priority.

The pre-war Japanese economy had depended heavily on imported raw materials, which accounted for as much as 60% of all imports. After the war, however, this proportion fell to 20–30%, while food imports increased dramatically in accordance with the above mentioned policy of SCAP. Foreign aid, particularly from the United States, was also crucial in this respect. Japan sustained large trade deficits during this period, which were met with US aid (Table 3.8); most of the aid came from a part of the budget of the US Department of the Army called GARIOA (Government and Relief in Occupied Areas).

Table 3.8. Trade deficits, 1946–1950 ($ million)

	1946	1947	1948	1949	1950
Current balance	– 78.1	46.4	74.8	207.1	476.3
Trade balance	– 238.0	– 267.4	– 284.3	– 194.8	34.4
Exports	65.3	181.6	262.3	533.3	920.3
Imports	303.3	449.0	546.6	728.1	885.9
Net transfers	194.5	404.8	461.6	513.5	429.4
Others	– 34.6	– 91.0	– 102.5	– 111.6	12.5

Source: Okura-sho (Ministry of Finance) (1978).

The trade policy of SCAP was revised as the objectives of the occupation shifted from disarmament and democratization to economic recovery. An early example is the permission given by SCAP for the import of heavy crude oil for steel production. This eventually became the starting-point for the Priority Production System or Keisha Seisan Houshiki, mentioned later. The clear turning-point, however, was the Johnston Report (*Report on the Economic Position and Prospects of Japan and Korea*, 26 April 1948). This report stated explicitly that imports should be permitted not only for the maintenance of a minimum standard of living, but also for economic reconstruction.[7] With this shift in trade policy, Japanese imports, heavily dominated by foodstuffs immediately after the war, gradually saw an increase in raw materials.

Fiscal Policy

Although the government cancelled all its wartime debts to the private sector except for the government bonds, it still ran huge deficits. The government debt relative to GNP is shown in Table 3.9. For three years, beginning in 1946, the budget ran an extremely large deficit, but in 1949 it suddenly became balanced and in 1950 ran a surplus. This surplus was brought about by an abrupt and drastic fiscal tightening known as the Dodge Plan, which will be discussed in greater detail in the next section.

Table 3.9. Government debts, 1946–1951 (¥ million)

Fiscal year	Total	Ratio to GNP (%)	General account total	Special account total	Food-stuff control	Trade	Communications	Railways
1946	65,888	13.9	99,437	– 33,55	3,280	1,400	3,406	9,487
1947	95,286	7.3	15,542	79,744	33,700	5,200	6,861	18,562
1948	163,781	6.1	28,578	135,204	78,000	18,400	13,004	20,624
1949	112,877	3.3	150,354	– 37,477	0	5,400	9,723	– 53,580
1950	– 83,278	– 2.1	– 44,029	– 39,249	0	– 30,400	0	0
1951	91,455	1.7	728	90,727	6,000	70,000	15,999	0

Source: Okura-sho (Ministry of Finance) (1978).

The budget deficits in 1946–8, particularly beginning in 1947, consisted mainly of transfers and subsidies. For example, in 1947

[7] The source of most of the aid for economic reconstruction was EROA (Economic Rehabilitation in Occupied Areas), a part of GARIOA.

more than 80% of the deficit resulted from payments to special accounts, two-thirds of which were used to provide subsidies for rice, railway construction and maintenance, etc. (Table 3.9).

During this period, the relative price of rice (relative, for example, to that of labour) sharply increased. Rice is such a basic food that the government purchased all the rice at an official price and distributed it under regulation to consumers at a lower price. Since the official price was lower than the black market price, there was a strong incentive for farmers to keep some back and sell it on the black market. Nevertheless, the regulated consumer price was almost equal to—and in 1945 and 1946 even lower than—the official purchase price. Thus, official transactions in rice incurred deficits for the government, which bore all the associated costs such as transportation and storage. In effect, this part of the government deficit served to mitigate the impact of the drastic change in income distribution by guaranteeing a certain amount of food to everyone at a low price. The same can be said of deficits in the national railway accounts: the government offered benefits by reducing the cost of the transportation service.

Monetary Policy

These public deficits were financed mainly by government bonds and loans from the Bank of Japan to the government. Since most government bonds were directly or indirectly purchased by the Bank of Japan, these two methods of financing the government debt were essentially the same: up to 1949, the public deficits were financed by high-powered money created by the Bank of Japan (Table 3.10). In 1949, for example, the Bank of Japan's loans to the government were four times as large as its loans to commercial banks.

Table 3.10. Accounts of the Bank of Japan, 1945–1950 (¥ million)

	1945CY	1946	1947	1948	1949	1950
Assets						
Loans to private sector	37,838	50,431	32,301	51,901	88,645	269,025
Loans to govt.	11,220	7,600	53,201	83,509	100,004	63,014
Govt. bonds	7,156	34,761	145,866	247,718	188,900	136,787
Liabilities						
Bank notes	55,440	93,397	219,141	355,280	355,311	422,063
Private deposits	4,159	10,869	20,953	22,660	22,126	25,062
Subtotal (HPM)	59,599	104,266	240,094	377,940	377,437	447,125
Govt. deposits	17,776	6,463	6,703	14,002	12,036	47,757

Source: Okura-sho (Ministry of Finance) (1978).

This sharp increase in the high-powered money financing of government deficits was clearly a major cause of the increase in the money supply, which in turn brought about high inflation: in 1949 the money supply (defined as currency plus deposits) was about five times as large as in 1946. As we saw in the previous section, parallel to this increase in money supply, the official wholesale price index increased from 464 in 1946 to 5,941 in 1949 (see Bank of Japan 1985).

On the other hand, from Table 3.11 we can also observe that an increase in the money supply was not the only cause of high inflation in this period. The table shows the 'quantity equation' in terms of the rate of change. During the war, when most commodities were rationed and money hoarding was encouraged by the government, the velocity of money was in continuous decline; in sharp contrast, in 1947 and 1948 the velocity increased substantially. A standard explanation for an increase in velocity is that people anticipate a depreciation of the real value of money during a period of high inflation. However, in addition to this expectational effect, it is possible that velocity increases when real output falls drastically, leading to a dire drop in the standard of living to minimum subsistence level. At this point, people can no longer afford to hold money as a store of value, for only those commodities that can be immediately consumed are valuable. In such a situation, even the transactions demand for money, a kind of inventory stock for contingent transactions, is kept to a minimum. Basically, whenever people obtain money, they quickly exchange it for the

Table 3.11. The quantity equation of money, 1939–1950 (%/year)

		Nominal GNP	Real GNP	Deflator	M2	Velocity
CY	1939	21.1	0.8	20.3	27.6	−6.5
	1940	17.5	−6.2	23.6	22.7	−5.3
	1941	13.1	1.6	11.5	19.7	−6.6
	1942	19.2	1.3	17.9	20.5	−1.3
	1943	16.0	−0.3	16.3	21.6	−5.6
	1944	15.5	−3.4	18.9	36.5	−21.0
FY	1947	101.6	8.1	93.5	65.8	35.8
	1948	71.1	12.2	58.9	61.9	9.2
	1949	23.6	2.2	21.4	26.9	−3.3
	1950	15.7	10.4	5.3	30.4	−14.7

Source: Somu-cho (Management and Co-ordination Agency) (1987).

commodities they need for their survival. So the velocity of money naturally increases.

In sum, a sharp increase in high-powered money to finance the government budget deficits, an increase in velocity, and a drop of production to the minimum subsistence level all contributed to the post-war Japanese hyperinflation.

Direct Control

In the post-war period, economic policies were not confined to standard fiscal and monetary policies; the government exerted direct control on almost every aspect of the economy.

During the Second World War, the Japanese government had produced a wide range of economic controls in order to manage the wartime economy.[8] After the war, these controls were kept in place in order to deal with the problems faced by the war-torn economy. Price controls were first implemented in 1939. From then on, prices were officially set by the government on the basis of the National General Mobilization Law (Kokka Sodoin Ho). After the war ended, there were discussions within the government to limit the range of goods whose prices were to be controlled. However, in March 1946 the government established a new statute called the Price Control Ordinance (Bukka Tosei Rei), which allowed price controls to continue for important commodities. Transactions conducted wherein prices exceeded the official rate in widespread black markets were considered illegal.

In conjunction with the incorporation of this Act, a systematic official price scheme was established. Cost calculations for each commodity were based on wages and the prices of rice and coal; using these base costs, official prices were calculated to make possible production on a commercial basis. However, increases in wages and the prices of non-regulated commodities made these official rates untenable, and the government revised its official price scheme on the basis of new cost calculations in July 1947. To avoid sharp price increases, the official prices were to be maintained by setting a ceiling for basic materials costs of 65 times the pre-war prices and subsidizing the difference between actual costs and this ceiling. Following the revision of the official price scheme, the amount of subsidies paid for the purpose of price adjustment increased.

[8] As to the Japanese wartime economic control, see Okazaki (1993).

Since the official prices were set lower than the prices that cleared the market, a second form of economic regulation was established in the form of quotas. The government was authorized to set quotas by the Temporary Law for Adjusting the Demand and Supply of Materials (Rinji Busshi Jukyu Chosei Ho) of November 1946, having lost that authority with the abolition of the 1938 National Mobilization Law. According to the 1946 Act, purchasers of specified goods were to present a Demand Request Form to the government. After taking into consideration the total amount demanded by the request on the one hand and forecasted supply on the other, the government was then to allot goods according to the importance of each purchaser to the recovery of the economy. This quota system was called the Materials Supply and Demand Plan (Busshi Jukyu Keikaku), and public corporations called *kodan* were established for actual handling and distribution of the allotted goods to the final purchasers.

This planning and rationing system was used to recover production in the Japanese mining and manufacturing industries, beginning at the end of 1946. It is known as the Priority Production System (Keisha Seisan Houshiki), or the policy giving first priority to the coal and steel industries. The primary purpose of the policy was to input as much as steel as possible into the coal mines and then, in return, to send coal back to the steel industry, to create a kind of virtuous circle between two industries (Kosai 1986: 44–53). Because the Japanese economy at that time was facing a serious shortage of raw materials, this policy was essentially an attempt to substitute domestic production of coal for lost imports, and it made sense, at least in theory. How successful the policy actually was remains questionable even today.

3.3 DISINFLATION: THE DODGE PLAN IN 1949

In the early stages of the occupation, the US government and SCAP were interested exclusively in the disarmament and democratization of Japan. However, as the Cold War intensified, they became increasingly interested in the reconstruction of the Japanese economy. The shift in the priority of occupational policy to economic reconstruction was confirmed finally by the US government in October 1948 ('NSC Recommendations with respect to US Policy toward Japan': NSC-13/2). The basic strategy for economic reconstruction chosen by the US government was to stop inflation in the first place.

To this end, in 1949 an American banker named Joseph Dodge, the former president of the Detroit Bank, came to Japan as the special advisor to the Japanese government, delegated by President Truman. Dodge put forward a plan to achieve rapid disinflation of the Japanese economy. Japan, which was still under occupation, had no power to veto this plan, which urged the government drastically to cut the deficit and to attempt to turn the budget to surplus. The Japanese government carried out this plan and was actually able to achieve a budgetary surplus by 1950 (Table 3.9).

Reflecting the drastic fall in the government budget deficit, the Bank of Japan's lending to the government, including its direct purchase of government bonds, declined by about one-third in 1950. Meanwhile, the policies prescribed by Dodge proved severely damaging to many industries, and in 1949 the unemployment rate began to rise. In order to alleviate the deflationary effect of the Dodge Plan, the Bank of Japan eased monetary policy. Consequently, the Bank's lending to commercial banks increased from ¥89 billion in 1949 to ¥269 billion in 1950 (Table 3.10). The drastic tightening of fiscal policy based on the Dodge Plan was matched by an easing of monetary policy in 1950. This policy mix successfully achieved the goal of rapid disinflation.

What was the mechanism for bringing about successful disinflation? As the next section will discuss in detail, the years 1946–9 were a period when labour conflicts intensified. In this economic climate, firms had agreed to any wage increase that workers demanded.[9] Losses created by these wage increases were then compensated for by all kinds of public subsidies and transfers, which in turn caused a government budget deficit. And as we observed above, this government deficit was at the heart of Japan's high inflation rate.

Establishment of a Single Exchange Rate

Dodge described the Japanese economy, armoured by many public subsidies and transfers, as an 'economy on stilts', and he urged the government to abolish them. In this respect, one of the most important policies in this period was the establishment of a single

[9] The problem is very similar to 'softening of the budget constraint' of firms in communist economies; see Kornai (1980: 299–322).

exchange rate of ¥360 to the dollar in April 1949. At first (in June 1948), the Young Report had recommended ¥300 per dollar. Dodge slightly changed this to ¥330. Then in March 1949 the National Advisory Council in Washington, under the strong influence of the State Department, finally urged SCAP to adopt ¥360 per dollar. It was at this time that the Chinese Communist Party was about to dominate the whole of mainland China. Beyond doubt, this political situation in east Asia influenced the adoption of the ¥360 rate rather than ¥300.

Whether the ¥360 rate was actually an overvaluation or undervaluation of the yen at the time remains an issue today.[10] If one emphasizes the fact that there was a recession in 1949, one may subscribe to the overvaluation theory. On the other hand, relative to the ¥330 rate, which at the time was widely held to be the 'equilibrium' rate, the ¥360 was an undervaluation. At any rate, the Japanese economy did not get stuck in a period of prolonged stagnation in subsequent years; in the light of this fact, the ¥360 rate seems to have been about right. What was really important at the time was the establishment of a single exchange rate. This in effect meant that the government abolished numerous subsidies relating to foreign trade.

To understand the relationship between the establishment of a single exchange rate and these subsidies, it is necessary to keep in mind the way trade was conducted up to 1948. During this time, Japanese trade was implemented through the yen-denominated Trade Fund Special Account (Boeki Shinkin Tokusetsu Kaikei), which was managed by the Japanese government on the one hand, and by the dollar-denominated accounts controlled by SCAP on the other. For instance, when a Japanese importer wanted to import a good, it would pay the domestic yen-denominated official price to the Trade Fund Special Account of the Japanese government, and SCAP would purchase the good from abroad at international prices using dollars from its dollar-denominated account. In the case of exports, the Japanese government would sell the good on the basis of the domestic official price; payment from abroad, on the other hand, would be in dollars and would be made to the SCAP

[10] Shinohara (1974) argues that the yen was undervalued at ¥360 per dollar from the beginning. That is why, he argues, almost all the Japanese manufacturing industries came to be export-dominated, and Japan enjoyed export-led growth. On the other hand, Fujino (1988) argues that the equilibrium rate in 1955 was about ¥450–490 per dollar, and therefore that the yen was highly overvalued in the beginning. See also Shinohara (1989) for his rejoinder to Fujino.

account. Thus, an exchange rate in the normal sense did not exist; the yen–dollar rate was determined *post hoc* for each trade transaction. Table 3.12 shows exchange rates for various commodities in January 1949. The exchange rate, in fact, differs significantly, from ¥67 per dollar for pig iron to ¥600 for glass, celluloid products, and china. On the whole, the yen rate for exports tends to be undervalued and that for imports, overvalued.

Table 3.12. De facto exchange rates for various commodities, January 1949 (yen per dollar)

Exports		Imports	
Cotton yarn	250	Iron ore	125
Silk	420	Pig iron	67
Woollen yarn	300	Bauxite	158
Cars	430	Coal	178
Bicycles	510	Heavy oil	284
Radios	550	Wheat	165
Steel	240	Sugar	177
Coal	320	Cotton for domestic use	80
Canned food	300	Cotton to be used for exports	250
Tea	330	Wool	120
Oranges	340	Rubber	154
Chemicals	200	Phosphate ore	154
Leather products	580	Potassium	82
Celluloid products	600	Wood	77
Cement	320	Medicines	300
Glass	600		
China	600		

Source: Keizai-antei Honbu, *The 1949 Economic Report of the Japanese Government.*

Table 3.13 shows a change in the average exchange rates for exports and imports, respectively. The divergence between the two is, in effect, equivalent to a subsidy, whereby the yen prices that Japanese nationals could receive for selling their exports abroad were high, and prices for purchasing imports were relatively low. The size of the implicit subsidy can be estimated from the difference between the dollar-denominated trade balance and the so-called yen-denominated trade balance, calculated from the Trade Fund Special Accounts (Table 3.14). While the dollar-denominated trade balance maintains a significant deficit, as noted above, the Trade Fund Special Accounts are roughly in balance. The difference between the two can be

Table 3.13. Average exchange rates, 1946–1950 (yen per dollar)

Calendar year	Exports[a]	Imports[a]
1946	21.9	13.3
1947	58.5	38.5
1948	328.8	88.1
1949	333.2	314.4
1950	363.4	357.4

[a] Exports or imports in terms of yen divided by that in terms of dollars.

Source: Okura-sho (Ministry of Finance) (1978).

interpreted as the amount of implicit subsidy. Using the average yen rate for exports and imports, we can change the SCAP dollar-denominated balance into the yen-denominated balance, and then take the difference between this converted SCAP trade balance and the Trade Fund Special Accounts of the Japanese government. The difference, which measures the amount of implicit subsidy by way of trade, is almost half of the explicit price adjustment subsidy paid from the General Government Account. The *de facto* subsidy expended on trade owing to the lack of a single exchange rate was quite substantial.

When the government subsidies and transfers were abolished, high wage increases would have pushed firms to the edge of bankruptcy. *In effect, a single exchange rate meant an enforced incomes policy, and cut the vicious cycle of wage and price increases.* Before the time of a single exchange rate, the Japanese government had attempted in vain to implement an incomes policy; for example in

Table 3.14. Estimation of subsidies by multiple exchange rates, 1946–1948 (¥ million)

	1946	1947	1948
(1) Deficit of trade balance	3,684	11,623	33,877
(2) Surplus of trade fund special account	− 7	1	818
(3) (1)− (2)	3,690	11,622	33,060
(4) Subsidies for price control	10,216	26,557	70,472
(3)/(4)	0.36	0.44	0.47

Note: (1) is based on calendar year; (2) and (4) on fiscal year. 'Deficit of trade balance' is converted into yen by the average exchange rate (the total trade in terms of yen divided by that in terms of dollars).

Source: Okura-sho (Ministry of Finance) (1978).

the calculation of official price schemes in July 1947, nominal wages were assumed to be only 28 times higher than the pre-war level, whereas the general price level was assumed to be 65 times higher. However, the government could not enforce effective wage control, because SCAP was maintaining a pro-labour standpoint at that time. In December 1948, SCAP issued a memorandum on wage stabilization to the Japanese government, prohibiting wage increases by means of subsidies. A single exchange rate was the effective means of achieving this goal. In parallel with the adoption of a single exchange rate, government subsidies were drastically cut in 1949 (Table 3.15); the only exception was the subsidy for food. In any case, a cut in the budget deficit *per se* would not have been enough to curb high inflation. The incomes policy aspect of the Dodge Plan, particularly the single exchange rate, was instrumental to disinflation.

We can also trace this disinflationary process in terms of the quantity equation in Table 3.11. The growth rate of money supply certainly declined to a considerable degree, from 61.9% in 1948 to 30.4% in 1950. But at the same time the velocity of money also declined, from 9.2% to –14.7%. To some extent, a decline in velocity is the result of disinflation through the standard expectation effect, but it can be a *cause* of further disinflation. A possible reason for a decline in velocity independent of expectations is that output had recovered sufficiently to move the economy up from the minimum subsistence level. As explained above, when output falls to the minimum subsistence level, velocity increases; conversely, velocity will decrease, independent of an expectation of disinflation, when output rises above the minimum subsistence level. I argue that an

Table 3.15. Decreases in government subsidies, 1949–1950 (¥ billion)

	1949	1950
Total	202.2	90.0
Coal	36.5	0.0
Steel	41.6	18.8
Copper	2.8	0.0
Fertilizer	17.4	13.7
Food	40.6	45.7

Source: Keizai-antei Honbu, *The 1950 Economic Report of the Japanese Government*.

increase in output, a real factor, contributed to disinflation along with a deceleration of the money supply and the effective 'incomes policy' in the Dodge Plan period. The relative importance of real and monetary factors in the process of disinflation remains a very important and as yet unresolved problem.

3.4 LABOUR–MANAGEMENT RELATIONS AND THE ORIGIN OF THE JAPANESE FIRM

Through the incessant turbulence of 1946–50, the so-called 'Japanese firm' emerged. The Japanese firm today is commonly celebrated for its distinctive features, in comparison with US and European firms. In particular, labour–management relations are characterized by lifetime employment, seniority wages, and enterprise unions, all allegedly unique to Japan. Just as in the case of the high Japanese household saving rate, some are quick to explain the phenomenon of the Japanese firm in terms of national characteristics and/or 'cultural' factors. The truth is, however, that the so-called Japanese firm has an historical origin. This section explains it by focusing on the labour–management relations in the period 1945–54.[11]

The pre-war Japanese firm did not have lifetime employment, seniority wages, or enterprise unions. It is true that long-term employment, seniority wages, and on-the-job training were first introduced into a few large firms after the First World War, mostly in heavy industry rather than, say, textiles (Hyodo 1965). The number of such firms was, however, very limited. In fact, employment responded very flexibly to changes in output. For example, Table 3.16 cites changes in employment and output during the 1929–31 depression. Remarkably, drops in employment were much greater than those in output in many industries, with machinery industry the only exception. This pattern is in distinct contrast to the one we observe for the post-1955 period. Lifetime employment was, therefore, not at all common but very exceptional in the pre-war Japanese firm.

The Second World War exerted a strong shock on Japanese society. The firm was no exception. In order to conduct the war,

[11] The best reference in English on history of the labour relations in Japan is A. Gordon (1985).

Table 3.16. The decline in employment and output in the 1929–31 depression (%)[a]

	Employment	Output
Cotton	– 24.2	– 9.6
Food	– 12.7	– 8.6
Machinery	– 13.7	– 31.3
Steel/nonferrous metals	– 16.5	– 13.9
Chemicals	– 13.5	– 1.0

[a] The percentages represent the extent of the drop from the 1929 levels.

Source: Employment: index of employed workers compiled by the Bank of Japan; output: index of production, compiled by the Nagoya High School of Commerce.

the government designed a planned economy, akin to the pre-*perestroika* Soviet economy. In this wartime economy, the firm was simply taken as a production unit and was reformed drastically. Thus, the rights of shareholders were strongly curtailed in favour of management, and the privileges of white-collar workers were diminished. Dividends were cut. The wages of blue-collar workers doubled relative to the salaries of white-collar employees, making them equal. And, in order to stabilize industrial relations, the firm-based organization, the Sangyo Hokoku Kai, or Sanpo, covering both white-collar and blue-collar workers, was established (Odaka 1993). Some attribute the origin of lifetime employment, seniority wages, and enterprise unions to this wartime economy (Okazaki 1993).

Despite drastic changes to the firm during the war, however, the Japanese firm at that time was not actually what we presently understand as 'the Japanese firm'. The morale of workers, for example, was very low; the rate of non-attendance rose steadily from the early 1930s until the end of the war (Tsuda 1983; and Odaka 1993). Seniority wages simply did not exist. Besides, as we will see shortly, the end of the war threw the firm into complete chaos. It is reasonable, therefore, to conclude that what we presently understand basically as the Japanese firm emerged by trial and error after the war.

When the war ended, chaos prevailed. At Toyota, for example, within a month after the end of the war, on 15 August 1945, 5,000 employees out of 8,000 were dismissed from the company. At Mitsubishi Heavy Industry, 340,000 blue-collar workers out of 390,000 thousand were dismissed. At Hitachi, 22,000 workers out of

29,000 were dismissed (Tsuda 1983). The list continues. Nothing like lifetime employment!

In this turmoil, SCAP encouraged the establishment of trade unions as a part of Japan's democratization. Thus, the Labour Union Law was proclaimed as early as December 1945. Unions spread rapidly. By the end of 1946, the number of unions had already exceeded 17,000, and the proportion of organized workers had reached 40%. With the tide of this strong labour movement, two nation-wide organizations were established in August 1946: Nihon Rodo Kumiai Sodomei, or Sodomei (Japan Federation of Labour) and Zen Nihon Sangyobetsu Rodo Kumiai Kaigi, or Sanbetsu (Japan Congress of Industrial Unions). Sodomei, covering 22% of all organized workers, was the most conservative of the union federations, whereas Sanbetsu, consisting of 21 industrial unions and covering 43% of organized workers, was under the leadership of the Japan Communist Party and was very militant. In 1946 and 1947, the militant Sanbetsu was more active than the conservative Sodomei, and real power resided in the militant national industry-wide and inter-industry federations, and not in the enterprise unions. (A. Gordon 1985; Yonekura 1993).

In these early years, one of the most important slogans of the union movement was 'production control' (*seisan kanri*), which referred to the call for worker management. In fact, in many firms, the unions extracted the promise that management would have to gain union consent for all discharges, hirings, transfers, penalties imposed, and promotions of workers. Against the background of the massive dismissals in 1945, unions naturally sought job security, and in most cases they got it. In some extreme cases, such as Ishikawajima Shipbuilding and Kobe Steel, they won 'no-dismissal' promises from management. Beyond job security, some unions even succeeded in taking over the factory and running it without managers; in the first half of 1946, 225 such incidents of worker-control took place. The power of management declined to a minimum in this period.

Interestingly, many unions demanded the abolition of the distinction between white-collar and blue-collar workers. One reason for this was that, under the Marxist influence, unions wished to take workers just as 'workers', whether white-collar or blue-collar, supposedly against 'capitalists'. But another reason, perhaps more important, was that, as explained in Section 3.1, both blue-collar and white-collar workers had lost out to the self-employed during this period. They shared common objectives, such as securing an equitable rationing of food, and unions played an important part in settling the distribution of rationed commodities.

These radical labour movements culminated in a national general strike on 1 February 1947, called by both Sanbetsu and Sodomei. SCAP, however, bewildered by the increasingly Marxist stance of the unions, had changed its labour policy, and prohibited the planned strike. The failure of this general strike marked a turning-point, and thereafter the extreme Marxist influence on the labour movement faded. Meanwhile, with support from SCAP, managers founded Nihon Keieisha Dantai Renmei, or Nikkeiren (the Japan Federation of Employers' Associations) in August 1948. The unions and management fought fiercely over wages, job security, and work control. In time, the pendulum gradually swung back and management regained power. And yet, it was not merely a matter of win-or-lose. This turbulent period saw the development of a new outlook which was to endure for years to come.

Particularly important during this period was the introduction of a new wage structure in the autumn of 1948 by Denki Sangyo Rodo Kumiai Kyogikai, or Densan (the Electric Power Industry Worker's Union). This Densan-style wage structure involved determining wages largely on the basis of age, family size, and standard of living; about 70% of wages consisted of 'livelihood guarantees' and 'regional allowances'. This approach opened the door to the eventual establishment of seniority wages. At the same time, it formally abolished status distinction between white-collar and blue-collar workers. The introduction of *kihon-kyu* (a base wage) to guarantee a minimum standard of living for all employees naturally facilitated monthly payments even for blue-collar workers, instead of the hourly or daily payments.

Job security was another major battlefield in labour–management relations during this period. As Section 3.3 explained, Dodge's deflationary policy in 1949, accompanied by a drastic cut in government subsidies, succeeded in reducing inflation. But in this process of disinflation, firms were urged to cut down on their excessive workforces. In fact, during the 1949 Dodge recession many small firms were wiped out, and even large firms began to dismiss employees. For example, between June 1949 and June 1950, three major car manufacturers, including Toyota and Nissan, dismissed 23% of their employees. Despite the Korean War boom, major dismissals for rationalization continued throughout the early 1950s. As might be expected, strikes were prolonged and bitter; particularly notorious were those at Toyota (1950), the coal miners (1952), Nissan (1953), the Muroran Mill of Nikko Steel, and Omi Silk (1954). The unions lost in these major strikes, and, one by one, radical unions were replaced by co-operative 'second unions'. But management was not really a winner, either. For example, even ignoring non-pecuniary costs, the 200-day strike cost Nikko Steel more than double its paid-in capital. In the process of enduring prolonged strikes during the period 1949–54, both management and unions learned a hard lesson: bitter confrontations are extremely costly to both parties. No major dismissals were attempted by management after 1954. (The only exception is the case of Miike Coal Mine in 1960.) Paradoxically, perhaps, the bitter labour relations in the early 1950s was actually instrumental in the establishment of enterprise unions in Japan.

These early post-war years saw not only many prolonged strikes but also a very high turnover of the work-force in large firms. Table 3.17, for example, records turnover at Yahata Steel, the then largest steel company. Workers in large steel companies were known for their high skills, but the table reveals a very high turnover of these skilled workers. Plainly, long-term employment was not practised even for skilled labour at large firms at the beginning of the 1950s. It developed gradually, perhaps half unintentionally, thanks to subsequent high economic growth.

Table 3.17. The turnover of blue-collar workers at Yahata Steel, 1947–1951

	New hirings	Job-leavers
1947	3,083	4,779
1948	9,882	2,387
1949	2,185	1,572
1950	3,569	1,603
1951	1,545	1,442

Source: *The Corporate History of Shin Nihon Steel.* This history makes the remark that, maladjusted to their 'poor' urban life, most job-leavers returned to their rural homes.

As A. Gordon (1985) correctly points out, 'to simply credit cultural traditions centered upon an ethic of loyalty with a major role in the creation of an employment system is to lose sight of the dialectic by which history unfolds'. Japanese labour relations—encompassing seniority wages, long-term employment, and co-operative enterprise unions—were created by painful trial and error in the post-war turbulent years.

3.5 THE KOREAN WAR AND PREPARATION FOR HIGH ECONOMIC GROWTH, 1950–1954

During the 1949 Dodge disinflation, many Japanese firms were on the verge of bankruptcy. Not only were profits squeezed, but massive dismissals provoked bitter strikes. Then, in June 1950 the Korean War broke out. The war created a huge demand for goods produced in Japan and salvaged the fragile economy, just as the First World War had done forty years earlier. During the period of the Korean War, the Japanese economy was able to prepare for high economic growth, which was about to start in 1955.

Despite the chaos that prevailed during the first five years following the Second World War, the Japanese economy managed to achieve an average growth rate of 8.6%. The most notable characteristics of the 1946–50 period are, first, that production recovered and grew in parallel with the supply of raw materials rather than with an increase in capital stock; and, second, that the increase in output was almost entirely absorbed by an increase in consumption: the level of investment hardly changed (Table 3.1). In sharp contrast, the Korean War period (1950–4) saw a high rate of investment and rapid technical progress.

Because of the war, Japan's exports jumped from $820 million in 1950 to $1,355 million in 1951, an increase of 65%, and they stayed at that level during 1951–3. The extra demand created by the war accounted for 45%–65% of total exports. This export boom led the Japanese economy into immediate recovery from the Dodge recession. The profit rate in manufacturing industry, for example, rose from 2.8% in 1950 to 10.6% in 1951. Most important, the boom contributed to a sustained growth of investment. Investment increased from ¥390 billion in 1950 to ¥800 billion in 1953.

The most important factor behind high investment during this period was the abundance of opportunities for introducing new technology. And yet, there is no denying that the Korean War encouraged firms to make such investment by providing the prospect of strong demand. By 1950, much of the existing capital stock had been outmoded; in 1951, for example, an American advisor to SCAP estimated total factor productivity of Japan's steel industry to be about 70% of its US counterpart. Investment was planned, above all, to bring in new technology.

The steel industry best symbolizes this period. Newly developed strip mills, the key innovation at the time, were expected to cut down on labour by 75%, energy by 60%, and time by 70%. A massive investment, amounting to 5% of total investment in the economy as a whole, was made to introduce strip mills during the period 1951–5. At the same time, investment was also made with the purpose of integrating the production of pig iron and steel. Kawasaki Steel took the initiative by constructing the Chiba mill, one of the most advanced mills in the world. It was opened in 1953. Two firms immediately followed Kawasaki, and by 1955 six integrated producers of iron and steel had achieved the second-highest productivity in the world: the total cost of producing a ton of pig iron in that year was $113.0 for the United States, $89.9 for Japan, and $75.9 for West Germany. In the same year, steel accounted for 13% of Japan's exports. Equipped with modern strip mills, the steel industry was ready to meet any growth of demand. As Chapter 2 explained, beginning 1955, domestic demand for steel started to grow, led by construction and the increased production of such consumer durables as refrigerators, washing machines, and most importantly, cars.

The technical progress brought about by new investment was, of course, not limited to the steel industry. Many firms aggressively introduced new technologies, both domestically developed and borrowed from abroad. Toray, a textile company, was ready to pay $3 million, well exceeding its paid-in capital, to Dupont for a patent on nylon in 1951. By 1955, the high rate of investment made during the early 1950s had borne the fruit of modernized capacity. Militant labour activity was giving way to co-operative enterprise unions. In short, the Japanese economy was ready to embark on a period of high economic growth.

3.6 CONCLUSION

A final word about this dramatic period in the history of Japan. Throughout the turbulent decade after the Second World War, Japan had succeeded in transforming itself into a much more equitable society than that of its pre-war years, perhaps one of the most equitable in the world. As Section 3.1 explained, land reform, inflation, and the 1946 wealth tax substantially equalized wealth distribution. The pre-war affluent disappeared. At the same time, income distribution was also made much more equitable. For example, according to the Japan Federation of Employers' Association, in 1927 the annual income of the president of a large firm was on average about 100 times as high as that of a newly hired white-collar employee; by 1963 it was only 12 times as high. As explained in Section 3.4, the wage gap between white-collar and blue-collar workers had already diminished during the war; Mizoguchi (1986) and Minami and Ono (1987) show that the Gini coefficient fell from 0.4 to 0.3 during this period. It continued to equalize in the years that followed.

Equality of income and wealth contributed to the growth of the post-war Japanese economy through various channels. First, a rise in the incomes of farmers and blue-collar workers, who made up 70% of the total work-force in 1950, enlarged the domestic market for manufactured products, thus making possible the domestic-demand-led growth that was to begin in 1955. Second, equality of income also provided equal opportunities for higher education in the post-war society, which in turn brought about an efficient accumulation of human capital. And finally, within the firm, income equality served to raise the morale of the majority of employees.

4

Keynesian Economics Survives Supply Shocks: Demand/Supply Constraints and Inventory

In Chapter 2, I argued that business cycles in post-war Japan were caused basically by fluctuations in effective demand. I also explained that the permanent deceleration in economic growth in the early 1970s was caused by changes in the internal structure of the Japanese economy, rather than by the oil embargo of 1973. It would be unreasonable to suppose, however, that a sharp increase in the real price of inputs would have no impact on the macroeconomy. In fact, motivated by two oil shocks in the 1970s, a number of attempts have been made to extend the demand analysis by introducing the 'supply' side; the best-known example would be Bruno and Sachs (1985). To introduce the 'supply' side is, in the present context, explicitly to consider firm (supplier of commodities) behaviour in the model. Firm profit maximization then implies the condition that marginal products are equated to real input prices for all the variable inputs. For convenience, I refer to this(these) condition(s) as supply constraint(s).

This consideration now leads us to conjecture that poor output performance, traditionally attributed to low aggregate demand, may in fact be due to poor incentives for firms to supply output because of high real input prices. In terms of unemployment, Malinvaud (1982) and Sachs (1983), among others, argue that high unemployment in the 1970s was caused by high real wages rather than aggregate demand deficiency. If unemployment is 'classical' in nature rather than Keynesian, then the traditional demand management would be not only ineffective, but also potentially harmful. The supply-side consideration, therefore, has very important policy implications.[1] We will consider the problems of the labour market in Chapter 5. In this chapter, we focus on goods market.

[1] The supply-side consideration, together with wage behaviour, has important implications for the effectiveness of monetary and fiscal policies under flexible

Given our findings in Chapter 2, we know that demand constraints have been very important in the Japanese economy. There is also some evidence that the decline in output in the United Kingdom in the 1970s was in fact due to both demand and supply factors: see Bruno and Sachs (1985).[2] It is therefore reasonable to suppose that both supply and demand constraints play their roles in the real economy, and that their relative importance has varied over time. Granted that both constraints are potentially important, the most serious problem is our difficulty in determining which constraint is binding in particular cyclical episodes.

There are basically two approaches to this problem. One is to suppose that each individual firm is subject to either a demand or a supply constraint at any one time, but that the changes in the proportion of firms subject to a demand constraint varies over time, and therefore the relative importance of demand/supply constraints in the macroeconomy also changes. This approach does not require any modification of the standard general disequilibrium or non-market-clearing model. The problem boils down to the aggregation of firms in two different regimes: the price-taking firm versus the demand-constrained firm. An example of empirical application of this approach is Artus *et al.* (1984).

The other approach is to assume that each firm is simultaneously subject to both demand and supply constraints. The assumption that goods markets are imperfectly competitive, for example, leads us to the conclusion that the firm's output responds to changes in both real input prices and demand. Hickman (1987) applied this idea to estimate the 'demand gap' unemployment and the 'wage gap' unemployment in the United States. In this framework, elasticities of output, with respect to input prices and demand, depend on the price elasticity of demand facing the firm and on input elasticities of the production function. So long as these elasticities remain the same,

exchange rates: see Sachs (1980). The basic issue is whether the economy is constrained by real demand or is in the Walrasian equilibrium.

[2] For example, their output supply equation reported in Table III has an inventory variable as a significant right-hand-side (RHS) variable together with variable factor prices and capital stock. It should not appear in the supply equation, however, if what we call the supply constraint is always binding. It is also reported (their Table V) that during the period 1973–8 raw material prices directly explain about 55% of the 15% decline in output per capital in the UK, and that the demand variable (inventory–output ratio) accounts for another 45%. On the other hand, Buiter and Miller (1981) attribute the poor output performance of the UK economy under the Thatcher government almost exclusively to demand factors, particularly tight monetary policy.

therefore, the response of output to changes in input prices and demand also remains unchanged. The relative importance of demand/supply constraints directly reflects the relative size of demand and input price (supply) shocks. Instead, this chapter presents another approach, in which each firm is subject simultaneously to both demand and supply constraints, and yet the relative importance of the two constraints varies over time. It provides a theoretical justification for using inventory variables to measure the relative importance of supply and demand constraints.

Section 4.1 develops a theoretical model of the firm with inventory stock. The firm is assumed to be constrained both by exogenous real input prices and by demand (sales) over time. Within this framework, I analyse how output responds to changes in real input prices and demand constraints. Under the assumption of nonlinear net marginal return on inventory, Section 4.2 shows that the relative importance of the two constraints depends crucially on the level of inventory stock. At one extreme, where the level of inventory stock is very high relative to future demand, only the demand (sales) constraint matters as a determinant of output, and the usual Keynesian analysis holds. At the other extreme, the firm determines its output through responding only to real input prices, and the neoclassical theory holds. In general, however, both constraints are binding at one time. Therefore, in the present case we do not have a switch of demand- and supply-constrained regimes, as is often postulated. Rather, the relative importance of two constraints varies continuously as the level of inventory changes. Section 4.3 then provides some evidence in the case of the Japanese manufacturing industry that both constraints are in fact binding and, moreover, that the importance of such constraints depends on inventory.

The inventory–sales ratio sharply rose following the two oil crises. Demand, therefore, must have played a very important role as a determinant of output. In fact, the behaviour of real GNP differed remarkably in the two comparable oil crises: the growth rate of real GNP fell from 5.3% to –0.2% during 1973–4, while it declined only slightly from 5.3% to 3.7% during 1979–80. Section 4.4 shows that the key factor in explaining this difference is investment, and therefore that demand is indeed an indispensable part of any reasonable explanation of the Japanese economy during the two oil crises. It thereby suggests that focusing on the impact of an increase in real factor prices on output through the production function is insufficient as an explanation of supply shocks.

4.1 THE MODEL OF THE FIRM

Assuming the firm to be quantity-constrained as well as a price-taker in the goods market, we analyse the relative importance of supply and demand constraints. If the firm is a price-taker without any quantity constraint, then only the supply constraint is binding. We next observe that, if the behaviour of the quantity-constrained firm is analysed in a one-period (static) model without inventory investment, then the problem of the relative importance of supply and demand constraints has a well-known solution; that is, the actual level of output is equal to the minimum of S^* and D. Here D is a demand (quantity) constraint and S^* is the desired supply of the firm given a price vector (input and output prices) alone. This kind of analytical setting is popular in non-Walrasian or general disequilibrium theory, as surveyed by Malinvaud (1977) and Negishi (1979). In this framework, only one of two constraints is binding at a time and, therefore, the goods market is characterized by two different regimes.

Introducing inventory investment in a similar but now dynamic framework, however, changes this characterization. To be specific, the well-known condition MC (marginal cost) = P (price) which determines S^* above no longer holds. This point was emphasized, for example, by Blinder (1982). Given these observations, in what follows we analyse the quantity-constrained firm in a dynamic model with inventory investment. Inventory is a crucial element in the present analysis.

The firm is assumed to maximize the present value of net cash flow:

$$\sum_{t=1}^{N} \alpha^{t-1}[D_t - w_t L_t - C(K_{t+1})] + \alpha^N \phi(K_{N+1}) \qquad 0 < \alpha < 1, \tag{1}$$

where α is a discount factor and is assumed to be between zero and one, and $D_t(t = 1,\ldots, N)$ is a perceived demand (quantity) constraint facing the firm and is exogeneously given. The price of the firm's product is normalized to be one, and therefore $w_t(t = 1 \sim N)$ is the real wage, which is also exogenously given. In what follows, we call w_t the 'real wage', and refer to a variable input L_t as 'labour' for convenience, but w_t and L_t can be vectors without changing the subsequent analysis. K_{t+1} is an inventory *stock*[3] and $C(K)$ is the cost of holding this inventory stock: storage costs, economic depreciation of products, etc. We assume that the $C(K)$ function is convex:

[3] Having K_{t+1} rather than K_t in C function is notational, not of any substance.

$$C(0) = 0, \;\; C'(K) > 0 \;\; C''(K) > 0 \qquad \text{for } K > 0. \tag{2}$$

$\phi(K_{N+1})$ is the valuation function of inventory stock at a terminal date and is assumed to be concave:

$$\phi(0) = 0, \;\; \phi'(K_{N+1}) > 0, \;\; \phi''(K_{N+1}) < 0 \qquad \text{for } K_{N+1} > 0. \tag{3}$$

The valuation function of inventory stock would reflect various motives for holding inventory, such as to minimize stock-out costs or to shorten delivery lags.

For technical reasons, we consider a finite-period problem: to have a well-defined infinite-period model, we would have to put some restrictions on $\{w_t, D_t\}$ $(t = 1,\ldots, N)$. Since N is arbitrary, $\phi(K_{N+1})$ does not significantly influence current $(t = 1)$ decisions of the firm too much. For technical reasons, again, we do not consider the problem of fixed investment in the present model: capital stock, assumed to be constant, is implicit in the production function.[4] Fixed investment of the demand-constrained firm will be analysed in Chapter 7.

The firm's decision is subject to the following constraint:

$$K_{t+1} - K_t + D_t = F(L_t), \tag{4}$$

where $F(L_t)$ is a production function and is assumed to satisfy the following conditions:

$$\begin{gathered} F(0) = 0, \;\; \lim_{L\to\infty} F(L) = \infty, \\ F'(L) > 0, \;\; F''(L) < 0 \;\text{ for } L > 0, \\ \lim_{L\to 0} F'(L) = \infty, \;\; \lim_{L\to\infty} F'(L) = 0 \end{gathered} \tag{5}$$

The firm is assumed to maximize its present value (1) subject to constraint (4) and the given initial inventory stock $K_1 > 0$ by choosing the appropriate time paths of L_t and K_t. We assume the existence of an internal solution to this problem and note that the solution, if it exists, is unique, thanks to the strict concavity property of the problem. The solution is best characterized by dynamic programming (see Bellman 1957), and the principle of optimality leads us to the following functional equation with respect to $J_t(K_t)$:

$$\begin{aligned} J_t(K_t) &= \max_{\{L_t\}} [D_t - w_t L_t - C(K_{t+1}) + \alpha J_{t+1}(K_{t+1})] \\ &= \max_{\{L_t\}} [D_t - w_t L_t - C(K_t + F(L_t) - D_t) \end{aligned} \tag{6}$$

[4] Introducing capital, which is a substitute for labour input, could affect some of the results obtained, especially those on the effects of changes in future demand.

$$+ \alpha J_{t+1}(K_t + F(L_t) - D_t)] \quad t = 1,\ldots, N$$

$$J_{N+1}(K_{N+1}) = \phi(K_{N+1}).$$

We solve this recursive equation with respect to $J_t(K_t)$ backwards. The first problem to be solved therefore is as follows:

$$\max_{\{L_N\}} [D_N - w_N L_N - C(K_N + F(L_N) - D_N) + \alpha\phi(K_N + F(L_N) - D_N)]. \quad (7)$$

Because of (5), L_N, which maximizes (7), is uniquely related to K_N; also, strict concavity of (7) with respect to K_N and L_N guarantees strict concavity $J_N(K_N)$:[5]

$$J_N'(K_N) > 0, \qquad J_N''(K_N) < 0. \quad (8)$$

This information about $J_N(K_N)$ is then used to derive $J_{N-1}(K_{N-1})$ by (6). In this way, solving (6) backwards leads us to the firm's current (t = 1) decision problem:

$$\max_{\{L_1\}} [D_1 - w_1 L_1 - C(K_2) + \alpha J_2(K_2)]. \quad (9)$$

Since the firm formulates a plan for $\{L_1,\ldots, L_N\}$ at $t = 1$ but puts into effect only the first period of this plan, what interests us is the firm's current (t = 1) decision. For this reason, in what follows we will concentrate on (9). One point to note is that in (9) J_2 is written as a function only of K_2, but actually it also depends on $\{D_2,\ldots, D_N\}$ and $\{w_2,\ldots, w_N\}$. We can show,[6] for example, that

$$\frac{\partial J_2(K_2)}{\partial D_t} > 0, \qquad \frac{\partial J_2'(K_2)}{\partial D_t} > 0, \qquad (t = 2,\ldots, N). \quad (10)$$

Since we focus on the firm's current decision, we omit time subscripts in the following analysis. Introducing inventory investment of the final product, I, (9) can be rewritten as follows:[7]

[5] See Lemma 1 of Bellman (1957: 21).

[6] Since (10) can be shown by induction, it suffices to show $\partial J_t/\partial D_t > 0$, and that $\partial J_t'/\partial D_t > 0$. From (6), due to the envelope theorem, $\partial J_t/\partial D_t = 1 - (\alpha J'_{t+1} - C') \geqq 0$: the net shadow price of inventory investment is not greater than the current price of the goods, 1. Also,

$$\frac{\partial J_t'}{\partial D_t} = \frac{(J''_{t+1} - C'')(J'_{t+1} - C')F''}{[(\alpha J'_{t+1} - C')F'' + (\alpha J''_{t+1} - C'')F'^2]} > 0.$$

[7] In the present model, inventory investment I means the producer's inventory investment of the final product. As Blinder and Maccini (1991) emphasize, however, this component does not actually share the major part of total inventory investment. For Japan, in 1989 the producer's inventory investments of (i) the final products, (ii) goods in process, (iii) raw materials, and (iv) the trader's inventory investment of the final product were, respectively, ¥637, ¥443, ¥455, and ¥1,618 bn. The share of the producer's inventory investment of the final product is only about 20%.

$$D - wL - C(\bar{K} + I) + \alpha J(\bar{K} + I; \tilde{D}). \tag{11}$$

Since all future demand constraints affect the firm's current economic environment in qualitatively similar ways ((10) above), we summarize them as $\tilde{D}$ in (11). Using I, we can also rewrite constraint (4) as

$$Q = F(L) = D + I. \tag{12}$$

I can be either positive or negative.

The firm's problem is now reformulated as maximizing (11) with respect to L and I subject to (12), given D, w, and $\tilde{D}$. The necessary condition for the assumed internal solution is

$$\alpha J'(\bar{K} + I) - C'(\bar{K} + I) = \frac{\mathrm{d}Lw}{\mathrm{d}F}. \tag{13}$$

The left-hand side of (13) is what can be called the *net marginal return of inventory stock*: the marginal contribution of inventory in terms of the firm's present value net of inventory holding costs. Therefore condition (13) requires that, for optimality, this marginal return of inventory stock be equated to the marginal production cost.

Equations (12) and (13) now simultaneously determine the equilibrium output, Q (or, equivalently, input demand, L) and inventory investment, I. Inventory investment in this model is, as a result of the firm's optimization, at the desired level. It can be negative (inventory decumulation) if the initial inventory stock is sufficiently high. Specifically, the following relation holds:

$$I \lesseqqgtr 0 \quad \text{when } \bar{K} \gtreqqless \tilde{K}, \tag{14}$$

where $\tilde{K}$ is K such that

$$[\alpha J'(\tilde{K}) - C'(\tilde{K})]\, F'(F^{-1}(D)) = w.$$

In the usual non-Walrasian model, the left-hand side of (13) is always one, and I is zero in (12), with respective equalities replaced by appropriate inequalities. In that case, only the demand or the supply constraint is binding at any one time, and therefore we have two different regimes characterizing the goods market. In the present model, however, both constraints are binding, and, as we will see in the next section, the relative importance of the two constraints depends crucially on the level of inventory stock.

4.2 CHANGES IN OUTPUT AND INVENTORY STOCK

In this section we study how output Q and inventory investment I change in response to changes in exogenous variables. Differentiating

(12) and (13) with respect to D (the current demand constraint), we first obtain the following results:

$$\frac{dQ}{dD} = \frac{-(\alpha J'' - C'')F'^2}{-(\alpha J' - C')F'' - (\alpha J'' - C'')F'^2} > 0 \tag{15}$$

and

$$\frac{dI}{dD} = \frac{(\alpha J' - C')F''}{-(\alpha J' - C')F'' - (\alpha J'' - C'')F'^2} < 0, \tag{16}$$

since $\alpha J'' - C''$ is negative ((2) and (8)). Equations (15) and (16) imply that, in general, an increase in current demand is met *partly* by a decrease in inventory investment but also by an increase in production. We emphasize the above result $0 \leq dQ/dD \leq 1$ since in the usual non-Walrasian framework $dQ/dD = 1$ when the economy is demand-constrained, and $dQ/dD = 0$ when it is supply-constrained. It is interesting then to ask ourselves when we obtain $dQ/dD = 1$, the simple Keynesian multiplier in (15). To consider this problem, we focus on $(\alpha J'' - C'')$.

The net marginal return of inventory stock, $(\alpha J' - C')$, is assumed to decline when K increases so that $(\alpha J'' - C'')$ is always negative. But it seems reasonable to assume that, when K is low enough relative to future demand conditions (note that $\alpha J'$ depends on future demand as well as inventory stock, (10)), the extent to which $\alpha J'$ declines when K increases is relatively small. On the other hand, when K is very high, a substantial decrease in the marginal return is supposed to make $-(\alpha J'' - C'')$ large. This assumption, which is somewhat akin to the so-called (S, s) policies, can be summarized as follows:

$$0 < -(\alpha J'' - C'') < +\infty.$$

$$\alpha J''' - C''' < 0.$$

In particular,

$$\begin{aligned} -(\alpha J'' - C'') &\simeq 0 && \text{when } K \text{ is small relative to } \tilde{D} \\ -(\alpha J'' - C'') &\simeq +\infty && \text{when } K \text{ is very high relative to } \tilde{D}. \end{aligned} \tag{17}$$

This can be visualized in Fig. 4.1. This *nonlinearity of the net marginal return on inventory* plays a crucial role in the subsequent analyses.

Under assumption (17), it is easy to see when we obtain the simple Keynesian multiplier in (15). That is, when K is very high relative to future demand, so that $-(\alpha J'' - C'') \simeq +\infty$, dQ becomes nearly equal to dD and we obtain the simple Keynesian multiplier. On the other hand, if $-(\alpha J'' - C'') \simeq 0$, then $dQ/dD \simeq 0$. In general,

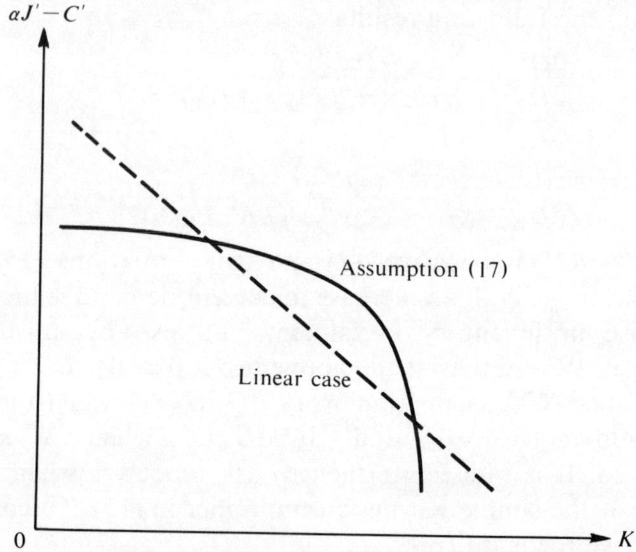

Fig. 4.1. Marginal return on inventory

however, when $0 < -(\alpha J'' - C'') < +\infty$, then $0 < \mathrm{d}Q/\mathrm{d}D < 1$ and as a consequence a part of the increase in current demand is met by a decrease in inventory investment.

We next study how output responds to changes in real input price, w. Differentiating (12) and (13) with respect to w, we obtain the following results:

$$\frac{\mathrm{d}Q}{\mathrm{d}w} = \frac{-F'}{-(\alpha J' - C')F'' - F'^2(\alpha J'' - C'')} < 0, \tag{18}$$

$$\frac{\mathrm{d}I}{\mathrm{d}w} = \frac{\mathrm{d}Q}{\mathrm{d}w} < 0. \tag{19}$$

Thus, an increase in real input prices induces the firm to cut its production and inventory investment. Under assumption (17), however, when inventory stock is very high relative to future demand and $-(\alpha J'' - C'') \simeq \infty$, $\mathrm{d}Q/\mathrm{d}w$ becomes almost zero. On the other hand, if K is low enough and $-(\alpha J'' - C'') \simeq 0$, then $-(\alpha J' - C')$ is almost constant and as a result the following holds:

$$\frac{\mathrm{d}Q}{\mathrm{d}w} \simeq \frac{F'}{F''} \,. \tag{20}$$

Note that F'/F'' is an output response to factor-price changes by the neoclassical firm facing only a price (or supply) constraint.

It is also of interest to see how the output of the firm responds to changes in the *perceived future* demand. This can be seen by differentiating (12) and (13) with respect to $\tilde{D}$:

$$\frac{\mathrm{d}Q}{\mathrm{d}\tilde{D}} = \frac{(\alpha \partial J'/\partial \tilde{D})F'^2}{-(\alpha J' - C')F'' - (\alpha J'' - C'')F'^2} = \frac{-\alpha J'' F'^2}{-(\alpha J' - C')F'' - (\alpha J'' - C'')F'^2} \tag{21}$$

$$\frac{\mathrm{d}I}{\mathrm{d}\tilde{D}} = \frac{\mathrm{d}Q}{\mathrm{d}\tilde{D}} > 0. \tag{22}$$

The second equality in (21) follows from the fact that $\partial J'/\partial \tilde{D} = -J''$. In general, $0 \leqq \mathrm{d}Q/\mathrm{d}\tilde{D} \leqq 1$. The effect of a change in future demand is very similar to that of a change in current demand though it is a little smaller. Just as in the case of a change in current demand, if inventory is very high relative to future demand and $-\alpha J'' \simeq \infty$, then $\mathrm{d}Q/\mathrm{d}\tilde{D}$ approaches one. Therefore in this case, perhaps in recessions, the output response, which is essentially a planned inventory investment of the firm anticipating changes in future demand conditions, becomes important. Focus on current demand and neglect of future demand are common practices in the simple Keynesian multiplier story. But this is not justified if $-\alpha J'' \simeq \infty$ holds in our model. Hicks (1981), for example, emphasized the importance of *future* demand as a determinant of current production.[8]

We can summarize these results as follows. First of all, in general, both demand and supply constraints are binding at one time in that changes in both current demand and real input price affect output. Under assumption (17), however, we can generate two polar cases. At one extreme, where the level of inventory stock is very high relative to future demand conditions, only demand affects output and the Keynesian multiplier holds. In this case, the firm's output supply is also affected by the *future* demand. This is a consequence of our assumption that the firm is subject to intertemporal demand constraints. At the other extreme, where the level of inventory is low relative to future demand, only real input price affects output; the demand constraint facing the firm is not effective, owing to inventory investment. The firm adjusts its output in the manner that the usual neoclassical model without inventory would predict.

[8] Yoshikawa (1982) presents a dynamic model of the firm in making a similar point.

Inventory Investment

Inventory investment plays such a crucial role in this analysis that it is appropriate to digress a little to discuss it. In macroeconomics, the most popular model of inventory investment is the production-smoothing model. If marginal costs in production are increasing and sales vary over time, a cost-minimizing strategy that equates marginal costs across time will smooth production relative to sales. Despite its popularity, however, the production-smoothing model fails to fit the US data. For example, production is more variable than sales, and sales and inventory investment normally are not negatively correlated in most industries. These stylized facts for the United States are clearly at odds with the production-smoothing model. (For these problems, see an excellent survey by Blinder and Maccini (1991).)

It is then interesting to check these 'stylized facts' for Japan. Using aggregate annual data, Fukuda and Teruyama (1988) demonstrate that for Japan production is actually *less* variable than sales, and sales and inventory investment were negatively correlated (Table 4.1). Plainly, Japan is an anomaly among developed countries, although according to Fukuda and Teruyama this pattern is very common among developing countries. Using physical quantity data for the 29 Japanese 3-digit industries, Beason (1993), too, finds that production is less variable than sales, and that sales and inventory investment are negatively correlated for almost all the industries he examines.

Does the Japanese firm, unlike the firm in other developed countries, really smooth production then? Not quite. Beason finds strong

Table 4.1. Output, sales, and inventory investment in Japan, 1965–1986[a]

	Var(y)/Var(s)	ρ (s, INV)
Japan	0.95	− 0.32
Canada	1.84	0.52
France	1.23	0.43
UK	1.82	0.48
USA	1.68	0.09
W. Germany	1.62	0.02

[a] Var(y) is the variance of detrended real GNP; Var(s) is the variance of final demand defined as real GNP less inventory investment; ρ(s, INV) is the correlation coefficient between final demand and inventory investment.

Source: Fukuda and Teruyama (1988).

co-movements between production and sales at seasonal frequencies. My own analysis of the seasonal cycle presented in Chapter 9 leads to the same conclusion. Since deterministic seasonal patterns in sales can be anticipated, they are the ones to be smoothed if marginal production costs are significantly increasing. As maintained in Chapter 1, strong co-movements between production and sales in the seasonal cycle suggest flat marginal costs and the unimportance of the production-smoothing.

The variances of output and sales, and the correlation between sales and inventory investment, depend on many things. For example, in the model presented above, output responds to changes in both current and future demand. Therefore, the extent to which output responds to *current* demand depends on how changes in current demand are translated into the revision of the firm's anticipation of future demand. This in turn would depend on the persistence of demand under the assumption of rational expectations. An inspection of equations (15) and (21) reveals that, depending on the relation between current demand D and future demand $\tilde{D}$, the variance of output can be either greater or smaller than the variance of sales. Likewise, a comparison of equations (16) and (22) shows that the correlation between current sales and inventory investment can be either positive or negative. This is beyond the present analysis, and we must await further study to explore the anomaly of the Japanese data (Table 4.1) from this perspective.

I must reiterate that the inventory investment in the present model is the desired one. In general, it is possible that the firm's inventory investment is at an undesired level. In terms of my model, this means that the firm's optimization in the previous section has a corner solution. As a result, condition (13) would be replaced by

$$\alpha J'(\bar{K}+I) - C'(\bar{K}+I) < \frac{w}{F'(\underline{L})} \qquad (23)$$

where $\underline{L} > 0$ is the lowest possible L allowed.[9] When inequality condition (23) holds, with $L = \underline{L}$ rather than equality condition (13), an increase in D is absorbed by a decrease in I (inventory liquidation). Hicks (1974), for example, emphasizes the possibility of this case by noting that the usual Keynesian multiplier process would be

[9] The optimization problem in this case has another constraint, $L \geqq \underline{L} > 0$. Lowering L below $\underline{L}$ incurs prohibitive costs to the firm. The existence of $\underline{L}$ would be due to various adjustments and/or fixed costs associated with extremely low levels of production. L cannot be zero unless we drop assumption (5): $\lim_{L\to 0} F'(L) = +\infty$.

'cut off' if an increase in demand were met by inventory liquidation in deep recessions. Unfortunately, it is difficult to integrate this 'corner-solution case' into our internal-solution case, and so it must await further investigation. My empirical analysis in the next section is therefore subject to this qualification.

4.3 AN EMPIRICAL STUDY

In this section, I conduct an empirical study based on the theoretical analysis advanced in the previous section. The major result obtained there is that output responds to changes in both current demand and real input price, but that the relative importance of the two variables depends on the level of inventory stock.

The Estimated Equation

Given this result, I estimate the following equation:

$$\Delta Q = \phi(S)\Delta w + \psi(S)\Delta D, \tag{24}$$

where ΔQ, Δw, ΔD are changes in output, real input price, and current demand, respectively, and S is an index of the level of inventory stock *relative to future demand conditions*. Our results in the previous section imply that

$$\begin{aligned} &\phi(S) < 0, \qquad \phi'(S) > 0 \\ &\lim_{S \to \bar{S}} \phi(S) = 0 \qquad \text{for some } \bar{S} \\ &\lim_{S \to \underline{S}} \phi(S) = \bar{\phi} < 0 \qquad \text{for some } \underline{S} \qquad (\bar{S} > \underline{S}) \end{aligned} \tag{25}$$

and

$$\begin{aligned} &\psi(S) > 0, \qquad \psi'(S) > 0 \\ &\lim_{S \to \bar{S}} \psi(S) = 1 \\ &\lim_{S \to \underline{S}} \psi(S) = 0. \end{aligned} \tag{26}$$

Using quarterly data for 1968(IV)–1981(IV), I estimate (24). ΔQ, Δw, and ΔD are indices of production of manufacturing industry, real wages defined as nominal wages deflated by the WPI, and shipments, respectively. When real energy prices were put into the equation simultaneously with real wages, they did not turn out to be significant, possibly because of multicollinearity.

To implement regression analysis, I first approximate $\phi(S)$ and $\psi(S)$ in the following way:

$$\begin{aligned} \phi(S) &= \alpha \exp(-\gamma_1 S), \\ \psi(S) &= \beta[1 - \exp(-\gamma_2 S)] \qquad (\alpha < 0;\ \beta \simeq 1;\ \gamma_1, \gamma_2 > 0) \end{aligned} \tag{27}$$

where α, β, γ_1, γ_2 are parameters to be estimated. It is easy to see that (27) satisfies (25) and (26). Thus, the equation to be estimated is actually

$$\Delta Q = \alpha \exp(-\gamma_1 S)\Delta w + \beta[1 - \exp(-\gamma_2 S)]\Delta D + \delta. \tag{28}$$

I include a constant term δ in (28). Equation (28) is of the first-difference form. Therefore a constant term reflects a time trend which presumably is due to such factors as population growth and capital accumulation, taken as exogenous for our purposes here.

To proceed further, we must find a proxy S. Conceptually, this reflects the excessiveness of the firm's current inventory stock *relative to future demand*. Here I simply use the modified inventory–sales ratio. This would be justified if (i) the firm forms its forecast of future sales using their past values, and (ii) the stochastic process of sales largely contains permanent shocks.[10] The data on the inventory–sales ratio Z is an index (1975 = 1.0) and varies from 0.6 to 1.1 in my sample period. I transform this Z into our modified inventory–sales ratio, S: $S = 1/(1.2 - Z)$. The idea behind this transformation is to assign a high value of S relative to an exponential function when the actual inventory–sales ratio approaches its historical high.

Strictly speaking, the net marginal return on inventory, and as a result, γ_1 in (28), depend on *future* real wages as well as on S. Therefore, (28) would be valid only if (i) expectations of real wages in the sample period do not change, or (ii) the net marginal return on inventory depicted in Fig. 4.1 shifts up and down in such a way that $\alpha J'' - C''$ remains the same for given K when expectations of

[10] Specifically, suppose that the demand (sales) variable D_t follows the stochastic process $D_t = \Sigma_{i=0}^{\infty} u_{t-i} + v_t$. Here the temporary shock v_t and the permanent shock u_t are mutually and serially uncorrelated with mean zero and variance σ_v^2 and σ_u^2, respectively. Then the forecast of D_{t+j}, D_{t+j}^e $(j = 1, 2, \ldots)$, which minimizes the error variance, is given by $D_{t+j}^e = (1 - \lambda)\,\Sigma_{j=0}^{\infty}\,\lambda^j D_{t-j}$, where λ is

$$\lambda = 1 + \frac{1}{2}\frac{\sigma_u^2}{\sigma_v^2} - \frac{\sigma_u}{\sigma_v}\sqrt{\left(1 + \frac{1}{4}\frac{\sigma_u^2}{\sigma_v^2}\right)}$$

When σ_u/σ_v is very large, λ becomes close to zero so that only D_t essentially matters in forecasting future demand, D_{t+j}. In this case, current demand is a good proxy for future demand. See Muth (1960).

future real wages vary. The following analysis is subject to these qualifications.

Using quarterly data (1968(IV)–1981(IV)) of ΔQ, Δw, ΔD, and S, I estimate (28). The estimation method is nonlinear least squares regression.[11] Some experimentation with two-stage nonlinear least squares did not result in any convergence. In the final two versions of estimations presented in Table 4.1, I estimate (28) under the restrictions of $\gamma_1 = \gamma_2$ and $\gamma_1 = 0$, respectively, since in nonlinear least squares we need to decrease the number of parameters to be estimated whenever possible. In each regression, the assigned initial values of the parameters are determined after some experimentation with ordinary least squares versions of the equation. For each parameter, ten different initial values within a reasonable range were tried, but the same convergence was achieved.

The Estimation Results

As for the estimation results presented in Table 4.2, we must first note that all the statistics, such as *t*-values and Durbin–Watson (DW), are meaningful only in the asymptotic sense. Under the assumption of normality (independent and identically distributed—i.i.d.) of the errors, nonlinear least squares and maximum likelihood estimates are identical. Furthermore, under suitable regularity conditions, the maximum likelihood estimator is consistent, asymptotically normally distributed with mean equal to the true parameter value, and also asymptotically efficient.[12] The subsequent discussions of the obtained results are therefore based on these large sample properties of the estimator.

Table 4.2. Output equation, 1968 (IV)–1981(IV) (53 observations)[a]

$$\text{(i) } \Delta Q = -\underset{(-1.19)}{0.44}[\exp(-\gamma S)]\Delta w_{-1} + \underset{(8.47)}{1.32}[1-\exp(-\gamma S)]\Delta D + \underset{(2.41)}{0.004}; \gamma = \underset{(3.26)}{0.51}$$

$$\text{(ii) } \Delta Q = -\underset{(-2.39)}{0.14}\Delta W_{-1} + \underset{(9.68)}{1.22}[1-\exp(-\gamma S)]\Delta D + \underset{(2.38)}{0.004}; \gamma = \underset{(3.15)}{0.64}$$

(i) $SE = 0.0089$, $DW = 2.14$, (ii) $SE = 0.0086$, $DW = 2.36$

[a] Dependent variable, ΔQ: index of industrial production (manufacturing: 1975 = 1.0).
Mean of $\Delta Q = 0.015$; standard deviation of $\Delta Q = 0.026$.
Numbers in parentheses are *t*-statistics.

[11] The particular version used is the Gauss–Newton method (see e.g. Maddala 1977: ch. 9).

[12] As for the nonlinear least squares estimation, the reader is referred to Goldfeld and Quandt (1972).

In both regressions, DW does not indicate significant serial correlation and a plot of the residuals does not reveal apparent heteroscedasticity. All the estimates of the parameters have correct signs and reasonable values. The estimate of the constant term, 0.004, for example, implies the annual rate[13] of 1.4%, which is due to exogenous factors. As for the effect of real wage, we determined that lagged rather than current real wage was more decisive for output supply. This is perhaps due to costs of adjustment in altering labour input and/or to the existence of periods of production.[14]

The estimate of α in the second equation, −0.14, implies a real-wage elasticity of −0.08 when it is evaluated at the sample averages of Q and w. This may appear too low, but actually it is not. Shinkai (1982) estimates this elasticity to be −0.23 for the Japanese manufacturing industry without any demand variable in his equation.[15] The estimation results of Bruno and Sachs (1985),[16] however, suggest that the estimate of this elasticity typically declines by a factor of 2 to 3 when some demand variable is added in their equation. In fact, when Ueda (1983) estimates similar output equations for the Japanese manufacturing industry (log-linear forms with quarterly data), using real energy prices, real wages, and the inventory–sales ratio as explanatory variables, he finds that neither real energy prices nor real wages are significant: his real-wage elasticity is estimated to be −0.28 in the equation—without any demand variables, though. Therefore, it is not really surprising for our estimate of the real-wage elasticity to be −0.08, which is significant in an equation with a demand variable. Note that, although this elasticity is commonly identified with a parameter of neoclassical production function, our analysis, in particular (18), shows that it depends crucially on the level of inventory stock. *With demand constraints, the real-wage elasticity changes not only for technological reasons, but also as a result of demand factors.*

Turning to the estimate of β, we find that 1.22 in the second equation of Table 4.2 is not significantly different from 1, its theoretical value, at the 0.05 level. The most interesting parameter,

[13] This is based on the sample mean of Q, i.e. 1.12.

[14] In a similar equation, estimated with *annual* data, Bruno and Sachs (1985) also report a one-period lag in factor prices for the UK economy.

[15] His estimation method is to classify the whole sample period into demand- and supply-constrained subperiods. Real factor prices affect output only in the supply-constrained period. As a result, the demand variable is omitted when the real-wage elasticity is estimated.

[16] In particular, see Table IV of their paper.

γ, turns out to be significant in both equations and has a reasonable value. Using point estimates of α, β, and γ, we display time series of $\alpha(\exp(-\gamma S))$ and $\beta(1-\exp(-\gamma S))$ together with the inventory–sales ratio in Fig. 4.2 and 4.3. The coefficient for the real wage, $\alpha(\exp(-\gamma S))$, varies from -0.18 to 0 when $\gamma > 0$ is imposed, but in this case α becomes insignificant. On the other hand, when $\gamma = 0$ is imposed in $\alpha(\exp(-\gamma S))$, α is estimated to be -0.14 and is significant. The real wage affects output supply independent of demand factors, but the nonlinearity is weak in our sample period. In contrast, the extent to which demand affects output supply depends on the level of inventory stock, as is shown in Fig. 4.3. In any case, demand constraints are always found to affect output. This result is consistent with our finding in Chapter 2 that aggregate demand is the key factor in explaining business cycles in Japan. Changes in output are determined basically by effective demand, but are occasionally modified by real input prices.

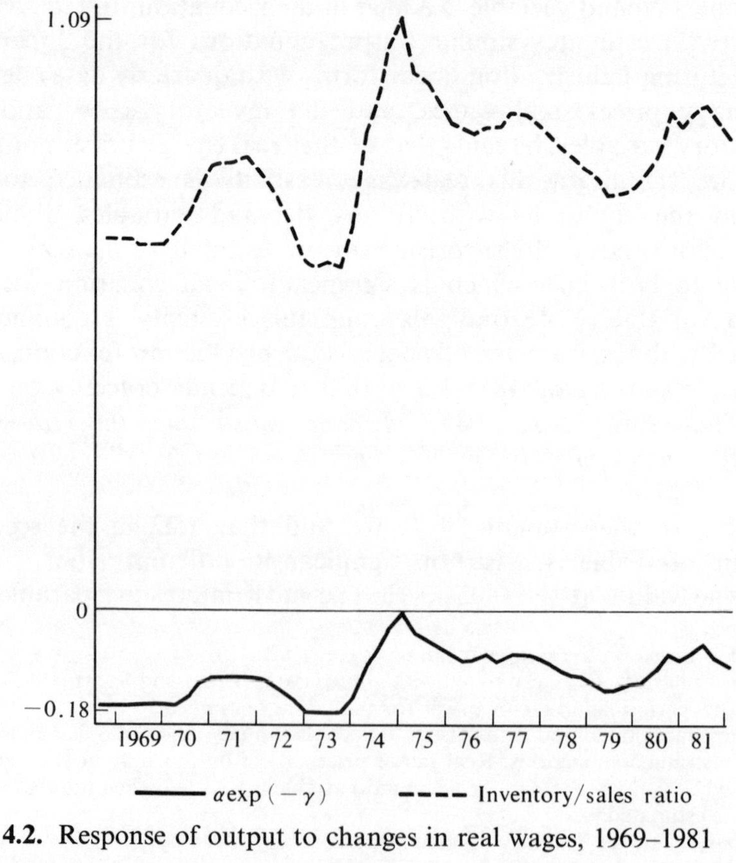

Fig. 4.2. Response of output to changes in real wages, 1969–1981

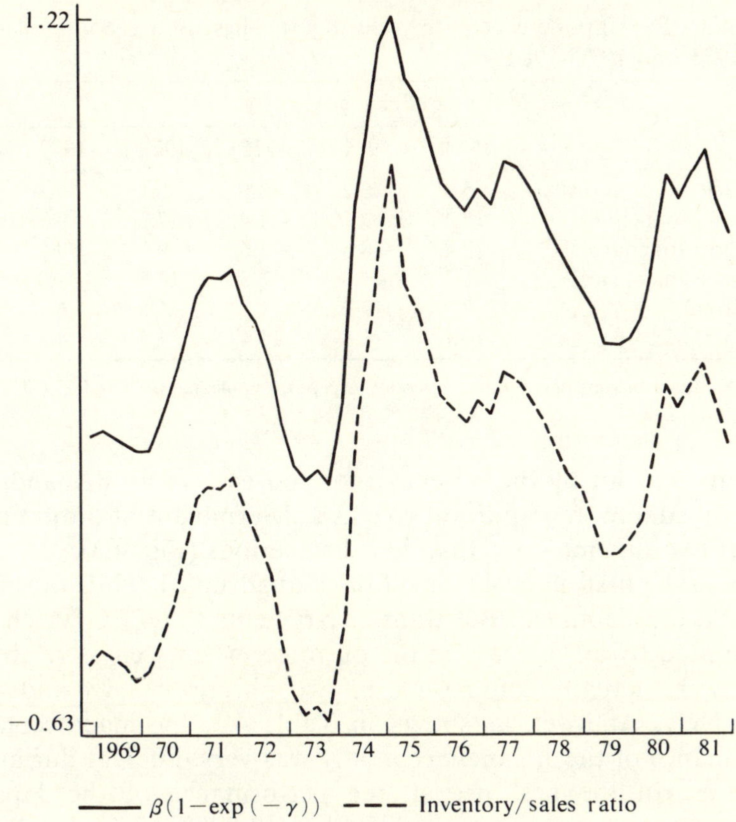

Fig. 4.3. Response of output to changes in demand

4.4 THE JAPANESE ECONOMY IN THE FIRST AND THE SECOND OIL CRISES

Given the analysis above, it is very interesting to compare the macroeconomic performance of the Japanese economy during the first and the second oil shock periods (1973–4 and 1978–80). These were times when the economy was hit by major supply shocks, and therefore they provide ideal opportunities to study the interactions of supply and demand in macroeconomics.

As Chapter 2 maintains, it is very hard to explain the experiences in the oil shock periods by focusing only on the production function and real factor prices. Indeed, the analysis in the previous section demonstrates that demand is an indispensable part of any reasonable explanation; the inventory–sales ratio sharply rose each time the

Table 4.3. The Japanese economy during the first and second oil crises, 1973–1975 and 1978–1980

	Rates of change (%)					
	1973	1974	1975	1978	1979	1980
Real GNP	5.3	−0.2	3.6	5.1	5.3	3.7
Industrial production	12.4	−9.7	−4.4	7.0	9.3	4.5
Private investment (real)	14.4	−8.5	−3.6	9.7	9.8	5.7
Public investment (real)	−6.3	−1.0	3.8	14.4	−1.0	−0.5
Export (real)	3.7	19.0	1.8	−5.5	6.1	17.1
Consumer price	16.1	21.8	10.4	3.4	4.8	7.8

Source: National Income and Product Account, except for consumer price index (CPI).

economy was hit by the oil embargo, and as a result demand must have played a more important role as a determinant of output at the time of two oil embargos than in other periods (Fig. 4.3).

During the first oil crisis the oil price quadrupled, while during the second it only doubled. But transfer payments to OPEC which were necessitated by an increase in the oil price, when seen as relative to GNP, were actually comparable in two oil crises: 3.8% and 4.1%, respectively. And yet, as shown in Table 4.3, the macroeconomic performance of the Japanese economy was very different during two oil crises. In the first period, the performance of the Japanese economy, inflicted as it was with both double-digit inflation and an unprecedented negative growth of real GNP, was actually the *worst* among OECD countries. In sharp contrast, during the second oil crisis, growth rate declined only slightly, and at the same time, inflation as measured by the consumer price index (CPI) was only 7.8% at its peak as against 21.8% in 1974. The 'good' macroeconomic performance of the Japanese economy during this second period became a widely discussed topic throughout the 1980s. We must recall, however, that the performance of the Japanese economy was the worst among OECD countries during the first crisis. The cause of such a significant difference for the macroeconomic performance in two comparable oil crises is clearly an interesting and important issue.

Two popular explanations which have gained wide currency in Japan emphasize the difference in the initial conditions on the one hand, and the 'learning effect' on the other. Regarding inflation, the difference in the initial conditions is evident. The Japanese government, unexperienced in the intricacies of floating exchange rates, had overestimated the deflationary effects of the appreciation of the yen in 1971–2, and mistakenly had allowed money supply (M2) to grow by 25% in 1972, at a time when real GNP was at its potential or 'natural' level. As expected, such a lax monetary policy generated very high inflation; *before the first oil embargo*, in the autumn of 1973, inflation as measured by the consumer price index (CPI) had already reached 12%. In contrast, in 1979 the CPI inflation rate had been only 3% before the second oil embargo. Wage settlements also contributed to a difference in inflation in two periods; these will be discussed in Chapter 5.

Putting aside inflation for the moment, I will focus on the real economy in what follows. The growth rate of real GNP fell from 5.3% to −0.2% during 1973–4 while it declined only slightly, from 5.3% to 3.7%, during 1979–80. The difference is much more pronounced for industrial production than for real GNP (Table 4.3). Unlike inflation, however, the difference in initial conditions is not evident for real GNP at all: it happens to be 5.3% for both 1973 and 1979. The preceding analysis in this chapter indicates the importance of demand as a determinant of output in the periods following two oil crises; the inventory–sales ratio rose substantially in both periods, and therefore demand is expected to have played a more important role in the determination of output than did real factor prices.

Table 2.24 shows the relative contribution of each demand component. Clearly, for the unprecedented negative growth in 1974, the contribution of private investment was by far the greatest influence. A decline in consumption was also a very unusual factor, which contributed to the deep recession. On the other hand, public expenditure, inventory investment, and, most of all, net exports all sustained growth. Table 4.3 shows the growth rates of investment and export in real terms.

For 1980, the growth rate of investment decelerated from 9.8% in the previous year to 5.7%. This decline was, however, much smaller than for 1974: 4.1% versus 22.9% during the earlier period. And this made the difference for the growth of real GNP during two oil crises. In both periods, the growth rate of exports was very high and comparable: 19.0% in 1974 and 17.1% in 1980. In 1974, however, the significant contribution of net exports was simply wiped out by the 23% decline in investment; in contrast, the high growth rate of exports was smoothly linked to a sustained growth in the second oil crisis. In sum, looked at from the perspective of demand, the key to understanding the difference in the growth rate of real

GNP in two oil crises lies in the difference in the behaviour of private investment.

The next question then is, what caused investment to behave so differently in two periods? First of all, by any measure, the real interest rate was much higher in the second oil shock period than in the first: roughly 3% versus 6%. If anything, therefore, the real interest rate cannot be an explanation for the higher rate of investment during the second oil crisis. Just as in the case of output, I turn now to demand and real factor prices.

Since the preceding analysis in this chapter suggests that most firms were demand-constrained during the two oil crises, demand is expected to have affected not only the firm's output but also its investment. In this respect, it is suggestive that in 1974 a decline in real investment was greater for the non-manufacturing sector, excluding electricity, than for the manufacturing sector: −14.4% and −9.4%, respectively, according to the Corporate Statistics Quarterly (*Hojinkigyo Tokei*) compiled by the Ministry of Finance. The non-manufacturing sector excluding electricity is much *less energy-intensive* on the supply side, while it is more responsive to consumption on the demand side, than the manufacturing industry. As pointed out above, a decline in consumption in 1974 was literally an unprecedented event. As will be explained in Chapter 6, high inflation during the first oil crisis most likely reduced the propensity to consume for at least two possible reasons. First, it significantly reduced the real value of financial assets, and as a result households were encouraged to save more (see equation (6) of Chapter 6). Second, the unprecedentedly high inflation also meant that greater uncertainty faced most households; under the convexity of marginal utility, the rational consumer is expected to make more precautionary savings in such circumstances. Whatever the reason, a sharp decline in consumption most likely contributed to a substantial decline in investment in the non-manufacturing sector.

On the other hand, the high rate of investment at the time of the second oil crisis was led by the manufacturing industry. As Section 2.3 explained, growth and business cycles of the Japanese economy from the early 1970s to the mid-1980s were dominated by exports. Investment was no exception. Fig. 4.4 demonstrates a positive correlation between the growth of capital and exports. In the second oil crisis, high investment was sustained in the manufacturing industry, particularly in the machinery industries, thanks to the high growth of exports.

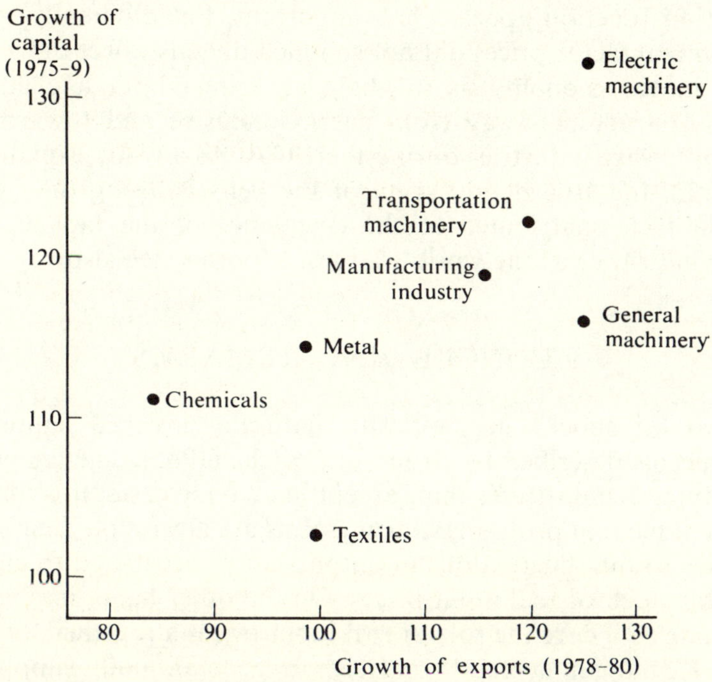

Fig. 4.4. Exports and the growth of capital
Source: Economic Planning Agency; *Capital Stock of Private Firms;* Ministry of Finance, *Customs Statistics.*

So much for demand. What about real factor prices as a determinant of investment? The effects of factor prices on investment depend crucially on whether or not the firm is demand-constrained. For the demand-constrained firm, higher real factor prices actually encourage investment to save labour/energy; just the opposite is true for the unconstrained firm. Chapter 7 will explain this in a formal model. According to the survey on the firm's investment regularly conducted by the Industrial Bank of Japan, the percentage of 'labour-/energy-saving' as a motive for firms in the manufacturing industry to invest rose from 19.6% in 1975 to 27.4% in 1980. The growing importance of labour-/energy-saving investment, in turn, suggests that most firms were demand-constrained.

In sum, to understand the Japanese economy during two oil crises, the most important factor is demand: not only demand as a determinant of output or real GNP, but also demand as a determinant of investment, the key component of GNP. Compared with demand, the impact of a sharp rise in real factor prices on output through the production function appears less important. Put differently, an increase in real factor prices did not so much directly affect the level of output in the economy as a whole as bring about a change in industrial structure, away from energy-intensive and towards less energy-intensive industries during the 1970s. As already explained in Chapter 2, the 10% depreciation of the yen following the first oil crisis, in fact, contributed to the emergence of the Japanese machinery industries as the world's largest exporter (see also Fig. 4.4).

4.5 CONCLUDING REMARKS

The two oil shocks in the 1970s naturally invoked supply-side economics as described by Bruno and Sachs (1985). The analysis of this chapter demonstrates that, except in extreme cases, it is misleading to assume that profit-maximizing firms are always on their supply schedules so that fluctuations in output can be attributed to changes in capital stock or real input prices. On the other hand, it is equally misleading to ignore the role of real input prices altogether, as in the simple Keynesian demand analysis. In general, both supply and demand factors are at work, and there is a theoretical justification for using inventory variables to measure the relative importance of these two factors.

During the two oil crises, the inventory–sales ratio rose sharply, and, contrary to common belief, demand actually played the major role as a determinant of output. In particular, the remarkable difference in the behaviour of real GNP during the first and second oil crises can be attributed mainly to the differing investment behaviour. Investment was, in turn, greatly affected by demand. Keynesian economics is well able to survive supply shocks.

5

The Japanese Labour Market

The labour market in Japan is said to differ in many respects from those of other advanced economies. Japanese workers, for example, seem to have much longer employment tenure—allegedly, 'lifetime' employment. The unemployment rate in 1994 was 3%, the highest it has been since 1950, and is generally very low by OECD standards. Wages of primary labour, though they are determined by union bargaining, are flexible. Characteristically, Japanese institutional factors such as enterprise unions, annual synchronized wage bargaining (the *Shunto*), and bonus payments are believed to sustain this flexibility of wages. Some economists, such as Komiya and Yasui (1984) and Taylor (1989), then argue that flexibility of wages is in fact the key factor in explaining the 'good' macroeconomic performance of the Japanese economy.

Chapter 3 showed how the so-called 'Japanese labour relations' emerged by painful trial and error in the first decade after the Second World War. This chapter, on the other hand, explains how the Japanese labour market works, and also evaluates its function. Sections 5.1–5.3 discuss employment, wage determination, and the unemployment rate, respectively. The Japanese labour market is shown to be two-tiered, in that the much celebrated system of long-term employment applies only to a portion of workers—the core workers—with the remaining portion of the labour force frequently moving between jobs and *out of* the labour force rather than into the unemployment pool during cyclical fluctuations. The burden of recessions, therefore, falls mainly on secondary labour. As a consequence, cyclical fluctuations do not threaten the core workers, and, in exchange for their job security, these core workers contribute to productivity of the firms. Section 5.4 then argues that (i) in Japan the unemployment rate is not a good measure of resource utilization, and also that (ii) flexibility of wages is *not* a key factor in explaining relatively small cyclical fluctuations of the Japanese economy. It also maintains that the sharp rise in labour's income share in the early 1970s was mainly the *result* of slower economic growth.

Finally, Section 5.5 offers a simple macroeconomic model to explain the 'stylized facts' of the Japanese labour market within the Keynesian framework. In this model, the firm's output depends on primary and secondary labour inputs. Unlike most efficiency wage models, the productivity of primary labour depends on perceived fairness, which in turn is linked to the share of wages within the firm. The firm maximizes its profits under these constraints as well as under the quantity constraint on sales. Considering the firm's maximization, we can derive demand functions of primary and secondary labour. The household, on the other hand, supplies the two kinds of labour, and consumes. The supply of primary labour is quantity-constrained by demand, which is determined by the firm. The supply of the secondary labour, however, is determined by the household in its utility maximization. The market of the secondary labour is competitive.

The general equilibrium model of the Japanese labour market generates the following outcomes. Changes in output keep the employment of the primary labour intact, and are absorbed by changes in the secondary labour. At the same time, changes in output bring about proportionate changes in real wages of primary labour, which in turn affect the household's income. And changes in the household's income affect its supply of secondary labour. Since both supply and demand shift in response to changes in output, the real wages of secondary labour change substantially. As a result, the relative wage of secondary labour becomes pro-cyclical; the wage differential between primary and secondary labour diminishes in booms and widens in recessions.

The equilibrium in this model depends ultimately on the level of exogenous demand. In general, there is underemployment, though no unemployment, in the sense that the household's utility increases when exogenous demand increases. Flexibility of real wages has nothing to do with the determination of output, nor thus with the level of welfare in the short run. Flexible real wages, however, make it possible for the firm to retain its primary labour force, particularly in such adversity as would otherwise make this impossible. This is expected to have contributed to the long-run productivity growth in the Japanese firm.

5.1 THE LABOUR FORCE AND EMPLOYMENT

Chapter 2 argued that a growth of unprecedented magnitude in the number of households in Japan, generated by internal migration from the agricultural to the industrial sector, was the fundamental factor that sustained the domestic-demand-led high growth from 1955–70. Table 5.1 shows that in 1950 the Japanese economy was, by international standards, still largely dominated by agriculture; it was like today's Indonesia, for example. By the late 1980s, however, it had become comparable in this respect to other advanced economies. This transformation necessarily involved a major reallocation of the the labour force. Table 5.2 traces this shift by showing changes in the labour force by three sectors in successive five-year periods beginning in 1951. Throughout the

Table 5.1. Total employment in primary, secondary, and tertiary occupations: Japan, USA, UK, and West Germany, 1950 and 1989 (%)

	Primary (agriculture and mining)	Secondary (manufacturing and construction)	Tertiary (services)
1950			
Japan	48.3	21.9	29.7
USA	12.4	35.3	49.7
UK	5.1	47.5	47.0
Germany	23.2	42.2	32.4
1989[a]			
Japan	7.6	33.8	58.1
USA	2.9	25.9	71.1
UK	2.4	29.0	68.6
Germany	4.9	38.4	55.3

[a] For UK and Germany, 1987.

Table 5.2. Changes in employment by sector, 1951–1955 to 1981–1985 (millions of workers)

	Primary (mainly agriculture)	Manufacturing	Tertiary
1951–5	−1	1	3
1956–60	−2	4	3
1961–5	−2	2	3
1966–70	−2	3	4
1971–5	−3	0	4
1976–80	−1	1	3
1981–5	−0.6	0	2.5

Source: Census.

period, employment in agriculture steadily decreased. Employment in manufacturing, on the other hand, increased during the high-growth period of 1956–70, but thereafter showed almost no increase. In contrast, employment in the service sector increased throughout the whole period. Beginning in the 1970s, therefore, the service sector became the sole absorber of labour in the Japanese economy.

In keeping with this process, more and more new school-leavers in rural agricultural areas, who once would have worked as farm-workers, moved to urban industrial areas and became employees in either manufacturing or the service sector. In 1955, for example, 33% of new school-leavers (15 years old) still found jobs in agriculture, whereas 43% became blue-collar workers in manufacturing; in 1965 the proportions had shifted to 9% and 72%, respectively. Not only new school-leavers but also unpaid family workers started to leave agriculture beginning in the early 1950s. This tendency continued throughout the 1980s. Eventually, when economic growth peaked in the 1960s, even landowners themselves started to abandon agriculture. All those who left rural agricultural areas became employees in urban industrial areas. Once there, did they share in the celebrated 'lifetime employment' of Japanese firms? Some certainly did, but not all of them.

According to 'conventional wisdom', Japanese firms seek to employ their workers for lifetime, training them on the job in order to help them acquire firm-specific human capital, and encouraging them to stay by paying seniority wages. In contrast—say in the United States or the European Union—firms do not attempt to develop firm-specific skills in workers, and workers in turn frequently change their jobs, often as a result of layoffs by firms. The OECD (1986), for example, estimates the percentage of job-leavers per year in 1980 as 0.14 for Japan, 0.48 for the United States, 0.30 for Germany, 0.25 for the United Kingdom, 0.14 for France, and 0.15 for Italy. For all qualifications, it seems true that *on average* Japanese workers do indeed have longer employment tenure than in other countries, particularly the United States. (See Hashimoto and Raisian (1985), and Mincer and Higuchi (1988) for a Japanese–US comparison.) This does not imply, however, that most Japanese workers are employed for life. In contrast with the core workers, there is a significant proportion of workers who do not enjoy lifetime employment or skill formation through on-the-job training (OJT).

According to the the Labour Force Survey (*Rōdōryoku Chōsa*), for example, 9.5% of total employees in the non-agricultural sector were temporary/seasonal workers in both 1960 and 1978. And the 1987 Employment Status Survey (*Shūgyō Kōzō Kihon Chōsa*) classifies 19.7% of workers in the private non-agricultural sector as '*not* formally employed (including part-time) workers'. One is tempted to assume that casually employed workers are concentrated in small service-sector firms and that there are few such workers in large manufacturing establishments. In fact, casually employed workers play an important role in large firms as well as small. Table 5.3 shows the number of new hirings of the Toyota motor company; the

Table 5.3. New hirings at Toyota Motor Company, 1956–1980

	(1) Formally employed	(2) Not formally employed (temporary, seasonal)	(3) Total	(4) % of temporary workers ((2)/(3))
1956	56	200	256	78.1
1957	133	362	495	73.1
1958	196	198	394	50.3
1959	213	1,465	1,678	87.3
1960	385	3,752	4,137	90.7
1961	616	3,366	3,982	84.5
1962	1,364	1,874	3,238	57.9
1963	1,846	4,444	6,290	70.7
1964	3,341	5,976	9,317	64.1
1965	3,701	2,259	5,960	37.9
1966	2,279	4,242	6,521	65.1
1967	3,750	5,467	9,217	59.3
1968	3,659	6,806	10,465	65.0
1969	4,320	6,508	10,828	60.1
1970	3,734	7,879	11,613	67.8
1971	5,927	3,717	9,644	38.5
1972	3,349	1,777	5,126	34.7
1973	3,283	4,265	7,548	56.5
1974	3,715	4,300	8,015	53.6
1975	2,812	158	2,970	5.3
1976	2,182	195	2,377	8.2
1977	2,513	189	2,702	7.0
1978	2,199	36	2,235	1.6
1979	1,869	1,052	2,921	36.0
1980	3,182	1,901	5,083	37.4

Source: Toyota.

percentage of workers *not* formally employed (i.e. temporary/seasonal) is in fact extraordinarily high.

The burden of cyclical fluctuations falls largely on the shoulders of such casually employed workers. Fig. 5.1 shows that cyclical fluctuations in the employment of part-time workers are much stronger than those for full-time workers. As a consequence, firms can afford to keep a group of workers semi-permanently as core workers and to invest in their firm-specific skills. In most countries, for white-collar workers such long-term employment and career-making is more or less prevalent. What is perhaps unique in Japan is the existence of core *blue-collar workers*, who are also employed for life, and who experience skill formation based on job rotation wider than that commonly found in other countries, and earn white-collar-like seniority wages (see Fig. 5.2). The above-mentioned 10%–20% figure for 'casually' employed workers

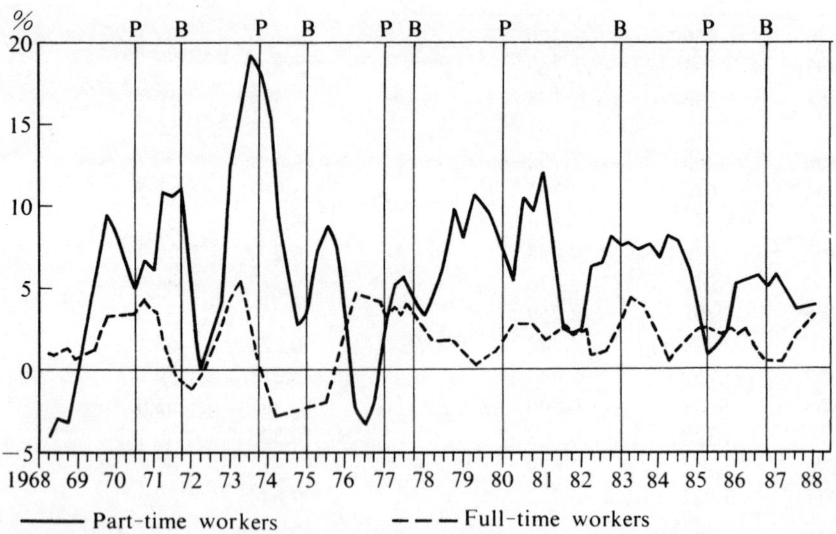

Fig. 5.1. Cyclical sensitivity of employment of full-time and part-time female workers, 1968–1988

The figures are the rates of change in employment (three quarters moving averages) for full-time workers working 35 hours or longer per week and part-time workers defined otherwise. P and B refer to the peak and bottom of the business cycle.

Source: Statistical Bureau, Management and Co-ordination Agency, *Labour Force Survey* (*Rōdōryoku Chosa*).

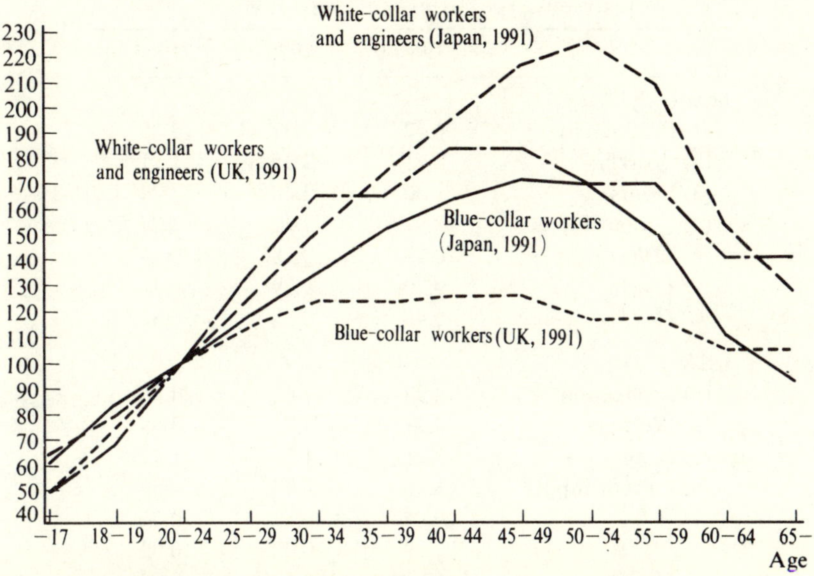

Fig. 5.2. Seniority wages, Japan and United Kingdom, 1991
For Japan, 'regular monthly payment' of male workers in manufacturing; for the UK, 'weekly real earnings' of male full-time workers in industry. The wage for age-group 20–4 is 100 for all types of worker.
Sources: Ministry of Labour, *Basic Statistics on Wage Structure* (Chingin Kozo Kihontokei Chosa); Ministry of Employment, *New Earnings Survey.*

would constitute the definite lower bound for the percentage of *non-core workers.* Koike (1991) roughly estimates the percentage of core blue-collar and white-collar workers who enjoy semi-lifetime employment and seniority wages in the total labour force in Japan as 40%.

Despite the widespread existence of casual employment, adjustment in the number of workers during cyclical fluctuations is still small in Japan by international standards (Table 5.4) (see also Abraham and Houseman 1989). One reason for it, of course, is that in post-war Japan potential growth was so strong (a decline in the level of real GNP occurred only once, in 1974) that it was rarely necessary for firms to cut their labour forces. Perhaps a more important factor is the flexibility of *real* wages, which enables firms to be able to afford to hoard workers over cyclical fluctuations.

Table 5.4 An international comparison of the labour input adjustment, 1961–1969 to 1980–1990[a]

	1961–9	1970–9	1980–90
Japan			
(1) Production	6.42	8.39	3.88
(2) Workers	3.41	2.35	1.11
(3) Hours	1.30	2.40	1.24
(4) Labour input	2.97	3.22	1.24
(2)/(1)	0.53	0.28	0.29
(3)/(1)	0.20	0.29	0.32
(4)/(1)	0.46	0.38	0.32
USA			
(5) Production	4.22	7.02	4.76
(6) Workers	2.71	4.71	3.39
(7) Hours	1.21	1.56	1.51
(8) Labour input	3.36	5.74	4.37
(6)/(5)	0.64	0.67	0.71
(7)/(5)	0.29	0.22	0.32
(8)/(5)	0.80	0.82	0.92
W.Germany			
(9) Production	5.32	4.95	3.65
(10) Workers	3.33	3.53	2.38
(11) Hours	1.93	1.78	1.11
(12) Labour input	4.83	4.49	2.63
(10)/(9)	0.63	0.71	0.65
(11)/(9)	0.36	0.36	0.30
(12)/(9)	0.91	0.91	0.72

[a] Figures are standard deviations of rates of change.

'Production', 'Workers', 'Hours', and 'Labour input' refer to production in manufacturing industry, the number of workers, hours worked per worker, and the product of the number of workers and hours worked per worker in the same sector, respectively.

Sources: Index of Industrial Production of MITI; Ministry of Labour, *Monthly Labour Survey* (Maitsuki Kinro Tokei Chosa); FRB, *Federal Reserve Bulletin*; US Department of Labor, *Monthly Labor Review*; Bundesbank, *Monthly Report*.

5.2 FLEXIBILITY OF REAL WAGES

Flexibility of real wages makes the extent of firms' necessary adjustment of labour input smaller than would otherwise be the case. Moreover, some economists, such as Komiya and Yasui (1984) and Suzuki (1985), argue that it is a key factor in explaining the 'good' macroeconomic performance of the Japanese economy. In the same vein, Bruno and Sachs (1985) argue that the 'wage gap' caused by an inflexibility of real wages is in fact responsible for the poor macroeconomic performance and high unemployment rate in OECD countries; in their view, 'the 1970's were characterized by extended periods of classical unemployment, with intervening periods of Keynesian recession'. Taylor (1989) also argues, within the framework of monetary models, that a flexibility of *nominal* wages accounts for the much smaller size of the fluctuations in real output in Japan compared with the United States. I will discuss these problems critically in Section 5.4. This section explains how wages are determined in Japan.

The extent to which wages in Japan are flexible by international standards is not immediately obvious. Bruno and Sachs (1985) classify Japan as a country of *medium* nominal-wage responsiveness, along with Germany. According to them, such responsiveness is high in the United Kingdom and low in the United States and Canada. Flexibility, or the responsiveness of wages, depends, of course, on the definition of the term. Branson and Rotenberg (1980), for example, formulated a model in which nominal wages respond to movement of 'target wages'. In their model, the 'target wages' are identified by price changes; as a consequence, the more flexible *nominal* wages are, the more inflexible *real* wages become, and vice versa. Using this framework, Branson and Rotenberg conclude that the US economy is characterized by inflexible nominal wages and flexible real wages, while the Japanese and European economies have inflexible real wages and flexible nominal wages.

R. J. Gordon (1982), on the other hand, attempted a more direct comparison among leading nations by looking at the standard deviations of changing rates of nominal and real wages. His results are shown in Table 5.5. According to the table, the Japanese and UK economies are more flexible in terms of both nominal *and* real wages compared with the United States. Ohtake (1986), who has doubts about the flexibility of real wages in Japan, also points out that the United Kingdom has the most flexible real wages out of Japan, UK, USA, Germany, and France. These results suggest, in passing, that, given the notorious 'British Disease' of the 1970s and early 1980s, it is premature to link the flexibility of real wages directly to 'good' macroeconomic performance. To be fair, economists have not yet reached a consensus regarding the flexibility

Table 5.5. Standard deviations of rates of change in nominal wages (w) and real wages ($w - p$) (quarterly data)[a]

	Nominal wages (w)	Real wages ($w - p$)
1963(I)–1980(III)		
USA	1.69	1.46
UK	5.29	3.86
Japan	4.84	2.78
1963(I)–1972(IV)		
USA	1.66	0.82
UK	3.40	1.74
Japan	2.83	2.50

[a] p is the rate of change in GNP deflator.

Source: R. J. Gordon (1982).

of real wages in Japan. Here I take Gordon's results shown in Table 5.5 as a loosely accepted standard; real wages in Japan are considerably more flexible than those in the United States, and real wages in the United Kingdom are as flexible as, or perhaps more flexible than, those in Japan.

It has been widely argued that flexibility of wages in Japan is sustained by two institutional factors: (i) *Shunto*, i.e. the annual synchronized wage determination, and (ii) the bonus system. Sachs (1979), R. J. Gordon (1982), and Freeman and Weitzman (1987) emphasize the role played by biannual bonus payments. Freeman and Weitzman, in particular, interpret it as the profit-sharing advocated by Weitzman (1986). As Ohashi (1989) and Taylor (1989) demonstrate, however, bonuses are actually closely tied to base wages, and changes in total wage payments are dominated by changes in base wages. Ohashi also shows that, although bonuses do respond to some extent to firm-specific factors such as profits, they cannot be properly interpreted as profit-sharing. The key factor in explaining wages in Japan is not bonus payments, but base wages.

Base wages in the primary sector are set at the annual synchronized union bargaining, called *Shunto*, which began in 1955. Although *Shunto* is economy-wide bargaining, it has been noted that there is a 'leading sector', such as the steel industry, which strongly influences the economy-wide base wages (see Shinkai 1980 and Sano 1981). It is also said that firm-specific factors such as profits affect the level of base wages of individual firms. Given these observations, I analyse the determination of wages using corporate-level microeconomic data. For reference, Table 5.6 shows prices, nominal wages, and real wages, together with the growth rate of real GNP. Not surprisingly, the growth of real wages significantly slowed after the first oil shock, in tandem with real GNP.

Table 5.6. Wages and prices, 1966–1991 (annual rates of change)

	Real GNP	Consumer price index (CIP)	Wholesale price index (WPI)	*Shunto* nomina l wages	Real wages (CPI)	Real wages (WPI)
1966	10.0	5.0	2.3	10.6	5.6	8.3
1967	10.4	3.9	1.8	12.5	8.6	10.7
1968	11.4	5.2	0.8	13.6	8.4	12.8
1969	11.4	5.1	2.1	15.8	10.7	13.7
1970	9.8	7.4	3.5	18.5	11.1	15.0
1971	4.3	6.0	− 0.7	16.9	10.9	17.6
1972	8.0	4.4	0.8	15.3	10.9	14.5
1973	7.4	11.2	14.7	20.1	8.9	5.4
1974	− 0.8	21.8	27.3	32.9	11.1	5.6
1975	2.9	11.2	3.0	13.1	1.9	10.1
1976	4.1	8.9	5.0	8.8	− 0.1	3.8
1977	4.7	7.7	1.9	8.8	1.1	6.9
1978	4.8	3.8	− 2.6	5.9	2.1	8.5
1979	5.4	3.5	7.0	5.8	2.4	− 1.2
1980	3.4	7.7	16.4	6.7	− 1.0	− 9.6
1981	3.4	4.8	1.4	7.7	2.9	6.3
1982	3.4	2.6	1.8	7.0	4.4	5.2
1983	2.8	1.8	− 2.2	4.4	2.6	6.6
1984	4.2	2.2	− 0.3	4.5	2.2	4.7
1985	5.0	2.0	− 1.1	5.0	3.0	6.2
1986	2.6	0.4	− 9.6	4.6	4.1	14.1
1987	4.2	− 0.2	− 3.8	3.6	3.8	7.4
1988	6.1	0.5	− 1.0	4.4	3.9	5.4
1989	4.7	2.2	2.5	5.2	3.0	2.6
1990	5.1	3.1	2.0	5.9	2.8	3.9
1991	4.4	3.4	0.2	5.7	2.2	5.5

Estimation of the Real-Wage Equation

Suppose that the following equation describes the determination of nominal wages:

$$\omega_{it} = f_{it} + \omega_t, \tag{1}$$

where ω_{it} is the rate of increase in nominal wages of firm i at time t. ω_{it} depends on both the microeconomic factor f_{it}, which is company-specific, and the economy-wide wage increase ω_t, which is, of course, the macroeconomic factor. If the labour market is completely homogeneous and no firm-specific factor is relevant in the wage determination, then f_{it} should not affect ω_{it}. The significance of f_{it} can therefore be interpreted as a measure of the heterogeneity of the labour market.

The data on wages are taken from the Bank of Japan's *Business Analysis of Main Enterprises in Japan*. Since the data are compiled on a fiscal-year basis, the wage equation is not estimated for each firm. To fill this gap, we prepared a panel of 297 corporations in 13 types of industry and then carried out our own estimations based on this panel. The sample period is 18 years, from 1968 to 1985.

The estimation equation consists of three factors: firm-specific factors, industry-specific factors, and economy-wide factors:

$$\omega_{it} = \mu + F'_{it}\,\beta_f + D'_{j(i)t}\,\beta_d + M'_t\,\beta_m + \varepsilon_{it}, \tag{2}$$

where ω_{it} denotes the rate of increase in nominal wages of firm i at time t, F_{it} is the vector of variables specific to firm i at time t, $D_{j(i)t}$ is the vector of variables specific to industry j to which firm i belongs at time t, and, finally, M_t is the vector of macroeconomic variables at time t. β_i $(i = f, d, m)$ is the corresponding coefficient vector, and ε_{it} is the error term. F_{it} corresponds to f_{it} in (1), of course, while $D_{j(i)t}$ and M_t are supposed to affect the economy-wide wage increase. The firm-specific variables are the rate of increase in the firm's real sales and the rate of profit. The industry-specific variable is the index of shipments for each industry. Finally, the macroeconomic variables are the unemployment rate, the expected rate of inflation, and the variance of the industry shipment indices. The last variable will be explained in more detail shortly.

All the firm-specific variables are taken from the *Business Analysis of Main Enterprises in Japan*, mentioned above. Nominal wages are taken from the 'Personnel expenses per employee' in the *Analysis* divided by 'Working hours per employee'. The shipment of each firm is the nominal sales deflated by the wholesale price index (WPI) of the respective industry to which the firm belongs.[1] The profit rate is the ratio of operating profits to total capital. And the shipment of each industry is taken from the 'Industrial shipment

[1] For the general machinery and precision machinery industries, the respective wholesale price indices are not separately available. Accordingly, the two industries are deflated by the same wholesale price index of the general and precision machinery industry.

index' (1980=100) compiled by the Ministry of International Trade and Industry.

After some experimenting, I decided to use the rate of increase in the consumer price index (CPI) as the expected rate of inflation. It is, of course, more desirable to generate the inflationary expectation in accordance with an explicit price equation. Such a framework would also enable us to analyse the interdependence of wages and prices. Here, however, for simplicity of analysis, I use the consumer price index without a lag as a proxy for inflationary expectations. The coefficient of the rate of increase in the CPI is not significantly different from zero in my preliminary estimation as commonly obtained for the Japanese wages equation. Therefore, in what follows I report only the *real*-wage equation.

It is well known that, in an analysis using panel data, there is a strong possibility of simultaneous correlation and heteroscedasticity in the error term. We cannot therefore assume that

$$E(\varepsilon_{is}\varepsilon_{jt}) = \begin{cases} \sigma^2 & (\textit{if } i = j \text{ and } s = t) \\ 0 & (\text{otherwise}), \end{cases} \tag{3}$$

which is the standard assumption in ordinary least squares (OLS) estimation. With this in mind, we use the generalized least squares (GLS) estimation with the following assumptions:[2]

(1) Mean zero $E(\varepsilon_{it}) = 0$

(2) Heteroscedasticity $E(\varepsilon_{it}^2) = \sigma_i^2$

(3) Contemporaneous correlation $E(\varepsilon_{is}\varepsilon_{jt}) = \begin{cases} \sigma_{ij} & (s = t) \\ 0 & (s \neq t) \end{cases}$

(4) First-order serial correlation $\varepsilon_{it} = \rho_i\varepsilon_{i,\,t-1} + \nu_{it}$

$\nu_{it} \sim WN(0, \phi_{ii})$.

$$E(\nu_{is}\nu_{jt}) = \begin{cases} \phi_{ij} & (s = t) \\ 0 & (s \neq t) \end{cases}$$

The estimation results are shown in Table 5.7. In equation (i), two microeconomic factors, the rate of increase in the sales S_{it} and the rate of profit R_{it} are both significant. Among macroeconomic factors, the unemployment rates U_t and σ_t, which measure the dispersion of sales over industries, are significant. U_t measures the demand–supply conditions in the external labour market. Considering the possible

[2] For details of the methods of estimation, see Fomby *et al.* (1984). What we use here is the TSCSREG procedure of the SAS/SUGI supplement.

Table 5.7. The real wage equation[a]

(i)	$\dot{W}_{it} = -0.042 + 0.19\dot{S}_{it} + 0.002R_{it} - 1.40\sigma_t + 0.11(1/U_t)$
	(24.3) (22.8) (8.8) (7.1) (38.8)
(ii)	$\dot{W}_{it} = -0.042 + 0.19\dot{S}_{it} - 0.01\sigma_t^i + 0.002R_{it} - 1.40\sigma_t + 0.11(1/U_t)$
	(24.4) (22.7) (0.11) (8.7) (6.5) (36.9)

[a] t-values are given in parentheses.

nonlinear effects, we put U_t into the equation in a reciprocal form. The expected sign of its coefficient is therefore positive.

More explanation is necessary for σ_t. Wages set by each firm depend heavily on the average wage prevailing in the economy as a whole. The economy-wide average wage is in turn significantly affected by the performances of industries. Suppose that the relationship between the rate of wage increase in each industry and that in sales in the respective industry is concave, as shown in Fig. 5.3. Under such conditions, the average wage increase declines when the dispersion of sales across industries becomes larger with the average rate of increase in sales, $\Sigma_{i=1}^{N}(\dot{S}_j/N)$ held constant. Fig. 5.3 explains it in the simple case where there are only two industries in the economy. When the rates of increase in sales of the two industries are both $\dot{S}_A$, the average rate of wage increase is ω_A. When the rates of increase in sales of the two industries are, respectively, $\dot{S}_B$ and $\dot{S}_C$, however, the average rate of wage increase $\omega_{BC} = (\omega_B + \omega_C)/2$ becomes smaller than

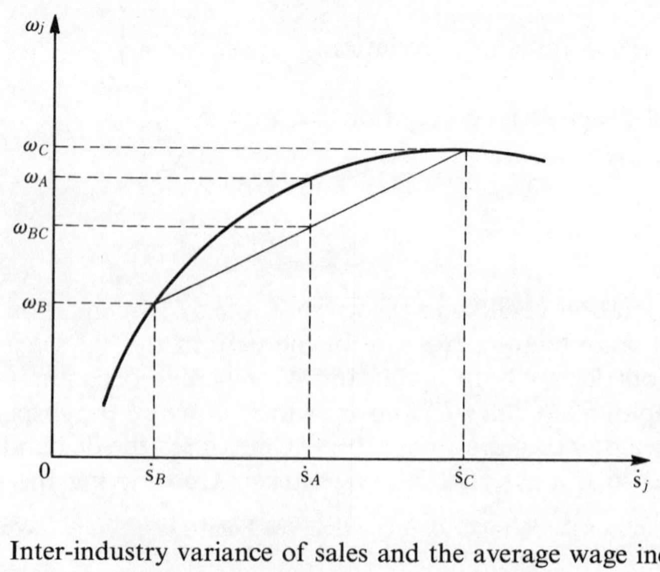

Fig. 5.3. Inter-industry variance of sales and the average wage increase

ω_A, even if the average rate of increase in sales remains the same ($\dot{S}_A = (\dot{S}_B + \dot{S}_C)/2$).

Since σ_t measures the dispersion of sales across industries, under this assumption, the coefficient of σ_t in the wage equation is expected to be negative. In this framework, the mean of $\dot{S}_j$ must, of course, have a positive effect on ω_j. In my estimations, however, a high correlation between the rate of increase in sales at the level of individual firm $\dot{S}_{it}$ and the mean of $\dot{S}_{jt}$ across industries caused a serious problem of multicollinearity.

In the estimation results shown in Table 5.7, the coefficient of σ_t has a significantly negative sign. The dispersion of sales *across industries*, therefore, suppresses the wage increase; the negative effects of declining industries dominate the positive effects of growing industries in *Shunto.* In contrast, the dispersion of sales across companies *in a single industry*, σ_t^i, turned out to be insignificant (equation (ii) in Table 5.7).

Table 5.8 shows relative contributions of four explanatory variables to changes in real wages for each year based on equation (i) of

Table 5.8. The relative contribution of four explanatory variables to changes in real wages, 1968–1985[a] (%)

	S_{it}	R_{it}	σ_t	U_t
1968	22.6	14.3	- 6.6	70.2
1969	22.6	15.4	- 2.6	73.0
1970	17.7	12.6	- 1.2	62.6
1971	9.6	15.3	- 3.2	98.5
1972	13.5	12.3	- 1.9	74.4
1973	8.9	14.2	- 3.1	61.5
1974	0.5	15.3	- 13.1	71.3
1975	28.9	- 21.6	17.0	- 186.1
1976	26.7	18.1	- 10.8	92.3
1977	11.5	11.1	- 6.2	61.7
1978	14.8	18.2	- 4.4	81.9
1979	11.1	18.2	- 4.9	62.0
1980	20.7	33.8	- 32.6	114.4
1981	14.1	21.2	- 4.5	79.8
1982	2.4	17.2	- 4.1	71.6
1983	10.5	15.9	- 8.3	62.6
1984	15.3	14.8	- 8.4	51.5
1985	10.3	12.9	- 5.2	54.3

[a] Based on equation (i) of Table 5.7; see the text for four explanatory variables.

Table 5.7. It shows, for example, that the dispersion of sales among industries contributed considerably to suppressing real wages at the time of the second oil crisis (see Table 5.6 for 1980). Although the relative contributions change considerably over years, we can roughly conclude that about 60%–70% of the wage increase can be attributed to macroeconomic factors, with the remainder to firm-specific factors. The significance of microeconomic factors indicates that the labour market is not a single homogeneous market but is segmented at the corporate level.

The importance of firm-specific factors in the determination of wages appears to have risen since the first oil crisis. Table 5.9 shows the coefficients of variation of real wages, real sales (both growth rates), and profit rates across 297 firms in our sample. We can observe that the dispersion of changes in real wages across firms rose after the first oil shock, reflecting the increased dispersion of the growth of real sales. *The Survey of Wage Determination*, compiled by

Table 5.9. Variation of real wages, sales, and profits across firms, 1966–1985[a]

	Real wages	Growth rate of real sales	Profit rate
1966	1.49	1.07	0.57
1967	0.82	0.67	0.48
1968	0.76	0.69	0.51
1969	0.56	0.66	0.62
1970	0.51	0.76	0.69
1971	1.35	2.83	0.90
1972	0.99	1.68	0.72
1973	0.99	2.27	0.54
1974	0.89	61.11	0.74
1975	2.82	3.55	2.26
1976	5.05	1.39	0.92
1977	1.52	2.17	1.06
1978	7.72	2.39	0.99
1979	2.69	2.33	0.62
1980	38.54	2.57	0.67
1981	2.97	2.21	0.74
1982	2.80	13.54	0.91
1983	3.72	2.83	0.80
1984	3.53	1.60	0.68
1985	1.78	2.47	0.85

[a] Inter-firm (297 firms) coefficient of variation (mean/s.d.).

the Ministry of Labour, also shows that the importance of the prevailing market wage significantly declined after the first oil shock, while the individual firm's performance became by far the most important factor in the determination of wages by firms (Fig. 5.4; see also Higuchi (1989), who documents that relative wages among different sectors in Japan have changed significantly during the past two decades).

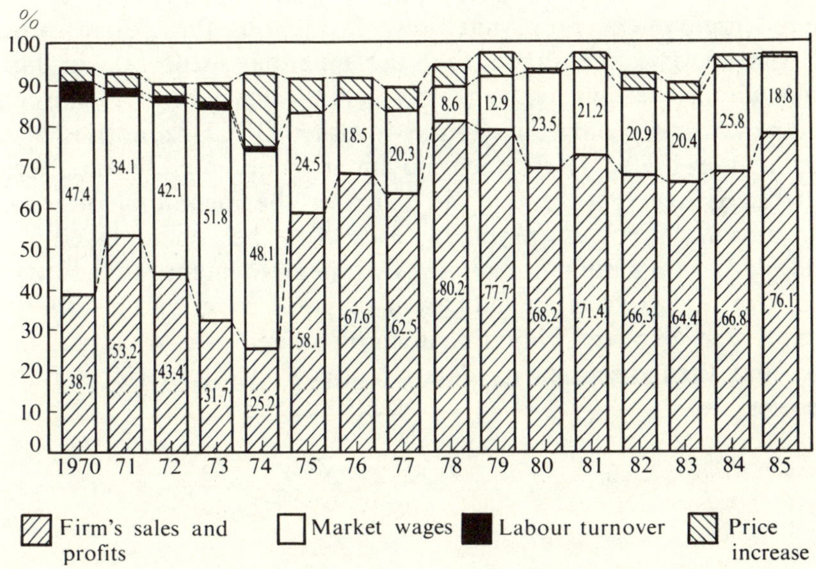

Fig. 5.4. Important determinants of wage settlements, 1970–1985
Source: Ministry of Labour, *A Survey of Wage Settlements in Large Firms,* ('Large firms' refer to firms with 1,000 or more employees in manufacturing industries.)

Flexibility of real wages in Japan is sustained *partly* by the annual synchronized wage determination, *Shunto.* But the flexibility also comes from the high responsiveness of wages to firms' performances such as the growth of sales at the level of the individual firm. If wages were perfectly flexible at the individual-firm level, synchronization of wage determination in the economy would not actually matter. In reality, of course, *Shunto* matters, but for flexibility of wages in Japan, as equally important as *Shunto* is perhaps flexibility of wages at firm level. I will explain the mechanism to sustain this flexibility of wages at individual firm level by a simple efficiency wage model in

Section 5.5. Contrary to the usual efficiency wage model, which purports to explain the *rigidity* of real wages, the 'Japanese efficiency wage model' presented in Section 5.5 explains the *flexibility* of wages.

5.3 UNEMPLOYMENT

Despite the significant reallocation of the labour force among sectors, and cyclical fluctuations, the Japanese economy managed to keep the unemployment rate quite low throughout the post-war period. Indeed, Fig. 5.5 shows that the unemployment rate in Japan looks almost flat at its very low level, and does not share the tendency to rise commonly found in other OECD countries beginning in the 1970s. High unemployment is not merely a reflection of reduced aggregate output; it increases the inequality of income distribution, involves psychic costs for the unemployed, and erodes a nation's human capital. Low unemployment in itself, therefore, can be taken as an indication of good economic health. This section first explains why the unemployment rate in Japan is so low, and then discusses its determinants in relation to alternative theories.

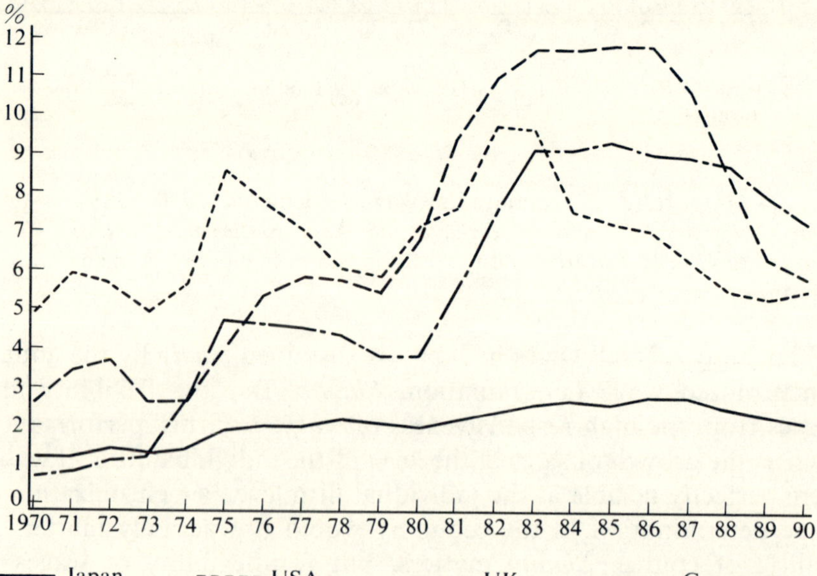

Fig. 5.5. Unemployment rates in Japan, USA, UK, and W. Germany, 1970–1990

Why is the Unemployment Rate in Japan So Low?

The first factor explaining the low unemployment rate is the definition of unemployment in Japan, compared with other countries (Table 5.10). For example, according to the stringent Japanese criterion, persons engaged in paid work *for an hour* or more during the last seven days of the previous month are not to be counted as unemployed, although those having very odd jobs are entitled to claim that they are 'without work' in the common sense. Taira (1983) argues that the unemployment rate in Japan is generally underestimated and that, on the basis of the US definition, the figure for 1978, for example, becomes 4.7% as against the official 2.6%. Taira's argument naturally invoked active controversy. One numerically important issue is whether new school university graduates waiting for their first jobs (mostly in March in Japan) should be counted as unemployed or should not yet be included in the labour force; Taira classifies them as the unemployed. Meanwhile, Sorrentino (1984) shows that the Japanese unemployment rate, as calculated on the basis of the US Bureau of Labor Statistics (BLS) method, is not very different from the official figure: for four years between 1977 and 1980, the BLS method gives 2.8%, 3.0%, 2.7%, and 2.3%, respectively, while the corresponding official figures are 2.4%, 2.6%, 2.5%, and 2.2%. For all technicalities, therefore, it seems reasonable to conclude that low unemployment in Japan is not simply a definitional artefact.

The unemployment rate in Japan is low because (i) on the demand side, the cyclical adjustment of employment is small, particularly in the downward direction (Table 5.4), and (ii) on the supply side, cyclical fluctuations in the labour force participation rate are large.

I have already discussed the demand side. On the labour supply side, it is well recognized in Japan that the labour force participation rate fluctuates pro-cyclically to a considerable extent, (Umemura 1961; Ono 1981). Since the unemployment rate is defined as $1 - (E/L^s)$ (where E is the number of the employed and L^s is the labour force), if L^s declines in parallel with a plunge in E, a change in the unemployment rate would be insignificant. According to Ono (1981), for example, those who stop looking for employment or who give up participating in the labour force in recessions accounted for 8.9% (or 2.87 million people) of the non-labour force in Japan in 1978. In the United States, the corresponding figure is only 1.4%. These 2.87 million people correspond to 4% or 5% of the total labour

Table 5.10. Definitions of unemployment in major countries[a]

	Japan	USA	UK	W. Germany	France	Italy	Canada
Institution	Statistics Bureau, Management and Co-ordination Agency	Department of Labor	Department of Employment	Federal Labour Office	Ministere des Affaires Sociales el de l'Emploi	Istituto Nazionale di Statistico (ISTAT)	Statistics Canada
Source	*Monthly Report on the Labor Force Survey*	*Monthly Labor Review*	*Monthly Digest of Statistics*	*Monthly Report of the Deutsche Bundesbank*	*Bulletin Mensuel de Statistique* (monthly)	*Bollettino Mensile di Statistica* (monthly)	*Canadian Statistical Review* (monthly)
Basic data	Sample surveys (about 40,000 households)	Sample surveys (about 60,000 households)	Registration data	Registration data	Registration data	Sample surveys (about 70,000 households)	Sample surveys (about 55,000 households)
Survey period	A week (the last seven days of every month)	A week (the week including the 12th of the month)	A day (in principle, the Thursday in the second week of the month)	A day (the last day of every month)	A day (the last day of every month)	A week (the first week of January, April, July, and October)	A week

+

Definition of 'unemployed'	Persons without work and currently available for work, who wish to work, and who actively sought or prepared for work (excl. those engaged in paid work for an hour or more during the survey period)	Persons who did not work during the survey week, but were available for work and had looked for jobs within the preceding 4 weeks	Persons claiming benefit (i.e. unemployment benefit, supplementary benefit, or national insurance credits of Unemployment Benefit Offices) Prior to October 1982, those who registered at a local employment office or careers service office	Persons without work and currently available for work who have been registered for at least 3 months for a job of 20 hours or more per week	Persons without work and currently available for work who want full-time job for more than 3 months and who also have registered with an employment office (excl. 60-year-old recipients of income maintenance benefits and incl. those who had made arrangements to take up a job but have not yet worked)	Persons without work and who were not engaged in work for more than one hour during the survey period, and are currently available and seeking work (incl. those who had made arrangements to take up a job but had not yet worked)	Persons without work and currently available for work who had sought work within the previous 4 weeks
Age	15 years of age and over	16 years of age and over	15 years of age and over	15 years of age and over	Irrespective	14 years of age and over	15 years of age and over
Layoffs	Excluded	Included	Excluded	Included	Included	Included	Included
New job hunters	Included	Included	Excluded	Included	Included	Included	Included
Formula for unemployment rate	[b]	[c]	[d]	[e]	[d]	[c]	[c]

[a] Labour force = Employed + self-employed + unemployed.

[b] $\dfrac{\text{Unemployed}}{\text{Labour force (incl. self–defence force)}} \times 100.$ [c] $\dfrac{\text{Unemployed}}{\text{Labour force (excl. armed forces)}} \times 100.$

[d] $\dfrac{\text{Unemployed}}{\text{Labour force (incl. armed forces)}} \times 100.$ [e] $\dfrac{\text{Unemployed}}{\text{Employed + unemployed (excl. armed forces)}}.$

force. I do not intend to argue that these people should all be included in the unemployed category, but I do argue that the difference between such people and the unemployed is very slight. In any case, the strong cyclical movements of some workers (mostly the non-core workers in Section 5.1) into and out of the labour force rather than the unemployment pool is a major factor in explaining the low unemployment rate in Japan.

Alternative Theories of Unemployment

Although the unemployment rate in Japan is much lower than in other OECD countries, it showed a moderately rising tendency beginning in the 1970s. In addition, as will be explained later, unemployment in Japan tends to be concentrated in a relatively small group of workers, particularly the aged, and as a consequence, the average *duration* of unemployment tends to be longer than in other countries. This is the reason why unemployment has been one of the major macroeconomic issues in Japan, despite its low level, just as it has in other OECD countries, where the levels of unemployment are much higher.

There are several alternative theories of unemployment. The Keynesian theory suggests that we look at demand deficiency in the goods market when we analyse the problem of unemployment/under-employment in labour market. Section 5.5 presents a Keynesian model to explain the 'stylized facts' of the Japanese labour market. Monetarism, on the other hand, on the basis of expectational errors (Lucas and Rapping 1969; Lucas 1972), blames unanticipated fluctuations in inflation generated by misguided monetary policy for a divergence between the natural and actual rates of unemployment. We saw in Chapter 1, however, that empirical studies mostly produce unfavourable evidence for this theory. My own analysis in Chapter 2 also demonstrates that the post-war Japanese experience does not support the theory. In any case, faded monetarism has lost its attraction as an explanation of changes in the unemployment rate. And yet, the notion of the natural rate of unemployment has survived. Some economists, indeed, attribute changes in the unemployment rate mainly to changes in the *natural* rate of unemployment.

Lilien (1982), for example, argues that about half of the post-war fluctuations of the US unemployment rate can be accounted for by changes in the natural rate, which are in turn caused by sectoral shifts in labour demand. He proposes the following measure of sectoral shifts:

$$\sigma_t = \left[\sum_{i=1}^{n} \frac{e_{it}}{e_t} (\Delta \log e_{it} - \Delta \log e_t)^2 \right]^{1/2}, \tag{4}$$

where e_{it} stands for employment in sector i at time t and e_t represents total employment in the economy as a whole; σ measures the variance of changes in employment across sectors. Lilien shows that the unemployment rate is highly correlated with σ, and then interprets this result as supporting the thesis that sectoral shifts in labour demand significantly raise the unemployment rate.

Abraham and Katz (1986), however, point out a serious flaw in Lilien's interpretation. The point of their criticism is that a possible negative correlation between *aggregate* demand and σ may have spuriously produced the observed correlation between the unemployment rate and σ. For example, suppose that there are two sectors in the economy. Changes in employment in the two sectors correspond, respectively, to changes in aggregate demand as drawn in Fig. 5.6. In sector 1, the growth rate of employment on trend $\Delta \log e_1$, which obtains when the growth of aggregate demand $\Delta \log y$ is equal to its natural growth $\Delta \log y^*$, is high, while the cyclical elasticity of growth of employment is small; the line is flatter in the figure. The opposite holds in sector 2. One might realistically interpret sectors 1 and 2 as services and manufacturing, respectively. Under this assumption, two

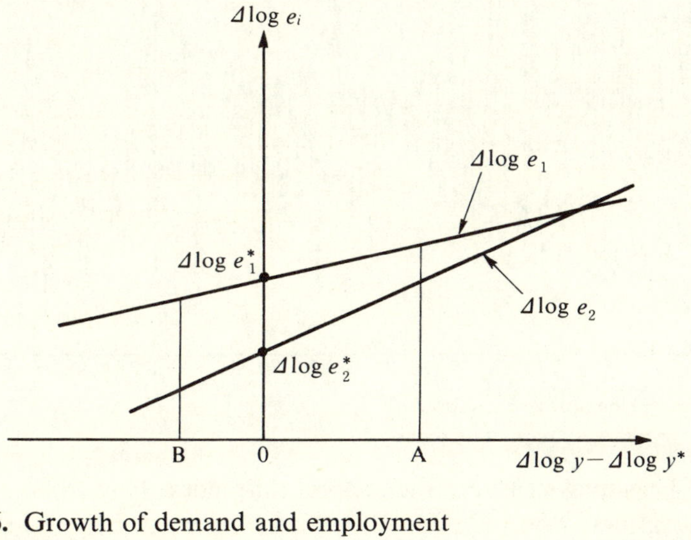

Fig. 5.6. Growth of demand and employment

situations A and B in the figure demonstrate that σ measured by the distance between the two lines increases when the growth of aggregate demand declines and vice versa. Therefore, even if the unemployment rate is determined basically by aggregate demand, as traditional Keynesian theory indicates, we would still find a positive correlation between Lilien's σ and the unemployment rate.

To sort out two alternative interpretations, Abraham and Katz calculate the correlation between σ and a measure of job offers. Under the Lilien thesis, σ must be positively correlated not only with the unemployment rate but also with a measure of job offers. It turns out that σ is negatively correlated with the measure of job offers. This is what one expects under the Keynesian theory. Under the Lilien thesis, the Beveridge curve must frequently shift up and down. The Abraham–Katz finding, however, implies that movements along the stable Beveridge curve dominate.

For Japan, Nishikawa (1989) formally tests the Lilien hypothesis. Fig. 5.7 depicts the time series of the sectoral shift index, σ, along

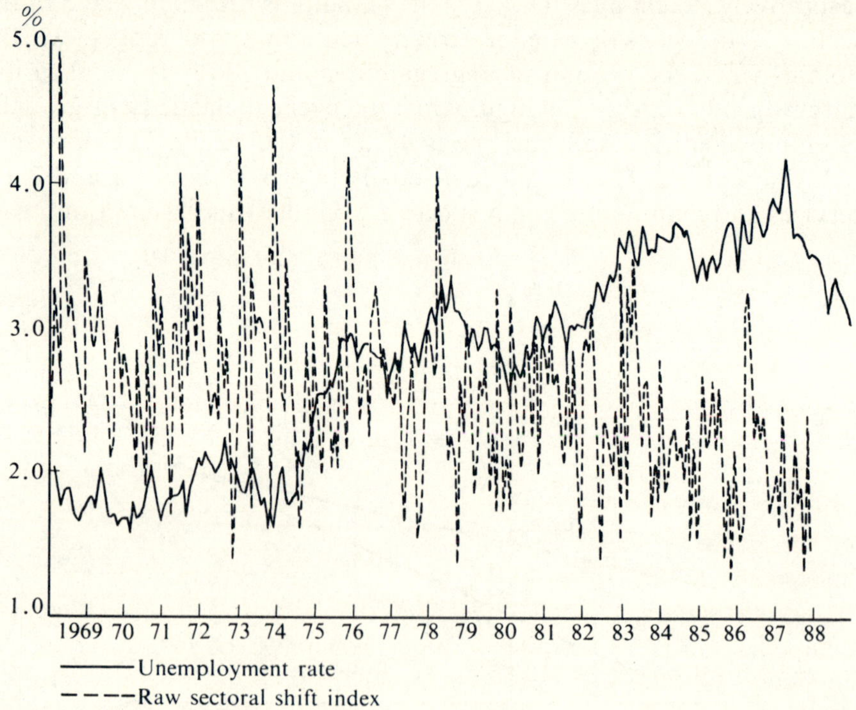

Fig. 5.7. Unemployment rate and sectoral shift index, 1969–1988
Source: Nishikawa (1989).

with the unemployment rate. Casual observation reveals that these are broadly *negatively* correlated. This impression is indeed borne out by formal regressions. For the Japanese economy, therefore, the Lilien hypothesis is rejected outright. And yet, the argument that beginning in the mid-1970s the natural rate of unemployment kept rising in Japan has persisted. In what follows, I will critically review some of the representative arguments.

Unemployment benefits are one of the major issues. Layard *et al.* (1991), on the basis of their massive work on OECD countries, conclude that 'unemployment will fall if unemployment benefits are of limited duration and subject to stronger job-search tests', although they are cautious enough to point out that, without active manpower policies, harsh benefits regimes have undesirable distributional effects.

The Japanese unemployment compensation which started in 1947 saw a major reform in 1974 (*Koyōhoken-hō*). Under this reform, unemployment compensation became more liberal. Also, in the old system the duration of compensation depended on the job tenure of the unemployed, while in the new system it depends on the age of the unemployed. (The 1984 reform combined age and job tenure of the unemployed for eligibility.) For example, to get compensation for 10 months, the unemployed person had to have worked for more than 20 years under the old system, but in the new system those aged 55 or older are eligible for 10 months' compensation regardless of their job tenure.

Fig. 5.8, taken from Shimada (1981), shows the duration of unemployment by age for 1973 and 1977, i.e. before and after the reform. We can observe that the duration of unemployment became uniformly longer in 1977 than in 1973. Shimada *et al.* then suggest that the 1974 reform of unemployment compensation might be responsible for this prolonged duration of unemployment. The problem, however, is that 1973 was the year of a cyclical peak, while 1977 was in a period of long recession following the first oil shock. For example, the job offer–job seeker ratio, which is known to be much more cyclically sensitive than the unemployment rate, was at its historically highest level of 1.74 in 1973, while it was 0.56 in 1977. Although separating the effects of the reform of unemployment compensation from the effects of cyclical fluctuations still remains a challenge, Ohtake (1987), analysing the cross-section data by prefecture, concludes that the effect of recession on unemployment is more dominant. It is often taken for granted that unemployment benefits raise the level of unemployment. It is worth noting, therefore, that

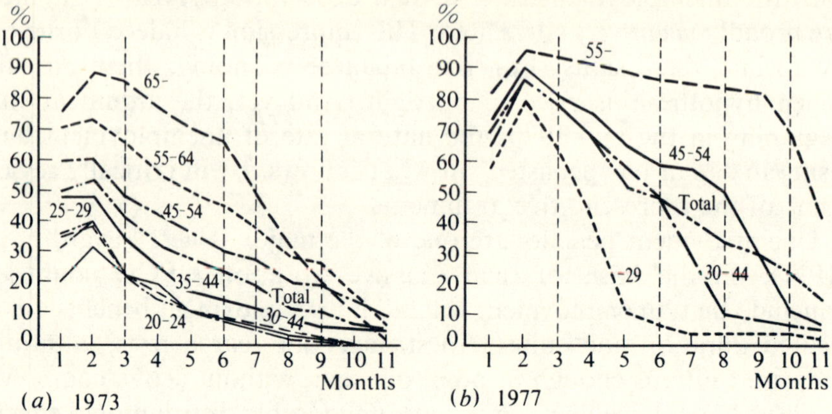

Fig. 5.8. Duration of unemployment by age, 1973 and 1977
The survival probability is measured vertically against the duration of unemployment in months for each age-group.
Source: Shimada *et al.* (1982).

the conclusions drawn about the effect of unemployment insurance may actually be reversed when account is taken of such aspects as the requirement for previous job tenure, or of the restricted coverage (see Atkinson *et al.* 1991).

Meanwhile, changes in unemployment U are determined by

$$\dot{U} = F - (U/d), \tag{5}$$

where F is the inflow into the stock of the unemployed and d is the average duration of unemployment. A steady-state approximation then gives us $U = dF$. Mizuno (1992) decomposes changes in the unemployment rate into changes in d and F. He finds that the relative contributions of Δd and ΔF to a steady rise in the unemployment rate are, respectively, 82.5% and 14.7% for 1975–8, and 21.2% and 77.6% for 1984–7. Based on other evidence as well as on the prolonged duration of unemployment after 1975, Mizuno concludes that the unemployment compensation reform did contribute to some extent to a rise in the unemployment rate in mid-1970s.

In passing, the average duration of unemployment in Japan in 1973–7 was about 3.6 months (Mizuno 1992), compared with 2.2 months in the United States in 1974 (Clark and Summers 1982); it rose to 5.3 months in Japan in 1987. It seems that, although the unemployment rate is much lower in Japan than in the United States, the *duration* of unemployment is actually longer in Japan. This fact partly reflects the relatively heavy concentration of unemployment on the aged in Japan: in 1987, about 43% of the unemployed were aged 55 or older.

Another branch of the argument that attributes a rise in the unemployment rate to a rise in the natural rate of unemployment blames higher turnover, resulting from a growing proportion of female and young workers in the Japanese labour market. As shown in Table 5.11, however, the fact is that the turnover rate was much higher in the high-growth period of 1960s, when the unemployment rate was lower, than in 1970s and 1980s. Turnover remained stable at the lower level throughout 1970s and 1980s. A high turnover rate cannot therefore be blamed for a rise in the unemployment rate beginning in the mid-1970s.

Perhaps we can go a step further and be sceptical even of the *notion* of the natural rate of unemployment. The natural rate of unemployment is defined by Milton Friedman (1968) as the level of unemployment 'that would be ground out by the Walrasian system of general equilibrium equations, provided that there is embedded in them the actual structural characteristics of the labor and commodity markets, including market imperfections, stochastic variability in demands and supplies, the costs of getting information about job vacancies and labor availabilities, the costs of mobility; and so on'. The crucial assumption underlying this definition is that job search is significantly more efficient when the searcher is unemployed. This can be explained by a simple example.

Suppose that a worker has two alternatives, A and B, in a two-period model (Table 5.12). For simplicity, he is assumed to be risk-neutral and interested in the present value of income stream. If he takes or keeps the present job with wages w_A (option A), the present value is $w_A + w_A/(1 + i)$ (i is the interest rate). If he chooses to be unemployed and search for a better job in the current period (option B), the present value is $pw_B/(1 + i)$, where p is the probability of success of finding a better job with wages $w_B(w_B > w_A)$. For simplicity, income is assumed to be zero when unemployed. Those workers who perceive $w_A + w_A/(1 + i)$ as greater than $p\,w_B/(1 + i)$ work, while those who perceive otherwise choose to be unemployed.

In this framework, unemployment is investment. Under the neoclassical assumption that real wages are equal to marginal products of labour, unemployment chosen by workers must be 'productive' for the economy as a whole, in the sense that it must

Table 5.11. Rates of job separation and accession, 1965–1986 (%)[a]

	All industries	Construction	Manufacturing industries	Utilities	Transportation and communications	Wholesale and retail	Finance	Services
Rate of job separation								
1965	31.9	71.1	26.9	15.2	22.1	34.8	34.4	
1970	32.2	64.9	30.3	14.0	23.5	36.1	34.9	22.2
1975	19.8	35.6	15.6	12.9	14.5	22.2	27.4	19.3
1976	18.8	35.3	16.2	12.4	12.7	21.4	25.0	18.9
1977	18.7	32.2	15.7	14.1	13.2	21.5	24.4	19.9
1978	17.6	29.2	14.6	13.4	12.5	20.0	23.6	19.6
1979	18.3	28.9	16.0	14.1	13.3	22.5	21.8	20.1
1980	19.3	25.6	17.3	13.6	14.7	22.6	22.9	20.5
1981	19.1	25.6	17.3	13.5	13.8	23.1	22.9	20.0
1982	18.9	29.4	15.9	15.1	14.6	22.4	23.1	20.6
1983	18.7	29.2	16.2	14.2	13.8	21.8	22.5	19.3
1984	19.0	28.2	17.0	13.1	14.8	20.8	23.5	19.6
1985	18.7	23.7	16.7	12.0	15.0	20.8	24.9	19.9
1986	19.1	23.3	15.8	14.4	17.4	21.9	26.7	20.8
Rate of job accession								
1965	30.8	66.2	27.8	14.3	20.6	32.0	30.2	
1970	29.7	59.2	27.9	14.4	22.4	33.1	31.0	20.7
1975	22.1	38.7	20.5	12.5	16.2	22.9	26.4	18.0
1976	19.8	35.3	17.8	11.8	13.5	22.7	24.5	17.6
1977	19.6	35.2	18.2	14.2	13.7	22.6	23.9	18.2
1978	18.6	29.3	17.3	11.9	13.6	21.8	22.8	18.4
1979	18.7	28.3	17.1	13.9	14.3	22.3	22.1	17.7
1980	18.9	28.8	16.8	13.3	14.4	22.6	23.0	18.8
1981	18.7	24.7	16.6	13.7	14.6	22.9	23.0	19.1
1982	18.8	27.9	16.0	14.7	14.8	22.3	23.2	18.9
1983	19.1	30.6	15.8	15.3	15.6	22.4	23.3	18.3
1984	18.9	30.1	15.9	15.4	17.1	21.7	24.4	18.2
1985	18.7	27.1	16.4	12.9	17.0	21.3	25.2	18.1
1986	19.4	23.8	16.9	14.9	20.3	21.3	25.7	19.3

[a] The figures are on annual basis obtained by multiplying the original monthly data by 12.

Source: Ministry of Labour, *Labour Statistics Monthly*.

raise the expected present value of marginal products of labour over time. If 'naturally' unemployed workers were somehow compelled to work, then this would have a Pareto-deteriorating effect.

Table 5.12. Job search

	Present	Future	Present value of expected earnings
(A)	W_A	W_A	$W_A + \frac{W_A}{1+i}$
(B)	0	$\begin{cases} W_B & (P) \\ 0 & (1-P) \end{cases}$	$\frac{PW_B}{1+i}$
(C)	W_A	$\begin{cases} W_B & (P) \\ 0 & (1-P) \end{cases}$	$W_A + \frac{PW_B}{1+i}$

The natural rate of unemployment generated this way is thus Pareto-optimal.

Suppose instead that workers can search for better jobs while keeping their present jobs; unemployment does not enhance the efficiency of job search. Then workers have alternative C in Table 5.12, which always dominates B. The natural unemployment vanishes. Even sophisticated models such as Lucas and Prescott (1974) cannot generate natural unemployment without the crucial assumption that job search is significantly more efficient when the searcher is unemployed.

Tobin (1972) expresses his doubts about this assumption by saying that 'members of our own profession are adept at seeking and finding new jobs without first leaving their old ones or abandoning not-in-labor-force status. We do not know how many quits and new hires in manufacturing are similar transfers, but some of them must be.' For Japan, Mizuno (1983) succeeds in decomposing the monthly accession data for 1981 by status of workers (Table 5.13). It seems that the overwhelming proportion of the Japanese workers change their jobs without first leaving their old ones and experiencing unemployment. Given this fact, the assumption that unemployment enhances the efficiency of job search must be rejected. Although the notion of the natural rate of unemployment contributes to an understanding of frictional unemployment and is valuable for some purposes, it is not so empirically well grounded as some economists might wish. It seems therefore premature for us to rely on this notion in our welfare judgement of the actual rate of unemployment.

If the rising natural rate of unemployment is not the answer to the question of why the Japenese unemployment rate rose montonically after the first oil shock, what is the answer? One reason must be

Table 5.13. Labour turnover 1981 ('000)[a]

Worker's status immediately before job acquisition	Male	Female
Unemployed	970	580
Employed in non-agricultural sector	11,820	7,490
Non-labour force	1,270	2,540
Employed in agriculture	680	420
Self-employed	1,590	1,320

[a] Total number of workers who acquired jobs as employees in the non-agricultural sector in 1981, classified by their previous status. If a worker changed his job three times during 1981, for example, he is counted three times.

Source: Mizuno (1983).

simply the persistent low economic growth. The average growth rate of the Japanese economy between 1974 and 1986 was 3.7%. This was still high among advanced industrial nations, but it was no comparison to the 10% or greater growth rate experienced in Japan in the 1950s and 1960s. Firms not confident enough to expand employment relied more heavily on extra working hours per worker; indeed, Kurosaka (1988) shows that the adjustment of hours became more dominant, compared with changes in employment, in the 1970s than in the 1960s. Fig. 5.9 also shows that the shortening of annual working hours per worker, which had continued since 1960s, stopped immediately after the first oil shock. When hiring, firms tended to seek casual employment in preference to formal full-time employment. This is reflected in the significant divergence between job offer–job seeker ratios of full-time and part-time workers (Fig. 5.10). Weak demand for labour over 1974–87 is perhaps the most important reason for the rising unemployment rate in this period; the cyclically sensitive job offer–job seeker ratio, which had been 1.76 in 1973, persistently stayed at the low level of 0.6 from 1975 to 1987.

The economic boom in 1987–91 dramatically changed the situation. The job offer–job seeker ratio, which had been about 0.6 for more than 13 years, turned upward, crossed the critical value of 1 in 1988, and reached 1.4 in 1990. In line with this change, the unemployment rate declined, from 2.9% in 1987 to 2.1% in 1990. Given this observation, hysteresis (Blanchard and Summers 1986) does not appear to apply to the Japanese unemployment rate. In typical models of hysteresis, negative shocks reduce the number of union members ('insiders') and increase unemployment. This impulse then has permanent effects, because the union takes this reduced number

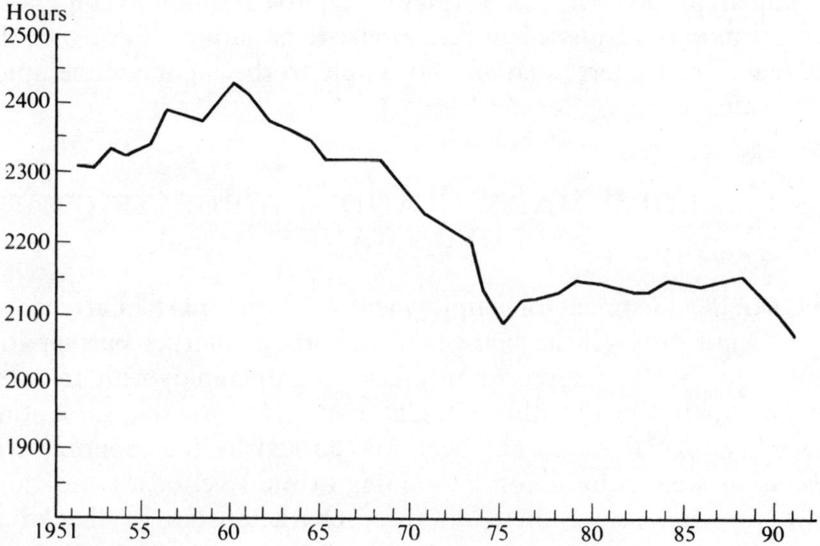

Fig. 5.9. Hours worked in Japan yearly, 1951–1990
Source: Ministry of Labour, *Labour Statistics Monthly* (Maitsuki Kinro Tokei).

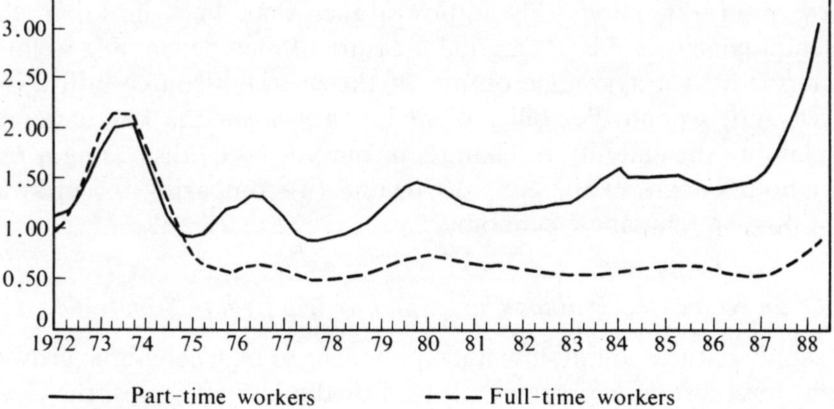

Fig. 5.10. Job offer/job-seeker ratios for full-time and part-time workers, 1972–1988
Source: Ministry of Labour, *Statistics of the Employment Office* (Shokugyō Antei Gyōmu Tōkei).

as the basis for its next wage negotiations. In Japan, however, as explained in Section 5.1, formally employed union members are not commonly dismissed in recessions. It is natural, therefore, that the theory of hysteresis should not apply to the Japanese unemployment rate.[3]

5.4 LABOUR MARKET AND MACROECONOMIC PERFORMANCE

The small adjustment of employment by firms, particularly downwards, and pro-cyclical changes in the labour market participation rate, help the Japanese economy keep the unemployment rate very low compared with other OECD countries. At the same time, flexibility of real wages has been maintained by the economy-wide *Shunto* as well as by union bargaining at the level of the individual firm. In what sense, then, do these characteristics of the labour market contribute to the macroeconomic performance of the Japanese economy?

In one sense, as mentioned earlier, low unemployment in itself signifies good economic health. It means a greater equality of income distribution than otherwise; it also allows the economy to avoid the erosion of human capital and the work incentives of labour. With these points in mind, this section argues that, first, in Japan the unemployment rate is *not* a good measure of macroeconomic welfare in terms of lost aggregate output or the overall resource utilization level, and, second, flexibility of real wages is *not* the key factor in explaining the stability of changes in output, by (i) discussing a rise in labour's share in the early 1970s and (ii) comparing the pre-war and post-war Japanese economies.

Okun's Law, the Phillips Curve, and the Aggregate Supply Curve

It is only natural to link low unemployment to high economic growth or a small loss of aggregate output. For the United States, the close relationship between the unemployment rate and the growth rate of output is in fact so stable that it is even called a law—Okun's law.

[3] Brunello (1990) argues that the theory of hysteresis holds for Japan: an increase in the Japanese unemployment rate in the 1970s and 1980s was small but persistent. What occurred around 1990, however, seems to contradict his argument.

Okun (1962) estimated several variants of the following equation for the United States:

$$\log(1 - u) = \alpha + \beta \ln Q + \gamma T + \varepsilon, \tag{6}$$

where u, Q, T, and ε are the unemployment rate, real GNP, and time and error terms, respectively. It turns out that the estimated β is very robust with respect to sample period and specifications of the equation and is about 1/3.

Hamada and Kurosaka (1984) estimate the same equation for Japan. The Okun coefficient, namely the inverse of β, turns out to be very unstable with respect to sample period, and also extraordinarily high: 18 for 1953–65, 32 for 1965–74, and 13 for 1974–82 as against 3 for the United States in the latter period. Table 5.14, from Kurosaka (1988), compares the Okun coefficient and its decomposition in terms of (i) the direct effect of changes in the unemployment rate, (ii) the effects of cyclical changes in labour participation rate, (iii) the number of hours worked per worker, and (iv) labour productivity, for six OECD countries. The extraordinarily high level of the estimated Okun coefficient simply means that the unemployment rate is not a good measure of resource utilization for Japan. It is in fact difficult to measure the extent of underemployment in Japan, where workers' movements into and out of the labour force

Table 5.14. Decomposition of the Okun coefficient[a]

Country	Sample period	(1) Direct effect of changes in the unemployment rate	(2) Effect of changes in labour participation rate	(3) Effect of changes in no. of hours worked per worker	(4) Effect of changes in labour productivity	(5) The Okun coefficient (1)+(2)+(3)+(4)
Japan	1960–72	1.01	2.51	8.11	25.27	36.9
	1973–85			29.52	3.86	
USA	1960–85	1.06	0.16	0.37	1.19	2.78
W. Germany	1960–72	1.02	0.35	0.86	1.38	3.61
	1973–83			2.38	−0.14	
UK	1960–83	1.03	0.54	0.51	0.08	2.16
France	1960–83	1.03	0.44	0.92	3.40	5.79
Italy	1960–83	1.06	−1.13	0.30	5.80	6.03

[a] The Okun coefficient in this table is the inverse of β of equaion (6) in the text.

Source: Kurosaka (1988).

are so frequent. The next section offers a conceptual framework to define underemployment.

Very small fluctuations of the unemployment rate and flexible wages also mean a steep short-run Phillips curve, compared with those for other countries (see e.g. Shimada 1981; Grubb *et al.* 1983). This fact is well known, but its implications deserve some discussion. A steep short-run Phillips curve has been frequently interpreted to imply that prices fluctuate more and quantities fluctuate less for a given demand shock, and therefore that demand management is ineffective in Japan. If changes in the unemployment rate precisely reflected the level of the economy's overall activities, this interpretation would be correct. As explained above, however, the unemployment rate is not a good indicator of the level of macroeconomic activity in Japan. In the United States, workers are laid off in accordance with a decline in output, which leads to a rise in the unemployment rate; in Japan, a similar drop in output will not cause the unemployment rate to rise comparably, because the necessary adjustment of labour input is made through a decrease in working hours or an increase in the percentage of the population not looking for work, i.e. 'disguised unemployment'. The difference in the levels of the unemployment rate in Japan and the United States, therefore, reflects mainly the difference in income distribution, i.e. in who bears the burdens of the decline in output. The problem of income distribution is very important, of course, but it is a different issue from that of macroeconomic activity. As an indicator of the level of macroeconomic activity, real GNP is actually a clearer and more appropriate concept than the unemployment rate.

Thus, it is necessary to consider the aggregate supply function, which shows the relation between real GNP and wages or prices. One is tempted to suppose that a steep Phillips curve automatically means a steep aggregate supply function. However, while the slope of the Phillips curve is $\Delta w/\Delta u$ (where w and u denote the rate of increase in wages and the unemployment rate, respectively), the slope of the aggregate supply function is $\Delta w/\Delta y$ (where y is real GNP):

$$\Delta w/\Delta y = (\Delta w/\Delta u)/(\Delta y/\Delta u). \qquad (7)$$

It is clear that large $\Delta w/\Delta u$ does not necessarily mean large $\Delta w/\Delta y$. $\Delta y/\Delta u$ in the equation is the Okun coefficient. We have already seen that it is extremely large in Japan. Therefore it is not only a logical possibility, but is in fact very likely, that a large $\Delta w/\Delta u$ coexists with a small $\Delta w/\Delta y$. Indeed, Table 5.15, from Kurosaka and Goto (1987), shows that the slope of the Japanese aggregate supply curve has the

Table 5.15. Slope of the aggregate supply curve: six countries

	Slope of Phillips curve	Inverse of Okun's coefficient	Slope of aggregate supply curve
Japan, 1960–85[a]	3.11 (7.64)	0.03	0.08 (0.21)
USA, 1960–85	0.61	0.38	0.23
W. Germany, 1960–83	1.09	0.28	0.30
UK, 1960–83	1.98	0.46	0.92
France			
1960–73	– 2.05	0.17	– 0.35
1974–84	2.81		0.49
Italy, 1960–83	3.93	0.17	0.65

[a] For Japan, the figure is based on estimated equation in Table 5.7. Kurosaka and Goto's original result is shown in parentheses.

Source: Kurosaka and Goto (1987).

smallest coefficient among the major countries. Since the Phillips curve estimated by Kurosaka and Goto does not include a measure of industry-wide dispersion σ_t (in our wage equation), the coefficient of the unemployment rate U_t is overestimated. With a linear approximation of the unemployment rate U_t in equation (i) of Table 5.6 and a mean value of 1.88% for U_t in the sample period, the coefficient becomes 3.11. The Japanese aggregate supply curve is even flatter than was estimated by Kurosaka and Goto. The short-run Phillips curve in Japan is steep, but the aggregate supply curve is in fact very flat compared with those of the other major countries. Demand shocks are not, therefore, liable to bring about inflation, but instead are likely to bring about relatively large quantity adjustment.

The Wage Gap and Labour's Income Share

There is still an argument that flexible real wages enhance the stability of the real economy (see e.g. Komiya and Yasui 1984; Suzuki 1985; and Bruno and Sachs 1985). This point is illustrated in Fig. 5.11. Suppose that the labour demand curve shifted downward for some reason and, as a result, the equilibrium point changed from A to B. If real wages are flexible, they would go down from W_A to W_B. As a consequence, the employment and production levels would remain unchanged. (For simplicity, the supply curve is set vertically.) In contrast, if real wages remain at the level of W_A, employment will go down to L_c and with it output will also decline. Therefore, the more

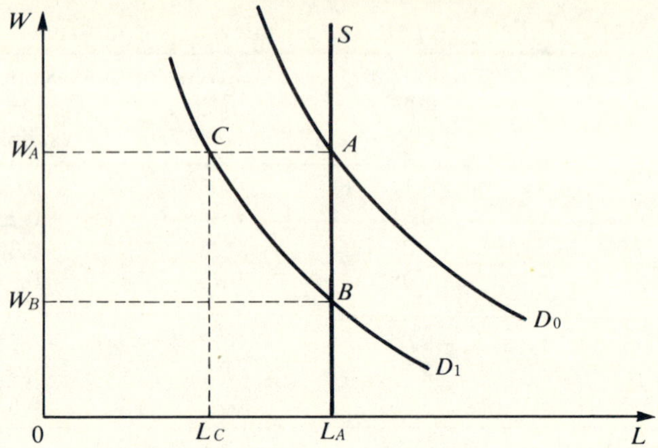

Fig. 5.11. The flexibility of real wages

rigid real wages are, the greater the fluctuations of output become. This is a natural conclusion obtained in the neoclassical paradigm, and illustrated by the well-known proposition, 'It is because prices are rigid that the Keynesian quantity adjustment occurs.'

One measure of the extent of disequilibrium caused by rigid real wages is $(W_A - W_B)/W_B$ in Fig. 5.11. This is called the 'wage gap' by Bruno and Sachs (1985) (For Japan, see also Lipschitz and Schadler 1984.) The problem of measuring the wage gap lies in estimating the marginal product of labour at full employment. In practice, therefore, the marginal product is approximated by the *average* product of labour. On the further simplifying assumption that the average product of labour at full employment is equal to labour's actual average product, the wage gap simply becomes labour's income share.

Bruno and Sachs (1985), among others, argue that the rising and persistent wage gap was responsible for high unemployment in Europe in the 1970s and 1980s. R. J. Gordon (1987), on the other hand, raises the question of how an increase in the wage gap could be a sign of classical unemployment. He notes that the wage gap approximated by labour's share increased far more in Japan than in either Europe or the United States, and yet this larger increase in the wage gap did not cause high unemployment in Japan (see Fig. 5.12). The unemployment rate, however, is not a good indicator of the utilization of labour input in Japan, and therefore, here again, the wage gap argument had better be cast in relation to output rather than unemployment.

Do too high real wages bring about a slower growth of output than otherwise? It is common practice to suppose that the economy is

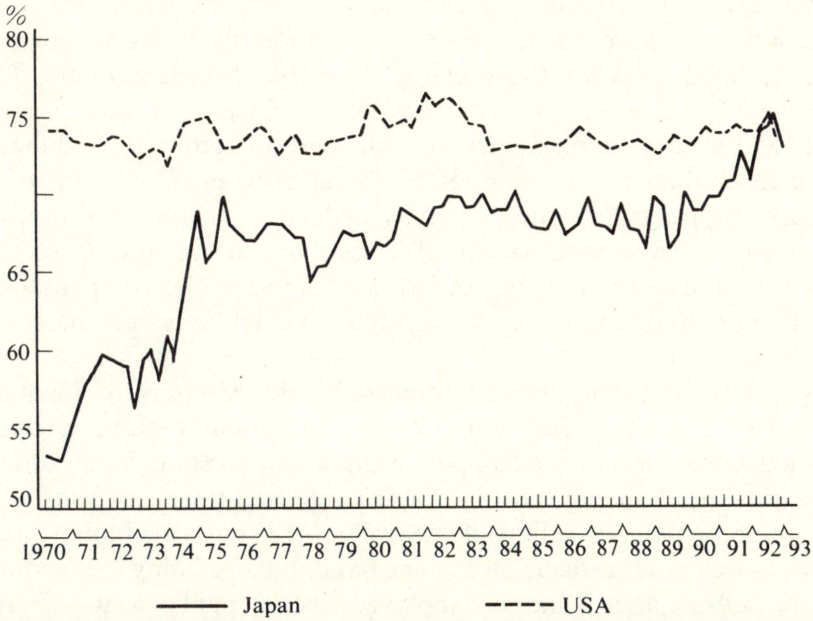

Fig. 5.12. Labour's share of national income, Japan and the United States, 1970–1993
Labour's share = (SNA compensation of employees)/(national income)
Source: Economic Planning Agency, *National Income and Product Accounts.*

either in the classical regime, where real wages affect output, or in the Keynesian regime, where output is determined by demand in the goods market. Within this standard framework, the wage gap argument makes sense only in the classical regime. Chapter 4, however, shows, both theoretically and empirically, that output is affected simultaneously both by goods demand and by real factor prices. It also shows that, for Japan, changes in output are determined basically by effective demand, but are occasionally modified by real input prices, including real wages. The wage gap, therefore, is expected to matter only to a limited extent in the Japanese economy. Still, given the fact that labour's income share markedly rose in Japan within a few years in the early 1970s, it is important to determine what caused this sharp increase.

The measurement of labour's share is not trivial. The difficulty lies, for example, in the treatment of the income of the self-employed, which the OECD calls 'household entrepreneurial income'.

R. J. Gordon (1987) adds the income of the self-employed to that of employees and treats it as part of labour's income share. He finds that labour's share so defined rose in the early 1970s but that it had declined back to the previous level by the early 1980s. The income of the self-employed, however, includes not only labour income but also capital income and rent on land; it is difficult to believe that the income of a shopkeeper in Tokyo or of a farmer cropping rice consists mainly of labour income. Yet another problem is the compensation of employees in the public sector. For the public sector, value added is imputed as the compensation for labour, and, therefore, by construction, labour's income share is 100%.

Statistics on Corporations, compiled by the Ministry of Finance, provides us with a clear-cut measure of labour's share of total income as the ratio of the compensation of employees to value added. This statistic, however, covers only private non-financial firms with the value of paid-in capital of ¥10 million or more. Including small firms as well as large firms on the one hand, but excluding the incomes of the self-employed and of employees in the public sector on the other, I estimate labour's share of income in private corporations as follows:

$$\text{Labour's Share} = \frac{\begin{pmatrix}\text{SNA comp-}\\\text{ensation}\\\text{of employees}\end{pmatrix} - (\text{Ratio}) \times \begin{pmatrix}\text{Compensation}\\\text{of self-}\\\text{employed}\end{pmatrix} - \begin{pmatrix}\text{Compensation}\\\text{of employees}\\\text{in the}\\\text{public sector}\end{pmatrix}}{\begin{pmatrix}\text{SNA income}\\\text{of private}\\\text{corporations}\end{pmatrix} + \begin{pmatrix}\text{SNA interest and}\\\text{dividends in Household's}\\\text{capital income}\end{pmatrix} + (\text{Nominator})} \tag{8}$$

The System of National Accounts (SNA) income of private corporations excludes interest and dividend payments and therefore is not 'profits'. To obtain 'profits', we need to add the interest and dividend income of households. 'Ratio' in (8) is the ratio of the income of employees to that of the self-employed in non-agricultural enterprises run by the self-employed (taken from the Statistics Bureau, Management and Co-ordination Agency's, *Statistics of Enterprise of Self-employed*). 'Compensation of employees in the public sector' is from the *Annual Statistics* of the Central Tax Agency (equivalent to the Inland Revenue Service in the United Kingdom).

Table 5.16. Labour's share of income, 1955–1990

	SNA[a]	SC[b]
1955	65.8	61.0
1956	69.3	59.5
1957	61.8	56.7
1958	66.7	60.9
1959	64.8	59.8
1960	57.8	56.5
1961	55.8	55.4
1962	61.1	59.5
1963	61.4	59.4
1964	59.9	61.0
1965	63.5	62.9
1966	62.1	61.8
1967	59.3	55.7
1968	58.2	61.8
1969	59.4	60.9
1970	59.1	62.6
1971	65.0	65.1
1972	65.4	64.8
1973	68.0	60.5
1974	71.5	64.9
1975	75.2	72.7
1976	74.4	70.8
1977	74.7	72.4
1978	72.4	72.4
1979	72.4	69.2
1980	71.1	68.4
1981	71.9	70.4
1982	72.2	72.3
1983	72.4	72.3
1984	71.3	71.6
1985	70.7	72.1
1986	71.0	72.8
1987	71.7	70.1
1988	71.5	68.1
1989	73.3	67.6
1990	73.9	67.3

[a] System of National Accounts. The SNA figures are my own estimates (equation (8)), as explained in the text.

[b] Statistics on Corporations.

My own estimates of labour's share in private corporations, based on SNA (8), and of labour's share in large firms, based on *Statistics on Corporations* (SC), are shown in Table 5.16. The two series coincide broadly with each other; roughly speaking, labour's share of income in Japan rose from 60% in the 1960s to 70% in the early 1970s. They do differ rather significantly in several years, however. For example, both SNA and SC labour's share rose by about 5% in 1971 but SC labour's share declined to the 1970 level by 1973 while SNA labour's share kept rising. As a consequence, for 1973 the two series differ by nearly 8%. The SC series makes the sharp rise in labour's share in 1975 much more pronounced than does the SNA series. Noting this difference, I refer to SC-based labour's share in what follows.

Before turning to data, it is useful briefly to discuss some theories of factor distribution. Suppose that we have the 'well-behaved' production function

$$Y = F(uK, eL), \tag{9}$$

where Y, K, and L are output, capital, and labour, respectively. Efficiency factors of capital and labour, u and e, represent either technological progress or the utilization level. Although we can easily introduce adjustment costs for changing factors of production (see Solow 1968 for such a model), I will discuss simple models as if there were no adjustment costs. I think that doing so is legitimate and useful, since my major purpose is to explain the permanent, rather than transitory, rise in labour's share which occurred in the early 1970s.

Straight neoclassical equilibrium theory indicates an increase in labour's share as

$$\left(\frac{1-\sigma}{\sigma}\right)\left[\left(\frac{\dot{K}}{K}-\frac{\dot{L}}{L}\right)-\left(\frac{\dot{e}}{e}-\frac{\dot{u}}{u}\right)\right], \tag{10}$$

where σ is the elasticity of substitution. Given σ less than one, labour's share increases when the capital–labour ratio increases or when capital-saving technical progress occurs ($\dot{e}/e < \dot{u}/u$). As observed above, labour's share of income in Japan increased from 0.6 to 0.7 in the early 1970s. The equilibrium theory then implies that, for $\sigma = 0.5$, the capital–labour ratio plus the capital-saving technical factor must have increased by 56%, whereas for $\sigma = 0.9$ it must have increased by 500%! It is very unreasonable, however, to suppose that an increase in the capital–labour ratio and the capital-saving technical factor of such magnitude occurred within a few years. It is difficult to explain a sharp increase in labour's share in the early 1970s within the framework of the equlibrium theory.

The wage gap theory, in contrast, argues that too high real wages, manifested in a sharp increase in labour's share, were resposible for the poor performance of output growth in the 1970s. Bruno and Sachs, for example, argue as follows:

In the late 1960s and early 1970s, a real wage explosion (particularly in Europe and Japan) caused a major shift in income distribution away from profits and toward labor. Even *before* the oil shocks, therefore, many OECD countries faced a major problem of declining profitability and slowing growth. In the second phase real wages did not decelerate (outside of the United States) to make room for the raw material price increases, so the profit squeeze intensified. In the third phase low profitability and rising unemployment slowed the rate of capital accumulation and productivity growth. Real wage increases *were* reduced, but so too was productivity growth, with the result that the excess of wages over full-employment productivity persisted into the early 1980s. (Bruno and Sachs 1985: 167)

Yet another approach is Keynesian. Kaldor (1956) is the best-known Keynesian theory of income distribution, in which the difference in the saving rates out of labour incomes and profits plays the crucial role. However, as Solow (1968) correctly points out, his famous equation is nothing but the goods market equilibrium condition, and therefore it is actually compatible with any theory, even neoclassical theory. What I call a Keynesian theory here has nothing to do with Kaldor (1956). It differs from the neoclassical theory of distribution in two important respects. First, it takes output Y as determined basically by demand. At the same time, real wages are not necessarily equal to the marginal product of labour. Given the production function (9), demand for labour must satisfy

$$\frac{\dot{Y}}{Y} = \frac{\partial Y}{\partial(uK)} \frac{(uK)}{Y} \left(\frac{\dot{K}}{K} + \frac{\dot{u}}{u}\right) + \frac{\partial Y}{\partial(eL)} \frac{(eL)}{Y} \left(\frac{\dot{L}}{L} + \frac{\dot{e}}{e}\right). \tag{11}$$

Since a change in labour's share Π is

$$\frac{\dot{\Pi}}{\Pi} = \frac{\dot{w}}{w} + \frac{\dot{L}}{L} - \frac{\dot{Y}}{Y}, \tag{12}$$

substituting $\dot{L}/L$ out, we obtain, from (11) and (12),

$$\frac{\dot{\Pi}}{\Pi} = \left(\frac{\dot{w}}{w} - \frac{\dot{e}}{e}\right) + \left(\frac{\beta}{1-\beta}\right)\left[\frac{\dot{Y}}{Y} - \left(\frac{\dot{K}}{K} + \frac{\dot{u}}{u}\right)\right], \tag{13}$$

where β is the elasticity of output with respect to capital service uK:

$$\beta = \frac{\partial Y}{\partial(uK)} \frac{uK}{Y}.$$

Thus, according to Keynesian theory, labour's share rises (i) when an increase in real wages exceeds labour-augmenting technical progress, and (ii) when the growth of effective demand Y exceeds changes in capital services, particularly capacity utilization rate. Since a substantial amount of labour is hoarded in Japanese firms, the necessary adjustment falls mainly on capital services when demand Y changes. As a consequence, uK becomes more variable than Y; the standard deviations of $\dot{Y}/Y$ and $\dot{K}/K + \dot{u}/u$ are in fact 2.6 and 6.1, respectively[4] (1969–90). This entails that the correlation between $(\dot{Y}/Y - (\dot{K}/K + \dot{u}/u))$ and $\dot{Y}/Y$ becomes negative, -0.41 for the Japanese economy. At the same time, labour hoarding means that a part of changes in e reflect changes in the utilization rate rather than pure technological change, and therefore the correlation between $\dot{e}/e$ and $\dot{Y}/Y$ is expected to be positive. All in all, these facts explain the counter-cyclical fluctuations in labour's share of income.

The wage gap and Keynesian theories both, naturally enough, predict that an autonomous increase in real wages, *ceteris paribus*, raises labour's share. According to the wage gap theory, too high real wages, manifested in a high share for labour, are the primary cause of poor macroeconomic performance such as a slowing of growth. Keynesian theory, on the other hand, emphasizes that it is more likely that a high share for labour is the *result* of slowing growth than the other way round. It is therefore important to determine which explanation is more plausible in the case of an increase in labour's share in Japan in the early 1970s. As shown in Table 5.16, labour's share in Japan rose from 60% in the late 1960s to 65% in 1971, and then to 75% in 1974–5. The critical years were 1971 and 1974–5.

The year 1971 was when the growth rate of real GNP fell to below 5% for the first time in more than two decades. President Nixon's statement on 15 August suspending the convertibility of the US dollar (called the 'Nixon Shock' in Japan) shook the Japanese economy, which had been on the verge of recovery from an ongoing recession. A sharp appreciation of the yen thereafter, from ¥360 per dollar to ¥308 in December 1971, discouraged exports, while uncertainty in foreign exchange market hindered investment. Meanwhile, the increase in real wages did not decelerate but kept at the then 'normal' pace (Table 5.6). As a consequence, labour's share rose significantly in 1971. In 1974–5, the Japanese economy, hit by the first oil embargo, fell into the most severe recession of its post-war

[4] Y is real GNP and K is the series of capital stock compiled by the EPA; u is the index of capacity utilization in manufacturing industry compiled by MITI.

era. Again, the increase in real wages did not significantly respond to the recession, and labour's share rose sharply; in (13), the two terms on the right-hand side both increased.

In both cases, there were clearly identifiable exogenous shocks to the Japanese economy: international monetary disorder in 1971 and the first oil embargo in 1974–5, both of which evidently caused severe recessions. On the other hand, increases in real wages in 1971 and 1974–5 were not disproportionately high *by the standard of the 1960s* (see Table 5.6). What happened in Japan in the early 1970s, therefore, was not that real wages were autonomously pushed up, as in late 1960s Europe, the so-called 'real wage explosion', but rather that an increase in real wages did not decelerate when faced with an unprecedented recession intensified by unforeseen exogenous shocks. The protection of real wages from the recession was not brought about easily, however. Table 5.17 shows pronounced increases in labour disputes in 1971 and 1974–5, although their level remained very low compared with other OECD countries.

In any case, it is not clear that recessions in 1971 and 1974–5 would have been milder if the increase in real wages had decelerated. In both episodes, low investment played the major role (see Section 4.4 above). As will be shown in Chapter 7, an increase in real wages theoretically entails an increase, rather than a decrease, in investment *if firms are demand-constrained in the goods market*. Since the Japanese firms were most likely demand-constrained in the early 1970s (see Chapter 4), slower growth of real wages is not expected to have saved the Japanese economy from slipping into severe recession.

In summary, the increase in labour's share of income in Japan was a result, rather than a cause, of severe recessions intensified by such unexpected shocks as the international monetary disorder and the first oil embargo in the early 1970s. Meanwhile, as explained in Chapter 2, the Japanese economy entered a new era of slower economic growth. Once settled, real wages responded to economic growth flexibly enough to keep labour's share stable at around 70% thereafter (Table 5.16).

The next section provides a Keynesian model to explain the flexibility of real wages which attains a stable share in income for labour.

A Comparison of the Pre-War and Post-War Japanese Economies

To consider the relationship between the flexibility of real wages and the stability of output from yet another angle, I compare Japan's

Table 5.17. Labour disputes, six countries, 1965–1989 (thousands of days lost)

	Japan	USA	UK	W. Germany	France	Italy
1965	5,669	23,300	2,925	49	980	–
1966	2,742	25,400	2,398	27	2,523	–
1967	1,830	42,100	2,787	390	4,204	–
1968	2,841	49,018	4,690	25	423	–
1969	3,634	42,869	6,846	249	2,224	–
1970	3,915	66,414	10,980	93	1,742	–
1971	6,029	47,589	13,551	2,599	4,388	–
1972	5,147	27,066	23,909	66	3,755	19,497
1973	4,604	27,948	7,197	563	3,915	23,419
1974	9,663	47,991	14,750	1,051	3,380	19,467
1975	8,016	31,237	6,012	69	3,869	27,189
1976	3,254	37,859	3,284	534	5,011	25,378
1977	1,518	35,822	10,142	24	3,666	16,566
1978	1,358	36,922	9,405	4,281	2,200	10,177
1979	930	33,000	29,474	483	3,172	27,530
1980	–	32,000	11,910	–	1,511	–
1981	543	16,908	4,266	58	1,442	10,527
1982	535	9,061	5,313	15	2,257	18,563
1983	504	17,461	3,754	41	1,321	14,003
1984	354	8,499	27,135	5,618	1,318	8,703
1985	257	7,079	6,402	35	727	3,831
1986	252	12,140	1,920	28	568	5,644
1987	256	4,469	3,546	33	501	4,606
1988	163	4,364	3,702	42	1,132	3,315
1989	176	16,996	4,128	100	805	4,436

pre-war and post-war economies. Table 5.18 shows the means, standard deviations, coefficients of variation, and autocorrelation of the nominal prices, nominal wages, real wages, and production indices in the pre-war (1905–38) and post-war (1966–85) periods. As the coefficients of variation clearly show, both nominal and real wages were three to four times more flexible in pre-war than in post-war Japan. A comparison of the autocorrelation coefficients shows that the persistence of real wages also increased during the post-war period. Nevertheless, the coefficients of variation of the production index are almost the same for both sample periods.[5] This

[5] A glance at the autocorrelation coefficient of the first degree, however, shows that the persistence of changes in the production index increased slightly after the Second World War. This point remains a subject for further investigation.

Table 5.18. Comparison of pre-war and post-war Japan: prices, wages, and output, 1905–1938 and 1966–1985

	(1) Mean (%)	(2) s.d. (%)	(3) Coefficient of variation ((2)/(1))	(4) 1st-order auto-correlation	(5) 2nd-order auto-correlation
1905–38					
Nominal price	2.2	12.0	5.45	0.45	−0.01
Nominal wages	4.9	9.8	2.00	0.64	0.30
Real wages	2.4	6.3	2.63	0.39	−0.12
Industrial production	6.8	6.9	1.01	−0.04	−0.15
1966–85					
Nominal price	4.1	7.3	1.78	0.28	−0.16
Nominal wages	10.7	5.6	0.52	0.76	0.54
Real wages	4.4	3.6	0.82	0.56	0.50
Industrial production	6.6	7.1	1.08	0.33	−0.00

Sources: Pre-war data are taken from Ohkawa *et al.* (1974–90). Post-war figures are from the Ministry of Labour, *Maitsuki Rodo Tokei Chosa Geppo* (Labour Statistics Monthly), the Bank of Japan, and MITI.

result leads us to question the widely accepted, yet not fully substantiated, proposition that rigid prices are the most important factor leading to output fluctuations.[6]

5.5 A MODEL OF LABOUR MARKET

We observed in Section 5.1 that the Japanese labour market is a dual market: a portion of workers are employed permanently or semi-permanently and earn seniority wages, while the rest frequently change their statuses between being in casual employment and out of the labour force. The base wages in the primary or core sector of the labour market are determined in the annual synchronized union bargaining called *Shunto*. While *Shunto* may be instrumental in maintaining the flexibility of wages in Japan, the flexibility of both nominal and real wages is also sustained at the level of the individual

[6] For the USA, a similar result is obtained by Taylor (1986). For comparisons between Japan, the USA, and other OECD countries, see Summers and Wadhwani (1987).

firm. And yet, this wage flexibility does not appear to be the key factor as far as fluctuations of output are concerned. Meanwhile, the importance of labour-hoarding by firms on the demand side and the continuous entries into and exits from the labour force on the supply side during cyclical fluctuations keep the Japanese unemployment rate very low, while making it difficult to measure the exact extent of underemployment. This final section offers a simple macroeconomic model to explain these 'stylized facts' of the Japanese labour market. The model is Keynesian in the sense that both firm and household are subject not only to given prices, but also to quantity constraints; and output in the economy as a whole is determined basically by demand. It also explicitly introduces a dual labour market.

The firm maximizes its profit,

$$\max_{\{L_1, L_2, w_1\}} \; Q - w_1 L_1 - w_2 L_2 - \delta(L_1 - L^*) \tag{14}$$

subject to

$$\bar{Q} = [\theta(w) L_1]^a L_2^b. \tag{15}$$

Output of the firm depends on two kinds of labour input, L_1 and L_2. Here, L_1, L_2 are the primary (core) and secondary labour inputs, respectively. The adjustment cost of L_1 will be explained shortly; ω is the share of the primary labour force L_1:

$$\omega = w_1 L_1 / Q. \tag{16}$$

I assume that the efficiency of primary labour depends upon this relative share, ω. Usual models of efficiency wages (Solow 1979; Katz 1986) attempt to explain the rigidity of real wages and to demonstrate that shocks facing firms are absorbed mostly through changes in labour input. Contrary to this, however, the Japanese firm facing various shocks tends to minimize the adjustment of labour input, in particular the size of its work-force (Table 5.4), while in exchange both union and management concede to the flexibility of real wages.

We can explain this characteristic of the Japanese firm by a simple efficiency wage model. For the sake of comparison, I first briefly explain the standard efficiency wage model. A firm maximizes profits,

$$\alpha F(\theta L) - wL, \tag{17}$$

by optimally choosing real wage w and labour input L. Here α is the exogenous demand/productivity shock. The efficiency factor of labour service, θ is assumed to depend on the level of real wage, w:

$$\theta = \theta(w) \qquad \theta'(w) > 0. \tag{18}$$

This is the crucial assumption in the model. Under this assumption, the necessary condition requires the elasticity of efficiency factor θ always to be one:

$$\frac{\mathrm{d}\theta(w)}{\theta(w)} \Big/ \frac{\mathrm{d}w}{w} = 1. \tag{19}$$

From (19), the optimally chosen real wage w becomes independent of exogenous shock α. Changes in α are absorbed totally by changes in L.

According to (18), efficiency of labour depends positively on the level of real wages, presumably because workers work harder when they are 'better' treated. This is not necessarily the most plausible assumption, however. One can argue alternatively that labour efficiency depends on workers' perceived 'fairness'. We assume that the labour efficiency of the primary labour force, θ, depends on a kind of distribution within the firm, ω, instead of on the level of real wage w itself:

$$\theta(\omega) \qquad \theta'(\omega) > 0 \qquad \theta''(\omega) < 0. \tag{20}$$

We assume that $|\theta''(\omega)|$ is very large at ω^*. This assumption means that marginal efficiency drastically changes in the neighbourhood of ω^*. If ω is raised higher than ω^*, an increase in efficiency is small; if ω falls lower than ω^*, on the other hand, a decrease in efficiency is substantial. In this sense, ω^* can be interpreted as the level of distributive share perceived as fair by workers.

The two assumptions, (18) and (20), have quite different implications, of course. According to (18), for example, labour efficiency always declines when the real wages decline. In contrast, (20) implies that it does not decline if real wages decline when the firm faces adversities. Alternatively, according to (18), efficiency stays the same whenever real wages are kept unchanged; assumption (20), on the other hand, implies that efficiency declines if real wages are unchanged when the firm faces favourable shocks. Assumption (20) assumes that labour efficiency depends on perceived 'fairness', which in turn is linked to the factor share within the firm.[7] As will be shown shortly, (20) leads to the flexible real wages, contrary to the result obtained under (18).

[7] An interesting survey conducted by Kahneman *et al.* (1986) does indeed suggest that nominal wage cuts by a firm that is losing money or theatened with bankruptcy do not violate standards of fairness; see also Okun (1981) on the role of fairness in the economy.

Primary and secondary labour differ not only in terms of their productivity in the production of current output, but also in their potential contribution to the firm's long-run growth. Primary labour, for example, is the core of the celebrated quality control (QC) circles which generate various innovations. The firm is assumed to have the desired level of primary labour L^*, which is determined by the firm's long-run considerations and is independent of the current output Q. The adjustment of the primary labour force L_1 away from L^* incurs a cost to the firm. This adjustment cost function, $\delta(L_1 - L^*)$, is assumed to have the following properties:

$$
\begin{aligned}
&\delta(0) = 0 \\
&\delta'(x) > 0, \quad \delta''(x) > 0, \quad \lim_{x \to +0} \delta'(x) = \delta_+ > 0 \quad \text{for } x > 0 \qquad (21) \\
&\delta'(x) < 0, \quad \delta''(x) > 0, \quad \lim_{x \to -0} \delta'(x) = \delta_- < 0 \quad \text{for } x < 0
\end{aligned}
$$

Koike (1984, 1991), in his justifiably influential works, argues that high productivity of the core *blue-collar* workers, which is sustained by on-the-job training (OJT), often involving job rotation, is the basis of the strength of the Japanese firm. Given the importance of his argument, it deserves a comment: namely, it is a misleading proposition that the contribution of engineers, many of whom have master's degrees these days, is relatively minor in the Japanese firm. What Koike has persuasively shown is that blue-collar workers on production lines do contribute to the high productivity of Japanese firms; the relative importance of the blue-collar workers on the one hand and engineers on the other is, of course, quite another issue. Nomura (1992), for example, argues that the contribution of engineers and foremen is much greater than that of blue-collar workers on production lines in generating high productivity in the Japanese firm. Plainly, engineers would be responsible for most product innovations, whose importance in the process of growth is explained in Chapter 10. L_1 in my model includes engineers, other white-collar employees, foremen, and the core blue-collar workers on production lines. Employment of L_1 is determined by the firm from the long-run perspective, and changes in L_1 incur substantial costs of adjustment.

The firm maximizes its profits with respect to L_1, L_2, and w_1, taking into account a sales constraint $\bar{Q}$, the dependence of the primary labour force's efficiency on its distributive share, and finally the adjustment cost for its primary work-force, L_1. Profit maximization then leads to the following conditions (λ is the Lagrange multiplier for a sales constraint):

$$w_1 + \delta'(L_1 - L^*) \lesseqgtr \lambda a(\theta L_1)^{a-1} L_2^b [\theta'(\omega)\omega + \theta(\omega)] \text{ for } L_1 \lesseqgtr L^*, \tag{22}$$

$$1 = \lambda a \left(\frac{\theta'(\omega)}{\theta(\omega)} \right), \tag{23}$$

$$w_2 = \lambda b(Q/L_2). \tag{24}$$

I assume that, for the change in Q under consideration, inequalities always hold in (4) so as to make L^* an optimum for L_1. This would be true if there were a substantial *marginal* adjustment cost at L^* and if the real wages w_1 were flexible enough to respond to changes in Q.

Under the assumption that $L_1 = L^*$, we obtain

$$L_2 = Q^{1/b}(\theta L^*)^{-(a/b)}. \tag{25}$$

Equations (23), (24), and (25) then lead to

$$\frac{w_2(b/a)\, L^{*(a/b)}}{Q^{(1/b)-1}} = \frac{\theta'(\omega)}{[\theta(\omega)]^{(a/b)+1}} = f(\omega). \tag{26}$$

Equation (26) determines optimum ω. Under the assumption that $|\theta''(\omega)|$ is very large at ω^*, the effect of changes in Q on ω is very small and, as a consequence, the distributive share ω is always in the neighbourhood of ω^*. This in turn means that the real wages of primary labour w_1 change proportionately with output Q:

$$w_1 \simeq \omega^* Q. \tag{27}$$

It also means that the demand for secondary labour, L_2 is highly elastic with respect to Q: (25) implies that the elasticity is 1/b, which is larger than one. When demand falls, for example, the firm keeps its primary labour force L_1 intact, while at the same time the firm and its work-force agree on the proportionate decline in real wages that leaves the share of the primary labour force unchanged; the burden of recession therefore falls solely on the shoulders of the secondary labour force.

To consider the general equilibrium, we must proceed to analyse the household's behaviour. The household is assumed to maximize

$$U = C^{\alpha}(1 - L_1)^{\beta}(1 - L_2)^{\gamma}, \tag{28}$$

with respect to L_2, and consumption C subject to

$$w_1 \bar{L}_1 + w_2 L_2 = C. \tag{29}$$

$$\bar{L} = L_1^d.$$

For simplicity, I ignore household savings: investment is financed by corporate profits. The household is subject to a quantity constraint with respect to its supply of the primary labour service, L_1. The actual size of L_1 is determined by demand for it, namely L^* and the household perceives L^* as a quantity constraint. In contrast, the supply of secondary labour services, L_2, is determined by the household in an optimizing way. Casual observation suggests that the choice of working hours by persons in the primary labour market such as prime-aged males is in fact very limited, whereas most workers in the secondary market can freely choose their working hours.

The supply function of L_2 is

$$L_2^S = \frac{\alpha}{\alpha + \gamma}\left(1 - \frac{\gamma}{\alpha}\frac{w_1 L^*}{w_2}\right). \tag{30}$$

If we define the income from the supply of primary labour $w_1 L^*$ as Y, then (30) can be rewritten as

$$L_2^S = \frac{\alpha}{\alpha + \gamma}\left(1 - \frac{\gamma}{\alpha}\frac{Y}{w_2}\right). \tag{31}$$

The supply function of secondary labour services, (31), is similar to those empirically estimated in many countries. In particular, the labour supply of married females is often reported to have the following characteristics:[8] (i) it is a *decreasing* function of the husband's income Y; while (ii) it is an *increasing* function of the own real-wage rate, w_2. Chapter 6 presents an estimation of the labour supply function of married females which shares these characteristics. I note that the husband's *income*, as distinct from the husband's *real wage*, w_1 would not properly enter the supply function L_2^S in a neoclassical framework. The income variable enters the wife's labour supply function only when the husband's labour supply is quantity-constrained.

In Japan, the labour participation rate of married females steadily declined until the mid-1970s, but has been on a steady increase since then (Fig. 5.13). The decline up to the mid-1970s is usually explained by the shrinkage of the agricultural sector, in which the female participation rate is much higher than in urban employee households. The increase since the mid-1970s, on the other hand, is due mainly to an increase in the participation rate in urban employee households, which is, in turn, caused by a deceleration of the husband's income, as equation (31) indicates. Growth accounting such as in Jorgenson (1988) often attributes a non-negligible part of the decline in the growth rate of income (GNP) in the 1970s to the falloff in upgrading the labour force, which in turn is allegedly caused by the rise in the female participation rate (see e.g. Table 2.17 above).

[8] For the case of Japanese labour market, see Shimada and Higuchi (1985); for other countries, see papers in the *Journal of Labour Economics*, 3, 1 (1985).

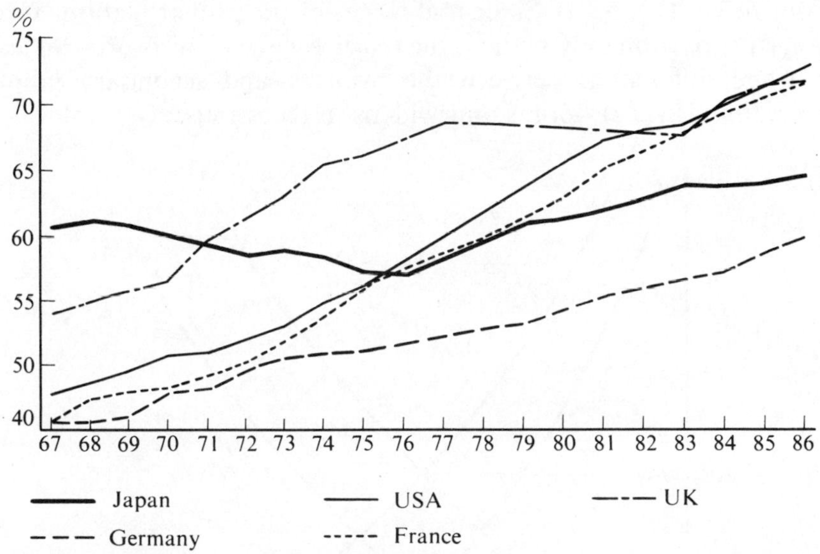

Fig. 5.13. Labour participation rates of married women aged 35–44, 1967–1986

However, as far as the rise in the female participation rate beginning in the mid-1970s is concerned, it is, at least in part, the result of slower economic growth.

The secondary labour market is assumed to work competitively, and demand is assumed equal to supply:

$$L_2^d = L_2^S \tag{32}$$

This assumption, again, is supported by a deal of empirical literature. The working of the secondary market is believed to be quite different from that of the primary labour market. Equations (25), (27), and (30) lead to

$$w_2 = \frac{\left(\dfrac{\beta}{\alpha+\beta}\right)\omega^* Q}{\left(\dfrac{\alpha}{\alpha+\beta}\right) - (\theta L^*)^{-(a/b)} Q^{1/b}}. \tag{33}$$

Equation (33) implies that the real wages of the secondary labour w_2 change more than proportionately with changes in output Q. When output falls, for example, real wages of the primary labour force proportionately decline. Since the income of the primary labour force falls, the supply of the secondary labour increases, while at the same time the firms' demand for the secondary labour declines. This brings about a substantial decrease in real wages of the secondary labour force (Fig. 5.14). Since real wages of the primary labour force change proportionately with Q, the *relative* wage w_2/w_2 is pro-cyclical; the wage differential between the primary and secondary labour forces diminishes in booms and widens in recessions.

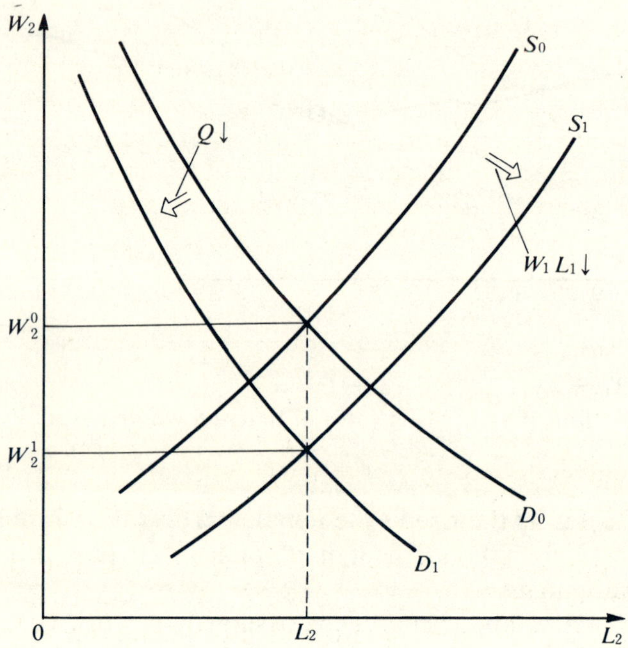

Fig. 5.14. The secondary labour market

Some of the results obtained here are similar to those derived by McDonald and Solow (1985). The major point of their paper is to explain two 'stylized facts' of the US economy: that the relative wage differential between the primary (core) and secondary (peripheral) sectors widens as the overall labour market weakens and narrows as it tightens; and that primary-sector employment fluctuates proportionately more than secondary-sector employment. The first 'fact' is empirically well confirmed in Japan and obtains in my model, too. On the other hand, just the opposite of the second 'stylized fact' holds in Japan: the primary labour force employment is stable, whereas employment of the secondary labour force fluctuates greatly.

In the McDonald–Solow model, the transition of a worker between the two labour markets is stressed. In recessions, for example, more workers in the secondary sector, discouraged from entering the primary sector to search for better jobs, make their positions worse in terms of wages paid, but at the same time this decline of relative wages keeps fluctuations of employment in the secondary sector smaller than they would otherwise be. In my model, in contrast, a worker does not move between the two sectors; rather, a household is assumed to have two types of worker, each moving between either the primary or secondary market and a non-market activity. In this sense, the out-of-labour-force status, a part of which is really disguised unemployment, is explicitly analysed in my model.

Up to this point, we have taken the level of output Q as given. We can now discuss how the level of output, Q, is determined. Since w_1, w_2, and L_2 are all functions of Q (equations (27), (30), (32), and (33)), consumption C, which is equal to $w_1L^* + w_2L_2$, also becomes a function of Q. To put this explicitly, we have

$$C = \frac{vQ[1 - (\theta L^*)^{-(a/b)}Q^{1/b}]}{\left[\left(\dfrac{\alpha}{\alpha+\gamma}\right) - (\theta L^*)^{-(a/b)}Q^{1/b}\right]} \qquad (v > 0), \tag{34}$$

where v is a constant which depends on a, b, α, and γ. The goods market equilibrium is kept as simple as possible:

$$Q = C + \bar{I}, \tag{35}$$

where $\bar{I}$ is exogenous demand such as private investment. It would be trivial to extend the model in the *IS–LM* manner by making I dependent upon the interest rate and introducing an asset market. The essential point is that the actual level of output Q is determined by effective demand.

Equations (34) and (35) generally have two roots or none at all (if I is large enough, for example). The larger root is unstable for natural dynamics. Focusing on the smaller root, we know that Q is uniquely determined as an increasing function of I. It is important to note that the level of output depends solely on I and is determined in goods market. *Real wages, which respond flexibly to changes in output, have nothing to do with the determination of output* (see also Negishi 1977); *flexible real wages do not so much mitigate fluctuations of output as bring about stable factor share to attain 'fairness' within the firm.*

It is interesting to check how the utility level of the representative household varies when the level of output changes. There exists Q^* such that, for Q smaller than Q^*, an increase in Q raises the utility level of the representative household. This level of Q, Q^*, which depends on the preference and technology parameters, can be called *the natural level of output*. Whenever the actual level of Q is lower than Q^*, there is underemployment of labour in the sense that the utility of a representative household is not maximized. The result gives us the welfare economic foundations for demand management policies in the model. Again, the utility level of the representative household depends ultimately on effective demand in the goods market. Flexibility of real wages has little to do with this utility level.

Thus, flexible real wages in Japan have more important implications for the economy in the context of the long run than the short run. They contribute to achieving 'perceived fairness' within the firm by stabilizing labour's share, as well as by protecting employment of the primary labour force from cyclical fluctuations. The primary labour force, under long-term employment, contributes to productivity growth in the long run. Meanwhile, the burden of cyclical fluctuations falls mainly on the shoulders of the secondary labour force. In any case, the macroeconomic performance of lost output or under-utilization of resources rests primarily on aggregate demand in the goods market. The cyclical performance of the economy, however, which depends upon demand, could have long-run implications. For example, the desired level of the primary labour force, L^* in our model, depends naturally on the prospects for growth. Persistent stagnation of the economy could lead to major adjustment in L^* and also could destroy the celebrated long-term employment of the primary labour force, which is instrumental for productivity growth. In this sense, the cyclical performance and institutional factors in the labour market are likely to be related to each other.

6

Household Saving

The saving rate in Japan has long attracted the attention of economists—in the 1950s and 1960s as a 'source' of rapid economic growth, and then in the 1980s as a 'cause' of huge current account surpluses. This chapter considers the household saving rate in Japan. The neoclassical theory actually implies that it is the aggregate saving rate that matters, not the household saving rate. But in the real world, the household saving rate appears to have a life of its own, and in any case broadly determines international differences in the aggregate saving rate.

Section 6.1 reviews the basic facts and representative works on the saving rate. It argues that the high growth rate of the economy is probably the most important factor in explaining the high saving rate in Japan, but at the same time stresses that a single factor cannot explain even the basic changes in the saving rate over time. In fact, many factors, such as the high rate of growth, the relatively low level of financial assets, the bonus system, and the extraordinary land prices prevailing, seem to go towards explaining the saving rate in Japan.

The life-cycle theory is perhaps the most important factor, predicting a positive relationship between growth and savings. As Section 6.1 explains, however, it has been challenged both theoretically and empirically. In particular, anticipated growth may actually discourage savings. In the light of this problem, it is a very important fact that high economic growth in the 1950s and 1960s was largely unforeseen by economic agents in Japan. On the one hand, this implies an unambiguously positive relationship between growth and savings, while on the other, it contradicts the neoclassical view that the saving rate is determined as if it were generated by a standard Ramsey optimization model.

Although the SNA-based household saving rate has declined since the mid-1970s, the saving rate of worker households did not decline so much as the life-cycle theory would predict and actually even rose in the 1980s. Section 6.2 considers the target savings for a house, which implies a *negative* relation between growth and savings. High land prices and a strong demand for owner-occupied housing have been long noted by many Japanese economists as a cause for the high saving rate. Section 6.2 explores a simple life-cycle model which takes housing demand explicitly into account. The younger, renting households may either make the target savings for a down payment or decide not to purchase a house. The effects of economic growth and land prices on the saving rate depends on tenure choice, while at the same time tenure choice itself depends, among other things, on growth and land prices. The relation between growth and savings among the younger households, therefore, is not simple. Section 6.2 also offers an empirical analysis based on this model. The estimation results show that the saving rate of the younger renters increases as the growth rate declines even if changes in tenure choice are taken into account. Although year-to-year changes in the growth rate of income were largely unforeseen, by the end of the 1970s everyone in Japan had fully recognized that the 10% average growth rate prevailing in the 1950s and 1960s was gone. The permanent deceleration of growth may have raised the target savings for down payment on a house among the young renters, and might explain, at least partly, why the saving rate did not decline as a simple life cycle-theory would predict, and even rose among worker households in the 1980s.

A crucial question surrounding savings is causality between economic growth and the saving rate. Although conditioned by many factors, the correlation between growth and the household saving rate is still seen to be broadly positive; and yet the issue of causality remains unresolved. Concluding remarks offer some speculation. (A formal model of growth is presented in Chapter 10.)

6.1 THE HOUSEHOLD SAVING RATE IN JAPAN

The household saving rate in Japan, measured on an SNA (System of National Account) basis, has been very high by international standards (see Table 6.1). There are, however, many conceptual differences among countries in the household saving rates reported in national income accounts. Hayashi (1986), for example, emphasizes the significance of the fact that depreciation is valued at replacement cost in the United States but at historical cost in Japan; this creates an upward bias in Japan's net saving during inflationary

Table 6.1. International comparison of household saving rate, 1970–1986

	Japan	USA	Canada	France	Sweden	UK
Saving rate as defined in SNA	23.0	14.3	16.5	17.7	7.8	10.4
Saving rate adjusted for consumer durables	26.1	23.6	27.3	24.6	16.8	19.0
Saving rate adjusted to include savings in social security funds	25.8	13.9	17.9	18.4	13.1	10.8
Saving rate of employee households (excl. self-employed)[a]	20.7	7.7	9.5	13.4	4.2	8.0

[a] For 1970–80, source is OECD, 'Alternative Measures of Saving', *OECD Economic Outlook, Occasional Studies*, June 1983.

Source: Blades (1989).

periods. According to Hayashi, this fact alone accounts for as much as two to three percentage points of the gap between the net household saving rates of Japan and the United States. Table 6.1 shows that, adjusted for the effect of service flows from consumer durables as a part of saving, Japan's rate becomes comparable to those in other well developed nations although it is still higher than most.

Obviously, it is important carefully to adjust official statistics for any conceptual differences and to decide which definition of saving rate to use before making international comparisons. Many of the adjustments appear to lead to a reduction in the gap between the saving rate of Japan and those of other countries. However, the difference in saving rates among nations becomes larger if calculated only for employee households. Japan's saving rate is extremely high under this definition. Since employees' income and expenditure are the most accurately measured of various components used in calculating the saving rate in any country, it would be reasonable to conclude that the saving rate in Japan is high, if not extremely high, by international standards.

In passing, it should be noted that the saving rate, when unadjusted for consumer durables, as is the case with the SNA, is *not meaningless*. In seeking to estimate the underlying utility function and/or the representative consumers' subjective discount rate, one needs the data on 'consumption', which includes not only expenditure on non-durables but also service flows from consumer durables. From the standpoint of the Keynesian theory of economic fluctuations, however, it is expenditure on consumer goods, e.g. the *purchase* of a car, rather than its use, that matters, regardless of whether it is classified as saving or consumption. The SNA saving rate based on expenditure rather than 'consumption' makes sense in this regard.

It is also necessary at the outset to discuss the relevance of the *household* saving rate. In the neoclassical theory, it is the aggregate saving rate of the country that counts, supposedly reflecting the intertemporal decision of the 'representative' household. According to this theory, fluctuations in the rate of household saving counteract movements in corporate and/or public savings, thus ensuring that the aggregate saving rate stays at its planned level. In particular, according to the Ricardian equivalence theorem (Barro 1974), government deficits, signalling an increase in households' future tax liabilities, force households to increase their saving in order to meet future tax payments. Therefore, deficits should be matched yen-for-yen by increased household saving, and vice versa.

There are, however, a number of theoretical arguments against the Ricardian equivalence (see e.g. Tobin 1980). In fact, a test by Modigliani (1990), based on the 22 OECD countries, indicates that the effect of government deficits on private saving is only partial; according to his estimates, a percentage increase in government deficits would increase private saving by only 0.4 percentage point and therefore would produce a net decline in national saving by 0.6 point.

For Japan, a careful analysis of the cohort data on employee households, from the 1970–84 *Kakeichosa* (Family and Expenditure Survey) by Homma *et al.* (1986), which is similar to Ashauer (1985) and Boskin and Kotlikoff (1985), rejects the Ricardian equivalence theorem. Beyond formal analysis, a glance at the data for the 1980s plainly suggests that government deficits do affect the national saving rate, which in turn implies that the household saving rate has a life of its own. Table 6.2, for example, shows that a steady increase in government saving in the 1980s was not at all matched by a decrease in household saving. In the United States, too, sudden and very large changes in government saving in the 1980s were in no way compensated by changes in private saving. Indeed, one could argue that the divergence of the national saving rates in Japan and the United States in the 1980s simply reflects the differences in fiscal policies between the two countries.

With regard to corporate saving, Ishikawa (1978) finds that the simple correlation between corporate and household saving rates

Table 6.2. Saving by sector in Japan, 1981–1989 (¥ trillion)

	Household	Government[a]	Non-financial corporations
1981	33.4	7.9	5.2
1982	31.8	7.6	5.8
1983	32.1	6.5	6.2
1984	33.2	9.7	8.7
1985	34.4	13.7	10.1
1986	37.0	13.7	12.3
1987	34.8	19.8	13.7
1988	35.5	25.4	15.7
1989	37.4	30.7	13.8

[a] Government saving is the sum of the budget surplus plus net government capital formation.

Source: SNA statistics.

(1955–76) is actually 0.3 (0.8 if calculated only for boom years), which is in sharp contrast to the value of –0.7 for the United States. It is therefore not surprising that the retained earnings variable turns out to be insignificant in his consumption function. In sum, there appears to be little substitutability between household and government/corporate savings in Japan. And it is household saving that largely determines the differences in the *levels* of the national saving rate among countries. This chapter therefore focuses on the household saving rate.

Two series of household saving rates are shown in Fig. 6.1. One is the 'household' saving rate on the SNA basis, which includes the self-employed; the other is the saving rate of employee households from the *Kakeichosa.* The two series are parallel from 1955 to 1975, their peak. From the late 1970s onwards, however, the SNA saving rate keeps declining, while the saving rate of employees stays at a high level and actually turns upward again in the 1980s. The divergence between the two series in the 1980s poses an interesting question. We will briefly discuss this in the next section, but for the moment we consider the SNA household saving rate.

The SNA household saving rate increased from 12% in 1955 to 16% in 1961, and then stayed at this level throughout the 1960s. In the early 1970s it sharply rose again, to its post-oil-shock peak of 23% in 1974–6. Since then it has steadily declined, to 14% in 1989.

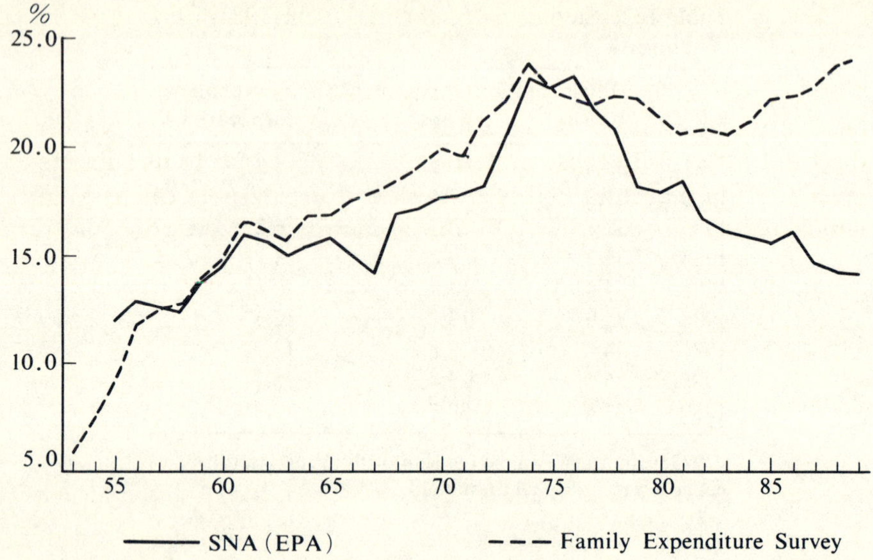

Fig. 6.1. Household saving rate in Japan, 1955–1985

Overall, the saving rate is hump-shaped with its peak in 1974–6. How can this hump-shaped saving rate be explained?

The Neoclassical Explanation

The neoclassical theory takes the *national* saving rate as the one to be explained. The time profile of the national saving rate, however, strongly resembles that of the household saving rate shown in Fig. 6.1, as it too is hump-shaped.

As explained in Chapter 1, mainstream macroeconomics of the 1980s attempted to explain everything by a standard neoclassical theory. In this case, a natural framework is optimum growth theory. One might like to work with a stochastic model, but it is the deterministic part of the model that determines the basic time profile of the saving rate. Does a standard optimum growth model (Cass 1965; Koopmans 1965) generate a hump-shaped time profile of the saving rate? The well-known answer is no. The standard model predicts that, starting with a low capital stock, the saving rate monotonically declines on the optimum path. It fails to account for the observed hump-shaped time pattern.

Noting this failure of the standard model, Christiano (1989) modifies it by slightly changing the objective function of the model as follows:

$$\int_0^\infty U(C_t - C^*)\mathrm{e}^{-\rho t}\mathrm{d}t \qquad (U' > 0,\ U'' < 0), \tag{1}$$

where C_t is per capita consumption and C^* is its minimum subsistence level. (C^* is zero in the standard model; $\rho > 0$ is the subjective discount rate.) With these preferences, as C_t declines to its subsistence level C^*, the marginal utility of consumption shoots off to infinity, which discourages saving. On the assumption that Japan's capital stock in 1946 was only 12% of its steady-state value, the model can generate a hump-shaped pattern of the saving rate on the optimum path. It is important to note, however, that the pattern of growth of the Japanese economy in the first decade after the war does not actually conform to this theory.[1]

Unforeseen Growth

The optimum growth model, with minimum subsistence consumption, could account for the basic time pattern of the Japanese post-war saving rate, at least qualitatively. This analysis, however, rests crucially on the premiss that the post-war growth was foreseen.

Table 6.3 shows the actual growth rate of real GNP, its forecast made by the Economic Planning Agency in the previous year, and the difference between the two. This table very clearly demonstrates that high growth in the 1950s and 1960s and deceleration in the 1970s were largely unforeseen. The high growth rates in the earlier period were consistently underestimated, while the relatively low growth rates in the 1970s and early 1980s were successively overestimated. The assumption of rational expectations is therefore decisively rejected.

The same feature applies to expectations held by the private sector. Ishikawa and Ueda (1984), for example, show the expected and actual values of bonus payments per average worker-household, reproduced here as Table 6.4. Again, growth of the bonus is successively underestimated. The fact that the lifetime profile of consumption in Japan is very steep—much steeper than in the United

[1] See Ch. 3 on the destruction of capital stock by the war. It is widely accepted that the interruption in the import of raw materials from abroad was much more damaging to the Japanese economy than the destruction of capital stock. The fact that GNP could increase by 40% without a corresponding increase in capital stock during 1946–50 suggests that the drop in capacity utilization arising from shortages in raw materials was much more serious than the wartime destruction of capital stock.

Table 6.3. Actual and expected GNP growth, 1955–1990

	Actual	Expected[a]	Difference
1955		4.5	
1956	6.3	4.2	−2.1
1957	8.2	6.5	−1.7
1958	6.7	3.0	−3.7
1959	11.0	5.5	−5.5
1960	12.0	6.6	−5.4
1961	11.5	9.2	−2.3
1962	7.6	5.4	−2.2
1963	10.0	6.1	−3.9
1964	9.7	7.1	−2.6
1965	6.3	7.5	1.2
1966	11.2	7.5	−3.7
1967	10.9	9.0	−1.9
1968	12.8	7.6	−5.2
1969	12.1	9.8	−2.3
1970	8.1	11.1	3.0
1971	5.2	10.1	4.9
1972	9.0	7.2	−1.8
1973	4.7	10.7	6.0
1974	−0.2	2.5	2.7
1975	4.0	4.3	0.3
1976	4.0	5.6	1.6
1977	4.8	6.7	1.9
1978	5.1	7.0	1.9
1979	5.5	6.3	0.8
1980	3.2	4.8	1.6
1981	3.2	5.3	2.1
1982	3.5	5.2	1.7
1983	3.0	3.4	0.4
1984	4.5	4.1	−0.4
1985	4.8	4.6	−0.2
1986	2.9	4.0	1.1
1987	4.9	3.5	−1.4
1988	5.9	3.8	−2.1
1989	4.8	4.0	−0.8

[a] 'Expected' is the forecast made by the Economic Planning Agency in the previous year.

Source: Economic Planning Agency.

Table 6.4. Expected and actual values of bonus payments per average worker household, 1966–1981 (¥ '000)

Year[a]	Expected	Actual
1966s	54.8	59.0
1966w	73.1	77.8
1967s	60.5	64.5
1967w	76.3	86.8
1968s	67.6	74.2
1968w	91.1	98.5
1969s	77.5	87.6
1969w	114.6	115.8
1970s	92.3	102.8
1970w	123.3	141.0
1971s	116.2	133.2
1971w	151.3	175.6
1972s	129.7	147.5
1972w	179.3	201.7
1973s	154.5	178.4
1976s	268.0	291.6
1976w	395.7	352.8
1977s	360.1	351
1977w	428	438
1978s	376	367
1978w	444	453
1979s	387	383
1979w	448	466
1980s	417	408
1980w	481	496
1981s	420	407
1981w	485	501

[a] s and w refer to summer and winter, respectively.

Source: Ishikawa and Ueda (1984) (original data: *Shohi Doko Chosa*).

States (Carroll and Summers 1991)—is also consistent with the fact that households in Japan were continuously surprised at their high income growth. *In sum, the high growth of the Japanese economy was largely unforeseen by economic agents, most of whom faced a long string of positive surprises in terms of the rate of growth of the economy, labour income, and rates of return.* Since rational expectations is a prerequisite for such a model, violation of rational expectations implies that the optimum growth model cannot be applied in interpreting the time pattern of the post-war Japanese saving rate.

After all, the post-war growth process explained in Chapter 2 (see Fig. 2.4 in particular) is, as an historical process, beyond rational calculation on the part of each economic agent. Viewed in this way, it is actually not surprising that economic agents faced a long string of either positive or negative surprises in the growth rate of income. This observation also casts a serious doubt on the flourishing Euler equation approach (Hall 1978; Flavin 1981) in the analysis of consumer behaviour. Hall proposes to test directly whether or not the data at hand satisfy the first-order condition for optimality (the Euler equation) in consumer's intertemporal maximization, on the *assumption* that expectations are formed rationally. The rejection of the hypothesis would imply either that a fraction of consumers do not satisfy the Euler equation, perhaps because they face liquidity constraints, or that expectations are not formed rationally.

The alleged advantage of Hall's approach is that it is not necessary to model explicitly how future values of possible determinants of consumption such as income are generated. This simplicity, however, comes at the cost of a heavy reliance on the strong assumption of rational expectations. Direct observations of forecasts as discussed above suggest that rational expectations on future income are, in fact, very unlikely. Beyond expectations, if households merely satisfy, or follow rules of thumb, one would hardly expect to find Euler equations satisfied by individual households, much less by aggregates of households. (See Deaton (1992) on the issue of aggregation.) Hayashi (1986), for example, employs the Euler equation approach on the Japanese cohort data to obtain the wrong signs for disposable income and the social security dummy. For the US data there are many works, but on the whole the attempts have not been very encouraging. Specifically, the underlying utility function is often estimated to be non-concave, which renders the analysis meaningless (Hansen and Singleton 1982). When labour supply is jointly taken into account, a key symmetry condition on the effect of relative prices on the labour supply and on commodity demand is violated (see Deaton 1985; Ando and Kennickell 1987).

Clearly, we need a more eclectic approach. Given the premiss that households follow rules of thumb, with previous plans being amended only when drastic changes in expectations occur, it would be much more productive to enquire, if imperfectly, as to what the important determinants of consumption have been and why expectations concerning those variables have changed significantly.

Various Explanations

A number of hypotheses have, in fact, been offered to explain post-war Japanese saving behaviour. (See Mizoguchi (1988) and Horioka (1990) for an extensive survey.) Among the candidates are (i) the high growth rate, (ii) the high proportion of the self-employed, whose saving rate is high, (iii) the relatively low level of financial assets–income ratio, (iv) the bonus payment system, and (v) high land prices, and a strong demand for owner-occupied housing.

As pointed out at the beginning of this chapter, the causality between saving and growth is an important and yet an unsettled issue. Most economists, however, agree that, if the causality is not unidirectional, the high growth rate of income is an important—perhaps the most important—factor in explaining Japan's saving behaviour. Modigliani (1970), for example, obtains the following cross-country equation for 22 countries for the period 1952–1969:

$$\underset{(3.5)}{S = 0.045} + \underset{(5.7)}{1.42\, g_{-1}}, \tag{2}$$

where S is the saving rate, g_{-1} is the growth rate of real GNP the year before, and the numbers in parentheses are t-values.[2] According to (2), for two countries with 10% and 4% growth rates, the saving rates are 19% and 10%, respectively. This calculation is, in fact, quite successful in explaining the difference in the SNA saving rates of Japan and the USA/UK (Table 6.1), for example.

There are many other studies that suggest a close link between growth and saving. Bosworth (1993), for example, in a comprehensive study of the determinants of saving rates in OECD countries from the 1960s to the 1980s, finds that the growth rate of income is the most important determinant of saving. From a longer-run perspective (1870–1950), Maddison (1992) also finds a close relation between growth and the saving rate;[3] the correlation is about 0.6.

[2] An update of the estimations by Modigliani (1990) led him to the results very similar to eq. (2).

[3] According to Maddison (1992), the US saving behaviour is quite exceptional in that the United States is the only country that experienced almost no increase in the growth rate of output over the 120-year period and at the same time whose saving rate was almost constant; there are pronounced upward trends in the saving rate with economic growth in other major countries.

Several alternative theories imply a substantial effect of growth on the rate of saving, but among them the most important is the life-cycle theory (Modigliani and Brumberg 1954; Modigliani 1986). In the life-cycle theory, the young save while at the same time the old dissave. If there were no productivity growth across generations, and no population growth, the saving of the young would exactly offset the dissaving of the old, and accordingly the net aggregate saving rate would be zero. Population growth, however, by way of making the saving of the young outweigh the dissaving of the old, produces the positive saving in the economy as a whole. In addition, productivity growth makes the young richer than the old, and as a result the young will save more than the old dissave. In fact, the stripped-down life-cycle model first advanced by Modigliani and Brumberg (1954) implies that it is only aggregate growth that matters for the saving rate, not whether it is population growth with a constant per capita income, or income growth in a constant population.

Justifiably influential as it is, the life-cycle theory has been challenged both theoretically and empirically. In theory, the positive relation between productivity growth and saving is not necessarily obtained. In a standard Ramsey model of consumption and saving, for example, the effective discount rate becomes $\delta + (\rho - 1)\lambda$, where δ is the subjective discount rate, ρ ($\geqq 1$) is the coefficient of relative risk aversion, and λ is the rate of labour-augmenting technical progress. The productivity growth raises the effective discount rate, the extent of which depends on the degree of the relative risk aversion or the elasticity of intertemporal substitution. It is, therefore, quite possible that saving declines when the productivity growth rises. Indeed, a simulation analysis of Carroll and Weil (1993) demonstrates that the medium-run relationship between growth and saving is negative under the assumption of $\rho = 1$ and $\rho = 4$, and that if $\rho = 4$ the long-run relationship is negative as well.

Empirically, since Mirer (1979)'s seminal work, research has questioned whether the old actually do dissave. Although the matter has hardly been settled yet, particularly for Japan, where the prevalence of the merged (three-generation) family creates an additional difficulty, the accumulated evidence suggests that the old do not dissave so much as the simple life-cycle theory would indicate. For the United States, for example, Ando and Kennickell (1987) conclude that 'most families save a relatively small portion of their income throughout the period of their active participation in the labor force, and after they retire, they dissave very little, keeping their assets more or less at the same level'. For Japan, Hayashi (1992) calls it a stylized fact that 'both the independent and dependent aged save until they get very old (about 80–85)'. A corollary of these findings is that there are non-negligible bequests.[4]

In summary, although a standard generational aggregation in the stripped-down life-cycle theory leads to a positive correlation between growth and savings, the matter is actually not so simple, either theoretically or empirically. Our own analysis in Section 6.2 provides another link between growth and saving in relation to housing demand.

In spite of all these qualifications, in general, a positive relation between growth and the saving rate in Japan remains as a matter of fact (Fig. 6.1). Within the framework of the life-cycle theory, we can possibly explain this positive correlation by focusing on the fact that high growth had been largely unanticipated in Japan. According to Tables 6.3 and 6.4, consumers experienced a long string of positive surprises in terms of their income growth. This could be interpreted as an unanticipated permanent rise in the *level* of income in each period. Suppose that, in the simple Modigliani–Brumberg (1954) model, the level of income rose permanently from 1 to $1 + g$. The lifetime gains from this unanticipated change depend, of course, on the age of consumer. With no population growth, the *aggregate* saving rate becomes

$$\frac{R}{L}\log\left(\frac{R+L}{R}\right)-\frac{R}{(1+g)\,(L+R)}, \tag{3}$$

where L and R are, respectively, the length of working and retirement periods. Expression (3) is positive and is an increasing function of g. Since the discount rate remains unchanged in this case, the saving rate unambiguously increases. In retrospect, we would observe a positive relation between the growth rate and the saving rate.

The life-cycle theory is not the only theory that predicts a positive relationship between growth and the saving rate. A variant of the Duesenberry (1949) relative income hypothesis has also been used to explain the dependence of the saving rate on growth. Suppose that consumption at time t, C_t, depends not only on current income, Y_t, but also on the maximum income level in the past; i.e.

[4] There is a lively debate on the role of bequests in saving and the accumulation of wealth. If Kotlikoff and Summers (1981) exaggerated the importance of bequests, their basic message that—bequests play a sizeable role in saving—still remains true. See Kotlikoff (1988), Modigliani (1988), and Kessler and Masson (1989) on the controversy, and Hayashi (1992) on the Japanese case.

$Y_t^* = \max\{Y_{t-k}, k = 1, 2, \ldots\}$. Then, $C_t = aY_t + bY_t^*$ $(a, b > 0)$. In a growing economy like Japan's, Y_t^* is simply Y_{t-1}, and therefore the saving rate becomes

$$\frac{S_t}{Y_t} = 1 - a - b + b\,\frac{Y_t - Y_{t-1}}{Y_t}. \tag{4}$$

In this case, the saving rate is an increasing function of growth rate of income, with a coefficient b, which measures the 'ratchet' effect in consumption over time.

Utilizing this framework, Shinohara (1958) explains the difference in saving behaviour between employee-households and farmers in the early 1950s. As explained in Chapter 3, in the turmoil following the Second World War, relative income shifted significantly in favour of farmers at the expense of employees. As a result, for farmers, Y_t^* would be simply Y_{t-1}, and their saving rate would be an increasing function of the growth rate. In contrast, for employees, Y_t^* during the early 1950s would remain at the pre-war peak level, $\tilde{Y}$, and therefore their saving rate would become, unlike (4), an increasing function of the *level* of income:

$$\frac{S_t}{Y_t} = 1 - a - \frac{b\tilde{Y}}{Y_t}. \tag{5}$$

A standard life-cycle model emphasizes that the saving rate is independent of the level of income (Modigliani 1970). Shinohara (1958), in contrast, argues that the saving rate of employee households during the early 1950s was a function of the level of income, not of the growth rate. However, in the mid-1950s, when high growth started, (so the argument goes), the level of employees' income recovered its pre-war peak, and afterwards the saving rate became a function of the growth rate. In passing, the saving rate of employees increased from 2% to 16.5% between 1951 and 1961.

With relatively minor qualifications, then, whatever the theoretical justification, a high growth rate, which was largely unforeseen by economic agents, still seems to be at the head of the list of explanations of Japan's post-war saving behaviour. It explains not only the high level of the rate of saving, but also its basic time pattern. The gradual decline in the saving rate beginning in the mid-1970s also accords broadly with the deceleration of growth. This conclusion is, of course, based on the premiss that causality runs from growth to savings rather than vice versa. We will come back to the issue of causality in the final section of this chapter.

In addition to growth, a number of alternative/additional explanations for the high rate of savings have been offered. For example, the *high proportion of the self-employed*, whose saving rate is high, is alleged to account for a high aggregate saving rate. It is true that, in the first decade after the war, the saving rate of the self-employed was much higher than that of employee households. Shinohara (1958) estimated household saving rates of the non-agricultural self-employed, farmers, and employees to be 36.3%, 7.7%, and 5.8%, respectively for 1951–5; in fact, by his estimation, two-thirds of total household saving came from the savings of the non-agricultural self-employed in this period. A glance at Fig. 6.1, however, reveals that, in the early 1960s, the saving rate of employee households began to *exceed* the SNA saving rate. To the extent that measurement errors do not alter the overall picture, this implies that the saving rate of the self-employed has been *lower* than that of employee households. The relatively high proportion of the self-employed, therefore, is not relevant in explaining Japan's high household saving rate.

The bonus payment system, unique to Japan, is another popular explanation for the high saving rate. Shinohara (1964, 1981) argues that the bonuses paid twice a year (23.5% of total income on average for 1958–79) are regarded by households as transitory income, and therefore a higher proportion of such income would be saved. Indeed, Fig. 6.2 shows that the share of bonus payment out of total income and the saving rate of employees rose in parallel until the mid-1970s and has declined in parallel since then; the simple correlation between the saving rate and the proportion of income accounted for by bonus is in fact a sweeping 0.92. Mizoguchi (1964), by comparing the *Kakeichosa* (Family and Expenditure Survey) data on workers' households for several years, also finds that the annual consumption expenditure of the households bears a remarkably stable relationship with the family head's regular income, with the ratio about 1.2. This implies that an increase in the ratio of 'temporary' income, including the incomes of other members of the household and bonus payments, in the family's total income is bound to raise the saving rate.[5]

[5] Mizoguchi's finding seems to hold only up to the early 1970s. There is some evidence that beginning in the 1970s the income of the housewife is perceived as a part of the family's 'regular' income together with that of the family head (see Mizoguchi 1988). For labour participation of married women, see Ch. 5 and the next section of this chapter.

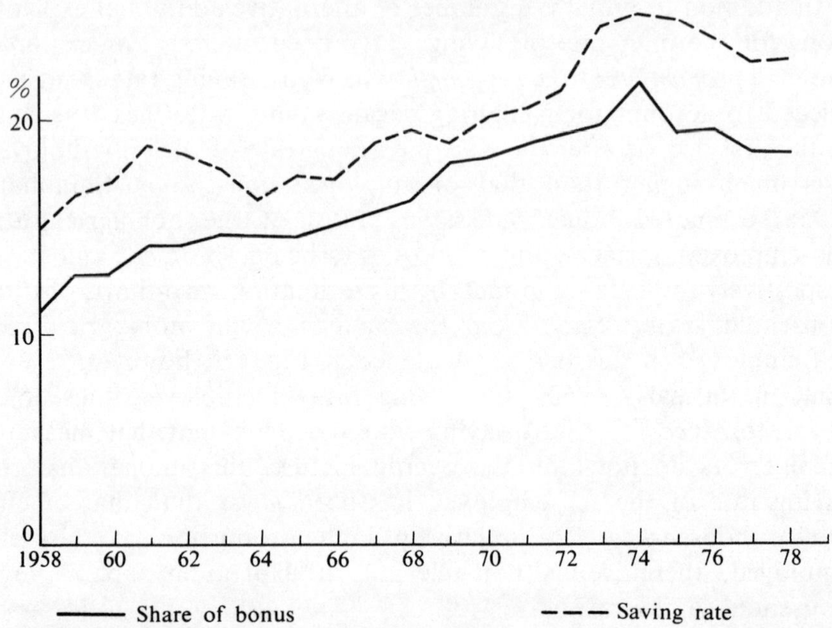

Fig. 6.2. The proportion of bonuses out of total income, and the saving rate, 1958–1978
Source: Ishikawa and Ueda (1984: 136, Fig. V-1); the original data are taken from *Kakeichosa* (Family Income and Expenditure Survey).

Critics, however, have found the hypothesis still unconvincing, because bonuses are paid twice a year on a regular basis and there is no reason for households to treat them as temporary or transitory. A crucial question is clearly to what extent bonuses are perceived as transitory by households.

The seasonally unadjusted monthly incomes of employee-households are shown in Fig. 6.3 (taken from *Kakeichosa*). Decomposing the detrended incomes into autoregressive and seasonal parts, I estimated standard deviations of error terms of two components for five income classes. These are given in Table 6.5. If we identify the seasonal component with bonuses, we can observe that bonuses, though regularly paid, are still much more unpredictable than other sources of income, particularly for relatively low-income-class households. How would bonuses affect savings, then?

Ishikawa and Ueda (1984) analyse this problem using the panel data of *Kakeichosa* for 1969–81. Somewhat surprisingly, they found, first, that the average time horizon of worker-households is only half a year. This means that the distinction between perma-

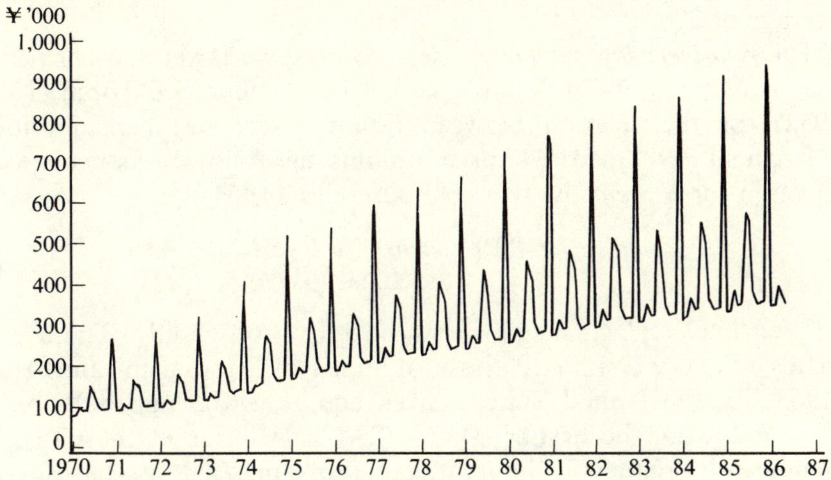

Fig. 6.3. Monthly incomes of worker households, 1970–1987
Source: *Kakeichosa* (Family Income and Expenditure Survey).

nent and transitory income does not play a major role in the behaviour of worker-households. Despite this finding, however, the marginal propensities to consume (MPC) out of regular income and out of bonuses appear to be significantly different; specifically, the MPC out of regular income is about 0.66, whereas the MPC out of bonuses is only about 0.4. The bonus payment system, therefore, does tend to raise the saving rate, whether bonuses are perceived as temporary or not. Their simulation predicts that, if there had not been the bonus payment system, Japan's

Table 6.5 Unpredictability of monthly incomes, 1970(I)–1986(IV)[a]

Income class	Autoregressive component	Seasonality
1	0.01	0.05
2	0.00	0.08
3	0.12	0.18
4	0.14	0.08
5	0.09	0.01

[a] The figures are standard deviations of error terms of autoregressive and seasonal components, fitted for the detrended logs of monthly incomes. The method used is Gersch and Kitagawa (1983).

aggregate saving rate would have been 3% lower than its actual average of 22%.

The *relatively low financial asset–income ratio* is yet another factor that may account for Japan's saving behaviour. (See Tobin (1951, 1952) for the relation between liquid assets and consumption.) Mizoguchi (1988), for example, obtains the following consumption function for *Kakeichosa* worker households, 1964–84:

$$C_t = \underset{}{90283} + \underset{(0.02)}{0.63 Y_t} + \underset{(0.009)}{0.05 A_t}, \tag{6}$$

where A_t is real financial assets held by households. These estimates are very similar to those obtained by Modigliani and Ando (1963) for the United States. Given equation (6), high inflation in 1974 following the first oil shock (23.2% in terms of the CPI), by significantly reducing the real value of financial assets, can be expected to have encouraged saving. This may partly account for the fact that the household saving rate peaked in the mid-1970s. It may also account for the decline in the saving rate in the 1980s, when Japan's financial asset–income ratio rose to an internationally comparable level.

High inflation in the early 1970s also meant that greater uncertainty faced most households. If marginal utility is a convex function, a mean-preserving increase in risk will increase the marginal utility of future consumption, so that current consumption will have to decrease in order to achieve intertemporal optimality. In this way, the convexity of marginal utility provides a rationalization for the precautionary saving. (See Deaton (1992) for an expository survey.) This precautionary motive for saving may also account for the peak in the household saving rate in the mid-1970s.

In summary, the growth rate is regarded by many as the most important factor explaining Japan's household saving behaviour. And yet, since growth was largely unforeseen, and households faced a long string of positive and negative surprises, the neoclassical optimum growth model cannot usefully be applied in interpreting Japan's saving behaviour. Beyond growth, many other factors, such as the bonus system and the relatively low financial asset–income ratio, probably also contribute to explaining saving behaviour. The next section will examine yet another aspect of Japan's household saving behaviour: namely, the relation between saving and the demand for owner-occupied housing and land prices.

6.2 AN ANALYSIS OF THE SAVING RATE AND HOUSING DEMAND

In order to understand patterns of Japanese household behaviour, the analysis in this section considers household savings, the labour supply of married women, and the demand for residential housing within a unified framework.

It is widely believed that two factors particular to the Japanese economy impose major constraints on households in Japan. First, the economy experienced a substantial deceleration of the real growth rate in the early 1970s (see Chapter 2). This necessarily led Japanese households to revise downward their perceived permanent income. Indeed, the previous section argues that the growth rate is perhaps the most important factor accounting for Japan's post-war saving behaviour. A simple life-cycle theory would then predict a decline in the saving rate. As Fig. 6.1 shows, there was indeed a decline in the SNA-based saving rate, but in contrast, the saving rate of worker-households actually rose in the 1980s. Secondly, the extremely high price of land and the heightened demand for owner-occupied housing impose other constraints. In fact, many Japanese economists have noted that the high price of land and the high demand for owner-occupied houses, together with capital market imperfections, put upward pressure on the household savings rate (see e.g. Ihara 1976, and Horioka 1987).

It is well known that, by international standards, housing and real estate prices are extremely high in Japan (Table 6.6). In the year 1986–7, the already high land prices in Tokyo more than doubled. Despite such high prices, however, there is a strong demand for owner-occupied housing in Japan. The most important reason for this is that owner-occupied and rental housing are very imperfect substitutes. The ratio of the average size of owner-occupied housing to that of rental housing is 2 to 1: to be precise, 95 m^2 versus 51 m^2 according to the 1984 National Survey of Family Income and Expenditure. If they were closer substitutes, a household's decision on whether to own or rent a house would depend mainly on marginal considerations such as differential tax treatment. In Japan, however, there are two very distinct types of housing, and therefore households are likely to be subject to a corner solution. This fact of life is made explicit in the analysis below.

The argument that high land prices and the high demand for owner-occupied houses raise the household saving rate, though

Table 6.6. An international comparison of the ratio of land and housing prices to per capita national income[a]

	1970	1975	1980	1983
UK	6.5	7.3	7.6	6.6
USA	5.4	6.1	6.4	6.1
West Germany	6.0	7.7	7.9	7.5
All Japan	8.1	10.5	11.2	13.7
Japan, three major metropolitan areas	9.3	11.9	12.8	16.3

[a] The figures are ratios of land and housing price to per capita national income.

Sources: For land and housing prices, *BSA Bulletin* (Building Societies Association, UK), *Statistical Abstract of the United States* (Department of Commerce, USA), *Bundes Baublatt* (W. Germany), *Kenchiku Tokei Nenpo* (Construction Yearbook) (Ministry of Construction, Japan); for national income per capita, *National Accounts Main Aggregates*, i, 1960–83, Dep. of Economics and Statistics, OECD.

popular and seemingly promising, has been made only casually so far. The analysis below, focusing on the younger households, pursues this idea in a formal model.

The Model

The model is a three-period life-cycle model in which a household maximizes the following objective function under appropriate budget constraints:

$$U = \sum_{t=1}^{3} \beta^{t-1} u(c_t, h_t, l_t), \tag{7}$$

where β is a discount factor, and c_t, h_t, and l_t are consumption exclusive of housing services, housing services, and the labour supply of married woman, respectively. There are two distinct types of housing service: rented housing, denoted by h, and owner-occupied housing, denoted by $H (H > h)$. For simplicity, the levels of H and h are assumed to be exogenously given. In period 1 all of the households consume h, but in period 2 a switch from h to H is available to households.

We have already seen that $H > h$. It is often argued that capital market imperfections raise the target savings for purchasing a house. If $H = h$, however, capital market imperfections would in fact become irrelevant as long as tax distortions were minor or absent. In Japan, tax considerations actually constitute a rather minor factor compared with the substantial difference in quality of housing that affects a household's house-ownership decision. Only about 20% of all households in Japan choose to rent a house permanently.

Before we solve the household's utility maximization problem, we must discuss tenure choice and bequests. There are two possible tenure choices open to households: to rent a house throughout life (strategy R), or to move into an owner-occupied house in period 2 (strategy O). As we will observe shortly, the lifetime budget constraints differ in each case. Let us denote the maximum utility in each case by U^R and U^O, respectively. It is clear that only if $U^O > U^R$ would the household decide to buy a house.

We next consider bequests. The role of bequests in asset accumulation has been intensively discussed in recent years by Kotlikoff and Summers (1981), Modigliani (1988), and Kotlikoff (1988). As pointed out in the previous section, older people in Japan, as well as in the United States, do not dissave as much as a standard life-cycle theory would predict. Ando and Kennickell (1987), for example, show that in Japan saving by independent older households outweighs the dissaving of older merged-with-younger households, and as a result the net worth by age group does not exhibit the classical hump-shaped pattern. Even in the group of older households that do dissave, at most only a half of their peak accumulation of net worth is dissaved before their deaths. Whether intended or unintended (because people do not know how long they will live), bequests cannot be ignored.[6] The 1993 households survey conducted by the Bank of Japan shows that 50.6% of 4,107 households actually have intentions to bequeath.

Bequests B can be easily introduced into the household's objective function (7):

$$U = \sum_{t=1}^{3} \beta^{t-1} u(c_t, h_t, l_t) + \phi(B) \qquad (B \geqq 0), \tag{8}$$

where $\phi(B)$ is a utility accruing from B. Then, with B, we can make the following classifications of the maximum lifetime utility.

The case of strategy R

R1: the maximum utility when the bequest of financial assets is zero (no bequest), U_R^1

[6] Ando and Kennickell (1987), however, demonstrate that whether or not retired persons dissave does not matter much in determining the *aggregate* savings rate when the growth rate of aggregate income is high.

R2: the maximum utility when the bequest of financial assets is positive, U_R^2

The case of strategy O

O1: the maximum utility when bequeathing only owner-occupied housing, U_O^1

O2: the maximum utility when bequeathing owner-occupied housing and some financial assets, U_O^2

O3: the maximum utility when selling owner-occupied housing and bequeathing some financial assets, U_O^3

O4: the maximum utility when selling owner-occupied housing and bequeathing no financial assets (no bequest), U_O^4.

In principle, six cases are possible, but here we focus on two cases which we believe are typical for Japanese households. First, for the household that chooses strategy R, we assume that $U_R^1 > U_R^2$ and that either (i) $U_R^1 > U_O^i$ ($i = 1$–4) or (ii) strategy O is not feasible. For the household that chooses strategy O, we assume that $U_O^1 > U_O^i$ ($i = 2$–4), $U_O^1 > U_R^i$ ($i = 1, 2$). These assumptions mean, among other things, that (i) there is no bequest of financial assets; (ii) the household that owns a house does not sell it during old age; and (iii) land and housing alone are left as bequests.

Several comments may be in order here. First, the above argument takes into account only the behaviour of the household bequeathing, not a history of bequests from the former generations. The assumption implies, of course, that the economy is not in the 'stationary state'. As explained in Chapter 3, virtually all of Japan's financial assets were wiped out by post-war hyperinflation, and most residential housing in big cities had been destroyed during the war. Post-war Japanese households, therefore, started from scratch with no assets. The current generation of workers is only the second generation since the war, and most workers moved from rural areas, where their parents had lived, to urban areas, where land prices were much higher, in the high-growth period of the 1950s and 1960s. These facts make our analysis tenable, although it takes into account only the behaviour of the household bequeathing and not the receipt of bequests. The application of the steady state in overlapping-generations models does not make much sense for the Japanese economy.

Secondly in Japan very few people, once they own a house, sell it and move into rental housing in their old age. This may be due to the fact that rented accommodation is a very poor substitute for owner-occupied housing. Also, land and housing account for the majority of bequests in Japan; according to the 1983 report of the Internal Revenue Service, about 70% of bequests consist of land and/or property.[7]

In fact, many older individuals choose to merge with younger households, thus contributing their land and house to the multiple-household and eventually bequeathing them to their children. About 70% of the population aged 65 or older live with their children. This fact was emphasized by Ando (1986) and Dekle (1987) as an important characteristic of the Japanese family. As is seen from Table 6.7, the pattern is certainly conspicuous by international standards. It is questionable, however, whether the merged household is a crucial element in explaining the high saving rate in Japan, simply because, in the high-growth period of the 1960s, the saving rate rose, while at the same time the ratio of the merged households consistently declined.

Under the assumptions stated above, we need to consider the household's maximization problem with the objective function (7), as

Table 6.7. 'Merged' households (younger and older generations living together): Japan, USA, UK, and France, 1983 (%)

Japan	USA	UK	France
52.0	3.4	2.4	9.1

if there were no bequests. In the case of strategy O, however, owner-occupied housing is actually bequeathed. The budget constraints we discuss shortly also reflect these assumptions.

We first consider the behaviour of households following strategy R. In this case, the lifetime budget constraint is

$$\sum_{t=1}^{3} \beta^{t-1}(y_t + w_t l_t - c_t - p_t^h h) = 0. \tag{9}$$

The price of consumption goods is normalized to be one; y_t is the husbands' (real) income at t and is taken as exogenously given. The assumption that the labour supply of husbands is not a choice variable seems realistic. w_t refers to the real wage for the wives'

[7] This statistic covers only those who must pay an inheritance tax; it therefore applies only to the relatively wealthy households.

labour services; p_t^h refers to housing rent. For simplicity, we consider the case where the interest rate in (9) is equal to the discount rate in (7).

Restricting the utility function (7) to the Cobb–Douglas type,

$$U = \sum_{t=1}^{3} \beta^{t-1} c_t^a h^b (1 - l_t)^c \qquad (a + b + c = 1,\ a,\ b,\ c > 0), \tag{10}$$

we can solve the maximization of (10) with respect to c_t and l_t under (9). Note that h is not a choice variable. In (10), we normalize the labour–leisure endowment to one. Labour supply l_t would be subject to the non-negative constraint, $l_t \geqq 0$, but since the $l_t = 0$ case does not provide a qualitatively different, comparative-static result, we will focus on the internal solutions ($l_t > 0$).

For simplicity, we assume $w_t = \overline{w}$. We also define a kind of 'permanent' husband's income Y as follows:

$$Y = \frac{y_1 + \beta y_2 + \beta^2 y_3}{1 + \beta + \beta^2}. \tag{11}$$

With the growth factor of income g, this permanent income can be written as

$$Y = \left(\frac{1 + \beta g + \beta^2 g^2}{1 + \beta + \beta^2} \right) y_1. \tag{12}$$

Then we obtain

$$c_t = \left(\frac{a}{a + c} \right) (Y + w - p^h h) \tag{13}$$

and

$$l_t = 1 - \left(\frac{a}{a + c} \right) \frac{1 + Y - p^h h}{w} \tag{14}$$

The labour supply of married women becomes an increasing function of w, but a decreasing function of Y. These properties are indeed typically observed for the labour supply of married women. Note that they are obtained only when the labour supply of husbands is quantity-constrained; otherwise, the labour supplies of both husband and wife become a function of the real wages (see also Chapter 5).

We can determine the saving rate for households in period 1 that follow the R strategy, S^R, as follows:

$$S^R = \frac{y_1 + wl_1 - c_1 - p^h h}{y_1 + wl_1} \tag{15}$$

$$= \frac{y_1 - Y}{y_1 + \left(\frac{a}{a+c}\right)w - \left(\frac{c}{a+c}\right)y_1 + \left(\frac{c}{a+c}\right)p^h h}.$$

We can easily determine that the saving rate is a decreasing function of Y and an increasing function of y_1.[8] In fact, with the positive growth rate, Y is larger than y_1 and therefore the saving rate of the young becomes negative. The expectations of lower economic growth reflected in a smaller Y would raise the saving rate. This negative relation between saving and growth for younger households is a standard result in life-cycle models.

In this case, the saving rate is of course, independent of P^H. Note that here we consider the effect of anticipated growth on the saving rate of younger households only. As explained in the previous section, a standard life-cycle theory predicts a positive relationship between the growth rate of incomes and the aggregate saving rate because high growth implies that younger cohorts have larger lifetime resources than older ones, and therefore their savings are larger than the dissaving of the poorer, retired cohorts. The *anticipated* growth of income, on the other hand, makes younger households less willing to save in their relatively poor life stage. Beyond that, unlike in a standard model, the present analysis also explicitly takes into account the wife's labour supply.

We next proceed to an analysis of households following the O strategy. The utility function in this case is also assumed to be of the Cobb–Douglas type:

$$c_1^a h^b (1 - l_1)^c + \beta c_2^a H^b (1 - l_2)^c + \beta^2 c_3^a H^b (1 - l_3)^c. \qquad (16)$$

The lifetime budget constraint, on the other hand, is

$$\sum_{t=1}^{3} \beta^{t-1} (y_t + wl_t - c_t) - p^h h - \beta \alpha P^H H - \beta^2 (1 - \alpha) P^H H = 0$$

$$(0 < \alpha < 1), \qquad (17)$$

where P^H is the price of land and owner-occupied housing, and α is the down-payment ratio which is about 0.4 for Japan compared with 0.25 for the United States. We assume that households are actually constrained by the down-payment requirement in the beginning of the second period. This means that they are subject to the following constraint in addition to (17):

[8] The saving rate is an increasing function of the *level* of the husband's current income y_1 because of the presence of the wife's labour supply and housing services in the model. Without w and h in (15), the saving rate becomes independent of y_1.

$$\beta^{-1}(y_1 + wl_1 - c_1 - p^h h) + y_2 + wl_2 - c_2 = \alpha P^H H. \tag{18}$$

Maximization of (16) with respect to c_t and l_t under constraints (17) and (18) leads us to

$$c_2 = \frac{H}{h} c_1 \tag{19}$$

$$l_1 = 1 - \frac{c}{a} \frac{c_1}{w} \tag{20}$$

$$l_2 = 1 - \frac{c}{a} \frac{c_2}{w}. \tag{21}$$

From these, we observe that $c_2 > c_1$ and $l_1 > l_2$. In contrast to what we obtained in the previous case of strategy R, consumption is lower and labour supply is larger in the first period than in the second.

Focusing on the first period, we explicitly derive c_1 and l_1:

$$c_1 = \frac{a}{a+c} \frac{1}{d} \left(y_1 + \beta y_2 + w + \beta w - p^h h - \beta \alpha P^H H \right), \tag{22}$$

$$l_1 = 1 - \frac{c}{a+c} \frac{1}{dw} \left(y_1 + \beta y_2 + w + \beta w - p^h h - \beta \alpha P^H H \right), \tag{23}$$

where d is defined as follows:

$$d = 1 + \beta \frac{H}{h}. \tag{24}$$

An increase in the price of owner-occupied housing lowers consumption and raises labour supply in period 1. We also note that the requirement of meeting the down payment effectively shortens the household's time horizon.

The saving rate of younger households that follow strategy O, S_1^0, is

$$\begin{aligned} S_1^0 &= \frac{y_1 + wl_1 - c_1 - p^h h}{y_1 + wl_1} \\ &= \frac{y_1 + w - p_h h - (1/d)\left(\tilde{Y} + \tilde{w} - p^h h - \beta \alpha P^H H\right)}{y_1 + w - [c/(a+c)]\,(1/d)\left(\tilde{Y} + \tilde{w} - p^h h - \beta \alpha P^H H\right)}, \end{aligned} \tag{25}$$

where $\tilde{Y}$ and $\tilde{w}$ are as follows:

$$\begin{aligned} \tilde{Y} &= y_1 + \beta y_2 \\ &= (1 + \beta g) y_1 \end{aligned} \tag{26}$$

$$\tilde{w} = w + \beta w. \tag{27}$$

We can find that the saving rate is a decreasing function of $\tilde{Y}$ or the growth rate of income, and an increasing function of y_1. The saving rate of younger households that plan to purchase a house is a decreasing function of income growth because the price of a house, $P^H H$, the target for saving, is independent of income growth in the present analysis. As Carroll and Weil (1993) argue, the assumption that the desired value of the house is a function of lifetime income would alter this result. Holding income in the first period of life, y_1, constant, the higher is the growth rate, the larger is lifetime income. The higher is lifetime income, in turn, the more expensive is the desired house, which will require a larger down payment, which will necessitate more saving in the early stage of life. In general, therefore, there are two competing effects of growth on the saving rate. The less responsive to growth is the price of the house to be purchased, the more likely is the saving rate to be a decreasing function of the growth rate; an empirical analysis below, in fact, suggests this negative relation.

The saving rate of younger households that plan to purchase a house is an increasing function of $P^H H$: the higher the price of the house to be purchased, the greater the required savings for the purchase.

If we compare S_1^0 with S_1^R for the same parameter values, we find that $S_1^0 > S_1^R$ is equivalent to the following inequality:

$$w + Y - p^h h - \frac{1}{d}(\tilde{Y} + \tilde{w} - p^h h - \beta\alpha P^H H) > 0 \qquad (28)$$

Now, as we observed above, $H/h \simeq 2$ and $\beta \simeq 0.8$ as a ten-year discount factor; therefore $H/h \simeq 1 + \beta$. In this case (28) is positive. We conclude that, for reasonable parameter values, S_1^0 becomes larger than S_1^R: the desire to own a house raises the saving rate of the young household. In this case, we can also show that $l_1^0 > l_1^R$.

We can summarize our analysis as follows. First, for simplicity, we made certain assumptions about bequests. The household maximizes lifetime utility conditional upon its house-ownership decision. We derived the saving function and the wives' labour supply function for two types of household. In the case of households that plan to own a house, the labour supply of married women is (i) a decreasing function of the husband's 'permanent' income, and (ii) an increasing function of real wages for the wife's labour services and the price of owning a house. Furthermore, in households that plan to own a house, for a reasonable set of parameter values, both the saving rate and the labour supply of married women are greater than in those households that do not have such a plan.

The house-ownership decision itself depends, among other things, on the permanent income or the growth rate of income and the price of owner-occupied housing. A decrease in the permanent income and/or an increase in the price of owner-occupied housing, for example, induces more households to choose strategy R. The net effects of a decrease in Y and/or an increase in P^H on the aggregate saving rate among younger households are therefore actually ambiguous. As observed above, a decrease in Y or a slower growth rate raises the saving rate of younger households as long as thcy keep their O or R strategy, but it actually induces more households to choose strategy R, in which case the aggregate saving rate among younger households becomes smaller.

We next carry out an empirical test of the model developed above, using microeconomic data from the 1984 National Survey of Family Income and Expenditure conducted by the Statistics Bureau, Management and Co-ordination Agency. We estimate the saving function and female labour supply function separately both for renters with a house purchase plan (O) and for renters without such a plan (R).

The Data

The National Survey of Family Income and Expenditure (*Zenkoku Shōhi Jittai Chōsa*; 'NSFIE data' for short) has been conducted every five years for the purpose of understanding the consumption patterns of all households in Japan, by investigating income and expenditure, assets and liabilities, the possession of durable goods, the tenure of dwellings, and house purchasing plans. It is a very large sample involving some 54,000 households, covering virtually all households in Japan.

Since our objective is to study the effect of housing strategy on the renter-households' saving behaviour, the sample is restricted to worker-households in rented accommodation aged 25–55. We deleted the observations with missing variables and households whose yearly disposable income was under ¥1 million. We assume that non-reporting is randomly distributed in the population. With the above defined working sample, we are left with 8,167 renter-households with a head aged 25–55. In this sample, 1,455 renter-households have plans to purchase a house.

Construction of the Variables

Permanent income of the household head (*PYHEAD*), the price of land (*LANDP*), and the wage rates for married women (*FW*) are variables not directly taken from the NSFIE, but constructed from the NSFIE and other sources.[9]

Permanent Income of the Household Head, PYHEAD

The expression for permanent income of the household head aged t is given by

$$\mathrm{PYHEAD_t} = \mathrm{LTLY_t}/(79 - t),$$

where $\mathrm{LTLY_t}$ is the estimated 'lifetime' labour income from the current period until retirement. (We assume that the household head will live until age 79.)

Price of Land, LANDP

We used the land prices for each city, town, and village reported in the Survey of Land Price (*Chika Kōji Chōsa*) conducted by the National Land Agency.

Wage Rates for Married Women, FW

FW is calculated based on the *Basic Survey on the Wage Structure*, published by the Ministry of Labour. We calculated the wage rate of full-time workers, both office workers and non-office workers, by age. For part-time workers, we used the average wage rate of part-time workers by prefecture.

Estimation Method

To test the implications obtained in our model, we estimated the saving function and female labour supply function for renters. In estimating the saving rate function, we had explicitly to take into account the households' tenure choices between strategy O and strategy R. For this purpose, we considered the following model:

$$\text{Strategy O:} \quad s_i = X_{1i}\beta_1 + u_{1i} \quad \text{if } U_i^O \geq U_i^R \tag{29}$$

$$\text{Strategy R:} \quad s_i = X_{2i}\beta + u_{2i} \quad \text{if } U_i^O \leq U_i^R \tag{30}$$

Here s_i is the saving rate, X_{1i} and X_{2i} are the explanatory variables of the saving rates for the respective groups, and u_{1i}, u_{2i} are residuals. U_i^O (U_i^R) is the maximum attainable utility when strategy O (R) is chosen by household i.

9 Details of the constructed data are given in Takayama *et al.* (1988).

We assume that U_i^O and U_i^R are described by the following equations:

$$U_i^O = Z_i \gamma^R - \varepsilon_i^O \tag{31}$$

$$U_i^R = Z_i \gamma^O - \varepsilon_i^R. \tag{32}$$

Z_i are the variables that determine U_i^j ($j =$ O, R). Then we obtain

$$U_i^O - U_i^R = Z_i (\gamma^R - \gamma^O) - (\varepsilon_i^O - \varepsilon_i^R) = Z_i \gamma - u_i. \tag{33}$$

We define a dummy variable as

$$\begin{aligned} I_i &= 1 \qquad \text{if } Z_i\gamma \geq u_i; \\ I_i &= 0 \qquad \text{otherwise.} \end{aligned} \tag{34}$$

Since we have I_i in our data, we can use the probit maximum likelihood (ML) to estimate the parameters γ. Because γ is estimable only up to a scale factor, we shall assume that $\mathrm{Var}(u_i) = 1$. We also assume that u_{1i}, u_{2i}, and u_i have a trivariate normal distribution, with mean vector zero and covariance matrix.

$$\Sigma = \begin{bmatrix} \sigma_1^2 & \sigma_{12} & \sigma_{1u} \\ \sigma_{12} & \sigma_2^2 & \sigma_{2u} \\ \sigma_{1u} & \sigma_{2u} & 1 \end{bmatrix}. \tag{35}$$

We use a two-step procedure to obtain consistent estimates (Heckman 1976; Maddala 1983). To obtain these estimates, we must determine the expected values of the residuals u_{1i} and u_{2i} in (29) and (30). The expected values are :

$$E(u_{1i} \mid Z_i \gamma \geq u_i) = -\sigma_{1u} \frac{\phi(Z_i\gamma)}{\Phi(Z_i\gamma)}, \tag{36}$$

$$E(u_{2i} \mid Z_i \gamma < u_i) = \sigma_{2u} \frac{\phi(Z_i \gamma)}{1 - \Phi(Z_i\gamma)}, \tag{37}$$

where ϕ refers to the standard normal density function and Φ refers to the cumulative normal.

Let us define, for convenience,

$$\lambda_{1i} = \frac{\phi(Z_i\gamma)}{\Phi(Z_i\gamma)} \qquad \text{and} \qquad \lambda_{2i} = \frac{\phi(Z_i\gamma)}{1 - \Phi(Z_i\gamma)}. \tag{38}$$

Then we can write (29) and (30) as

$$s_i = X_{1i} \beta_1 - \sigma_{1u} \lambda_{1i} + \varepsilon_{1i} \qquad \text{for } I_i = 1 \tag{39}$$

and

$$s_i = X_{2i} \beta_2 + \sigma_{2u} \lambda_{2i} + \varepsilon_{2i} \qquad \text{for } I_i = 0 \tag{40}$$

where ε_{1i} and ε_{2i} are the residuals with zero conditional means, which are defined as follows:

$$\varepsilon_{1i} = u_{1i} + \sigma_{1u}\lambda_{1i} \tag{41}$$

$$\varepsilon_{2i} = u_{2i} - \sigma_{2u}\lambda_{2i} \tag{42}$$

To sum up, in the two-step procedure, we first obtain the estimate of γ in (33) and (34) using the probit ML method, with observations I_i. Call this $\hat{\gamma}$. We then obtain estimates of λ_{1i} and λ_{2i}, $\hat{\lambda}_{1i}$ and $\hat{\lambda}_{2i}$, respectively. The second step is to estimate equations (39) and (40) by ordinary least squares (OLS), substituting $\hat{\lambda}_{1i}$ and $\hat{\lambda}_{2i}$ for λ_{1i} and λ_{2i}. In this way, we are able to obtain the consistent estimates of β_1, β_2, σ_{1u}, and σ_{2u}.

We estimate the labour supply function of married women by a similar method. Here, however, there is a problem with sample selection bias, since only 35% of married women are labour-force participants in our data.[10] Because of this, we have the following estimation model:

$$\text{Strategy O: } l_i = X_{3i}\beta_3 + u_{3i} \qquad \text{if } U_i^O \geq U_i^R,\ l_i \geq 0 \tag{43}$$

$$\text{Strategy R: } l_i = X_{4i}\beta_4 + u_{4i} \qquad \text{if } U_i^O < U_i^R,\ l_i \geq 0 \tag{44}$$

$$\text{Strategy R: } I_i' = Z_2\gamma_2 - u_i' \tag{45}$$

where

$$I_i' = 1 \qquad \text{if } l_i \geq 0$$

$$I_i' = 0 \qquad \text{otherwise.}$$

The X in (43) and (44) is the variable that affects the amount of labour supply when the married woman works. Z_2, on the other hand, is the variable that affects the decision to participate in the labour market. For simplicity, we assume the covariance of u_i in (33) and u_i' in (45) is zero.[11] On this assumption, we can obtain the consistent estimates of β_3, β_4, and σ by using the following two step-procedure:

$$l_i = X_{3i}\beta_3 - \sigma_{3u}\lambda_{1i} - \sigma_{3u'}\lambda_{3i} + \varepsilon_{3i} \qquad \text{for } I_i = 1,\ I_i' = 1, \tag{46}$$

$$l_i = X_{4i}\beta_4 + \sigma_{4u}\lambda_{2i} - \sigma_{4u'}\lambda_{3i} + \varepsilon_{4i} \qquad \text{for } I_i = 0,\ I_i' = 1, \tag{47}$$

where

[10] The labour-force participation rate of married women in this data-set is lower than that in the economy as a whole, for the following reasons. First, the married women of the owner-occupied households have higher labour-force participation rate than the renters. Second, households with working married women are misrepresented with a downward bias in the NSFIE.

[11] It is, of course, theoretically more desirable to assume the correlation between u_i and u_i', and to use the bivariate probit for the first-step estimation.

$$\lambda_{3i} = \frac{\phi(Z_{2i}\,\hat{\gamma}_2)}{\Phi(Z_{2i}\,\hat{\gamma}_2)}.$$

Results

The descriptive statistics of the variables in our estimations are shown in Table 6.8. Overall, our estimation results are consistent with the model developed above. The estimated first-step probit equation for tenure choice is shown in Table 6.9. The explanatory

Table 6.8. Descriptive statistics of variables[a]

	Whole sample		Strategy O		Strategy R	
SRATE	0.078	(0.268)	0.124	(0.256)	0.068	(0.270)
DY	398.4	(141.5)	435.2	(139.8)	390.4	(140.6)
DYHEAD	369.7	(137.0)	395.7	(133.0)	364.1	(136.0)
PYHEAD	250.3	(85.9)	272.1	(83.2)	245.6	(85.7)
ASSETS	446.2	(496.0)	595.2	(555.1)	413.6	(475.9)
LANDP	14.2	(13.6)	13.8	(10.9)	14.3	(14.2)
NCHILD	0.46	(0.64)	0.51	(0.65)	0.45	(0.64)
EPHOUSE	0.27	(0.44)	0.3	(0.46)	0.26	(0.44)
NOLD	0.046	(0.23)	0.038	(0.21)	0.047	(0.24)
DCITY	0.54	(0.49)	0.54	(0.50)	0.54	(0.50)
MEMBER	3.57	(0.96)	3.52	(0.94)	3.58	(0.97)
AGE 25–29	0.16	(0.37)	0.19	(0.39)	0.15	(0.36)
AGE 30–34	0.29	(0.45)	0.31	(0.46)	0.28	(0.44)
AGE 35–39	0.24	(0.43)	0.25	(0.43)	0.24	(0.43)
AGE 40–44	0.15	(0.36)	0.13	(0.34)	0.15	(0.36)
AGE 45–49	0.09	(0.29)	0.07	(0.25)	0.09	(0.29)

[a] Figures in parentheses are standard deviations.

SRATE	Saving rate
DY	Disposable income of household
DYHEAD	Disposable income of household head
PYHEAD	Permanent income of household head
ASSETS	Net financial assets
LANDP	Price of land
NCHILD	Number of children under 3 years
EPHOUSE	Employer provided house
NOLD	Number of dependent old
DCITY	Dummy for 3 metropolitan areas
MEMBER	Number of household members
AGE 26–29	Age dummy for 25–9
AGE 30–34	Age dummy for 30–4
AGE 35–39	Age dummy for 35–9
AGE 40–44	Age dummy for 40–4
AGE 45–49	Age dummy for 45–9

Table 6.9. Probit estimates[a]

	Probability of having a plan to purchase a house or land	Probability for renters of married females working
Constant	– 1.36268	0.26943
	(– 13.4)	(– 3.263)
Permanent income of head (¥'000)	0.00010804	– 0.00039944
	(4.33)	(– 15.63)
Net assets (¥'000)	0.00005669	0.00000705
	(14.4)	(1.80432)
Price of land (¥'000)	– 0.00075798	– 0.0000996
	(– 3.67)	(– 0.5708)
EPHOUSE	0.0624651	– 0.184637
	(– 1.56)	(– 4.391)
No. of household members	0.0434303	0.138558
	(2.09)	(7.218)
No. of children under 3 years	0.0369531	– 0.653929
	(1.17)	(– 17.95)
No. of dependent elderly	– 0.0202198	– 0.23249
	(– 0.268)	(– 3.324)
Age 25–9	0.30148	0.6429
	(3.23)	(7.79)
Age 30–4	0.25311	0.310013
	(2.88)	(4.06)
Age 35–9	0.21602	0.0929
	(2.52)	(1.26)
Age 40–4	0.16634	0.1147
	(1.89)	(1.54)
Age 45–9	0.32420	0.209
	(0.342)	(2.71)
Log likelihood	– 3663.95	– 3897.80

[a] Asymptotic *t*-statistics in parentheses; 8,168 observations.

variables in the probit equation include total net assets (*ASSETS*), permanent income of household head (*PYHEAD*), price of land (*LANDP*), employer-provided housing dummy (*EPHOUSE*), number of household members (*MEMBER*), number of children under 3 years (*NCHILD*), number of dependent elderly (*NOLD*), and age dummies. The probability of having a plan to purchase an owner-occupied house (choosing strategy O) is an increasing function of the permanent income of the household head and net assets. The price of land is found to have negative effects on the probability of choosing strategy O.

Table 6.10 shows the estimation results of the saving functions for households that choose strategy O and those that choose strategy R.

The explanatory variables in the saving functions include most of the variables in the probit equation plus the inverse of the household disposable income ($1/YD$), disposable income of household head ($DYHEAD$), the dummy for the three largest metropolitan areas ($DCITY$), and $\hat{\lambda}_1$, $\hat{\lambda}_2$. The inverse of the household disposable income ($1/YD$) corresponds to the constant term in the level form of the saving equation.

The saving rate is found to be an increasing function of the disposable income of the household head and a decreasing function of permanent income of the household head both for O and R. The effects of the price of land on the savings rate, however, are different for the two types of household. For the O households, the saving rate is an increasing function of the price of land. For the R households, on the other hand, the coefficient of the price of land is not significant and its sign is negative. These results are consistent with our theory.

We next turn to labour supply equations. The first-step probit equation for the labour supply decision is shown in Table 6.9. The participation rate of married women is a decreasing function of the permanent income of the household head and the number of children under 3 years of age. The coefficient of the price of land is not significant. The net assets have a positive effect on the labour supply. This positive effect may be spurious in that it actually captures the causality running from female labour supply to the level of assets.

Table 6.11 shows the estimation results of the labour supply equations for the two types of household. The explanatory variables in the labour supply equations include most of the variables in the probit equation plus $\hat{\lambda}_i$. The labour supply of married women is an increasing function of the price of land and the wage rate for the O household; however, for the R household labour supply is a decreasing function of the wage rate and the coefficient of the price of land is not significant.[12]

[12] The possible explanations of the unexpected sign of the coefficient for the wages are as follows. First, since the wage rate variables are constructed data, there is a problem of measurement error. Second, the dominance of the income effects over the substitution effects may account for the observed sign of the wage term.

Table 6.10. Saving functions

	Renters with purchase plans (strategy O)	Renters without purchase plans (strategy R)
Constant	1.94	0.264
	(6.40)	(10.36)
$1/DY$	– 159.2	– 114.1
	(– 13.4)	(– 29.5)
DYHEAD	0.000162	0.000287
	(1.216)	(6.74)
PYHEAD	– 0.000990	– 0.000580
	(– 5.17)	(– 7.84)
ASSETS	– 0.000268	– 0.0000404
	(– 3.95)	(– 1.86)
Price of land	0.00421	– 0.00010
	(2.97)	(– 0.260)
EPHOUSE	0.0818	0.295
	(4.94)	(4.133)
No. of dependent elderly	0.0422	– 0.0107
	(1.49)	(– 0.905)
DCITY	– 0.0412	– 0.0155
	(– 2.49)	(– 2.309)
Age 25–9	– 0.111	0.0948
	(– 1.96)	(4.89)
Age 30–4	– 0.0723	0.0983
	(– 1.48)	(5.82)
Age 35–9	– 0.0733	0.0912
	(– 1.72)	(5.96)
Age 40–4	– 0.0164	0.0715
	(– 0.437)	(5.01)
Age 45–9	– 0.0616	0.0506
	(– 1.699)	(3.58)
λ_1	– 0.763	
	(– 4.74)	
λ_2		0.346
		(3.94)
ADJ R-SQ	0.268	0.302
SE	0.229	0.224
Sample	1,455	6,697

Elasticities of the Saving Rate

The model estimated above allows us to calculate the elasticities of the saving rate with respect to the exogenous variables. We must note, however, that, since the permanent income of the household

Table 6.11. Labour supply functions of married women

	Renters with purchase plans (strategy O)	Renters without purchase plans (strategy R)
Constant	3666.6	3022.58
	(5.47)	(9.73)
DYHEAD	− 2.75	− 0.588
	(− 4.22)	(− 2.16)
PYHEAD	6.037	3.951
	(3.13)	(4.64)
FW	0.407	− 0.442
	(1.37)	(− 3.43)
LANDP	12.55	− 1.408
	(2.31)	(− 0.613)
NCHILD	550.37	603.4
	(1.69)	(4.21)
NOLD	606.2	688.5
	(2.43)	(6.18)
EPHOUSE	− 141.14	56.86
	(− 1.00)	(0.977)
Age 25–9	− 1266.85	− 654.2
	(− 3.27)	(− 3.99)
Age 30–4	− 953.7	− 437.2
	(− 3.48)	(− 3.87)
Age 35–9	− 862.5	− 224.0
	(− 3.59)	(− 2.42)
Age 40–4	− 516.3	− 208.9
	(− 2.28)	(− 2.42)
Age 45–9	− 425.9	− 76.64
	(− 1.83)	(− 0.872)
λ_3	− 941.5	− 1119.9
	(− 1.95)	(− 5.35)
λ_1	− 480.6	360.9
	(− 1.98)	(1.69)
$\bar{R}^2$	0.0705	0.0480
s.d.	955.5	875.1
Sample	561	2,251

head, the price of land, and the level of assets are all included in both the probit and the saving rate equations, a change in these variables has two effects. First, it alters the probability that a household will choose O strategy. Secondly, conditional upon having O strategy, it changes the saving rate. To capture the actual effects of a change in the exogenous variables on the saving rate, therefore, we must take into account the fact that *some households switch their strategies*. The elasticities based on the estimated coefficients in the second-step regressions are calculated on the assumption that all the households originally choosing O will maintain strategy O; in fact, some households will change their strategy from O to R when the exogenous variables change. In this sense, the elasticities based on the estimated coefficients (β_j) are only notional or partial. We call these elasticities, non-switching elasticities (NSEs). They are shown in Table 6.12.

Table 6.12. Elasticities of saving rate

	Permanent income of household head	Price of land	Assets
Households planning to buy a house			
Non-switching elasticity	– 2.17	0.47	– 1.29
Elasticity with switching	0.86	0.003	0.22
Households without plans to buy a house			
Non-switching elasticity	– 2.09	– 0.021	– 0.25
Elasticity with switching	– 2.01	– 0.06	– 0.018
Aggregate saving rates among renters			
Non-switching elasticity	– 2.11	0.08	– 0.46
Elasticity with switching	– 1.37	– 0.07	0.08

The switching elasticities (SEs) in Table 6.12, on the other hand, are those that take into account the switching effects. They are calculated as follows:

$$\frac{X_j}{s}\frac{\partial E(s \mid Z\gamma \geq u_i)}{\partial X_j} = \frac{X_j}{s}\left[\beta_j + \gamma_j \sigma_{1u} \frac{\phi(Z\gamma)}{\Phi(Z\gamma)}\left(Z\gamma + \frac{\phi(Z\gamma)}{\Phi(Z\gamma)}\right)\right], \tag{48}$$

where X_j and Z are the same variables included in both the probit and the saving equations, β_j and γ_j are the coefficients of the variables in those equations, and σ_{1u} is the covariance of residuals between the saving equation and probit equation.

The last term in the square brackets of (48) captures the switching effect on the saving rate. For example, when the permanent income of the household head increases by 1%, the saving rate for an O household would decrease by 2.17% if there were no switching from strategy R to O. In fact, however, some households will switch their strategy from R to O when the permanent income of the household head increases. These households will have a relatively higher saving rate in strategy O compared with the saving rate of households that originally chose strategy O, because the residuals of the saving rate equation for O and those of the probit equation are positively correlated in these estimation results. In this case, the switching from R to O will have a positive effect on the saving rate for O. This switching effect is actually so large that SE, with respect to the permanent income of the household head, takes a positive value of a little more than 0.8.

The effect of the price of land on the saving rate is as follows. When the price of land increases, the saving rate for O will increase if there is no switching from O to R. However, when the price of land increases, some households that would have an extremely high saving rate if they were to keep to O strategy are discouraged from buying a house, and switch from O to R. Therefore the observable effect of the increase in the price of land on the saving rate for O households becomes much smaller than NSE would imply. Table 6.12 shows that, for households with O strategy, the switching effect is so large that the value of the elasticity decreases from 0.47 to almost zero when the switching effect is taken into account. The table also shows that, for households with R strategy, the switching effects are relatively small compared with the potential effects of the exogenous variables. There are no changes in the signs of the elasticities between SE and NSE for households without a purchase plan.

Next, we examine the aggregate saving rate among renters, S. Renters are classified into two groups, O and R. We denote the average income, saving rate, and number of households in each group by Y^O, Y^R, S^O, S^R, N^O, and N^R, respectively. Then, by definition, we obtain

$$\begin{aligned} S &= \frac{S^O Y^O N^O + S^R Y^R N^R}{Y^O N^O + Y^R N^R}, \\ &= \frac{S^O(n^O, X)\, n^O \sigma^O + S^R(n^O, X)\,(1 - n^O)\,(1 - \sigma^O)}{n^O \sigma^O + (1 - n^O)\,(1 - \sigma^O)}, \end{aligned} \tag{49}$$

where

$$n^O = \frac{N^O}{N^O + N^R} \qquad \text{and} \qquad \sigma^O = \frac{Y^O}{Y^O + Y^R}. \tag{50}$$

We note that the average saving rate in each group depends on the relative share of households belonging to each group.[13] The effects of a change in an exogenous variable, X on S, therefore, can be determined as follows:

$$\begin{aligned}\frac{\partial S}{\partial X} &= \frac{n^O\sigma^O}{n^O\sigma^O + (1-n^O)(1-\sigma^O)}\left(\frac{\partial S^O}{\partial X} + \frac{\partial S^O}{\partial n^O}\frac{\partial n^O}{\partial X}\right)\\ &+ \frac{(1-n^O)(1-\sigma^O)}{n^O\sigma^O + (1-n^O)(1-\sigma^O)}\left(\frac{\partial S^R}{\partial X} + \frac{\partial S^R}{\partial n^O}\frac{\partial n^O}{\partial X}\right)\\ &+ \frac{\sigma^O(1-\sigma^O)(S^O - S^R)(\partial n^O/\partial X)}{[n^O\sigma^O + (1-n^O)(1-\sigma^O)]^2},\end{aligned} \tag{51}$$

where

$$\frac{\partial n^O}{\partial X} = \frac{\partial \Phi(X\gamma)}{\partial X} = \gamma \cdot \phi(X\gamma) \cdot.$$

We can calculate the elasticity of the aggregate savings rate $X/S \cdot \partial S/\partial X$ for renters by using (51), evaluating at the sample mean. In evaluating the elasticities of the aggregate savings rate, there are two types of elasticities, as before. First, we can calculate the elasticities under the assumption of no switching between O and R, $\partial n^O/\partial X = 0$ in (51). We call this NSE, as before. Secondly, the elasticities that take account of the switching effect can be calculated using (48) and (51). We call this SE again. The elasticities that we can actually observe are the latter.

Table 6.12 shows the aggregate elasticities of the saving rate with respect to exogenous variables. If households were to keep to the same strategy, a 1% increase in the price of land would raise the aggregate saving rate by 0.08%. In this sense, the high price of land in Japan has a potential role in explaining the high saving rate. Similarly, the increase in the household head's permanent income and assets has a potentially negative effect on the aggregate saving rate. We must note that the above results are obtained under the assumption that the household cannot change its housing strategy.

If we take into account the switching effect, however, the sign of the elasticities for the price of land change from positive to negative.

[13] On the other hand, we take it that the dependence of σ on n is less important, and so ignore it in our analysis.

When the price of land increases, the effect of switching from O to R is so large that the aggregate saving rate for renters decreases. Similarly, an increase in assets has large switching effects from R to O. The households that switch from R to O have higher saving rates in the new strategy regime than households originally choosing the O strategy. Thus, the actually observable aggregate saving rate is positively correlated with the level of assets. On the other hand, the switching elasticity of the aggregate saving rate among younger households with respect to the permanent income is negative (−1.37), though the absolute value declines compared with the non-switching elasticity (−2.11).

To see the quantitative importance of these effects, we conducted a simulation analysis using the estimated equations. The results are shown in Table 6.13. The base run in the first row corresponds to the actual values of the respective variables in 1984 where the explanatory variables such as *PYHEAD*, *LANDP*, and *ASSET* are normalized to be one. In rows 2–8, we can see the effects of changes in *PYHEAD*, *LANDP*, and *ASSET* on S^O, S^R and the aggregate saving rate among the renters. The values of *PYHEDA*, *LANDP*, and *ASSET* in row 8 are the actual values of these variables in 1972.

Table 6.13. Simulation results

	PYHEAD	*LANDP*	*ASSET*	S^O	S^R	Aggregate saving rate
Base (1984 = 1)	1.00	1.00	1.00	0.329	0.164	0.209
1	0.80	1.00	1.00	0.342	0.184	0.226
2	1.00	0.10	1.00	0.323	0.182	0.227
3	1.00	0.50	1.00	0.323	0.174	0.220
4	1.00	3.00	1.00	0.318	0.126	0.168
5	1.00	10.00	1.00	0.267	0.032	0.047
6	1.00	1.00	1.50	0.334	0.177	0.229
7	1.00	1.50	1.50	0.334	0.167	0.219
8 (1972)	1.34	0.84	0.64	0.282	0.124	0.170

Rows 4, 5, and 6 show, for example, that the aggregate saving rate among renters is a decreasing function of the land price. As explained above, this is caused by the switching effect from O to R. The effect of a decrease in permanent income on the saving rate can be seen by comparing the base run and row 1. A decrease in the permanent income by 20% would raise the aggregate saving rate from 20.9% to 22.6%. Row 8 shows that, if the economic conditions in 1984 had been the same as those in 1972, the aggregate saving rate would have been 17% compared with its actual value of 20.9%. A decrease in the permanent income by 25% seems to be a crucial factor in explaining why the saving rate of younger households stayed high at the level of 20% in 1984.

Summary

This section examined personal saving and female labour supply in Japan in relation to housing demand. The possible relation between the personal saving rate and housing demand has been long noted by many Japanese economists; some have positive views, others negative. Following their lead, we considered a model in which owner-occupied housing has a special role. Again, it must be emphasized that owner-occupied and rental housing are very imperfect substitutes in Japan. An important point of the model is that some households are discouraged from seeking to move into owner-occupied housing when, for example, the husbands' permanent income declines and/or the price of land increases. The converse move is, of course, possible, but in either case a change in the household's tenure choice brings about a substantial change in consumption/saving behaviour.

To examine this point, we focused on renters in this section. Not surprisingly, higher land prices and/or lower husbands' permanent income were found to induce more households to give up a house purchase plan. To consider the effects of the price of land on saving, we must pay adequate attention to a possible change in the household's house purchase plan.

According to our estimation results, a rise in the price of housing raises the saving rate among renters with an elasticity of 0.08 *if a change in tenure choice is not to occur*. On the other hand, a rise in house prices lowers the saving rate among renters with an elasticity of –0.07 *when a change in tenure choice is taken into account*; it lowers the saving rate because more households are induced to give up their plan to buy a house and thus can spend more on other consumables. With the estimated elasticity of –0.07, we obtain the result that the doubled land/housing price as actually occurred in 1986–7 would lower the initial saving rate of 20% to 18.6%. As Fig. 6.4 shows, the percentage of renter-households that have house purchase plans has

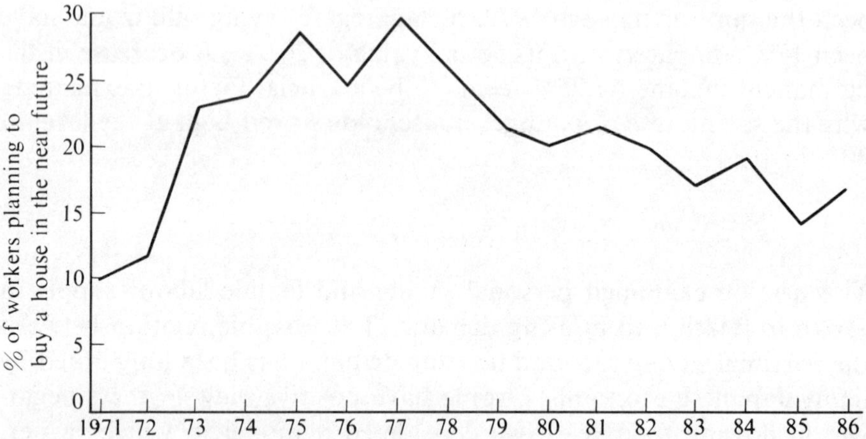

Fig. 6.4. Households with house purchase plans, 1971–1986
Source: Statistical Bureau, Management and Co-ordination Agency, *Family Saving Survey.*

indeed changed over the years. The survey on land/house purchase plans conducted by *Sorifu* in March 1991 revealed that about 56% of renters had given up their house purchase plans after the extraordinary increase in the price of land in 1986–7.

The switch of tenure choice among renters is important. Our analysis focuses only on renters of working age. Ando and Kennickell (1987), however, demonstrate that, when the growth rate of aggregate income is high, it is the saving rate of those of working age that determines the aggregate saving rate: the saving behaviour of the retired does not matter much.

A sharp increase in the relative price of land in the 1970s and 1980s may, therefore, be a factor in explaining the decline in the personal saving rate since 1974. On the other hand, a decrease in permanent income is a factor that raises the saving rate *ceteris paribus* with an estimated elasticity of −1.37. This would make a decline in the saving rate less marked than otherwise. As Fig. 6.1 showed, beginning in the mid-1970s, the saving rate of worker-households did not decline so much as a simple life-cycle theory would predict, and actually even rose in the 1980s. The importance of the target savings for a house may explain this fact, at least in part. In any case, evidence has been presented showing that in the Japanese economy tenure choice and housing demand significantly affect the target savings of younger households. It qualifies a positive relationship between growth and saving predicted by the standard life-cycle theory.

6.3 CONCLUDING REMARKS

For all the qualifications that have been made, the analysis of this chapter reconfirms a close link between saving and growth. An important and yet unsettled question is *causality* between growth and saving. The life-cycle theory implies that growth affects saving, while in the standard neoclassical growth theory a higher saving rate raises the growth rate out of steady state. The matter has not been settled yet, but Carroll and Weil (1993), for example, argue that the causality runs from growth to saving, rather than the other way round. Their Granger causality test, based on the panel data for 22 OECD countries in 1960–87, shows that growth Granger-causes saving with a positive sign. Their single-country case studies of Japan, Korea, Singapore, and Hong Kong also demonstrate that in all four cases growth was high early, and saving was high later. In none of the countries they examine does it appear to be the case that large increases in the saving rate were reflected in subsequent high growth.

For Japan, it would be wrong to argue that the high saving rate did not contribute to high growth in the 1950s and 1960s because, without high saving, the growth generated by high investment would have soon reached the ceiling of foreign reserves and been aborted by tightened monetary policy (see Chapter 9). But this is different from saying that high savings were the generating force of high growth; it is compatible with the argument that high growth caused high savings.

In passing, growth actually affects not only the household saving rate but also the public saving rate. A steady rise in the macro saving rate in Japan in the 1980s was caused basically by a sharp decline in the public deficits, which had turned to surpluses by the end of the decade. An increase in the government surpluses, in turn, was (by way of tax revenues) caused by growth rather than by intentional cuts in expenditure or changes in tax code.

Granted that high growth causes high saving, the next question facing us is, what generates growth? The life-cycle theory taking the growth rate exogenous is silent on this issue. Chapter 10 presents an explicit model in which are discussed the ultimate factors determining the growth rate.

7

Investment

Investment has always played a central role in both the growth of and the fluctuations in the Japanese economy. It is the most volatile component of aggregate demand, but on the other hand, it is only through investment that economic growth is made possible. In the process of economic growth, investment not only determines the rate of capital accumulation, but also leads to technical progress, since most modern technological innovations are embodied in new capital goods. On the other hand, as was observed in Chapter 2, business cycles in Japan were basically investment-led during the high-growth period of the 1950s and 1960s (see also Table 9.7 below). Clearly, it is essential to understand the behaviour of investment in order to grasp the movements of the Japanese economy in both the short run and the long run.

Section 7.1 starts by briefly discussing why the Japanese firms invest so much. It emphasizes the importance of real factors compared with the (possibly) low cost of capital. There then follows an overview of investment in Japan. An important point to note is that investment has almost always been higher in Japan than in other developed countries. Equally notable, however, is the fact that investment experienced a 'structural' change around 1970. Drawing upon the analysis in Chapter 2, factors that can account for these important facts are then explored.

Despite its importance, it is notoriously difficult to pin down how investment is determined. Accordingly, Section 7.2 considers theories of investment. It is shown that under reasonable conditions the usual q theory of investment does *not* hold. It then becomes possible to explain why real factors such as current sales or profits are often found to be more important than changes in the discount factor in empirical investment functions. The relationship between the stock market and investment is discussed, and the proposition that stock prices can be 'too volatile' relative to investment decisions, is clarified.

Finally Section 7.3 estimates industry investment functions based on the theoretical analysis in Section 7.2. The estimation results are on the whole in accord with our theory. In particular, the significant effects of shipments and the positive effects of real factor prices imply that firms were demand-constrained during the 1970s and 1980s.

7.1 OVERVIEW

The level of investment, measured for convenience as a proportion of GNP, has been high in Japan by international standards (Table 7.1). In fact, in 1988 Japan outran the United States even in terms of the absolute amount of investment, despite the fact that the Japanese economy is roughly just one-half the size of US economy in terms of both population and GNP. Given this situation, at one of the so-called 'Structural Impediments Initiative' meetings held in Washington (on 3 November 1989), US officials went so far as to urge Japan to curb investment for fear of the possibility that greater investment might create overcapacity, which in turn could put pressure on the already 'excessive' Japanese exports.

Why Do Japanese Firms Invest So Much?

A natural question arises as to why the Japanese firms invest so much. US businessmen and policy-makers are fond of blaming the relatively low US investment on the fact that American firms must pay a higher cost of capital than their Japanese rivals. Despite extensive research, however, evidence on the differeces in the cost of capital across the two countries is not clear-cut. A careful analysis by Ando and Auerbach (1988), for example, led to the following weak conclusion: 'The cost of capital in Japan may be fairly close to its

Table 7.1. Investment: an international comparison

	Japan	USA	W. Germany	UK
Investment/GNP (%)				
1975–81	15.2	11.1	8.1	11.5
Investment in 1988[a]				
US$ billion	498.0	488.4	147.7	114.8
Investment/GNP (%)	17.4	10.0	12.2	13.5

[a] Nominal base.

Source: National Income and Product Accounts.

counterpart in the United States or it may be substantially lower than it is in the United States, and if it is lower, we are quite uncertain of its maginitude.' In any case, it would be an issue in its own right if the cost of capital differed significantly and persistently across countries in the age of free international capital mobility.

On top of the ambiguity concerning the magnitude of the differences in the cost of capital between Japan and the United States, it is also very unclear how significantly the cost of capital affects investment. Section 7.2 will explain that real factors are likely to be much more important than financial factors, including the cost of capital as a determinant of investment.

Real factors that are suppossed to sustain high investment in Japan are several. As was fully explained in Chapter 2, the high growth of domestic demand was perhaps the most important factor during the 1950s and 1960s. In the 1970s and 1980s, an increase in the real prices of inputs such as labour and energy on the one hand and IC-based innovations on the other induced Japanese firms to make labour-/energy-saving investments (see Section 7.3). There are also several factors on the part of the firm that have contributed to high investment.

The good labour relations enjoyed in Japanese firms, for example, is often mentioned as a factor facilitating labour-saving investment, for the characteristically Japanese job rotations (*haichi tenkan*) make it possible to avoid labour dismissals. A dramatic example is the introduction of the computerized printing system by newspaper companies. In Japan, Asahi Shimbun started the development of the new computerized system in collaboration with IBM in 1965, and finally completed it in 1980. During the nine years between 1972 and 1980, management and labour had more than 250 meetings. There were no dismissals of workers: 716 out of 1,336 workers were moved to other jobs, while the remainder were left engaged in the production of magazines using the old system. In contrast, an attempt to introduce a computerized printing system by *The Times* of London in 1986 provoked workers to a long and bitter strike.

The long-term horizons of Japanese management are another often mentioned factor which supposedly contributes to vigorous investment. In contrast, US management is blamed for its short-term horizons. Dertouzos *et al.*, for example, in *Made in America*, argue as follows:

> The disparity in time horizons is caused by more than a difference in interest rates and required dividend yields. There is evidence, difficult to quantify

but ultimately convincing to us, that other forces also drive American business to excessive preoccupation with immediate profit, even to the sacrifice of long-term opportunities. . . . They [business executives] say they feel themselves pushed in the short-sighted direction, against their own better judgment, by the fear that development and investment policies oriented toward the long term will be undervalued by the market and leave their firm vulnerable to takeover. We are persuaded by the argument that the wave of hostile takeovers and leveraged buyouts has contributed to an exaggerated focus on short-term returns. . . . We have found no shortage of executive bonuses geared to yearly or even semiannual performance. (Dertouzos *et al.* 1989: 53, 62)

The opposite holds for Japanese management. Hostile take-overs and leveraged buyouts are very rare, and tend to be regarded almost as indecent acts in Japan. An increase in share prices, in fact, does not rank high in surveys of corporate objectives. Hayes and Abernathy (1980), in their interesting article entitled 'Managing our Way to Economic Decline', point out that 'our experience suggests that, to an unprecedented degree, success in most industries today requires an organizational commitment to compete in the market place on technological grounds—that is, to compete over the long run by offering superior products'. This simple rule is exactly the motto of most Japanese firms, particularly in manufacturing industry.

In passing, Hayes and Abernathy maintain that what they call the 'new management orthodoxy' is responsible for a pervasive myopia in American industry:

During the past two decades American managers have increasingly relied on principles which prize analytical detachment and methodological elegance over insight, based on experience, into the subtleties and complexities of strategic decisions. As a result, maximum short-term financial returns have become the overriding criteria for many companies. . . . This preoccupation with control draws support from modern theories of financial portfolio management. Originally developed to help balance the overall risk and return of stock and bond portfolios, these principles have been applied increasingly to the criterion and management of corporate portfolios—that is, a cluster of companies and product lines assembled through various modes of diversification under a single corporate umbrella. (Hayes and Abernathy 1980: 70–1).

The warning of Hayes and Abernathy echos what Keynes said forty years earlier:

Most, probably, of our decisions to do something positive, the full consequences of which will be drawn out over many days to come, can only be taken as a result of animal spirits—of a spontaneous urge to action rather than inaction, and not as the outcome of a weighted average of quantitative benefits multiplied by quantitative probabilities. Enterprise only pretends to itself to be mainly actuated by the statements in its own prospectus, however candid and sincere. Only a little more than an expedition to the South Pole, is based on an exact calculation of benefits to come. Thus, if the animal spirits are dimmed and the spontaneous optimism falters, leaving us to depend on nothing but a mathematical expectation, enterprise will fade and die;—though fears of loss may have a basis no more reasonable than hopes of profit had before. (Keynes 1936: 161–2)

Right, or wrong, most Japanese firms in manufacturing are very committed to the object of manufacturing. And vigorous investment is a manifestation of their 'animal spirits'. Having explained some of the microeconomic factors that most likely sustain the high rate of investment of the Japanese firm, we return to macroeconomic overview.

Investment and the Japanese Economy

Fig. 7.1 makes it possible to see changes in the investment–GNP ratio in Japan in a long-term perspective. Compared with the experience of the United States, investment in Japan has been much higher on average, but more volatile. Table 7.2 shows the

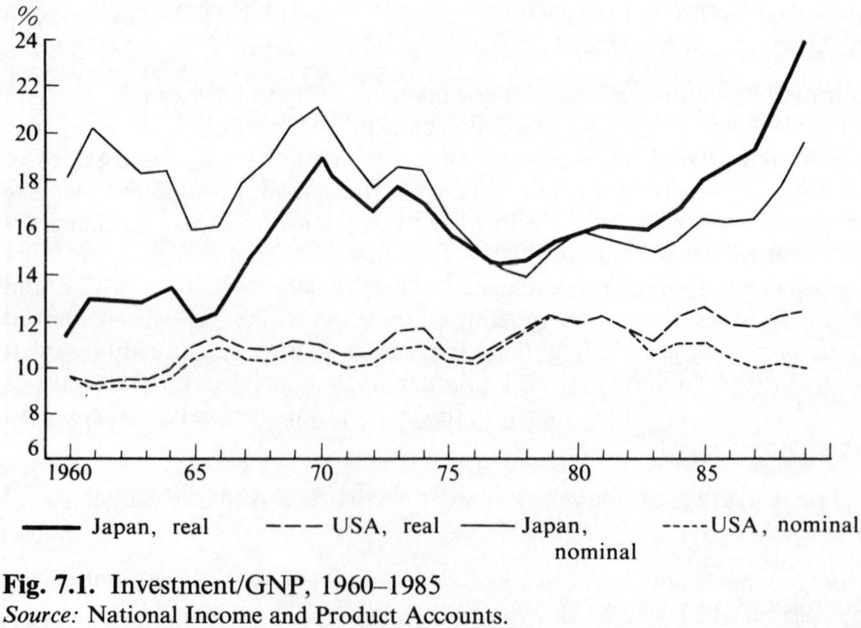

Fig. 7.1. Investment/GNP, 1960–1985
Source: National Income and Product Accounts.

Table 7.2. Means and standard deviations of fixed investment/GNP, Japan and the United States, 1960–1986

	(1) Means (%)	(2) s.d. (%)	(3) (2)/(1)
Japan			
Nominal			
1960–86	17.0	2.0	0.118
1960–73	18.5	1.5	0.081
1974–86	15.5	1.1	0.071
Real			
1960–86	15.3	2.1	0.137
1960–73	14.7	2.4	0.163
1974–86	16.0	1.2	0.075
United States			
Nominal			
1960–86	10.5	0.9	0.086
1960–73	10.0	0.6	0.060
1974–86	11.1	0.7	0.063
Real			
1960–86	11.0	0.9	0.082
1960–73	10.5	0.7	0.067
1974–86	11.6	0.7	0.060

Source: SNA.

standard deviations and variation coefficients of investment–GNP ratios of Japan and the United States. The standard deviations (1960–86, real terms), for example, are 2.1% for Japan and 0.9% for the United States. Japan's investment is much more volatile than its US counterpart.

Fig. 7.1 also reveals that the nominal and real investment–GNP ratios diverged much more markedly in Japan throughout the period than in the United States. The differences between these two series reflects the fact that the price index of capital goods and the GNP deflator changed at different rates. The pattern of the divergence shown in Fig. 7.1 indicates that the relative prices of capital goods in Japan kept declining, particularly in the 1960s and 1980s. This continuous decline in the relative price of capital goods is thought to have been a factor encouraging Japanese investment. At the same time, the significant decline in the relative price of capital goods can be interpreted as a fall of the price of tradables against that of non-tradables. Its implications for the equilibrium exchange rate will be fully explained in Chapter 8.

In both nominal and real terms, the investment–GNP ratio peaked in 1970, but in 1960 the figure was much higher in nominal terms than in real terms. As a result, the effect of the 1965 recession appears more clearly in nominal terms. In the 1980s, the ratio began to appear higher in real terms than in nominal terms, and from 1987 onwards, it exceeded the 1970 peak in real terms. Somewhat counter to our intuition, the average investment ratio was in fact higher for the low-growth period of 1974–87 than for the high-growth period of 1960–73.

Although the level of investment has on average been high even after the Japanese entered the 'age of low growth' in the 1970s, volatility in the level of investment significantly diminished in comparison with the high-growth period (Table 7.2). The decline in volatility is more significant in real terms than in nominal terms.

Chapter 2 has already explained why this decline in volatility occurred. To recapitulate the analysis in that chapter, it is argued that the single most important determinant of investment has been final demand. In the 1950s and 1960s, high growth in the domestic demand for consumer durables was the key factor. This demand for consumer goods was in turn supported by a rapid increase in the number of households in Japan, arising from the process of urbanization and/or industrialization, as well as by simultaneous increases in income on the one hand and decreases in the prices of consumer goods, brought about by technological progress and/or capital accummulation, on the other. In this macroeconomic 'virtuous cycle', economy-wide factors spurred investment, and as a result, strong parallels in investment across industries are observed (Table 2.14 above). Necessarily, the variance of aggregate investment was large.

This 'virtuous cycle' of high investment and high growth in domestic demand disappeared as the 'reserve army' in the agricultural sector dried up and most households became 'saturated' with the then-existing consumer durables in the late 1960s. The steel industry, which led the Japanese economy during the 1950s and 1960s, best illustrates the rapid economic growth and its end. Fig. 7.2 shows investment (in real terms) in the Japanese steel industry. As in the case of the petrochemical industry (Table 1.3 above), the steel industry too had faced 'structural change' during the years preceding the first oil shock in 1973.

The level of investment in the economy as a whole continued to be high in the low-growth period beginning in the 1970s. Investment in this period, however, was driven by different factors from those

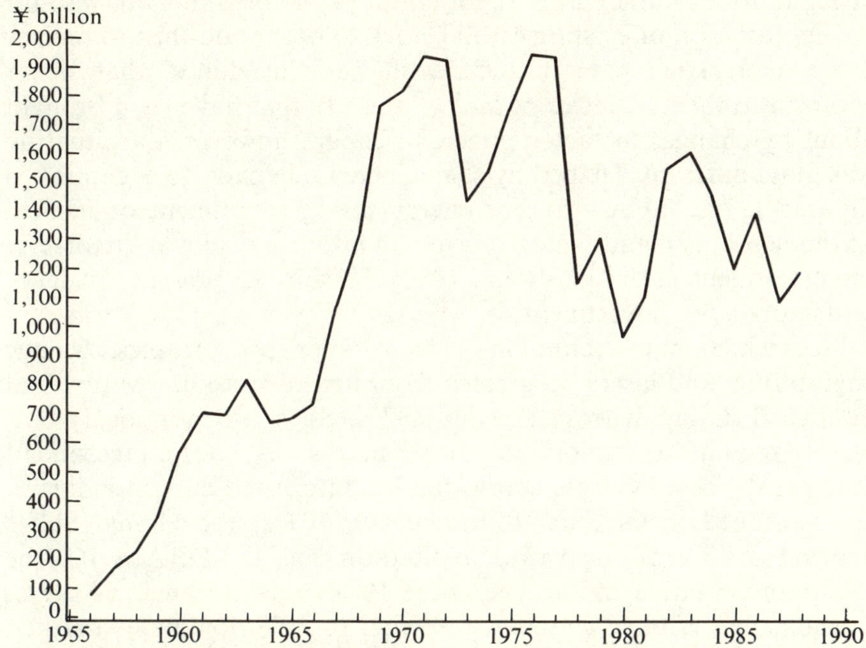

Fig. 7.2. Investment in the steel industry, 1955–1990
Billions of yen in 1980 constant prices.
Source: Economic Planning Agency.

operating in the high-growth period of the 1950s and 1960s. First, firms in many industries, facing demand constraints in the goods market, raised the level of investment in order to save on rising real labour/energy costs (see Section 7.3). Certainly, increases in demand helped in this regard too, though during this period the demand was not domestic but to a large extent export-led. Indeed, the VAR analysis in Chapter 2 (Table 2.25) suggests that the high level of investment in this period was most likely triggered by an increase in exports centring on the machinery industries. The reason for this close relationship between factor substitution and demand growth lies in the 'putty–clay' technology: before a piece of capital is built and put into use, there may be a substantial degree of substitutability between labour and capital, but after the capital is put into place, there may be very limited substitutability.[1] With no increase in

[1] See Johansen (1959) and Bischoff (1969, 1971). Bischoff shows that, even with a unitary elasticity of substitution, the putty–clay technology can explain why we find that investment responds more quickly to changes in output than to changes in the cost of capital in empirical Jorgensonian neoclassical models of investment.

demand, for example, firms might find it profitable simply to wait for the depreciation of existing capital stock to occur and then to replace those depreciated capital items with new 'machines' that better conform to the new levels of factor intensity that have been brought about by changes in factor prices. In Japan, however, the situation was quite different. Helped by sharp increase in exports beginning in the mid-1970s, labour- and/or energy-saving investment flourished. In this sense, demand factors played an important role in factor-saving investment in the 1970s and 1980s. Section 7.3 presents evidence on factor-saving investment.

Meanwhile, new technologies such as microelectronics, genetic engineering, and lasers progressed from invention to innovation and flourished in Japan from the mid-1970s. Such a continuously outwardly moving technological frontier necessarily boosts investment. Perhaps the best example here is the IC (integrated circuit) industry, as mentioned in Chapter 2. In the late 1970s, the United States controlled 85% of the world market for the 4K DRAM IC, the then-representative model. Japanese IC companies such as NEC, Toshiba, and Hitachi, in seeking to enter this US-dominated market, maintained very high levels of investment: the average investment–sales ratio was 25% in Japanese firms compared with 17% in their US counterparts during 1977–86. In 1984, investment in the Japanese IC industry amounted to some ¥800 billion ($3 billion) and for the first time exceeded investment in the steel industry, which throughout the post-war period had maintained the highest level of investment of any manufacturing industry. Because of this massive investment, the Japanese IC companies were able to achieve virtual domination of the world market by the end of the 1980s: whereas in 1982 the world market share of 64K IC was Japan 55% *v.* the USA 40%, in 1988, with 1M ICs, it became Japan 90% *v.* the USA 5%. Investment of the Japanese IC companies peaked in 1990, however. Thereafter, amid the deep recession beginning 1991, the Japanese firms curtailed their investment by 30%–50%. Meanwhile US and Korean firms carried out vigorous investment, and in 1992 INTEL became the world's largest IC producer once again. Investment is always and everywhere the key for competitiveness.

In any case, such driving forces of investment as technological progress and increases in factor prices have been largely industry-specific, as industries began to differ more and more in terms of their technology and factor intensity. As a result, inter-industry covariances of changes in investment became smaller or even negative in the low-growth period compared with the relatively high positive values in the 1950s and 1960s (see Table 2.14 above). This meant that changes in investment among industries tended to cancel each other out, making *aggregate* investment more stable in the 1970s and 1980s than it had been in the 1950s and 1960s. This is in spite of the fact that the level of aggregate investment was on average about the same in the two periods.

The macroeconomic overview of investment presented here has put the main emphasis on *real* factors, such as aggregate demand, technological progress, and real factor prices. The next section attempts to explain why real factors can be expected to be more important than financial factors in the investment decisions of firms.

7.2 THE THEORY OF INVESTMENT

Despite its importance, it is notoriously difficult to explain satisfactorily how investment is determined. Keynes's *General Theory* (1936) provides a suitable starting-point for an examination of the modern theory of investment. In Chapter 11 of the *General Theory*, Keynes argued that the level of investment is determined in such a way that the marginal efficiency of capital is equated with the market rate of interest. In this case the marginal efficiency of capital is defined as the rate of discount that would make the present value of the series of returns expected from the capital asset during its life just equal to its replacement cost.

Keynes's theory was later criticized by Lerner (1944) and Haavelmo (1960) for its crucial confusion of investment with capital stock. This criticism also applies to the neoclassical model of investment developed by Jorgenson (1963). Jorgenson's model explicitly introduces the production function and factors prices into the analysis, but, resting on the concept of the 'desired capital stock', it fails to derive the investment function.

Perhaps not surprisingly, a satisfactory investment function can be derived only by taking into account the cost of adjusting capital. In particular, the convex adjustment cost function concept is meant to capture the notion that, the more rapid is an increase in a firm's capital stock, the higher is the marginal adjustment cost associated with this investment. This idea was first formalized by Eisner and Strotz (1963) and then later elaborated as explicit models by Lucas (1967), Gould (1968), and Uzawa (1969). In these models, the optimal investment for a firm is determined in such a way that the shadow price of capital is equal to the marginal adjustment cost.[2]

The q *Theory*

Meanwhile, building on the idea put forward by Keynes in chapter 12 of the *General Theory*, Tobin (1969) advanced the *q* theory. This theory can be summarized as follows:

> The neoclassical theory of corporate investment is based on the assumption that the management seeks to maximize the present net worth of the company, the market value of the outstanding common shares. An investment project should be undertaken if and only if it increased the value of the shares. The securities markets appraise the project, its expected contributions to the future earnings of the company and its risks. If the value of the project as appraised by investors exceeds the cost, then the company's shares will appreciate to the benefit of existing stockholders. That is, the market will value the project more than the cash used to pay for it. If new debt or equity securities are issued to raise the cash, the prospectus leads to an increase of share prices. (Tobin and Brainard 1977: 242)
>
> [Thus] the rate of investment—the spread at which investors wish to increase the capital stock—should be related, if to anything, to *q*, the value of capital relative to its replacement cost. (Tobin 1969: 330)
>
> Economic logic indicates that a normal equilibrium value for *q* is 1 for reproducible assets which are in fact being reproduced, and less than 1 for others. Values of *q* above 1 should stimulate investment, in excess of requirements for replacement and normal growth, and values of *q* below 1 discourage investment. (Tobin and Brainard 1977: 238)

It was subsequently pointed out by Abel (1979) and Yoshikawa (1980), among others, that the *q* theory is formally equivalent to the dynamic models of Lucas (1967), Gould (1968), and Uzawa (1969). The shadow price of capital obtained in a standard model is nothing but the marginal *q*.

One issue surrounding the theory is a possible divergence between the marginal *q*, which is relevant for investment decisions and the average *q*, which can be constructed by using asset prices observable in the market. Hayashi (1982*a*) derived conditions under which average *q* and marginal *q* are equal. The Hayashi conditions, for resting on the fact that integration is a linear operator, require that, for average *q* and marginal *q* to be equal, both the revenue func-

[2] See excellent surveys of investment theory by Nickell (1978) and Abel (1990).

tion and the adjustment cost function must be linearly homoegenous in the variables involved. Among other things, the Hayashi conditions imply that the production function must be homogeneous of degree one, and also that imperfect competition must be ruled out in the goods market. Under these conditions, the equality of average q and marginal q holds if *disembodied* technical progress occurs.

On the other hand, it is easy to show that the equality of average q and marginal q is not obtained when *embodied* technological progress occurs. Note that the standard model that Hayashi worked with rules out embodied technical progress. Embodied technology makes it possible for the marginal q, which provides the incentive for investment, even to move in the opposite direction from average q. A good example is the sharp increase of energy prices after the oil embargo, which reduced quasi-rents on existing energy-intensive capital goods, and thereby average q, but stimulated investment in new, more efficient capital. All in all, it seems unlikely that marginal q and average q are equal. But on the other hand, one might expect average q and marginal q to move on average in the same direction, to the extent that the stock market and investment are positively correlated.

In any case, Tobin's q theory has gained substantial popularity as a theory of investment in recent years, and in several countries a number of empirical investment equations embodying the q approach have been estimated.[3] There are at least two reasons for this popularity. First, all the information relevant for investment decisions is conveniently summarized in a single variable called q. Moreover, aside from the difficulty of possible divergences between marginal and average q, this q can be constructed by using asset prices observable in the market. Thus, the q approach has the merit of possessing a simple theoretical structure, and it also easily lends itself to empirical implementation. Secondly, the q theory is formally equivalent to dynamic models of investment and therefore has a solid microeconomic foundation.

Despite these appealing features, several puzzles and problems associated with the q approach have arisen in empirical studies.

1. Without exception, empirical q equations contain lagged qs, or they show low Durbin–Watson statistics if no lags in q are

[3] See Ciccolo (1975), von Furstenberg (1977), and Summers (1981), among others, for the USA; Oulton (1981) and Bruno and Sachs (1982) for the UK; and Asako and Kuninori (1989) and Hayashi and Inoue (1991) for Japan.

introduced.[4] Note that only current q should matter in the ordinary q theory.

2. The performance of empirical q equations is often reported to be 'poorer' than simple accelerator-type models (see Clark 1979).
3. In many countries investment is known to be highly correlated with *current* 'real' variables such as profits, output, or capacity utilization rate. Abel and Blanchard (1983*a*), for example, include the profit rate together with q in their investment equations and find that current profit rate is always quite significant and that in some cases q even turns out to be insignificant. Fig. 7.3 shows investment relative to capital stock together with the profit rate for the Japanese manufacturing industry. A glance at the figure reveals that they are highly correlated: the correlation coefficient is in fact 0.49. Jorgenson (1971), surveying a number of empirical investment equations, writes: 'real output emerges as the single most important determinant of investment'. His verdict is indeed borne out by Table 7.3, which shows investment demand functions for seven OECD countries. On the whole, output is very significant, whereas the cost of capital is often insignificant and/or has the wrong sign.

Problem 1 above and the Abel–Blanchard finding in problem 3 lead to a reconsideration of the conventional q theory unless one resorts to measurement errors in the data and/or the constructed q variables as a source of explanation. Problems 2 and 3 are obviously related to each other and do not necessarily contradict the q theory, but at least they beg an explanation within the context of the q theory.

Liquidity Constraints

Traditionally, problems 2 and 3 have been explained by the existence of liquidity constraints including increasing costs of external borrowing (see Kalecki 1937; Meyer and Kuh 1957; Steigum 1983). With a constraint on external borrowing, investment would be determined basically by the availability of funds, and therefore would be highly correlated with current profits.

Earlier studies of investment and cash flow such as Meyer and Kuh (1957), however, suffered from a serious drawback because shocks to current profits signal two things: an increase in current liquidity on

[4] See e.g. von Furstenberg (1977); Hayashi (1982*a*); Bruno and Sachs (1982).

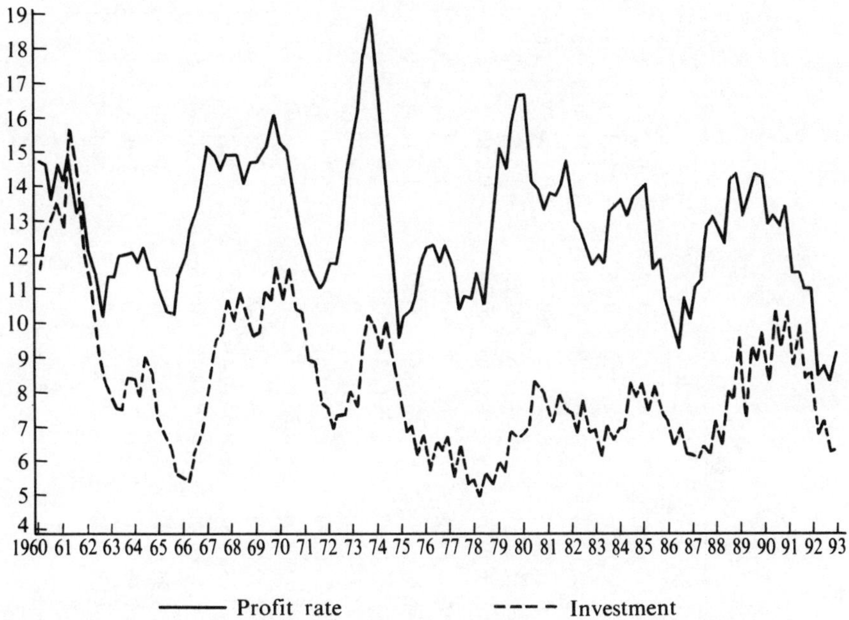

Fig. 7.3. Investment and the profit rate, 1960–1993
Source: Ministry of Finance, *Statistics on Corporations* (Hojinkigyo Tokei Kiho).
Data are for manufacturing industry. The profit rate is defined as the sum of operating profit and depreciation divided by fixed tangible assets outstanding at the end of the previous quarter. Investment is gross investment relative to fixed tangible assets outstanding at the end of the previous quarter.

the one hand, and an improved expectation of future profitability on the other. In fact, in the Economic Planning Agency survey, firms' expectations on future sales are found to be very highly correlated with current sales (Nakamura 1970). Therefore the significance of current profits or sales in the investment function does not necessarily endorse the liquidity constraint hypothesis. In attempting to avoid this problem, recent studies, such as Fazzari *et al.* (1988) and Hoshi *et al.* (1991), explicitly introduce firm heterogeneity ('small' *v.* 'big' firms) into the analysis and show that cash flow variables do indeed substantially improve investment functions. Specifically, they find that cash flow plays a more important role in the investment decisions of small firms, most of which are outside *Keiretsu* (Japanese industrial groups). This finding resurrects Shinohara's argument (1961) that, in the 'dual' structure of the Japanese financial market, small firms, unlike big firms, are subject to liquidity constraints.

Table 7.3. Investment demand functions

Dependent variable: first difference of the log of the capital stock

	DQ	*DQ*(−1)	*DU*[a]	DU(−1)[a]	DK(−1)[b]	*DK*(−2)	Adj.R^2	AR[c]	Chow[d]
USA	0.076 (8.8)	—	0.008 (4.4)	—	1.07 (1.4)	—	0.92	0.9 (0.8)	0.1
	0.064 (9.4)	—	0.005 (3.6)	—	1.38 (5.5)	− 0.38 (5.5)	0.96	− 1.6 (1.5)	0.4
	0.062 (8.2)	0.01 (1.2)	0.005 (3.5)	0.0 (0.2)	1.27 (2.2)	− 0.26 (1.9)	0.96	− 1.8 (1.4)	0.6
Japan	0.094 (5.3)	—	− 0.0 (0.7)	—	0.91 (4.0)	—	0.98	0.8 (0.8)	1.6
	0.077 (4.4)	—	− 0.0 (0.8)	—	1.23 (2.1)	− 0.31 (2.8)	0.98	− 1.3 (0.9)	0.7
	0.093 (5.2)	0.037 (1.9)	− 0.002 (2.2)	0.003 (3.4)	1.06 (0.5)	− 0.18 (1.6)	0.99	0.4 (0.3)	1.1
Germany	0.047 (5.2)	—	− 0.0 (0.8)	—	0.94 (2.0)	—	0.96	1.8 (1.8)	0.4
	0.043 (5.5)	—	− 0.0 (1.6)	—	1.34 (3.0)	− 0.40 (3.6)	0.97	1.6 (1.4)	0.5
	0.044 (5.4)	0.008 (0.8)	− 0.0 (1.7)	0.0 (0.2)	1.26 (1.8)	− 0.34 (2.4)	0.97	− 2.0 (1.0)	0.8
France	0.069 (9.0)	—	− 0.0 (0.3)	—	0.93 (3.8)	—	0.99	0.9 (0.8)	0.4
	0.068 (9.9)	—	− 0.0 (1.0)	—	1.20 (2.4)	− 0.28 (3.3)	0.99	− 0.3 (0.4)	1.0
	0.067 (9.4)	0.012 (1.0)	− 0.0 (0.4)	− 0.0 (1.6)	1.09 (0.6)	− 0.18 (1.3)	0.99	(0.3)	3.0
Italy	0.061 (9.4)	—	− 0.0 (1.2)	—	0.89 (4.2)	—	0.97	1.3 (1.2)	0.5
	0.060 (8.8)	—	− 0.0 (1.2)	—	0.93 (0.8)	− 0.04 (0.4)	0.97	1.3 (1.1)	1.4
	0.062 (8.4)	− 0.013 (1.0)	− 0.0 (1.0)	0.0 (0.6)	1.07 (0.4)	− 0.16 (1.1)	0.97	(2.0)	0.9
UK	0.031 (3.4)	—	− 0.0 (0.3)	—	0.94 (1.4)	—	0.93	1.0 (0.8)	0.5
	0.031 (3.4)	—	− 0.0 (0.4)	—	1.16 (1.0)	− 0.21 (1.5)	0.93	− 2.2 (0.9)	0.8
	0.028 (3.0)	0.01 (0.9)	− 0.0 (0.4)	− 0.0 (0.6)	1.08 (0.4)	− 0.14 (0.8)	0.93	(0.1)	0.6

Canada	0.040 (2.4)	—	0.0 (0.5)	—	0.97 (0.3)	—	0.78	4.3 (4.8)	2.2
	0.024 (1.8)	—	−0.001 (0.9)	—	1.49 (3.8)	−0.62 (4.9)	0.86	2.1 (1.9)	2.2
	0.024 (1.6)	−0.02 (1.0)	−0.0 (0.5)	−0.0 (0.2)	1.52 (3.9)	−0.69 (4.7)	0.86	1.5 (0.9)	1.7

Definition of variables: Q is real business sector output: U is the (user) cost of capital; K is the business sector capital stock. All variables are in logarithms except U, which is in levels for Italy (because some observations are negative). D indicates the first difference.

All regressions have a constant term.

Sample period: 1968 (I)–1988 (II) (semi-annual data).

Absolute values of t-statistics are given in parentheses.

[a] Numbers reported as 0.0 or −0.0 are less than 0.001 in absolute value.

[b] The t-statistics in this column refer to the null of 1, rather than the customary null of 0. Thus, in the first regression for the USA, the coefficient on $DK(-1)$ is not significantly different from 1 (although it is significantly different from 0) at 5%.

[c] This column reports two tests for first-order autocorrelation. The first figure is the Durbin-h (represented by an ellipsis if it is imaginary, as in the third regression for France). The figure in parentheses is from an alternative test involving a regression of the investment equation residuals against their own lag and all explanatory variables. The figure reported is the absolute value of the t-statistic of the coefficient on the lagged residual, which, if significant, indicates autocorrelation.

[d] This column reports the F-statistics for a break in 1978 (I). Critical values at 5% are $F(4,30) = 2.7$; $F(5,30) = 2.5$; $F(6,30) = 2.4$.

Source: Ford and Poret (1990).

The finding that cash flow plays a role in the investment decisions of small firms is also consistent with the often propounded theory of why many US firms in the IC industry have gone out of business since the mid-1970s. In Japan, ICs are produced by big electric companies like NEC, Toshiba, and Hitachi. In the United States, however, except for TI, integrated circuits are produced mainly by small venture capital business in Silicon Valley, California.[5] The IC industry has experienced very severe four-year cycles called 'silicon cycles'. The theory is that, when the industry is hit by deep recession, Japanese firms, being of sufficient size, can continue to carry out investment; small US firms, by contrast, suffer from liquidity shortages and have to go out of business. This hypothesis underlines the potential importance of liquidity constraints facing small firms.

Without denying the possibility that some firms, particularly small firms, are subject to liquidity constraints, it is argued that this constraint may be of only secondary importance when the economy is seen as a whole.

First, liquidity constraints should pertain to stocks, not to flows. Fig. 7.4 shows firms' liquidity positions defined as the sum of cash, deposits, and net trade credit balances relative to quarterly *gross* investment. (This ratio becomes higher, of course, if it is taken relative to net investment.) In the 1970s and 1980s, on average, the ratio was greater than 10. Is it then reasonable to suppose that firms holding liquid assets ten times their gross investment (on a quarterly basis) are forced to curtail investment because of liquidity shortages?

Secondly, on more micro level, Ruggles (1993) points out that for the United States 'the balance sheets of many enterprises indicate that they have financial resources available to undertake capital formation in periods when nevertheless they are contracting their capital outlays'. Thus, he concludes that 'the willingness of enterprises to undertake capital formation is, in most periods, a more important determinant than the availability of funds'.

Thirdly, the liquidity constraint hypothesis suggests two possible ways in which changes in investment are generated in macroeconomic models. An obvious candidate is a monetary, or *LM*, shock. Another possibility would be that some demand components other than investment itself fuel the economy, and thereby eventually boost investment through increased sales. The analysis from Chapter 2, however, indicates that real shocks have been more important than

[5] IBM and other big US firms do produce ICs but only for internal use.

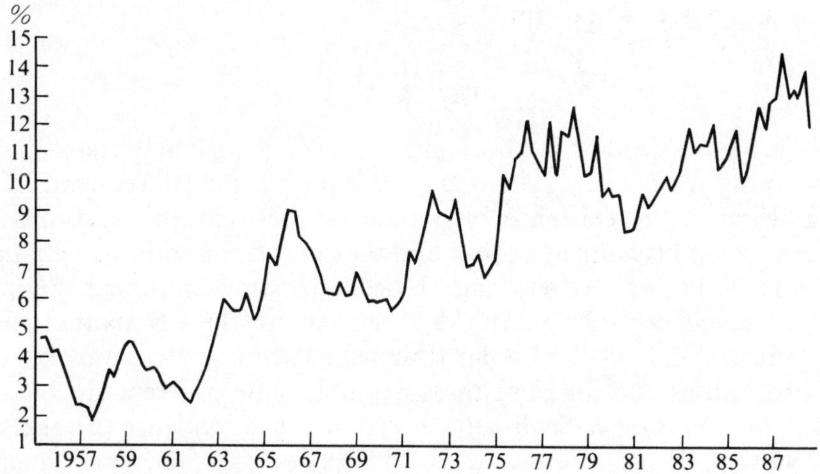

Fig. 7.4. Firms' liquidity, 1957–1987

$$\text{Liquidity} = \frac{\text{Firm's cash and deposit holdings + net inter-firm credit}}{\text{Net investment}}$$

Source: Ministry of Finance, *Statistics of Corporations* (quarterly).

monetary shocks in post-war Japanese business cycles. Also, in the second case, one would expect investment to tend to lag behind aggregate economic activities. But in fact, unlike in the United States, fixed investment in Japan, measured by order of equipment, *leads* aggregate economic activities.[6] This fact lends credence to the view that changes in real demand other than investment affect investment decisions, through anticipations of future profitability rather than liquidity.

Finally, the correlation between investment and operating profits is higher than that between investment and current profits: for 1983(II)–1990(IV), the figures are 0.32 and 0.08, respectively. The importance of a liquidity constraint would indicate otherwise. Once again, the evidence suggests that profits affect investment through the firm's expectations of future sales rather than its liquidity position.

All in all, it is here maintained that real factors play a more important role than liquidity constraints in determining investment decisions. Therefore, without denying the possible importance of liquidity constraints in certain firms or groups of firms, a different

[6] Equipment order is a leading indicator in the Japanese diffusion index of business cycles compiled by the Economic Planning Agency. Shipment of equipment is a lagging indicator.

approach to explaining the above-mentioned problems surrounding the q theory seems warranted.

The Model

For this purpose, I wish to emphasize two important observations concerning investment and its determinants in the subsequent analysis. First is the existence of a time lag between the decision to undertake an investment project and the completion of it, namely the 'time-to-build' or delivery lag. Indeed, existing empirical studies suggest seven- to eight-quarter delivery lags for the US manufacturing industry.[7] The second point is that the two basic determinants of q—profit rates and discount rates—exhibit quite different stochastic properties. More specifically, there is some casual evidence (presented below) that the time series of profit rates contains more permanent as opposed to temporary movements than does the time series of discount rates.

The introduction of these two features—delivery lags for capital and differences in the time-series properties of profit rates and discount rates—leads to a crucial modification of the standard q theory of investment. First, the existence of delivery lags results in an investment equation that depends on a distributed lag of q. Secondly, to the extent that the time-series properties of profit rates and discount rates are different, investment depends on the distributed lags of profit rates and discount rates *separately*. Thirdly, investment is correlated more with profit rates than with discount rates if profit rates contain more permanent movements than discount rates. These results not only solve the above-mentioned problems of the existing q theory, but they also provide a reasonable interpretation of the often loosely stated view that the stock market is 'too volatile'.

We consider investment decisions of the firm in the stochastic model. The starting-point of the model is the following one-period return to the firm's equity:

$$\frac{V_{t+1} + D_t}{V_t} = 1 + R_t \,, \tag{1}$$

where V_t is the stock value of the equity-financed firm at the beginning of the period t; stockholders are assumed to receive

[7] See e.g. Hall (1977) and Mayer (1960). Abel and Blanchard (1983*b*) present some evidence suggesting that, except for the petroleum industry, delivery lag structures are very similar across sectors. Time-to-build and delivery lags are emphasized by Kydland and Prescott (1982) in their model of aggregate fluctuation.

dividend D_t at the *end* of period t; then R_t defined by (1) is the *ex post* rate of return on a firm's share from t to $t + 1$. We assume that all variables are measured in real terms. Naturally, R_t is not known at the beginning of period t.

Letting the information set available to stockholders at the *beginning* of period t (end of $t - 1$) be Ω_{t-1}, we can derive the *ex ante* rate of return as follows:

$$\frac{E(V_{t+1} + D_t|\Omega_{t-1})}{V_t} = 1 + E(R_t|\Omega_{t-1}) \tag{2}$$

Note that $V_t \in \Omega_{t-1}$ but R_t, V_{t+1}, $D_t \notin \Omega_{t-1}$. Solving (2) recursively forward gives the value of the firm's equity at the beginning of t:

$$V_t = E\left(\sum_{j=0}^{\infty}\left\{\prod_{i=0}^{j}[1 + E(R_{t+i}|\Omega_{t+i-1})]^{-1}\right\}D_{t+j}|\Omega_{t-1}\right). \tag{3}$$

For notational simplicity, we define the compound discount factor ρ_τ^j as follows:

$$\rho_\tau^{j+1} = \prod_{i=0}^{j}[1 + E(R_{\tau+i}|\Omega_{\tau+i-1})]^{-1}\ (j = 0, 1, 2, \ldots, \tau = t, t+1, \ldots). \tag{4}$$

We note that

$$\begin{aligned} &\rho_t^1 \in \Omega_{t-1},\ \rho_t^{j+1} \notin \Omega_{t-1} && \text{for } j > 0 \\ &\rho_{t+i}^j \notin \Omega_{t-1}, && \text{for all } i, j > 0. \end{aligned} \tag{5}$$

Turning to dividend D_t, we assume that it is, in real terms, equal to the following cash flow of the firm:

$$D_{t+j} = r_{t+j}K_{t+j} - (\rho_{t+i}^1)^{-1}\,\phi(I_{t+j-k}). \tag{6}$$

The first term in (6) is profit, which is the product of the profit rate r_{t+j} and capital stock K_{t+j} at the end of $t + j$. Such a profit function would be justified if the production function exhibited constant returns to scale and capital were the only fixed input.[8] The profit rate r_{t+j} is taken as stochastic (($r_{t+j} \notin \Omega_{t-1}$ for all $j \geqslant 0$). The second term in (6) is investment expenditure including adjustment costs. The presence of $(\rho_{t+j}^1)^{-1}$ simply indicates that payment on investment

[8] It can be derived in the following situation, too. Suppose that the firm faces constraint on its sales with an individual demand curve $X = \theta P^{-\eta}(\eta > 0)$, where X, P, and θ denote sales, product price, and a stochastic shift parameter, respectively. Assuming that capital is the only input and that quantity produced is equal to sales, we have $X = K^\gamma$. Profits in this case would be $PX = \theta^{1/\eta}K^{\gamma(1-1/\eta)}$. Therefore, to the extent that capital exhibits increasing returns to scale ($\gamma > 1$), $\gamma(1 - 1/\eta) \simeq 1$ is possible, and this generates a type of profit function assumed in the text. Changes in profit rate r in this case are, of course, caused by fluctuations in the demand condition θ.

goods is made at the beginning of the period $t + j$.[9] The function ϕ, reflecting increasing adjustment costs, is assumed to be convex:

$$\phi(0) = 0, \qquad \phi' > 0, \qquad \phi'' > 0. \tag{7}$$

An important feature of the model is the existence of a time-to-build or delivery lag (k periods). That is, we assume that the technology of the investment goods industry is of point input–output type. Therefore, I_{t+j-k}, the order of investment goods in period $t + j - k$ for delivery in period $t + j$, enters the ϕ function in period $t + j$. Here, for expository simplicity, it is assumed that investment expenditure is made when the project is completed and starts being productive, i.e. starts to become a part of K_{t+j}. More general patterns of investment expenditure do not change the basic point of our analysis.

Noting the existence of the k-period time-to-build, we have the following equation for capital accumulation:

$$K_{t+j} = K_{t+j-1} + I_{t+j-k}. \tag{8}$$

Using (3), (4), and (6), we can rewrite the value of the firm's stock, V_t, as follows:

$$V_t = E\left\{\sum_{j=0}^{\infty} \rho_t^{j+1}[r_{t+j}K_{t+j} - (\rho_{t+j}^1)^{-1}\phi(I_{t+j-k})] | \Omega_{t-1}\right\}. \tag{9}$$

The firm is assumed to maximize V_t subject to equation (8), the initial capital stock, K_{t-1}, the known function ϕ, and the stochastic processes of r_{t+j} and ρ_t^j. This problem is analytically equivalent to the one analysed by Hartman (1972). To solve it, we consider the following Lagrangean form:

$$L = E\left\{\sum_{j=0}^{\infty} \rho_t^{j+1}[r_{t+j}K_{t+j} - (\rho_{t+j}^1)^{-1}\phi(I_{t+j-k})] + \sum_{j=0}^{\infty} E(\rho_t^j | \Omega_{t-1}) q_{t+j}(K_{t+j-1} + I_{t+j-k} - K_{t+j}) | \Omega_{t-1}\right\}. \tag{10}$$

We will clarify the meaning of the costate variables shortly. Assuming the existence of an internal solution, we note that it is unique. For optimality, the following must hold:

$$\phi'(I_t) = E(q_{t+k} | \Omega_{t-1}) \tag{11}$$

[9] Abel and Blanchard (1983*b*) present some evidence suggesting payments in equal instalments between the quarter following the order and the quarter of delivery. Essential parts of our analysis, however, will not change so long as *some* of the payments are made after order.

$$q_{t+i} = E\left(\sum_{j=0}^{\infty} \rho_{t+i}^{j+1} r_{t+i+j} | \Omega_{t+i-1}\right) \qquad (i = 0, 1, 2, \ldots) \qquad (12)$$

Equation (12) says that q_{t+i} is the marginal contribution of K_{t+i} in terms of the expected present value evaluated at the beginning of $t + i$. The costate variable in (10), $E(\rho_t^j | \Omega_{t-1}) q_{t+j}$, is therefore this marginal contribution evaluated at the beginning of period t. Note that $q_t \in \Omega_{t-1}$ but $q_{t+i} \notin \Omega_{t-1}$ for $i > 0$.

When there is no time-to-build ($k = 0$), (11) and (12) reduce to the usual q theory of investment. That is, from (11), I_t depends on q_t, which is known at the beginning of t. With significant time-to-build, however, the q theory must be modified in the way indicated by (11) and (12). In particular, the current investment *decision* I_t depends on a future marginal q expected at the beginning of t. Alternatively, investment *expenditure* (or simply investment, in the usual sense of the term) at t, $\phi(I_{t-k})$, depends on current q_t expected at the beginning of $t - k$, rather than on current q_t itself.

The Implication of the Model

We now proceed to discuss the implications of the modified q theory of investment for empirical investment equations. The major feature of our model as derived in the last section is that *investment orders depend on the expectation of a future q rather than on today's q.* Consequently, any empirical estimator of the individual equation boils down to modelling the expectations formation of future q. Depending on the way this is done, we obtain different investment equations. We shall see that features of the investment equations derived from our model conform very well to the stylized facts about investment summarized above.

In order to discuss the expectations formation process, we must first specify the information set possessed by the firm and asset-holders.[10] In what follows we shall deal with two cases: (i) the case where the information set includes observations of current and past q only; (ii) a more reasonable case where the information set includes current and past profit rates and discount rates in addition to q. The analysis of the first case will show that running investment on *current* q only produces inconsistent estimates and that lagged values of q as well as current q must be included in investment equations. The analysis of the second case will reveal that an investment equation

[10] We shall not here pursue the implications of the possibly divergent information held by the firm and asset-holders.

including current and past profit rates and discount rates separately produces a better fit than an equation with current and past q only.

We first restrict the information set of the firm to $\tilde{\Omega}_{t-1} = (q_t, q_{t-1}, \ldots)$ and analyse the appropriate specification of the investment equation under this assumption. We further assume that q_t has the following moving average representation (this is legitimate if q is stationary):

$$\begin{aligned} q_t &= a_0 u_t + a_1 u_{t-1} + \ldots \\ &= (a_0 + a_1 L + \ldots .)u_t \qquad (13) \\ &= A(L)u_t, \end{aligned}$$

where L is the one-period lag operator, u_t is a white-noise process, and A(L) is assumed to have a one-sided inverse. Then the expectation of q_{t+k} given $\tilde{\Omega}_{t-1}$ can be calculated as follows:

$$\begin{aligned} E(q_{t+k}|\tilde{\Omega}_{t-1}) &= E[A(L)u_{t+k}|\tilde{\Omega}_{t-1}] \\ &= a_k u_t + a_{k+1} u_{t-1} + \ldots \\ &= \tilde{A}(L)u_t \qquad (14) \\ &= \tilde{A}(L)A^{-1}(L)q_t \\ &= B(L)q_t \\ &= b_0 q_t + b_1 q_{t-1} + \ldots, \end{aligned}$$

where $B(L) = \tilde{A}(L)A^{-1}(L)$. Using (14) in (11) and assuming that ϕ is quadratic, we obtain

$$I_t = C_0 + C_1 B(L) q_t. \qquad (15)$$

Equation (15) shows that *current investment orders are a function of current and past* q *instead of a function of current* q *only*. Similarly, current investment expenditure, $X_t(= I_{t-k})$, can be written as

$$X_t = C_0 + C_1 B(L) q_{t-k}. \qquad (16)$$

In either case, we see that investment depends on a distributed lag of q and that an investment equation that includes only current q is mis-specified.[11] Thus, (15) and (16) are consistent with the stylized fact that lagged q as well as current q are important in empirical investment equations.

[11] It might be noted that (11) can be directly estimated by assuming rational expectations and using an *ex post* value of q and some instruments for it. However. by proceeding as in the text, we can see clearly why lagged q should be significant in an equation with current and lagged q.

We next observe that, if a variable Z_t in the information set is not perfectly correlated with q but is correlated with q_{t+k}, it will be significant when added to (15). Also, the fit of this equation, including the Z variable, is better than that of (15). As reasonable candidates for such variables, we consider the profit rate and the discount rate.

Roughly speaking, q can be decomposed into two parts, one that depends on expectations of future profit rates and one that depends on expectations of future discount rates. When there are no delivery lags, q is a sufficient statistic; i.e. it summarizes all the information necessary for determining the level of investment. However, when the expectation of a future q determines investment because of the presence of delivery lags, q will no longer be a sufficient statistic. As we shall see below, using current and past profit rates and discount rates separately yields a better forecast of future q than using merely current and past q.

Formally, we assume that the information set is $\Omega_{t-1} = (q_t, q_{t-1}, \ldots, r_{t-1}, r_{t-2}, \ldots, \rho_t^1, \rho_{t-1}^1, \ldots)$. For notational simplicity, we define

$$\beta_S = \rho_S^1 = \frac{1}{1 + E(R_S|\Omega_{S-1})}. \tag{17}$$

Then,

$$q_t = E\left[\sum_{j=1}^{\infty}\left(\prod_{i=0}^{j}\beta_{t+i}\right)r_{t+j}|\Omega_{t-1}\right]. \tag{18}$$

By linearizing this around $(\bar{q}, \bar{\beta}, \bar{r})$, we obtain

$$\begin{aligned} q_t &= \bar{q} + \frac{\bar{r}}{1-\bar{\beta}}\sum_{i=0}^{\infty}\bar{\beta}^i E(\beta_{t+i} - \bar{\beta}|\Omega_{t-1}) + \sum_{i=0}^{\infty}\bar{\beta}^{i+1} E(r_{t+i} - \bar{r}|\Omega_{t-1}), \\ &= \bar{q} + L_t(\beta) + L_t(r), \end{aligned} \tag{19}$$

where $L_t(\beta)$ and $L_t(r)$ are defined by the equation.[12] Therefore, we obtain

$$\begin{aligned} E(q_t|\Omega_{t-k-1}) &= \bar{q} + E[L_t(\beta)|\Omega_{t-k-1})] + E[L_t(r)|\Omega_{t-k-1}]. \qquad (20) \\ &= \bar{q} + \frac{\bar{r}}{1-\bar{\beta}}\sum_{i=0}^{\infty}\bar{\beta}^i E(\beta_{t+i} - \bar{\beta}|\Omega_{t-k-1}) \\ &\quad + \sum_{i=0}^{\infty}\bar{\beta}^{i+1} E(r_{t+i} - \bar{r}|\Omega_{t-k-1}) \end{aligned}$$

[12] Abel and Blanchard (1983*a*) report that (19) provides a reasonable approximation to q_t. Shiller (1981) uses a similar approximation.

Consequently, X_t depends on the right-hand side of (20) and I_t on the same formula advanced by k periods. If the stochastic processes β and r are stationary, expectations of future β and r can be written as functions of past β and r. Hence investment is a function of past β and r. However, one might think that, if we rearrange it in an appropriate way, such an expression could be written as a function of past q only. We now show, by using a simple example, that in general this is not the case. That is, investment cannot be written as a function of q only.

Consider the case where r and R (or β) are represented by the following stochastic processes:

$$\begin{aligned} r_t &= r_t^* + \varepsilon_t^1 + \rho_1 \varepsilon_{t-1}^1 \qquad & r_t^* &= r_{t-1}^* + u_t^1 \\ R_t &= R_t^* + \varepsilon_t^2 + \rho_2 \varepsilon_{t-1}^2 \qquad & R_t^* &= R_{t-1}^* + u_t^2, \end{aligned} \tag{21}$$

where $(u^1, u^2, \varepsilon^1, \varepsilon^2)$ are i.i.d. and are uncorrelated at all lags.[13] The crucial assumption we make is that firms observe r_t and R_t but not $(u_t^1, u_t^2, \varepsilon_t^1, \varepsilon_t^2)$ directly; therefore, they must infer the values of these from observations of r_t and R_t. Note that (17) can be linearized to yield

$$\beta_S = 1 - E(R_s|\Omega_{s-1}).$$

Therefore,

$$\beta_s = 1 - ({}_{s-1}R_{s-1}^* + \rho_2\, {}_{s-1}\varepsilon_{s-1}^2), \tag{22}$$

where a subscript in front of a variable indicates the date at which the expectation of the variable is taken. (Thus, for example, ${}_sX_t = E(X_t|\Omega_s)$. Note also that

$$\begin{aligned} {}_t r_{t+1} &= {}_t r_t^* + \rho_1\, {}_t\varepsilon_t^1 \\ {}_t r_{t+j} &= {}_t r_t^* \qquad \text{for } j > 2 \\ {}_t \beta_{t+j} &= -\, {}_{t-1}R_{t-1}^* \qquad \text{for } j > 1 \end{aligned} \tag{23}$$

Formulae (22) and (23) show that u^1 and u^2 are permanent shocks to r and R, while the ε are temporary shocks.

Using (22) and (23), we can calculate q_t and $E(q_t|\Omega_{t-k-1})$ as follows:

[13] In general, u^1 and u^2 on the one hand, and ε^1 and ε^2 on the other, might be correlated. This will make the analysis more complicated. However, there will be no essential changes in the qualitative aspects of the conclusions.

$$q_t = \bar{q} + L_t(\beta) + L_t(r).$$

$$= \bar{q} + \frac{\bar{r}}{(1-\bar{\beta})^2}(-{}_{t-1}R^*_{t-1}) - \frac{r\rho_2}{(1-\bar{\beta})}\,{}_{t-1}\varepsilon^2_{t-1} \tag{24}$$

$$+ \frac{1}{(1-\bar{\beta})}\,{}_{t-1}r^*_{t-1} + \rho_1\,{}_{t-1}\varepsilon^1_{t-1}$$

$$E(q_t|\Omega_{t-k-1}) = \bar{q} + E[L_t(\beta)|\Omega_{t-k-1})] + E[L_t(r)|\Omega_{t-k-1}]$$

$$= \bar{q} + \frac{\bar{r}}{(1-\bar{\beta})^2}(-{}_{t-k-1}R^*_{t-k-1}) + \frac{1}{(1-\bar{\beta})}({}_{t-k-1}r^*_{t-k-1}) \tag{25}$$

For later purposes, it is important to note that q_t contains the expectations of temporary disturbances ε^1 and ε^2 while $E(q_t|\Omega_{t-k-1})$ does not; that is, q_t is affected by temporary movements in the profit and discount rates. On the other hand, investment, which depends on $E(q_t|\Omega_{t-k-1})$, is not affected by these movements.

There remains the task of expressing the right-hand side of (25) in terms of realized values of R (or β) and r. We assume that agents use the Kalman filter technique to infer R^* and r^* given past observations of R and r. The exact formulae are shown in Appendix 1, where it may be seen that, after a large number of observations,

$$\begin{aligned} {}_tr^*_t &= \sum_{i=0}^{\infty} A^1_i r_{t-i} \\ {}_t\varepsilon^1_t &= \sum_{i=0}^{\infty} B^1_i r_{t-i} \\ {}_tR^*_t &= \sum_{i=0}^{\infty} A^2_i R_{t-i} \\ {}_t\varepsilon^2_t &= \sum_{i=0}^{\infty} B^2_i R_{t-i}. \end{aligned} \tag{26}$$

Substituting (26) into (25), and noting that X_t depends on $E(q_t|\Omega_{t-k-1})$, we obtain

$$X_t = C^1_0 + \frac{C_1\bar{r}}{(1-\bar{\beta})^2}\sum_{i=0}^{\infty}(-A^2_i)R_{t-k-1-i} + \frac{C_1}{(1-\bar{\beta})}\sum_{i=0}^{\infty}A^1_i r_{t-k-1-i}. \tag{27}$$

Thus, *investment is a function of past values of the profit rate and the discount rate*. This means that an investment equation containing only

q (such as equation (16)) is mis-specified so long as the information set of the firm contains observations of R and r. This, in turn, implies that, if either R or r is added to an equation containing only q, it will turn out to be significant. This result is consistent with the third empirical regularity about investment equations summarized above. This observation does not mean, however, that the q theory is incorrect. Our theory of investment is essentially based on the q approach. What we have shown, rather, is that *q will no longer be a sufficient statistic for investment as soon as delivery lags are introduced.*

Testing the Model

A natural way to test our model is to estimate equation (11) directly. We could run a future q on current investment and other variables such as profits; if the model is correct, only the current investment variable would be significant. However, such a regression cannot be easily carried out in practice because the length of delivery lags is not the same across industries.[14]

Let us then accept the modified q approach as the basic framework for the study of investment, and proceed to examine what must be shown in order to explain the empirical regularities of investment discussed previously. Among the regularities mentioned, the most important seems to be the significance of real variables such as profits (see Fig. 7.3). Once the modified q approach is accepted, showing the importance of profits in explaining the behaviour of investment boils down to showing that the profit rate contains more permanent movements than the discount rate.

More precisely, the relative importance of the two variables in the investment equation is reflected in the coefficients A_i^1 and A_i^2. Differences in these coefficients in turn reflect differences between the stochastic processes of the discount and profit rates. Therefore, we now present a rather casual but still suggestive empirical analysis to check the stochastic properties of the two variables. For this purpose, we have constructed the two variables in the following way. (Precise definitions are given in Appendix 2.) The profit rate is current profits divided by the value of capital stock (manufacturing sector, Japan).

[14] When the length of the delivery lag is different across industries, current investment would be a weighted average of the expectations of future q. One could then test the model by running a future q on a distributed lag of q, current investment, and other variables. However, the power of such a test would be quite low unless good instruements are chosen and the q on the left-hand side has a large weight in the determination of current investment.

The discount rate is a weighted average of *ex post* equity and debt discount factors where the weights reflect the debt–equity ratio of the Japanese manufacturing sector. The *ex post* equity discount factor is the one-period rate of return on equity consisting of the dividend–price ratio and the rate of capital gain. The *ex post* debt discount factor is the one-period return on long-term Japanese Telephone and Telegraph Company bonds. This one-period return also includes capital gains or losses. The sample period is 1964(II)–1981(IV) on a quarterly basis.

The two variables are plotted in Figs. 7.5 and 7.6. It is at once apparent that the discount rate exhibits much more variation than the profit rate. What is important for our purpose, however, is the *expected* discount rate rather than the discount rate itself. (Recall that q depends on *expected* one-period discount rates.) Also, the coefficients in (27) are determined by the relative importance of temporary and permanent fluctuations of the variables. The more permanent (temporary) the majority of the fluctuations of a variable, the more (less) important is the variable in the investment equation. This is because the right-hand side of (27) is the expectation of the permanent components of the discount and profit rates.

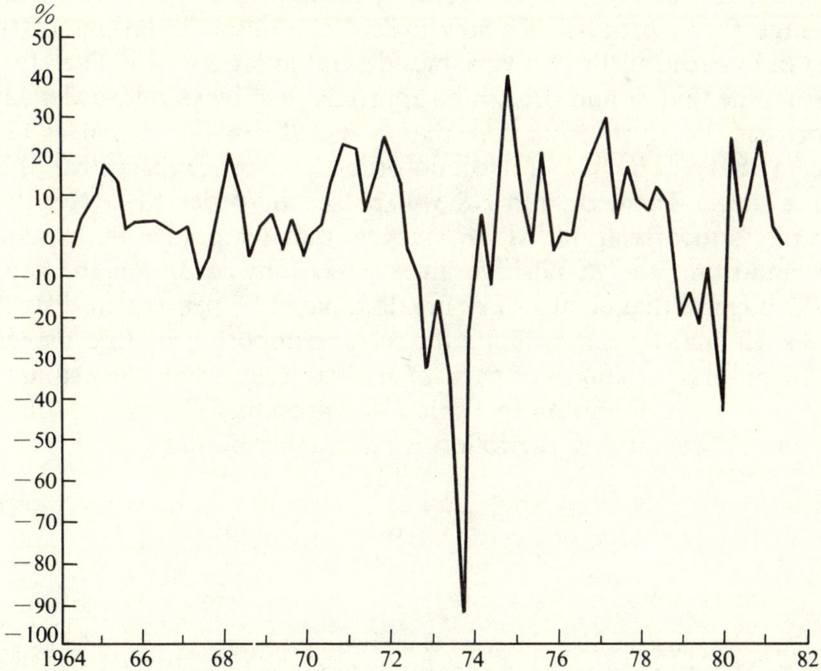

Fig. 7.5. Movements of the discount rate, 1964–1982

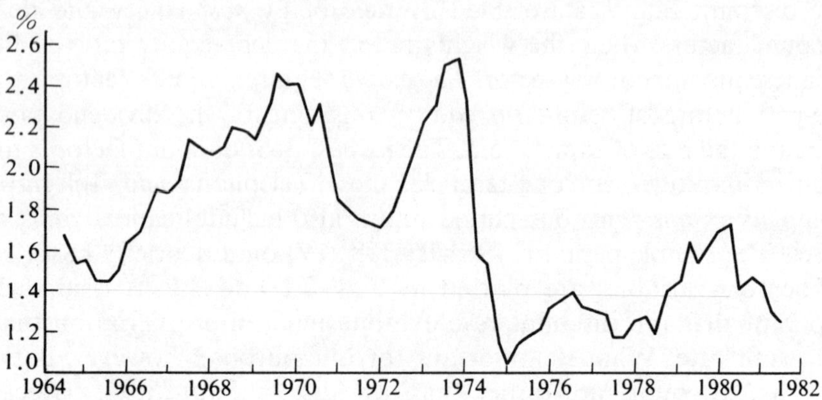

Fig. 7.6. Movements of the profit rate, 1964–1982

Sample autocorrelations of the variables and the first differences of the variables are presented in Table 7.4. The pattern of the autocorrelations of the profit rate is quite close to that of a random walk process (see Nelson and Plosser 1982: table 2). The autocorrelations of the discount rate die out quickly, indicating that it is a moving average (MA) process of a low order. The autocorrelations of the first differences of the two variables die out at lag 3 or 4.[15] Therefore, we assume that Δr and ΔR can be approximated by second-order MA processes. We further assume that r and R can be written as (21) except that u_t^1 and u_t^2 are second-order MA processes rather than white noise. Then, Δr and ΔR will be second-order MA. Negative sample autocorrelations of ΔR, suggest that temporary fluctuations are important for R; positive autocorrelations of Δr, on the other hand, suggest that changes in r are dominated by permanent disturbances. In fact, we can estimate the relative importance of permanent and temporary changes of each of the variables using the estimates of ρ_1 and ρ_2 for Δr and ΔR in Table 7.4. Appendix 3 shows that, under reasonable conditions, the following inequality holds:

$$\frac{\sigma_{\varepsilon^1}^2}{\sigma_{u^1}^2} < \frac{\sigma_{\varepsilon^2}^2}{\sigma_{u^2}^2}, \tag{28}$$

[15] Assuming that the first differences of the two variables are second-order moving average (MA) processes, we can test the significance of higher-order autocorrelations (the Bartlett test): see e.g. Nelson (1973). It turns out that ρ_3 and ρ_4 and most of the higher-order autocorrelations of ΔR and Δr are insignificant.

where notations in (21) are used and σ^2 stands for variances. That is, the profit rate contains more permanent (less temporary) fluctuations than the discount rate.

We have thus presented a piece of evidence that the profit and discount rates possess different stochastic properties and that *fluctuations in the profit rate can be regarded as more permanent than those of the discount rate.* This has an important implication for the explanatory power of the two variables in the investment equation (27). In order to see this more clearly, let us take the extreme case of (28), where the profit rate contains only permanent shocks and the discount rate contains only temporary shocks. That is,

$$\frac{\sigma_{u^1}^2}{\sigma_{\varepsilon^1}^2} \to \infty, \quad \frac{\sigma_{u^2}^2}{\sigma_{\varepsilon^2}^2} \to 0. \tag{29}$$

In Appendix 1 it is shown that, under (29), we obtain[16]

$$\begin{aligned} &A_0^1 \to 1,\ A_i^1 \to 0, \quad (\text{for } i > 1), \quad B_i^1 \to 0, \quad (\text{for all } i) \\ &A_i^2 \to 0, \quad (\text{for all } i), \quad B_0^2 \to 1,\ B_i^2 \to 0, \quad (\text{for } i > 1). \end{aligned} \tag{30}$$

Therefore, *the investment equation (27) will contain only the profit rate; the discount rate will have no explanatory power in the equation.*[17]

Table 7.4. Sample autocorrelations of profit and discount rates, 1964(II)–1981(IV)[a]

	DR	ΔDR	PR	ΔPR
T	71	71	71	71
ρ_1	0.47	−0.32	0.93	0.25
ρ_2	0.27	−0.16	0.83	0.24
ρ_3	0.25	0.22	0.70	0.10
ρ_4	−0.01	−0.01	0.56	0.01
ρ_5	−0.26	−0.29	0.41	−0.34
ρ_6	−0.20	0.13	0.32	−0.31
ρ_7	−0.28	−0.07	0.26	−0.28
ρ_8	−0.29	−0.13	0.24	−0.01

[a] DR, discount rate; PR, profit rate; Δ, first difference operator; T, number of observations.

[16] Here, we are assuming again that the permanent shocks u^1 and u^2 are serially uncorrelated.

[17] The analysis here can be interpreted as an extension of the Birch–Siebert (1976) 'permanent income' model of investment to the two-variate (profit and discount rates) case.

This extreme case would not be literally true, but it shows very clearly why the profit rate is often found to be more highly correlated with investment than is the discount rate. For one thing, the profit rate may contain more permanent fluctuations than the discount rate, as argued above. For another, the existence of delivery lags makes temporary fluctuations of the variables irrelevant in the determination of the level of investment.[18]

I must emphasize that delivery lags play a different role than adjustment costs. As is well recognized, the presence of adjustment costs makes the level of investment determinate. It also makes investment depend on the long-term interest rate or the entire term structure of interest rates, contrary to Hall (1977)'s argument that investment should depend only on the short-term interest rate. Even with the presence of adjustment costs, however, rationally determined investment must respond to transitory shocks, no matter how transitory they are, if there are no delivery lags: a standard stochastic model with adjustment costs such as Lucas and Prescott (1971) leads to the usual q theory. *It is the presence of delivery lags that makes transitory shocks irrelevant for investment decisions.* To the extent that the profit rate consists relatively more of permanent shocks than the discount rate, as suggested by the present analysis, it points to the relative importance of profit rate and other real variables in empirical investment equations.[19] To reiterate, the q theory does not hold in this case.

Financial Volatility and Investment

It is appropriate to discuss the relationship between financial volatility and investment in light of the present analysis. As a matter of theory, the q theory established a close link between stock price and investment. Some economists, however, have expressed concern

[18] Abel and Blanchard (1983*a*) report that temporary movements in the discount rate do not have sizeable impact of q even in the absence of delivery lags. This is because q or $L(\beta)$ in (19) is the sum of expected *future* discount rates. However, they simply estimate a low-order autoregressive model for the discount rate. This procedure might have resulted in underestimation of the importance of temporary movements in the discount rate and their contribution to q.

[19] This point is related to a difference in the effects of sales (quantity) constraints and capital costs on investment—a topic much debated in the literature on the neoclassical theory of investment: see Bischoff (1969). Bischoff has emphasized the importance of putty–clay technology. Our model, which emphasizes differences in the stochastic properties of the profit and discount rates, can be regarded as another explanation of differential impacts of quantity and capital cost variables on investment.

about using asset prices to construct q. Malinvaud, for example, argues as follows:

> The fundamental reason why Tobin's q might appear as a factor of investment behaviour is as a proxy for profitability. But we may fear that it is a poor proxy. Referring to Keynes's *General Theory*, chapter 12, we may say that q would be a good proxy if stock market evaluations would depend only on 'enterprise', i.e. on the 'state of long-term expectations', but that it is likely to be a poor proxy because these evaluations reflect also, to an unknown extent 'speculation'. (Malinvaud 1982: 12)

This point is, of course, related to the long-held view that the stock market is 'too volatile'.

Since Shiller's (1981) demonstration of the excess volatility of stock prices, many have studied the issue of the possible presence of 'bubbles' in financial markets, i.e. whether asset prices are rationally determined only by 'fundamentals'.[20] The weak point of this empirical research programme, however, lies in the treatment of the asset's rate of return. The return on assets or the discount factor is not usually included in the list of 'fundamentals' and is often merely assumed to be constant as in Shiller (1981). But, to the extent that the discount factor reflects, at least partly, the 'real interest rate', it also qualifies as a fundamental.

Despite this difficulty, a growing literature on financial volatility and bubbles, both theoretical and empirical, still suggests that stock prices can be, and are in fact, influenced not only by 'fundamentals' but also by 'fads', 'fashions', and 'investor sentiment'.[21] 'Investor sentiment' is able to affect stock prices because investors are largely concerned not with making superior long-term forecasts of the probable yield of an investment over its whole life, but with forecasting changes in the conventional basis of valuation a short time ahead of others. These short-term horizons of investors are the product of a well-developed financial market. The point is vividly illustrated by Keynes (1936: 151): 'It is as though a farmer, having tapped his barometer after breakfast, could decide to remove his capital from the farming business between 10 and 11 in the morning and reconsider whether he should return to it later in the week.' The source of possible trouble is of course that this sort of liquidity, available to

[20] For theory of financial bubbles, see Blanchard (1979), Harrison and Kreps (1978), and Tirole (1982).

[21] See e.g. Shiller (1984) and de Long *et al.* (1990).

asset-holders thanks to a well-developed financial market, is not available to real investment.

Given the possibility that financial bubbles are in fact present in the market, the important question then becomes one of determining how investment is affected by 'investor sentiment'. One may be tempted to argue, as Malinvaud (1982) (cited above) does, that share prices are too volatile to be closely related to investment. Although this argument is fairly widespread, it is usually put rather casually. Volatility stems from movements in the discount rate (see Shiller 1981; Grossman and Shiller 1981). But if there is no time-to-build, then investment decisions must actually follow this volatile discount rate. As long as investment is made in the interests of shareholders, companies must take account of the rate of return required by them, however volatile this discount rate may be (see Fisher and Merton 1984). This means that volatility of the discount rate *in itself* should not weaken the relationship between asset price and investment as long as rationality on the part of asset-holders and firms' managers is assumed. The assumption of time-to-build, however, entails a significant modification. We showed above that if (i) a time-to-build or delivery lag exists, and (ii) variations in the discount rate are dominated by temporary components, then investment is determined in such a way as to ignore temporary fluctuations in the discount rate.

Note that investment is still made in the interests of stockholders. With time-to-build, however, investment ordered today starts being productive only after a certain interval, and therefore rational investment decisions must regard temporary fluctuations in the discount rate as irrelevant. In contrast, asset-holders rationally respond to short-lived information if their time horizon is short enough. *Therefore stock prices can be 'too volatile' relative to investment decisions.* In order for this argument to hold, the assumption of time-to-build is crucial.

To the extent that 'investor sentiment' is short-lived, it is not expected to affect investment. It should be noted, however, that changes in share prices based on short-lived information are not necessarily 'bubbles'. Even when share prices are not 'too volatile', in the sense that they are determined as a discounted present value of a future dividend stream, they can still be called 'too volatile' relative to investment decisions. Conversely, 'investors' sentiments' or 'bubbles', if they persist long enough, should affect investment.

In any case, Morck *et al.* (1990) reports that, to a first approximation, swings in the stock market appear to be irrelevant for investment decisions by firms. Also, in a January 1988 survey, more than three-quarters of US top executives said that the stock market crash of October 1987 had not affected their investment plans. To the extent that changes in stock price were perceived largely as transitory by market participants, these findings are consistent with our analysis.

This section has explained why real factors are often found to be more important than financial factors in determining firms' investment decisions. In suggesting an important role for real factors in investment, the analysis here is consonant with the conclusion of Chapter 2.

7.3 FACTOR PRICES AND INVESTMENT

In the 1970s and 1980s, investment in Japan was much affected by rising real wages and energy prices. This section focuses on the relationship between real factor prices and investment. For this purpose, a theoretical model of investment built on the analysis in Section 7.2 is first presented, and then estimates are made of the investment functions for Japanese manufacturing industries.

The Model

The model presented below is similar to the one in the previous section and is based on the observation that the distinction between permanent and transitory shocks in the determinants is important. Using this model, the importance of sales, real wages, and real energy casts in determining investment in Japan is explored.

For this purpose, instead of (6), we first write net cash flow D_t in (3) as follows:

$$D_t = F(K_t, L_t) - W_t L_t - [1 + E(R|\Omega_{t-1})]^{-1}\phi(I_{t-k}), \tag{31}$$

where $F(K_t, L_t)$ is the amount of output or sales, and K_t and L_t are capital stock and variable input, respectively. Production function F is assumed to have the usual neoclassical properties; W_t is the real input price of L_t. As usual, both W_t and L_t can be vectors. The last term in (31) is investment expenditure including adjustment costs. The presence of the discount factor simply indicates that payment on investment goods is made at the beginning of period t. Because of a time-to-build or delivery lag (k periods), I_{t-k}, the order of investment goods for delivery in period t enters the ϕ function in period t. Here, just for expository simplicity, it is assumed that investment expenditure is made when the project is completed and starts being productive, i.e. when it starts to become a part of K_t. Noting the existence of a k-period time-to-build, we have equation (8) for capital accumulation.

Next, we assume a possible quantity constraint on the firm's sales:

$$Q_t > F(K_t, L_t), \tag{32}$$

where Q_t is exogenous stochastic sales. When the above inequality strictly holds the firm is said to be in the neoclassical regime, whereas with an equality it is in the quantity-constrained (or perhaps Keynesian) regime. As explained in Chapter 4, instead of two regimes, we can actually conceive that the relative importance of demand and supply constraints for the firm continuously changes depending on the level of inventory stock. Unfortunately, it is extremely difficult to integrate the analysis of Chapter 4 with the theory of investment. For simplicity of analysis, therefore, we assume two regimes.

The firm maximizes (3) under constraints (8), (31), and (32) with respect to I_t and L_t. W_t, R_t and Q_t, all stochastic, are taken as exogenous, together with suitable initial values of K_t. In general, the optimizing firm would anticipate a switch, or even switches of two regimes, in future. In the deterministic model, this possibility is explored by Precious (1985). In the stochastic model, however, it is simply too difficult to analyse to obtain interesting implications. In what follows, therefore, we assume that the firm is in either the neoclassical or the quantity-constrained regime. We must analyse these two possible regimes separately. As is usual, when the solution exists, it is unique under the strict concavity assumption.

Quantity-Constrained Economy

In this case, equality holds in constraint (32). The optimality condition for investment is given by

$$\phi'(I_t) = E(q_{t+K} | \Omega_{t-1}), \tag{33}$$

where the variable q_{t+k} can be interpreted as Tobin's marginal q, and is defined as follows:

$$q_{t+k} = E\left[\sum_{i=0}^{\infty} \rho_{t+k}^{i+1} \frac{W_{t+k+i} \dfrac{\partial F}{\partial K_{t+k+i}}}{\dfrac{\partial F}{\partial L_{t+k+i}}} \middle| \Omega_{t+k-1} \right]. \tag{34}$$

The marginal q for (34) is the discounted sum of future savings in labour costs arising from capital accumulation. In the present quantity-constrained regime, the firm can reduce labour costs while producing the same amount of output by increasing its capital stock. Note that q_{t+k} is stochastic as of time t. The optimality condition (33) then says that investment is determined in such a way that the expected value of q_{t+k} conditional on Ω_{t-1} is equal to the marginal adjustment cost of investment, $\phi'(I_t)$. Only in the degenerate case when $k = 0$, i.e. when there is no delivery lag or gestation period for investment (time-to-build), do we obtain the usual optimality condition involving the current non-stochastic q. With a time-to-build, however, the current investment decision I_t depends on the expected value of *future* marginal q evaluated at the beginning of time t. Alternatively, investment expenditure (or simply investment, in the usual sense of the term) at t, $\mathrm{INV}_t = \phi(I_{t-k})$, depends on the *expected value* of q_t evaluated at the beginning of $t - k$, rather than on current q_t itself:

$$\mathrm{INV}_t = \phi(I_{t-k}) = \psi[E(q_t|\Omega_{t-k-1})] \quad (\psi' > 0). \tag{35}$$

Our investment function is given by (34) and (35). To proceed further, it is useful to use the Cobb–Douglas illustration. Assume that the production function F is of the Cobb–Douglas type:

$$F(K, L) = K^{\alpha}L^{1-\alpha} \qquad (0 < \alpha < 1). \tag{36}$$

Then the marginal q, for (34) becomes

$$q_t = E\left[\left(\frac{1}{1-\alpha}\right)\sum_{i=0}^{\infty}\left(\prod_{j=0}^{i}\beta_{t+j}\right)W_{t+i}\left(\frac{Q}{K}\right)_{t+i}^{1/(1-\alpha)} \;\middle|\; \Omega_{t-1}\right], \tag{37}$$

where, for notational simplicity, we define

$$\beta_s = \rho_s^1 = \frac{1}{1 + E(R_s|\Omega_{s-1})}. \tag{38}$$

Although the right-hand side of (37) is a nonlinear function of β_t, W_t, Q_t, and K_t, we know that its linearization is not a bad approximation (see e.g. Abel and Blanchard 1986). Choosing the stable solution, and substituting K_t out by (8), the linearized q_t becomes

$$q_t = \bar{q} + \sum_{i=0}^{\infty}[a_i E(\beta_{t+i} - \bar{\beta}|\Omega_{t-1}) + b_i E(W_{t+i} - \bar{W}|\Omega_{t-1})$$
$$+ c_i E(Q_{t+i} - \bar{Q}|\Omega_{t-1})]. \qquad (a_i, b_i, c_i > 0 \text{ for all } i). \tag{39}$$

From (35), therefore, investment as of time t, INV_t, depends on

$$E(q_t|\Omega_{t-k-1}) = \bar{q} + \sum_{i=0}^{\infty} [a_i E(\beta_{t+i} - \bar{\beta}|\Omega_{t-k-1}) + b_i E(W_{t+i} - \bar{W}|\Omega_{t-k-1}) + c_i E(Q_{t+i} - \bar{Q}|\Omega_{t-k-1})]. \tag{40}$$

The important point is that investment is affected by only those parts of β_t, W_t, and Q_t that were *anticipated* k periods before. In other words, if Ω_{t-k-1} contains current and past values of β_t, W_t and Q_t, i.e. β_{t-k-i}, W_{t-k-i} and $Q_{t-k-i}(i \geqslant 1)$, then it is *not* β_{t-k-i}, W_{t-k-i}, and Q_{t-k-i}, but only the persistent or 'permanent' components of these variables, that affect investment. We also note that, in the quantity-constrained regime, an increase in the discount factor (or a decrease in the discount rate), an increase in the real price of variable input, and/or an increase in demand, if 'permanent', all *raise* investment. The empirical investment functions we will estimate are based on these observations.

The Neoclassical Economy

In this regime, inequality (32) holds strictly and the firm takes only the real factor price W_t and the discount factor β_t as given. The optimality condition (33) remains unchanged, and therefore we obtain the same investment function (35). However, the marginal q in this case is

$$q_t = E\left(\sum_{j=0}^{\infty} \rho_t^{j+1} \frac{\partial F}{\partial K_{t+j}} \,\middle|\, \Omega_{t-1}\right). \tag{41}$$

Here again we will use the Cobb–Douglas illustration. With the Cobb–Douglas production function, after linearization, (41) becomes

$$q_t = \bar{q} + \sum_{i=0}^{\infty} [d_i E(\beta_{t+i} - \bar{\beta}|\Omega_{t-1}) - e_i E(W_{t+i} - \bar{W}|\Omega_{t-1})]. \tag{42}$$

$$(d_i,\ e_i > 0 \text{ for all } i).$$

As explained previously, investment at time t, INV_t, depends on $E(q_t|\Omega_{t-k-1})$:

$$E(q_t|\Omega_{t-k-1}) = \bar{q} + \sum_{i=0}^{\infty} [d_i E(\beta_{t+i} - \bar{\beta} \mid \Omega_{t-k-1}) + e_i E(W_{t+i} - \bar{W}|\Omega_{t-k-1})]. \tag{43}$$

Note that, in the neoclassical regime, a permanent increase in W_t *lowers* investment. This result is in sharp contrast to that obtained in the quantity-constrained regime. In the quantity-constrained regime, the firm is on a particular isoquant; therefore an increase in W_t makes the firm substitute capital for labour and as a consequence raises investment. In the neoclassical regime, on the other hand, the firm is on a particular factor price frontier. In this case, an increase in W_t lowers profits and thereby discourages investment. *Changes in the real price of a variable input have opposing effects on investment, depending on whether the firm is in the quantity-constrained or neoclassical regime.*

Estimation of Investment Functions

On the basis of the theoretical analysis above, I estimated investment functions for Japanese manufacturing industries. The investment function is equation (35). The expected marginal q in (35) is given by (40) in the case of quantity-constrained regime and by (43) in the case of the neoclassical regime.

Our theoretical model indicates the importance of the distinction between permanent and transitory shocks in Q_t, W_t and β_t. In current practice, there is no generally accepted method of carrying out such decompositions. The approach used here is the Beveridge–Nelson (1981) decomposition. I assumed that the firm's information set Ω_{t-k-1} contains β_{t-k-i}, W_{t-k-i}, and Q_{t-k-i} $(i \geqslant 1)$ and also that in its investment decisions the firm responds only to what it perceives as the permanent components of the relevant variables. There is no knowing how the firm actually extracts the permanent components from the observed series. I simply applied the Beveridge–Nelson decomposition to the explanatory variables.

I estimated investment functions for Japanese manufacturing industries using quarterly data (1971(I)–1985(II)). Since investment in the 1970s and 1980s appears to have been governed by micro-specific factors, as argued in Chapter 2 and Section 7.1, it makes sense to estimate industry investment equations rather than an aggregate equation. Investment, I_t, is taken from the 'newly acquired fixed assets' series compiled by the Ministry of Finance. For demand variable Q_t, I used an index of shipments, S_t, published by the Ministry of International Trade and Industry. I identified labour and energy as variable inputs and defined the real wage, RW_t, and the real energy price, RE_t, as follows:

$$RW = \frac{(\textit{Index of total payment in cash to regular employees})}{(\textit{Index of total working hours of regular employees})} \qquad (44)$$
$$\times (\text{WPI } \textit{of domestic manufactured products})$$

$$RE = \frac{(\textit{Index of prices of imported oil, coal,} \text{ and } \textit{natural gas})}{(\text{WPI } \textit{of domestic manufactured products})} \qquad (45)$$

I also used the relative price of investment goods, *PI*, as an explanatory variable:

$$PI = \frac{(\text{WPI } \textit{of investment goods})}{(\text{WPI } \textit{of domestic manufactured products})}. \qquad (46)$$

Note that *PI* is implicit in function ψ in (35), and that investment is a decreasing function of *PI*. For simplicity, I assumed that *RE* and *PI* are the same across industries. I tried several cost-of-capital or interest-rate variables, corresponding to β, in my preliminary set of estimations; however, the results were not satisfactory, and therefore I dropped them from the final set of estimations presented below.

As the first step, I applied the Beveridge–Nelson decompositions to S_t, RW_t, RE_t, and PI_t. For this purpose, I first fitted the ARIMA (autoregressive integrated moving average) models to *S*, *RW*, *RE*, and *PI*. All the variables including *I* are in *natural logarithms*. The same notation is used for the logs of the variables. The final models were selected by Akaike's Information Criterion (AIC). It turned out that all the variables are first-order-integrated. Therefore only the ARMA parts are shown in Table 7.5.

Based on these models, I decomposed S_t, RW_t, RE_t, and PI_t into the Beveridge–Nelson permanent components denoted by S^*_t, RW^*_t, RE^*_t, PI^*_t, and the transitory components, $\tilde{S}_t$, $\tilde{RW}_t$, $\tilde{RE}_t$, $\tilde{PI}_t$. For reference, RW^*, $\tilde{RW}$, S^*, $\tilde{S}$ of the nonferrous metal

Table 7.5. ARIMA model of *S*, *RW*, *RE*, and *PI* [a]

Industries	*S*	*RW*	*RE*	*PI*
Nonferrous metals	MA (3)	AR (2)		
Chemicals	MA (4)	AR (2)		
Machinery	AR (4)	White noise		
Electrical machinery	MA (3)	MA (2)		
Transportation equipment	MA (2)	ARMA (3,1)	MA (3)	AR(4)
Paper, pulp	MA (4)	ARMA (2,1)		

[a] All variables were transformed with $\ln X_t - \ln X_{t-1}$ ($X = S_t$, RW_t, RE_t).

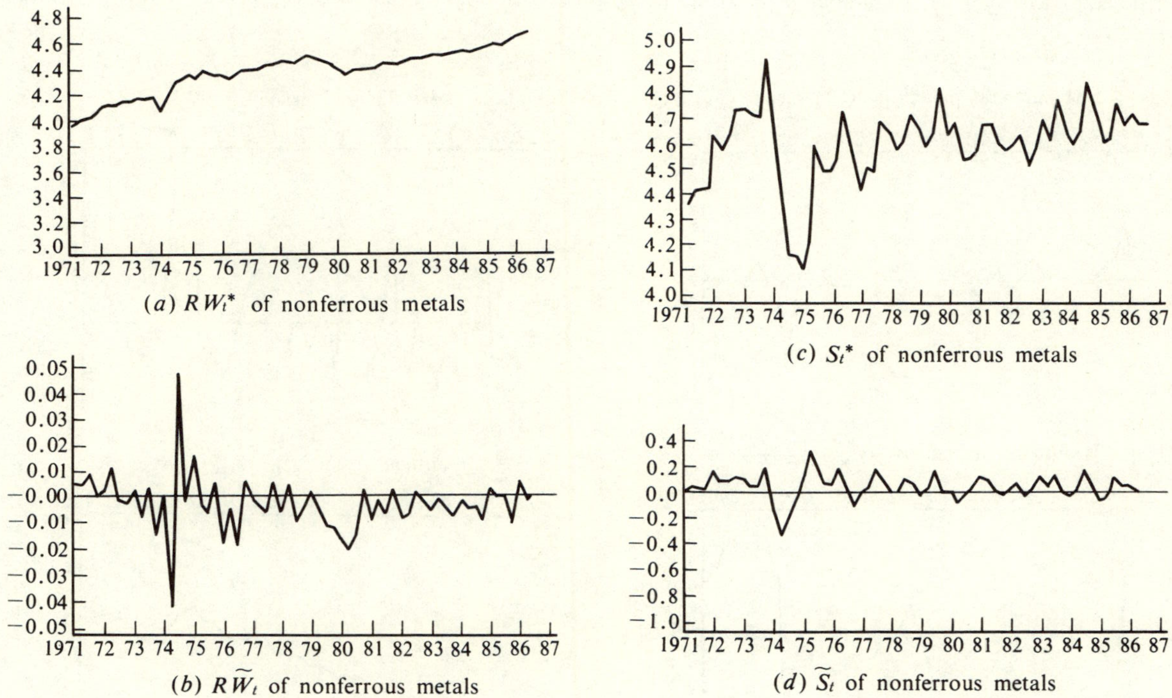

Fig. 7.7.
(*a*) RW_t^* of non-ferrous metals (*b*) $R\tilde{W}_t$ of non-ferrous metals (*c*) S_t^* of non-ferrous metals (*d*) $\tilde{S}_t$ of non-ferrous metals

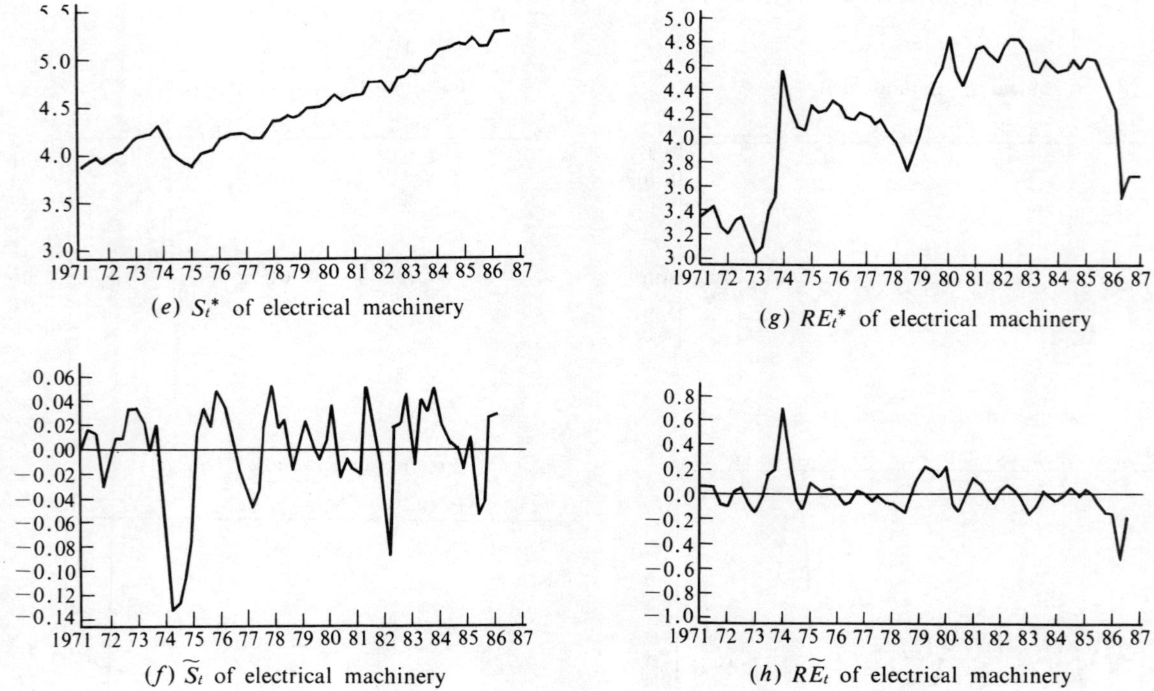

Fig. 7.7. (*Contd*)
(e) S_t^* of electrical machinery (*f*) $\tilde{S}_t$ of electrical machinery (*g*) RE_t^* of electrical machinery (*h*) $R\tilde{E}_t$ of electrical machinery

industry and S^*, $\tilde{S}$, RE^* and $\tilde{R}\tilde{E}$ of the electric machinery industry are illustrated in Fig. 7.7.

In the second step, I estimated industry investment equations using S_t^*, $\tilde{S}_t$, RW_t^*, $\tilde{R}\tilde{W}_t$, etc., rather than S_t, RW_t, RE_t, PI_t as explanatory variables. In addition to the six industries we have here, the steel and textile industries were included in the preliminary set of estimations. However, I did not succeed in obtaining satisfactory results for these two industries. It is interesting that these were proto-typical declining industries over the sample period. For example, the Japanese steel industry's capacity was 100 million tons in 1971; thereafter, the industry never tried to expand its capacity and has consistently suffered from overcapacity. The situation is very similar in the textile industry.

The final equations estimated for the six industries are shown in Table 7.6. In every case, I tried lags of from one to six periods. These lags correspond to delivery lags, k. The existing empirical studies suggest a lag of from a year to a year and a half. The method of estimation is generalized least squares; to be specific, full transform estimation (cf. Harvey (1981: ch. 6)) was employed.

Table 7.6. Estimated investment functions

(*a*) Non-ferrous metals

$$I_t = -1.36 + 1.54S^*_{t-4} - 1.81\tilde{S}_{t-4} + 0.18RE^*_{t-4} + \varepsilon_t$$

(− 0.79) (3.98) (− 3.63) (1.90)

$\hat{\rho} = 0.55,\ R^2 = 0.75$

(*b*) Chemicals

$$I_t = 3.55 + 0.82S^*_{t-4} - 0.85\tilde{S}_{t-4} + 0.15RE^*_{t-1} + \varepsilon_t$$

(3.36) (3.23) (− 1.40) (2.25)

$\hat{\rho} = 0.79,\ R^2 = 0.89$

(*c*) Machinery

$$I_t = -4.37 + 0.58RW^*_{t-3} + 1.83S^*_{t-3} + 0.22\tilde{S}_{t-2} + 0.16RE^*_{t-1} + \varepsilon_t$$

(− 5.42) (2.93) (9.06) (0.39) (2.26)

$\hat{\rho} = 0.19,\ R^2 = 0.91$

(*d*) Electrical machinery

$$I_t = -1.52 + 0.61RW^*_{t-3} - 2.70\tilde{R}\tilde{W}_{t-3} + 1.48S^*_{t-3} - 0.64\tilde{S}_{t-3} + \varepsilon_t$$

(− 1.98) (2.35) (− 2.26) (11.0) (−1.43)

$\hat{\rho} = 0.62,\ R^2 = 0.98$

(*e*) Transportation equipment

$$I_t = 12.1 + 1.00RW^*_{t-5} + 1.67S^*_{t-5} - 0.47RE^*_{t-5} - 0.90\tilde{R}\tilde{E}_{t-5} - 2.99PI^*_{t-5} + \varepsilon_t$$

(1.50) (2.80) (5.25) (− 2.72) (3.05) (−1.82)

$\hat{\rho} = 0.56,\ R^2 = 0.91$

(*f*) Paper, pulp

$$I_t = 0.87 + 0.79RW^*_{t-4} + 0.42S^*_{t-1} - 0.84\tilde{S}_{t-4} + 0.11RE^*_{t-1} + \varepsilon_t$$

(0.54) (2.57) (1.13) (− 0.99) (1.20)

$\hat{\rho} = 0.69,\ R^2 = 0.77$

Except for the pulp and paper industry, permanent shipments, S^*, has significant effects on investment; the elasticity is 0.8 for the chemical industry, but for other industries it is about 1.5. In theory, transitory shipments, $\tilde{S}$, should not affect investment. Consistent with this prediction, on the whole, only S_t^* is significant. The exception is the nonferrous metal industry. Note, however, that $\tilde{S}$ based on the Beveridge–Nelson decomposition does not exactly correspond to its counterpart in theory.

As for real factor prices, their effects on investment are mostly positive. This is consistent with the above result that shipments significantly affect investment. Together, these two results suggest that firms were in the quantity-constrained regime over the sample period. An increase in real wages raises investment in the three labour-intensive machinery industries and the pulp and paper industry, with the elasticities ranging from 0.6 to 1.0. An increase in real energy costs, on the other hand, raises investment in such energy-intensive industries as nonferrous metals, chemicals, general machinery, and transportation machinery. The elasticities in this case are smaller than the wage elasticities and are about 0.2.

The estimation results are on the whole in accord with our theory. In particular, the significant effects of shipments and the positive effects of real factor prices imply that firms were demand-constrained. Shapiro (1986), in the spirit of real business cycle theory, argues that, if the production function is subject to technological shocks, then output and profits and hence also investment all simultaneously increase. In this case, shipments may appear to drive investment even if the firm is in fact in the neoclassical regime. I argue, however, that (i) the important technological improvements are embodied in new investment, and (ii) the short-run fluctuations of labour productivity are demand-induced, given the firm's labour hoarding. Therefore it is more reasonable to interpret these results as indicating that firms are on the whole demand-constrained. This result is consistent with the conclusion of Chapter 2 that real shocks are important, but in business cycles in Japan they are mostly demand shocks rather than supply-side technological shocks.

7.4 CONCLUDING REMARKS

Investment is the key to understanding the Japanese economy, both in the short run and the long run. Although money plays an important role in the business cycle (see Chapter 9), it is a 'stylized fact' that real factors such as output, profit rates, and capacity utilization affect investment much more significantly than financial factors such as interest rates or cost of capital. Section 7.2 explained theoretically why this is so. In the presence of delivery lags, to the extent that the profit rate consists relatively more of permanent shocks than does the discount rate, as suggested by our analysis here, it points to the relative importance of the profit rate and other real variables in empirical investment equations.

At the level of the individual firm, it certainly makes sense simply to say that growth of output (sales) or anticipation thereof affects investment. In the economy as a whole, however, investment in turn affects growth of output. Some economists argue for a unilateral causality running from one variable to the other. De Long and Summers (1991), for example, maintain that equipment investment determines the growth rate. Chapter 2 explains, however, that the De Long–Summers thesis does not apply to the Japanese economy. And in opposition to De Long and Summers, Blomström *et al.* (1993) argue that increases in growth precede rises in rates of capital formation, and that fixed investment is not the main source of ignition for economic growth.

The issue is not simple. The simultaneity of the determination of investment and the growth rate of output then leads us to enquire into the ultimate determinants of these two variables in the macroeconomy. This problem will be taken up in Chapter 10.

APPENDIX 1

The coefficients in (26) can be derived in the following way. The formal structure of the problem is exactly the same as that analysed by Mussa (1975). Since the problem being analysed is a typical Kalman filter problem, we obtain

$$\begin{aligned} {}_t r_t^* &= {}_{t-1}r_{t-1}^* + a_1(t-1)[r_t - ({}_{t-1}r_{t-1}^* + \rho_1\, {}_{t-1}\varepsilon_{t-1}^1)]. \\ {}_t\varepsilon_t^1 &= b_1(t-1)[(r_t - ({}_{t-1}r_{t-1}^* + \rho_1\, {}_{t-1}\varepsilon_{t-1}^1)] \end{aligned} \qquad \text{(A1)}$$

After a large number of observations,

$$a_1(t-1) \to a_1,$$
$$b_1(t-1) \to b_1, \tag{A2}$$

where

$$a_1 = \frac{\sigma_{u^1}^2 + \phi_{\beta\beta}^* + \rho_1 \phi_{\beta\delta}^*}{\sigma_{\varepsilon^1}^2 + \sigma_{u^1}^2 + \phi_{\beta\beta}^* + 2\rho_1 \phi_{\beta\delta}^* + \rho_1^2 \phi_{\delta\delta}^*},$$
$$b_1 = \frac{\sigma_{\varepsilon^1}^2}{\sigma_{\varepsilon^1}^2 + \sigma_{u^1}^2 + \phi_{\beta\beta}^* + 2\rho_1 \phi_{\beta\delta}^* + \rho_1^2 \phi_{\delta\delta}^*} \tag{A3}$$

and $\phi_{\beta\beta}^*$, $\phi_{\beta\delta}^*$, $\phi_{\delta\delta}^*$ are defined by

$$\phi_{\beta\beta}^* = \frac{1}{\Delta}[(\sigma_{u^1}^2 + \phi_{\beta\beta}^*)\Delta - (\sigma_{u^1}^2 + \phi_{\beta\beta}^* + \rho_1 \phi_{\beta\delta}^*)^2],$$
$$\phi_{\beta\delta}^* = \frac{1}{\Delta}[-\sigma_{\varepsilon^1}^2(\sigma_{u^1}^2 + \phi_{\beta\beta}^* + \rho_1 \phi_{\beta\delta}^*)], \tag{A4}$$
$$\phi_{\delta\delta}^* = \frac{1}{\Delta}[\sigma_u^{21}(\sigma_u^{21} + \phi_{\beta\beta}^* + 2\rho_1 \phi_{\beta\delta}^* + \rho_1^2 \phi_{\delta\delta}^*)],$$
$$\Delta = \sigma_{\varepsilon^1}^2 + \sigma_{u^1}^2 + \phi_{\beta\beta}^* + 2\rho_1 \phi_{\beta\delta}^* + \rho_1^2 \phi_{\delta\delta}^*$$

Similarly,

$${}_tR_t^* = {}_{t-1}R_{t-1}^* + a_2(t-1)[R_t - ({}_{t-1}R_{t-1}^* + \rho_{2\,t-1}\varepsilon_{t-1}^2)]. \tag{A5}$$
$${}_t\varepsilon_t^2 = b_2(t-1)[R_t - ({}_{t-1}R_{t-1}^* + \rho_{2\,t-1}\varepsilon_{t-1}^2)]$$

and $a_2(t-1)$, $b_2(t-1)$ will converge to a_2 and b_2 as $t \to \infty$. The limits a_2 and b_2 are defined by the same formulae as (A3) and (A4) except that ε_1, u_1, and ρ_1 are replaced by ε_2, u_2, and ρ_2.

Solving the difference equations (A1) and (A5) (with $a_i(t-1) = a_i$, $b_i(t-1) = b_i$), we obtain

$${}_tr_t^* = \sum_{i=0}^{\infty} A_i^1 r_{t-i},$$
$${}_t\varepsilon_t^1 = \sum_{i=0}^{\infty} B_i^1 r_{t-i}, \tag{A6}$$
$${}_tR_t^* = \sum_{i=0}^{\infty} A_i^2 R_{t-i},$$
$${}_t\varepsilon_t^2 = \sum_{i=0}^{\infty} B_i^2 R_{t-i},$$

where

$$\begin{bmatrix} A_i^1 \\ B_i^1 \end{bmatrix} = M^i \begin{bmatrix} a_1 \\ b_1 \end{bmatrix}, \qquad M = \begin{bmatrix} 1-a_1 & -a_1\rho_1 \\ -b_1 & -b_1\rho_1 \end{bmatrix},$$

$$\begin{bmatrix} A_i^2 \\ B_i^2 \end{bmatrix} = N^i \begin{bmatrix} a_2 \\ b_2 \end{bmatrix}, \qquad N = \begin{bmatrix} 1 - a_2 & -a_2\rho_2 \\ -b_2 & -b_2\rho_2 \end{bmatrix}. \tag{A7}$$

Let us now see what will happen to A_i^1, B_i^1 when $\sigma_{u1}^2/\sigma_{\varepsilon 1} \to \infty$. From (A3) and (A4), it can be easily seen that $a_1 \to 1$, $b_1 \to 0$ as $\sigma_{u1}^2/\sigma_{\varepsilon 1}^2 \to \infty$. It then follows from (A7) that $A_0^1 = 1$, $A_i^1 = 0 (i \geqslant 1)$, and $B_j^1 = 0 (j \geqslant 0)$. By the same reasoning, we obtain the remaining results in (30).

APPENDIX 2

The data used in Section 7.2 are as follows.

The *profit rate* r is calculated as

$$r = \frac{(1-t)\pi}{p_w K},$$

where

- $\pi =$ total operating profits of all industries (Statistical Survey of Incorporated Enterprises: Ministry of Finance)
- $p_w =$ wholesale price index of investment goods (Bank of Japan)
- $K =$ capital stock of private enterprises, all industries, 1975 prices (Economic Planning Agency)
- $t =$ corporate income tax rate

The *expost discount rate* R is

$$R = \alpha x_1 + (1-\alpha) x_2,$$

$$x_1 = (1-t)\left(i - \frac{i_{+1} - i}{i_{+1}} \times 400 \right) - \frac{\dot{p}}{p},$$

$$x_2 = R_E - \frac{\dot{p}}{p},$$

where

- $\alpha =$ ratio of fixed liabilities to fixed liabilities plus equities
- $i =$ the interest rate on the Japanese Telephone and Telegraph Company
- $\dot{p}/p =$ rate of increase of wholesale price index (manufactured goods)
- $R_E =$ average rate of return on equities (Tokyo Stock Exchange)

APPENDIX 3

We assume that Δr and ΔR can be represented by the following stochastic processes:

$$\begin{aligned}\Delta r_t &= u_t^1 + \theta_1 u_{t-1}^1 + \theta_2 u_{t-2}^1 + \varepsilon_t^1 - (1-\rho_1)\varepsilon_{t-1}^1 - \rho_1 \varepsilon_{t-2}^1 \\ \Delta R_t &= u_t^2 + \phi_1 u_{t-1}^2 + \phi_2 u_{t-2}^2 + \varepsilon_t^2 - (1-\rho_2)\varepsilon_{t-1}^2 - \rho_2 \varepsilon_{t-2}^2.\end{aligned} \tag{A8}$$

We also assume that the parameters θ_1, θ_2, ϕ_1, ϕ_2, ρ_1, $1-\rho_1$, ρ_2, and $1-\rho_2$ are all positive and that there is no correlation between u^1 and ε^1 and between u^2 and ε^2 at all lags. Finally, we assume that the permanent part of the Δr_t process is invertible; that is, the roots of $1 + \theta_1 x + \theta_2 x^2 = 0$ lie outside the unit circle. Using these assumptions and the estimates of the first- and second-order autocorrelation coefficients of Δr and ΔR reported in Table 7.4, we can now see that the inequality (28) holds true. First, we shall find a lowerbound for $\sigma_{\varepsilon^2}^2/\sigma_{u^2}^2$. Note that, given (A8), the first- and second-order moments of ΔR can be written as

$$\rho_{\Delta R}^1 = \frac{\phi_1(1+\phi_2)\sigma_{u^2}^2 - (1-\rho_2)^2\sigma_{\varepsilon^2}^2}{(1+\phi_1^2+\phi_2^2)\sigma_{u^2}^2 + (1+\rho_2^2+(1-\rho_2)^2)\sigma_{\varepsilon^2}^2} \tag{A9}$$

$$\rho_{\Delta R}^2 = \frac{\phi_2\sigma_{u^2}^2 - \rho_2\sigma_{\varepsilon^2}^2}{(1+\phi_1^2+\phi_2^2)\sigma_{u^2}^2 + (1+\rho_2^2+(1-\rho_2)^2)\sigma_{\varepsilon^2}^2}. \tag{A10}$$

Since $\rho_{\Delta R}^1 = -0.32$ from Table 7.4, we have

$$\rho_{\Delta R}^1 < -0.25. \tag{A11}$$

Using (A9) and (A11), we obtain

$$\sigma_{\varepsilon^2}^2[2(1-\rho_2)^2 + 2(1-\rho_2) - 2] > \sigma_{u^2}^2(1+\phi_1^2+\phi_2^2+4\phi_1+4\phi_1\phi_2). \tag{A12}$$

Given that $\phi_1, \phi_2 > 0$, (A12) implies that

$$\sigma_{\varepsilon^2}^2 \cdot 2[(1-\rho_2)^2 + (1-\rho_2) - 1] > \sigma_{u^2}^2. \tag{A13}$$

The inequality (A13) implies that $(1-\rho_2)^2 + (1-\rho_2) - 1 > 0$; i.e.,

$$1-\rho_2 > \frac{-1+\sqrt{5}}{2} = 0.618. \tag{A14}$$

Next, note that

$$\rho_{\Delta R}^2 < -0.15. \tag{A15}$$

Then, from (A10) and (A15), we have (after some rearrangements)

$$\sigma_{\varepsilon^2}^2 2\cdot[7 - 7(1-\rho_2) - 3(1-\rho_2)^2] > \sigma_{u^2}^2(3+3\phi_1^2+3\phi_2^2+20\phi_2). \tag{A16}$$

This means $7 - 7(1-\rho_2) - 3(1-\rho_2)^2 > 0$; i.e.,

$$1-\rho_2 < \frac{-7+\sqrt{113}}{6} = 0.755. \tag{A17}$$

We can calculate a lower bound for $\sigma_{\varepsilon 2}^2/\sigma_{u2}^2$ by using the inequalities (A13), (A16), (A14), and (A17). Namely, from (A15), $\sigma_{\varepsilon 2}^2/\sigma_{u2}^2$ is smallest when $1 - \rho_2 = 0.755$. This bound turns out to be 1.538. From (A16), $\sigma_{\varepsilon 2}^2/\sigma_{u2}^2$ is smallest when $1 - \rho_2 = 0.618$. This bound turns out to be 0.982. By combining the two, we have

$$\sigma_{\varepsilon 2}^2/\sigma_{u2}^2 > 1.538. \tag{A18}$$

Second, let us obtain an upperbound for $\sigma_{\varepsilon 1}^2/\sigma_{u1}^2$. Let us first use the assumption that the roots of $1 + \theta_1 x + \theta_2 x^2 = 0$ lie outside the unit circle. The roots of the equation are

$$x = \frac{-\theta_1 \pm \sqrt{(\theta_1^2 - 4\theta_2)}}{2\theta_2}.$$

When $\theta_1^2 > 4\theta_2$, the roots are real and their absolute values must be larger than one. When $\theta_1^2 < 4\theta_2$, the roots are imaginary and

$$\frac{(-\theta_1)^2}{2\theta_2} + \frac{4\theta_2 - \theta_1^2}{(2\theta_2)^2} > 1 \tag{A19}$$

must hold. Next, using the inequality $\rho_{\Delta r}^2 > 0.20$, we obtain

$$\sigma_{u1}^2(5\theta_2 - 1 - \theta_1^2 - \theta_2^2) > [5\rho_1 + 1 + \rho_1^2 + (1 - \rho_1)^2]\sigma_{\varepsilon 1}^2. \tag{A20}$$

We first note that, given $\rho_1 > 0$, $5\theta_2 - 1 - \theta_1^1 - \theta_2^2$ must be positive. It can be easily seen that this is negative or zero when $\theta_1^2 > 4\theta_2$. Therefore, $\theta_1^2 < 4\theta_2$ and (A19) must hold. An upper bound for $\sigma_{\varepsilon 1}^2/\sigma_{u1}^2$ can be found by obtaining a maximum of

$$\frac{5\theta_2 - 1 - \theta_1^2 - \theta_2^2}{5\rho_1 + 1 + \rho_1^2 + (1 - \phi_1)^2}.$$

Given (A19) and $\theta_1^2 < 4\theta_2$, it can be easily seen that the numerator has a maximum of 3 when (θ_1, θ_2) is equal (or infinitely close) to (0, 1). The denominator, given $0 < \rho_1 < 1$, has a minimum, of 2. Hence,

$$\sigma_{\varepsilon 1}^2/\sigma_{u1}^2 < 1.5. \tag{A21}$$

By combining (A18) and (A21), we obtain the inequality (28) in the text.

8

Trade Imbalance and the Exchange Rate

Current account imbalances among major countries significantly widened during the 1980s, and have become the major economic problem today. Table 8.1 shows the record for Japan, the United States, (West) Germany, and the United Kingdom. In 1980 Japan's current account was in deficit after the second oil embargo the previous year, while that of the United States was in surplus. The situation reversed in 1982, and the gap abruptly widened in 1983–4. These imbalances continued throughout the 1980s. The prolonged boom in Japan in the late 1980s caused the current account surplus relative to GNP to decline to 1% by 1990, but then the subsequent recession once again forced it back above 3%. Germany (then West Germany) also kept its current account surplus at a high level—above 4% as a ratio relative to GNP—in the late 1980s; the Unification, however, turned it to deficit.

It is now commonplace worldwide for politicians, policy-makers, and even economists to talk about the 'Japan Problem'. Trade frictions between Japan and the United States worsened in the 1980s and again in the 1990s. The 1980s also saw a sharp appreciation of the yen. In the early 1980s \$1 was worth ¥240; a decade later it had dropped to ¥100 (Fig. 8.1). In fact, the decade of the 1980s was to provide students of international macroeconomics with a wonderful opportunity to test competing theories.

This chapter discusses current account imbalances and the exchange rate. It surveys competing theories which enjoyed wide currency in the 1980s. Both the neoclassical saving–investment balance approach and the updated Mundell–Fleming model can reasonably explain what happened in the early 1980s regarding (i) the worldwide high real interest rate, (ii) the sharp appreciation of the dollar, and (iii) the emergence of current account imbalances among Japan, the United States, and Europe. These theories deservedly enjoyed popularity in the 1980s. However, they cannot adequately

Table 8.1. Current accounts of major countries, 1980–1993 (US$ billion)[a]

	Japan	USA	West Germany	UK
1980	– 10.8	1.5	– 13.8	6.5
	(– 1.1)	(0.1)	(– 1.7)	(1.2)
1981	4.8	8.2	– 3.6	13.5
	(0.4)	(0.3)	(– 0.5)	(2.6)
1982	6.9	– 7.0	5.1	8.1
	(0.7)	(– 0.2)	(0.8)	(1.6)
1983	20.8	– 44.3	5.3	5.7
	(1.8)	(– 1.3)	(0.8)	(1.2)
1984	35.0	– 104.2	9.8	2.5
	(2.8)	(– 2.8)	(1.6)	(0.6)
1985	49.2	– 112.7	16.4	4.2
	(3.6)	(– 2.8)	(2.6)	(0.9)
1986	85.9	– 133.3	39.5	0.1
	(4.3)	(– 3.1)	(4.4)	(0.0)
1987	87.0	– 143.7	45.7	– 6.3
	(3.6)	(– 3.2)	(4.0)	(– 0.9)
1988	79.6	– 126.6	50.3	– 26.8
	(2.8)	(– 2.6)	(4.2)	(– 3.2)
1989	57.2	– 105.9	55.4	– 34.2
	(2.0)	(– 2.0)	(4.8)	(– 4.1)
1990	35.8	– 92.1	47.9	– 27.6
	(1.2)	(– 1.7)	(2.8)	(– 2.8)
1991	72.6	– 8.6	– 20.7	– 7.8
	(2.1)	(– 0.2)	(– 1.2)	(– 0.8)
1992	93.3	– 53.4	– 14.1	– 14.9
	(2.6)	(– 0.9)	(– 0.8)	(– 1.4)
1993	138.6	– 81.0	– 29.0	– 26.8
	(3.3)	(– 1.3)	(– 1.6)	(– 3.0)

[a] Current account/GDP in parentheses (for Japan and Germany, in % of GNP)

Source: IMF, *World Economics Outlook, 1993.*

explain why the dollar has fallen by half against the yen during the years following the 1985 Plaza Accord. The fundamental problem of existing open-economy macro theories is their tacit assumption that the equilibrium real exchange rate is constant or that its change is very slow. The final section of this chapter proposes a new definition of the equilibrium exchange rate which emphasizes the role of the international differential in productivity growth in addition to the more traditional price differential variables. Using this definition, I estimate the long-run equilibrium yen–dollar rate during the period of 1973–87. This calculation demonstrates that the actual

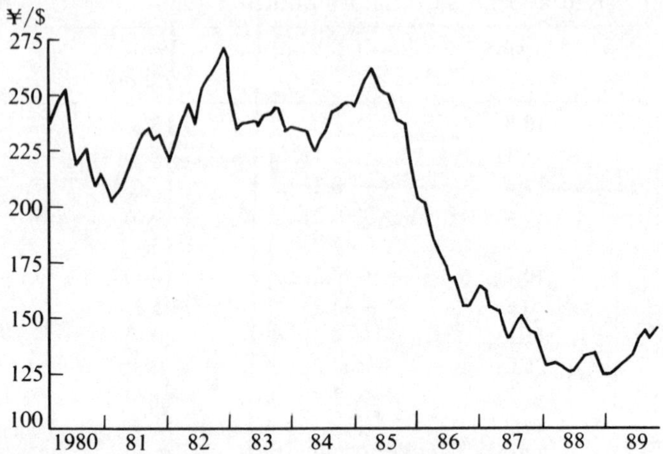

Fig. 8.1. The yen/$ exchange rate, 1980–1989

exchange rate broadly coincides with the movement of my equilibrium rate, and that real factors, most notably labour productivity, have been much more important than the nominal wages differential in determining the long-run trend of the yen–dollar rate from 1973 to 1987.

I begin my discussion by looking at Japan's current account from a long-run perspective.

8.1 THE LONG-RUN THEORY OF CURRENT ACCOUNT

On average, the current account of Japan had been in balance for more than two decades up to the end of the 1960s. In fact, as Fig. 8.2 illustrates, it had tended to be in balance during the pre-war period as well. It is fair to say that the century-long development of the modern Japanese economy depended primarily upon domestic savings, and little on foreign capital.[1] From the late 1960s, however, Japan's current account has tended to be in surplus. While the two oil embargos of the

[1] Despite this fact, contemporary policy-makers in pre-war Japan often held the view that foreign capital inflow was essential for the development of the Japanese economy. For example, to secure credibility for foreign creditors, Japan returned to the gold standard at the pre-WWI parity in January 1930, at the very outset of the Great Depression. It was then very well recognized that the pre-war parity was highly overvalued.

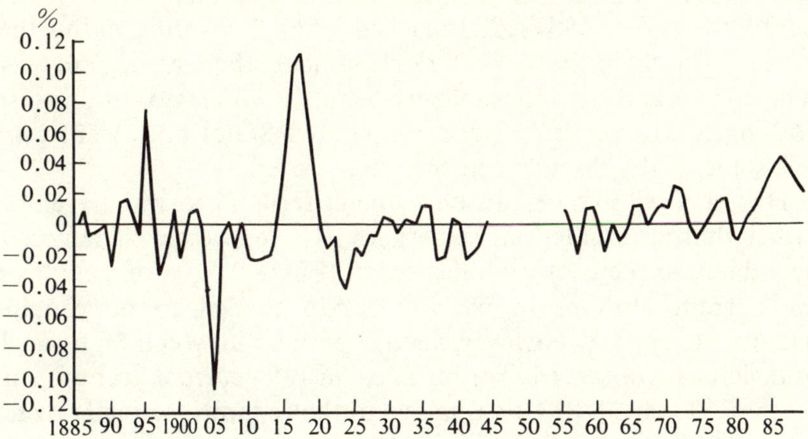

Fig. 8.2. Japan's current account/GNP: historical perspectives, 1885–1985
Source: Ohkawa *et al.* (1974).

1970s resulted in temporary deficits, Japan's surplus soared to an unprecedented level in the 1980s. Some economists explain this trend in Japan's current account in the context of long-run theory.

Stages of Balance of Payments

Some maintain that, just like an individual household, a country goes through various stages in its balance of payments during the course of economic development. (See Onitsuka (1974) for a formal model.) According to this 'life-cycle' theory, a 'young' country starting with small capital stock first keeps the level of investment higher than that of domestic saving, causing the current account at this stage of development to be in deficit. As capital accumulates, the country's trade balance, and then its current account, turn to surplus. Eventually, the country whose marginal product of capital declines sufficiently relative to the world's average changes from being a debtor to being a creditor, with net foreign assets. Finally, it may even reach the stage where it decumulates its foreign assets with current account deficits.

For example, the United States, which imported foreign capital in the nineteenth century, later became a capital-exporting country with current account surpluses; its average current account surplus during the period 1911–40 amounts to 2.4% of GNP. Similarly, the average ratio of current account surplus to GNP of the United Kingdom during the period 1851–1925 reached 3.5%. According to this theory, Japan is simply in the stage of development where its current account is in surplus and foreign assets are being accumulated. In this respect, nothing is wrong; Britain and the United States both went through this stage of development in the past.

This theory revolves around longer-term historical development rather than a decade-long experience. Its relevance, therefore, must be judged on the century-long record (Fig. 8.2). As indicated earlier, the current account in pre-war Japan tended to be roughly in balance. There are, however, several periods in which high surpluses or deficits are observed. For instance, in 1895 current account surplus reached 8% of GNP. This was due to the reparations made by China after the Sino-Japanese War—not due to trade surplus, but to transfer payments. The 1905 deficits, which amounted to 11% of GNP, were caused by the Russo- Japanese War. Massive amounts of government bonds, denominated in sterling and US dollars, were issued to finance the war. At the beginning of the 1910s, Japan actually had some difficulty in serving its foreign debt, as do some of today's developing nations, but then the First World War broke out. During 1915–18, Japan experienced an unprecedented export boom, with its current account surplus reaching almost 12% of GNP at its peak. In normal times this would certainly have caused trade frictions, but the other leading nations were too busy fighting the war. Finally, the deficits around 1923 were due to the reconstruction of Tokyo after the 1923 earthquake.

Viewed in this way, major current account imbalances in pre-war Japan were caused either by war or by earthquake. They have little to do with capital accumulation and the accompanying changes in productivity/time preference emphasized by the 'life-cycle theory' of the balance of payments. I conclude, therefore, that it is difficult usefully to apply this theory to the Japanese experience.[2]

[2] Actually it is doubtful that the 'life-cycle theory' holds even in the case of Britain, which has supposedly gone through typical stages of balance of payments. For almost a century up to 1914, Britain had kept its current account in surplus. And yet its trade balance had been in deficit throughout this period. A current account surplus was made possible by maritime incomes (the most important item up to the 1870s), incomes from foreign trading, and interest on foreign assets. Behind these factors was the domination of the British navy over the seven seas. However, when Britain lost its naval power, it had to face current account deficits during the inter-war period. Again, capital accumulation and the accompanying changes in productivity/time preference which the 'life-cycle theory' emphasizes have little to do with this British experience.

An Optimal Growth Model in an Open Economy

A kind of 'life-cycle theory' based explicitly on a representative household's optimization is the open-economy Ramsey optimal growth model which was developed by Hamada (1967) and others. In the 1960s, no one took such a model as a descriptive model: rather, it was taken as a normative model, supposedly to provide guidance for government policy. As explained in Chapter 1, however, in the 1980s many economists began to use the optimal growth model as a descriptive model. Blanchard and Fischer (1989), for example, call this model 'the basic organizing model in macroeconomics', and present a small-country model for an open economy.

In this Ramsey model, the representative household facing the constant worldwide interest rate r maximizes

$$\int_0^\infty u(C_t)e^{-rt}dt \qquad (u' > 0,\ u'' < 0), \tag{1}$$

under the budget constraint

$$\dot{B}_t = C_t + I_t\left[1 + \phi\left(\frac{I_t}{K_t}\right)\right] + rB_t - F(K_t) \quad (\phi' > 0,\ \phi'' > 0,\ F' > 0,\ F'' < 0), \tag{2}$$

$$\dot{K}_t = I_t, \tag{3}$$

where C_t, I_t, K_t, and B_t are consumption, investment, capital stock, and foreign debt, respectively. For investment, the convex adjustment cost ϕ is assumed. (See Chapter 7, however, for the limitation of this standard framework which leads to the q theory.)

In an open economy, the total domestic demand $C + I$ is not necessarily equal to domestic product $F(K)$. The difference between the two is met by a change in foreign debts/assets net of interest payments, $\dot{B} - r\dot{B}$. Since the subjective discount rate is assumed for simplicity to be equal to the interest rate r, the optimal consumption is constant. The trade balance, therefore, is basically determined by investment and domestic product, which in turn depend on capital stock. A country poorly endowed with capital stock first incurs trade deficits, but then, as capital accumulates, it eventually becomes a net exporter.

This model is a kind of the 'life-cycle' theory, its basic mechanism being the interaction between capital accumulation and the accompanying diminishing returns. As explained earlier, to the extent that the model is taken as a long-run model encompassing a century, it has little relevance for the Japanese experience. However, incorporating exogenous shocks, the model could be interpreted as a medium-run model. Following Blanchard and Fischer, we now consider unanticipated productivity shocks.

The production function is modified as

$$(1 + e_0)F(K) + e_1, \tag{4}$$

where e_0 and e_1 indicate productivity shocks; e_0 affects the marginal product of capital $(1 + e_0)F'(K)$, and thereby the optimal capital accumulation, whereas e_1 does not. Then *any* pattern of trade balance can be generated within the model. Permanent additive productivity shock e_1, for example, leaves the trade balance unchanged; on the other hand, temporary positive shock e_1 raises the trade surplus. Permanent positive multiplicative shock e_0 brings about trade deficits. The important question, therefore, is how relevant each case is for the experience of the 1980s.

To account for Japan's trade surpluses and the US trade deficits, permanent multiplicative shock e_0 would have to have been greater in the United States than in Japan. But in fact, in the 1980s investment relative to GNP remained at the level of 10% in the United States, whereas in Japan it had risen from 15% in 1980 to 20% by the end of the decade (see Chapter 7). Therefore, positive shocks to profits rates, e_0 on the part of the United States, cannot be a plausible explanation.

Additive shocks e_1, on the other hand, may be a promising factor when interpreted as government deficits. A temporary increase in deficits (a decline in e_1) on the part of the United States and a temporary decrease in deficits (an increase in e_1) in Japan generate the observed pattern of trade imbalances. In passing, it is worth recalling that, within the Ramsey framework, a permanent increase in government deficits must entail an equivalent decrease in consumption while keeping the trade balance unchanged. It is a matter of judgement whether a significant increase in the US government deficits in the 1980s is to be interpreted as (semi-) permanent or temporary.

In any case, if the Ramsey model is to be applicable to the experiences in the 1980s, the trade imbalances are simply the outcome of economic agents' optimization and therefore should not be any 'problem'. Also, the relevant factors are not long-run factors such as capital accumulation and accompanying changes in profit rates, but rather *temporary* changes in government deficits. Given this observation, we now turn to the less formal and yet more tractable medium-run models.

8.2 THEORIES FOR THE 1980s

Alternative models have been offered to account for the experiences in the 1980s: the neoclassical saving–investment balance approach, the Branson model, and Keynesian approaches such as the Mundell–Fleming model.

The Neoclassical Saving–Investment Balance Approach

This approach is a medium-run neoclassical model, assuming full employment but ignoring the effects of capital accumulation. It assumes that home goods and foreign goods are imperfect substitutes, and explicitly introduces the real exchange rate or the terms of trade. Examples are the 1984 US *Economic Report of the President*, Feldstein (1986), and Ueda (1988*b*).

Consider a two-country model. Equilibrium in the goods market for Japan is

$$S(Y; A_1) = I(r; A_2) + G + TB(e, Y, Y^*; B). \tag{5}$$

The similar equation for the rest of the world (or simply the United States, for convenience) is

$$S^*(Y^*; A_1^*) = I^*(r^*; A_2^*) + G^* - TB(e, Y, Y^*; B^*), \tag{6}$$

where S, I, G, and TB are savings, investment, government expenditure, and the trade balance, respectively (an asterisk indicates that the variable pertains to the foreign country, say the United States); real GNP, Y, is determined by production function and supplies of production factors, and is taken as given; r and e are the real interest rate and the exchange rate in terms of home currency (the inverse of the terms of trade); and A_1, A_2, and B are exogenous shift parameters (for example, A_2 would be the expected profit rate, and B the international competitiveness of exportables or the marginal propensity to import). In the two-country framework, the US trade balance is equal to $-TB$. For simplicity, the difference between the trade balance and the current account is ignored. This assumption is innocuous for the Japanese economy.

When both home and foreign bonds are freely traded, the following equation holds:

$$i = i^* + \left(\frac{\dot{E}}{E}\right)^{ex}, \tag{7}$$

where i is the nominal interest rate and $(\dot{E}/E)^{ex}$ is the expected rate of change in the nominal exchange rate. For simplicity, the risk premium is ignored.

Given the real exchange rate e, which is to be determined shortly, the nominal exchange rate E changes, reflecting the differential in inflation π between two countries:

$$\frac{\dot{E}}{E} = \pi - \pi^*. \tag{8}$$

Rational expectations then imply

$$\left(\frac{\dot{E}}{E}\right)^{ex} = \hat{\pi} - \hat{\pi}^*, \tag{9}$$

where $\hat{\pi}$ denotes the rationally expected inflation. From (7) and (9), we observe that the real interest rate r is equated across two countries:

$$r = r^*. \tag{10}$$

With $r = r^*$, goods market equilibrium equations for Japan and the United States, i.e. (5) and (6), determine two unknowns e and r, the real exchange rate and the world real interest rate. The two equations actually have a recursive structure.[3] Summing (5) and (6) leads us to

$$S(Y; A_1) + S^*(Y^*; A_1^*) = I(r; A_2) + I^*(r^*; A_2^*) + G + G^*. \tag{11}$$

This is the goods market equilibrium condition for the world as a whole. The world as a whole is a closed economy, and therefore the trade balance disappears. Equation (11) determines the world real interest rate; see Barro (1992) for empirical analysis based on this theory.

Given the real interest rate, either (5) or (6) determines the real exchange rate. Equation (5), for example, can be rewritten as

$$TB(e, Y, Y^*; B) = S(Y; A_1) - I(r; A_2) - G. \tag{5'}$$

Since the right-hand side of (5′) is independent of the real exchange rate e, the trade balance is independent of e. Causality runs from

[3] The recursive structure of the system derives from the independence of saving S and investment I from the real exchange rate e. If S and I depend on e, then equations (5) and (6) simultaneously determine r and e. The dependence of S and I on e is often referred to as the Metzler–Laursen effect (Metzler and Laursen 1950). A change in the real exchange rate, for example, would affect the value of foreign assets in terms of home currency and therefore in general through the wealth effect affect S.

trade balance to the real exchange rate within this framework, e being determined in such a way that it is consistent with the level of the trade balance, which in turn is determined by savings and investment.[4]

It is necessary to understand not only the results of comparative-static analysis but also the mechanism by which a particular result obtains in this framework. Take an increase in Y arising from either capital accumulation or productivity growth. In this case, by way of an increase in world savings, the real interest rate declines (equation (11)). Since a decline in the world interest rate raises investment in both countries, net saving or the trade surplus in the home country increases. For the trade surplus to increase, the real exchange rate must depreciate. In sum, growth of the Japanese economy brings about an *increase* in the trade surplus and at the same time makes the yen depreciate against the dollar. As a partial effect, an increase in Y raises imports and thereby brings about trade *deficits*, $\partial TB/\partial Y < 0$. And yet in equilibrium trade surplus rises as Y increases. The larger the marginal propensity to import (the absolute value of $\partial TB/\partial Y$), the larger is the extent of depreciation of the yen when Y increases. It has been occasionally pointed out that the differential in growth rate (higher in the United States than in Japan) during the 1980s was responsible for the observed trade imbalances. This argument, however, clearly does not hold within the present framework. This conclusion is in sharp contrast to the one obtained in the Keynesian approach.

An exogenous decrease in savings A_1, and/or an increase in government expenditure G, raises the world real interest rate and also the trade deficits of the country where the changes occurred, so long as the interest elasticity of investment does not differ significantly in the two countries. To take government deficits as a cause of trade deficits, of course, implicitly assumes that the Ricardian equivalence does not hold.

A rise in the expected profit rate A_2 also raises the world interest rate. Since by assumption S, S^*, G, and G^* all remain unchanged, $I + I^*$ also remains unchanged. Therefore, an increase in I is met by an equivalent decline in I^*. A domestic investment boom crowds out investment in the foreign country by raising the world interest rate. The trade balance in the home country turns to deficit, and accordingly the exchange rate appreciates.

[4] This strong result, however, obtains only in the absence of the Metzler–Laursen effect: see fn. 3.

Finally, consider the case where the international 'competitiveness' of exportables strengthens. *TB* rises for the same levels of *e*, *Y*, and Y^* as parameter *B* changes. Since the right-hand side of (5′) is independent of *B*, the trade balance actually remains unchanged in the new equilibrium after *B* changes. Thus, *the augmented international competitiveness of exportables is completely absorbed by the appreciation of the real exchange rate.* A popular argument that the strong international competitiveness of the Japanese exportables, which consist mainly of broadly defined machinery, is a cause of Japan's trade surplus does not make sense in this framework.

Table 8.2 shows the record for the world economy in the first half of the 1980s: (i) current account deficits in the United States accompanied by current account surpluses in Japan and then West Germany; (ii) real appreciation of the US dollar, and (iii) the high worldwide real interest rate. The neoclassical saving–investment balance approach explains these phenomena as primarily the result of substantial government deficits in the United States and surpluses in Japan and Europe. Some economists also mention the US investment boom as a cause for the strong dollar, the high real interest rate,

Table 8.2. The world economy in the early 1980s (%)

Current account/GNP	1980	1985	Change
USA	0.1	– 2.8	– 2.9
Japan	– 1.1	3.6	+ 4.7
W. Germany	– 1.7	2.6	+ 4.3
Government deficits/GNP		**Change from 1979 to 1985**	
USA		– 4.3	
Japan		+ 3.6	
W. Germany		+ 1.3	
		1979	**1985**
US gross investment/GNP		18.2	16.5
US private gross saving/GNP		17.8	17.2
Effective real US$		98.9	142.8
US real interest rate[a]		– 1.3	3.6

[a] Real interest rate = (TB rate) – (CPI inflation in the previous year).

Source: US *Economic Report of the President*, 1987.

and the US current account deficit; Blanchard and Summers (1984), for example, observing rising stock price in the early 1980s, argue this thesis. The dollar appreciated, however, even during the 1982 recession, and in any case, there was in fact no such investment boom in the United States as occurred in Japan in the 1980s (see Fig. 7.1 above).

After all, the main player in this theory is US government deficits. From an historical perspective, however, changes in the macro saving rate caused by an increase in government deficits would not necessarily entail current account deficits. With the 1960–74 average data, Feldstein and Horioka (1980) run the following cross-sectional regression for 15 OECD countries:

$$\left(\frac{I}{Y}\right)_i = \alpha + \beta\left(\frac{S}{Y}\right)_i \qquad (i\text{: country}). \tag{12}$$

They find that $\beta = 1$ cannot be rejected. Most subsequent works updating the regression basically reconfirm the central message of Feldstein and Horioka. On average, changes in the macro saving rate tend to be accompanied by parallel changes in the domestic investment rate rather than in the current account.

Feldstein and Horioka interpret their own finding as suggesting a limited international capital mobility. There are, however, several other reasons why the Feldstein–Horioka result, $\beta = 1$ in (12), might obtain even under perfect international capital mobility. Some attempt to identify a third factor which causes long-term averages of both saving and investment to move together. Tesar (1991), for example, shows that the fraction of the population aged 15–64 is positively related to both saving and investment rates. Chapter 2 has demonstrated that in Japan, population flow and the resulting high rate of household formation were fundamental factors behind the high investment rate and economic growth during the 1950s and 1960s. At the same time, as explained in Chapter 6, high growth was also an important factor behind the high saving rate in Japan. The Tesar argument, therefore, is quite plausible in the case of Japan.

Another plausible explanation for the Feldstein–Horioka finding is systematic current account targeting by governments (Summers 1988*b*). Chapter 9 will show that in Japan monetary policy has, indeed, aimed to limit external imbalances. Along these lines, the Feldstein–Horioka finding can be plausibly interpreted separate from international capital mobility. In any case, it implies that major current account imbalances caused by the US government deficits in the 1980s were exceptional by historical or cross-sectional standards.

Coming back to the neoclassical saving–investment balance approach, the extent to which changes in government deficits are transmitted into changes in the current account depends primarily on the interest elasticities of investment. This elasticity, however, is typically found to be small for most countries, as well as for most sample periods. Beyond that, without a significant change in the US government deficits, the post-Plaza period witnessed a decline in the real interest rate, a sharp depreciation of the dollar, and persistent current account imbalances. The saving–investment balance approach, while it explains well the experiences in the first half of the 1980s, fails as an explanation for the post-1985 period.

The Branson Model

Branson (1985) offers a hybrid model of the US economy. It is classical in that output Y is always at the full-employment level; on the other hand, the real exchange rate e and the real interest rate r, determined in the asset market rather than in goods market, can deviate from the equilibrium values.

Goods market equilibrium is

$$S(Y) = I(r) + G + TB(e) \qquad (TB'(e) > 0). \tag{13}$$

Here Y is given at the full-employment level. Equilibrium in the asset market requires the equality of rates of return, adjusted for the risk premium ρ, on domestic (i.e. US) and foreign bonds:

$$r = r^* + \left(\frac{\dot{e}}{e}\right)^{ex} + \rho(B) \qquad (\rho'(B) > 0), \tag{14}$$

where B is the amount of US bonds held by foreigners. The risk premium ρ is assumed to go up as B increases. Expectations for the real exchange rate are stable in the sense that it is always expected to fill the gap towards the equilibrium rate, e^*:

$$\left(\frac{\dot{e}}{e}\right)^{ex} = \theta(e^* - e) \qquad (\theta > 0). \tag{15}$$

Branson defines the equilibrium exchange rate as the one that keeps the current account in balance at the full-employment GNP. (Section 8.4 offers a different definition of the equilibrium exchange rate.)

Equations (14) and (15) lead us to

$$e = e^* - \frac{1}{\theta}[r - r^* - e(B)]. \tag{16}$$

In the short run, given Y, e^*, r^*, and $\rho(B)$, (13) and (16) determine the real exchange rate e and the real interest rate r. On the e, r plane, the saving/investment curve, *IS*, a combination of e, r that satisfies (13), is upward-sloping. The *FM* curve derived from (16) is, on the other hand, downward-sloping. The determination of e and r in this framework is shown in Fig. 8.3.

An increase in US government deficits makes the saving/investment curve shift up from saving/investment (*IS*) to saving/investment′ (*IS′*). At the new equilibrium, E_1 in the figure, the real interest rate goes up, the dollar appreciates, and the US current account deficit increases. This result broadly captures what happened in the first half of the 1980s.

Persisting current account deficits in E_1, however, necessarily raise B, the amount of US bonds held by foreigners, and thus the risk premium ρ eventually starts to rise. The *FM* curve shifts up from *FM* to *FM′* in the figure. Along the path towards the new equilibrium E_2, the dollar depreciates, while at the same time the real interest rate keeps rising. This process continues until the dollar depreciates enough to restore the current account balance.

Branson correctly rejected the then popular idea that appreciation of the dollar reflected the mounting confidence in the 'strength' of the United States in the early 1980s. He pointed out that confidence in the United States might bring about the strong dollars, but at the

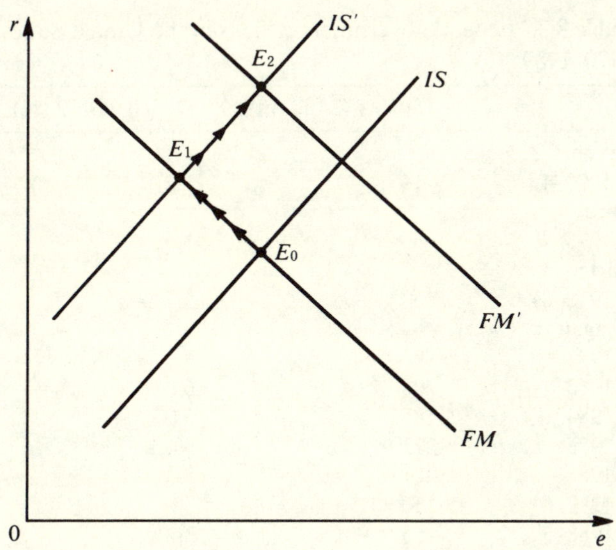

Fig. 8.3. Real interest rates and real exchange rates

same time it would have lowered the interest rate through a decline in the risk premium on US bonds. He argued that it was the US government deficit that was primarily responsible for the strong dollar and high real interest rates.

The 'structural' government deficits, however, appear to have risen significantly only after 1983. The high deficit in 1982 was due to the worst recession in the post-war period (Table 8.3). Branson maintained that the 1981 Economic Recovery Tax Act under the Reagan administration produced, through an increase in the *expected* government deficits, a strong dollar and high real interest rates as early as in 1981.

As an explanation for the first half of the 1980s, the Branson story is qualitatively similar to the neoclassical saving–investment balance approach. In his model, however, the strengthened dollar begins to depreciate as the persistent US current account deficit eventually raises the risk premium on US bonds. In fact, the dollar started to depreciate in 1985, but at the same time real interest rates declined. In this respect, the Branson model also fails as an explanation for the latter half of the 1980s.

The Mundell–Fleming Approach

The final candidate is an updated version of the Mundell–Fleming approach. Krugman (1991) ostentatiously calls it the 'Massachusetts

Table 8.3. Federal government deficits in the United States, 1970–1989

	Deficits ($ billion)	Deficits/GNP (%)
Nixon		
1970–4	14	1.2
Ford		
1975–7	60	3.5
Carter		
1978–81	63	2.4
Reagan		
1982	128	4.1
1983	208	6.3
1984	185	5.0
1985	212	5.4
1986	221	5.3
1987	150	3.4
1988	155	3.2
1989	151	3.1

Avenue model'. Its popularity spread from Massachusetts Avenue to Tokyo during the 1980s.

The model is Keynesian in that output is determined by demand. Take an investment boom as an example. In this model, an increase in investment raises output. And it is primarily this increase in output or growth that transforms the investment boom into changes in the trade balance, the interest rate, etc. In the neoclassical approach, on the other hand, apart from the eventual effect of an increase in capital stock, the investment boom is taken as a change in intertemporal resource allocation, in which the necessary adjustment is achieved primarily through the real interest rate.

Consider a small open economy. The model consists of three equations. Goods market equilibrium is the same as in other approaches:

$$S(Y; A_1) = I(r; A_2) + G + TB(e, Y, Y^*; B), \tag{17}$$

where the foreign output Y^* is given.

Asset-holders hold three assets in their portfolios: money, domestic bonds, and foreign bonds. In 'the beginning-of-period equilibrium' (see Foley 1975 for this concept), the Walras law with respect to stock makes only two of the equations for asset market equilibrium independent.

There is no equation for capital flow in this model,[5] but only an export/import function, *TB* in (17). Demand for assets is instantaneously adjusted in terms of stock. Note that the equalization of interest rates across countries has nothing to do with international capital flows. Niehans (1984: 120–31) gives the most lucid discussion on this point:

> Under the pressure of arbitrage, the equalization of interest rates will be virtually instantaneous. It requires no net capital movements, no savings (or dissavings) and no investment (or disinvestment). Its speed has nothing to do with the mobility of net capital flows. A few telephone calls are all that is necessary. (Niehans 1984: 121)

In contrast to the instantaneous equalization of interest rates on paper assets across the borders (equation (14)), profit rates on real capital are not necessarily equalized. Thus, despite a liberalization of and technological advancement in international financial transactions, Tobin's *q* in the two economies differs and so do investments.

[5] In 'the end-of-period equilibrium' model, there is an equation representing capital flow.

This difference (among other factors) affects exports and imports, entailing trade imbalances. Trade imbalances implicitly determine capital flows.

Asset prices or interest rates are instantaneously determined so as to equilibrate supply and demand in the asset market. In the present model, two equations characterize the asset market equilibrium. One is the money market equation:

$$M = L(r, Y). \tag{18}$$

Demand for money L is equal to money supply M. For simplicity, the price is normalized to be one, and the expected rate of inflation is assumed to be zero. The nominal interest, therefore, is equal to the real interest rate r. The nominal exchange rate is also identified with the real exchange rate. As will be shown, in the 1980s, changes in the nominal exchange rate broadly reflected changes in the real rate.

The other equation is (16). The crucial assumption behind (16) is that the exchange rate is expected to converge to equilibrium. Frankel and Froot (1987) actually demonstrate that the market expectations revealed in survey do not necessarily satisfy this assumption. For investors' horizons of less than three months, expectations are in fact unstable: θ in (15) is not positive but negative. Only for horizons longer than three months is the assumption of positive θ in (15) satisfied. For example, if the yen has appreciated by 10%, the market still expects the yen to appreciate by 2.4% next week, but expects it to *depreciate* by 3.4% in a year.[6] The Mundell–Fleming model is a medium-run model which does not intend to analyse weekly or monthly changes, but rather quarterly or annual changes. The assumptions of positive θ and equation (16), therefore, perhaps make sense in this approach.

The model consists of three equations, (16), (17), and (18), which determine Y, r, and e. Exogenous variables are M, G, Y^*, r^*, A_1, A_2, B, and e^*. The model, when empirically implemented, can actually accommodate various dynamics arising, for example, from the gradual adjustment of prices (the Phillips curve). They are not essential for our purpose, however.

[6] The sign of θ determines whether or not international transactions in the financial market augment the stability of the exchange rate: see Frankel and Meese (1987). Tobin (1978), arguing that 'excessive speculation' in the market destabilizes the exchange rate, proposes an introduction of tax on foreign exchange transactions. The Tobin tax reduces the volatility in the exchange rate only when θ in (15) is negative. Given the Frankel–Froot analysis of market survey, the Tobin tax stabilizes the exchange rate in the short run, but may actually destabilize it in the long-run.

In this model, an increase in government deficits raises the real interest rate and at the same time brings about an appreciation of the exchange rate. This result is qualitatively the same as in the neoclassical saving–investment balance approach or the Branson model. The mechanism at work, however, is, very different in the Mundell–Fleming model. In the Keynesian approach, an expansionary fiscal policy will raise domestic demand for goods and services, leading to an expansion in output; as output rises, the demand for money increases and, given money supply, the interest rate goes up. In the neoclassical model, an increase in government deficits, taken as a shift of demand away from future goods to present goods, raises the real interest rate as the intertemporal price.

Trade deficits also increase as government deficits rise, in all three approaches. In the neoclassical and the Branson models, the key variable is the exchange rate, while in the Mundell–Fleming approach an increase in output plays an important role on the top of the exchange rate. Another difference is that monetary policy affects the real interest rate and the real exchange rate in the Keynesian approach. This prediction is, of course, in sharp contrast to the neoclassical approach.

Another interesting case is the strengthening of Japan's competitiveness of exportables: a shift of parameter B in (17). In the neoclassical saving–investment balance approach, in the absence of the Metzler–Laursen effect, a strengthened competitiveness is to be wholly absorbed by an appreciation of the yen, and the current account is to remain unchanged. In contrast, the Keynesian model predicts that a strengthened competitiveness leads to a surge in exports, entailing a current account surplus.

8.3 THE EXPERIENCES IN THE 1980s

In the 1980s, the world economy saw vast changes in the exchange rates and the emergence of current account imbalances on an unprecedented scale. Today, students of international macroeconomics find in this decade a wonderful opportunity to test competing theories. To this end, it is convenient to divide the 1980s into two sub-periods.

The First Half of the 1980s

The early 1980s is characterized by the worldwide high real interest rates, an appreciation of the dollar, and the emergence of current account imbalances among major economies (Table 8.2 and Fig. 8.1). As explained in the previous section, most theories ascribe these features mainly to a substantial increase in the US government deficit. However, the 'structural' government deficits in the United States increased from 1983 onwards; and yet the real interest rate went up, and the dollar started appreciating, as early as 1981. To resolve this inconsistency, Branson introduces anticipations of future increases in government deficits beginning in 1981. A more reasonable explanation, however, would be a major change in the US monetary policy.

In October 1979, the Federal Reserve led by Paul Volker made a formal announcement effectively indicating that the Fed would adopt a more monetarist policy, seeking to keep the growth rate of monetary aggregates such as M1 within pre-announced target zones. This 'new monetary policy', which lasted for nearly three years until the summer of 1982, in effect meant an extremely tight monetary policy. From Table 8.4, it can be seen that the growth rate of real M1 was negative for three consecutive years beginning in 1979. Naturally enough, the interest rate, both nominal and real, rose sharply. And the high interest rates produced the worst recession in the post-war history of the United States. The pattern of this recession, triggered by a tight monetary policy, was of an almost textbook type: first, residential construction was hit hard, then eventually, a decline in fixed investment deepened the recession in 1982 (Table 8.5).

High interest rates entail an appreciation of the dollar. The high interest rates, recession, and appreciation of the dollar are all well accounted for by the Mundell–Fleming approach. The point is that, for 1980–2, the major exogenous change was monetary

Table 8.4. The 'new monetary policy' in the United States, 1979–1982 (%)[a]

	1978	1979	1980	1981	1982	1983
M1	8.2	7.6	6.8	6.5	8.5	9.6
GNP deflator	7.3	8.9	9.0	9.7	6.4	3.9
Real M1	0.9	– 1.3	– 2.2	– 3.2	2.1	5.7
TB rate	7.2	10.0	11.5	14.0	10.7	8.6
Real TB rate[b]	– 0.1	1.1	2.5	4.3	4.3	4.7
Real GNP	5.3	2.5	– 0.2	1.9	– 2.5	3.6

[a] Rate of change except for interest rates.

[b] Real TB rate = (TB rate) – (inflation in GNP deflator in the same year).

Table 8.5. The 1982 recession in the United States (%)[a]

	1980	1981	1982				1983	
			I	II	III	IV	I	II
Real GNP	−0.2	1.9	−5.5	1.0	−1.0	−1.3	2.6	8.7
Consumption	0.5	2.7	2.4	3.1	0.9	3.6	2.9	10.0
Fixed investment	−2.4	5.2	−5.9	−14.3	−8.8	−6.6	−1.5	4.6
Residential construction	−20.4	−5.2	−28.5	17.9	−13.0	53.2	57.3	61.1
Industrial production	−3.6	2.6	−11.7	−6.6	−3.4	−8.1	9.9	17.8

[a] Annual rate of change in seasonally adjusted figures.

policy. The government deficit in 1982 was simply the *result* of the deep recession.

High interest rates and the accompanying deep recession in the United States produced a serious debt problem in developing countries, which were facing a fall in the price of oil and other raw materials from 1981 onwards. As the debt problem of Mexico surfaced in the summer of 1982, the Federal Reserve abandoned the 'new monetary policy' without any formal announcement. Monetary policy returned to expansion—and yet the real interest rate remained high. The reason is that the 'structural' government deficits increased beginning in 1983.

A summary of the US economy in the first half of the 1980s is shown in Fig. 8.4. In 1980–2, tight monetary policy moved the economy from *A* to *B*. Beginning in 1983, a mix of expansionary fiscal and monetary policies moved the economy from *B* to *C*. The real interest rate remained high, but growth of the economy was also high. Meanwhile, in Japan government deficits inherited from the 1970s had been squeezed throughout the 1980s (see Table 8.6). In 1983 and 1984, the growth rate of the United States was, in fact, higher than that of Japan (Table 8.7); in particular, 6.8% (1984) was the highest US growth rate since the Korean War (1951). As expected in a Keynesian model, current account deficits soared between 1983 and 1984.

The updated Mundell–Fleming model explains the appreciation of the exchange rate by the differential in real interest rates across countries, the extent of which depends on the parameter representing the adjustment speed in expectations, θ in (15). With a small θ, the

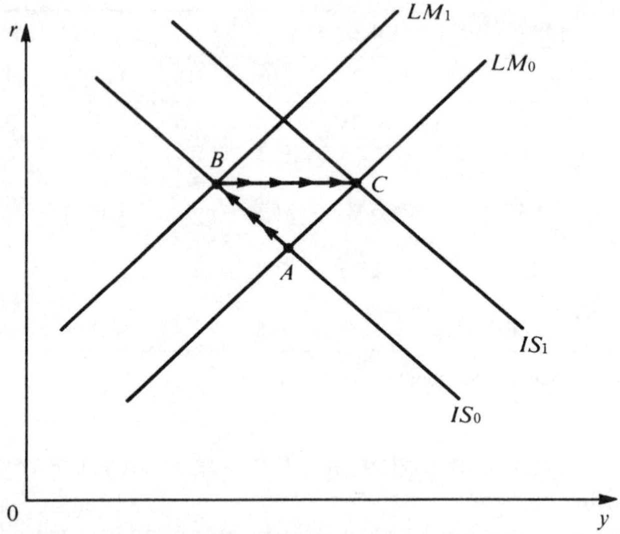

Fig. 8.4. The US economy in the early 1980s

real interest rate differential and/or the risk premium easily causes the exchange rate to deviate from its equilibrium value. In the early 1980s, a number of equations similar to (16) were estimated with reasonable results. (For the yen–dollar rate, see Fukao 1983.) There is, however, the problem of whether the exchange rate that is consistent with equation (16) is really 'rational' from the 'long-run' viewpoint. Krugman (1985), for example, questioning whether the strong dollar in the early 1980s was 'sustainable', made the following calculation.

Denoting current account, trade balance, and foreign debt, all relative to GNP, by CA, T, and D, we obtain

$$CA = T - rD, \tag{19}$$

$$\dot{D} = - CA - gD = - T + (r - g)D, \tag{20}$$

for the United States, where r and g are the real interest rate and growth rate, respectively. The trade balance is assumed to depend only on the deviation of the exchange rate, e, from its equilibrium value, e^*:

$$T = \gamma(e^* - e) \qquad (\gamma > 0). \tag{21}$$

This assumption is very strong in that the implied income elasticity of the trade balance is one, actually contradicting Houthakker and Magee (1969). In any case, (20) and (21) lead us to

Table 8.6. Japanese government deficits, 1970–1991 (¥ trillion)[a]

	Central government	Ratio relative to GDP (%)	Local government	Ratio relative to GDP (%)	Social security	Ratio relative to GDP (%)	Total	Ratio relative to GDP (%)
1970	– 0.02	– 0.03	– 0.31	– 0.42	1.73	2.30	1.39	1.85
1971	– 0.80	– 0.97	– 0.87	– 1.05	2.15	2.60	0.48	0.58
1972	– 1.06	– 1.10	– 1.09	– 1.13	2.39	2.48	0.24	0.25
1973	0.46	0.39	– 1.15	– 0.98	3.11	2.67	2.43	2.08
1974	– 1.98	– 1.43	– 1.74	– 1.25	3.79	2.74	0.07	0.05
1975	– 6.10	– 4.00	– 3.26	– 2.14	3.85	2.52	– 5.52	– 3.62
1976	– 7.39	– 4.31	– 2.70	– 1.58	4.12	2.41	– 5.97	– 3.48
1977	– 9.51	– 5.00	– 3.45	– 1.81	5.22	2.75	– 7.74	– 4.07
1978	– 10.09	– 4.84	– 3.60	– 1.72	5.12	2.45	– 8.57	– 4.11
1979	– 12.76	– 5.67	– 3.05	– 1.36	5.80	2.57	– 10.02	– 4.45
1980	– 13.25	– 5.40	– 3.15	– 1.28	6.48	2.64	– 9.92	– 4.04
1981	– 13.67	– 5.24	– 3.24	– 1.24	7.24	2.78	– 9.67	– 3.71
1982	– 14.12	– 5.16	– 2.56	– 0.94	7.35	2.69	– 9.33	– 3.41
1983	– 13.86	– 4.85	– 2.17	– 0.76	7.64	2.68	– 8.39	– 2.94
1984	– 12.27	– 4.02	– 1.82	– 0.60	8.51	2.79	– 5.58	– 1.83
1985	– 11.81	– 3.64	– 0.89	– 0.27	10.21	3.15	– 2.49	– 0.77
1986	– 10.24	– 3.03	– 0.83	– 0.25	10.00	2.96	– 1.07	– 0.32
1987	– 6.83	– 1.93	– 0.37	– 0.11	9.60	2.71	2.39	0.68
1988	– 4.19	– 1.11	0.26	0.07	12.14	3.22	8.21	2.18
1989	– 4.88	– 1.21	2.42	0.60	13.15	3.27	10.70	2.66
1990	– 1.40	– 0.32	1.35	0.31	15.38	3.56	15.33	3.54
1991	– 1.14	– 0.25	– 0.34	– 0.07	17.33	3.81	15.85	3.48

[a] Deficit (–), surplus (+).

Table 8.7. Differential in growth rate of real GNP between Japan and the United States, 1980–1989 (%)

	(1) Japan	(2) USA	Difference ((1) – (2))
1980	4.3	– 0.2	4.5
1981	3.7	1.9	1.8
1982	3.1	– 2.5	5.6
1983	3.2	3.6	– 0.4
1984	5.1	6.8	– 1.7
1985	4.9	3.4	1.5
1986	2.5	2.7	– 0.2
1987	4.6	3.7	0.9
1988	5.7	4.4	1.3
1989	4.9	2.5	2.4
1960–9	10.7	4.1	6.6
1970–9	5.1	2.8	2.3

$$\dot{D} = \gamma(e - e^*) + (r - g)D. \qquad (22)$$

Ignoring the risk premium, the market expectations for the exchange rate are

$$\left(\frac{\dot{e}}{e}\right)^{ex} = r^* - r. \qquad (23)$$

Therefore, assuming the initial value of $e_0 - e^*$ to be 0.33 (the dollar overvalued by 33% relative to e^* at the beginning), $r - r^*$ to be 0.024 (the US real interest rate higher than that in foreign country by 2.4%), r to be 0.08, g to be 0.03, and γ to be 0.1, (22) and (23) make it possible to calculate the path of D. Krugman's calculation demonstrates that the foreign debt–GNP ratio D reaches 45.7% at its peak, a level comparable to those in Mexico or Brazil. Krugman argues that such a high debt–GNP ratio is not politically acceptable for the United States, that in this sense, therefore, the strong dollar is not rational from the long-run perspective.

The Post-Plaza Period: 1985–1990

Whether or not the strong dollar in the early 1980s was 'rational' from the long-run perspective, the tide turned dramatically in the autumn of 1985. On 22 September 1985, the G5 agreed on the desirability of a depreciation of the US dollar, and to achieve this goal co-ordinated intervention in the foreign exchange market. Immediately before this 'Plaza Accord', the dollar was at ¥241; only a week later, the dollar had already depreciated to ¥220, and by the beginning of November it had fallen to ¥207: a 15% depreciation in a month. Since then, the dollar has depreciated close to ¥100 (in the summer of 1993). In particular, during the short period spanning the two years following the Plaza Accord, the dollar fell by nearly half against the Japanese yen (Fig. 8.1).

It is difficult to explain this sharp revaluation of currencies by such conventional theories as described in the previous section. In the very short run, in October 1985, immediately after the Plaza Accord, the interest rate differential between Japan and the United States actually widened, which in itself was a factor leading to an *appreciation* of the dollar. From the medium-run perspective, the dollar depreciated while the Japanese and US current account imbalances persisted.

The fundamental problem of existing open-economy macro theories is their tacit assumption that the 'equilibrium' real exchange rate, such as e^* in (16), is constant or that its change is very low. In the trade balance equation (17), TB should also explicitly read '$TB\ (e/e^*, Y, Y^*: B)$' rather than '$TB(e, Y, Y^*; B)$'. Krugman, for example, defending the Massachusetts Avenue model, argues that

> the trend (in the 'equilibrium' real exchange rate) is fairly slow, on the order of 2 percent or less annually. This can amount to a lot over the course of a decade, but it does not make the short- and medium-run response of trade to the exchange rate either unpredictable or irrelevant. (Krugman 1991: 21–2)

Contrary to Krugman's argument, the next section demonstrates that the change in the value of the dollar during the period by and large reflected changes in the 'equilibrium' exchange rate. This fact is consistent with another: namely, that the huge change in the exchange rate did not necessarily diminish current account imbalances even if it contributed to this end to some extent.

The Keynesian approach assigns a more important role in explaining the current account to changes in output than to changes in exchange rates: specifically, to (i) the growth rate of the economy relative to the foreign counterpart, (ii) whether growth is led by domestic demand or exports (the relative contribution of net exports to growth), and (iii) the levels of and changes in the marginal propensity to import. Indeed, Houthakker and Magee (1969) emphasize the importance of differences in income elasticities of exports/imports across countries. For Japan, their finding is that the export elasticity is nearly three times the import elasticity: 3 versus 1. Very similar estimates are obtained by Ueda (1988*b*) for the period 1970–87. They imply that a differential in growth rates easily brings about a sizeable change in the trade balance. To be specific, a change in the trade balance due to growth differentials is

$$\frac{\mathrm{d}TB}{TB} = \left(\frac{X}{TB}\right)\eta_X g^* - \left(\frac{M}{TB}\right)\eta_M g,$$

where the trade balance TB is the difference between exports X and imports M; η_X and η_M are income elasticities of Japan's exports and imports and are estimated by Houthakker and Magee (1969) and Ueda (1988*b*) to be 3 and 1, respectively; and, finally, g^* and g are growth rates of the foreign (US) and Japanese economies. Then, for example, since TB, X, and M are $18, $138, and $120 billion for 1982, a percentage change in Japan's trade balance due to growth differentials would be $24g^* - 7g$.

Table 8.7 compares the growth rates of real GNP of Japan and the United States. On the whole, the growth rate in Japan tends to be higher, but remarkably, in 1983–4 the order is reversed. With the 1984 figures of 6.8% for the USA and 5.1% for Japan, $24g^* - 7g$ becomes 127%. One expects Japan's trade surplus to have more than doubled. Beyond that, as shown in Table 2.24, the relatively low growth of the Japanese economy during this period was export-led. It is natural that trade imbalances suddenly soared in 1983–4. The simulation analysis by Ueda (1988*b*) basically bears this out, concluding that the growth differential is a much more important factor in explaining the surge in Japan's current account surplus in the early 1980s than the real exchange rate. Similarly, the most important factor in explaining a gradual decrease in Japan's current surplus during 1987–90 is the domestic-demand-led high growth of the Japanese economy. As the recession deepened in Japan during 1991–3, the current surplus once again rose (see Table 8.1).

For the 1987–90 boom, behind the high growth of domestic demand were such factors as (i) a high rate of investment based on technological progress (see Chapter 7), (ii) high stock/land prices triggered by low interest rates, and (iii) income generated by improvement in the terms of trade. Here we focus on the third factor. Appreciation of the yen from ¥240 to ¥130 per dollar during the three-year period following the Plaza Accord brought about a sizeable improvement in Japan's terms of trade. The gains arising from this terms-of-trade improvement can be measured as follows.

First we consider exports. During 1985–7, the quantity of Japan's exports remained unchanged. From 1985 to 1986, the yen appreciated from ¥240 to ¥170, by 30%, while exports in terms of US dollars rose from $180 billion to $210 billion. This means that, given the same quantity of exports, the dollar price of Japan's exportables rose by 15%, whereas the yen price declined by 15%. This decline in the yen price of Japan's exportables in response to the appreciation of yen is known as 'pricing to market' (see Marston 1990 and Knetter 1993). A decline in exports, in yen terms, amounted to ¥8 trillion. This was the major factor behind the 1986 recession.

On the other hand, substantial gains arose from the import side. In 1985, Japan's imports in dollar terms were about $120 billion; by 1988 they had increased to $180 billion. At the same time, the quantity of Japan's imports also increased, by nearly 50%. The dollar price of Japan's importables on average remained unchanged. Appreciation of the yen, therefore, brought about a one-for-one decline in the yen price of importables. Savings in financing the same quantity of imports as in 1985 amounted to ¥10 trillion for 1986, ¥12 trillion for 1987, and ¥15 trillion for 1988. Cumulative savings measure up to almost ¥40 trillion, equivalent to more than one-tenth of GNP! These gains were a major factor, perhaps more important than the oft-cited high asset prices, contributing to a four-year-long boom (1987–90) of the Japanese economy.

In passing, Japan's net foreign assets, amounting to $130 billion in 1985, did not suffer capital losses *in real terms* despite the 50% appreciation of the yen during the period 1985–8. The reason is that, first, importables and domestic goods are imperfect substitutes, and, second, depreciation of the dollar was not caused by US inflation, and the dollar price of Japan's importables remained basically unchanged. Therefore, Japan's net foreign assets in terms of importables were left intact.

In any case, domestic-demand-led growth diminished Japan's current account surplus; it fell to $33 billion dollars in 1990, about 1% of GNP. It also turned government deficits to surpluses, perhaps unintentionally on the part of the government (Table 8.6). Subsequently, however, the Japanese economy entered a period of severe recession beginning in 1991, and this recession once again raised the current account surplus—to $120 billion, the highest ever, and amounting to more than 3% of GNP. Meanwhile, the dollar kept depreciating, from ¥140 in 1990 to ¥110 in 1993.

Again, what happened during this period contradicts existing theories. The reason why the continuing appreciation of yen accompanied the surge in Japan's trade surplus in the 1980s is that, for the exchange rate, the movement of the yen has broadly reflected a change in the 'equilibrium' rate.

8.4 THE EQUILIBRIUM EXCHANGE RATE

Conventional theories, as surveyed in Section 8.2, cannot adequately explain the almost 60% appreciation of the yen that occurred during the period 1985–93 so long as they take the equilibrium exchange rate as constant. As will be seen shortly, the appreciation of the yen during this period broadly reflected changes in the 'equilibrium' rate.

There are many definitions of the equilibrium exchange rate in the literature. One may define it as the exchange rate that is consistent with the neoclassical saving–investment balance. Or, taking the longer perspective, one might prefer to define it as the exchange rate that makes the current account or the trade balance zero; Branson (1985) and Krugman (1985), among others, use this definition. Another major definition of the equilibrium exchange rate is purchasing power parity (PPP), advanced by Cassel (1922) and Keynes (1923).

This section proposes a new definition of the long-run equilibrium exchange rate that emphasizes the role of the supply factors in addition to the more traditional price differential variables. Using this definition, I estimate the long-run equilibrium yen–dollar rate during the period 1973–87. This calculation demonstrates that supply-side factors are in fact very important determinants of the long-run movement of the exchange rate.

Despite the central role that exchange rates play in the economy, economists often seem to doubt their own ability to explain, let alone predict, exchange rate movements. This is because in many cases structural exchange rate equations based on such economic theories as those explained in Section 8.2 do not significantly outperform various other models that do not appeal to economic theory, such as the random walk (see e.g. Meese and Rogoff 1983). While I share this pessimism concerning our ability to forecast exchange rates in the short run (intra-daily to monthly or quarterly), I argue that it is possible reasonably to *explain*, if not predict, long-run movements.

The long-run equilibrium rate is most often thought to be determined by purchasing power parity (PPP), which tends to focus only on price differentials. Medium-run divergences of the exchange rate from the long-run equilibrium are therefore commonly identified with fluctuations in the inflation-adjusted real exchange rate. The subsequent analysis demonstrates, however, that the *simple* PPP is unsatisfactory because it emphasizes only the inflation differential. In the more elaborated theory of purchasing power parity, of course, the potential importance of supply-side *real* factors as critical determinants of the exchange rate has been well recognized (see e.g. Keynes 1923, Dornbusch *et al.* 1977). Nevertheless, in empirical applications and policy discussions, these supply-side real factors have been curiously ignored. (To my knowledge, an exception is Hsieh 1982.) The main point of this section is to show that these supply-side factors have actually been very important determinants of the yen–dollar rate over the period 1973–87.

The Definition of the Equilibrium Rate

In formulating a definition of the long-run equilibrium exchange rate, I start by considering the tradables sector of the Japanese economy. I assume that two inputs, labour and natural resources (including energy), are necessary for production. For simplicity, I also assume a fixed-coefficient production function. Accordingly, the production process can be characterized by two parameters, a and b, which are, respectively, the labour input and the natural resources input necessary to produce one unit of the tradable good.

Under the assumption of perfect competition, we are led to the following relationship:

$$wa + p_R b = p, \tag{24}$$

where p and p_R are the domestic (yen) prices of tradables and natural resources, respectively, and w is the nominal wage rate. For simplicity, I have assumed zero profits in (24), although this assumption is not essential to our analysis. If we allow for a normal rate of profit and call it r, we need only to add rp to the left-hand side of (24). As long as we hold the normal rate of profit r constant, this inclusion will not affect our analysis.

Assume that Japan exports manufactured products and imports the natural resources that are necessary for the production of such tradables. In 1980, for example, 96% of Japan's exports consisted of manufactured products, whereas 70% of imports were raw materials including oil. Recently, however, the percentage of manufactured products in Japan's imports has steadily risen; by 1990, the proportion of raw materials including oil had declined to 36%.

I take as given (in dollars) both p^*, the international price of the tradable good, and p^*_R, the international price of the natural resources. Since most manufactured products are more or less differentiated, the 'law of one price' does not exactly hold. Observed pricing to market (Marston 1990; Knetter 1993) is a clear indication of this point. We would therefore expect the following relation between p and p^*:

$$p = ep^*/\varepsilon, \tag{25}$$

where e is the nominal exchange rate (yen–dollar) and ε is random deviations reflecting such factors as changes in the relative demand for Japan's exportables and/or strategic pricing to market. I assume that the expected value of ε, $E(\varepsilon)$, is one. For the natural resources, we have

$$p_R = ep^*_R. \tag{26}$$

With (25) and (26), (24) can be rewritten as

$$wa + ep^*_R b = ep^*/\varepsilon. \tag{27}$$

If we set p^* at US unit costs, we have

$$p^* = w^*a^* + p^*_R b^* = w^* \left[a^* + \frac{p^*_R}{w^*} b^* \right], \tag{28}$$

where a^* and b^* are the labour and energy coefficients and w^* is the nominal US wage rate. When (28) is substituted into (27), we obtain

$$e = \varepsilon \left(\frac{w}{w^*} \right) \frac{a/(1 - bt^*)}{a^* + (p^*_R/w^*)b^*}, \tag{29}$$

where $t^* = \varepsilon p^*_R/p^*$ is the relative price of natural resources in terms of Japan's exportables. Since $E(\varepsilon) = 1$, we finally obtain

$$e^* = E(e) = \frac{w}{w^*} \frac{a/(1 - bt^*)}{a^* + (p^*_R/w^*)b^*} \tag{30}$$

for a long-run trend of the yen–dollar exchange rate. The equilibrium exchange rate e^* defined in (30) depends on the following factors:

1. the relative nominal wage levels in Japan and the United States;
2. the terms of trade (the relative price of natural resources such as oil, and of manufactured goods in the international market);
3. the labour and energy coefficients (productivities) of the Japanese export sector.

The simple PPP tends to emphasize the price differential, which in this case is factor 1, or the nominal wage differential. In constrast to factor 1, factor 2, the terms of trade, and factor 3, the productivities, are real factors.

At this point, it is appropriate to clarify the meaning of the above equilibrium exchange rate. The long-run equilibrium rate defined by (30) is the exchange rate at which the profit rate of the Japanese export sector remains constant, given exogenous movements of wages, productivity, terms of trade, and export prices. It is certainly compatible with a variety of different models. The appendix offers a classical model in which this equilibrium rate is embedded.

The equilibrium exchange rate proposed here does not guarantee current account balance. Since the relation between this equilibrium exchange rate and the current account is a very important point, it will be discussed in the appendix. The equilibrium rate is, in fact, simply one version of PPP by which we can measure the relative importance of monetary and real factors in determining the long-run movement of the exchange rate.

Given this equilibrium rate, we observe the following relationship between the domestic and foreign prices of the *tradables*:

$$E(e)p^*/p = 1. \tag{31}$$

This means that, in order to hold constant the competitiveness of both foreign and domestic countries with regard to the tradables sector, the p-adjusted real exchange rate must be one.

However, the real exchange rate calculation is often based on more broadly defined price deflators, such as the GNP deflator or the CPI. In such instances, if we let $\hat{p}$, $\hat{p}^*$ represent the domestic and foreign deflators, respectively, (31) is violated for $\hat{e}$, even though (32) holds:

$$\hat{e}\,\hat{p}^*/\hat{p} = 1. \tag{32}$$

To be more specific, the GNP deflators of home (Japan) and foreign (the USA) countries are, respectively, defined as

$$\hat{p} = \delta p + (1 - \delta)p_N \tag{33}$$

and

$$\hat{p}^* = \delta^* p^* + (1 - \delta^*)p_N^*, \tag{34}$$

where p_N and p_N^* are the domestic and foreign prices of non-tradables, and δ and δ^* are the expenditure shares of tradables in Japan and the United States, respectively.

Under the condition

$$\delta + (1 - \delta)\frac{p_N}{p} > \delta^* + (1 - \delta^*)\frac{p_N^*}{p^*}, \tag{35}$$

(32) holds, but we have

$$p < \hat{e}\, p^*. \tag{36}$$

If $\delta^* = \delta$, (35) boils down to

$$\frac{p}{p_N} < \frac{p^*}{p_N^*}. \tag{37}$$

Therefore, if high productivity in Japan makes tradables relatively cheaper in Japan than in the United States, Japan's competitiveness is increased even though the real exchange rate in terms of the GNP deflator remains constant. The point was raised many years ago by Balassa (1964) and is recently emphasized by Marston (1987) and Ohno (1986).

The Estimation of the Equilibrium Rate

In what follows, I estimate the equilibrium yen–dollar exchange rate on the basis of equation (30). I adopt the two-country framework, using Japan as the home country and the United States as the foreign country. My analysis is limited in the sense that I take into account only one trading partner.

First, a and b are calculated from the input coefficients (annual data) of 13 manufacturing industries as categorized by the SNA, which are used in the Economic Planning Agency's medium-term multi-sector model. I identify Japan's export industries as fibres, chemicals, primary metals, general machinery, electrical equipment, transportation equipment, and precision equipment. Using the export volume of each industry, X_i, $(i = 1, 2,\ldots, 7)$, the weights are calculated as follows:

$$\sigma_i = X_i / \sum_{j=1}^{7} X_j \qquad (i = 1, 2,\ldots, 7), \tag{38}$$

where X_i refers to exports (in dollar terms) after passing customs. Data are taken from the Ministry of Finance's *Foreign Trade Outlook*. Using these weights,

$$a = \sum_{i=1}^{7} \sigma_i a^i, \tag{39}$$

where a^i is each industry's labour input coefficient.

Similarly, b is calculated as follows:

$$b = \sum_{i=1}^{7} \sigma_i (b_{io} + b_{i,PETRO} b_{PETRO,O}), \tag{40}$$

where b_{io} is the ith industry's input coefficient for oil and natural gas, and $b_{i,\,PETRO}$ and $b_{PETRO,O}$ are, respectively, the ith industry's input coefficient for petroleum products, and the petroleum products sector's input coefficient for oil and natural gas. Using this method, a and b are prepared annually. The annual series for 1973–87 are shown in Table 8.8. We observe that, in the 10^+-year period after the first oil shock, the labour coefficient and the energy–natural resources coefficient of Japan's exporting industry were down to about 1/2 and 1/6, respectively.

Next, t^* was calculated from the contract-based (mostly dollar-based) export price of manufactured goods and the import prices of oil, gas, and coal. The data source for this calculation is the Bank of Japan's *Annual Statistics of Prices*. w is the nominal wage in Japan's manufacturing industry, and is taken from the Bank of Japan's *Monthly Economic Statistics*.

Finally, to obtain the equilibrium rate defined by (30), we must measure the US unit costs of the products that correspond to Japan's exportables. To calculate these unit costs, we start with the following definition:

$$\text{Unit cost} = \frac{w^* L^* + p_M^* M^*}{Q^*}, \tag{41}$$

Table 8.8. Labour and energy coefficients in Japan's export industries, 1973–1987

	Labour coefficient	Energy coefficient
1973	0.089	0.026
1974	0.081	0.030
1975	0.087	0.024
1976	0.079	0.020
1977	0.074	0.018
1978	0.067	0.016
1979	0.061	0.017
1980	0.058	0.017
1981	0.056	0.012
1982	0.054	0.010
1983	0.053	0.009
1984	0.049	0.008
1985	0.049	0.008
1986	0.044	0.006
1987	0.041	0.004

where w^* and p^*_M are the nominal wage and price of materials and energy, and L^*, M^*, and Q^* are US labour, material inputs, and output, respectively. *The Annual Survey of Manufactures: Statistics for Industry Groups and Industries*, compiled by the US Department of Commerce, provides the necessary data. Using these data, the unit cost is calculated as follows:

$$\text{Unit cost} = p^* \frac{w^*L^*}{P^*Q^*} + p^* \frac{p^*_M M^*}{P^*Q^*}, \tag{42}$$

where w^*L^*, $p^*_M M^*$, and P^*Q^* are, respectively, the payroll of all employees, the cost of materials, and the sum of the cost of materials and value added by manufactures. p^* in (42) is the producer price index in the *Survey of Current Business*, which is equivalent to the wholesale price index for Japan. I prepared this unit cost on an annual basis for the above-mentioned seven industries, which correspond to Japan's export industries, and then, with weights (38), calculated the economy-wide unit cost. This is the unit cost $w^*a^* + p^*_R b^*$ in (30).

To calculate the equilibrium yen–dollar exchange rate from (30), we need a base year. Here I consider two cases: the first presumes that the actual exchange rate was close to (30) before the first oil shock (i.e. the first quarter of 1973), and the second uses 1975, when the Japan's current account was nearly in balance.

The estimated long-run equilibrium rates are shown in Table 8.9. They correspond to the two different base years. For the sake of comparison, the table also shows simplc PPP rates based on economy-wide wages which are supposed to reflect general inflation differential but do not take into account any productivity differential. In addition, the table lists the actual yen–dollar exchange rate. These are all shown in Figures 8.5 and 8.6.

My equilibrium rate differs substantially from the simple PPP rate based on economy-wide wages only. Since my rate broadly tracks the trend of the actual exchange rate, I argue that the supply-side factors such as labour and energy productivity are very important determinants of the exchange rate in the long run. The results obtained are reasonably robust with respect to changes in the base year.

We can measure the relative impact of each factor on the equilibrium rate by calculating the hypothetical rate. In order to do this, I assume that one factor remains constant at the base-year level. These hypothetical rates for the constants a, b, the US unit labour cost, and

Table 8.9. Wage-adjusted rates and equilibrium exchange rates, 1973–1987

		Base year 1973		Base year 1975	
	Actual rate	Equilibrium rate	Wage-adjusted rate	Equilibrium rate	Wage-adjusted rate
1973	271.70	271.70	271.70	284.37	228.30
1974	292.08	271.79	324.83	284.46	272.95
1975	296.79	283.56	353.21	296.79	296.79
1976	269.55	278.10	370.25	291.07	311.11
1977	268.51	269.02	373.39	281.57	313.75
1978	210.44	240.43	367.82	251.64	309.08
1979	219.14	217.15	361.96	227.28	304.15
1980	226.74	199.70	359.84	209.01	302.37
1981	220.54	182.93	348.47	191.46	292.81
1982	249.08	176.63	347.12	184.87	291.68
1983	237.51	175.68	339.78	183.87	285.51
1984	237.52	166.04	337.53	173.79	283.62
1985	238.54	156.58	339.27	163.89	285.08
1986	168.52	148.13	342.18	155.04	287.52
1987	144.64	140.53	339.95	147.08	285.65

the US energy cost are shown, together with the equilibrium rate for the 1975 base-year case, in Table 8.10. We can see, for example, that the equilibrium rate would have been ¥303.77 per dollar in 1987 if the labour coefficient in Japan had remained unchanged at the 1975 level. However, as we can see from Table 8.8, the labour coefficient in Japan declined sharply between 1975 and 1987, and therefore the equilibrium rate was ¥147.08 per dollar. The divergence between the equilibrium rate and the hypothetical rate for the constant b, the Japanese energy coefficient, is rather small, which means that the effect of changes in b on the equilibrium rate is not substantial. Thus, overall, an increase in labour productivity in Japan is by far the most important factor behind the long-run appreciation of the yen. Conversely, on the US side, an increase in unit energy and material costs seems to be a more important determinant of the dollar's depreciation than an increase in the unit labour cost.

8.5 CONCLUDING REMARKS

The Mundell–Fleming approach does a good job of explaining trade imbalances in the 1980s. A growth differential across countries plays

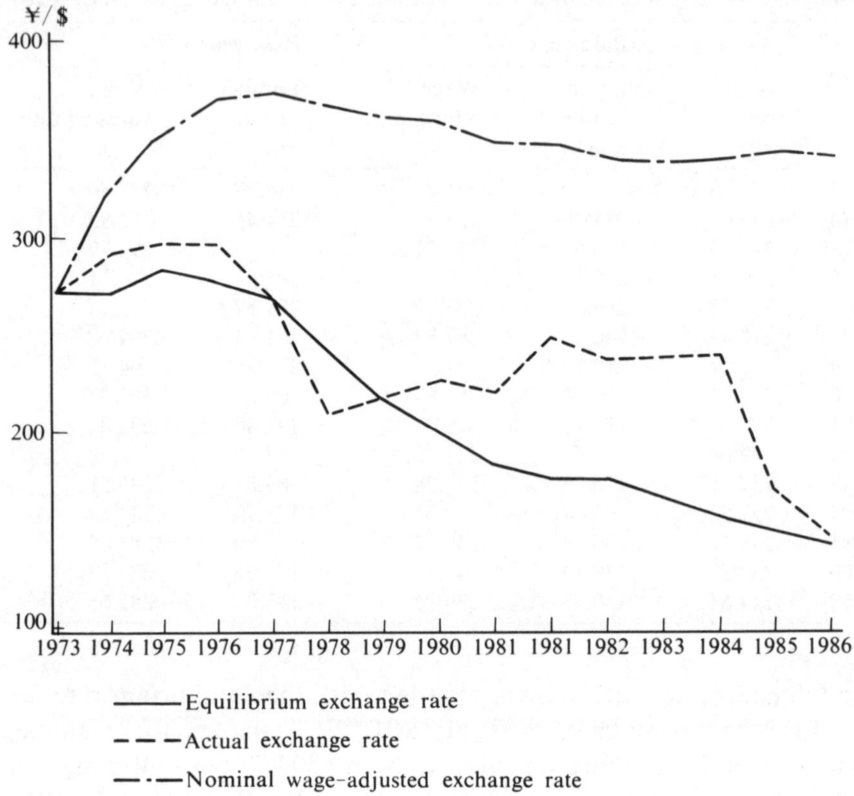

Fig. 8.5. Equilibrium and actual exchange rates, 1973–1987
Base year: 1973.

the major role in this explanation. High and/or low growth rates of the economies are caused by, among other factors, *both monetary and fiscal policies*, although the surge in US fiscal deficits beginning in 1983 was a major factor.

The Mundell–Fleming approach, however, fails to account for the continuing appreciation of the yen during the 1980s, and other theories are no more successful. A dollar was worth ¥240 in 1985 but fell to ¥110 in 1993. The key factor in explaining this sharp appreciation of the yen is a significant change in the 'equilibrium' exchange rate, which is tacitly assumed to be constant in existing open-macroeconomy theories.

In this chapter, I proposed a definition of the long-run equilibrium yen–dollar rate and attempted to estimate it using Japanese and US data. The long-run equilibrium rate defined by (30) is based on three

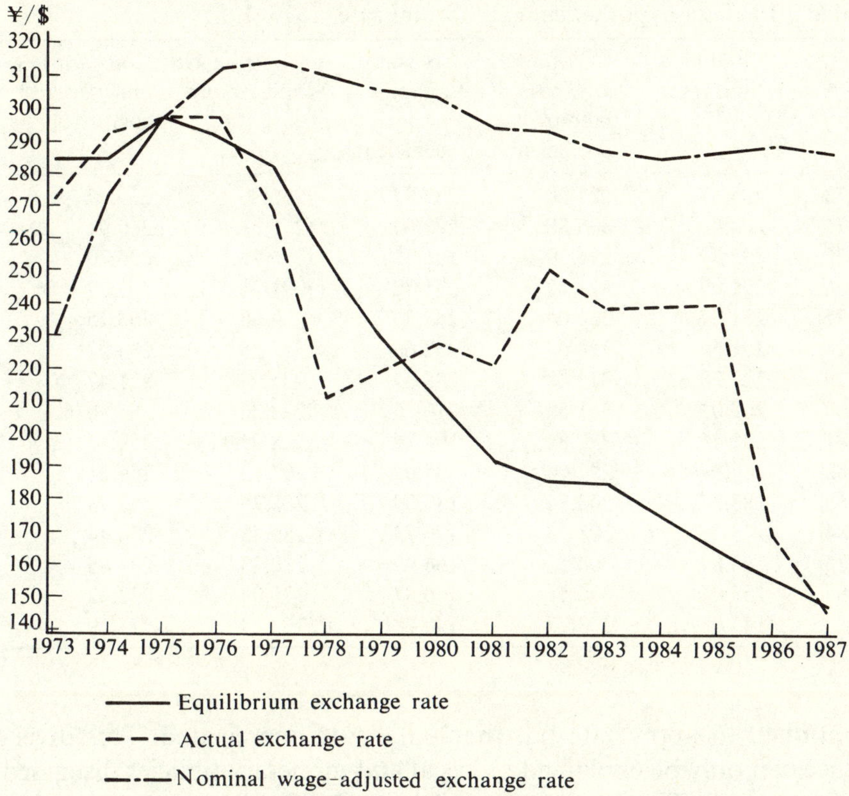

Fig. 8.6. Equilibrium and actual exchange rates, 1973–1987
Base year: 1975.

factors: (i) the (wage) inflation differential between Japan and the United States; (ii) the real-world price of natural resources, such as oil, in terms of manufactured goods (Japan's terms of trade); and (iii) the labour and energy coefficients in both Japan and the United States for Japan's export sector. As a variation of PPP, this approach allows us to explore the relative importance of monetary and real factors in determining the long-run trend of the exchange rate.

From 1973 to 1987, the trend in the actual exchange rate broadly coincides with the movement of this equilibrium rate. On occasion, however, the actual exchange rate diverges from its long-run equilibrium value for fairly long periods. For example, the yen was greatly overvalued in 1978, and the dollar was overvalued for more than four years from 1981 to 1985. During most of the period of the dollar's overvaluation (1981–4), the equilibrium yen–dollar exchange rate

Table 8.10. The hypothetical equilibrium rate, 1973–1987

	Equilibrium rate	Constant Japanese labour coefficient	Constant Japanese energy coefficient	Constant US unit labour cost	Constant US unit material cost
1973	284.37	277.20	283.97	266.30	239.77
1974	284.46	305.88	283.45	276.36	260.91
1975	296.79	296.79	296.79	296.79	296.79
1976	291.07	321.82	291.72	291.21	302.67
1977	281.57	331.04	282.56	283.68	305.75
1978	251.64	324.64	252.66	257.35	285.27
1979	227.28	323.48	228.37	235.92	271.47
1980	209.01	311.55	210.76	223.26	265.90
1981	191.46	297.84	194.34	208.09	257.47
1982	184.87	297.64	188.02	204.73	250.41
1983	183.87	300.94	187.09	202.75	253.93
1984	173.79	308.33	176.73	189.43	246.44
1985	163.89	308.53	166.89	180.23	234.65
1986	155.04	306.21	156.87	171.04	222.42
1987	147.08	303.77	148.88	163.14	213.19

continued to appreciate but the actual rate depreciated. This divergence can only be explained by fiscal and monetary policies discussed in Section 8.3. The depreciation of the dollar from 1985, on the other hand, signalled a return to the equilibrium value.

My analysis demonstrates that real factors, most notably changes in labour productivity, have been much more important than the nominal wages differential in determining the long-run trend of the yen–dollar exchange rate from 1973 to 1987. As mentioned above, most empirical works concerning the long-run equilibrium exchange rate have tended to focus on the price differential and have largely ignored productivity. Meanwhile, statistical evidence indicates that changes in both nominal and real exchange rates can be approximated by the random walk, and therefore that they tend to be nearly permanent. Because changes in real and nominal exchange rates are very highly correlated and have similar variances, it is consistent with the view that most changes in nominal exchange rates are due to real shocks with a large permanent component. Purely statistical analyses leading to this conclusion, however, cannot explain what kind of real shocks are in fact important. This section identified increases in labour productivity in Japan's export industries as the most important factor in explaining the long-run trend of the yen–dollar rate from 1973 to 1987.

As Norsworthy and Malmquist (1983) show, this increase in labour productivity can in turn be attributed to capital investment in Japanese manufacturing, particularly in the machine industries. Since the first oil shock in 1973, the Japanese economy has developed what can be called the 'machinery bloc' through the high rate of investment which has been concentrated in the machinery sector (see Chapters 2 and 7).

Finally, it is interesting to update, if only casually, the equilibrium exchange rate presented in this section. During 1985–91, the producer price index of manufactured products rose by 13% in the United States. The fact that the CPI rose by 26% implies that productivity growth was much higher in the US manufacturing sector than in the non-manufacturing sector. In Japan, however, the WPI of exportables *declined* by 20%, as against a 10.1% increase in CPI during the same period. As a result, the cumulative differential in the price increase in Japan's exportables amounts to 33% for the period 1985–91. Starting with ¥160 per dollar as the equilibrium rate for 1985 (Table 8.9), therefore, we obtain ¥107 for 1992. The actual yen–dollar rate was about ¥108 in mid-1993.

About half of this change (17% out of 33%) is to be attributed to a differential in productivity growth between the Japanese and US manufacturing industry rather than to a differential in increases in the general price level such as CPI. Productivity growth remains a very important factor in determining the nominal/real exchange rate. This implies that, despite a widespread nostalgia, particularly among policy-makers and businessmen (e.g. Volcker and Gyohten 1992), maintaining fixed exchange rates is impossible in today's world.

APPENDIX

This appendix presents a simple classical model which, incorporating the Japanese trade structure, embeds the equilibrium exchange rate given in the main text. On the basis of this model, we consider the relation between the equilibrium exchange rate and the current account.

Model

The country under consideration (let us say, Japan) is a small country, and it produces and consumes two types of good: non-tradables (domestic goods) and tradables. The consumption pattern is determined by a representative consumer's maximization of the Cobb–Douglas utility function with respect to two goods, c_1 and c_2:

$$u(c_1, c_2) = c_1^{\delta_1} c_2^{\delta_2} (\delta_1, \delta_2 > 0, \delta_1 + \delta_2 = 1) \tag{A1}$$

under the budget constraint

$$p_1 c_1 + p_2 c_2 = w\bar{L}. \tag{A2}$$

In (A2), p_1 and p_2 are the prices of the two goods (nominal prices in yen terms), w is the nominal wage, and $\bar{L}$ is the given labour endowment. Labour service is the only domestic input, and therefore wL can be thought of as the gross domestic product (GDP). The optimization of the consumer leads to the following demand functions for the two goods:

$$p_1 c_1 = \delta_1 w\bar{L} \tag{A3}$$

$$p_2 c_2 = \delta_2 w\bar{L}. \tag{A4}$$

For the production of the two goods, two inputs, labour and natural resources (including energy), are necessary. For simplicity, a fixed coefficient production function is assumed. Therefore, the production process can be characterized with four parameters, a_i, b_i ($i = 1, 2$). a_i is the labour input necessary to produce one unit of good i, and b_i is the necessary natural resources input to produce one unit of good i.

Under the assumption of perfect competition, the following relationships hold:

$$wa_1 + p_R b_1 = p_1, \tag{A5}$$

$$wa_2 + p_R b_2 = p_2, \tag{A6}$$

where p_R is the domestic price of natural resources. For simplicity, zero profits are assumed in (A5), (A6), though this assumption is not essential to the present model. As pointed out in the main text, if we allow for a *normal* rate of profit and call it r, we need only add rp_1 and rp_2 to the left-hand sides of both equations. As long as we treat the normal rate of profit r as exogenous, the analysis that follows is kept intact. This assumption, however, excludes 'pricing to market', or the strategic changes in the mark-up in response to changes in real exchange rates.

The input equations are

$$a_1 Q_1 + a_2 Q_2 = \bar{L}, \tag{A7}$$

$$b_1 Q_1 + b_2 Q_2 = R, \tag{A8}$$

where Q_1 and Q_2 refer to the supply of the first and second good, respectively, and therefore (A7) shows that the supply and demand of labour service are in equilibrium. Equation (A8), on the other hand, shows the relationship between the amount of natural resources required, R, and Q_1, Q_2.

By the definition of non-tradables, the domestic supply of good 1 must equal the domestic consumption of good 1:

$$Q_1 = C_1. \tag{A9}$$

Since the second good is a tradable good, such a relationship as (A9) does not hold. For simplicity, I assume for the moment that there is no saving or investment. This assumption means that the current account is always in balance. Saving and investment are introduced into the model later.

The country exports the tradable good 2, and imports the natural resources R that are necessary for the production of the two goods. p_2^* is the international price of tradable good 2, and p_R^* is the international price of natural resources. These prices are considered as given. From here on, we will call p_2^* and p_R^* the dollar price of each good. Under these assumptions, the volume of trade is given by

$$p_2^* (Q_2 - c_2) = p_R^* R. \tag{A10}$$

Let e be the exchange rate in terms of domestic currency; we then obtain

$$p_2 = ep_2^*, \tag{A11}$$

$$p_R = ep_R^*. \tag{A12}$$

This leads to

$$p_2(Q_2 - c_2) = p_R R \tag{A13}$$

as another form for (A10).

From (A13), (A2), and (A9), we can observe that wL is GDP:

$$wL = p_1 Q_1 + P_2 Q_2 - p_R R. \tag{A14}$$

Lastly, to model the asset market, the simplest form of the quantity theory is assumed:

$$\bar{M} = kw\bar{L} = k(p_1 Q_1 + p_2 Q_2 - p_R R), \tag{A15}$$

where the nominal money supply M is exogenous, and k is the Marshallian k. This completes the model. Equations (A3)–(A9), (A11), (A12), and (A15) determine the ten variables p_1, p_2, w, p_R, c_1, c_2, Q_1, Q_2, R, and e. This system is in fact recursive, and therefore the determination of each variable is straightforward.

With (A15), we can first determine w:

$$w = \bar{M}/k\bar{L} \tag{A16}$$

The quantity theory strictly applies to the nominal wage level w. Next, from (A6), (A11), and (A12), we obtain

$$wa_2 + ep_R^* b_2 = ep_2^* \tag{A17}$$

and

$$e = wa_2/(p_2^* - b_2 p_R^*). \tag{A18}$$

The w in the RHS of (A18) is already determined by (A16). Leaving aside the exchange rate for the moment, I first discuss the determination of the other variables.

Equations (A5) and (A12) give

$$p_1 = wa_1 + ep_R^* b_1. \tag{A19}$$

Substituting (A18) for this equation then leads to

$$p_1 = wa_1 + wa_2 b_1 p_R^*/(p_2^* - b_2 p_R^*). \tag{A20}$$

On the other hand, from (A11) and (A18), we obtain

$$p_2 = wa_2 p_2^*/(p_2^* - b_2 p_R^*). \tag{A21}$$

Since we assumed fixed coefficients of production, the prices are determined independently of the domestic demand functions (δ_1, δ_2).

The consumption of the domestic good, of course, depends on p_1; from (A3) we obtain

$$c_1 = \delta_1 w\bar{L}/p_1. \tag{A22}$$

By assumption, consumption is equal to production Q_1. In the same manner, the domestic consumption of the second good is, from (A4),

$$c_2 = \delta_2 w\bar{L}/p_2. \tag{A23}$$

On the other hand, the production of good 2 is derived from equations (A7), (A9), and (A22).

$$Q_2 = (\bar{L} - a_1 Q_1)/a_2 = [L - (a_1 \delta_1 w \bar{L})/p_1)]/a_2. \tag{A24}$$

Finally, the production level of the two goods Q_1 and Q_2 determines the consumption level of natural resources:

$$R = b_1 Q_1 + b_2 Q_2$$

$$= \frac{b_2}{a_2}\bar{L} + \frac{\dfrac{b_2}{a_2}\bar{L}\left(\dfrac{b_1}{b_2} - \dfrac{a_1}{a_2}\right)\delta_1}{\left[\left(\dfrac{a_1}{a_2}\right) + \dfrac{b_1\,(p_R^*/p_2^*)}{1 - b_2\,(p_R^*/p_2^*)}\right]}. \tag{A25}$$

This R is, by assumption, equal to the total volume of trade in units of natural resources. Equation (A25) implies that

$$\partial R/\partial a_2 < 0. \tag{A26}$$

The trade volume increases as the tradable sector's labour productivity grows. This is broadly what actually happened in post-war Japan.

The equilibrium exchange rate given by (A18) can be rewritten as

$$e = (w/p_2^*)\,[a_2/(1 - b_2 t^*)]. \tag{A27}$$

This is essentially equivalent to (30) in the main text.

The Equilibrium Exchange Rate and the Current Account

In the preceding model, as in the main text, the assumption of perfectly substitutable foreign and domestic tradable goods plays a crucial role in deriving the equilibrium exchange rate. More specifically, the model allows unlimited exports at the given price; the home country faces a horizontal demand curve for its exports. In this case, the 'competitiveness' of foreign and domestic producers is fixed by definition—or, rather, such a concept is irrelevant. In what follows, I clarify the meaning of the equilibrium exchange rate under the assumption that the tradable goods are not perfectly substitutable. I also incorporate saving and investment into the model.

When the foreign and domestic tradables are perfect substitutes, the small country's exports are automatically equal to the difference between domestic production of the second good and domestic expenditure, $Q_2 - C_2 - D$, where D is exogenous domestic expenditure on tradables other than consumption.[7] In contrast, under the assumption of incomplete substitutability, the home country faces the foreign country's downward-sloping demand curve for the home country's exportables X^d. X^d can be written as

$$X^d = X^d(\tau, Y^*), \tag{A28}$$

where τ is defined by

$$\tau = p_2/ep_2^*. \tag{A29}$$

It measures the 'competitiveness' of the foreign and domestic producers of the second good. Since, as τ increases, the export competitiveness of this country declines, X^d is a decreasing function of $\tau\,(\partial X^d/\partial\tau < 0)$. Y^* is the shift parameter for the export demand function, e.g. the foreign country's real GNP ($\partial X^d/\partial Y^* > 0$).

[7] If savings and investment are introduced, the home country's GDP remains wL or $P_1Q_1 + P_2Q_2$. Domestic expenditure, on the other hand, necessarily includes some expenditure D other than consumption. For example, D would be $I(r) + G$, where G is government expenditure and I investment. I may depend on the real interest r, determined in the world market. As long as D is exogenous, the equilibrium exchange rate remains unchanged. The major change is that there no longer is a need for the current account to be balanced. In yen terms, the current account is $P_2\,(Q_2 - C_2 - D) - p_R R$. It is a decreasing function of D.

Since the model has three varables that resemble each other, it is useful to ascertain their differences before further analysis. The three variables are t^*, τ, and Japan's terms of trade. First, $t^* = p_R^*/p_2^*$ is the relative price of the natural resources with respect to the manufactured goods in the world market, and is exogenously given. Next, this country's export competitiveness τ is endogenously determined, as will be seen shortly. Finally, terms of trade is defined as

$$p_2/ep_R^* = (p_2/ep_2^*)\,[1/(p_R^*/p_2^*)] = \tau/t^*. \tag{A30}$$

Since t^* is exogenously given, there is a one-to-one correspondence between the terms of trade and τ, but the two are conceptually different. In the text, τ is assumed to be one, and therefore t^* is equivalent to the terms of trade.

From (A6), (A11), (A12), and (A29), we obtain

$$e = wa_2/[p_2^*(\tau - b_2t^*)]. \tag{A31}$$

This is the equilibrium exchange rate in this generalized model, though τ at this stage is as yet an undetermined variable. With τ as an undetermined variable, the price of the non-tradable good, p_1, is

$$p_1 = wa_1 + wa_2b_1/[(\tau/t^*) - b_2]. \tag{A32}$$

Therefore, the consumption (= production) of the non-tradables, the consumption and the production of the tradables, and finally the exports of this country, given by $Q_2 - C_2 - D$, are all functions of τ. Writing exports X^s for convenience, we obtain

$$X^s = Q_2 - C_2 - D = X^s(\tau, D), \tag{A33}$$

where X^s is a decreasing function of τ and D: $\partial X^s/\partial\tau < 0$, $\partial X^s/\partial D < 0$.

The country's 'competitiveness' in export τ is determined in such a way that the following holds:

$$X^d(\tau, Y^*) = X^s(\tau, D). \tag{A34}$$

This completes the model.

The determination of τ by (A34) is best understood from Fig. 8.7. It can be seen that competitiveness τ and the export volume X, which are dependent on such variables as D and Y^*, are simultaneously determined. For example, if for some reason the demand for the home country's exportables increased, in Fig. 8.7 X^d would shift to the right, thus strengthening the competitiveness (τ would go down), and at the same time the export volume would increase. If such a change resulted from the increase in the budget deficit of a 'large country' such as the United States, the real interest rate r would rise, as determined by the world saving–investment balance equation or the asset market equation, and D would decrease. Therefore, under this scenario the rightward shift of X^d would be accompanied by a downward shift of X^s. As a result, Japan's competitiveness would be strengthened, and the export volume and the current account would be in surplus.

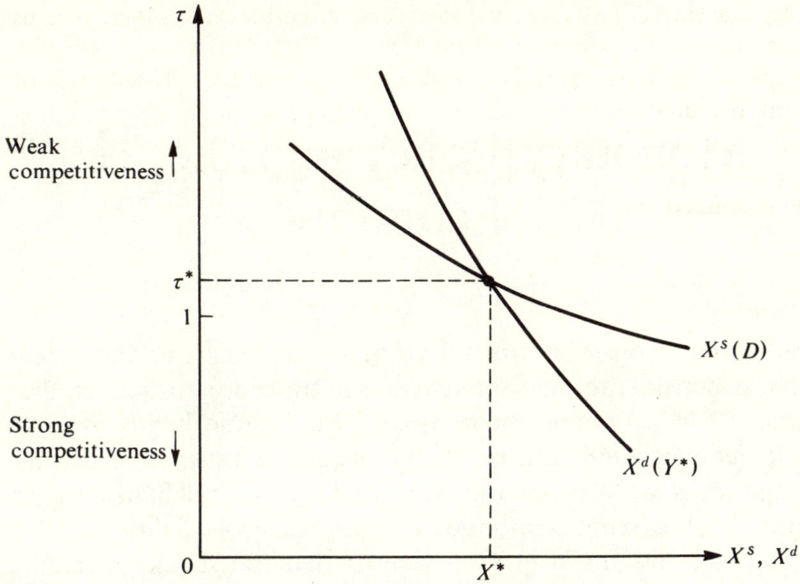

Fig. 8.7. Determination of international competitiveness τ

With τ thus determined, the equilibrium exchange rate is also determined by (A31). From Fig. 8.7, we observe that the equilibrium competitiveness τ, the exchange rate e, and the current account are all dependent on such variables as D and Y^*. For example, an increase in Y^* and/or a decrease in D would lead to a depreciation of the exchange rate, a strengthening of competitiveness, and an increase in the surplus of the current account.

As explained Section 8.1, the balance in the current account is by no means necessary for equilibrium from the theoretical viewpoint of intertemporal resource allocation across the economies. The practical question, however, is whether or not continued deficits are sustainable. Continued current account surpluses are necessarily accompanied by continued current account deficits elsewhere. I maintain that a prolonged divergence of τ from 1 is not sustainable in the long run.

Note that there is no need for the current account to be in balance even if τ is 1. It is reasonable, however, to maintain that a prolonged divergence of τ from 1, distorting international competitiveness in tradables, would make continued current account deficits unsustainable. The logic underlying this argument is simply the economic rationale for PPP as the long-run equilibrium. When τ is 1, (A31) boils down to our definition of the long-run equilibrium exchange rate (30) in the main text.

9

Monetary Policy and the Real Economy

This chapter considers the role that money plays in the economy. There is considerable disagreement among economists over the role of money in economic fluctuations. On the one hand, monetarists (M. Friedman 1968; Lucas 1972) consider unanticipated changes in the money supply exogenously caused by central banks to be the major shock driving economic fluctuations. As explained in Chapter 1, 'new' Keynesians also often identify demand shocks with exogenous money supply shocks in their theoretical and empirical works; in their view, money supply shocks translate into real shocks because prices are inflexible. This idea motivates attempts to explain nominal price/wage rigidities.

On the other hand, real business cycle theorists argue that macroeconomic fluctuations are set off by technological shocks such as changes in total factor productivity, and that the propagation of these shocks through the economy is due to non-monetary factors, such as optimal consumption-smoothing by individuals and lags in the construction of new capital. According to this theory, money does not play a major role either as a shock or as a propagation mechanism: money is nothing but a veil (King and Plosser 1984; Plosser 1990).

Between these two polar views, 'old' Keynesians hold that both real demand and monetary shocks are important in business cycles. Chapter 2 has demonstrated that neither rational-expectations-based monetarism nor real business cycle theory can reasonably explain post-war business cycles in Japan, maintaining instead that real demand shocks played the major role. This chapter focuses on money and considers its role in economic fluctuations.

To understand fully the role that money plays in the economy, it is essential to grasp precisely how monetary policy is conducted. Irrespective of the views expressed by their authors, most macroeconomic analyses, both theoretical and empirical, assume either that the money supply is exogenous or that very simple feedback rules guide monetary policy. These simplifying assumptions make calculations of equilibrium that are consistent with rational expectations easy, but it is rarely questioned whether the assumptions made are a good approximation of how monetary policy is actually conducted in the real world.

This chapter maintains that the money supply very often becomes endogenous, passively reflecting various shocks to the economy. The basic reason why money becomes endogenous is that central banks smooth the nominal interest rate. Occasionally, however, central banks do change the money supply independently or exogenously, thus affecting the real economy ('dynamic operations' in Roosa's (1956) terminology). Monetary policy, therefore, follows *time-varying* nominal interest-rate-smoothing, and consists of a regime somewhere between the two polar cases of interest-rate-pegging and dynamic operations.

Section 9.1 demonstrates the endogeneity of the money supply using a simple model. To shed light on the role of money in economic fluctuations, Section 9.2 analyses monetary policy in seasonal fluctuations. The analysis of the seasonal cycle demonstrates that the Bank of Japan (BOJ hereafter) smoothes the call rate by systematically reacting to output, price, or money demand shocks with a lag of less than one month. Fluctuations in money supply over the seasonal cycle are therefore nothing but the mirror-image of output and other shocks. The analysis of the seasonal cycle also reveals another important fact: namely, the fact that production and shipments broadly move together in the seasonal cycle contradicts the notion of increasing short-run marginal costs and suggests a flat marginal cost curve.

Section 9.3 studies monetary policy at business cycle frequencies. A careful examination of the chronology of Japanese monetary policy demonstrates that the nominal interest rate is very often smoothed. The money supply, therefore, very often becomes endogenous in the business cycle as well as in the seasonal cycle. This section also analyses the proximate targets the Bank of Japan has pursued in its policy-making. Finally, it demonstrates that monetary policy affects real output.

Section 9.4 deals with the transmission mechanism of monetary policy. The experiences of Japan over a 30-year period are examined and then compared with those of the United States. For Japan, investment is the key variable. And yet, the interest elasticity of investment demand is notoriously insignificant (see Chapter 7). This section examines precisely how changes in the call rate translate into changes in investment. The appendix presents a model of the Japanese financial market, and discusses some technical issues concerning monetary policy in Japan.

9.1 NOMINAL INTEREST-SMOOTHING AND THE ENDOGENOUS MONEY SUPPLY

Monetarists and 'new' Keynesians take changes in the money supply to be exogenous. As will be shown below, however, this is not a good description of observed changes in the money supply, because the Bank of Japan very often smooths the nominal interest rate. Of course, another issue is whether nominal interest-smoothing is a desirable policy, but the fact is that such policies *have* been adopted by the BOJ. When the BOJ smooths the nominal rate—specifically, *the call rate* in the case of Japan (equivalent to the US federal funds rate)—the money supply must change endogenously in response to real disturbances. In this case, changes in the money supply become nothing but mirror-images of real shocks. Keeping this point in mind, I first consider the relationship between the money supply and the real economy in a simple macroeconomic model. This model will form the basis for discussion in subsequent sections.

Although the basic points I want to make in Sections 9.2 and 9.3 are not model-specific, to facilitate explanation I consider a simple Taylor-type macroeconomic model (Taylor 1979, 1980). Here no attempt to elaborate on the financial sector is made; a more detailed analysis of the Japanese financial market is offered in the appendix. The model consists of the following five equations:

$$Y_t = -\gamma(W_t - P_t) \qquad (\gamma > 0), \tag{1}$$

$$Y_t = -a[i_t - E(P_{t+1} \mid \Omega_t) + P_t] + \tilde{u}_t \qquad (a > 0), \tag{2}$$

$$W_t = \alpha E(P_{t+1} \mid \Omega_{t-1}) + (1-\alpha)P_{t-1} + \tilde{\eta}_t \qquad (0 < \alpha < 1), \tag{3}$$

$$M_t - P_t = Y_t - \beta i_t + \tilde{v}_t \qquad (\beta > 0), \tag{4}$$

$$M_t = d(i_t - i_t^*) + \tilde{\varepsilon}_t, \tag{5}$$

where Y is real GNP, P is the price level, W is nominal wages, and M is the nominal money supply (all measured in logs); $E(x \mid \Omega)$ denotes taking the expected value of x conditional on information set Ω; and $\tilde{u}$, $\tilde{\eta}_t$, $\tilde{v}$ and $\tilde{\varepsilon}$, are disturbances in each equation.

The BOJ is assumed to smooth the nominal interest rate i around the target rate i^*. The extent of nominal interest-rate-smoothing is expressed by parameter d in (5). When d becomes large, the nominal interest rate is virtually pegged. On the other hand, when d is zero, money supply is equal to the disturbances ε, which is supposed to reflect changes in the BOJ's policy stance, and in this case the nominal rate i becomes an endogenous variable. Note that this characterization of the BOJ's behaviour implicitly assumes that the BOJ systematically reacts to income, price, or money demand shocks *within a period.*[1] In fact, the analysis of the seasonal cycle that follows suggests that the BOJ systematically reacts to various shocks with a lag of less than one month.

The model is otherwise standard and needs no explanation. Output Y, the price level P, the money supply M, and the nominal interest rate i in this model are determined as follows (for simplicity, i^* is taken to be zero):

$$Y_t = \frac{1}{A}\,[\gamma a(\phi^2 - bc)P_{t-1} - \gamma ab\tilde{\eta}_t + \gamma a(b-1)(\tilde{\varepsilon}_t - \tilde{v}_t) + \gamma\tilde{u}_t], \tag{6}$$

$$P_t = \frac{1}{A}\,\{\gamma c[(b-1)a+1] + a\phi^2\}P_{t-1} + \frac{1}{A}\,\{\gamma[(b-1)a+1]\tilde{\eta}_t + (b-1)a(\tilde{\varepsilon}_t - \tilde{v}_t) + \tilde{u}_t\}, \tag{7}$$

$$M_t = \frac{1}{(1+\beta/d)A}\,\{[cA + (\gamma+1)a(\phi^2 - bc)]P_{t-1} + [A - (\gamma+1)ab]\tilde{\eta}_t + (\gamma+a)\tilde{v}_t + [\beta A/d + (\gamma+1)(b-1)a]\tilde{\varepsilon}_t + (\gamma+1)\,\tilde{u}_t\}, \tag{8}$$

$$i_t = \frac{1}{(d+\beta)A}\,\{[cA + (\gamma+1)a(\phi^2 - bc)]P_{t-1} + [A - (\gamma+1)ab]\tilde{\eta}_t$$

[1] McCallum (1983) argues that in VAR systems, monetary policy surprises may be more accurately represented by interest rates than by money stock innovations if the monetary authority aims at the money supply target but uses an interest rate instrument. His analysis, however, rests on the assumption that the monetary authority does not systematically react to income, price, or money demand shocks within a period. The analysis of the seasonal cycles below suggests that the BOJ does systematically react to various shocks with a lag of less than one month.

$$+ (\gamma + a)\tilde{v}_t - (\gamma + a)\tilde{\varepsilon}_t + (\gamma + 1)\tilde{u}_t\}, \tag{9}$$

where

$$A = \gamma\left(1 + \frac{a}{\beta + d}\right) + \frac{a}{\beta + d} + a$$

$$b = 1 + \frac{1}{\beta + d} \qquad (b > 1)$$

$$c = \alpha\phi^2 + (1 - \alpha) \quad (0 < c < 1),$$

and $\phi(0 < \phi < 1)$ is a root of the following characteristic equation of the system:

$$f(X) = \left[\frac{a}{(b-1)a + 1} + \gamma\alpha\right]X^2 - \left[\frac{ab}{(b-1)a + 1} + \gamma\right]X + \gamma(1 - \alpha) = 0. \tag{10}$$

The basic message is that, in general, changes in money supply M_t contain various shocks; price shocks η, real demand shocks u, portfolio shocks v, and changes in the BOJ's policy stance ε. Monetarism and 'new' Keynesian economics take it for granted that the ε are by far the most dominant shocks.

Before I proceed to the empirical analysis, I will consider some special but important cases of the solutions (6)–(9).

When the BOJ smooths the nominal interest rate to a considerable degree ($d \to \infty$), we obtain

$$Y_t = \frac{1}{(\gamma + a)}\,[\gamma a(\phi^2 - c)P_{t-1} - \gamma a\tilde{\eta}_t + \gamma\tilde{u}_t], \tag{11}$$

$$P_t = \frac{1}{(\gamma + a)}\,[(\gamma c + a\phi^2)P_{t-1} + \gamma\tilde{\eta}_t + \tilde{u}_t], \tag{12}$$

$$M_t = \frac{1}{(\gamma + a)}\,\{[c(\gamma + a) + (\gamma + 1)a(\phi^2 - c)]P_{t-1} + \gamma(1 - a)\tilde{\eta}_t \tag{13}$$

$$+ (\gamma + a)\tilde{v}_t + (\gamma + 1)\tilde{u}_t\},$$

$$i_t = i^*. \tag{14}$$

Real output Y and the price level P become independent of portfolio shocks v, whereas money supply responds to v one-for-one.

Under the same assumption that d is large, if we further assume that the marginal cost curve is fairly flat ($\gamma = \infty$), then we obtain

$$Y_t = a(\phi^2 - c)P_{t-1} - a\tilde{\eta}_t + \tilde{u}_t, \tag{15}$$

$$P_t = cP_{t-1} + \tilde{\eta}_t \tag{16}$$

$$M_t = [c + a(\phi^2 - c)]P_{t-1} + (1 - a)\tilde{\eta} + \tilde{v}_t + \tilde{u}_t. \tag{17}$$

If a, the interest elasticity of aggregate demand, is small, output is virtually determined by real demand shock u. On the other hand, real demand shocks do not affect price. Price is affected only by price shocks η.

We next consider the other extreme case, where the BOJ does not attempt to smooth the nominal interest rate ($d = 0$). In this case, we obtain

$$Y_t = \frac{1}{\gamma[(b-1)a+1] + (b-1)a + a}[\gamma a(\phi^2 - bc)p_{t-1}$$

$$- \gamma ab\tilde{\eta}_t + \gamma a(b-1)(\tilde{\varepsilon}_t - \tilde{v}_t) + \gamma\tilde{u}_t], \tag{18}$$

$$P_t = \frac{1}{\gamma[(b-1)a+1] + (b-1)a + a}\{[\gamma c((b-1)a+1) + a\phi^2]p_{t-1}$$

$$+ \gamma((b-1)a+1)\eta_t + (b-1)a(\tilde{\varepsilon}_t - \tilde{v}_t) + \tilde{u}_t\}, \tag{19}$$

$$M_t = \tilde{\varepsilon}_t, \tag{20}$$

$$i_t = \frac{1}{\beta A'}\{[cA' + (\gamma+1)a(\phi^2 - b'c)]P_{t-1}$$

$$+ \gamma(1-a)\tilde{\eta}_t + (\gamma+a)\tilde{v}_t - (\gamma+a)\tilde{\varepsilon}_t + (\gamma+1)\tilde{u}_t\}, \tag{21}$$

where

$$A' = \gamma(1 + a/\beta) + a/\beta + a \quad \text{and} \quad b' = 1 + 1/\beta.$$

Output is affected by ε, the independent change in the money supply. This corresponds to Roosa's (1956) 'dynamic operations'.

With different degrees of interest-rate-smoothing d, observed changes in the money supply either passively reflect various shocks to the economy (13), or embody exogenous changes in the BOJ's policy stance (20). The relative importance of the exogenous component ε in the variance of money supply M, $\sigma_\varepsilon^2/\sigma_m^2$, is

$$\frac{[(\beta A/d) + (\gamma+1)(b-1)a]^2\sigma_\varepsilon^2}{[A - (\gamma+1)ab]^2\sigma_\eta^2 + (\gamma+a)^2\sigma_v^2 + [(\beta A/d) + (\gamma+1)(b-1)a]^2\sigma_\varepsilon^2 + (\gamma+1)^2\sigma_u^2}. \tag{22}$$

$\sigma_\varepsilon^2/\sigma_m^2$ approaches 1 or 0 as d vanishes or becomes infinite, respectively.

With these results, I turn to the empirical analyses, in which monetary policy in both the seasonal and the business cycles is examined.

9.2 MONEY SUPPLY AND THE SEASONAL CYCLE

Although seasonal cycles have long been recognized, until very recently most research on macroeconomic fluctuations used seasonally adjusted data, treating seasonal fluctuations as unworthy of study. It was against this current of research that Barsky and Miron (1989) and Yoshikawa (1989) began to study seasonal cycles in the United States and in Japan, respectively. Although the main interest here is in the role of money in business cycles, much information can be obtained by studying seasonal cycles.

Fluctuations of monthly real output (in the index of industrial production (IIP) compiled by MITI) and of the money supply (M2 + CD) in Japan are shown in Fig. 9.1 (in rates of change relative to the previous month). They are highly periodic and regular. This initial impression is confirmed by examining the spectrum of these variables (Fig. 9.2 and 9.3); it is seen that real output and the money supply do indeed show very similar patterns of seasonal fluctuation. The peaks and troughs of the deterministic seasonality of the two variables, however, do not exactly coincide (Table 9.1).[2] The rate of change in the money supply peaks in December, is high in March and June, and bottoms out in January and February. On the other hand, the rate of change in IIP peaks in March, is high in September, bottoms out in January, and is low in August or April and May. This difference in the timing of fluctuations is most likely due to two facts: (i) industrial production is not equal to expenditure, and (ii) there is a lag between production and other transactions on the one hand,

[2] The seasonality shown in Table 9.1 refers to the *deterministic* seasonality captured by 12 monthly dummies. An estimated coefficient for the monthly dummy can be interpreted as the average rate of change in each month. A tacit assumption is that the variance of errors around the average is the same from January to December. Although stochastic seasonality exists, Barsky and Miron (1989) report that deterministic seasonality is quantitatively much more important than stochastic seasonality in the majority of the economic variables they examined.

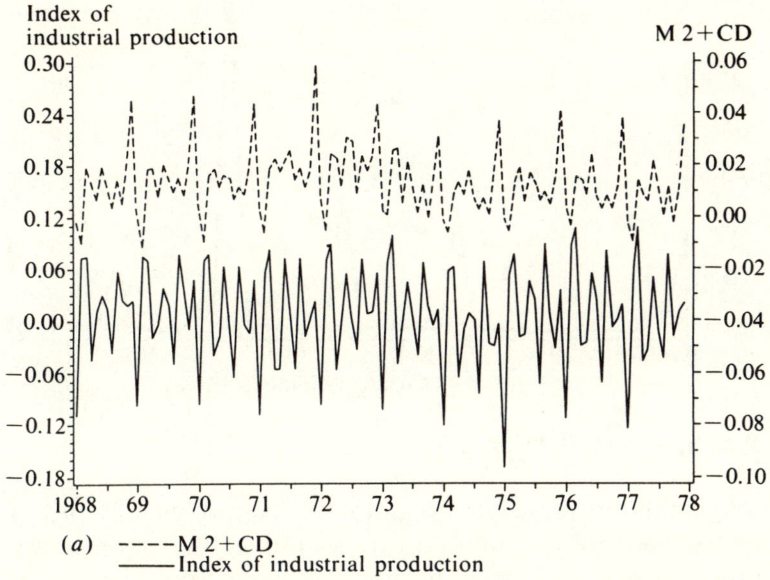

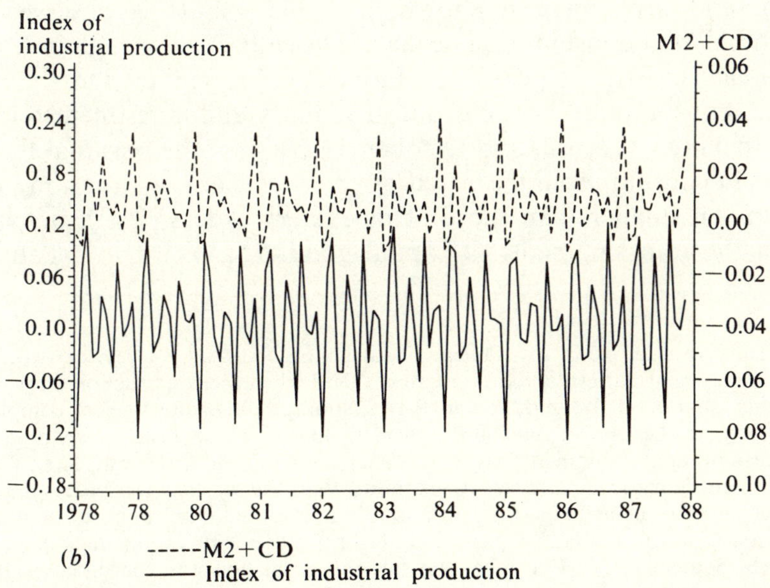

Fig. 9.1. Money and production, 1968–1978

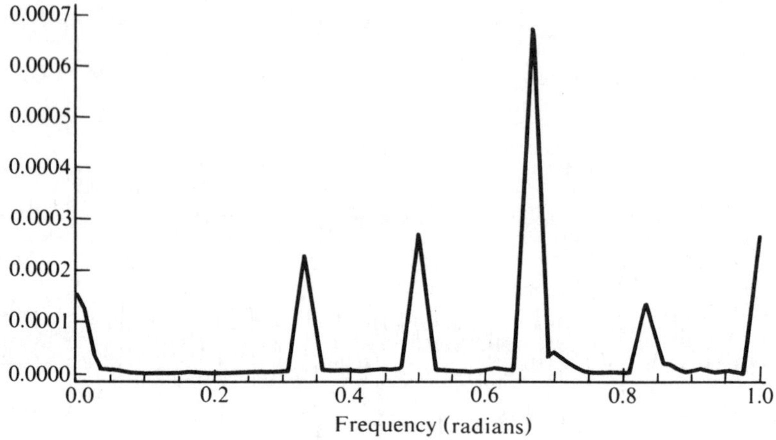

Fig. 9.2. Spectrum of M2 + CD

and payments on the other.[3] The money supply usually increases in December because consumption peaks during that month, and also because customary payments such as inter-firm settlements and wages also peak then.

For reference, the deterministic seasonality in income, consumption, and investment is shown in Table 9.2. It is observed, for example, that consumption peaks in December and is high in March, whereas investment peaks in March and September. On the other hand, consumption bottoms out in January and investment bottoms out in January, April, and October. In passing, the seasonal fluctuations in consumption, measured by the coefficient of variation (31.7), are much smaller than those of machinery orders (71.3), but larger than those in shipments of capital goods (15.9). Finally, Table 9.2

[3] Take an example of investment. Construction could take a year or two, and a typical payment pattern is that a quarter is paid when the construction work starts, another quarter in the middle, and the remaining half at the time of completion. Similarly, in the case of machinery, there is, first of all, a three- to six-month lag between order and shipment; payment is then made three to six months later. Finally, if payment is made by a three- to six-month bill, the lag between orders and final settlements can be at longest a year and a half. An additional point to be noted in the case of Japan is that, by custom, inter-firm settlements are made at the end of March, September, or December. So far, the discussion has concerned payments made by firms that order investment goods. When firms that produce investment goods take orders and start production, it soon becomes necessary for them to pay for labour and raw materials. The lags for those payments are much shorter than those for investment orders.

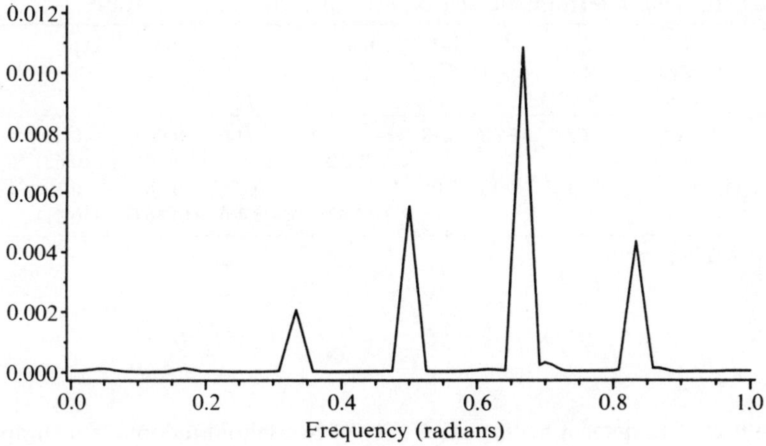

Fig. 9.3. Spectrum of index of industrial production

also shows that household income peaks in December and June, a consequence of the celebrated bonus system.

Aside from a peak in consumption in December, therefore, production and expenditure tend to move concurrently over the seasonal cycle; both increase in June and September and decrease in January.[4] A comparison of indices of production, shipments, and inventory stocks (Table 9.3), in fact, shows that there is little production-smoothing. The variance of shipments (0.76) is slightly greater than that of production (0.62), but the difference is fairly marginal. As a result, seasonal fluctuation in inventory stocks is small. Substantial production-smoothing is observed only in December: the high consumption in December is met by a decumulation of inventory stocks. The fact that production and shipments move broadly together contradicts the notion of an increasing short-run marginal cost curve and suggests a flat marginal cost curve. This case is strengthened by the fact that seasonal fluctuations in expenditure are largely anticipated by producers.

Aside from timing, money and real output show very similar seasonal fluctuations. As noted at the beginning of this chapter, it is a matter of much dispute whether the high correlation between money and real output over the business cycle reflects a causal mechanism running from money to output, or the other way round. In contrast to the case of business cycles, however, it is absurd to

[4] Indices of industrial production in all industries except for food peak in March and September; production in the food industry peaks in December.

Table 9.1. The deterministic seasonality of money and output[a]

	(1) Mean (× 10)	(2) s.d. (× 10)	(3) (2)/(1)	(4) SE	Jan.	Feb.	Mar.	Apr.	May
IIP	0.05	0.62	12.40	0.18	− 1.20	0.66	0.90	− 0.41	− 0.24
					(− 30.29)	(17.08)	(23.32)	(− 10.63)	(− 6.26)
M2 + CD	0.10	0.13	1.30	0.06	− 0.04	− 0.07	0.18	0.12	0.06
					(− 3.43)	(− 5.45)	(14.66)	(10.21)	(4.57)

[a] *t*-values in parentheses.

Table 9.2. The deterministic seasonality of household income, consumption, and investment[a]

	(1) Mean (× 10)	(2) s.d. (× 10)	(3) (2)/(1)	(4) SE	Jan.	Feb.	Mar.	Apr.
Household income	0.07	4.44	63.43	0.30	− 10.17	0.12	1.37	− 0.72
					(− 155.54)	(0.89)	(21.01)	(− 10.98)
Consumption	0.06	1.90	31.67	0.24	− 4.13	− 0.58	1.99	− 0.44
					(− 73.93)	(− 10.02)	(34.71)	(− 7.65)
Orders of machinery	0.04	2.85	71.25	1.21	− 2.90	1.34	4.80	− 3.78
					(− 10.48)	(4.71)	(16.89)	(− 13.29)
Shipment of capital goods	0.08	1.27	15.88	0.43	− 1.28	1.14	2.32	− 1.77
					(− 13.26)	(12.13)	(24.68)	(− 18.84)

[a] *t*-values in parentheses.

Sources: Income and consumption are from *Kakei-chosa* (Survey of Household Expenditures). Orders of machinery are compiled by Economic Planning Agency. Shipment of capital goods are compiled by MITI.

Table 9.3. The deterministic seasonality of production, shipments, and inventory stocks[a]

	(1) Mean (× 10)	(2) s.d. (× 10)	(3) (2)/(1)	(4) SE	Jan.	Feb.	Mar.	Apr.
Production (IIP)	0.05	0.62	12.40	0.18	− 1.20	0.66	0.90	− 0.41
					(− 30.29)	(17.08)	(23.32)	(− 10.63)
Shipments	0.05	0.76	15.20	0.20	− 1.59	0.72	1.23	− 0.60
					(35.06)	(16.23)	(27.68)	(− 13.47)
Inventory stocks	0.05	0.23	4.60	0.16	0.43	0.15	− 0.21	0.05
					(12.04)	(4.40)	(− 5.91)	(1.43)

[a] *t*-values in parentheses.

Jun.	Jul.	Aug.	Sep.	Oct.	Nov.	Dec.	Sample period
0.46	0.08	− 0.68	0.81	− 0.05	− 0.02	0.25	1967(2)–
(11.89)	(2.11)	(− 17.68)	(21.12)	(− 1.21)	(− 0.63)	(6.43)	1987(12)
0.18	0.12	0.04	0.10	0.01	0.13	0.39	1967(2)–
(14.77)	(9.71)	(3.44)	(8.56)	(1.23)	(10.99)	(32.46)	1988(1)

May	Jun.	Jul.	Aug.	Sep.	Oct.	Nov.	Dec.	Sample period
0.03	4.81	− 0.89	− 2.92	− 0.87	0.18	0.13	9.80	1967(2)–
(0.52)	(73.57)	(− 13.59)	(− 44.64)	(− 13.34)	(2.73)	(1.97)	(149.83)	1988 (1)
− 0.48	0.26	0.75	− 0.46	− 0.75	0.59	− 0.19	4.19	1969(10)–
(− 8.39)	(4.52)	(13.07)	(− 8.00)	(− 13.08)	(10.63)	(− 3.38)	(74.99)	1988(1)
− 0.40	0.81	− 0.92	− 0.08	4.18	− 3.50	− 0.58	1.61	1969(5)–
(− 1.43)	(2.94)	(− 3.32)	(− 0.28)	(15.11)	(− 12.67)	(− 2.11)	(5.81)	1988(1)
− 0.55	0.69	0.06	− 0.27	1.63	− 1.39	− 0.17	0.46	1967(2)–
(− 5.80)	(7.30)	(0.69)	(− 2.89)	(17.32)	(− 14.79)	(− 1.86)	(4.87)	1987(12)

May	Jun.	Jul.	Aug.	Sep.	Oct.	Nov.	Dec.	Sample period
− 0.24	0.46	0.08	− 0.68	0.81	− 0.05	− 0.02	0.25	1967(2)–
(− 6.26)	(11.89)	(2.11)	(− 17.68)	(21.12)	(− 1.21)	(− 0.63)	(6.43)	1987(12)
− 0.24	0.38	0.16	− 0.64	0.87	− 0.22	− 0.02	0.49	1967(2)–
(− 5.50)	(8.61)	(3.51)	(− 14.44)	(19.67)	(− 4.86)	(− 0.45)	(11.09)	1987(12)
0.05	0.09	0.08	− 0.03	− 0.09	0.17	0.11	− 0.26	1967(2)–
(1.54)	(2.58)	(2.14)	(− 0.77)	(− 2.51)	(4.90)	(3.19)	(− 7.30)	1987(12)

Table 9.4. The deterministic seasonality of monetary aggregates[a]

	(1) Mean (× 10)	(2) s.d. (× 10)	(3) (2)/(1)	(4) SE	Jan.	Feb.	Mar.	Apr.	May
M2 + CD	0.10	0.13	1.30	0.06	− 0.04	− 0.07	0.18	0.12	0.06
					(− 3.43)	(− 5.45)	(14.66)	(10.21)	(4.57)
High-powered money	0.09	0.70	7.78	0.18	− 1.42	0.17	0.43	− 0.09	− 0.29
					(− 34.40)	(4.07)	(10.13)	(− 2.18)	(− 6.81)
Cash	0.09	0.75	8.33	0.14	− 0.94	− 0.76	0.40	− 0.01	− 0.12
					(− 30.70)	(− 24.81)	(12.96)	(− 0.40)	(− 4.00)
Reserves	0.12	0.58	4.83	0.54	− 0.10	− 0.29	0.55	0.12	− 0.01
					(0.82)	(− 2.45)	(4.72)	(1.06)	(− 0.08)
BOJ's lending	0.08	3.29	41.13	2.72	0.52	− 0.16	0.31	− 3.55	− 1.93
					(0.82)	(− 0.25)	(0.49)	(− 5.69)	(− 3.09)

[a] *t*-values in parentheses.

argue that seasonal fluctuations in real activities are caused by similar fluctuations in money; they clearly reflect real factors such as weather or social customs (for example, New Year's Day in Japan or Christmas in the West). In other words, there is an 'identifying restriction' that fluctuations in real output are independent of money in the case of seasonal cycles.

It is theoretically possible, in the context of models in which agents are solving intertemporal optimization problems, that seasonal power in output is due in part to a white noise monetary shock. This possible effect is not very important, however, because real variables such as outputs in various industries, consumption, and investment have similar spectral patterns but different seasonal patterns of peaks and troughs (Tables 9.2, 9.3). To the extent that (as a first approximation) all agents are subject to the same monetary shocks, it is difficult to understand that the optimum responses of agents to a *common* monetary shock produce changes in real variables that have similar spectral patterns but at the same time different seasonal patterns of peaks and troughs. It is more reasonable to consider that taste and technology show their own idiosyncratic seasonal fluctuations, which are conditioned by weather and custom. Therefore, I argue that the 'identifying restriction' that fluctuations in real variables be independent of money in the case of seasonal cycles is, if not definite, at least quite reasonable.

The reason why money fluctuates similarly to real variables is that the money supply responds endogenously to seasonal fluctuations in real activities. If the the money supply did not so respond, then

Jun.	Jul.	Aug.	Sep.	Oct.	Nov.	Dec.	Sample period
0.18	0.12	0.04	0.10	0.01	0.13	0.39	1967(2)–
(14.77)	(9.71)	(3.44)	(8.56)	(1.23)	(10.99)	(32.46)	1988(1)
0.62	– 0.12	– 0.17	0.13	– 0.13	0.35	1.60	1969(10)–
(14.62)	(– 2.93)	(– 3.93)	(3.19)	(– 3.18)	(8.58)	(38.88)	1988(1)
0.62	– 0.12	– 0.17	– 0.38	0.07	0.10	2.14	1967(2)–
(7.70)	(15.82)	(– 2.94)	(– 12.48)	(2.13)	(3.29)	(70.01)	1988(1)
0.28	– 0.09	0.05	0.44	– 0.24	0.14	0.42	1967(2)–
(2.39)	(– 0.76)	(0.41)	(3.75)	(– 2.04)	(1.18)	(3.58)	1988(1)
1.55	0.63	– 0.27	2.18	– 0.56	– 1.87	4.16	1966(10)–
(2.48)	(1.01)	(– 0.43)	(3.50)	(– 0.90)	(– 3.00)	(6.67)	1987(12)

interest rates would show seasonal fluctuations. In fact, the BOJ intentionally responds to real shocks in order to smooth the nominal interest rate.[5] It can be observed that changes in the money supply broadly coincide with changes in high-powered money and BOJ lending rather than with changes in the reserve ratio or the currency–deposit ratio (Table 9.4); they all peak in December and are high in March and June, bottoming out in January and February.

Cash moves slightly differently from money. It peaks in December but is also high in July. The July peak coincides with high consumption, and confirms that cash is used mostly by consumers rather than by firms.

As a digression, it would be interesting also to examine the other component of money—bank deposits. In December 1988, cash amounted only ¥31.5 billion of (M2 + CD), which totalled ¥409.3 billion. Demand deposits and time deposits are ¥80.3 billion and ¥297.5 billion, respectively. Table 9.5 shows the seasonal cycles of the demand and time deposits of individuals and firms. Time deposits do not exhibit any clear seasonal movements, but demand deposits do. Demand deposits of household and firms, however, show quite different seasonal patterns. For households they are high in the second and fourth quarters; evidently this reflects the bonus payments (Table 9.2). In contrast, the demand deposits of firms peak in

[5] In the USA, the Federal Reserve also smooths the nominal interest rate at seasonal frequencies. Indeed, one of the major objectives of the Federal Reserve System since its establishment in 1914 was to smooth the nominal interest rate (see e.g. Shiller 1980 and Miron 1986).

Table 9.5. The deterministic seasonality of deposits[a]

	Firm's demand deposit	Firm's time deposit	Household's demand deposit	Household's time deposit
(1) Mean (× 10)	0.23	0.31	0.28	0.33
(2) s.d. (× 10)	0.58	0.29	0.47	0.16
(3) (2)/(1)	2.52	0.94	1.68	0.48
(4) SE	0.48	0.27	0.30	0.12
Quarter				
I	0.38 (3.45)	0.11 (1.80)	− 0.09 (− 1.27)	0.16 (5.74)
II	− 0.26 (− 2.40)	0.46 (7.52)	0.50 (7.33)	0.31 (10.89)
III	0.66 (6.06)	0.28 (4.57)	− 0.07 (− 1.05)	0.37 (13.03)
IV	0.14 (1.34)	0.38 (6.37)	0.77 (11.53)	0.46 (16.53)
Sample period	1968(IV)–1987(IV)	1968(IV)–1987(IV)	1968(IV)–1987(IV)	1968(IV)–1987(IV)

[a] *t*-values in parentheses.

the third quarter and reach a trough in the second quarter. This seasonal pattern is broadly consistent with that of production.

Coming back to the main argument, we see that, as a result of the BOJ's actions, seasonal fluctuations in the nominal interest rate are substantially weakened. Indeed, the spectrum of the call rate does not show any significant seasonality (Fig. 9.4).

Interest-rate-smoothing or the money supply accommodation would make changes in real output greater than otherwise, which is not a fault of this policy in the case of the seasonal cycle, since seasonal fluctuations of real activities are mostly desirable. As argued above, agents' intertemporal optimization, which produces the smoothing of consumption or production, makes much less sense

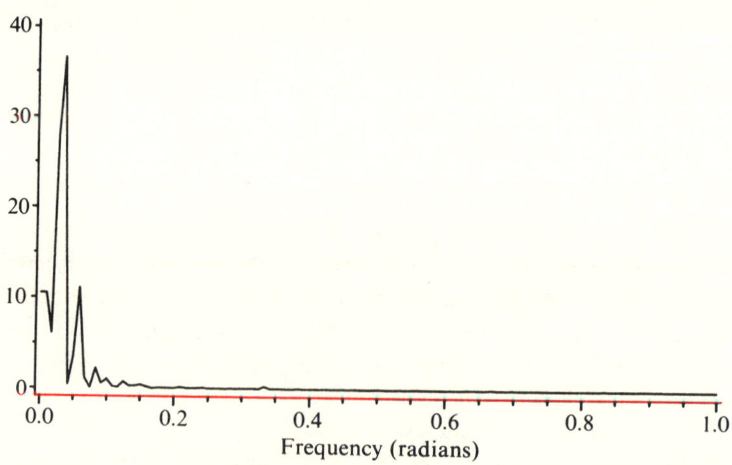

Fig. 9.4. Spectrum of the call rate

over the seasonal cycle than over the business cycle or the life cycle of an individual. Tastes and technology, which are usually taken as stable in intertemporal optimization models, fluctuate during the seasonal cycle. As the example of a fall in construction activities during the rainy season shows, seasonal fluctuations in real activities are mostly desirable.

Seasonal fluctuations in interest rates, on the other hand, can be a disturbance to the real economy. Miron (1986), for example, argues that in the United States, before the foundation of the Federal Reserve System in 1914, seasonal fluctuations in the nominal interest rate often created financial panic, whereas the number of such financial panics substantially decreased after 1914, when the Fed started smoothing the nominal interest rate at seasonal frequencies. This is a standard argument for seasonal nominal interest-smoothing.

In terms of the model in Section 9.1, therefore, the BOJ's behaviour at seasonal frequencies corresponds to $d \cong \infty$. The call rate does not fluctuate much, but the money supply does. Then, to what shocks does the money supply respond? First, it is also observed here that price movements do not show any significant seasonality (Fig. 9.5). Output fluctuates, but prices do not. Comparing equations (11) and (12) with (15) and (16), one can conclude that the marginal cost curve is fairly flat ($\gamma = \infty$) and that price shocks are

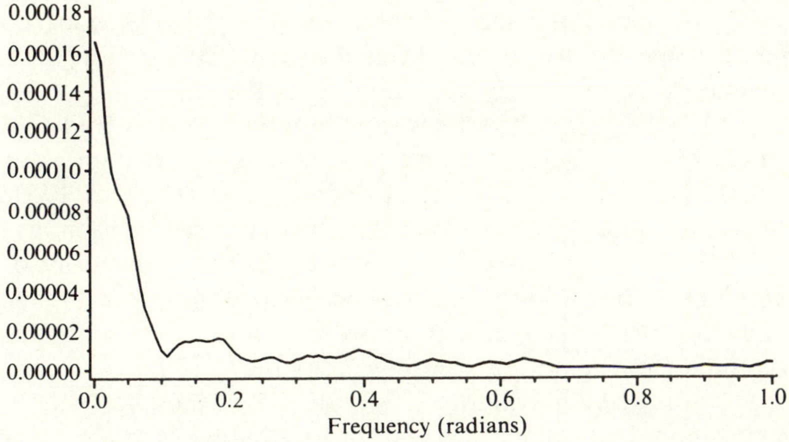

Fig. 9.5. Spectrum of price inflation (WPI)

not significant ($\eta = 0$) at seasonal frequencies. As noted above, a comparison of the seasonal cycles of production and shipments also indicates that the marginal cost curve is flat. From (17), therefore, it becomes apparent that seasonal changes in the money supply simply reflect portfolio shocks v (such as sharp increases in the demand for cash in December), and real demand shocks u, one-for-one. There is little exogenous component (ε) in money. Monetarism, both old and new, and 'new' Keynesian economics, therefore, make no sense in explaining seasonal cycles.

Barsky and Miron (1989) obtain similar results for the US economy, and make the following argument. If it is accepted that the seasonal co-movements of money and output reflect the endogeneity of money, does this allow us, by analogy, to draw any inference about similar high correlations associated with the conventional business cycle? Application of the principle of parsimony suggests that money is endogenous rather than causal with respect to business cycles as well as seasonal cycles. Of course, one might take the position that two different mechanisms are operative in generating the observed correlations over seasonal and business cycles. None the less, the similar co-movement of money and output at the two sets of frequencies is at the very least suggestive of an endogenous money supply.

9.3 THE MONEY SUPPLY AND THE BUSINESS CYCLE

It was found that, in the seasonal cycle, the money supply endogenously responds to portfolio and real demand shocks. This section examines the relation between money and output over the business cycle.

A fairly high correlation between the money supply and GNP is observed over the business cycle, though it is not as high as in the seasonal cycle. Monetarists (e.g. Friedman and Schwartz 1963*a*, *b*) contend that changes in the money supply have been 'exogenous' and have been determined largely by autonomous policy decisions of the central bank. They also find that the velocity of money or the money demand function is stable, and accordingly argue that money is the causal factor in explaining economic activities.

Economists such as Kaldor (1970) argue the other way round: the money supply 'accommodates itself' to the needs of trade, rising in response to an expansion, and vice versa, just as in a seasonal cycle. According to their view, the relative stability in the demand for money is merely a reflection of the instability in its supply; if the supply of money had been kept more stable, the velocity of money would have been more unstable.[6] In short, income causes endogenous changes in money.

The issue has been analysed using a causality test (Granger 1969; Sims 1972). Sims's original finding, that causality running from money to income cannot be rejected, was soon discovered to be not robust by Y. Mehra (1978), and this was reconfirmed by Sims (1980). Extending the original bivariate model to a model that included money, industrial production, the WPI, and the short-term nominal interest rate, these authors found that the exogeneity of money dramatically declines. Subsequent works (Bernanke 1986; and Stock and Watson 1989) also show that the results of the test are not quite robust with respect to such technical matters as the treatment of seasonality or the method used to make variables stationary.

The causality test has been applied to Japanese data by a number of economists. A typical result for the Japanese data (see e.g. Suzuki *et al.* 1988) is that the call rate is exogenous, and causality runs from the call rate to money. In the second stage, the causality runs from money to high-powered money and output. This result is taken by some BOJ officials as being consistent with the view that changes in high-powered money are the result rather than the cause of changes in more broadly defined monetary aggregates such as (M2 + CD), and that the BOJ cannot control the money supply simply by controlling high-powered money. In addition, the finding of causality running from money to income is often taken as evidence in support of the monetarist view that the stability of the money supply necessarily contributes to the stability of output.

Aside from a lack of robustness in the test with respect to the sample period or such technical matters as mentioned above, the most serious problem of the causality test is that it can falsely indicate causality in certain cases. For example, suppose that stock prices are determined by the present value of future profits. If expectations of future profits embodied in the price of stock contain

[6] Kaldor (1970), for example, mentions a comparison of the US and Canadian experience during the Great Depression (Friedman and Schwartz 1963*a*: 352) as evidence for this argument. In Canada there were no bank failures at all during the Great Depression; the contraction in the money supply was much smaller than in the USA—only two-fifths of that in the USA, or 13% *versus* 33%—yet the contraction in nominal GNP was nearly the same. The difference in the change in the money supply was largely offset by differences in the decline in the velocity of money: in the USA it fell by 29%, in Canada by 41%.

more information than is contained in the series of past profits, then the stock price would Granger-cause profits even though the truth is, in fact, the opposite. The appendix provides a model that produces spurious causality in the money–output relation. Since the demand for loans depends on the future interest rate as well as on the current interest rate, the quantity of money depends on expectations of future output. One must, therefore, be cautious in interpreting the results of causality test.

Given these consideration, how does one approach the money–output relationship in the business cycle? My initial view was that the BOJ often smooths the nominal interest rate over the business cycle just as it does over the seasonal cycle, and therefore that the money supply is endogenous during those interest-smoothing periods. There is an important difference between the two cycles, however. In the case of the business cycle, the BOJ does not always smooth the nominal rate, and as a result the money supply often reflects exogenous changes in the BOJ's policy stance (nonzero ε).

The basic problem is that there is no simple feedback rule that governs the money supply, but rather one that involves *a shift in regime*: the BOJ *often* accommodates various shocks to smooth the nominal interest rate, but not *always*. This makes it extremely difficult to use productively such conventional econometric methods as vector autoregressions (VARs), which 'flatten' shifts in regime and see only the averages. Still, it is desirable to identify the circumstances under which the BOJ either smooths the nominal interest rate or actively changes the money supply. As a first step, I have simply plotted the data. By plotting monthly data on money, output, and the nominal interest rate, we can at least identify those times when the BOJ smoothed the nominal rate, making changes in the money supply largely endogenous as in the seasonal cycle, and we can also determine what kinds of shock drove the money supply in each period.

In Fig. 9.6, monthly rates of change in money, output, and inflation are plotted against the level of the nominal interest rate. (Only a few examples are shown here.) The measures of money, output, inflation, and the nominal interest rate are (M2 + CD), IIP compiled by MITI, CPI inflation, and the call rate, respectively. To correct for seasonality, the rate of change of each variable is calculated relative to the same month of the previous year.

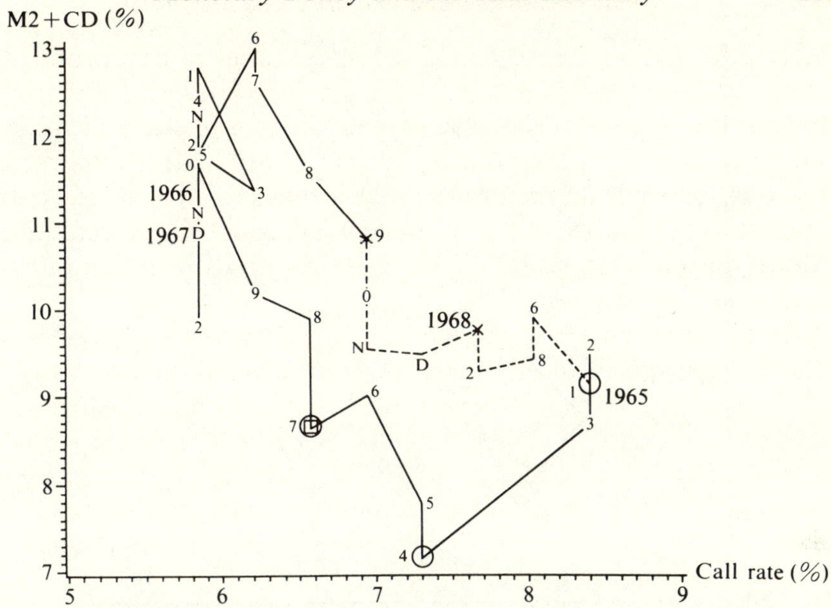

(*a*) Easy money: 1965(1)—1967(8) Tight money: 1967(9)—1968(7)

× The discount rate raised △ The reserve ratio raised

○ The discount rate lowered □ The reserve ratio lowered

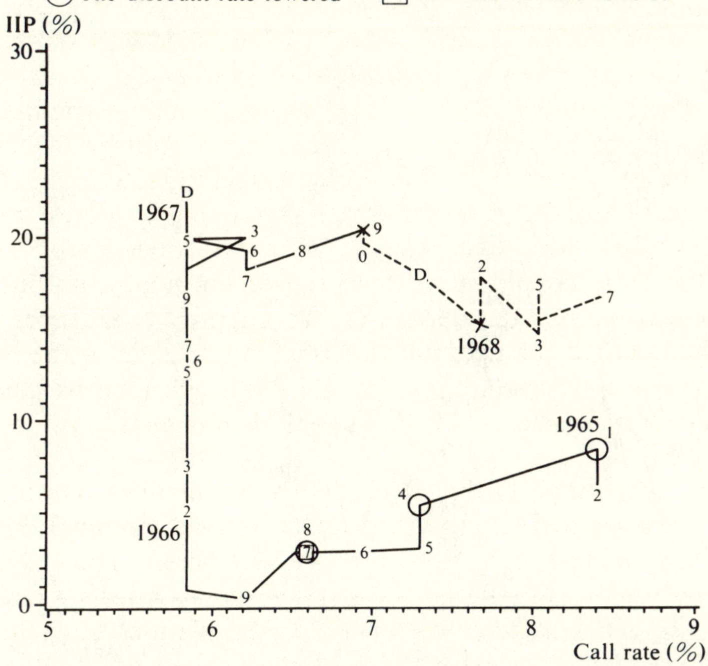

(*b*) Easy money: 1965(1)—1967(8) Tight money: 1967(9)—1968(7)

Fig. 9.6. Chronology of monetary policy

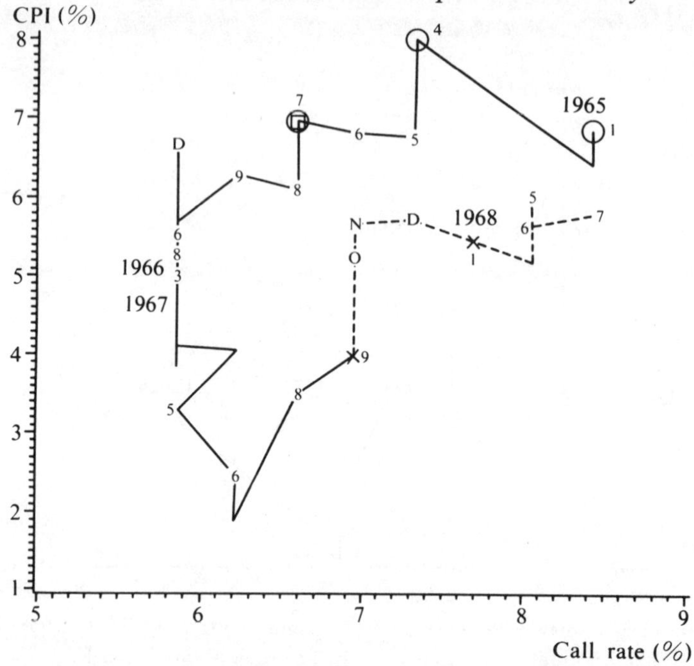

(*c*) Easy money: 1965(1)—1967(8) Tight money: 1967(9)—1968(7)

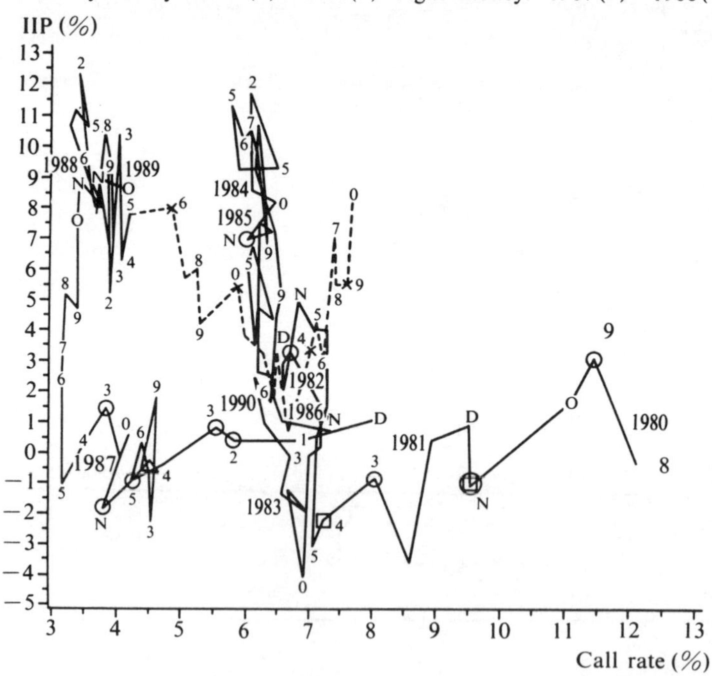

(*d*) Easy money: 1980(8)—1989(4) Tight money: 1989(5)—1990(10)

Fig. 9.6. (*Contd*)

Each figure corresponds to a pair of 'easy'- and 'tight'-money periods. The beginnings of 'easy'- and 'tight'-money periods are identified as the months in which the discount rate was *first* either lowered or raised, respectively. This method of identifying the beginnings or ends of easy- and tight-money periods is not altogether satisfactory, but is used for convenience. With the help of Fig. 9.6, the chronology of Japanese monetary policy is traced for the 30-year period from June 1958 to October 1990. This exercise is rather monotonous but is essential for the subsequent argument; readers may prefer to skip to the end of the chronology, and come back to it whenever necessary.

Chronology of Japanese Monetary Policy: June 1958–October 1990

1. *June–November 1958 (6 months)* At the trough of the recession, in June 1958, the discount rate was lowered. During this period both output and money increased, and at the same time the interest rate declined. An easy monetary policy was actively pursued. The stable price level suggests that price shocks were absent and the marginal cost curve was flat ($\gamma = \infty$) in this period.
2. *December 1958–November 1959 (12 months)* Output increased while the interest rate was smoothed. The increase in money in this period reflected mainly output shocks. The stable price suggests the absence of price shocks and flat marginal costs.
3. *December 1959–July 1960 (8 months)* The discount rate was raised in December 1959. Output peaked and started to decline, while inflation began to accelerate. The BOJ continued to smooth the interest rate, which implies that the decrease in money during this period reflected mainly the decline in output.
4. *August 1960–June 1961 (11 months)* The discount rate was lowered in August 1960. Output continued to decline, albeit slightly. The interest rate was basically pegged. Changes in money during this period, therefore, reflected mainly output shocks.
5. *July 1961–September 1962 (15 months)* The discount rate was raised in July 1961. Money growth continued to fall during this period. The interest rate was raised, although only slightly—from 8.4% to 8.8%. Output still declined. Inflation accelerated from June to December 1961 and started to decelerate in May 1962. The decrease in money reflected mainly output and price shocks.
6. *October 1962–April 1963 (7 months)* Output hit the trough and started rising. Inflation sharply accelerated, but an easy monetary

policy was still actively pursued. Money increased and the interest rate was lowered. (Note that the call rate in December 1962 is clearly abnormal, perhaps because of the BOJ's failure to accommodate the seasonal increase in the demand for money.)

7. *May–November 1963 (7 months)* Output continued to climb while inflation stayed high. The interest rate was virtually pegged. Changes in money during this period therefore reflected mainly output and price shocks.

8. *December 1963–June 1964 (7 months)* Output stayed high while inflation decreased. A tight monetary policy was actively pursued, which drove the interest rate up.

9. *July–December 1964 (6 months)* Output fell while inflation accelerated. The interest rate was pegged. The decrease in money during this period reflected mainly output and price shocks.

10. *January–October 1965 (10 months)* The discount rate was lowered in January 1965. Output growth kept decelerating while inflation stayed high. The interest rate was sharply lowered. The increase in money during this period suggests that an easy monetary policy was actively pursued.

11. *November 1965–May 1967 (19 months)* Output kept rising while inflation kept decelerating. The interest rate was pegged. Therefore changes in money basically reflected output and price shocks.

12. *June 1967–July 1968 (14 months)* Output started to decrease while inflation accelerated. The money supply was actively lowered, raising the interest rate.

13. *August–December 1968 (5 months)* Output kept decreasing and at the same time inflation decelerated. The interest rate was actively lowered.

14. *January–June 1969 (6 months)* Output began to increase while inflation also accelerated. The interest rate was smoothed.

15. *July–September 1969 (3 months)* Both output and inflation stayed high. The growth rate of the money supply was kept stable, allowing the interest rate to rise. In September the discount rate was raised.

16. *October 1969–September 1970 (12 months)* The interest rate was basically pegged. During the first six months (October 1969–March 1970), output stayed high and inflation sharply accelerated. Afterwards (April–September 1970) output fell, and inflation also decelerated. Changes in money during this period reflected mainly output and price shocks.

17. *October 1970–July 1972 (22 months)* During this period, the interest rate was sharply lowered by allowing the money supply to grow. Until January 1972 output fell, but it hit its trough in December 1971 and a recovery began. Inflation continued to decelerate.

18. *August–December 1972 (5 months)* The interest rate was pegged. Output kept growing while inflation was stable at the 5% level.

19. *January 1973–October 1974 (22 months)* The interest rate was sharply raised from below 5% to above 12% by reducing the money supply. Inflation accelerated, from 6% (January 1973) to the unprecedented level of 26% (February 1974), and finally started to decelerate (October 1974). Output stayed high for most of 1973, then sharply declined from 14% (November 1973) to –11% (October 1974).

20. *November 1974–March 1975 (5 months)* The interest rate was basically pegged. Inflation kept decelerating, from 25% to 14%. Output also decelerated, from –13% to –18%.

21. *April 1975–January 1976 (10 months)* The interest rate was actively lowered by increasing the money supply. During this period inflation decelerated from 13% to 9% while output rose steadily from – 14% to 6%.

22. *February 1976–February 1977 (13 months)* The interest rate was basically pegged. Output stayed high at 12% until November 1976 and then started decelerating, while inflation also stayed high, at 9%. Changes in the money supply reflected output shocks.

23. *March 1977–1978 (13 months)* The interest rate was actively lowered from 7% to 4.5%. Output continued to fall, while inflation started to decelerate from 9.5% to 5%.

24. *April 1978–March 1979 (12 months)* The interest rate was basically pegged. During this period, output stayed high at 7% while inflation continued to decelerate, from 5% to below 3%.

25. *April 1979–July 1980 (16 months)* The interest rate was actively raised from 5% (April 1979) to 12.5% (July 1980) by reducing the money supply. Output was fairly stable at around 10% and started to decelerate in April 1980. On the other hand, inflation was stable during the first six months of this period, then accelerated from 4% (October 1979) to 7.5% (February 1980) and stayed at that level afterward.

26. *August 1980–April 1981 (9 months)* The interest rate was actively lowered from 12% to 5% by increasing the money supply.

Output continued to decline below zero while inflation decelerated from 8% to 5%.

27. *May 1981–December 1985 (56 months)* The interest rate was kept stable at around 6%–7%. Output first recovered, from – 4% (May 1981) to 5% (November 1981), but then declined, from 5% to –5% (October 1982). Afterward (November 1982–October 1984) it rose from –5% to 12% and declined again to zero (December 1985). In the same period, inflation continued to decline, from 5% (May 1981) to 2% (November 1982); it remained at about that level thereafter. The growth of the money supply changed irregularly, reflecting output and price shocks.

28. *January 1986–April 1987 (16 months)* The interest rate was actively lowered. The yen sharply appreciated in real terms after the Plaza Accord in September 1985, and the subsequent decline in exports caused a recession in 1986. Output growth continued to decline to below zero. The bottom of this recession occurred in December 1986. Inflation declined, owing partly to the sharp appreciation of the yen.

29. *May 1987–March 1989 (23 months)* The interest rate was basically pegged at 3%. Output growth recovered from –1% (May 1987) to 11% (March 1988) and stayed high thereafter. Throughout this period, inflation was very stable. Changes in the money supply therefore reflected mainly output shocks.

30. *April 1989–October 1990 (19 months)* The interest rate was actively raised. Output growth declined from 7% (May 1985) to zero (March 1990) but recovered to 8% (October 1990) again. Inflation was stable at 3% during this period.

Summary

The above findings can be summarized as follows.

First of all, in 195 out of 389 months in the sample period June 1958–October 1990, the interest rate was either pegged or tightly smoothed. During those periods in which it was substantially smoothed, money, output, and inflation all fluctuated widely. It is very unlikely that real output and inflation respond within a month to exogenous changes in the money supply in such a way as to keep the interest rate unchanged. In contrast, it is known from the study of the seasonal cycle that the BOJ can accommodate output, price, and portfolio shocks to wipe out monthly movements in the interest rate. The conclusion, therefore, is that, in about half of the 30-year period, changes in the money supply were endogenous and simply reflected output, inflation, and/or portfolio shocks just as they did over the seasonal cycle. This fact alone implies that monetarism, both new and old, is very misleading in interpreting the observed changes in money supply and therefore in explaining the business cycle.

This fact also means that monetary models, which emphasize nominal rigidities arising from temporary wage and price stickiness (Taylor 1989; Fischer 1977), are likewise untenable to the extent that they take exogenous money supply shocks to be the major impulses behind economic fluctuations. As Chapter 1 pointed out, the literature on monetary models with nominal rigidities, however, which is sometimes referred to as 'Keynesian' or 'new' Keynesian, flourishes. In theory, attempts to explain nominal price rigidities are clearly motivated by the premiss that exogenous money supply shocks are the major disturbances to the economy.

Empirical works also abound. Blanchard and Quah (1989), for example, assume the existence of a 'demand shock' that has no permanent effect on real variables in their VAR analysis. They use this assumption as an identifying restriction and then interpret 'demand shocks' as money supply innovations. Taylor (1989) also assumes that money supply shocks are the major disturbances in the economy, and he emphasizes differences in price/wage flexibility (specifically, the synchronized wage-setting known as *Shunto*) as the key factor in explaining the differences in output variability between Japan and the United States. He argues, that, thanks to *Shunto*, nominal wages are much more flexible in Japan than in the United States, and therefore nominal money supply shocks do not translate into real shocks, thereby making real output in Japan more stable than in the United States.

A brief review of the post-war record of monetary policy in Japan reveals, however, that the interest rate was very often (about half the time) either pegged or substantially smoothed, suggesting, therefore, that the money supply innovations during those periods simply reflect output, price, and portfolio shocks. The fact that changes in output fluctuate considerably during periods of interest-smoothing suggests the importance of real shocks in explaining the business cycle. Whether these real shocks are the supply (productivity) shocks emphasized by the real business cycle theorists or the real demand shocks emphasized by the Keynesians is, of course, another issue. Chapter 2 has demonstrated that, for the postwar business cycle in Japan, real *demand* shocks were the major disturbances.

The BOJ's ability to peg or smooth the interest rate from month to month over the business cycle as well as the seasonal cycle necessarily implies that changes in the interest rate reflect the BOJ's policy stance. This is the case whether the BOJ actively changes the interest rate in the absence of other shocks or allows the interest rate to change when the shocks do not originate in the actions of the BOJ. Bernanke and Blinder (1992) also attempt to show that changes in the federal funds rate reflect the US Federal Reserve's policy stance, by estimating the interest elasticity of the reserve supply function. The point of their estimation is to find a proper instrument to identify the supply function. I make a similar argument by showing that the call rate was very often pegged or tightly smoothed from month to month by the BOJ.

When the interest rate changes consistently and substantially between months, it reflects the BOJ's policy stance. In this sample, in 96 out of 389 months the interest rate was raised, while it was lowered in 98 months. The question is whether there is any systematic feedback rule guiding the BOJ's choice either to smooth or to change the interest rate. Since the data contain many zero or close-to-zero values for the rate of change in the interest rate, one would have to resort to an estimation method involving probit (like the one used in Chapter 6) to take into account a regime shift in monetary policy. In what follows, however, as a preliminary exercise, a VAR is used simply to explore the policy reaction function of the BOJ.

The BOJ's Policy Targets

For the United States, Papell (1989) argues that a rule which stabilizes the rate of growth of nominal GNP provides a good description of monetary policy since 1973. Bernanke and Blinder (1992) also estimate a VAR with three variables and show that the federal funds rate responds positively to an inflation shock and negatively to an unemployment shock (during the pre-October 1979 period). This result is broadly consistent with Papell (1989). In the United States, monetary policy appears to have been conducted as a standard stabilization policy.[7]

[7] Examination of Federal Reserve records (Romer and Romer 1989) confirms that during the post-war era the Federal Reserve appears to have made deliberate decisions to sacrifice real output to lower inflation (in October 1947, September 1955, December 1968, April 1974, August 1978, and October 1979).

In Japan, the case is not as simple. A previous review of the records, for example, shows that, in the period October 1962–April 1963 (period 6 in the above chronology), the interest rate was successively lowered while output was rising and inflation was rapidly accelerating to 9%. During this period (particularly March and April 1963), the BOJ explicitly stated that the purpose of the reduction of the discount rate was not stabilization, but rather a strengthening of the international competitiveness of Japanese industry by encouraging investment (BOJ 1986). Anticipating the liberalization of capital import regulations in April 1964, when Japan became a member of OECD, policy-makers as well as businesspeople in those days regarded international competitiveness as one of the most important policy targets.

In the 1980s, the interest rate was substantially lowered between December 1985 and May 1986. Although 1986 was a recession year, it is widely believed that these reductions of the interest rate were aimed mainly at assisting the smooth appreciation of the yen, which the G5 countries agreed upon at the Plaza in September 1985. These examples and my previous discussion both suggest that the BOJ's policy objective is not simply stabilized output, but rather is multi-valued.

Within the confines of stabilization, the nominal interest-rate-smoothing often pursued by the BOJ complicates matters. Consider, for example, the following feedback rule:

$$M_t = -\alpha Y_t - \beta P_t + \varepsilon_t. \tag{23}$$

If the authority attempts to stabilize Y and P, we would expect α and β in (23) to be positive. As mentioned above, this seems to be the kind of rule that the US Federal Reserve pursues. When the BOJ smooths the interest rate, however, α and β are *negative* in (23). Since the BOJ does in fact attempt to stabilize the interest rate at times, even the signs of α and β are time-varying in the BOJ's policy reaction function.

How can we characterize the BOJ's policy reaction governing nominal interest-rate-smoothing? To answer this question, we confine our discussion to real output, Y. Let the 'natural', 'potential', 'non-inflation-accelerating', or 'full-employment' output be denoted by Y^*. The BOJ seems to pursue the following rule: raise the interest rate if $Y_t > Y_t^* - \varepsilon$; smooth or peg the interest rate if $Y_t^* - \varepsilon \geqq Y_t \geqq Y_t^* - \delta$; lower the interest rate if $Y_t^* - \delta > Y_t$ $(\delta > \varepsilon > 0)$.

The important point is that Y_t^* cannot be found by mechanical methods such as estimating a time trend. Indeed, it would not be an exaggeration to say that one of the major tasks of the BOJ is to grasp current Y^* as soon and as accurately as possible. No monetary authority would attempt to curb economic growth simply because output exceeded its trend line. Rather, growth would always be welcomed and accommodated, just as are seasonal cycles, provided that it did not fuel inflation or conflict with other important policy objectives such as exchange rate or balance of payment targets. The point is that Y_t^* cannot be measured accurately enough using past data to make it feasible for monetary policy to be described as a stable, time-invariant feedback rule. Given this caveat, I nevertheless checked the response functions of the call rate on the basis of VARs.

For this purpose, I first estimated a four-variable VAR with the call rate, the rate of change in IIP, CPI inflation, and a net export variable, NEX. The last variable is defined as nominal net export divided by CPI × IIP. The whole sample period is July 1958–November 1990, but I also estimated VARs for two sub-sample periods: July 1958–December 1972 and January 1973–November 1990. In Table 9.6, the impulse response functions of the call rate to shocks to other variables are shown in the first column.

The results look like a plausible response function. Output shocks drive up the call rate, though only mildly, with the peak effect coming after 20 months and then decaying very slowly. In a very similar fashion, inflation shocks also drive up the call rate for the January 1973–November 1990 period, but then push it in the opposite direction during January 1958–December 1972. Judging from this result, we can conclude that the anti-inflation stance of the BOJ was much stronger in the post-oil-shock period than in the 1950s and 1960s. Finally, for the entire period, the call rate responds negatively to an increase in the trade balance. The response of the call rate to net export shocks is more substantial than its response to output and inflation shocks, and the peak effect comes after 20 months. In Japan the trade balance or current account has always been one of the main targets of monetary policy. Put differently, Japan's 'potential' output has been effectively constrained by the supply of raw materials, which constitute the bulk of the country's imports.

Irrespective of its objectives, when the BOJ changes its policy stance, how does this affect the economy? Table 9.6 shows that innovations in the call rate very strongly drive down output, with the peak effect coming after 12–15 months. Since it has already been observed that innovations in the call rate mainly reflect changes in the BOJ's policy stance, one can conclude that monetary policy does

Table 9.6. Responses to a one-standard-deviation shock

Lag	Call	IIP	CPI	NEX
		1958(7)–1990(11)		
		Call		
1	0.451915	− 0.251948E-01	− 0.261513E-01	0.348897
2	0.390639	− 0.174553	0.463459E-01	− 0.306428
3	0.403578	− 0.277046	0.127254	0.115980E-01
4	0.472020	− 0.494240	0.199149	0.463057E-01
5	0.446735	− 0.508574	0.227798	0.705311E-01
6	0.432520	− 0.671324	0.222736	− 0.188166
7	0.410158	− 0.719435	0.214346	0.539650E-01
8	0.386531	− 0.714655	0.190505	0.399531E-01
9	0.340379	− 0.769521	0.162276	− 0.485095E-01
10	0.302258	− 0.744029	0.134719	0.656681E-01
11	0.263490	− 0.711218	0.983827E-01	0.569025E-01
12	0.219125	− 0.675445	0.577705E-01	0.564377E-01
13	0.179454	− 0.610880	0.207843E-01	0.842084E-01
14	0.141253	− 0.541397	− 0.164786E-01	0.102610
15	0.104908	− 0.465697	− 0.523441E-01	0.107114
16	0.713187E-01	− 0.382622	− 0.843619E-01	0.117829
17	0.414448E-01	− 0.298199	− 0.113807	0.131045
18	0.146865E-01	− 0.213365	− 0.140072	0.133669
19	− 0.892036E-02	− 0.130393	− 0.162467	0.138640
20	− 0.289494E-01	− 0.509359E-01	− 0.181221	0.142830
21	− 0.458361E-01	0.239390E-01	− 0.196503	0.143427
22	− 0.597504E-01	0.925754E-01	− 0.208267	0.143235
23	− 0.707750E-01	0.154704	− 0.216755	0.142219
24	− 0.791732E-01	0.209643	− 0.222275	0.139862
		IIP		
1	0.000000	1.93870	− 0.404968	− 0.174424
2	− 0.719107E-03	1.45175	− 0.361983	0.276811E-01
3	− 0.741255E-02	1.49619	− 0.325161	0.271821E-03
4	0.182094E-01	1.95114	− 0.316685	− 0.110917
5	− 0.165459E-01	1.74494	− 0.273859	− 0.115514
6	0.311224E-02	1.84962	− 0.275887	− 0.849986E-01
7	0.167063E-01	1.80767	− 0.252514	− 0.122911
8	0.936477E-02	1.70544	− 0.225727	− 0.123965
9	0.253457E-01	1.65916	− 0.203541	− 0.146173
10	0.313907E-01	1.53202	− 0.174542	− 0.114822
11	0.378390E-01	1.42451	− 0.152298	− 0.140559
12	0.463838E-01	1.30670	− 0.129983	− 0.146584
13	0.527668E-01	1.17971	− 0.107660	− 0.122549
14	0.593096E-01	1.06187	− 0.891609E-01	− 0.139172
15	0.640610E-01	0.939334	− 0.71145E-01	− 0.131411
16	0.683418E-01	0.826103	− 0.549967E-01	− 0.122894
17	0.716155E-01	0.718813	− 0.416513E-01	− 0.123838
18	0.734911E-01	0.617120	− 0.297332E-01	− 0.116448
19	0.746518E-01	0.526084	− 0.197923E-01	− 0.110994
20	0.748184E-01	0.442428	− 0.118207E-01	− 0.105699
21	0.740112E-01	0.367823	− 0.535052E-02	− 0.995787E-01
22	0.725173E-01	0.302483	− 0.460963E-03	− 0.937104E-01
23	0.703327E-01	0.245195	0.305770E-02	− 0.875551E-01
24	0.675603E-01	0.196399	0.539831E-02	− 0.818328E-01

Table 9.6. (*Contd*)

Lag	Call	IIP	CPI	NEX
		CPI		
1	0.000000	0.000000	0.807994	− 0.301015E-01
2	0.246178E-01	− 0.220914	0.900214	− 0.471669E-01
3	0.446420E-01	− 0.142202	0.901251	− 0.128321
4	0.599440E-01	− 0.144987	0.885858	− 0.239186
5	0.109790	− 0.255200	0.840905	− 0.128907
6	0.134779	− 0.317590	0.861784	− 0.192851
7	0.146244	− 0.471135	0.864394	− 0.215257
8	0.164498	− 0.606159	0.858800	− 0.187376
9	0.176348	− 0.720153	0.845387	− 0.195476
10	0.183705	− 0.861891	0.823085	− 0.208762
11	0.189032	− 0.973177	0.802277	− 0.193269
12	0.191293	− 1.07546	0.778606	− 0.180609
13	0.189401	− 1.16999	0.752247	− 0.179483
14	0.185650	− 1.24075	0.724205	− 0.166131
15	0.180028	− 1.29809	0.693791	− 0.153202
16	0.172312	− 1.33788	0.661660	− 0.144332
17	0.163337	− 1.36066	0.628850	− 0.132507
18	0.153265	− 1.36894	0.595539	− 0.120042
19	0.142446	− 1.36246	0.561908	− 0.109881
20	0.131103	− 1.34368	0.528513	− 0.995305E-01
21	0.119580	− 1.31367	0.495576	− 0.893083E-01
22	0.108109	− 1.27409	0.463344	− 0.805144E-01
23	0.968169E-01	− 1.22684	0.432149	− 0.722240E-01
24	0.859424E-01	− 1.17324	0.402165	− 0.646859E-01
		Net exports		
1	0.000000	0.000000	0.000000	2.02431
2	− 0.587840E-01	0.124346E-01	0.878078E-02	0.233568
3	− 0.861485E-01	− 0.168360	− 0.160674E-01	0.649400
4	− 0.474438E-01	− 0.213482	− 0.489064E-01	1.00044
5	− 0.818597E-01	− 0.227968	− 0.120922	0.546051
6	− 0.108454	− 0.358756	− 0.146262	0.677360
7	− 0.123530	− 0.369464	− 0.152667	0.759102
8	− 0.142656	− 0.413756	− 0.187364	0.677630
9	− 0.168890	− 0.464972	− 0.212614	0.645373
10	− 0.186441	− 0.449452	− 0.238842	0.687676
11	− 0.201860	− 0.456929	− 0.267572	0.664819
12	− 0.220897	− 0.444802	− 0.290309	0.643405
13	− 0.234655	− 0.417372	− 0.310508	0.646648
14	− 0.246967	− 0.389299	− 0.329377	0.637699
15	− 0.257960	− 0.349251	− 0.346223	0.620754
16	− 0.266657	− 0.307440	− 0.360011	0.610413
17	− 0.273219	− 0.261140	− 0.371428	− 0.601013
18	− 0.277966	− 0.212757	− 0.380533	0.584513
19	− 0.281153	− 0.165172	− 0.386955	0.571008
20	− 0.282385	− 0.117048	− 0.391156	0.557342
21	− 0.282140	− 0.710436E-01	− 0.393295	0.541400
22	− 0.280552	− 0.275637E-01	− 0.393374	0.525994
23	− 0.277602	− 0.132165E-01	− 0.391630	0.510394
24	− 0.273552	0.502881E-01	− 0.388265	0.494504

Table 9.6. (*Contd*)

Lag	Call	IIP	CPI	NEX
		1958(7)–1972(12)		
		Call		
1	0.463816	0.154725	– 0.129125	0.268250
2	0.235975	0.887188E-01	– 0.617366E-01	– 0.169161
3	0.265744	– 0.356279E-01	0.353317E-01	0.512376E-02
4	0.341445	– 0.190919	0.708389E-01	0.625894E-01
5	0.255041	0.947892E-01	0.430471E-01	– 0.209170E-01
6	0.223765	– 0.778355E-01	0.306688E-02	– 0.834157E-01
7	0.217228	– 0.152236	0.450199E-01	– 0.294483E-01
8	0.193465	– 0.143778	0.307972E-01	– 0.254329E-01
9	0.144985	– 0.290790	0.356738E-01	– 0.756735E-01
10	0.138428	– 0.349881	0.630513E-01	– 0.534878E-01
11	0.123604	– 0.399172	0.622603E-01	– 0.455309E-01
12	0.948564E-01	– 0.456257	0.627437E-01	– 0.491060E-01
13	0.869052E-01	– 0.504200	0.687061E-01	– 0.473857E-01
14	0.747465E-01	– 0.522382	0.682926E-01	– 0.378897E-01
15	0.606252E-01	– 0.531811	0.634109E-01	– 0.300621E-01
16	0.526266E-01	– 0.552265	0.628454E-01	– 0.259016E-01
17	0.448870E-01	– 0.545410	0.609817E-01	– 0.195882E-01
18	0.362380E-01	– 0.532505	0.561452E-01	– 0.137695E-01
19	0.297233E-01	– 0.523928	0.537104E-01	– 0.740348E-02
20	0.241575E-01	– 0.502043	0.505111E-01	– 0.348843E-02
21	0.176786E-01	– 0.476048	0.462929E-01	– 0.377441E-03
22	0.123580E-01	– 0.450362	0.429800E-01	0.394644E-02
23	0.786032E-02	– 0.420751	0.396008E-01	0.670167E-02
24	0.294365E-02	– 0.389142	0.359865E-01	0.819396E-02
		IIP		
1	0.000000	2.02244	– 0.514355	– 0.134834
2	0.393852E-01	1.60244	– 0.394727	– 0.857447E-01
3	0.504268E-01	1.34394	– 0.329176	– 0.439390E-03
4	0.962156E-01	1.76283	– 0.306749	– 0.137799
5	0.726187E-01	1.50776	– 0.207829	– 0.119309
6	0.119329	1.60323	– 0.179729	– 0.849393E-01
7	0.130386	1.57640	– 0.169717	– 0.130615
8	0.119192	1.47825	– 0.145454	– 0.143366
9	0.141387	1.45684	– 0.137533	– 0.138143
10	0.148468	1.32492	– 0.114989	– 0.131499
11	0.148927	1.21368	– 0.101715	– 0.141715
12	0.160013	1.08473	– 0.823503E-01	– 0.143263
13	0.165089	0.942478	– 0.625884E-01	– 0.131534
14	0.168117	0.816103	– 0.511506E-01	– 0.130465
15	0.170653	0.671366	– 0.361767E-01	– 0.127861
16	0.171983	0.543799	– 0.238889E-01	– 0.119909
17	0.171271	0.420757	– 0.151552E-01	– 0.113035
18	0.168861	0.295410	– 0.517689E-02	– 0.106245
19	0.165839	0.185203	0.301902E-02	– 0.994921E-01
20	0.160963	0.816758E-01	0.100145E-01	– 0.917810E-01
21	0.155003	– 0.144939E-01	0.165168E-01	– 0.837865E-01
22	0.148399	– 0.995036E-01	0.219774E-01	– 0.767762E-01
23	0.140504	– 0.174712	0.265715E-01	– 0.696628E-01
24	0.132090	– 0.240101	0.303423E-01	– 0.623115E-01

Table 9.6. (*Contd*)

Lag	Call	IIP	CPI	NEX
		CPI		
1	0.000000	0.000000	0.727932	0.692156E-01
2	– 0.611066E-01	– 0.210813	0.726385	– 0.523411E-01
3	– 0.644215E-01	0.144553	0.632892	– 0.583901E-01
4	– 0.385368E-01	0.174354	0.569543	– 0.495216E-01
5	– 0.703329E-01	0.169784	0.448898	– 0.978552E-01
6	– 0.828531E-01	0.138884	0.406792	– 0.899858E-01
7	– 0.501309E-01	– 0.104655	0.401509	– 0.504198E-01
8	– 0.446885E-01	– 0.203637	0.368807	– 0.530313E-01
9	– 0.349783E-01	– 0.353044	0.351953	– 0.555566E-01
10	– 0.167156E-01	– 0.529760	0.339718	– 0.263476E-01
11	– 0.597528E-02	– 0.605113	0.311745	– 0.126225E-01
12	– 0.398661E-02	– 0.715755	0.284744	– 0.760553E-02
13	0.154712E-02	– 0.801617	0.262863	0.866628E-02
14	0.481747E-02	– 0.855074	0.238227	0.219776E-01
15	0.980013E-03	– 0.913187	0.216745	0.305345E-01
16	– 0.157717E-02	– 0.949302	0.198593	0.388319E-01
17	– 0.570577E-02	– 0.969120	0.181533	0.468921E-01
18	– 0.133162E-01	– 0.975717	0.164844	0.532465E-01
19	– 0.205402E-01	– 0.969565	0.149742	0.576458E-01
20	– 0.284744E-01	– 0.950769	0.135803	0.614965E-01
21	– 0.372512E-01	– 0.918928	0.121944	0.644094E-01
22	– 0.455415E-01	– 0.880119	0.109314	0.664468E-01
23	– 0.533962E-01	– 0.832504	0.976385E-01	0.676738E-01
24	– 0.608669E-01	– 0.777076	0.863228E-01	0.680235E-01
		Net exports		
1	0.000000	0.000000	0.000000	1.11223
2	– 0.497889E-01	– 0.965139E-01	0.396278E-01	0.213031
3	– 0.743544E-01	– 0.229250	– 0.204372E-01	0.342844
4	– 0.406194E-01	– 0.183668	– 0.194451E-01	0.470098
5	– 0.928896E-01	– 0.462482	– 0.320531E-01	0.441305
6	– 0.133481	– 0.616518	– 0.527506E-02	0.275186
7	– 0.181845	– 0.494707	– 0.531743E-02	0.242348
8	– 0.187594	– 0.584694	– 0.962022E-02	0.325647
9	– 0.229062	– 0.600060	– 0.237193E-01	0.242996
10	– 0.251499	– 0.525763	– 0.265802E-01	0.187954
11	– 0.265562	– 0.480013	– 0.318457E-01	0.201723
12	– 0.271219	– 0.389776	– 0.402269E-01	0.205579
13	– 0.277078	– 0.321000	– 0.484172E-01	0.169139
14	– 0.279292	– 0.204199	– 0.534016E-01	0.152805
15	– 0.270581	– 0.848766E-01	– 0.616230E-01	0.157815
16	– 0.263603	0.165947E-01	– 0.687443E-01	0.146958
17	– 0.254542	0.135710	– 0.754149E-01	0.128885
18	– 0.241697	0.247423	– 0.806925E-01	0.120610
19	– 0.227779	0.350651	– 0.854246E-01	0.115726
20	– 0.213229	0.444307	– 0.896696E-01	0.103038
21	– 0.198507	0.528040	– 0.919035E-01	0.906959E-01
22	– 0.182631	0.603152	– 0.935124E-01	0.824911E-01
23	– 0.166812	0.663012	– 0.943535E-01	0.732438E-01
24	– 0.151451	0.711039	– 0.940334E-01	0.623556E-01

Table 9.6. (*Contd*)

Lag	Call	IIP	CPI	NEX
		1973(1)–1990(11)		
		Call		
1	0.345314	– 0.521271E-01	0.358766E– 02	0.643173
2	0.430163	– 0.244549	0.764083E-01	– 0.483027
3	0.438019	– 0.327619	0.115689	0.655225E-01
4	0.441549	– 0.331405	0.144017	– 0.762214E-01
5	0.422529	– 0.606613	0.170416	0.262974
6	0.417857	– 0.708228	0.191912	– 0.300318
7	0.405033	– 0.751015	0.181749	– 0.101941
8	0.392066	– 0.833962	0.140724	0.109706
9	0.347660	– 0.781982	0.972191E-01	– 0.810666E-01
10	0.307137	– 0.808896	0.656081E-01	0.176427
11	0.267147	– 0.775428	0.284819E-01	0.155407
12	0.222534	– 0.704136	– 0.247099E-01	0.139488
13	0.180585	– 0.659767	– 0.770748E-01	0.211247
14	0.138194	– 0.557412	– 0.134020	0.245367
15	0.955394E-01	– 0.457188	– 0.189025	0.270406
16	0.522549E-01	– 0.359419	– 0.237836	0.297365
17	0.127891E-01	– 0.245657	– 0.284997	0.327480
18	– 0.247366E-01	– 0.135112	– 0.329287	0.335237
19	– 0.596628E-01	– 0.254738E-01	– 0.370063	0.349588
20	– 0.906605E-01	0.847574E-01	– 0.406071	0.362119
21	– 0.118816	0.188853	– 0.436915	0.371074
22	– 0.143685	0.286277	– 0.462200	0.373520
23	– 0.165011	0.376025	– 0.481849	0.376195
24	– 0.182709	0.456068	– 0.496425	0.376888
		IIP		
1	0.000000	1.57782	– 0.257672	– 0.124713
2	– 0.668887E-02	0.834421	– 0.204889	0.709747E-01
3	– 0.992714E-02	1.01760	– 0.104790	0.867949E-01
4	0.648149E-02	1.27487	– 0.175380E-01	– 0.450686E-01
5	– 0.351863E-01	0.947907	0.393420E-01	– 0.133210
6	– 0.218546E-01	0.940310	0.727841E-01	– 0.212827E-01
7	– 0.505374E-02	0.832118	0.131935	– 0.201965E-02
8	– 0.349703E-03	0.651661	0.175440	– 0.156930E-01
9	0.114719E-01	0.554080	0.223555	– 0.626642E-01
10	0.217078E-01	0.365298	0.270992	0.114335
11	0.313481E-01	0.217277	0.303804	0.201918E-01
12	0.391063E-01	0.798225E-01	0.332629	0.987168E-02
13	0.511784E-01	– 0.848074E-01	0.354301	0.990174E-01
14	0.591249E-01	– 0.190821	0.364297	0.366230E-01
15	0.637336E-01	– 0.307999	0.370328	0.644456E-01
16	0.676416E-01	– 0.410498	0.371557	0.831050E-01
17	0.689509E-01	– 0.478718	0.364303	0.683073E-01
18	0.680475E-01	– 0.546494	0.352609	0.731334E-01
19	0.656954E-01	– 0.589107	0.335643	0.730029E-01
20	0.619555E-01	– 0.612374	0.313867	0.715058E-01
21	0.560879E-01	– 0.624883	0.289447	0.681586E-01
22	0.491835E-01	– 0.619441	0.262670	0.654898E-01
23	0.414553E-01	– 0.601935	0.234396	0.624247E-01
24	0.328702E-01	– 0.573943	0.205206	0.565270E-01

Table 9.6. (*Contd*)

Lag	Call	IIP	CPI	NEX
		CPI		
1	0.000000	0.000000	0.807020	− 0.410476E-01
2	0.673291E-01	− 0.821613E-01	0.915074	− 0.631172E-01
3	0.111601	− 0.260953	0.944603	− 0.796559E-01
4	0.105739	− 0.235262	0.908378	− 0.363744
5	0.192335	− 0.353933	0.874586	− 0.138283
6	0.232553	− 0.395178	0.906294	− 0.192817
7	0.246533	− 0.574410	0.950325	− 0.282032
8	0.252260	− 0.703436	0.988558	− 0.304969
9	0.258885	− 0.863333	1.00479	− 0.142415
10	0.262989	− 0.999266	1.00073	− 0.358269
11	0.268271	− 1.10463	0.988139	− 0.296260
12	0.275344	− 1.20465	0.969256	− 0.224240
13	0.270114	− 1.25324	0.941028	− 0.289692
14	0.262668	− 1.31378	0.913144	− 0.234901
15	0.254426	− 1.34649	0.880573	− 0.225515
16	0.244270	− 1.34943	0.838561	− 0.243400
17	0.232683	− 1.34761	0.794052	− 0.238564
18	0.220316	− 1.31887	0.746325	− 0.225739
19	0.206566	− 1.27434	0.697249	− 0.226662
20	0.191098	− 1.22232	0.649195	− 0.225056
21	0.176012	− 1.15732	0.601707	− 0.220878
22	0.161031	− 1.08407	0.555039	− 0.223167
23	0.146327	− 1.00607	0.509976	− 0.224709
24	0.132492	− 0.923065	0.467457	− 0.225515
		Net exports		
1	0.000000	0.000000	0.000000	2.32720
2	− 0.865343E-01	0.711964E-01	− 0.139190E-01	0.311834
3	− 0.135694	− 0.752655E-01	− 0.308229E-01	0.701730
4	− 0.883904E-01	− 0.207102	− 0.580918E-01	1.23770
5	− 0.115579	− 0.504608E-01	− 0.139423	0.414948
6	− 0.145850	− 0.145090	− 0.181230	0.756236
7	− 0.168843	− 0.144832	− 0.191985	0.939649
8	− 0.199989	− 0.739442E-01	− 0.230280	0.767357
9	− 0.230690	− 0.112180	− 0.256277	0.682070
10	− 0.247004	− 0.698565E-01	− 0.292984	0.774259
11	− 0.259240	0.586466E-02	− 0.341853	0.707556
12	− 0.280053	0.566298E-01	− 0.381175	0.659603
13	− 0.293665	0.123205	− 0.411597	0.696789
14	− 0.305525	0.201987	− 0.439251	0.656171
15	− 0.317145	0.267430	− 0.464475	0.611368
16	− 0.323959	0.337496	− 0.485212	0.583736
17	− 0.327311	0.410010	− 0.503360	0.565395
18	− 0.329195	0.476209	− 0.516911	0.522976
19	− 0.329002	0.537379	− 0.524176	0.493730
20	− 0.325686	0.591070	− 0.526417	0.472400
21	− 0.320595	0.638540	− 0.524594	0.433319
22	− 0.313327	0.676171	− 0.518447	0.403288
23	− 0.303681	0.705494	− 0.508323	0.376830
24	− 0.292434	0.727257	− 0.494887	0.346518

affect real output.[8] Accordingly, it is possible to reject the real business cycle theorist's view, which holds that money is nothing but a mirror-image of real shocks and plays no role in the business cycle (King and Plosser 1984; and Plosser 1990). This point can also be confirmed, though more casually, just by looking at Fig. 9.6. Inflation also negatively responds to call rate shocks, but its response is much weaker than the response of output, and the lags are longer.

By focusing on the periods of interest-rate-smoothing, I have argued that real shocks are important in the business cycle. When the BOJ changes its policy stance, however, it also affects the real economy.

9.4 THE TRANSMISSION OF MONETARY POLICY

Monetary policy affects the real economy. What is the transmission mechanism of monetary policy? As a preliminary step to answering this question, Table 9.7 summarizes, for the post-war business cycle, the extent to which different demand components have accounted for different proportions of the change in GNP.

Since the Japanese economy has been growing rapidly, almost all the variables increased in absolute terms, even during recessions. I therefore first calculated the change in each variable, measured from trough to peak in case of a recovery, and from peak to trough in case of a growth recession. I then subtracted the latter from the former to obtain the difference. Table 9.7 reports the relative contribution of each demand component, for each post-war cycle, to this cyclical difference in the change in real GNP. B. Friedman (1990) presents a similar but slightly different table for post-war US recessions. For the sake of comparison, I present results for the United States, based on the method described above, in Table 9.8.

In Japan, throughout the whole period, the relative contribution of fixed investment has been the greatest of all the demand components: 60% of GNP on average. In contrast, in the United States fixed investment accounts for only 25% on average of the change in real GNP. The relative contribution of inventory and housing invest-

[8] Romer and Romer (1989) put a dummy variable (which identifies the six months when the Federal Reserve made the decision to seek to induce a recession in order to reduce inflation) into the univariate autoregressive equation for industrial production. They found that this dummy variable has a significantly negative effect on industrial production. The dummy variable constructed from Federal Reserve records, however, does not indicate the length of the shocks caused by the Fed, nor does it differentiate the shocks by size. I believe that changes in the call rate identify the timing and size of changes in the BOJ's policy stance.

Table 9.7. The relative contribution of demand components to the business cycle in Japan

Peak	Trough	Peak	GNP %	II	D	IH	IF	C
1957(II)	1958(II)	1961(IV)	100	60.955	39.045	2.8816	56.7851	47.9378
1961(IV)	1962(IV)	1964(IV)	100	71.822	78.178	14.9896	46.1396	45.3235
1964(IV)	1965(IV)	1970(III)	100	5.270	94.730	1.6540	62.5451	35.8547
1970(III)	1971(IV)	1973(IV)	100	− 10.643	110.643	27.2298	77.9559	90.6800
1973(IV)	1975(I)	1977(I)	100	6.754	93.246	41.2309	29.2053	37.8202
1977(I)	1977(IV)	1980(I)	100	30.916	69.084	− 9.1070	81.1159	74.5326
1980(I)	1983(I)	1985(II)	100	22.322	77.678	1.3227	73.6131	8.9868
1985(II)	1986(IV)	1990(III)	100	12.840	87.160	11.8504	67.5603	35.8865
Average %			100	15.7818	84.218	16.6272	58.237	45.0169

Peak	Trough	Peak	CD	CND	NEX	EX	IM	G
1957(II)	1958(II)	1961(IV)	—	—	− 62.257	7.492	− 69.75	− 6.302
1961(IV)	1962(IV)	1964(IV)	—	—	− 45.338	6.863	− 52.20	− 32.937
1964(IV)	1965(IV)	1970(III)	—	—	− 11.176	10.953	− 22.13	5.851
1970(III)	1971(IV)	1973(IV)	8.8544	81.8256	− 82.482	− 5.144	− 77.34	− 2.741
1973(IV)	1975(I)	1977(I)	15.4472	22.3729	− 21.105	2.321	− 23.43	6.095
1977(I)	1977(IV)	1980(I)	44.6072	29.9255	2.901	60.069	− 57.17	− 80.357
1980(I)	1983(I)	1985(II)	14.0854	− 5.0986	10.281	63.956	− 53.67	− 16.525
1985(II)	1986(IV)	1990(III)	10.6049	26.5199	− 5.124	87.435	− 92.56	− 23.013
Average %			18.0807	35.8718	− 24.065	27.780	− 51.845	− 11.598

Table 9.8. The relative contribution of demand components to the business cycle, United States

Peak	Trough	Peak	GNP %	II	D	IH	IF	C
1957(III)	1958(I)	1960(I)	100	34.0739	65.9261	8.5508	17.0499	27.1248
1960(I)	1960(IV)	1969(III)	100	52.5561	47.4439	15.7570	15.9706	33.2836
1969(III)	1970(II)	1973(IV)	100	28.2595	71.7405	24.4541	21.9450	13.9530
1973(IV)	1975(I)	1980(I)	100	31.5844	68.4156	21.5106	25.4131	35.2068
1980(I)	1980(II)	1981(III)	100	8.6601	91.3399	31.0866	31.4134	53.9011
1981(III)	1982(III)	1990(III)	100	19.7589	80.2411	13.2042	27.2770	25.5607
Average %			100	24.2747	75.7253	20.7552	25.1305	35.4643

Peak	Trough	Peak	CD	CND	NEX	EX	IM	G
1957(III)	1958(I)	1960(I)	7.7241	19.4007	15.397	15.9907	− 0.465	− 2.2991
1960(I)	1960(IV)	1969(III)	7.8344	25.4492	− 18.225	0.5729	− 18.679	0.6577
1969(III)	1970(II)	1973(IV)	11.9637	1.9893	− 7.534	4.5817	− 12.116	18.9436
1973(IV)	1975(I)	1980(I)	13.8456	21.3612	− 12.426	10.7646	− 23.191	− 1.2044
1980(I)	1980(II)	1981(III)	34.1299	19.7712	− 18.791	5.5147	− 24.306	− 6.4134
1981(III)	1982(III)	1990(III)	10.8982	14.6625	9.814	27.3771	− 17.463	4.2434
Average %			17.8298	17.6345	− 6.059	11.4677	− 17.496	0.36471

ments is greater in the United States than in Japan. Changes in housing investment in Japan are not really systematic over the business cycle. On the other hand, until the mid-1960s, inventory investment had a large impact on Japanese business cycle: a 60%–70% contribution. A substantial portion of the inventory, however, was raw materials—which were also imports. Therefore, the contribution of inventory investment and imports almost cancelled each other. As a result, fixed investment retained its importance. As a long-term trend, the role of inventory investment in the business cycle seems to have diminished in both Japan and the United States.

Net exports have been counter-cyclical in Japan's business cycle except for the years 1977–85, in which economic growth was export-led. In particular, imports have been very counter-cyclical: the fraction of output was −52% on average, compared with −17% in the United States. Until very recently, the bulk of Japanese imports consisted of raw materials and therefore moved, very mechanically, in parallel with the level of aggregate economic activity.

The contribution of consumption to GNP seems in large part to be similar in the two countries, although the contribution of non-durables is substantially higher in Japan. As for government expenditure, we find this counter-cyclical for Japan (−12% of GNP on average), but neutral (0.4%) for the United States.

In sum, the major differences between Japan and the United States lie in the fact that fixed investment plays a much larger role in the business cycle in Japan, and that net exports and government expenditure are much more counter-cyclical in Japan. These findings help us identify the important components in the Japanese business cycle. Yet it remains to be seen how they are related to monetary policy. With this objective, I ran a set of bivariate VARs using the call rate and each component of expenditure. (All the variables except inventory investment are log-differenced; inventory investment is differenced.) We can see from Figs. 9.7–9.12 that investment and imports are the components that respond substantially to innovations in the call rate. There are lags of two to three quarters before changes in the call rate have an impact on these variables.

Summing up these findings, I conclude that monetary policy, represented by changes in the call rate, exerts substantial effects on real output in Japan mainly through its effect on fixed investment and imports. Since imports were almost identical to inventory investment in the 1950s and 1960s, one can also say that inventory investment was a major channel of monetary policy in those days. This finding,

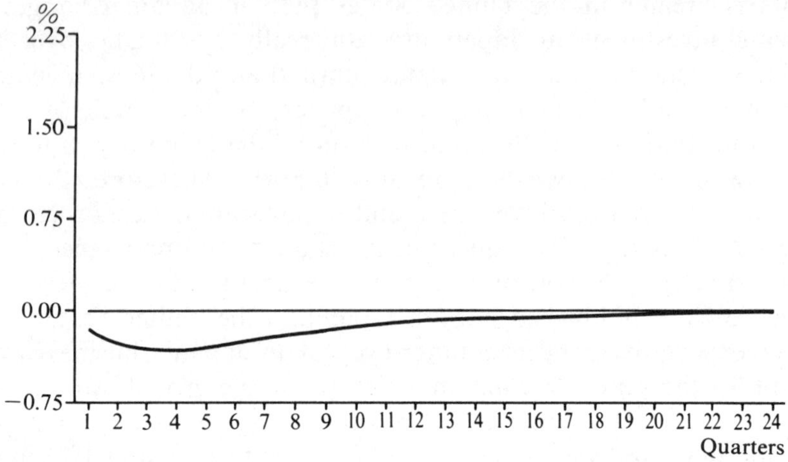

Fig. 9.7. Responses of consumption to changes in the call rate

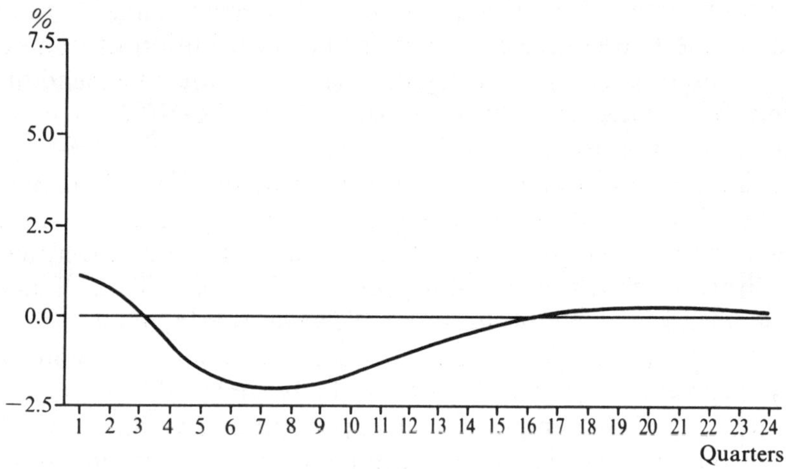

Fig. 9.8. Responses of fixed investment to changes in the call rate

however, presents a puzzle, because fixed investment is typically found to be interest-inelastic. As fully explained in Chapter 7, investment is very strongly affected by changes in output, which presumably proxy the prospective sales and profits, but is *not* significantly affected by the cost of capital. Investment, therefore, must be explained by real rather than financial factors. To solve this puzzle, I advance the following proposition.

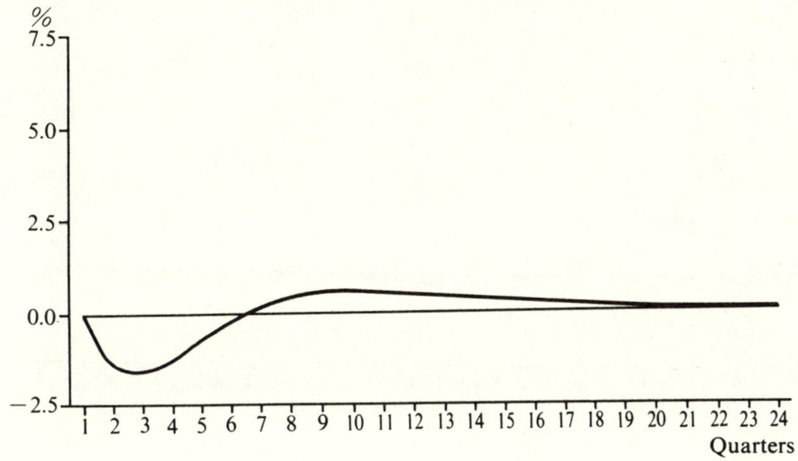

Fig. 9.9. Responses of housing investment to changes in the call rate

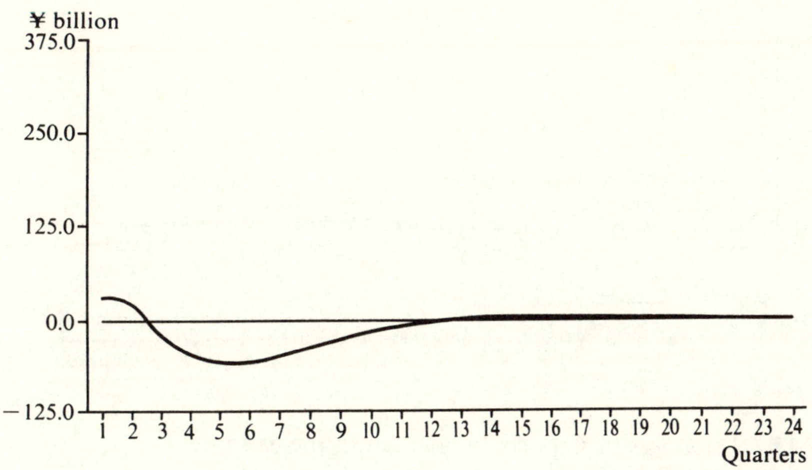

Fig. 9.10. Responses of inventory investment to changes in the call rate

In his *General Theory*, Keynes (1936) took the effect of the long-term interest rate on fixed investment as the major channel of the monetary transmission mechanism. Hawtrey (1937), on the other hand, criticized Keynes and argued strongly that it was the fluctuation in the amount of inventory stocks that was responsible for the

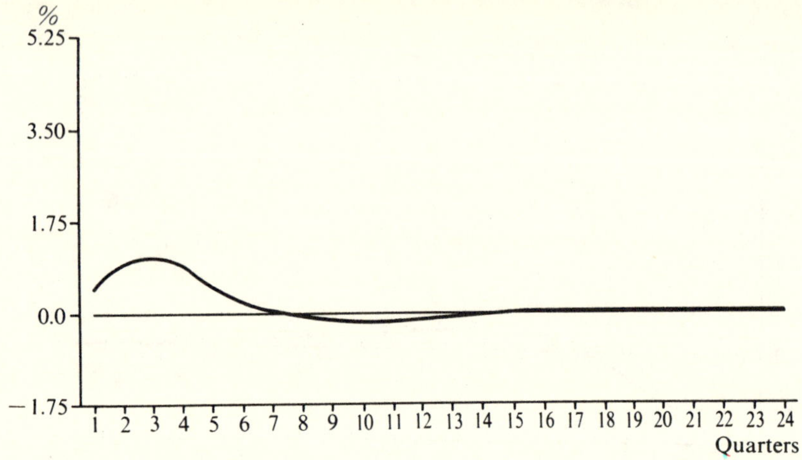

Fig. 9.11. Responses of exports to changes in the call rate

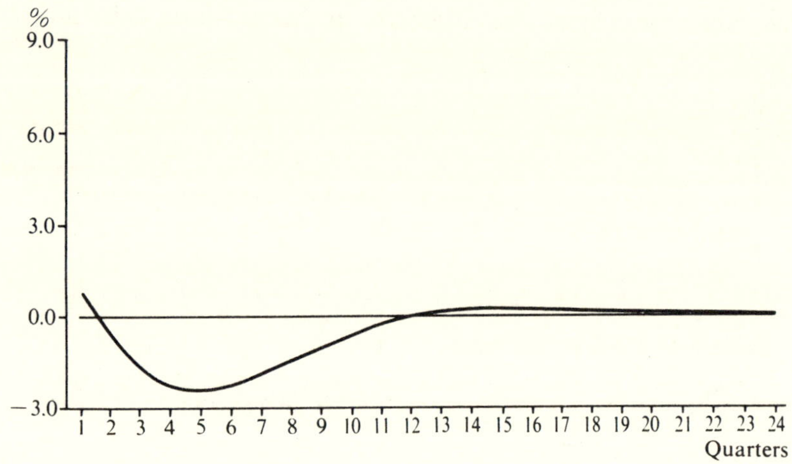

Fig. 9.12. Responses of imports to changes in the call rate

ups and downs of business; and it was the behaviour of the short-term interest rate that was responsible for those fluctuations. We might call this mechanism the *Hawtrey mechanism*.

Coupling the Hawtrey mechanism to such typical investment functions as shown in Table 7.3 above, according to which output affects investment much more significantly than does the interest rate, one obtains the monetary transmission mechanism in which first the interest rate affects inventory investment/output, and then changes in output, including anticipated changes, eventually affect fixed investment. In this way, we can reconcile a typical investment function with the fact that fixed investment is by far the most important demand component in the Japanese monetary transmission mechanism.

To test this hypothesis empirically, I ran a four-variable VAR with the call rate, loans for working capital, production (IIP), and machinery orders for the period January 1976–January 1987. The analysis in the previous section indicates that a change in monetary policy is best captured by a change in the call rate. Table 9.9 and Fig. 9.13 demonstrate that the Granger causality runs from the call rate to production, and then from production to investment. As one might expect, the direct causality from the call rate to investment is rejected.

Table 9.10 seeks to check out what kind of production is most strongly affected by changes in the call rate. Industries where production is very significantly affected by changes in the call rate are metal, paper and pulp, ceramics, chemicals, and so on. Broadly speaking, they are intermediate goods. On the other hand, in such industries as food, textiles, iron and steel, precision instruments, and motor vehicles, production is not significantly affected by changes in the call rate.

Similarly, Fig. 9.14(*a*)–(*d*) show the impulse response functions of IIP to a one-standard-deviation shock in the call rate, based on bivariate VAR for four different kinds of goods: construction materials, intermediate goods, machinery, and consumption goods. These charts demonstrate clearly that the production of construction materials and intermediate goods is most significantly affected by a

Table 9.9. VAR of the call rate, bank loans for working capital, production and Machinery Orders, January 1976–January 1987

Explanatory variable	Left-hand-side variable: Investment	Production	Call rate	Loan
P-values for Granger causality				
Investment	0.00006	0.19547	0.46961	0.27231
Production	0.00004	0.00000	0.77740	0.00590
Call rate	0.84979	0.04834	0.00000	0.00280
Loan	0.00120	0.00006	0.10581	0.00000
Variance decomposition (%)				
Investment	50.51	24.59	37.78	26.64
Production	23.92	37.91	14.59	17.78
Call rate	11.56	33.99	35.46	37.69
Loan	13.99	3.49	12.15	17.87

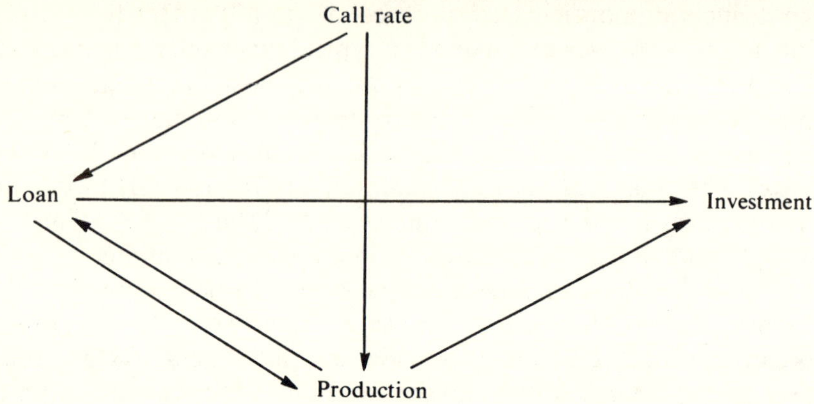

Fig. 9.13. The call rate, bank loans for working capital, production, and machinery orders
Arrows indicate the causality flows significant at the 10% level.

change in the call rate with the shortest lag. The production of machinery is also significantly affected, but with much longer lags. Finally, the effect of a change in the call rate on the production of

Table 9.10. The effects of the call rate on production (IIP) by industry, based on bivariate VAR

Industry	Causality test	Variance decomposition	
	(*P-values*)	Call	IIP
Metal	0.00002	62.23	37.76
Paper and pulp	0.00110	70.62	29.37
Ceramics	0.00164	70.62	29.37
Furniture	0.00201	51.08	48.91
Chemicals	0.00222	69.09	30.90
Rubber	0.00453	39.34	60.65
Wood	0.00460	66.47	33.52
Plastic	0.00732	47.50	52.49
Nonferrous metals	0.02529	45.19	54.80
Leather	0.07506	21.06	78.93
Food	0.08835	31.94	68.05
Petroleum	0.19923	34.92	65.07
Textiles	0.29446	39.14	60.85
Iron and steel	0.41940	33.05	66.94
Precision instruments	0.64133	4.89	95.10
Motor cars	0.78566	7.46	92.53

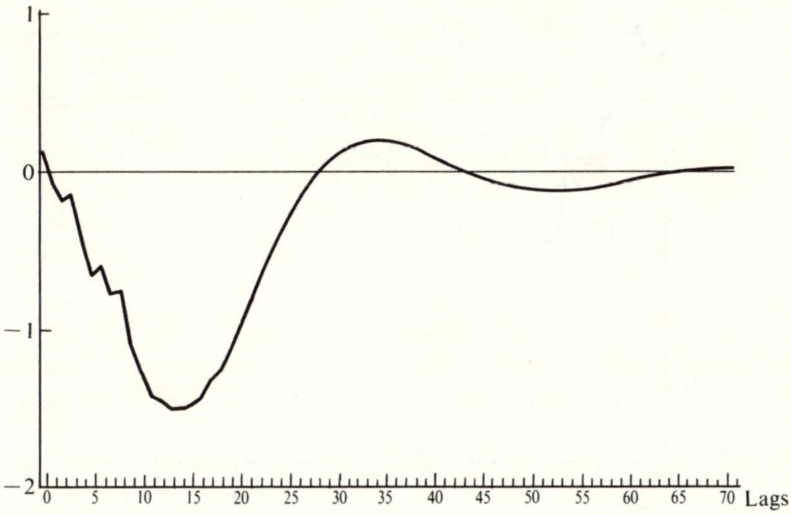

(*a*)

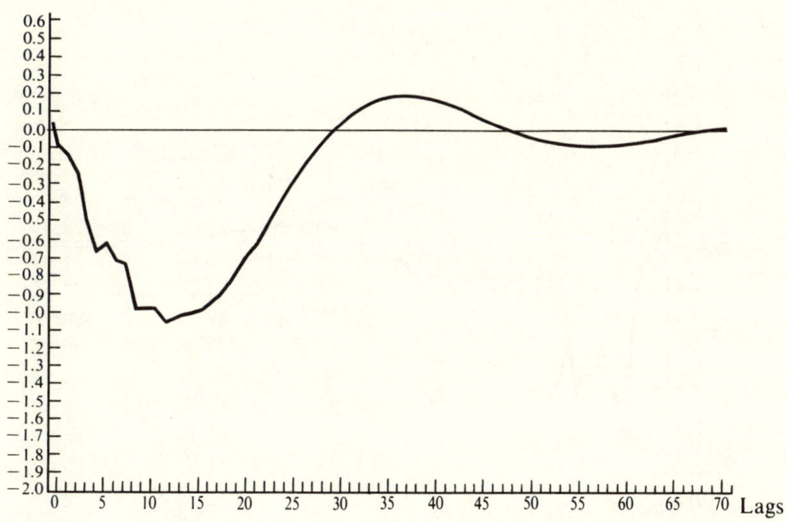

(*b*)

Fig. 9.14. (a) The impulse response function of IIP to a shock in the call rate: construction materials (b) call rate: intermediate goods (c) call rate: machinery (d) call rate: consumption goods

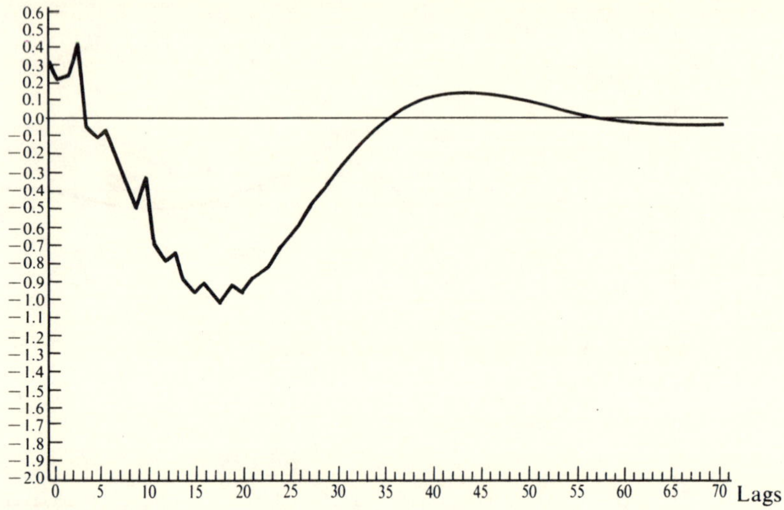

(*c*)

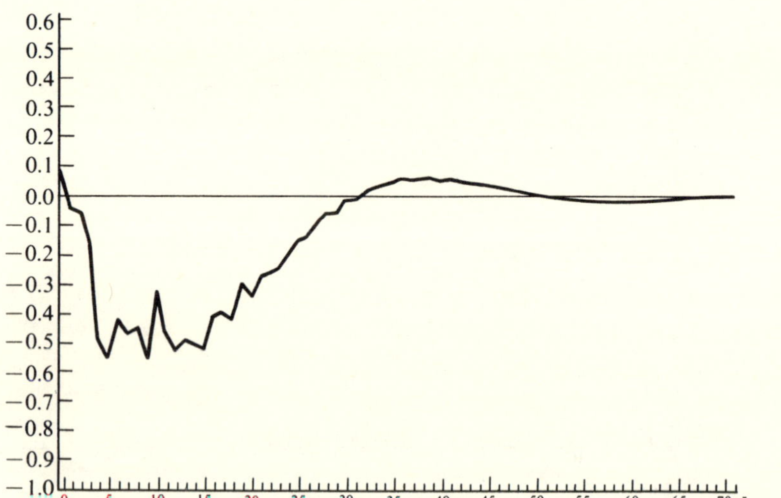

(*d*)

Fig. 9.14. (*Contd*)

consumption goods is small. (Note that the vertical scale for part (*d*) is different from those for parts (*a*)–(*c*) of Fig. 9.14.)

In summary, monetary policy, defined as a systematic change in the call rate, first affects the production of construction materials and intermediate goods (the Hawtrey mechanism); changes in production in those sectors eventually affect fixed investment, and at this stage the effects of monetary policy spread over the economy as a whole. In retrospect, fixed investment is the most important demand component in accounting for the Japanese business cycle.

9.5 CONCLUDING REMARKS

Economists often assume an exogenous money supply in both theoretical and empirical works. Monetarism, both old and new, and 'new' Keynesian economics all rest crucially on this assumption. In this chapter I have shown that this assumption is highly misleading. In Japan, over the seasonal cycle, changes in the money supply are actually nothing but mirror-images of the changes in real output and/or portfolio preferences. This is because the Bank of Japan either pegs or smooths the nominal interest rate. The same observation applies to the business cycle—even in the 1980s—and leads us to reject an array of monetary models of the business cycle such as monetarism, both new and old, and monetary models with nominal rigidities. To the extent that the money supply responds endogenously to real output through interest-rate-smoothing, it is not at all surprising that nominal money and real output are highly correlated. From this viewpoint, I find that the distinction between anticipated and unanticipated changes in the money supply (Barro 1977) is not very important.

There is an important difference between the seasonal and business cycles, however. The BOJ does not always accommodate output, price, and portfolio shocks, but instead allows the interest rate to change, and at times even actively changes the interest rate during the business cycle ('dynamic operations' in Roosa 1956). The BOJ's policy response function, therefore, involves a kind of regime shift between interest-smoothing and dynamic operations. My simple VAR analysis suggests, however, that the trade balance has always been the main target of monetary policy. In the 1950s and 1960s the anti-inflation stance of the BOJ seems to have been much weaker than during the post-oil-shock period.

When the BOJ changes its policy stance, it affects real output. Accordingly, I reject the real business cycle theorist's view, which holds that money shocks are always nothing but the mirror-image of real shocks and that money therefore plays no role in the business cycle. The analysis in Section 9.4 suggests that monetary policy has substantial impacts on real output, mainly through fixed investment and imports in Japan. The transmission mechanism is that, first, monetary policy directly affects output through working capital, particularly in those industries producing construction materials and other intermediate goods such as metal, ceramics, and paper/pulp; and then, with some lags, investment responds to changes in output and anticipations thereof. In retrospect, *investment* is the most important demand component in accounting for the Japanese business cycle.

APPENDIX: A MODEL OF THE JAPANESE FINANCIAL MARKET

This chapter has considered the role of money in economic fluctuations, abstracting from details of the financial market. Here I discuss some technical problems concerning monetary policy in Japan in a model of the Japanese financial market.

Built on Tobin's (1969) general equilibrium approach, standard models of Japanese financial market are all *static*; this appendix offers a dynamic model and shows that some of the standard results must be qualified in such a model. For institutional details of the Japanese financial market, readers are referred to Suzuki (1987).

The Model

The economic agents of this model are the Bank of Japan (hereafter BOJ), the banking sector, and the non-financial private sector (households and non-financial firms). Correspondingly, the assets explicitly considered are bank deposits, the banks' reserves at the BOJ, *call* (interbank lending), bank loans, and 'bonds'. As usual, the 'bonds' in the model can be interpreted to include all the long-term bonds and equity. The model can be easily extended, however, to allow imperfect substitutability between long-term bonds and equity.

Cash is abstracted away, and therefore banks' reserves at the BOJ are equal to high-powered money. Likewise, 'money' consists only of bank deposits. At the end of 1991, (M2 + CD) outstanding amounted to ¥516.3 trillion, out of which cash accounted for ¥38.0 trillion, about 7.4% of the total; more than 90% of 'money' in Japan consists of bank deposits. Again, it is easy to introduce cash into the model without changing the major results.

I assume that the reserves are met by the BOJ's lending. As a result, the balance sheet of the BOJ is the BOJ's lending (supply of reserves), R^s which is equal to the banks' reserves (demand for reserves), R^d. Assets of banks consist of loans L^s, reserves R^d, and call lending C^s, whereas their liabilities are deposits D, the BOJ lending R^s, and call borrowing C^d. For simplicity, banks are assumed not to hold bonds, B.

Finally, the non-financial private sector holds deposits, D^d, and bonds, B^d, as assets. Its liabilities consist of bank loans L^d and net worth. Net worth is 'capital stock' and corresponds to long-term bonds and equity, that is, the 'bonds' B in the model. The model abstracts itself from the government sector, and therefore there are no government bonds.

On normalization of units of capital or the number of shares, the supply of bonds at time t, B_t^s becomes

$$B_t^s = \rho_t^e / r_t^B, \tag{A1}$$

where ρ_t^e is the (statically) expected profit rate, taken as exogenous, and r_t^B, the rate of return on bonds, determined in the financial market.

In this model, assets are: deposits (money), reserves (high-powered money), call, bank loans, and bonds. Thanks to the Walras law with respect to assets and liabilities, therefore, only four equilibrium conditions are independent. Besides, the interest rate on bank deposits r_t^d is under regulation, and there is a persistent excess supply of deposits: banks are willing to take whatever is demanded at a given interest rate on deposits. Therefore we need explicitly to consider three market equilibrium conditions. Specifically, the interest rate for loans r_t^L, the call rate r_t^c, and the bond return r_t^B are determined by these three conditions. In what follows, we will consider the market equilbria of bonds, bank loans, and reserves (high-powered money).

Demand for bonds, as usual, depends on an array of interest rates:

$$\log B_t^d = -b_1 r_t^d + b_2 r_t^B - b_3 r_t^L \qquad (b_i > 0,\ i = 1, 2, 3), \tag{A2}$$

where r_t^d is exogenous. Rearranging (A1), we obtain

$$\log B_t^s = \log \rho_t^e - b_4 r_t^B \qquad (b_4 > 0). \tag{A3}$$

Equality of demand for and supply of bonds ((A2) and (A3) above) leads us to

$$r_t^B = \frac{1}{b_2 + b_4} (\log \rho_t^e + b_1 r_t^d + b_3 r_t^L). \tag{A4}$$

Given r_t^d and ρ_t^e, there is a one-to-one correspondence between r_t^B and r_t^L.

We next turn to demand for and supply of bank loans. The demand function for bank loans is assumed to be

$$\log L_t^d = l_1 + l_2 r_t^B - l_3(r_{t+1}^B - r_t^B) + l_4(r_{t+1}^L - r_t^L) - l_5 r_t^L + l_6 \log Y_t \quad (l_i > 0,\ i = 1,\ldots, 6) \qquad \text{(A5)}$$

Borrowings from banks increase when the 'one-period' return on bonds rises.[9] Also, flows of real economic activities Y_t, here taken as exogenous for simplicity, raise the demand for bank loans. It could represent the textbook transaction demand for money, a kind of inventory stock against contingencies in payments; but perhaps more comfortably it would reflect *finance motives* of money demand (Robertson 1937; Keynes 1937*b*), for, unlike transaction demand, most loans are demanded and approved by banks against specific plans for payment.

Demand for bank loans is of course a decreasing function of the loan rate r_t^L, but it is an increasing function of the *expected* rise in the loan rate, $r_{t+1}^L - r_t^L$. Results of many surveys (e.g. Fujino 1986) reveal that the level of the loan rate does not substantially affect loan demand ($l_5 \cong 0$), but that expectations about changes in the loan rate do ($l_4 > l_5$). This makes the model dynamic.

Substituting (A4) into (A5), we obtain the following equation (constant term ignored):

$$\log L_t^d = \frac{l_2}{b_2 + b_4}(\log \rho_t^e + b_1 r_t^d) + \left(l_4 - \frac{l_3 b_3}{b_2 + b_4}\right)(r_{t+1}^L - r_t^L) - \left(l_5 - \frac{l_2 b_3}{b_2 + b_4}\right) r_t^L + l_6 \log Y_t. \qquad \text{(A6)}$$

We assume that

$$l_4 - \frac{l_3 b_3}{b_2 + b_4} > 0, \qquad l_5 = \frac{l_2 b_3}{b_2 + b_4} > 0. \qquad \text{(A7)}$$

These assumptions imply that, in the demand function for loans, the elasticity with respect to the loan rate is larger than that with respect to the bond rate. The converse holds for the demand function for bonds. Equation (A6) can be rewritten as

$$\log L_t^d = \alpha + a\left(r_{t+1}^L - r_t^L\right) - c r_t^L + \eta \log Y_t \qquad (\alpha, a, c, \eta > 0). \quad \text{(A8)}$$

The constant term α is an increasing function of the exogenous r^d and ρ^e.

Given the budget constraint for the non-financial private sector, i.e. $D^d + B^d = L^d + B^s$, (A2), (A3), and (A5) implicitly determine the demand for bank deposits D^d. In equilibrium, $B^s = B^d$ holds, and therefore the budget constraint also means that $D^d = L^d$. In this model, cash is assumed

[9] The 'one-period' return of long-term bonds is $r_t^B - (r_{t+1}^B - r_t^B)/r_t^B$. This can be linearly approximated by $r_t^B - (r_{t+1}^B - r_t^B)/r^*$ where r^* is constant.

away and 'money' M_t consists of bank deposits. Money is thus equal to bank loans in equilibrium.

The supply function of bank loans, on the other hand, is

$$\log L_t^s = \beta_t + b(r_t^L - r_t^c) \qquad (b > 0). \tag{A9}$$

It is an increasing function of the difference between the loan rate and the call rate. The constant term β_t is the BOJ's policy variable, which captures the extent of the *window guidance*.

Equilibrium in the loan market implies that

$$\log L_t^d = \log L_t^s = \log M_t. \tag{A10}$$

It is much disputed whether or not the loan market in Japan is in equilibrium (see Ueda 1985; Asako and Uchino 1987 for a survey). The evidence so far is mixed. On the one hand, some economists emphasize the fact that the interest rate on bank loans has been under regulation, and they argue that excess demand has persisted in the loan market. On the other hand, it is well known that the compulsory deposits relating to loans make the effective interest rate higher than the nominal loan rate. Even if movements in the nominal loan rate appear sluggish, the effective interest rate could, in fact, change with sufficient flexibility to keep the market in equilibrium. In what follows, it is assumed that the loan market is in equilibrium.

Finally, it is necessary to consider the market equilibrium of high-powered money. In this model demand for high-powered money is nothing but demand for reserves:

$$\log R_t^d = \log M_t + \log \gamma_t, \tag{A11}$$

where γ_t is the required reserve ratio. Equation (A11) implies that banks hold no excess reserves. Unlike in the United States, this is indeed the case in Japan. In the period September 1980–January 1988, for example, reserves totalled ¥2,658 billion, whereas excess reserves were only ¥2 billion.

Reserves are supplied by the BOJ:

$$\log R_t^s = \log \bar{R}_{t_t} + d(r_t^c - r_t^*) \qquad (d > 0). \tag{A12}$$

They are changed by independent actions of the BOJ (changes in log $\bar{R}_t$), but also, the BOJ seeks to stabilize the call rate r_t^c around its target r_t^*. The former corresponds to the dynamic operations, and the latter, the defensive operations in Roosa (1956). The stabilization of the call rate makes the supply of reserves endogenous. The parameter d indicates the extent of the stabilization. As shown in the main text, d is quite large in the seasonal cycle, and is often so in business cycle, as well. For simplicity, $r_t^* = 0$ is assumed in (A12).

The market equilibrium for reserves or high-powered money means that

$$\log R_t^d = \log R_t^s. \tag{A13}$$

Equations (A8)–(A13) determine r_t^c, r_t^L, R_t, and L_t $(=M_t)$. In what follows, M_t is used for L_t. From (A8), (A9), and (A10), we obtain

$$\log M_t = \frac{b\alpha_t + b\eta \log Y_t + [(a+c) - aL^{-1}]\,(\beta_t - br_t^c)}{(a+b+c)\left[1 - \left(\dfrac{a}{a+b+c}\right)L^{-1}\right]}, \tag{A14}$$

$$r_t^L = \frac{\alpha_t - \beta_t + br_t^c + \eta \log Y_t}{(a+b+c)\left[1 - \left(\dfrac{a}{a+b+c}\right)L^{-1}\right]}, \tag{A15}$$

where L^{-1} is the lead operator, defined as $L^{-i}x_t = x_{t+i}$ $(i = 1, 2, 3,\ldots)$.

Equations (A14) and (A15) are not yet final forms, however, since r^c is an endogenous variable. Final forms for M_t and r_t^c are obtained with (A11)–(A15) as follows:

$$\log M_t = \left\{ db\alpha_t + d(a+c)\left[1 - \left(\frac{a}{a+c}\right)L^{-1}\right]\beta_t + db\eta \log Y_t + b(a+c) \times \left[1 - \left(\frac{a}{a+c}\right)L^{-1}\right](\log \bar{R}_t - \log \gamma_t)\right\} \Big/ \{[(a+c)(b+d) + bd]\,(1 - AL^{-1})\}, \tag{A16}$$

$$r_t^c = \left\{ b\alpha_t + (a+c)\left[1 - \left(\frac{a}{a+c}\right)L^{-1}\right]\beta_t + b\eta \log Y_t + (a+b+c) \times \left[1 - \left(\frac{a}{a+b+c}\right)L^{-1}\right](\log \gamma_t - \log \bar{R}_t)\right\} \Big/ \{[(a+c)(b+d) + bd]\,(1 - AL^{-1})\}, \tag{A17}$$

where

$$A = \frac{a(b+d)}{(a+c)(b+d) + bd} \qquad (0 < A < 1). \tag{A18}$$

Equation (A16) shows that the money supply at time t is a function of real economic activity Y, the window guidance β, the interest rate on bank deposits α, the expected profit rate, also α, the BOJ lending $\bar{R}$, and the required reserve ratio γ. The equation is in stock terms, but clearly, a similar equation holds for rates of change. We discuss the implications of this equation in what follows.

Implications

1. *Causality test* Current money supply depends on expectations of future economic activities, Y. Therefore, as long as the information set for

predicting future Y contains variables other than past Y, money will Granger-cause Y. In this model, Y causes M in fact, but money can spuriously Granger-cause Y since demand for loans depends on expectations of future interest rates. The causality test does not make sense for this model.[10]

2. *Lead of money ahead of income* In the model, Y causes M but M leads ahead of Y.[11] The mean lead time of $\Delta \log M$ ahead of $\Delta \log Y$ is

$$\frac{A}{1-A} = \frac{a(b+d)}{c(b+d)+bd}. \tag{A19}$$

The mean lead time depends on various interest elasticities.

3. *Supply of high-powered money* High-powered money is assumed here to be supplied only through the BOJ lending. In reality, however, there are several ways in which the BOJ can supply high-powered money to the market. One example would be open-market operations. Are interest rates and the money supply affected differently by the way high-powered money is supplied, independently of its amount? Most economists such as Horiuchi (1980), who use a *static* general equilibrium model, say that the answer is no: only the amount of high-powered money matters, and how it is supplied is irrelevant. In a static model, this answer is inevitable.

In a dynamic model, however, current money supply and interest rates depend not only on current policy variables but also on expectations of future policy. Therefore, to the extent that the way in which high-powered money is currently supplied conveys some information about the future policy stance of the BOJ to the market, it does affect current money supply and interest rates, independently of the amount of high-powered money. For example, outright purchases of long-term bonds and purchases of bonds with the repurchase contract would affect the financial market differently, even if the amount of high-powered money supplied were the same. This is because they send different signals about the future supply of high-powered money.

Another good example concerns the adjustment of the *progress ratio of reserve deposits*. To make this mechanism understandable, a brief explana-

[10] The example given in the text is a bivariate case, but the basic point holds in a multivariate case containing M and Y.

[11] Tobin (1970) demonstrates the possibility that, even if money does not affect income, it systematically leads ahead of income. In his model, demand for money depends on income Y and wealth. As far as transaction demand is concerned, there is no lead-lag relation between Y and M. However, when Y increases, tax revenue also increases, and this reduces government deficits. As a result, the amount of outstanding government bonds starts to decline. Then, through the wealth effect, money demand starts declining as well. Since money demand depends on both Y and wealth, the rate of change in M leads ahead of Y even though Y is independent of M in his model. In my example, money leads income simply because demand for money (loans) depends on future interest rates as well as current interest rates.

tion of required reserves is necessary. Financial institutions subject to reserve requirements must place with the BOJ the legally required reserve deposits: cash-in-vault is not counted as reserve assets.[12] Required reserves are set equal to the product of the required reserve ratio and the *average* outstanding balance of deposits during one month, while a 'maintenance period' of reserve deposits begins on the sixteenth day of that month and ends on the fifteenth of the next month. The Japanese reserve requirement system is therefore a combination of a 'lagged reserve system' and a 'contemporaneous reserve system'.[13] Banks must make the required amount of deposits at the BOJ *in the cumulative sense* by the end of a 'maintenance period', given the average deposits in the previous month. Individual financial institutions may attempt to meet their requirements by using the call market. But transactions in the call market are mutually offsetting, and therefore in the market as a whole reserves must be ultimately supplied by the BOJ. The *reserve progress ratio* is the ratio of reserve deposits accumulated from the first day of a 'maintenance period' to total cumulative reserve deposits required for that period. The ratio would increase by 3.3% a day in a 'standard' path, along which required reserve deposits are equally maintained every day during a given 'maintenance period' (30 days).

Now the BOJ curbs the reserve progress ratio relative to the standard path by supplying less high-powered money (i.e. providing less BOJ lending) when it intends to follow a tight monetary policy stance; in contrast, it raises the reserve progress ratio when it follows an easy monetary policy stance. The amount of high-powered money (reserves) supplied by the last day of a 'maintenance period' is, however, in all ways equal to the amount required under a predetermined 'lagged reserve system'. Put another way, the reserve progress ratio of the last day of lodging is 100% in any event. Taking a month as a unit of time, therefore, one can observe the same amount of high-powered money supplied, and yet observe significantly different time paths of the reserve progress ratio within a month.

As noted above, a time path of the reserve progress ratio conveys a signal to the market of the BOJ's intended current and near-future policy stances. A manipulation of the reserve progress ratio is in fact taken as a very important tool of monetary policy. Suzuki *et al.* (1988), for example, regard

[12] In the USA, reserve assets include vault cash possessed by financial institutions as well as deposits with Federal Reserve banks. The German system has also included vault cash since March 1978, as long as the share of vault cash in the required reserve does not exceed 50% on a monthly basis.

[13] Under the US Reserve Requirements System in place since February 1984, reserve deposits related to the settlement of accounts have been lodged 'contemporaneously' (strictly speaking, with a two-day lag), while reserve deposits related to (i) time deposits possessed by non-individuals and (ii) the Euro-market debts have been lodged with lags. In the German minimum reserve requirements system (Mindestreservepolitik), reserve deposits are lodged both 'contemporaneously' and 'with lags', just as in the Japanese reserve requirements system. For more details on the Japanese reserve requirement system, see Suzuki (1987: 322).

this policy instrument as an important ingredient of the BOJ's skill in policy-making. This is an example of the case in which the way high-powered money is supplied does affect the market independently of the amount of money supplied. It does not make sense in static models, but can be easily understood in a dynamic model, for in such a model the money supply and interest rates depend not only on the current amount of high-powered money, but also on its future values: see (A16) and (A17).

4. *Window guidance* It has been a matter of dispute whether window guidance is effective in controlling the *total* amount of bank loans. Horiuchi (1977), for example, argues that window guidance to big commercial banks (*Toshiginko*) does not affect the total amount of loans made by financial institutions as a whole, but simply entails reallocation among different institutions. As Furukawa (1981) reports, the conclusion depends crucially on the interest elasticity of bank reserves. If bank reserves are interest-elastic, the BOJ's window guidance affects the amount of loans through a change in the call rate.

This problem has usually been analysed by two-financial-sector models, with big commercial banks, subject to strong window guidance, and the other financial institutions. The model in this appendix has only one financial sector, but the supply function of loans (equation (A9)) consists of two parts, one independent of and the other dependent on interest rates. Therefore one can interpret the first term of (A9) as representing the behaviour of big commercial banks subject to window guidance, and the second term as the behaviour of the other financial institutions. From there, one can analyse the effects of window guidance, β, on the amount of loans or the money supply.

One can easily see, then, that the effect of a change in β on money is nonzero only if $d > 0$ in (A12). Window guidance can affect the money supply only if the BOJ elastically supplies reserves so as to smooth the call rate. As pointed out, Japanese financial institutions hold little excess reserves, and demand for reserves is not so interest-elastic. However, to the extent that *supply* of reserves is interest-elastic, window guidance can affect the money supply. Other instruments of monetary policy, such as changes in the required reserve ratio or open-market operations, do of course affect the money supply, but they simultaneously affect the call rate. As far as the BOJ finds the smoothness of interest rate (the call rate, in particular) a worthwhile objective, window guidance has its own role.

Such is the effectiveness of window guidance as a means of affecting the total amount of loans or the money supply. Meanwhile, many economists, both Japanese and foreign, have criticized the fact that window guidance coupled with the BOJ lending is liable to entail uneven treatment of financial institutions by the BOJ. Big commercial banks accepted window guidance, but in exchange they enjoyed the BOJ lending which was *de facto* subsidy, since the discount rate was lower than the call rate. In any event, this compromise was reached not in the open market, but behind closed doors. Perhaps reacting to foreign pressure for more 'openness' and 'transparency' in the Japanese financial market, the Bank of Japan finally decided to abolish window guidance in the third quarter of 1991.

5. *Liberalization of the interest rate on deposits* In the model, the interest rate on deposits is assumed to be regulated and is taken as exogenous. The gradual liberalization of the Japanese financial market meant a *de facto* increase in the interest rate on deposits. One can analyse the effect of an increase in the interest rate on deposits (an increase in α) on the the money supply by looking at (A16).

An increase in the deposit rate brings about an increase in the the money supply only if (i) the banks' supply function of loans is interest-elastic ($b > 0$, in (A9)), *and* (ii) the supply of reserves by the BOJ is also elastic with respect to the call rate ($d > 0$ in (A12)). An increase in the interest rate on deposits causes shifts in both deposits and loan demand, but the extent to which new loans are made depends on the interest elasticity of the supply function. Also, if the BOJ does not mitigate an increase in the call rate, but instead sticks to a given amount of high-powered money ($d = 0$), then the effect of an increase in the interest rate on deposits is wholly absorbed by an increase in the call rate and no change in the the money supply is brought about. It is noted that exactly the same result is obtained in the case of an increase in stock prices (an increase in ρ^e).

The growth rate of (M2 + CD) in Japan was 8.4% in 1985, but it accelerated to 11.2% by 1988. It was a popular argument then that the sky-rocketing stock prices raised the demand for money while at the same time an increase in the interest rate on deposits made money a more attractive asset, and that these were the major factors accounting for a growth in the the money supply during the period (see e.g. BOJ 1988). It is worth pointing out, however, that these factors can cause an increase in the money supply only when the BOJ attempts to smooth the nominal interest rate ($d > 0$). If the BOJ desires, it can keep the the money supply from accelerating under the same circumstances by making $d = 0$, but, of course, in that case interest rates would have to rise.

6. *Endogenous money supply* When d is positive, the money supply reflects both changes in real economic activities, Y, and the BOJ's dynamic operations, $\log \bar{R}_t - \log \gamma_t$ (equation (A16)). As observed in the main text, the extent of interest-rate-smoothing, d, itself varies from time to time. Having noted this fact, we calculate the relative contribution of Y in accounting for changes in the money supply on the simplifying assumption that both $\Delta \log Y_t$ and $\Delta(\log \bar{R}_t - \log \gamma_t)$ follow identically and independently distributed processes.

Under this assumption, the relative contribution of $\Delta \log Y$ in accounting for the variance of $\Delta \log M_t$ (call it S_y) is

$$S_y = \frac{d^2\eta^2\sigma_y^2}{d^2\eta^2\sigma_y^2 + (a+c)^2\left[1 - 2A\,\dfrac{a}{a+c} + \left(\dfrac{a}{a+c}\right)^2\right]\sigma_R^2}, \qquad \text{(A20)}$$

where σ_y^2 and σ_R^2 are the variances of $\Delta\log Y$ and $\Delta(\log\bar{R}_t - \log\gamma_t)$, respectively. As expected, S_y is an increasing function of d and approaches one as $d \to \infty$. In a seasonal cycle, d is in fact quite large and S_y is close to one.

BOJ (1977), explicitly taking into account expectations of changes in interest rates in the money demand function of firms, provides estimates of the parameters in (A20): $a = 0.15$, $c = 0.10$, $\eta = 1.0$. Ueda (1985) also provides estimates of short-run and long-run elasticities: $c = 0.005$ and 0.25; $\eta = 0.25$ and 2.5; $b = 0.003$ and 0.008. On the assumptions of $a = 0.15$, $b = 0$, $c = 0.10$, and $\eta = 1.0$, (A20) becomes

$$s_y = \frac{d^2\sigma_y^2}{d^2\sigma_y^2 + (0.04)\sigma_R^2}. \qquad \text{(A21)}$$

The variances of IIP and high-powered money (monthly change relative to 12 months before for January 1968–December 1987) happen to be equal, i.e. 0.005. Substituting this value for σ_y^2 and σ_R^2 in (A21), we obtain

$$S_y \cong \frac{d^2}{d^2 + 0.04}. \qquad \text{(A22)}$$

Equation (A22) indicates that $S_y = 0.5$ when $d = 0.2$. In this chapter we observed that, even in business cycles, the BOJ very often smooths the interest rate. The above calculation is meant to be only illustrative, but it still demonstrates that observed changes in the money supply can reflect changes in real economic activities to a large extent when the BOJ smooths nominal interest rates such as the call rate.

10

Demand Constraint, Technical Progress, and Economic Growth: A Model of Demand-Led Growth

The foregoing chapters have attempted to establish, from various angles, that real demand constraint is an essential factor in the macroeconomy. This final chapter argues that real demand constraint is essential not only in the short run, but also for the long-run growth of the economy. I put forward a new demand-led growth model, and with it analyse the rapid growth and slowdown of the post-war Japanese economy.

In the 1950s and 1960s, following the pioneering works of Harrod (1939, 1948) and Domar (1947), growth theories flourished. By the 1970s, research interest among economists had shifted away from growth towards fluctuations, despite the paramount importance of the growth issues. Today, however, progress in the world economy has once again stimulated renewed work on growth. Continuing differential in growth rates between Japan and the United States, for example, may drastically change the world economic atlas in the next century: with growth rates for Japan and the United States of 4% and 2.5%, respectively, by the year 2010 the level of real per capita income in the United States will be two-thirds of that of Japan. The remarkable economic growth of East Asia, which the World Bank (1993) calls 'the East Asian miracle', is another example; it is estimated that by 2002 the GNP of the greater China, including Hong Kong and Taiwan, will exceed that of the United States.

It is clearly crucial to understand why an economy grows and why growth rates differ. In attempting to answer these questions, all the hitherto existing growth models, including recent 'endogenous' growth models, focus on the supply side, ignoring demand constraints. Real demand constraint, however, is the key to understanding the process of economic growth.

It is often held that demand constraints, if they *are* important, make an impact only in the short run. Economics, then, falls into two parts, which deal, respectively, with the short-run fluctuations and long-run growth. Real business cycle theory has attempted to achieve the sought-after integration of the short run and the long run by ignoring the problem of demand deficiency altogether. Unfortunately, in my judgement the outcome of that attempt is unrealistic (see Chapter 2). The problem of combining the long run and short run is still a challenge to macroeconomics. Solow, for example, in his Nobel lecture, argues as follows:

> Growth theory was invented to provide a systematic way to talk about and to compare equilibrium paths for the economy. In that task it succeeded reasonably well. In doing so, however, it failed to come to grasp adequately with an equally important and interesting problem: the right way to deal with deviations from equilibrium growth. One possible solution strikes me as wrongheaded: that is to deny the existence of an analytical problem by claiming that 'economic fluctuations' are not deviations from equilibrium growth at all. . . .
>
> It will not do simply to superimpose your favorite model of the business cycle on an equilibrium growth path. That might do for very small deviations, more in the nature of minor slightly autocorrelated 'errors.' But if one looks at substantial more-than-quarterly departures from equilibrium growth, as suggested for instance by the history of the large European economies since 1979, it is impossible to believe that the equilibrium growth path itself is unaffected by the short- to medium-run experience. In particular, the amount and direction of capital formation is bound to be affected by the business cycle, whether through gross investment in new equipment or through the accelerated scrapping of old equipment. . . . So a simultaneous analysis of trend and fluctuations really does involve an integration of long run and short run of equilibrium and disequilibrium. . . . As you would expect, an important role is played by the investment function. (Solow 1988: 311–12)

This chapter follows Solow's suggestion and sets out an alternative theory to explain economic growth. My theory emphasizes two important points that are largely ignored by existing growth models. First, there is the *real demand constraint* as an important factor determining the long-run performance of the economy. This constraint is, just like factor endowment, *exogenous* to the macroeconomy, in the sense that it is not necessarily an outcome of economic agents' optimization. Wars would be an obvious example; for the century-long development of the Japanese economy, the First World

War and the Korean War were the major positive demand shocks that immediately revived the fragile economy, and at the same time left a lasting impact. The neoclassical theory simply ignores this demand constraint. Keynes's theory, of course, emphasizes real demand constraints, but merely in the context of the short run, where capital stock is unchanged. This chapter maintains that the real demand condition facing the economy, on top of technological progress on supply side, is the key ingredient of any reasonable theory of economic growth and fluctuation. Young goes so far as to argue that

> It is dangerous to assign to any single factor the leading role in that continuing economic revolution which has taken the modern world so far away from the world of a few hundred years ago. But is there any other factor which has a better claim to that role than the persisting search for markets? No other hypothesis so well unites economic history and economic theory. (Young 1928: 536)

The search for markets has no place in standard neoclassical theory, but it is, in fact, vital for growth of the economy. This leads to the second point of my theory, namely the nature of technical progress.

Most economists agree that technical progress is a key factor in explaining economic growth. In the standard neoclassical model, on top of population growth, the Harrod-neutral or labour-augmenting technical progress is an ultimate determinant of the growth rate. In his famous article, Solow (1957) attributes about nine-tenths of an increase in the US per capita GNP during the 40-year period up to the mid-1950s to technical progress, and only one-tenth to an increase in the capital–labour ratio. More recently, Grossman and Helpman (1991) endogenize the growth rate by, essentially, postulating that spending more resources on R&D will bring about a *proportionate* increase[1] in technical progress factor A for the production function $AF(K, L)$; though their model is much more sophisticated. Technical progress is the all-time winner in growth theory.

Technical progress in the existing literature, however, concerns only the supply side; that is, it is customarily identified as something that augments the capacity of the firm on the supply side. We

[1] If spending more resources on R&D generates only an *absolute* increase in A instead of a *proportionate* increase, then growth is not sustained. Thus, as Solow (1994) points out, endogenous growth generated in this way rests crucially on the arbitrary assumption.

normally say that technical progress has occurred when we obtain more output than before for the same amount of inputs. This chapter maintains, however, that technical progress really has two aspects: one is the traditional concept on the supply side; the other, neglected, aspect is that technical progress also augments prospects for demand by way of introducing new products, quality changes, and/or reduction of prices. As we will see shortly, in the demand-constrained economy, this *demand-creating technical progress* is a crucial determinant of the growth rate.

Now technical progress, which augments capacity and at the same time raises growth of demand for the firm's products, is mostly embodied in investment. Thus, investment is the carrier of technical progress. But, as Chapter 7 explains, investment in turn is greatly affected by demand. It is therefore essential to analyse explicitly how investment is determined by the demand-constrained firm.[2] I will consider the firm's investment decisions by taking into account real demand constraint on the one hand, and technical progress on the other. To make clear the role of the investment function in growth theory incorporating demand constraint, Section 10.1 begins by commenting on the well-known Harrod–Domar model. It then presents a model in which the demand-constrained firm invests while recognizing that the investment it makes embodies the demand-creating technical progress. This model provides the basis for my growth theory.

Drawing on the results of Section 10.1, Section 10.2 discusses the growth of the macroeconomy: aggregation, the sources of growth of demand, and the high growth of the Japanese economy during the period 1955–70. The steady-state growth rate in my model is the growth rate of exogenous demand divided by one minus what I call the demand-creating power of investment. Given this steady-state growth rate, the growth of demand for labour is not necessarily equal

[2] Criticizing the standard growth accounting, Grossman and Helpman (1994) correctly point out the endogeneity of investment. Asking themselves whether the Solow residual in standard growth accounting really measures the full contribution of technological change to the expansion in output, they argue as follows: 'Evidently not. After all, technological improvements typically raise the productivity of capital and thereby induce additional investments. In such cases, the resulting capital formation ought not to be considered as an independent spur to output, but rather as a facilitator of the growth that is due ultimately to the innovation.' They naturally focus on the effects of technological change on the supply side in the neoclassical framework. In this chapter, I emphasize the effects of demand-creating technological change on investment in the demand-constrained economy.

to the growth of labour supply or the natural rate of growth. This outcome would be readily taken by many theorists as a serious shortcoming of the model, for it allegedly implies ever-increasing or falling unemployment rates. Section 10.3 shows, however, that the Lewisian endogenous mobilization of the disguised unemployed in stagnant sectors of the economy equates growth rates of labour supply and demand in growing sectors. It demonstrates that this mechanism worked for the Japanese economy during the period 1950–85. Contrary to common belief, the Lewisian mechanism applies not only to developing economies but also to well developed economies. Section 10.3 also discusses productivity and the role of increasing returns in demand-led growth.

A comment before we proceed. In what follows, I will not make use of the currently fashionable intertemporally optimizing representative household,[3] because I believe that firms, by way of investment, play a much more active and dominant role than households in the process of economic growth. In contrast, in neoclassical theory firms are nothing but veils, in that, given an exogenous technological possibility set, households' preferences ultimately determine the outcomes of the economy. As reviewed in Chapter 1, in recent years more and more emphasis has been put on households' utility maximization. The optimum growth model, once understood as a normative model, is now taken as a descriptive model of the economy. As a consequence, the saving rate or the time preference of the representative consumer is supposed to play the dominant role in the process of economic growth. And yet, as Chapter 6 explained, personal saving is, if anything, determined by, rather than determining, the growth rate. Growth itself is generated by investment.

Chapter 2 demonstrates that post-war business cycles in Japan are also caused by fluctuations in investment. Since investment is much more volatile in Japan than in the United States, so is output. Referring to neoclassical theory, one would have to argue that the Japanese have a higher elasticity of substitution over time than the Americans. Similarly, observing that the Japanese economy became

[3] Solow is one of a few economists who do not subscribe to the representative agent model: 'I cannot say the same [nice things] about the use made of the intertemporally-optimizing representative agent. Maybe I reveal myself merely as old-fashioned, but I see no redeeming social value in using this construction, which Ramsey intended as a representation of the decision-making of an idealized policy-maker, as if it were a descriptive model of an industrial capitalist economy. It adds little or nothing to the story anyway, while encumbering it with unnecessary implausibilities and complexities.' (Solow 1994: 49)

more stable beginning in the 1970s, one would have to conjecture that the elasticity of intertemporal substitution somehow declined substantially during this period. Yet such an attempt to explain the nature and causes of business cycles in terms of consumers' preferences seems far-fetched. I maintain that the consumers' elasticity of intertemporal substitution actually has little impact. In the process of growth and fluctuation, firms play a much more dominant role than households. In this respect, I follow Schumpeter:

> To be sure, we must always start from the satisfaction of wants, since they are the end of all production, and the given economic situation at any time must be understood from this aspect. Yet innovations in the economic system do not as a rule take place in such a way that first new wants arise spontaneously in consumers and then the productive apparatus swings round through their pressure. We do not deny the presence of this nexus. It is, however, the producer who as a rule initiates economic change, and consumers are educated by him if necessary; they are, as it were, taught to want new things, or things which differ in some respect or other from those which they have been in the habit of using. (Schumpeter 1934: 65)

10.1 THE ROLE OF DEMAND CONSTRAINT AND TECHNICAL PROGRESS IN ECONOMIC GROWTH

In a standard neoclassical model of economic growth (Solow 1956, 1957), supply factors such as population growth and the rate of technological progress ultimately determine the growth rate of the economy. Out of the steady state, an increase in the saving rate also accelerates the growth rate. Growth in population or in the labour force, however, is not actually quite so fundamental in explaining economic growth. By itself, population increase will not suffice to fuel growth, as is amply illustrated both in history and in the world today. The same applies to the saving rate. If there is a positive correlation between the growth rate and the saving rate, there are many works, such as Blomström *et al.* (1993), which provide more evidence that increases in growth precede rises in the *ex post* saving/investment rate than that increases in the saving rate precede increases in growth. What neoclassical theory lacks is, as is often pointed out, an independent investment function (Sen 1965) and the feedback of changes in demand to investment. These factors are indispensable ingredients for a theory to explain economic growth when examined at least over a decade or two, if not over a century.

In passing, it is often useful to make explicit the time span a particular growth theory purports to explain. In my view, it is plainly too much for any mathematical model usefully to explain a century-long growth experience without resorting to *exogenous* shocks such as wars. In what follows, I take a decade or two as a relevant time span for my growth theory. Since a century is nothing but a succession of decades, the model would have something to say for growth over a century. In any case, no economy has achieved average growth of 10% for more than two decades, but quite a few, including Japan and Asian NIEs, have achieved it for a decade or longer. And such decades of high economic growth are crucial for the development of those countries. It is therefore very important to understand why such economies grow so fast over 10–20 years. Clearly, a decade is an important time span for growth theory.

Naturally, investment is the key variable for such a growth theory. It was almost half a century ago when Domar (1946) argued that the relationship between investment and output is two-sided: investment augments production capacity on the supply side, but at the same time it must be accompanied by a level of demand sufficient to require the resulting increase in capacity. Studies on growth since then, however, have focused largely on the supply side—that is, the production function. As far as future demand to meet augmented capacity is concerned, it is normally taken for granted that supply creates its own demand. Unlike the neoclassical model, the Harrod–Domar model explicitly contains investment, and also takes into account the demand constraint of the economy. It is therefore appropriate to begin by commenting on this well-known model.

The Harrod–Domar Model

The mechanics of the model run something like this. Current investment I augments capacity by I/v, given a capital coefficient v. In order for demand and supply to be equal, demand must increase by I/v. Given the saving rate s, aggregate demand would increase by $\mathrm{d}I/s$ when investment increased by $\mathrm{d}I$; through the multiplier, an increase in investment by $\mathrm{d}I$ generates sufficient income to create $\mathrm{d}I/s$ of aggregate demand. Along the equilibrium path, therefore, investment and GNP both grow at the rate s/v.

A crucial assumption of the model is that the whole of demand, other than investment itself, depends on income and is generated by investment through the multiplier process. In this model, it is as if firms make investment decisions today by anticipating that enough demand will be created if they invest enough tomorrow. It makes more sense to introduce some exogenous demand into the model. Suppose, then, that there is some exogenous demand X which is independent of income Y, and is thus independent of I. On the supply side, as in the standard model, current investment I augments capacity by

$$\mathrm{d}Y = I/v \tag{1}$$

Demand, on the other hand, increases by

$$\mathrm{d}Y = \frac{\mathrm{d}I + \mathrm{d}X}{s} \tag{2}$$

rather than $\mathrm{d}I/s$.

Using the notations

$$\sigma_I = \frac{I}{I + X},$$

$$\sigma_X = \frac{X}{I + X},$$

we obtain

$$\frac{\mathrm{d}I}{I} + \frac{\sigma_X}{\sigma_I}\frac{\mathrm{d}X}{X} = \frac{s}{v}. \tag{3}$$

From $sY = I + X$, we also have

$$\frac{\mathrm{d}Y}{Y} = \sigma_I \frac{\mathrm{d}I}{I} + \sigma_X \frac{\mathrm{d}X}{X}. \tag{4}$$

Equations (3) and (4) lead to

$$\frac{\mathrm{d}Y}{Y} = \sigma_I \frac{s}{v}. \tag{5}$$

This is the warranted growth rate for output. If there is no exogenous demand other than investment ($\sigma_I = 1$), it becomes s/v.

When X grows at $g_X(= \mathrm{d}X/X)$, investment grows as follows:

$$\frac{\mathrm{d}I}{I} = \frac{s}{v} - \frac{\sigma_X}{\sigma_I} g_X. \tag{6}$$

If this $\mathrm{d}I/I$ happens to be equal to g_X, then Y also grows at g_X. The warranted growth rate in this case is g_X. In general, however, the growth rate of investment (6) may not be equal to g_X. If growth rates of I and X differ, σ_I changes over time and so does the warranted growth rate of output $\sigma_I(s/v)$. It is easy to show that, when the initial growth rate of output $\sigma_I(s/v)$ is lower than g_X, the warranted growth rate $\sigma_I(s/v)$ asymptotically approaches 0, whereas when the initial $\sigma_I(s/v)$ is higher than g_X, it converges to s/v. Thus, the warranted growth rate itself changes over time, even though v and s are constant, and it converges to either 0 or s/v. The constant warranted growth rate of output is independent of s and v, and equal to the growth rate of the exogenous component of demand g_X, though this is possible only when the initial level of investment is appropriately set.

Introduction of exogenous demand entails a significant modification of the conclusion. The model actually produces a rather strange outcome for the warranted growth rate. Part of the reason for this lies in an awkward feature of the implicit investment function in the Harrod–Domar analysis, equation (6): the *higher* the growth of exogenous demand, the *lower* the growth of investment. The reason is that, since there is no explicit investment function, the greater is exogenous demand, the less investment is necessary to generate a given income through the multiplier. In fact, even the Harrod–Domar model, let alone neoclassical models, considers the growth path on which the shadow price of the demand constraint for investment is zero, despite the fact that the multiplier theory on which it relies presumes the contrary for production. An explicit analysis of the investment decisions of firms under a demand constraint is necessary. Indeed, Chapter 7 demonstrates that the demand constraint is important for investment that is, in fact, the engine for economic growth.

The Demand Creating Technical Progress and Investment

To introduce investment into the theory of growth, I consider the investment decisions of a firm. The model is actually very similar to the one put forward in Chapter 7, except for one thing: the firm is demand-constrained, but to some extent the growth of demand depends on technical progress embodied in current investment.

Investment is customarily identified as something that augments the production capacity of the firm on the supply side. I argue, however, that investment embodies *the demand-creating technical progress*, and thus raises the growth of demand for the firm's product to some extent. Specifically, investment would expand future demand for the firm's product, perhaps through the introduction of new products (*product innovations*), an improvement in the quality of existing products, or a reduction of their prices (*process innovations*).

This demand-creating aspect of investment is not confined to R&D investment. When blueprints of innovations are ready, to the extent that the demand-creating technical progress is embodied in new investment, such investment creates future demand while it augments present capacity.

Table 10.1 shows the importance of the introduction of new products for economic growth. In the decade beginning 1960, for example, the average growth rate of production of pre-1950 products was only 18.9%, while products invented in the 1960–4 period saw an almost 700% annual growth rate! The proportion of new products is naturally small, and not all new products would enjoy such high growth. However, Table 10.1 still demonstrates that the introduction of new products can be an important source of economic growth; without new products, the growth rate of the economy is bound to decelerate. And the introduction of such new products is made possible not only by R&D investment, but also by ordinary investment which embodies innovations. The same argument holds for process innovations.

It must be clear that this demand-creating aspect of investment does not refer to the fact that investment raises *current* effective demand. It is also conceptually wholly different from the capacity-augmenting aspect of investment, since the former concerns the market for the product and the latter, the technology or production

Table 10.1. Growth through the introduction of new products, 1950–1969

	Contribution to production by				
	Pre-1950 products	Products invented in 1951–4	Products invented in 1955–9	Products invented in 1960–4	Total
1950[a]	1.00				1.00
1955	2.05	0.15	0.01		2.21
1960	4.14	0.65	0.28	0.03	5.10
1965	6.65	1.19	0.93	0.38	9.15
1969	11.19	2.43	2.56	1.90	18.28
Avg. annual growth rate, 1960–9 (%)	18.9	30.4	90.5	692.6	28.7

[a] Total production in 1950 is normalized to be 1.0.

Source: *The 1970 White Paper of the Japanese Government*, p. 211; original data are from MITI, *Statistics of Industrial Production*.

function. In reality, of course, the two can be related. The introduction of new products, for example, often necessitates the adoption of new machines and/or the construction of new factories which augment production capacity. Investment, therefore, can augment future demand, and at the same time enlarge present production capacity. Most likely investment embodies capacity-augmenting technical progress as well as demand-creating technical progress. Embodied technical progress on the supply side, however, has been extensively studied in the literature.[4] In what follows, therefore, the model abstracts from embodied technical progress on the supply side, and assumes disembodied technical progress in this respect (equation (12) below). On the other hand, it presumes that the demand-creating technical progress is actually embodied in investment.

The firm maximizes the following discounted sum of net cash flow:

$$\int_0^{\infty}(D_t - w_tL_t - \phi(\alpha_t)K_t)e^{-\rho t}dt, \tag{7}$$

where D_t, w_t, L_t, K_t, and ρ are, respectively, demand for the firm's product, real wages, labour, capital stock, and the discount rate, α_t is the growth rate of capital stock:

$$\alpha_t = \dot{K}_t/K_t. \tag{8}$$

I ignore depreciation for simplicity.

As in Chapter 7, the adjustment cost is assumed to be convex:

$$\begin{aligned} \phi'(\alpha) > 0, \qquad & \phi''(\alpha) > 0, \\ \phi(0) = 0, \qquad & \phi(0) = 1. \end{aligned} \tag{9}$$

At each moment in time, demand D_t is given. Demand grows exogenously at the rate of θ, but its growth also depends on current investment:

$$\dot{D}_t = (\theta + \gamma\alpha_t)D_t \qquad (0 < \gamma < 1). \tag{10}$$

Equation (10) captures the demand-creating technical progress embodied in investment, its degree measured by parameter γ. The strength of this demand-creating technical progress depends on many

[4] Solow (1962) shows that the stock of surviving capital goods of different vintage and productivity can be summarized for production-function purposes in an 'equivalent stock of capital'. This equivalent stock of capital can be constructed by adding up the survivors of each vintage after weighting them by the appropriate productivity improvement factor.

factors—the vigour of the creation of new products, the extent of cost reductions and quality improvements of existing products, and their income and price elasticities in both domestic and world markets. For the economy as a whole, even the structural adjustment among industries is a factor that determines γ. These factors are so complex that they cannot easily be taken into a formal model. There are in fact many models that explicitly introduce the representative consumer's utility maximization under the assumption of many commodities with quality changes (e.g. Grossman and Helpman 1991). Unfortunately, to make the analysis tractable, the Cobb–Douglas utility function is assumed in most cases. This implies, among other things, that the income and price elasticities of all the products are the same: namely, one. It therefore completely misses the essential point: that each product or industry has a different growth prospectus (θ and γ). Rather than pursuing a superficial formality, I represent them by a single strategic parameter, γ. The larger γ is, the stronger are the firm's product and process innovations and/or the responsiveness of market. For simplicity, I assume that γ is independent of θ. However, the product life-cycle approach to international trade actually emphasizes that innovation of new products and processes is more likely to occur near a market where there is a strong demand for them than in a country with little demand. In the present model, γ is likely to be an increasing function of θ (see Linder 1961 and Wells 1972). In any case, as will be seen shortly, γ is a fundamental determinant of the growth rate in the present model.

Normalizing the units in such a way that $D_0 = K_0^\gamma$, we obtain

$$D_t = e^{\theta t} K_t^\gamma. \tag{11}$$

Employment and Investment Decisions

On the supply side, output Y_t (equal to D_t) is assumed to be produced according to the Cobb–Douglas production function,

$$Y_t = D_t = \Lambda_t L_t^a K_t^b, \tag{12}$$

where Λ_t is the *capacity-augmenting* technical progress factor. It is simply the technical progress factor in the usual terminology, but I refer to Λ_t as the capacity-augmenting technical progress to distinguish it from the demand-creating technical progress measured by γ.

This production function does not have to exhibit constant returns to scale ($a + b = 1$); in fact, later I will underline the importance of increasing returns ($a + b > 1$). I do assume, however, that b is larger than γ, i.e. the capital elasticity is greater on the supply side than on the demand side. As γ approaches b from below, the demand constraint becomes virtually non-existent.

Since D_t and K_t are both given at time t, employment of labour is determined as follows:

$$L_t = \Lambda_t^{-1/a} D_t^{1/a} K_t^{-b/a}. \tag{13}$$

The marginal product of labour at this level of employment is given by

$$\frac{\partial D}{\partial L} = a\Lambda_t L_t^{a-1} K_t^b. \tag{14}$$

$$= a\Lambda_t^{1/a} K_t^{[b+(a-1)\gamma]/a} \exp\left[\frac{(a-1)\theta t}{a}\right].$$

This is assumed to exceed the real wage, since labour employment is constrained by the demand for products. The neoclassical theory, in contrast, having no such demand constraint, equates real wages w_t to this marginal product of labour. If they are equal, $w_t L_t$ becomes aD_t and the labour's share is a. Therefore the factor share becomes independent of the technical progress Λ. This is the well-known result obtained under the assumption of Hicks-neutral technical progress. I, however, assume that real wages grow in parallel with the marginal product of labour as capital accumulates, but that their *levels* are below the marginal product. In this case, the factor share depends on the technological progress Λ even though Λ is Hicks-neutral.

Specifically, I assume that

$$w_t = \hat{w}_t K_t^{[b+(a-1)\gamma]/a} \exp\left[\frac{(a-1)\theta t}{a}\right], \tag{15}$$

where $\hat{w}_t$ is taken as exogenous and is assumed to satisfy

$$\hat{w}_t < a\Lambda_t^{-1/a}. \tag{16}$$

Given w_t, we obtain

$$w_t L_t = \hat{w}_t \Lambda_t^{-1/a} e^{\theta t} K_t^{\gamma}. \tag{17}$$

$$= \hat{w}_t \Lambda_t^{-1/a} D_t$$

The capital share $R = 1 - \hat{w}_t \Lambda_t^{-1/a}$ is defined as a ratio of profits to sales. This capital share depends on $\hat{w}_t$ and Λ_t. An increase in real wages with an unchanged Λ, of course, lowers the capital share. On the other hand, capacity-augmenting technical progress (an increase in Λ) raises the capital share *only to the extent that it is not fully reflected in an increase in real wages*. As noted above, with technical progress, the marginal product of labour increases by $\Lambda^{1/a}$, and therefore, if real wages increase proportionally, the capital share R is left unchanged. Since sales D_t are demand-constrained (equation (11)) rather than supply-side-determined (equation (12)), in such a case profits RD_t are not affected by technical progress, either.

In Chapter 5, we found that in Japan real wages tend to be determined so as to stabilize the factor share, although not always; the major exception is the early 1970s. Chapter 5 also provides some theoretical justification for stable factor share in the modified efficiency wage model; if labour productivity depends on a kind of factor share, the efficiency wage becomes flexible enough to entail the stable factor share. In any case, it is important to note that there is no necessity that the factor share is related to a parameter of production function in the demand-constrained economy.

Using (7), (11), and (17), we obtain

$$\int_0^\infty (Re^{\theta t}K_t^\gamma - \phi(\alpha_t)K_t)e^{-\rho t}dt \tag{18}$$

as the objective function which the firm maximizes under constraint (8) and the initial stock of capital. Assuming the existence of the solution, we know that it is unique, and we can characterize it as follows.

The optimum level of investment $\alpha_t K_t$ satisfies

$$\phi'(\alpha_t) = q_t, \tag{19}$$

where the marginal q_t is defined as

$$q_t = \int_t^\infty (R\gamma K_\tau^{\gamma-1} - \phi(\alpha_\tau))\exp\left[-\int_t^\tau (\rho - \alpha_v)dv\right]d\tau. \tag{20}$$

q_t itself depends on the time path of α, or investment. On the assumption of the existence of an optimum path, the simultaneous determination of q and investment can be analysed in the following way. We first define k_t by

$$k_t = K_t^{1-\gamma}e^{-\theta t}, \tag{21}$$

which is nothing but the capital–output ratio or the capital coefficient K_t/D_t. Then the necessary conditions for optimality consist of

$$\dot{k}_t = [(1-\gamma)\alpha(q_t) - \theta]k_t. \tag{22}$$

and

$$\dot{q}_t = (\rho - \alpha(q_t))q_t - \frac{R\gamma}{k_t} + \phi(\alpha(q_t)). \tag{23}$$

The optimum path that satisfies the transversality condition is unique and is drawn by a bold line in the phase diagram (Fig. 10.1). *In the long-run stationary state, the growth rates of capital and output both converge to* $\theta/(1-\gamma)$. The long-run q is equal to

$$q^* = \phi'\left(\frac{\theta}{1-\gamma}\right) > 1. \tag{24}$$

The long-run capital–output ratio k^* satisfies

$$\frac{R\gamma}{k^*} = \left(\rho - \frac{\theta}{1-\gamma}\right)\phi'\left(\frac{\theta}{1-\gamma}\right) + \phi\left(\frac{\theta}{1-\gamma}\right). \tag{25}$$

This relation is shown with respect to the adjustment cost function in Fig. 10.2. Since $R\gamma/k^*$ is the profit rate on investment $R\Delta y/\Delta K$, then, *the higher is the long-run growth rate* $\theta/(1-\gamma)$, *the higher is the profit rate.* Accordingly, given the capital share, R, and the demand-creating power of investment, γ, *the higher the long-run growth rate* $\theta/(1-\gamma)$ *is, the lower is the long-run capital–output ratio.*

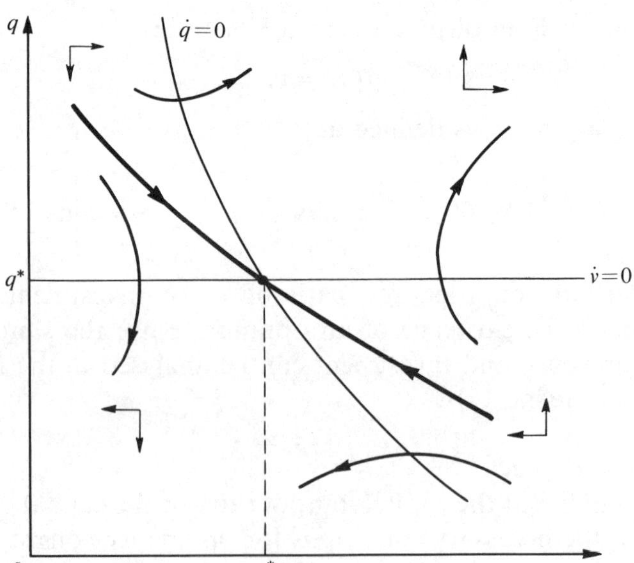

Fig. 10.1. Determination of the optimal path

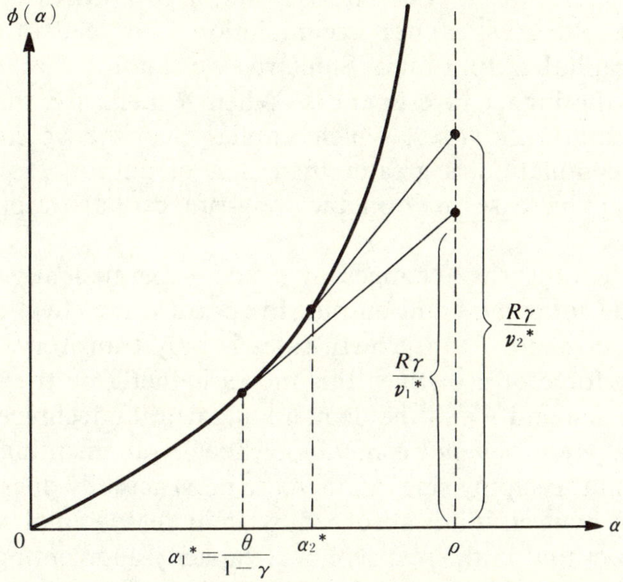

Fig. 10.2. The growth rate, profit rate, and capital coefficient

These results are qualitatively similar to those obtained in the standard neoclassical growth model, but the mechanism is very different. In the standard neoclassical model, the growth rate is ultimately equal to the growth rate of the population. When population growth accelerates, the economy is endowed with more labour; thus, real wages decline while profit rates rise, and labour is substituted for capital. Given the production function, a lower capital–labour ratio means a lower capital–output ratio. The basic mechanism is substitution between capital and labour when the growth rate rises as a result of population growth. In the present model, on the other hand, the substitution between capital and labour has little impact. Specifically, (22) and (23), which determine the dynamics of the capital–output ratio k, do not involve the production function. Since increasing returns ($a + b > 1$) are allowed in production function (12), there is no one-to-one correspondence between the capital–output ratio and the capital–labour ratio in the steady state.

The time paths of capital accumulation and output growth depend on γ, and R. Using the phase diagram, we can establish the following results. When θ increases, for example, the $\dot{k} = 0$ schedule shifts up while the $\dot{q} = 0$ schedule remains unchanged. As a result, given the current capital stock, investment rises. But in this process, the growth of output outpaces capital accumulation and leads to a lower long-run capital–output ratio. Similarly, we can find that, the higher γ or R is, the higher investment is. When R increases, the long-run capital–output ratio rises, which implies that the acceleration of capital accumulation is greater than that of output. However, the effect of an increase in γ on the long-run capital–output ratio is ambiguous.

Finally, I note that changes in θ and γ permanently affect the growth rates of capital and output. In contrast, the effect of changes in the factor share R on growth rates is only transitory. The main generating force of growth in this model is therefore the exogenous growth of demand θ and the demand-augmenting technical progress γ. In fact, *given demand conditions*, capacity-augmenting technical progress on the supply side (an increase in Λ) actually does not affect investment by itself if it is absorbed by an increase in real wages. One might expect that in the real economy capacity-augmenting technical progress would raise investment. This intuitively appealing result is obtained either if technical progress not only augments efficiency on the supply side but also augments the growth rate of demand, or if it raises the capital share. The kind of new technology which brings about the introduction of new products or improvement on the quality of existing products would certainly meet the first requirement.

10.2 GROWTH OF THE MACROECONOMY

The preceding analysis of firm behaviour can naturally be carried forward to a theory of growth of the macroeconomy. Above all, it leads us to focus on investment as the key variable. It also suggests that the most important ultimate factors in explaining economic growth are the growth of exogenous demand θ, and the demand-augmenting technical progress which is embodied in investment γ. The long-run growth rate of the economy is $\theta/(1 - \gamma)$.

Aggregation

On the micro level of an individual firm, the demand-augmenting effect of investment γ rests largely on the firm's own innovations such as the introduction of new products. On the macroeconomic level, investment by any firm also generates income through the multiplier, which augments the exogenous growth of demand for products of all firms, perhaps mostly firms other than the one that did the investing.[5] I can illustrate aggregation in the case of the steady state, where all the firms share the same values of θ and γ.

For firm $i (i = 1, \ldots, n)$, output Y_i is constrained by $e^{\theta t} K_i^{\gamma}$:

$$Y_i = e^{\theta t} K_i^{\gamma}, \tag{26}$$

where K_i is the stock of capital of firm i.

The demand share of each firm σ_i is

$$\sigma_i = \frac{Y_i}{Y} = \frac{K_i^{\gamma}}{\sum_i K_i^{\gamma}} \tag{27}$$

Total output $Y = \Sigma_i Y_i$ must be equal to total demand. For the sake of illustration, I assume the simple multiplier for aggregate demand as in the Harrod–Domar model. Therefore we have

$$Y = (I + X)/s, \tag{28}$$

where s is the *marginal* propensity to save. I and X are, respectively, total investment, and other expenditure which is independent of income Y.

In the steady state,

$$I = \sum_i \alpha_i K_i = \sum_i \left(\frac{\theta}{1-\gamma}\right) K_i \cdot \tag{29}$$

For X, we assume that

$$X = c e^{\theta t} \left(\sum_i K_i\right)^{\gamma}, \tag{30}$$

where c is the scale factor, defined later.

I next assume that each firm is small enough that it does not take into account the effects on aggregate variables of its own investment. For example, when a firm makes investment decisions, it does not anticipate an increase in demand for its own product due to a rise in income that would be generated by its own investment. On this assumption, in the steady state we have

$$\frac{I + X}{s} = \frac{\left[K_0\left(\frac{\theta}{1-\gamma}\right) + c K_0^{\gamma}\right] \exp\left[\left(\frac{\theta}{1-\gamma}\right) t\right]}{s}, \tag{31}$$

[5] These aggregate demand spillovers are, in fact, emphasized by Murphy, *et al.* (1989) in relation to the 'big push' by government for industrialization.

where the initial values of K_i is K_0/n, and

$$\sigma_i = \frac{K_i^{\gamma}}{n\left(\dfrac{K_0}{n}\right)^{\gamma} \exp\left[\left(\dfrac{\theta\gamma}{1-\gamma}\right)t\right]} . \tag{32}$$

Therefore, when the scale factor c in (30) is appropriately set to be equal to

$$c = sn^{1-\gamma} - \left(\frac{\theta}{1-\gamma}\right)K_0^{1-\gamma}, \tag{33}$$

demand for products, and accordingly output of firm i, Y_i, becomes

$$Y_i = \sigma_i Y = \frac{\sigma_i(I + X)}{s} = e^{\theta t}K_i^{\gamma}, \tag{34}$$

as is assumed in the model. However, since the firm's objective function (18) is not homogeneous of degree one with respect to K, we do not obtain the above steady state for arbitrary K_0. From equations (28), (29), (30), and (33), K_0 must be equal to $k^{*[1/(1-\gamma)]}n$.

Although the *marginal* saving rate s is exogenous, the *average* saving rate $\hat{s}$ is endogenous.[6] It is equal to I/Y, and therefore equals $[\theta/(1-\gamma)]k^*$. Since k^* is a decreasing function of the growth rate $\theta/(1-\gamma)$, *it is ambiguous whether the average saving/investment rate is increasing in the growth rate or not.* The less convex is the adjustment function of investment ϕ, the more likely is the average investment/saving rate an increasing function of the growth rate. It is important to note that in this model the causality runs from the growth rate to the average saving/investment rate. Growth rate in turn is determined by two ultimate factors, θ and γ: see Chapter 6 for the relation between growth and savings.

We have seen above that under certain conditions aggregation is possible for the steady state, so that the foregoing analysis of the firm can be translated into a theory of steady-state growth of the

[6] The exogenous *marginal* saving rate s cannot be arbitrary, however. Since c must be positive, s must be greater than $[\theta/(1-\gamma)]k^*$. For example, if the capital–output ratio is 2, and the growth rate is 0.04, the marginal saving rate must be greater than 0.08 in steady state. Within the limit of this inequality, the *marginal* saving rate does not affect the steady-state capital–output ratio k^*. k^* is uniquely determined by the growth rate of the economy, given the adjustment cost function ϕ and the capital share R (see (25)). In the standard neoclassical growth model (Solow 1956), the exogenous *average* saving rate positively affects the steady-state capital–output ratio k^*. There, the saving rate affects the steady-state factor intensity, and substitution between capital and labour changes the capital–output ratio. In the present model, the exogenous marginal saving rate is not linked directly to investment. Substitution between capital and labour has nothing to do with the choice of capital–output ratio. As is explained in the text, the average saving rate is endogenous.

macroeconomy. In this economy, aggregate demand depends on total investment and the other demand component X, which is independent of income. Growth of X in turn depends partly on investment; but at the same time, X grows exogenously at the rate of θ. This is the case for each firm as well, but in addition a firm's growth also depends on current investment. Firms realizing this demand-creating technical progress embodied in their own investment, in addition to demand constraints, make their investment decisions. It is shown that in the steady state the firm's optimal rate of capital accumulation is $\theta/(1-\gamma)$. Therefore the steady-state growth rates of capital and output also become $\theta/(1-\gamma)$ in the economy as a whole.

This analysis sheds some light on an alleged puzzle of the production function estimate of elasticity of output with respect to capital. In the neoclassical approach, under the assumption of perfect competition, this elasticity would be equal to the capital's share and therefore would be around 0.3. In time-series regressions, however, one often obtains a much higher value for this elasticity. P. Romer (1987), for example, using low-frequency data (decade data from the 1890s to 1970s) for the United States, obtains 1.0, and then, on the basis of this estimate, goes on to argue that the positive externality associated with capital accumulation generates endogenous growth. For Japan, even with annual data, one obtains a high value for this elasticity. Shinohara and Asakawa (1974) estimate the elasticity for 21 manufacturing industries over 1960–71; for the Japanese manufacturing industry as a whole, their estimate is 1.06.

The estimate of 1.0 for the 'capital elasticity' is certainly a puzzle from the viewpoint of the neoclassical production function approach. In the present analysis, however, factor share has little to do with a technological parameter characterizing the production function. Moreover, demand-constrained output Y grows as

$$\frac{\dot{Y}}{Y} = \theta + \gamma\left(\frac{\dot{K}}{K}\right).$$

With the growth rate of exogenous demand θ as a fundamental shock, *optimally chosen* $\dot{K}/K$ is approximately equal to $\theta/(1-\gamma)$. And therefore the regression coefficient of $\dot{Y}/Y$ on $\dot{K}/K$, $\mathrm{Cov}(\dot{Y}/Y, \dot{K}/K)/\mathrm{Var}(\dot{K}/K)$, becomes 1. Table 10.2, taken from Shinohara and Asakawa (1974), shows the growth of output, capital, and labour by industry; we are bound to obtain 1 for the capital elasticity. The point is that in the present model, (i) output is determined by demand, and (ii) both output and investment respond

Table 10.2. Growth by industry, 1960–1971 (%)[a]

	Output	Capital[b]	Labour[b]
Flour milling	11.3	12.0	1.4
Edible oils	9.1	12.7	2.2
Cotton spinning	7.6	7.6	− 1.0
Synthetic fibres	15.2	12.6	0.0
Paper/pulp	9.0	9.4	− 0.9
Synthetic chemistry	14.2	14.5	− 1.3
Pharmaceuticals	17.9	15.8	5.5
Glass	14.9	13.2	3.0
Cement	8.8	10.7	− 0.9
Oil refining	9.5	14.0	1.1
Blast furnace	12.7	15.2	2.0
Regular steel	10.6	17.0	2.6
Special steel	10.8	12.9	1.0
Nonferrous metals	7.6	11.9	− 5.6
Electric cables	11.0	14.3	1.5
Machine tools	9.2	12.3	1.8
Ball and roller bearings	14.8	15.4	0.7
Motor cars	22.8	24.3	10.0
Heavy electrics	15.3	11.8	4.5
Consumer electrics	22.0	17.2	5.0
Optical machinery	23.3	21.1	7.1
Total	14.1	14.2	2.2

[a] Figures are average annual growth rates.

[b] Capital and labour are adjusted for capacity utilization and working hours.

Source: Shinohara and Asakawa (1974).

to the same exogenous shock θ. In fact, an attempt to estimate the contribution of exogenously determined capital accumulation to output growth does not make much sense in the present analysis, because investment is endogenously determined by the growth of demand. In passing, as already noted, the capital elasticity of output as a technological parameter has no bearing on the factor share in this model.

The Sources of Growth of Demand

The engine of economic growth in this economy is investment determined by demand-constrained firms. The ultimate determinants, then, are θ and γ. As discussed earlier, the demand-creating power of investment γ depends on the rate at which new products are being created, the extent of cost reductions and quality improvements of existing products, and their income and price elasticities in both domestic and world markets. Here I will discuss θ.

At firm level, a part of the exogenous growth of demand for a product comes from the growth of the economy as whole. For the macroeconomy, what are the sources of growth of demand θ? I argue that historically the following sources of demand growth were important in many countries, including Japan: (i) population growth, (ii) Lewisian dual structure, and (iii) exports.

First, at least in a well-organized economy, population growth is expected to augment the growth of demand. I have already argued that population growth will not by itself suffice to fuel growth; in fact, population growth contributes to economic growth only by raising demand (θ in the present analysis). However, it is certainly reasonable to conceive that under certain circumstances population growth will augment the growth of demand.

Some economists think that the fact that employment always seems to return to a level pretty close to the size of the labour force, preventing unemployment from becoming arbitrarily large in the long run, demonstrates that the forces of supply and demand lead to factor-market-clearing, and that output is determined by the supply of these factors of production. I will later discuss this problem in greater detail, but for the moment I must point out that employment increases roughly in parallel with population *partly* because population growth normally sustains the growth of demand. Keynes, for example, argued that

> An increasing population has a very important influence on the demand for capital. Not only does the demand for capital—apart from technical changes and improved standard of life—increase more or less in proportion to population. But, business expectations being based much more on present than on prospective demand, an era of increasing population tends to promote optimism, since demand will in general tend to exceed, rather than fall short of, what was hoped for. Moreover a mistake, resulting in a particular type of capital being in temporary oversupply, is in such conditions rapidly corrected. But in an era of declining population the opposite is true. (Keynes 1937a: 125–6)

Young (1928) also maintains that, 'under most circumstances, though not in all, the growth of population still has to be counted a factor making for a larger *per capita* product'. (This is, incidentally, exactly contrary to the prediction of the neoclassical growth model.) A. Hansen (1939), in his presidential address to the American

Economic Association, discussed the implications of population growth on demand. He argued that the American prosperity in the 1920s was sustained by high population growth; then, regarding the 1930s, he went on to express his 'conviction that the combined effect of the decline in population growth, together with the failure of any really important innovations of a magnitude sufficient to absorb large capital outlays, weighs very heavily as an explanation for the failure of the recent recovery to reach full employment' (p. 11). The important point is that population growth affects economic growth only to the extent that it raises or lowers the growth rate of demand.

Secondly, the Lewisian dual structure contributes to the growth of demand. In the Lewisian model (Lewis 1954), an unlimited supply of labour is available at a 'subsistence' wage determined in the 'traditional' sector. Capital formation and technical progress in the modern capitalist sector therefore result not in raising real wages, but in raising the share of profits, which in turn entails further investment. Instrumental in this cycle is a high profit rate sustained by low real wages. This analysis, however, lacks the perspective on demand. In the modern sector, growth of demand for products is implicitly assumed to meet the growth of productive capacity. In reality, demand does not grow automatically. And herein lies the problem with this theory.

According to the Lewisian theory, population is supposed to flow continuously from the rural agricultural sector to the urban industrial sector, as actually happened in Japan. Among Asian developing countries, however, this Lewisian population flow in fact occurred substantially in only a few NIES countries; the Lewisian theory does not actually hold for many developing countries, including the Phillippines and Indonesia. To repeat, the basic problem of the theory is that the growth of the modern industrial sector is sustained by high profits guaranteed by repressed real wages, while the demand for products in the modern industrial sector is assumed to emerge automatically as production grows. In reality, demand does not automatically emerge.

There are, obviously, two sources of demand: domestic and foreign. The role of the Lewisian dual structure in the process of growth differs depending on whether growth is led by domestic demand or by exports. For domestic-demand-led growth, the low real wages emphasized by Lewis (1954) are not so important as some other factors, such as household formation accompanying population flow. In Chapter 2, I argued that this mechanism worked in the case of post-war Japanese growth. I will shortly explain it using the model presented above.

Finally, exports can be a substantial source of growth of demand θ. 'Export-led growth' is in fact a much discussed subject (see Beckerman 1962, 1966; Lamfalussy 1963; Thirlwall 1979; and Kaldor 1989). The neoclassical two-sector model, focusing on the supply side, would indicate that trade accelerates the growth rate of the economy if it lowers the relative price of investment goods (see Corden 1971). Here, instead, I focus on exports as a source of growth of effective demand.

In this regard, the record of the Japanese economy during the First World War provides an instructive example. In the 1910s, Japan imported most of its technologically advanced investment goods such as spinning machines. The war interrupted imports of such machines from Europe, and as a result their prices sharply rose; in some cases supplies were completely cut off. The war was therefore a major *negative* supply shock to the Japanese economy. And yet, Japan enjoyed high growth during the war, taking advantage of an unprecedentedly sharp increase in exports; the average growth rate of real GNP in 1915–18 was 7.6%, while that of real exports was 19.2%. This example well illustrates export-led growth, which overwhelmed the large negative supply shock caused by the war.

As pointed out above, low real wages in the Lewisian economy are not necessarily advantageous for economic growth, but they can certainly be a contributing factor in the case of export-led growth. Today's NIEs and pre-war Japan are typical examples of such export-led growth. Song (1990), for example, estimating the contribution of demand components to South Korean growth in the 1963–73 period, finds 33% of growth generated by exports compared with 31% generated by domestic final demand. The same story applies to the pre-war Japanese economy (see Shinohara 1961 and Yoshikawa and Shioji 1990). We observed in Chapter 2 that real wages in pre-war Japan were often stagnant, a distinctively different pattern from that in the post-war period.

Misalignment of the exchange rate can also play an important role for export-led growth. The persistent deflationary effect of the overvalued pound in the inter-war period is well documented. In contrast, Japan managed to 'escape' almost completely the Great Depression by taking advantage of the high growth of exports driven by the undervalued yen (Fig. 10.3). Under the fixed-exchange-rate

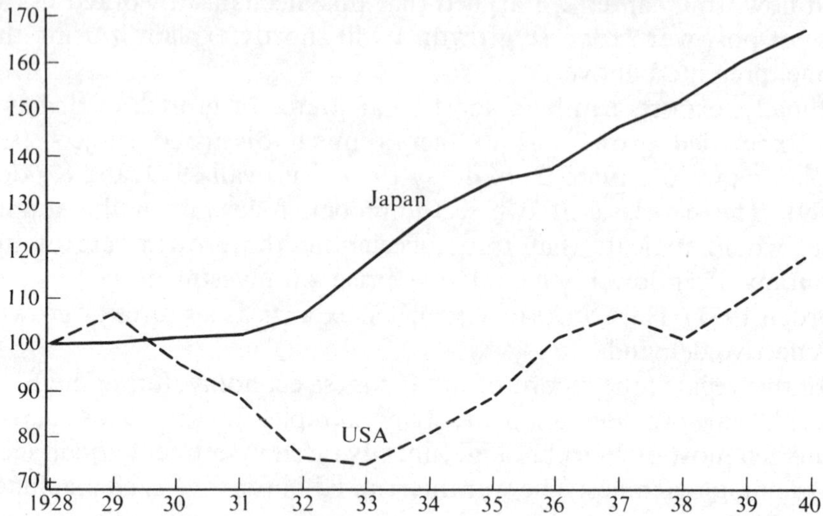

Fig. 10.3. Real GNP, 1928–1940

regime, the problem turns to the balance-of-payments constraint on growth. Thirlwall, for example, argues as follows:

The importance of a healthy balance of payments for growth can be stated quite succinctly. If a country gets into balance of payments difficulties as it expands demand, before the short term capacity growth rate is reached, then demand must be curtailed; supply is never fully utilised; investment is discouraged; technological progress is slowed down, and a country's goods compared to foreign goods become less desirable so worsening the balance of payments still further, and so on. A vicious circle is started. By contrast, if a country is able to expand demand up to the level of existing productive capacity, without balance of payments difficulties arising, the pressure of demand upon capacity may well raise the capacity growth rate. There are a number of possible mechanisms through which this may happen: the encouragement to investment which would augment the capital stock and bring with it technological progress; the supply of labour may increase by the entry into the workforce of people previously outside; the movement of factors of production from low productivity to high productivity sectors, and the ability to import more may increase capacity by making domestic resources more productive. It is this argument that lies behind the advocacy of export-led growth, because it is only through the expansion of exports that the growth rate can be raised without the balance of payments deteriorating at the same time. Believers in export-led growth are really postulating a balance of payments constraint theory of why growth rates differ. (Thirlwall 1979: 46)

According to this argument, the high growth of exports, by lifting the ceiling of the balance-of-payments constraint, encourages other expenditure, particularly investment, and thereby raises the growth rate of the economy. In the United Kingdom things worked the other way; Beckerman, for example, notes that

> in the United Kingdom, although the average *pressure* of demand over the whole period has not been low by international standards, experience has taught all but the most ill-informed entrepreneurs that, however high may be the *rate of growth* of demand in the short-run, it will not persist, since the external balance soon deteriorates, thereby requiring measures of demand restraint. [They are] also aware, more or less vaguely, that this is related to the United Kingdom's poor performance in export markets, and that this, in turn, is connected with the country's failure to prevent a continuous rise in relative prices by means of repeated doses of demand restraint. (Beckerman 1962: 917)

Under certain simplifying assumptions, the constraint that the balance of payments must be zero leads us to the simple formula $y = x/m$, where y, x are the growth rates of GNP and exports, respectively, and m is the income elasticity of the demand for imports. Thirlwall (1979), comparing $y = x/m$ across countries, argues that the growth of exports is a crucial determinant of the growth rate of the economy as a whole.

International competitiveness with respect to quality and price is obviously very important for the growth of exports. It is often postulated, by analogy with industrial organization, that a lower price contributes only to a once-and-for-all increase in the market share, and not to a higher *growth*. This may be true for a firm in one industry but not true for the economy as a whole. Suppose that there are two goods in the world market, one with a high growth of demand and the other a low growth, depending on the difference in income elasticities. If, offering lower price or higher quality, a country captures the larger share of the world market for the high-growth product, it can achieve higher *growth*. Exports may not be a necessary condition for high growth, as some economists who believe in a strong form of export-led growth might argue, but it can be sufficient to sustain high growth for a decade or two by raising θ in my model.

No doubt, the growth of demand is, in part, endogenously generated. I maintain, however, that, for any economy in any period, there are macroeconomic constraints which condition the growth of demand beyond economic agents' optimization. In my model, they are summarized by a single parameter θ.

The Japanese Economy: A Case Study

We can once again explain post-war Japanese economic growth using our model. As described in Chapter 2, the Japanese economy in the late 1950s and 1960s enjoyed high θ and, as a consequence, a very high growth rate of the economy. The economic growth in this period was led basically by domestic demand. The factors behind high θ were (i) an unprecedentedly high growth in the total number of households (much higher than population growth), which was generated by internal migration in the Lewisian dual economy, and (ii) the introduction of many consumer durables at progressively lower prices. Internal migration, by generating an unprecedentedly high growth in the number of households, sustained a high growth of domestic demand. As the pool of labour in the rural agricultural sector was exhausted, however, internal migration subsided and, accordingly, the increase in the number of households decelerated. Meanwhile, the domestic market for the then existing consumer durables was becoming saturated. These factors not only restrained the growth of those industries producing consumer durables but also, through input–output channels, affected the whole of the manufacturing industry, including iron and steel and chemicals, which had led the rapid economic growth beginning in 1955. In this way, both θ and γ substantially declined, signalling the end of the rapid growth period around 1970.

This whole process can be illustrated with a simple model. The growth rate of the economy is $\theta/(1-\gamma)$. Noting that internal migration sustains high a growth of domestic demand, I assume that

$$\theta = g + \dot{f}, \tag{35}$$

where g is a constant and f is the percentage of population in urban areas.

f changes in a logistic way, but its rate of change depends positively on the growth rate of the economy; high growth accelerates migration from rural to urban areas (see Minami 1970). Thus, we have

$$\dot{f} = \left[\beta + \delta\left(\frac{\theta}{1-\gamma}\right)\right](1-f)f \qquad (0 < \delta < 1,\ 0 < \beta). \tag{36}$$

From (35) and (36), we obtain

$$\theta = \frac{\beta(1-f)f + g}{1 - \left(\dfrac{\delta}{1-\gamma}\right)(1-f)f}, \tag{37}$$

where

$$\frac{\partial \theta}{\partial f} \gtreqqless 0 \quad \text{as} \quad f \lesseqqgtr \frac{1}{2} \tag{38}$$

and

$$\theta \rightarrow g \quad \text{as} \quad f \rightarrow 1.$$

Therefore, as f monotonically approaches one, both internal migration and the growth rate of the economy first accelerate and then decelerate. This is shown in Fig. 10.4. I maintain that this is the basic mechanism of the high growth of the Japanese economy in the 1950s and 1960s, which ended around 1970.

In growth accounting, the positive effect of the contraction of agriculture on growth is often taken into account (Denison 1967; Maddison 1987). However, this positive effect arises only because of the different pace of technical progress between the agricultural and industrial sectors. Here, I argue instead that the unprecedentedly high growth in the number of households generated by internal migration was much more important to sustaining high economic growth, by way of raising domestic *demand* in the post-war Japanese economy.

For a sharp decline in the growth rate beginning in the 1970s, it is often argued that, given the Harrod–Domar warranted growth rate s/v, it was brought about by an increase in capital–output ratio v. In my model, however, the capital–output ratio v is an endogenous

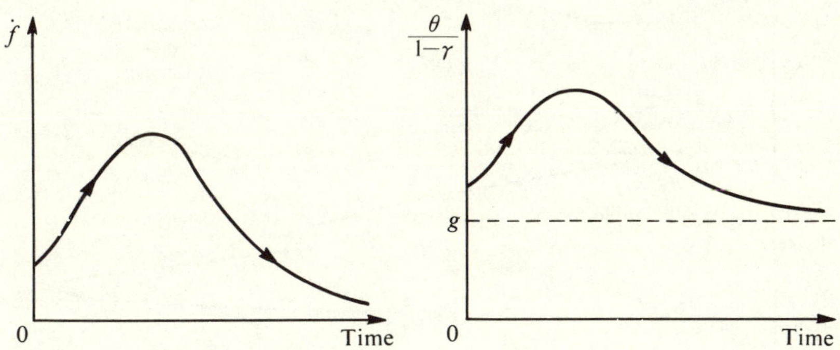

(*a*) Change in % of population of urban areas

(*b*) Growth rate

Fig. 10.4. Growth and internal migration

variable determined by the long-run growth rate $\theta/(1-\gamma)$. The higher the growth rate, the lower the capital–output ratio. Fig. 10.5, in fact, shows that the capital–output ratio was about 1 in the high-growth period of the 1960s, but then rose to about 1.6 in the 1970s when the growth rate decelerated from 10% to 4%. According to my model, an increase in the capital–output ratio is the *result* of the slower economic growth, not the other way round.

10.3 EMPLOYMENT, PRODUCTIVITY, AND INCREASING RETURNS

The growth rate of the economy is determined basically by investment, which in turn is induced by the prospective growth of demand, both exogenous and created by firms (θ and γ). Growth of employment is then determined in accordance with production function (13):

$$\frac{\dot{L}}{L} = l = \frac{1}{a}\left[(1-b)\left(\frac{\theta}{1-\gamma}\right) - \lambda\right], \tag{39}$$

where $\dot{Y}/Y$ and $\dot{K}/K$ are equal to $\theta/(1-\gamma)$ in the long run. Here λ is the rate of Hicks-neutral capacity-augmenting technical progress Λ. Given demand-constrained output, its major role is to save labour.

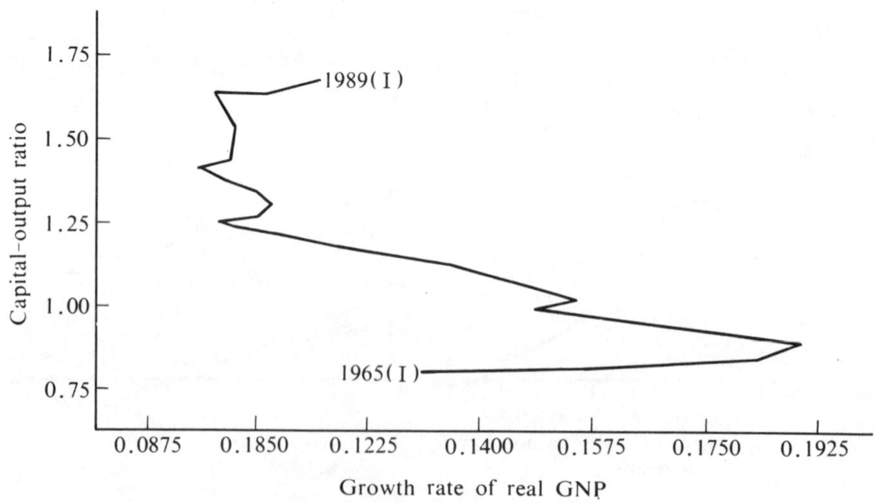

Fig. 10.5. Growth rate and capital-output ratio, 1965(I)–1989(I)
Source: Economic Planning Agency, National Income and Product Accounts

The Labour Market

Plainly, the growth rate of employment l given by (39) is not necessarily equal to the 'natural' growth rate of labour force, n. Now a divergence between the growth rates of labour supply and demand is readily taken by many theorists as a serious shortcoming of any model. Under this condition, such economies should spend most of their time experiencing either prolonged episodes of increasing or falling unemployment rates and/or prolonged periods of rising or falling capacity utilization. As Solow (1994) observed, 'this is not what the record of the main capitalist economies looks like'. This apparently formidable argument is, however, actually not so tight as it first appears.

Thanks to Lewis (1954), the 'the dual economy' is well established in the literature. In such a dual economy, when the economy grows at a higher rate than its labour force, more workers come out of the 'jungle' to meet the demand for labour in the growing 'modern' sector; when the opposite occurs, more workers return to or stay in the 'jungle' to equate labour supply and demand. Solow would say that, if this is true, then it is true for a developing country. Not quite. In what follows, I will show that the generalized Lewisian mechanism works for developed countries as well.

Let us first look at the record for Japan. Table 10.3 shows the growth of real output and labour by sector for two periods, 1950–70 and 1970–85. Plainly, the growth of the Japanese economy throughout the period as a whole was led by the manufacturing and service sectors; the contribution of agriculture was negligible during 1950–70, and was literally nil during 1970–85.

How did the growing sectors, i.e. manufacturing and services, obtain their necessary labour? For the 1950–70 period, labour force in those sectors increased by 25 million. Out of the 25 million, 17 million are accounted for by a growth of the labour force during the period, whereas the remaining 8 million came from the agricultural sector. The proportion of workers who moved into the labour force from the 'jungle' out of the total increase in the labour force demanded by the growth sectors is, therefore, one-third. Put another way, the average annual increase in labour in the growth sectors of the Japanese economy was 6.6%, of which 4.5% was met by an increase in the total labour force, or by natural growth, and 2.1% by the intersectoral move of workers. The Lewisian 'jungle mechanism' for equating labour supply and demand in the growth sectors clearly worked in the Japanese economy. This may not be very surprising

Table 10.3. The growth of output and labour by sector, 1950–1970 and 1970–1985

	Real output (¥ trillion)[a]						Labour (million)					
	(1) 1950	(2) 1970	(3) Δ(1970/ 1950)	(4) 1970	(5) 1985	(6) Δ(1985/ 1970)	(7) 1950	(8) 1970	(9) Δ(1970/ 1950)	(10) 1970	(11) 1985	(12) Δ(1985/ 1970)
Total (real GNP/total labour force)	3.3	34.8	31.5	172	320	148	36	53	17	53	58	5
Agriculture	0.9	2.8	1.9	10	10	0	18	10	− 8	10	5	− 5
Manufacturing	1.0	14.0	13.0	64	121	57	8	18	10	18	19	1
Tertiary	1.4	18.0	16.6	79	170	91	10	25	15	25	34	9

[a] Since real GNP is not available for 1950 in SNA data, 'real GNP' for 1970 in col. (2) is constructed by deflating nominal GNP by WPI; 'real GNP' in cols. (1) and (2) are, therefore, constant 1950 WPI GNP. Real GNP in cols. (4) and (5), on the other hand, are constant 1985 price GNP taken from SNA.

Source: SNA for output, and Census for labour.

for the 1950–70 period; Chapter 2 and the foregoing analysis in this chapter repeatedly emphasize the Lewisian mechanism in Japan's high-growth period. Japan in 1970, however, had become an 'advanced' capitalist economy by any measure. For our purposes, therefore, it is interesting to examine the record for the 1970–85 period.

During this latter period, the labour force employed in the growth sectors of the economy increased by 10 million, or 1.6% per year. Out of this 10 million, just half was accounted for by the 'natural' growth of labour, and the other half by intersectoral moves. This demonstrates the importance of the Lewisian mechanism even for well-developed economies.

Note that the Lewisian 'jungle' is not confined to agriculture; agriculture is only an extreme case. Even well developed economies usually have many 'jungles'. In the neoclassical theory, under the assumptions of decreasing returns and perfect competition, marginal value products of labour are equal in all sectors. I maintain that this is not actually the case in a real economy. Although the relative prices of products in the high-productivity growth sectors tend to decline and vice versa,[7] the differentials in the marginal value products of labour remain, because output of the growth sectors is constrained by demand. As a result, the economy consists of growing high-productivity sectors on the one hand, and stagnant low-productivity sectors on the other. Since the stagnant sectors or 'jungles' are not one but many, with stepwise labour productivities, the economy is not 'dual' but actually a 'multi-jungle' economy. Growth of the economy as a whole is, of course, led by the growth sectors. When this 'multi-jungle economy' grows faster than the natural growth rate, not only does the unemployment rate decline, but workers move from stagnant sectors to growth sectors. In the opposite case, where the growth of the economy is lower than the natural rate, not only does the unemployment rate rise, but also the stagnant sectors enlarge, absorbing workers who would otherwise be employed in the growing sectors.

In this way, the growth rate of the economy necessarily affects industrial structure, while industrial structure in turn affects the

[7] Ch. 8 shows, e.g., that the significant differential in productivity growth between the tradable and non-tradable sectors in the Japanese economy resulted in a change in the relative prices, which in turn brought about a sharp appreciation of the yen during the 1980s, despite a relatively small differential in inflation across countries.

growth rate.[8] For the purpose at hand, it suffices to understand that the growth rate of the economy can deviate from the natural growth rate n for a considerably long time with a wide margin; the generalized Lewisian mechanism equates growths of labour supply and demand.[9] We saw in Table 10.3 that this mechanism certainly worked in the Japanese economy during the 35-year period from 1950 to 1985. It is worth emphasizing once again that this mechanism would not cease to work if the population in the agricultural sector were exhausted, for the economy has many 'jungles' in which both marginal value products of labour and the growth rate are much lower than those in the growth sectors.

The foregoing argument can be formalized as follows. Supply of labour L^s is

$$L^s = PN, \tag{40}$$

where N is the size of the population whose growth rate n is exogenous. 'Effective participation rate' P, on the other hand, is endogenous. P stands not only for participation rate in the usual sense, but also for mobilization of the 'disguised unemployed' in the 'jungles'. In the process of growth, the latter is much more important than the former. We observed above that growth of P in this sense played a significant role in the Japanese economy.

The growth rate of P, $p = \dot{P}/P$, is assumed to be endogenous. Specifically, I assume that

$$p = -\phi(u - u^*) \qquad (\phi > 0) \tag{41}$$

where u is the unemployment rate and u^* its 'natural' rate. According to (41), the lower the unemployment rate, the higher the rate of

[8] For example, in the economy that does not have a well-developed domestic machinery industry, an increase in investment may not raise the growth rate but may instead result in an increase in imports. This is what happened in the pre-war Japanese economy and in some Asian NIEs today.

[9] Endogenous labour-saving technical progress could be another mechanism that equates growths of labour supply and demand. The idea that technical progress may be stimulated by a scarcity of labour relative to demand has been put forward by many; e.g. Robinson (1963) argues that, 'when the urge to accumulate ("animal spirits") is high relative to the growth of the labour force, technical progress has a tendency to raise the "natural" rate of growth to make room for it, so that near-enough steady growth, with near-enough full employment, may be realized'. Kennedy (1964) emphasizes the importance of induced bias in innovation and argues that it is the fundamental determinant of the factor share. It has been also a popular topic in economic history; e.g. Kendrick (1961) identifies an increase in the trend rate of productivity growth in the USA in the years following the First World War, and interprets it as a response to the labour shortages and increased wages brought on by restrictions on immigration.

mobilization of workers in the stagnant sectors (see Table 5.14 for decomposition of the Okun coefficient).

Given the definition of the unemployment rate,

$$u = \frac{L^s - L}{L^s}, \tag{42}$$

we obtain

$$l - n - p = -\left(\frac{\dot{u}}{1 - u}\right). \tag{43}$$

Equations (41) and (43) then lead us to

$$\dot{u} = -(1 - u)[\phi u - (\phi u^* + n - l)]. \tag{44}$$

It is easy to show that this differential equation is globally asymptotically stable for $0 < u < 1$; u converges to its long-run equilibrium $\hat{u}$:

$$\begin{aligned} \hat{u} &= u^* + \left(\frac{n - l}{\phi}\right) \\ &= u^* + \frac{n}{\phi} + \frac{1}{\phi a}\left[\lambda - (1 - b)\left(\frac{\theta}{1 - \gamma}\right)\right]. \end{aligned} \tag{45}$$

When u is equal to $\hat{u}$, the growth rates of labour supply and demand are equal (equation (44)). They are, of course, equated to each other through the endogenous growth of the labour supply which is based on the mobilization of workers in the stagnant sectors.

The equilibrium unemployment rate $\hat{u}$ is of some interest. It depends on the 'natural' unemployment rate u^*, the natural growth rate n, the rate of labour-saving technical progress λ, and the growth rate of the economy $\theta/(1 - \gamma)$. $\hat{u}$ is not necessarily equal to u^*, and is affected by the growth rate of the economy. A large ϕ in (41) means that a divergence between the growth rate of labour demand and the natural growth rate is mostly absorbed by changes in the disguised unemployment in the stagnant sectors rather than by changes in the official unemployment rate. Therefore, the larger is ϕ, the smaller is the effect of the growth rate of the economy $\theta/(1 - \gamma)$ on the equilibrium unemployment rate $\hat{u}$. It is certainly impossible to explain only by the growth rate why the unemployment rate in Spain, for example, has been above 15% throughout the 1980s, often reaching 20%. For international differences in the average unemployment rate, u^* is the major factor. However, on top of u^*, the average growth rate also affects the equilibrium unemployment rate, its effect depending on ϕ. Chapter 5 explains that in Japan u^* is very low, and ϕ is large.

Productivity

Growth of labour productivity is determined as follows:

$$\frac{\dot{Y}}{Y} - \frac{\dot{L}}{L} = \frac{\lambda}{a} + \left(\frac{a+b-1}{a}\right)\left(\frac{\theta}{1-\gamma}\right). \tag{46}$$

Since the capital–output ratio is constant in the long run, the capital–labour ratio grows at the same rate, as given by (46). Growth of total factor productivity, or the Solow residual, is

$$\frac{\dot{Y}}{Y} - \sigma\frac{\dot{L}}{L} - (1-\sigma)\frac{\dot{K}}{K} = \frac{\sigma}{a}\left[\lambda + (a+b-1)\left(\frac{\theta}{1-\gamma}\right)\right], \tag{47}$$

where σ is the relative share of labour. In the standard model with constant returns to scale ($a + b = 1$), where the labour share is assumed to be equal to a, (47) becomes λ.

Suppose that λ is exogenous. Even in this case, aside from exogenous productivity growth λ, productivity grows as the economy grows when there are increasing returns to scale ($a + b > 1$). Higher growth of demand θ and the demand-creating power of investment γ, through encouraging investment, bring about a higher growth in total factor productivity. To be sure, as was discussed in Section 10.1 in some detail, γ is actually a parameter which reflects an aspect of technical progress and would be closely related to λ. Therefore it is not correct to say that productivity growth based on increasing returns is demand-driven. The point is simply that increasing returns in the economy cannot be taken advantage of unless demand grows. Kaldor, in his famous inaugural lecture, made this point:

> The usual hypothesis is that the growth of productivity is mainly to be explained by the progress of knowledge in science and technology. But in that case, how is one to explain the large differences in the *same* industry over the *same* period in different countries? How can the progress of knowledge account for the fact, for example, that in the period 1954–60, productivity in the German motor-car industry increased at 7 per cent a year and in Britain only 2.7 per cent a year? Since large segments of the car industry in both countries were controlled by the same American firms, they must have had the same access to the improvements in knowledge and know-how. This alternative hypothesis is tantamount to a denial of the existence of increasing returns which are known to be an important feature of manufacturing industry. (Kaldor 1966: 13)

To make the economy-wide increasing returns compatible with the assumption of competitive equilibrium, the Marshallian externality is often postulated (see P. Romer 1986, 1987). Increasing returns at individual firm or industry level are, however, very common in manufacturing industries.

Perhaps the best-known classical example is the Silberston curve for the production of motor cars. Maxy and Silberston (1959), analysing the British car industry, concluded that the unit cost of producing a car declined by 40% as production increased from 1,000 cars per year to 50,000; the unit cost was found to decline by a further 13% when production increased from 100,000 cars per year to 400,000. For Toyota, the unit cost of producing a car, adjusted for WPI, was ¥760,000 in 1954, when 22,000 cars were produced, and only ¥420,000 in 1967, when 830,000 cars were made (Okada 1969).

For many manufacturing industries, engineers have used the equation $\log C = a + b\log X$ (where C is the total cost and X is the level of production) to find b close to 0.6. This result is known as 'the six-tenths factor', or 'the two-thirds factor', by which the average cost declines by about 30% – 40% when production doubles. Here we refer to Haldi and Whitcomb (1967). Based on their survey of engineers' estimates of the scale coefficient b, they conclude that, 'out of a total of 687 scale coefficients, 618 (90.0 per cent) show increasing returns, and 50 (7.3 per cent) show constant returns. Only 19 (2.8 per cent) observed [that] scale coefficients reflect decreasing returns.' They report that in process plants, operating expenses for labour, supervision, and maintenance also show significant economies of scale. Consumption of utility services and raw materials, on the other hand, generally shows few economies of scale. These results for the US economy are very similar to those for the Japanese economy reported in Echigo (1969). Such economies of scale arise from the indivisibility of plant equipment and from a family of geometric relationships that relate the material required for the building of equipment to the equipment's capacity. The amount of material required for 'containers', for example, depends principally on the surface area, whereas capacity depends on the volume enclosed.

Yet another example is the case of integrated circuits. The unit cost of an IC is believed to decline by 27.6% when its *cumulative* production doubles:

$$C_t = \left(\int_{-\infty}^{t} y_\tau \, \mathrm{d}\tau \right)^{-0.276}, \tag{48}$$

where C_t is the unit cost and y_t is the production of an IC at t. To be precise, this is an example of the learning curve rather than of increasing returns, but it also brings about the advantage of greater production.

By the mid-1960s, the Japanese producers were ready to produce ICs, but, unlike the United States, Japan lacked the military demand for the product. Instead, in the late 1960s and early 1970s, the most important source of demand for ICs in Japan was pocket calculators. In 1969, more than 50% of Japanese-made ICs were used for pocket calculators, whereas 28.6% were for computers. This order was not reversed until 1976, when the share of ICs going to computers became 27.3% and the share used in pocket calculators fell to 18.5%. The point is that the growth of the Japanese IC industry was possible only because there was enough domestic demand for pocket calculators to sustain the growth of demand for ICs. Technical progress, rather than a purely supply-side phenomenon, was able to lead to growth because it succeeded in boosting demand for ICs through a particular final product, the pocket calculator. Increasing returns, or the learning curve, materialized as the *result* of growth.

When increasing returns are taken advantage of by demand-led growth, productivity growth becomes a result as well as a cause of economic growth. The very well attested correlation between the rate of growth of productivity and the rate of growth of production, between industries as well as between countries, has been reported (see e.g. Salter 1960 for the United Kingdom). For Japan, in the cross-industry regression of total factor productivity (TFP) growth (1960–71) on the growth rate of output for 21 manufacturing industries, Shinohara and Asakawa (1974) obtain 0.4 (significant) for the coefficient. This estimate happens to be almost exactly the same as the 0.45 found by Verdoon (1949), which is known as the Verdoon's law. Yoshioka (1989) obtains a similar result using more recent data.

As shown in Fig. 10.6, there is a positive correlation between growth rates of the economy as a whole and of TFP. These figures are for Japan, but the qualitatively same result is obtained for any advanced economy. A standard explanation is that high TFP growth brings high economic growth and vice versa. Given increasing returns, however, TFP may be not solely a *cause* of growth, but, at least in part, a result of demand-led growth. In fact, Fase and Van den Heuvel (1988), using Dutch manufacturing data on labour productivity and output (1968(I)–1987(IV)), ran causality tests and concluded that the causality from output growth to productivity growth cannot be rejected.

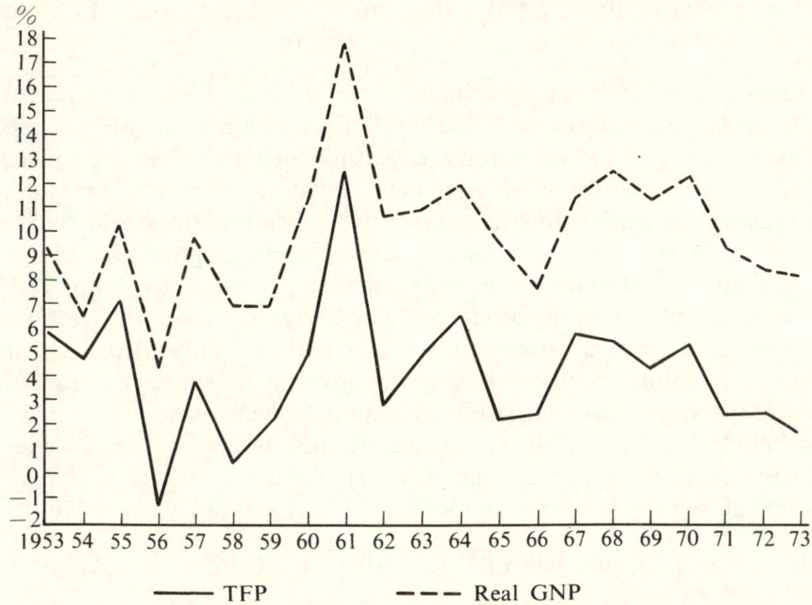

Fig. 10.6. Growth rates of real GNP and total factor productivity
Source: Yoshioka (1989: 110)

Costello (1993), estimating productivity growth for five major industries in six countries, also found that productivity growth is correlated more across industries within a country than across countries within one industry. To the extent that technology is more uniform across countries within one industry than across industries within one country, this finding casts a serious doubt on interpreting total factor productivity as a reflection only of pure technological advance. It points to the significant effect of economy-wide growth on the measured productivity.

Once this point is granted, we are led to the possible 'virtuous' and 'vicious' circles of output and productivity growth in an open economy, because TFP growth driven by output growth is most likely to entail a reduction of relative price. Houthakker (1969) in fact reports the significantly negative correlation between changes in output and relative prices on the industry level for the United States. For Japan, Shinohara and Asakawa (1974), in regressing average price changes on TFP growth (1960–71) for 21 manufacturing industries, obtain a significant −0.49 for the coefficient.

Lamfalussy supports the thesis of virtuous and vicious circles of output and productivity growth to explain the different growth performances of the United Kingdom and the European Economic Community in the 1950s:

> we found a close link between the export performance and the increase in productivity. It seems extremely likely that the faster growth of EEC exports can be ascribed to the more rapid expansion of output per head in EEC industries. This rounds off the argument and shows the 'virtuous' circle of Continental Europe's growth: competitive advantage in world markets, leading to faster growth of exports; export-oriented growth, raising the share of investment in the national product; higher investment ratio, calling forth a faster growth in the productivity of labour and leading, therefore, to renewed competitive advantage in world markets. A competitive *dis*advantage, on the other hand, depresses the investment ratio, and therefore prevents productivity from rising fast enough; hence Great Britain's 'vicious' circle. The two orbits will remain distinct so long as money wages in the EEC do not rise fast enough to offset the advantage the area derives from its more rapidly increasing productivity. (Lamfalussy 1963: 116–17)

In terms of my model, TFP growth rate t is given by (47), which can be rewritten as

$$t = \frac{\sigma}{a}\left[\lambda + (a + b - 1)\left(\frac{\theta}{1 - \gamma}\right)\right] \tag{49}$$

To the extent that growth of demand depends on TFP growth t, we obtain the following relationship between $\theta/(1 - \gamma)$ and t:

$$\frac{\theta}{1 - \gamma} = g(t) \qquad (g(0) > 0,\ g'(t) > 0) \tag{50}$$

It is then possible, depending on $g(t)$, to obtain multiple equilibria of 'virtuous' and 'vicious' circles of high/low growths of output and productivity, points A and C in Fig. 10.7.

10.4 CONCLUDING REMARKS

It is widely believed that the Keynesian problem of demand deficiency is relevant, if at all, only in the short run. This chapter argues, to the contrary, that demand constraints matter even in the process of long-run economic growth.

Theory is supposed to help us identify particularly important *exogenous* factors. The neoclassical growth model, focusing on the supply side, naturally leads us to factor endowments; the growth rate of the population is a fundamental determinant of economic growth in this model. The considerable industry-wide variation of labour

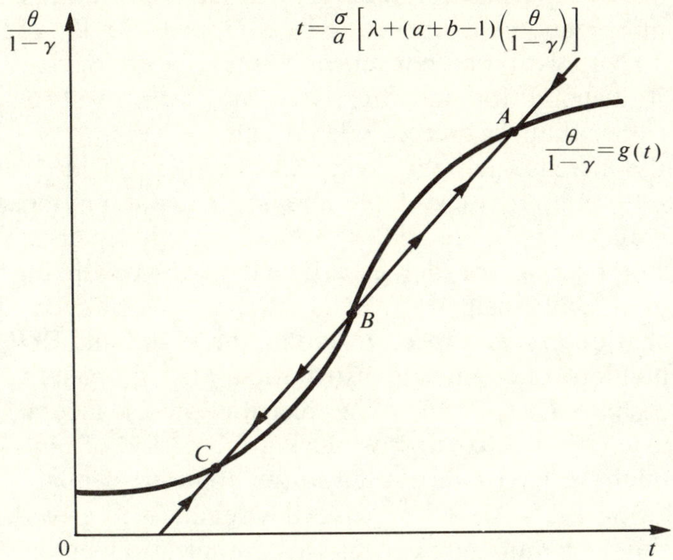

Fig. 10.7. Total factor productivity and growth rate

input shown in Table 10.2, however, suggests that we must explain the growth of output by something other than the growth of labour input. The model of this chapter accordingly approaches the problem of growth from a different angle. It postulates that the engine of economic growth is investment, and that investment in turn is constrained by the expected growth of demand, both exogenous and that created by firms' own efforts. Thus, in terms of causality, investment and the rate of growth are simultaneously determined by two primary factors: the growth rate of exogenous demand θ and the strength of the demand-creating power of investment γ. I emphasize that exogeneity is an attribute of the chosen framework of thought, not an attribute of the events themselves. Recent 'endogenous' growth theories lead us to certain *exogenous* factors such as factor endowment as ultimate determinants of economic growth. My model focuses on θ and γ.

The growth rate of demand depends on many factors, some of which may even be accidental to the economy. In this book I have maintained that the high growth in the number of Japanese households generated by internal migration from the rural agricultural sector to the urban industrial sector in the post-war period was the ultimate source of high growth of demand θ. Particularly important products for the purpose of such growth were consumer durables. The Japanese economy happened to be equipped with the productive capacity to supply those consumer durables; otherwise, the high growth of demand for such items would have resulted in high imports, rather than high economic growth.

A steady increase in real wages in the 1950s and 1960s also contributed to high θ by enabling more households to purchase those consumer durables. While for export-led growth lower real wages may sustain high θ, for domestic-demand-led growth higher real wages can actually help to raise θ. Income distribution deserves special attention in this respect. In Japan, the 1946 Land Reform had a substantial impact on income distribution, and enlarged the domestic market (see Chapter 3). The distribution of income among individuals continued to improve during the period of high growth, and is thought to have contributed to the domestic-demand-led high growth during 1955–70. In any case, the demand-led growth cannot be seen simply as an outcome of the optimization of the 'representative' consumer. In particular, a low rate of time preference, and/or high intertemporal elasticity of substitution, have little bearing on the high growth rate of the Japanese economy in the 1960s.

The second factor determining the long-run growth rate of the economy is the strength of the demand-creating power of investment, γ in the model. γ is essentially a measure to gauge the neglected aspect of technical progress on the demand side, such as the introduction of new products. It has been well understood since Solow (1957) that technical progress plays the crucial role in economic growth. The new 'endogenous growth theory' such as propounded by Grossman and Helpman (1991) once again underlines technical progress as the mainspring of economic growth. In all the hitherto existing theories of growth, however, technical progress simply means the augmentation of productive capacity on the supply side. It is taken for granted that, when the economy is able to produce more, given the same amount of inputs, it will succeed in selling its increased output. Endogenizing technical progress by focusing on the supply side leads us naturally to identify, in addition to the time preference, the endowment of factors used intensively in R&D as the ultimate *exogenous* factor explaining economic growth. Thus, in Grossman and Helpman (1991), for example, *exogenously given* inputs that are used intensively in R&D are conducive to innovation and growth, while inputs that are used intensively in the manufacturing of traditional goods may discourage innovation and growth.

In contrast, in the present model the rate of growth depends crucially on the effect of technical progress on prospects of demand. Here, if technical progress occurred on the supply side *under unchanged prospects of growth of demand*, it would mainly change the real wages, labour employment, and the factor share, *not* the growth rate of the economy. In reality, however, technical progress embodied in new investment would not only augment productive capacity but also enhance the growth of demand. Technical progress on the supply side, for example, would lower production costs and thus prices if it were not totally absorbed in the increase in real wages. To the extent that lower prices enable the country to capture the market for the product, the demand for which is growing widely in the world economy, technical progress on the supply side leads to rising prospects of a growth in demand. In the model, Λ increases while at the same time γ increases.

Since increasing returns can be taken advantage of when demand grows, the initial technological advance on the supply side in one country *could* create 'virtuous' and 'vicious' circles of high/low growths of output and productivity across countries. Whether such a circle will in fact occur depends, among other things, on the degree of increasing returns, the price elasticity of the products, and the growth rates of total demand for the products in the world economy. In any case, the present analysis does not imply convergence over time in the levels of per capita income across countries. Moreover, we can easily explain that a country *outgrows* another, as in the case of Japan and the United Kingdom in the post-war period.[10] It is difficult to explain this phenomenon by increasing returns without demand constraints (P. Romer 1986, 1987), for in such a model the latecomer would never be able to catch up with the more developed nation. Nor is it so reasonable to explain it by such drastic changes in factor endowment within a decade or two.

The model of economic growth presented in this chapter indicates that the key for growth is demand. This has obvious policy implications. To raise the growth rate, the economy must augment its

[10] Brezis *et al.* (1993) present a model in which the international leadership shifts in response to occasional major changes in technology. In their model, efficiency of a technology is assumed to depend on cumulative production. Thus, initially, a new technology may well seem inferior to older methods to those who have extensive experience with those older methods, despite the fact that such 'inferior' technology may have more potential in the long run. Their analysis focuses on cost structures. In contrast, here I argue that the interactions between demand-led growth and increasing returns could lead to a shift in international leadership.

prospects of growth in demand. For this purpose, it is first essential to identify the kinds of product for which demand is growing rapidly in the world economy. In every period in history, there have been certain key products for which demand is growing fast the world over while production is also enjoying increasing returns—e.g. cotton, steel, motor cars, and perhaps currently IC-based broadly electrical machinery. Historically, those products (except perhaps for the case of the American automobile) eventually saturated the domestic market, and had to find foreign markets to maintain a high θ. That is why export-led growth is often found to occur even if it is not a logical necessity for high economic growth.

The strength of demand-creating technical progress, γ is related to the product life-cycle theory of international trade (Akamatsu 1956 and Vernon 1966). It is often found that a country's export strength lies in industries enjoying a high rate of new product development (see e.g. Gruber *et al.* 1967, and Wells 1972). Exports of goods that have high income–price elasticities in the world market help the economy attain high economic growth.

The free market may not necessarily enable a country to develop such high-growth industries. Increasing returns is an obvious factor which can lead to market failure; capital market imperfection may impede the development of an infant industry; and the supply of factors intensively used in growth industries are not necessarily provided only by motivations of private profit. Chapter 1, for example, shows that in the late 1950s the Japanese system of higher education was significantly restructured towards science and technology. Nineteenth-century Germany experienced the same restructuring. In both cases, the government played a very important role; the reformation was not merely the outcome of the private agents' optimization. Obviously, supply-side policies are important for economic growth. However, those supply-side policies must be effectively designed with due consideration to the prospects of demand, θ and γ in my model.

Finally, the model of demand-led growth, although it is still in the early stage of development, can be much more smoothly integrated with the Keynesian theory of short-run fluctuations than can the neoclassical growth model.

11

Conclusion

This book has argued that real demand constraint is essential to an understanding of the macroeconomy. No doubt, a part of demand is determined endogenously within any given period, but there is always an exogenous component in real aggregate demand which constrains the economy as a whole. Wars are obviously exogenous real demand shocks (though they are supply shocks as well), without which we cannot reasonably explain the century-long developments of any advanced country. Exports are another example. The Keynesian approach begins with exogenous real demand.

On the other hand, in addition to preferences and technology, the neoclassical theory takes factor endowments as a fundamental determinant of the economy. It then determines prices and quantities in such a way that all the factors are 'fully employed'. This implies, among other things, that the marginal value products of labour in all the sectors are equated. I contend that this is a poor characterization of the economy even in the long run, let alone the short run. I imagine that the most advanced economy consists of many Lewisian 'jungles' with stepwise marginal products; some sectors enjoy even increasing marginal products; but all the sectors are constrained by demand. Demand determines the utilization of factors.

The law of supply and demand evidently explains the microeconomic problem of choice well: choice between orange and apple, or labour and machine, or one kind of labour and another. However, the neoclassical general equilibrium theory claims much more than that. For macroeconomics, the issue is whether real factor prices are determined in such a way that all the factors are 'fully employed'. I have argued that even an advanced economy is a Lewisian '*multi*-jungle' economy with rising sectors on the one hand and stagnant sectors on the other. In such an economy, exogenous demand determines quantities. Some economists would think that exogenous demand is intrinsically inferior to endogenous demand. But recall that exogeneity is an attribute of the chosen framework of thought, not an attribute of the events themselves. In fact, through the exogeneity of real aggregate demand, leaving macroeconomic *theory*, we enter the realm of history. In any case, as far as quantity is concerned, 'Hamlet without the prince' is truly the best characterization of macroeconomics without the principle of effective demand.

All this, of course, is not to say that supply factors are not important. Supply is obviously as important as demand. Innovations are, after all, supply-side phenomena, though they may be induced by demand, as proponents of product life-cycle theory emphasize. However, innovations bear fruit only through investment, and investment is always constrained by demand. Contrary to common belief, therefore, demand affects the economy in the long run. Plainly, it is necessary to consider supply-side factors with demand in a different way from that ordinarily adopted in neoclassical theory. Toward this goal, I introduced the notion of demand-creating technical progress in Chapter 10. In any case, the nexus between supply and demand is investment.

The field of neoclassical economics has been fully cultivated. No matter how dynamic or 'endogenized' models are, their basic logic remains the same. The experience of the Japanese economy would seem to recommend pursuit of an approach to macroeconomics that is not based on neoclassical logic.

References

Works published in English

Abel, A. (1979), *Investment and the Value of Capital*, Garland, New York.

—— (1981), 'Dynamic Adjustment in a Putty–Putty Model: Implications for Testing the Putty–Clay Hypothesis', *International Economic Review*, February.

—— (1990), 'Consumption and Investment', in B. Friedman and F. Hahn (eds.) *Handbook of Monetary Economics*, ii, North-Holland, Amsterdam.

—— and Blanchard, O. (1983*a*), 'An Intertemporal Model of Saving and Investment', *Econometrica*, May.

—— —— (1983*b*), 'Investment and Sales: An Empirical Study', paper presented at NBER Macroeconomics Conference, July.

—— —— (1986), 'The Present Value of Profits and Clynical Movements in Investment', *Econometrica*, March.

Abraham, K. and Katz, L. (1986), 'Cyclical Unemployment: Sectoral Shifts or Aggregate Disturbances?' *Journal of Political Economy*, June.

—— and Houseman, S. (1989), 'Job Security and Work Force Adjustment: How Different are US and Japanese Practices?' *Journal of Japanese and International Economies*, December.

Akerlof, G. and Yellen, J. (1985), 'A Near-Rational Model of the Business Cycle, with Wage and Price Inertia', *Quarterly Journal of Economics*, Supplement.

Altonji, J. (1982), 'Intertemporal Substitution Model of Labour Market Fluctuations: An Empirical Analysis', *Review of Economic Studies*, Special Issue.

—— and Ashenfelter, O. (1980), 'Wage Movements and the Labour Market Equilibrium Hypothesis', *Economica*, August.

—— and Ham, J. (1986), 'Variation in Employment Growth in Canada: The Role of External, National, Regional and Industrial Factors', NBER Discussion Paper no. 1816, January.

Ando, A. (1986), 'Comment on Hayashi's Paper', in S. Fischer (ed.), *NBER Macroeconomics Annual*, MIT Press, Cambridge, Mass.

—— and Auerbach, A. (1988), 'The Cost of Capital in the United States and Japan: A Comparison', *Journal of Japanese and International Economies*, June.

—— and Kennickell, A. (1987), 'How Much (or Little) Life Cycle Is There in Macro Data? The Cases of the United States and Japan', in R. Dornbusch, S. Fischer, and J. Bossons (eds.), *Macroeconomics and Finance: Essays in Honor of Franco Modigliani*, MIT Press, Cambridge, Mass.

Andrews, M. and Nickell, S. (1982), 'Unemployment in the UK since the War', *Review of Economic Studies*, Special Issue.

Artus, P., Laroque, G. and Michel, G. (1984), 'Estimation of a Quarterly Macroeconomic Model with Quantity Rationing', *Econometrica*, November.

Asako, K. and Uchino, Y. (1987), 'Bank Loan Market of Japan: A New View of the Disequilibrium Analysis', Bank of Japan, *Monetary and Economic Studies*, May.

Ashauer, D. (1985), 'Fiscal Policy and Aggregate Demand', *American Economic Review*, March.

Atkinson, A. B. and Micklewright, J. (1991), 'Unemployment Compensation and Labor Market Transitions: A Critical Review', *Journal of Economic Literature*, December.

Balassa, B. (1964), 'The Purchasing Power Parity Doctrine: A Reappraisal', *Journal of Political Economy*, December.

Ball, L., Mankiw, N. G. and Romer, D. (1988), 'The New Keynesian Economics and the Output–Inflation Tradeoff', *Brookings Papers on Economic Activity*, no. 1.

Bank of Japan (1986), *A Centennial History of the Bank of Japan*, Tokyo.

Barro, R. (1974), 'Are Government Bonds Net Wealth?' *Journal of Political Economy*, November/December.

—— (1977), 'Unanticipated Money Growth and Unemployment in the United States', *American Economic Review*, March.

—— (1989*a*), 'Interest-Rate Targeting', *Journal of Monetary Economics*, January.

—— (1989*b*), 'New Classicals and Keynesians, or the Good Guys and the Bad Guys', NBER Working Paper no. 2982, May.

—— (1992), 'World Interest Rates and Investment', *Scandinavian Journal of Economics*, no. 2.

—— and Grossman, H. (1971), 'A General Disequilibrium Model of Income and Employment', *American Economic Review*, March.

Barsky, R. and Miron, J. (1989), 'The Seasonal Cycle and the Business Cycle', *Journal of Political Economy*, June.

Bean, C. R. (1981), 'An Econometric Model of Manufacturing Investment in the UK', *Economic Journal*, March.

Beason, R. (1993), 'Tests of Production Smoothing in Selected Japanese Industries', *Journal of Monetary Economics*, June.

Becker, G. and Barro, R. (1988), 'A Reformulation of the Economic Theory of Fertility', *Quarterly Journal of Economics*, February.

Beckerman, W. (1962), 'Projecting Europe's Growth', *Economic Journal*, December.

—— (1965), *British Economy in 1975*, Cambridge University Press.

—— (1966), 'The Determinants of Economic Growth', in P. Henderson (ed.), *Economic Growth in Britain*, Weidenfeld & Nicolson, London.

Bellman, R. (1957), *Dynamic Programming*, Princeton University Press, Princeton, NJ.

Benhabib, J. and Nishimura, K. (1985), 'Competitive Equilibrium Cycles', *Journal of Economic Theory*, April.

Bernanke, B. (1986), 'Alternative Explanations of the Money–Income Correlation', *Journal of Monetary Economics*, Supplement (Carnegie–Rochester Conference Series 25).

—— and Blinder, A. (1992), 'The Federal Funds Rate and the Channels of Monetary Transmission', *American Economic Review*, September.

Beveridge, S. and Nelson, C. (1981), 'A New Approach to Decomposition of Economic Time Series into Permanent and Transitory Components with Particular Attention to Measurement of the Business Cycles', *Journal of Monetary Economics*, March.

Bils, M. J. (1985), 'Real Wages over the Business Cycle: Evidence from Panel Data', *Journal of Political Economy*, August.

Birch, E. M. and Siebert, C. D. (1976), 'Uncertainty, Permanent Demand, and Investment Behavior', *American Economic Review*, March.

Bischoff, C. (1969), 'Hypothesis Testing and the Demand for Capital Goods', *Review of Economics and Statistics*, August.

—— (1971), 'The Effect of Alternative Lag Distributions', in G. Fromm (ed.), *Tax Incentives and Capital Spending*, Brookings Institution, Washington DC.

Blades, D. (1989), 'Household Saving Ratios for Japan and Other OECD Countries', in Economics Research Institute (Economic Planning Agency), *Paper and Proceedings of the Fifth EPA International Symposium*, Tokyo.

Blanchard, O. (1979), 'Speculative Bubbles, Crashes and Rational Expectations', *Economics Letters*, no. 3.

—— (1981), 'What is Left of the Multiplier Accelerator?' *American Economic Review*, May.

—— and Fischer, S. (1989), *Lectures on Macroeconomics*, MIT Press, Cambridge, Mass.

—— and Kiyotaki, N. (1987), 'Monopolistic Competition and the Effects of Aggregate Demand', *American Economic Review*, September.

—— and Quah, D. (1989), 'The Dynamic Effects of Aggregate Demand and Supply Disturbances', *American Economic Review*, September.

—— and Summers, L. (1984), 'Perspectives on High World Real Interest Rates', *Brookings Papers on Economic Activity*, no. 2.

—— —— (1986), 'Hysteresis and the European Unemployment Problem', *NBER Macroeconomics Annual*, MIT Press, Cambridge, Mass.

Blinder, A. (1982), 'Inventories and Sticky Prices: More on the Microfoundations of Macroeconomics', *American Economic Review*, June.

—— (1987), 'Keynes, Lucas, and Scientific Progress', *American Economic Review*, May.

Blinder, A. and Maccini, L. (1991), 'Taking Stock: A Critical Assessment of Recent Research on Inventories', *Journal of Economic Perspectives*, Winter.

Blomström, M., Lipsey, R. and Zejan, M. (1993), 'Is Fixed Investment the Key to Economic Growth?' NBER Working Paper no. 4436, August.

Boskin, M. and Kotlikoff, L. (1985), *Public Debt and United States Saving: A New Test of the Newtrality Hypothesis*, Carnegie–Rochester Conference Series on Public Policy no. 23, North-Holland, Amsterdam.

Bosworth, B. (1993), *Saving and Investment in a Global Economy*, Brookings Institution, Washington, DC.

Branson, W. (1985), 'Causes of Appreciation and Volatility of the Dollar', in *The US Dollar: Recent Developments, Outlook, and Policy Options*, Federal Reserve Bank of Kansas City.

—— and Rotemberg, J. J. (1980), 'International Adjustment with Wage Rigidity', *European Economic Review*, May.

Brezis, E., Krugman, P. and Tsiddon, D. (1993), 'Leapfrogging in International Competition: A Theory of Cycles in National Technological Leadership', *American Economic Review*, December.

Brock, W. and Mirman, L. (1972), 'Optimal Economic Growth and Uncertainty: The Discounted Case', *Journal of Economic Theory*, June.

Brunello, G. (1990), 'Hysteresis and "the Japanese Unemployment Problem": A Preliminary Investigation', *Oxford Economic Papers*, July.

Bruno, M. (1986), 'Aggregate Supply and Demand Factors in OECD Unemployment: An Update', *Economica*, Supplement.

—— and Sachs, J. (1981), 'Supply versus Demand Approaches to the Problem of Stagflation', in *Macroeconomic Policies for Growth and Stability*, Institut für Weltwirtschaft, Kiel.

—— —— (1982), 'Input Price Shocks and the Slowdown in Economic Growth: the Case of UK Manufacturing', *Review of Economic Studies*, Special Issue.

—— —— (1985), *Economics of Worldwide Stagflation*, Harvard University Press, Cambridge, Mass.

Buiter, W. and Miller, M. (1981), 'The Thatcher Experiment: What Went Wrong?' *Brookings Papers on Economic Activity*, no. 2.

Campbell, J. Y. and Mankiw, N. G. (1987), 'Are Output Fluctuations Transitory?' *Quarterly Journal of Economics*, November.

—— and Perron, P. (1991), 'Pitfalls and Opportunities: What Macroeconomists Should Know about Unit Roots', in O. Blanchard and S. Fischer (eds.), *NBER Macroeconomics Annual*, MIT Press, Cambridge, Mass.

—— and Shiller, R. (1987), 'Cointegration and Tests of Present Value Models', *Journal of Political Economy*, October.

Carroll, C. and Summers, L. (1991), 'Consumption Growth Parallels Income Growth: Some New Evidence', in B. Bernheim and J. Shoven (eds.), *National Saving and Economic Performance*, University of Chicago Press.

—— and Weil, D. (1993), 'Saving and Growth', NBER Working Paper no. 4470.

Cass, D. (1965), 'Optimum Growth in an Aggregative Model of Capital Accumulation', *Review of Economic Studies*, January.

Cassel, G. (1916), 'The Present Situation of the Foreign Exchanges', *Economic Journal*, March.

—— (1918), 'Abnormal Deviations in International Exchanges', *Economic Journal*, September.

—— (1922), *Money and Foreign Exchange after 1914*, Oxford University Press.

Caves, R. (1970), 'Export-Led Growth: Post-War Industrial Setting', in W. Elitis *et al.* (eds.), *Induction, Growth, and Trade: Essays in Honour of Sir Roy Harrod*, Clarendon Press, Oxford.

—— (1971), 'Export-Led Growth and New Economic History', in J. Bhagwati *et al.* (eds.), *Trade, Balance of Payments and Growth*, North-Holland, Amsterdam.

Chenery, H. B., Shishido, S. and Watanabe, T. (1962), 'The Pattern of Japanese Growth, 1914–54', *Econometrica*, January.

Chipman, J. (1971), 'International Trade with Capital Mobility: A Substitution Theorem', in J. Bhagwati *et al.* (eds.), *Trade, Balance of Payment and Growth*, North-Holland, Amsterdam.

Christiano, L. (1988), 'Money does Granger-Cause Output in the Bivariate Money–Output Relation', *Journal of Monetary Economics*, March/May.

—— (1989), 'Understanding Japan's Saving Rate: The Reconstruction Hypothesis', Federal Reserve Bank of Minneapolis *Quarterly Review*, Spring.

—— and Eichenbaum, M. (1989), 'Unit Roots in GNP: Do We Know and Do We Care?' in *Carnegie–Rochester Conference Series on Public Policy*, North-Holland, Amsterdam.

Ciccolo, J. H. (1975), 'Four Essays on Monetary Policy', Ph.D. thesis, Yale University.

Clark, P. K. (1979), 'Investment in the 1970s', *Brookings Papers on Economic Activity*, no. 1.

—— (1987), 'The Cyclical Component of US Economic Activity', *Quarterly Journal of Economics*, November.

—— and Summers, L. (1982), 'Unemployment and Labor Market Transition', in M. N. Baily (ed.), *Workers, Jobs and Inflation*, Brookings Institution, Washington, DC.

Clay, H. (1928), 'Unemployment and Wage Rates', *Economic Journal*, March.

Clower, R. (1965), 'The Keynesian Counterrevolution: A Theoretical Appraisal', in F. H. Hahn and F. P. R. Brechling (eds.), *The Theory of Interest Rates*, Macmillan, London.

Cochrane, J. H. (1988), 'How Big is the Random Walk in GNP?' *Journal of Political Economy*, October.

Cooley, T. and LeRoy, S. (1985), 'A Theoretical Macroeconometrics', *Journal of Monetary Economics*, November.

Corden, W. (1971), 'The Effects of Trade on the Rate of Growth', in J. Bhagwati, *et al.* (eds.), *Trade, Balance of Payments and Growth*, North-Holland, Amsterdam.

Costello, D. (1993), 'A Cross-Country, Cross-Industry Comparison of Productivity', *Journal of Political Economy*, April.

Cuddington, J. T. and Winters, L. A. (1987), 'The Beveridge–Nelson Decomposition of Economic Time Series: A Quick Computational Method', *Journal of Monetary Economics*, January.

Davis, S. (1987), 'Allocative Disturbances and Specific Capital in Real Business Cycles Theories', *American Economic Review*, May.

Deaton, A. (1985), 'Life Cycle Models of Consumption: Is the Evidence Consistent with the Theory?' paper presented at the Fifth World Congress of the Econometric Society, Cambridge, Mass., 16–23 August.

—— (1992), *Understanding Consumption*, Clarendon Press, Oxford.

Dekle, R. (1987), 'Do the Japanese Elderly Reduce their Total Wealth?' mimeo, Raischauer Institute of Japanese Studies, Harvard University, November.

DeJong, D. N., Nankervis, J. C., Savin, N. E., and Whiteman, C. H. (1992), 'Integration Versus Trend Stationarity in Time Series', *Econometrica*, March.

De Long, J. B. and Summers, L. (1986), 'Is Increased Price Flexibility Stabilizing?' *American Economic Review*, December.

—— —— (1991), 'Equipment Investment and Economic Growth', *Quarterly Journal of Economics*, May.

—— Shleifer, A., Summers, L. and Waldmann, R. (1990), 'Noise Trader Risk in Financial Markets', *Journal of Political Economy*, August.

Denison, E. (1967), *Why Growth Rates Differ*, Brookings Institution, Washington, DC.

Dertouzos, M., Lester, R. and Solow, R. (1989), *Made in America*, MIT Press, Cambridge, Mass.

Diamond, P. (1982), 'Aggregate Demand Management in Search Equilibrium', *Journal of Political Economy*, October.

—— (1984), 'Money in Search Equilibrium', *Econometrica*, January.

Dickey, D. and Fuller, W. (1979), 'Distribution of Estimators for Autoregressive Time Series with a Unit Root', *Journal of American Statistical Association*, June.

Doeringer, P. and Piore, M. (1971), *Internal Labor Markets and Manpower Analysis*, D.C. Heath, Lexington, Mass.

Domar, E. (1946), 'Capital Expansion, Rate of Growth, and Employment', *Econometrica*, April.

—— (1947), 'Expansion and Employment', *American Economic Review*, March.

Dornbusch, R. (1976), 'Expectations and Exchange Rate Dynamics', *Journal of Political Economy*, December.

—— (1984), 'The Overvalued Dollar', *Lloyds Bank Review*, April.

—— (1986), *Dollars, Debts, and Deficits*, MIT Press, Cambridge, Mass.

—— (1989), 'Real Exchange Rate and Macroeconomics: A Selective Survey', *Scandinavian Journal of Economics*, no. 2.

—— Fischer, S. and Samuelson, P. (1977), 'Comparative Advantage, Trade and Payments in a Ricardian Model with a Continuum of Goods', *American Economic Review*, December.

Duesenberry, J. (1949), *Income, Saving and the Theory of Consumer Behavior*, Harvard University Press, Cambridge, Mass.

Dunlop, J. T. (1938), 'The Movement of Real and Money Wage Rates', *Economic Journal*, September.

Eichenbaum, M. and Singleton, K. (1986), 'Do Equilibrium Business Cycle Theories Explain Post-War Business Cycles?' in S. Fischer (ed.), *NBER Macroeconomics Annual*, MIT Press, Cambridge, Mass.

Eisner, R. and Strotz, R. (1963), 'Determinants of Business Investment', in *Impacts of Monetary Policy: Commission on Money and Credit,* Prentice-Hall, Englewood Cliffs, NJ.

Engle, R. F. and Granger, C. W. J. (1987), 'Cointegration and Error Correction: Representation, Estimation, and Testing', *Econometrica*, March.

Fair, R. (1989), 'A Book review of *Model of Business Cycles* by Robert Lucas', *Journal of Economic Literature*, March.

Fase, M. and Van den Heuvel, P. J. (1988), 'Productivity and Growth: Verdoon's Law Revisited', *Economics Letters*, no. 2.

Fazzari, S., Hubbard, R. and Petersen, B. (1988), 'Financing Constraints and Corporate Investment', *Brookings Papers on Economic Activity*, no. 1.

Feldstein, M. (1986), 'The Budget Deficit and the Dollar', in S. Fischer (ed.), *NBER Macroeconomics Annual, 1986*, MIT Press, Cambridge, Mass.

—— and Horioka, C. (1980), 'Domestic Saving and International Capital Flows', *Economic Journal*, June.

Fellner, W. (1976), *Towards a Reconstruction of Macroeconomics*, American Enterprise Institute, Washington, DC.

Fischer, S. (1977), 'Long-Term Contracts, Rational Expectations, and the Optimal Money Supply Rule', *Journal of Political Economy*, February.

—— and Merton, R. (1984), 'Macroeconomics and Finance: The Role of the Stock Marker', NBER Working Paper no. 1291, March.

Fisher, I. (1930), *The Theory of Interest*, Macmillan, New York.

Flavin, M. (1981), 'The Adjustment of Consumption to Changing Expectations about Future Income', *Journal of Political Economy*, October.

Foley, D. (1975), 'On Two Specifications of Asset Equilibrium in Macroeconomic Models', *Journal of Political Economy*, April.

Fomby, T. B., Hill, R. C. and Johnson, S. R. (1984), *Advanced Econometric Methods*, Springer, Berlin.

Ford, R. and Poret, P. (1990), 'Business Investment in the OECD Economies: Recent Performance and Some Implications for Policy', OECD, Department of Economics and Statistics, Working Paper no. 88, November.

Frankel, J. and Froot, K. (1987), 'Short-Term and Long-Term Expectations of the Yen–Dollar Exchange Rate: Evidence from Survey Data', *Journal of Japanese and International Economies*, September.

—— and Meese, R. (1987), 'Are Exchange Rates Excessively Variable?' in S. Fischer (ed.), *NBER Macroeconomics Annual 1987*, MIT Press, Cambridge, Mass.

Freeman, R. B. and Weitzman, M. L. (1987), 'Bonuses and Employment in Japan', *Journal of Japanese and International Economies*, June.

Friedman, B. (1988), 'Monetary Policy without Quantity Variables', *American Economic Review*, May.

—— (1990), 'Changing Effects of Monetary Policy on Real Economic Activity', NBER Working Paper no. 3278, March.

Friedman, M. (1968), 'The Role of Monetary Policy', *American Economic Review*, March.

—— and Schwartz, A. (1963*a*), *A Monetary History of the United States, 1867–1960*, Princeton University Press, Princeton, NJ.

—— —— (1963*b*), 'Monetary and Business Cycles', *Review of Economics and Statistics*, February.

Frisch, R. (1933), 'Propagation Problems and Impulse Problems in Dynamic Economics', in *Economic Essays in Honour of Gustav Cassel*, Allen & Unwin, London.

Fukuda, S. and Teruyama, H. (1988), 'Some International Evidence of Inventory Fluctuations', *Economics Letters*, no. 3.

Fuller, W. A. and Battese, G. E. (1974), 'Estimation of Linear Models with Crossed-Error Structure', *Journal of Econometrics*, May.

von Furstenberg, G. (1977), 'Corporate Investment: Does Market Valuation Matter in the Aggregate?' *Brookings Papers on Economic Activity*, no. 6.

Gersch, W. and Kitagawa, G. (1983), 'Prediction of Time Series with Trends and Seasonalities', *Journal of Business and Economic Statistics*, July.

Goldfeld, S. and Quandt, R. (1972), *Nonlinear Methods in Econometrics*, North-Holland, Amsterdam.

Gordon, A. (1985), *Evolution of Labor Relations in Japan*, Harvard University Press, Cambridge, Mass.

Gordon, R. A. (1951), 'Cyclical Experience in the Interwar Period: The Investment Boom of the Twenties', in *Conference on Business Cycles*, National Bureau of Economic Research, New York.

Gordon, R. J. (1982), 'Why US Wages and Employment Behaviour Differs from that in Britain and Japan', *Economic Journal*, March.

—— (1987), 'Productivity, Wages, and Prices Inside and Outside of Manufacturing in the US, Japan, and Europe', *European Economic Review*, April.

—— and Veitch, J. (1986), 'Fixed Investment in the American Business Cycle, 1919–83', in R. Gordon (ed.), *The American Business Cycle*, University of Chicago Press.

Gould, J. P. (1968), 'Adjustment Costs in the Theory of Investment of the Firm', *Review of Economic Studies*, January.

Grandmont, J. (1985), 'On Endogenous Competitive Business Cycles', *Econometrica*, no. 2.

—— (1989), 'Keynesian Issues and Economic Theory', *Scandinavian Journal of Economics*, no. 2.

Granger, C. W. J., (1969), 'Investigating Causal Relations by Econometric Models and Cross-Spectral Methods', *Econometrica*, July.

Greenwald, B. and Stiglitz, J. (1988), 'Examining Alternative Macroeconomic Theories', *Brookings Papers on Economic Activity*, no. 2.

Greenwood, J., Hercowitz, Z. and Huffman, G. (1988), 'Investment, Capacity Utilization, and the Real Business Cycle', *American Economic Review*, June.

Grossman, G. M. and Helpman, E. (1991), *Innovation and Growth in the Global Economy*, MIT Press, Cambridge, Mass.

—— (1994), 'Endogenous Innovation in the Theory of Growth', *Journal of Economic Perspectives*, Winter.

Grossman, H. (1972), 'A Choice-Theoretic Model of an Income–Investment Accelerator', *American Economic Review*, September.

Grossman, S. and Shiller, R. (1981), 'The Determinants of the Variability of Stock Market Prices', *American Economic Review*, May.

Grubb, D., Jackman, R. and Layard, R. (1983), 'Wage Rigidity and Unemployment in OECD Countries', *European Economic Review*, March/April.

Gruber, W., Mehta, D. and Vernon, R. (1967), 'The R&D Factor in International Trade and International Investment of the US Industries', *Journal of Political Economy*, February.

Haavelmo, T. (1960), *A Study in the Theory of Investment*, University of Chicago Press.

Habakkuk, H. J. (1962), *American and British Technology in the Nineteenth Century*, Cambridge University Press.

Haberler, G. (1964), *Prosperity and Depression*, 5th edn., Harvard University Press, Cambridge, Mass.

Haldi, J. and Whitcomb, D. (1967), 'Economies of Scale in Industrial Plants', *Journal of Political Economy*, August.

Hall, R. (1977), 'Investment, Interest Rates and the Effects of Stabilization Policies', *Brookings Papers on Economic Activity*, no. 1.

—— (1978), 'Stochastic Implications of the Life Cycles Permanent Income Hypothesis—Theory and Evidence', *Journal of Political Economy*, December.

Hall, R. (1986), 'Market Structure and Macroeconomics Fluctuations', *Brookings Papers on Economic Activity*, no. 2.

—— (1988), 'The Relation between Price and Marginal Cost in US Industry', *Journal of Political Economy*, October.

—— (1991), *Booms and Recessions in a Noisy Economy*, Yale University Press, New Haven, Conn.

—— and Mishkin, F. (1982), 'The Sensitivity of Consumption to Transitory Income: Estimates from Panel Data on Households', *Econometrica*, March.

Hamada, K. and Kurosawa, Y. (1984), 'Relationship between Production and Unemployment in Japan: Okun's Law in Comparative Perspective', *European Economic Review*, June.

Hamilton, J. (1983), 'Oil and the Macroeconomy since World War II', *Journal of Political Economy*, April.

Hansen A. (1939), 'Economic Progress and Declining Population Growth', *American Economic Review*, March.

Hansen L. and Singleton, K. (1982), 'Generalized Instrumental Variables Estimation of Nonlinear Rational Expectations Models', *Econometrica*, September.

Harrison, J. and Kreps, D. (1978), 'Speculative Investor Behavior in a Stock Market with Heterogeneous Expectations', *Quarterly Journal of Economics*, May.

Harrod, R. (1939), 'An Essay in Dynamic Theory', *Economic Journal*, March.

—— (1948), *Towards a Dynamic Economics*, Macmillan, London.

Hart, O. (1982), 'A Model of Imperfect Competition with Keynesian Features', *Quarterly Journal of Economics*, February.

Hartman, R. (1972), 'The Effects of Price and Cost Uncertainty on Investment', *Journal of Economic Theory*, October.

Harvey, A. C. (1981), *Econometric Analysis of Time Series*, Philip Allan, Oxford.

—— (1985), 'Trends and Cycles in Macroeconomic Time Series', *Journal of Business and Economic Statistics*, July.

Hashimoto, M. and Raisian, J. (1985), 'Employment Tenure and Earnings Profiles in Japan and the United States', *American Economic Review*, September.

Hawtrey, R. (1937), *Capital and Employment*, Longmans, London.

Hayashi, F. (1982*a*), 'Tobin's Marginal *q* and Average *q*: A Neoclassical Interpretation', *Econometrica*, January.

—— (1982*b*), 'The Permanent Income Hypothesis: Estimation and Testing by Instrumental Variables', *Journal of Political Economy*, October.

—— (1986), 'Why is Japan's Saving Rate So Apparently High?' *NBER Macroeconomics Annual*, i, MIT Press, Cambridge, Mass.

—— (1989), 'Is Japan's Saving Rate High?' Federal Reserve Bank of Minneapolis *Quarterly Review*, Spring.

—— (1992), 'Explaining Japan's Saving: A Review of Recent Literature', Bank of Japan *Monetary and Economic Studies*, November.

—— and Inoue, T. (1991), 'The Relation between Firm Growth and *q* with Multiple Capital Goods: Theory and Evidence from Panel Data on Japanese Firms', *Econometrica*, May.

—— Ito, T. and Slemrod, J. (1988), 'Housing Finance Imperfections, Taxation, and Private Saving: A Comparative Simulation Analysis of the United States and Japan', *Journal of Japanese and International Economies*, September.

Hayes, R. and Abernathy, W. (1980), 'Managing Our Way to Economic Decline', *Harvard Business Review*, July/August.

Heckman, J. J. (1976), 'The Common Structure of Statistical Models of Truncation, Sample Selection and Limited Dependent Variables and a Simple Estimation for Such Models', *Annuals of Economic and Social Measurement*, Fall.

Hickman, B. (1974), 'What Became of the Building Cycle?' in P. David and M. Reder (eds.) *Nations and Households in Economic Growth*, Academic Press, New York.

—— (1987), 'Real Wages, Aggregate Demand, and Unemployment', *European Economic Review*, December.

Hicks, J. (1960), 'Thoughts on the Theory of Capital: The Corfu Conference', *Oxford Economic Papers*.

—— (1974), *The Crisis in Keynesian Economics*, Basic Books, New York.

—— (1977), 'The Mainspring of Economic Growth', in his *Economic Perspectives*, Clarendon Press, Oxford.

—— (1981), '*IS–LM*: An Explanation', *Journal of Post-Keynesian Economics*, Winter.

Higuchi, Y. (1989), 'Japan's Changing Wage Structure: The Impact of Internal Factors and International Competition', *Journal of Japanese and International Economies*, December.

Hill, T. (1979), *Profits and Rates of Return*, Paris, OECD.

Horie, Y., Naniwa, S. and Ishihara, S. (1987), 'The Changes of Japanese Business Cycles', Bank of Japan *Monetary and Economic Studies*, December.

Horioka, C. (1990), 'Why is Japan's Household Saving Rate So High? A Literature Survey', *Journal of Japanese and International Economies*, March.

—— and Magee, S. (1969), 'Income and Price Elasticities in World Trade', *Review of Economics and Statistics*, May.

Hoshi, T., Kashyap, A. and Scharfstein, D. (1991), 'Corporate Structure, Liquidity and Investment: Evidence from Japanese Industrial Groups', *Quarterly Journal of Economics*, February.

Houthakker, H. (1979), 'Growth and Inflation: Analysis by Industry', *Brookings Papers on Economic Activity*, no. 1.

Horioka, C. and Magee, S. (1969), 'Income and Price Elasticities in World Trade', *Review of Economics and Statistics*, May.

Hsiao, C. (1986), *Analysis of Panel Data*, Cambridge University Press.

Hsieh, D. (1982), 'The Determination of the Real Exchange Rate', *Journal of International Economics*, May.

Inada, K., Sekiguchi, S., and Shoda, Y. (1992), *The Mechanism of Economic Development*, Clarendon Press, Oxford.

Ishikawa, T. and Ueda, K. (1984), 'The Bonus Payment System and Japanese Personal Savings', in M. Aoki (ed.), *Economic Analysis of the Japanese Firm*, North-Holland, Amsterdam.

Ito, T. (1987), 'Intradaily Exchange Rate Dynamics and Monetary Policies after the Group of Five Agreement', *Journal of Japanese and International Economies*, September.

Iwamoto, Y. and Kobayashi, H. (1992), 'Testing for a Unit Root in Japanese GNP', *Japan and the World Economy*, May.

Johansen, L. (1959), 'Substitution versus Fixed Production Coefficients in the Theory of Economic Growth', *Econometrica*, April.

Jorgenson, D. (1963), 'Capital Theory and Investment Behavior', *American Economic Review*, May.

—— (1971), 'Econometric Studies of Investment Behavior: A Survey', *Journal of Economic Literature*, December.

—— (1988), 'Productivity and Economic Growth in Japan and the United States', *American Economic Review*, May.

Kahneman, D., Knetsch, J. and Thaler, R. (1986), 'Fairness as a Constraint on Profit Seeking: Entitlements in the Market', *American Economic Review*, September.

Kaldor, N. (1956), 'Alternative Theories of Distribution', *Review of Economic Studies*, no. 6.

—— (1961), 'Capital Accumulation and Economic Growth', in F. Lutz (ed.), *The Theory of Capital*, Macmillan, London.

—— (1966), *Causes of the Slow Rate of Economic Growth of the United Kingdom*, Cambridge University Press.

—— (1970), 'The New Monetarism', *Lloyds Bank Review*, July.

—— (1989), 'The Role of Increasing Returns, Technical Progress and Cumulative Causation in the Theory of International Trade and Economic Growth', *Economie Appliquée*, no. 4; also in his *The Essential Kaldor*, Duckworth, London, 1989.

—— and Trevithick J. (1981), 'A Keynesian Perspective on Money', *Lloyds Bank Review*, January.

Kalecki, M. (1937), 'The Principle of Increasing Risk', *Economica*, November.

—— (1944), 'Professor Pigou on "The Classical Stationary State" ', *Economic Journal*, April.

—— (1954), *Theory of Economic Dynamics*, George Allen & Unwin, London.

Katz, L. (1986), 'Efficiency Wage Theories: A Partial Evaluation', *NBER Macroeconomics Annual*, MIT Press, Cambridge, Mass.

Kawagoe, T. (1993), 'Land Reform in Postwar Japan', in J. Teranishi and Y. Kosai (eds.), *The Japanese Experience of Economic Reforms*, Macmillan, London.

Kendrick, J. (1961), *Productivity Trends in the United States*, Princeton University Press, Princeton, NJ.

Kennedy, C. (1964), 'Induced Bias in Innovation and the Theory of Distribution', *Economic Journal*, September.

Kessler, D. and Masson, A. (1989), 'Bequest and Wealth Accumulation: Are Some Pieces of the Puzzle Missing?' *Journal of Economic Perspectives*, Summer.

Keynes, J. M. (1923), *A Tract on Monetary Reform*, Macmillan, London.

—— (1936), *The General Theory of Employment, Interest and Money*, Macmillan, London.

—— (1937*a*), 'Some Economic Consequences of a Declining Population', *Eugenics Review*, April; also in D. Moggridge (ed.), *The Collected Writings of John Maynard Keynes*, xiv, *The General Theory and After: Part II*, (Macmillan, London, 1937).

—— (1937*b*), 'The "*Ex Ante*" Theory of the Rate of Interest', *Economic Journal*, December.

Kindleberger, C. (1967), *Europe's Postwar Growth*, Harvard University Press, Cambridge, Mass.

—— (1989), 'The Iron Law of Wages', in his *Economic Laws and Economic History*, Cambridge University Press.

King, R. and Plosser, C. (1984), 'Money, Credit and Prices in a Real Business Cycle', *American Economic Review*, June.

—— and Rebelo, S. (1988), 'Production, Growth and Business Cycles: I, The Basic Neoclassical Model; II, New Directions', *Journal of Monetary Economics*, March/May.

Kiyotaki, N. (1988), 'Multiple Expectational Equilibria under Monopolistic Competition', *Quarterly Journal of Economics*, November.

Knetter, M. (1993), 'International Comparisons of Pricing-to-Market Behavior', *American Economic Review*, June.

Koike, K. (1984), 'Skill Formation Systems in the US and Japan', in M. Aoki (ed.), *The Economic Analysis of the Japanese Firm*, North-Holland, Amsterdam.

Komiya, R. and Yasui, K. (1984), 'Japan's Macroeconomic Performance since the First Oil Crisis: Review and Appraisal', *Carnegie–Rochester Conference Series on Public Policy*, Spring.

Koopmans, T. (1947), 'Measurement without Theory', *Review of Economic Statistics*, August.

Koopmans, T. (1965), 'On the Concept of Optimal Economic Growth', in his *The Economic Approach to Development Planning*, Rand McNally, Amsterdam/Chicago.

Kornai, Y. (1980), *Economics of Shortage*, North-Holland, Amsterdam.

Kosai, Y. (1986), *The Era of High-Speed Growth*, University of Tokyo Press.

Kotlikoff, L. (1988), 'Intergenerational Transfers and Savings', *Journal of Economic Perspectives*, Spring.

—— and Summers, L. (1981), 'The Role of Intergenerational Transfers in Aggregate Capital Accumulation', *Journal of Political Economy*, August.

Krugman, P. (1985), 'Is the Strong Dollar Sustainable?' in *The US Dollar: Prospects and Policy Options*, Federal Reserve Bank of Kansas City.

—— (1991), *Has the Adjustment Process Worked*? Institute for International Economics, Washington, DC.

Kuroda, M., Yoshioka, K. and Jorgenson, D. (1984), 'Relative Price Changes and Biasis of Technical Change in Japan', *Economic Studies Quarterly*, August.

Kydland, F. and Prescott, E. (1982), 'Time to Build and Aggregate Fluctuations', *Econometrica*, November.

Lamfalussy, A. (1963), *The United Kingdom and the Six*, Macmillan, London.

Landes, D. (1969), *The Unbound Prometheus*, Cambridge University Press.

Layard, R., Nickell, S. and Jackman, R. (1991), *Unemployment*, Oxford University Press.

Lerner, A. (1944), *The Economics of Control*, Macmillan, New York.

Lewis, W. Arthur (1954), 'Economic Development with Unlimited Supplies of Labour', *Manchester School of Economic and Social Studies*, May.

Lilien, D. (1982), 'Sectoral Shifts and Cyclical Unemployment', *Journal of Political Economy*, August.

Linder, S. (1961), *An Essay on Trade and Transformation*, Almqvist & Wiksell, Stockholm.

Lipschitz, L. and Schadler, S. M. (1984), 'Relative Prices, Real Wages, and Macroeconomic Policies: Some Evidence from Manufacturing in Japan and United Kingdom', *IMF Staff Papers*, June.

Litterman, R. and Weiss, L. (1985), 'Money, Real Interest Rates, and Output: A Reinterpretation of Postwar US Data', *Econometrica*, January.

Long, J. and Plosser, C. (1983), 'Real Business Cycles', *Journal of Political Economy*, February.

Lucas, R. (1967), 'Adjustment Costs and the Theory of Supply', *Journal of Political Economy*, August.

—— (1972), 'Expectation and the Neutrality of Money', *Journal of Economic Theory*, April.

—— (1973), 'Some International Evidence on Output–Inflation Tradeoffs', *American Economic Review*, June.

—— (1977), 'Understanding Business Cycles', in K. Brunner and A. H. Meltzer (eds.), *Stabilization of the Domestic and International Economy*, North-Holland, New York.

—— (1987), *Models of Business Cycles*, Basil Blackwell, New York.

—— and Prescott, E. (1971), 'Investment under Uncertainty', *Econometrica*, September.

—— —— (1974), 'Equilibrium Search and Unemployment', *Journal of Economic Theory*, February.

—— and Rapping, L. (1969), 'Real Wages, Employment and Inflation', *Journal of Political Economy*, September/October.

—— —— (1970), 'Real Wages, Employment, and Inflation', in E. Phelps (ed.), *Microeconomic Foundations of Employment and Inflation Theory*, W. W. Norton, New York.

Maddala, G. S. (1971), 'The Use of Variance Components Models in Pooling Cross Section and Time Series Data', *Economcetrica*, March.

—— (1977), *Econometrics*, McGraw-Hill, New York.

—— (1983), *Limited Dependent and Qualitative Variables in Econometrics*, Cambridge University Press.

Maddison, A. (1987), 'Growth and Slowdown in Advanced Capitalist Economies: Techniques of Quantitative Assessment', *Journal of Economic Literature*, June.

—— (1992), 'A Long-run Perspective on Saving', *Scandinavian Journal of Economics*, no. 2.

Malinvaud, E. (1977), *Theory of Unemployment Reconsidered*, Basil Blackwell, Oxford.

—— (1982), 'Wages and Unemployment', *Economic Journal*, March.

—— (1983), 'Notes on Growth Theory with Imperfectly Flexible Prices', in J. Fitoussi (ed.), *Modern Macroeconomic Theory*, Basil Blackwell, Oxford.

—— (1984), *Mass Unemployment*, Basil Blackwell, New York.

Mankiw, N. G. (1985), 'Small Menu Costs and Large Business Cycles: A Macroeconomic Model of Monopoly', *Quarterly Journal of Economics*, May.

—— (1989), 'Real Business Cycles: A New Keynesian Perspective', *Journal of Economic Perspectives*, Summer.

—— and Romer, D. (1991), *New Keynesian Economics*, i and ii, MIT Press, Cambridge, Mass.

—— Rotemberg, J. and Summers, L. (1985), 'Intertemporal Substitution in Macroeconomics', *Quarterly Journal of Economics*, February.

Marsh, T. and Merton, R. (1986), 'Dividend Variability and Variance Bounds Tests for the Rationality of Stock Market Prices', *American Economic Review*, June.

Marston, Richard C. (1987), 'Real Exchange Rates and Productivity Growth in the United States and Japan', in J. D. Richardson and S. Arndt (eds.), *Real Financial Linkages in Open Economy*, MIT Press, Cambridge, Mass.

—— (1990), 'Pricing to Market in Japanese Manufacturing', *Journal of International Economics*, November.

Matthews, R., Feinstein, C. and Odling-Smee, J. (1982), *British Economic Growth*, Stanford University Press, Stanford, Calif.

Maxy, G. and Silberston, A. (1959), *The Motor Industry*, Allen & Unwin, London.

Mayer, T. (1960), 'Plant and Equipment Lead Times', *Journal of Business*, April.

McCallum, B. T. (1983), 'A Reconsideration of Sim's Evidence Concerning Monetarism', *Economics Letters*, no. 2.

—— (1993), 'Unit Roots in Macroeconomic Time Series: Some Critical Issues', NBER Working Paper no. 4368, May.

McDonald, I. and Solow, R. (1981), 'Wage Bargaining and Employment', *American Economic Review*, December.

—— —— (1985), 'Wages and Employment in a Segmented Labor Market', *Quarterly Journal of Economics*, November.

Meese, R. and Rogoff, K. (1983), 'Empirical Exchange Rate Models of the Seventies: Do They Fit Out of Sample?' *Journal of International Economics*, February.

Mehra, R. and Prescott, E. (1985), 'The Equity Premium: A Puzzle', *Journal of Monetary Economics*, March.

Mehra, Y. (1978), 'Is Money Exogenous in Money-Demand Equations?' *Journal of Political Economy*, April.

Metzler, L., and Laursen, S. (1950), 'Flexible Exchange Rates and the Theory of Employment', *Review of Economics and Statistics*, November.

Meyer, J. and Kuh, E. (1957), *The Investment Decision*, Harvard University Press, Cambridge, Mass.

Minami, R. (1968), 'The Turning Point in the Japanese Economy', *Quarterly Journal of Economics*, August.

—— (1986), *The Economic Development of Japan: A Quantitative Study*, St Martin's Press, London.

Mincer, J. and Higuchi, Y. (1988), 'Wage Structures and Labor Turnover in the United States and Japan'. *Journal of Japanese and International Economies*, June.

Mirer, T. (1979), 'The Wealth–Age Relationship among the Aged', *American Economic Review*, June.

Miron, J. (1986), 'Financial Panics, the Seasonality of the Nominal Interest Rate, and the Founding of the Fed', *American Economic Review*, March.

Modigliani, F. (1944), 'Liquidity Preference and the Theory of Interest and Money', *Econometrica*, January.

—— (1970), 'Life Cycle Hypothesis of Saving and Intercountry Differences in the Saving Ratio', in W. Eltis, M. Scott, and J. Wolfe (eds.), *Induction, Growth, and Trade: Essays in Honour of Sir Roy Harrod*, Oxford University Press.

—— (1986), 'Life Cycle, Individual Thrift, and the Wealth of Nations', *American Economic Review*, June.

—— (1988), 'The Role of Intergenerational Transfers and Life Cycle Saving in the Accumulation of Wealth', *Journal of Economic Perspectives*, Spring.

—— (1990), 'Recent Declines in the Saving Rate: A Life Cycle Perspective', *Rivista di Politica Economia.*

—— and Ando, A. (1963), 'The "Life-Cycle" Hypothesis of Saving: Aggregate Implications and Tests', *American Economic Review*, March.

—— and Brumberg, R. (1954), 'Utility Analysis and the Consumption Function: An Interpretation of Cross-Section Data', in K. Kurihara (ed.), *Post-Keynesian Economics*, Rutgers University Press, New Brunswick, NJ.

Morck, R., Schleifer, A. and Vishny, R. (1990), 'The Stock Market and Investment: Is the Market a Sideshow?' *Brookings Papers on Economic Activity*, no. 2.

Morishima, M. (1958), 'Prices, Interest and Profits in a Dynamic Leontief System', *Econometrica*, July.

Morley, R. (1979), 'Profit, Relative Prices and Unemployment', *Economic Journal*, September.

Murphy, K., Shleifer, A. and Vishny, R. (1989), 'Industrialization and the Big Push', *Journal of Political Economy*, October.

Mussa, M. (1975), 'Adaptive and Regressive Expectations in a Rational Model of the Inflationary Process', *Journal of Monetary Economics*, October.

Muth, J. (1960), 'Optimal Properties of Exponentially Weighted Forecasts', *Journal of American Statistical Association*, June.

Nakamura, T. (1981), *The Postwar Japanese Economy*, University of Tokyo Press.

Negishi, T. (1977), 'Existence of an Under-Employment Equilibrium', in G. Schwödiauer (ed.), *Equilibrium and Disequilibrium in Economic Theory*, Reidel, Dordrecht.

—— (1979), *Microeconomic Foundations of Keynesian Macroeconomics*, North-Holland, Amsterdam.

Nelson, C. R. (1973), *Applied Time Series Analysis for Managerial Forecasting*, Holden Day, San Francisco.

Nelson, C. R. and Kang, H. (1981), 'Spurious Periodicity in Inappropriately Detrended Time Series', *Econometrica*, May.

Nelson, C. R. and Plosser, C. I. (1982), 'Trends and Random Walks in Macroeconomic Time-Series: Some Evidence and Implications', *Journal of Monetary Economics*, September.

Nickell, S. (1978), *The Investment Decisions of Firms*, Cambridge University Press.

Niehans, J. (1984), *International Monetary Economics*, Johns Hopkins University Press, Baltimore.

Nishikawa, M. (1989), 'Sectoral Shifts and Unemployment in Japan', Ph. D. dissertation, University of Hawaii.

Norsworthy, J. R. and Malmquist, D. H. (1983), 'Input Measurement and Productivity Growth in Japanese and US Manufacturing', *American Economic Review*, December.

OECD (1986), *Employment Outlook*, Paris.

Ogawa, K. (1987), 'Household Saving Rates and Demand for Housing: Some Evidence in Japan', *JCIF Policy Study Series*, no. 8.

Ohashi, I. (1989), 'On the Determinants of Bonuses and Basic Wages in Japanese Manufacturing Industries', *Journal of Japanese and international Economies*, December.

Ohkawa, K. and Rosovsky, H. (1973), *Japanese Economic Growth*, Stanford University Press, Stanford, Calif.

Ohno, Ken-ichi (1986), 'Yen–Dollar Rate Misalignments: A New Purchasing Power Parity Criterion', mimeo, Stanford University, May.

Oi, W. (1962), 'Labor as a Quasi-Fixed Factor', *Journal of Political Economy*, December.

Okazaki, T. (1993), 'The Japanese Firm under the Wartime Planned Economy', *Journal of Japanese and International Economies*, June.

Okina, K. (1986), 'Relationship between Money Stock and Real Output in the Japanese Economy: Survey on the Empirical Tests of the LSW Proposition', Bank of Japan *Monetary and Economic Studies*, April.

Okun, A. (1962), 'Potential GNP: Its Measurement and Significance', in *Proceedings of the Business and Economic Statistics Section, American Statistical Association*, Washington DC.

—— (1973), 'Upward Mobility in a High-Pressure Economy', *Brookings Papers on Economic Activity*, no. 1.

—— (1981), *Prices and Quantities: A Macroeconomic Analysis*, Brookings Institution, Washington, DC.

Onitsuka, Y. (1974), 'International Capital Movements and the Patterns of Economic Growth', *American Economic Review*, March.

Oulton, N. (1981), 'Aggregate Investment and Tobin's *q*: the Evidence from Britain', *Oxford Economic Papers*, July.

Papell, D. (1989), 'Monetary Policy in the United States under Flexible Exchange Rates', *American Economic Review*, December.

Perron, P. (1989), 'The Great Crash, the Oil Price Shock, and the Unit Root Hypothesis', *Econometrica*, November.

Pigou, A. C. (1927), 'Wage Policy and Unemployment', *Economic Journal*, September.

—— (1936), 'Mr J. M. Keynes' General Theory of Employment, Interest and Money', *Econometrica*, May.

—— (1937), 'Real and Money Wage Rates in Relation to Unemployment', *Economic Journal*, September.

Plosser, C. (1989), 'Understanding Real Business Cycles', *Journal of Economic Perspectives*, Summer.

—— (1990), 'Money and Business Cycles: A Real Business Cycle Interpretation', NBER Working Paper no. 3221, January.

Precious, M. (1985), 'Demand Constraints, Rational Expectations, and Investment Theory', *Oxford Economic Papers*, December.

Reder, M. (1955), 'Theory of Occupational Wage Differentials', *American Economic Review*, December.

Robertson, D. H. (1937), 'Alternative Theories of the Rate of Interest: A Rejoinder', *Economic Journal*, September.

Robinson, J. (1963), 'Findlay's Robinsonian Model of Accumulation: A Comment', *Economica*, November.

Romer, C. and Romer, D. (1989), 'Does Monetary Policy Matter? A New Test in the Spirit of Friedman and Schwartz', in O. Blanchard and S. Fischer (eds.), *NBER Macroeconomics Annual 1989*, MIT Press, Cambridge, Mass.

Romer, P. (1986), 'Increasing Returns and Long-Run Growth', *Journal of Political Economy*, October.

—— (1987), 'Crazy Explanations for the Productivity Slowdown', in S. Fischer (ed.), *NBER Macroeconomics Annual 1987*, MIT Press, Cambridge, Mass.

Roosa, R. (1956), *Federal Reserve Operations in the Money and Government Securities Market*, Federal Reserve Bank of New York.

Rose, A. (1986), 'Four Paradoxes in GNP', *Economics Letters*, no. 2/3.

Ruggles, R. (1993), 'Accounting for Saving and Capital Formation in the United States, 1947–1991', *Journal of Economic Perspectives*, Spring.

Runkle, D. E. (1987), 'Vector Autoregressions and Reality', *Journal of Business and Economic Statistics*, October.

Sachs, J. (1979), 'Wages, Profits, and Macroeconomic Adjustment: A Comparative Study', *Brookings Papers on Economic Activity*, no. 2.

—— (1980), 'Wages, Flexible Exchange Rates, and Macroeconomic Policy', *Quarterly Journal of Economics*, June.

—— (1983), 'Real Wages and Unemployment in the OECD Countries', *Brookings Papers on Economic Activity*, no. 1.

—— and Roubini, N. (1988), 'Sources of Macroeconomic Imbalances in the World Economy: A Simulation Approach', in Y. Suzuki and M. Okabe (eds.), *Toward a World of Economic Stability*, University of Tokyo Press.

Salter, W. (1960), *Productivity and Technical Change*, Cambridge University Press.

Schor, J. B. (1985), 'Changes in the Cyclical Pattern of Real Wage: Evidence from Nine Countries, 1955–80', *Economic Journal*, June.

Schumpeter, J. (1934), *Theory of Economic Development*, Harvard University Press, Cambridge, Mass.

—— (1939), *Business Cycles*, McGraw-Hill, New York.

Sen, A. (1965), 'The Money Rate of Interest in the Pure Theory of Growth', in F. Hahn and F. Brechling (eds.), *The Theory of Interest Rates*, Macmillan, London.

Shapiro, M. (1986), 'Investment, Output and the Cost of Capital', *Brookings Papers on Economic Activity*, no. 1.

—— (1987), 'Are Cyclical Fluctuations in Productivity Due More to Supply Shocks or Demand Shocks?' *American Economic Review*, May.

Shea, J. (1993), 'Do Supply Curves Slope Up?' *Quarterly Journal of Economics*, February.

Shiller, R. (1980), 'Can the Fed Control Real Interest Rates?' in S. Fischer (ed.), *Rational Expectations and Economic Policy*, University of Chicago Press.

—— (1981), 'Do Stock Prices Move Too Much to be Justified by Subsequent Changes in Dividends?' *American Economic Review*, June.

—— (1984), 'Stock Prices and Social Dynamics', *Brookings Papers on Economic Activity*, no. 2.

Shimada, H., and Higuchi, Y. (1985), 'An Analysis of Trends in Female Labor Participation in Japan', *Journal of Labor Economics* (Pt. 2), January.

Shinkai, Y. (1980), 'Spillovers in Wage Determination: Japanese Evidence', *Review of Economics and Statistics*, May.

—— (1982), 'Oil Crises and the Stagflation in Japan', in K. Yamamura (ed.), *Policy and Trade Issues of the Japanese Economy*, University of Washington Press, Seattle, Wash.

Sims, C. (1972), 'Money, Income and Causality', *American Economic Review*, September.

—— (1980), 'Comparison of Interwar and Postwar Business Cycles: Monetarism Reconsidered', *American Economic Review*, May.

Singleton, K. (ed.) (1993), *Japanese Monetary Policy*, University of Chicago Press.

Solow, R. (1956), 'A Contribution to the Theory of Economic Growth', *Quarterly Journal of Economics*, February.

—— (1957), 'Technical Change and the Aggregate Production Function', *Review of Economics and Statistics*, August.

—— (1962), 'Technical Progress, Capital Formation and Economic Growth', *American Economic Review*, May.

—— (1968), 'Distribution in the Long and Short Run', in J. Marchal and B. Ducros (eds.), *Distribution of National Income: Proceedings of IEA Conference*, Macmillan, London.

—— (1979), 'Another Possible Source of Wage Stickiness', *Journal of Macroeconomics*, Winter.

—— (1986), 'Unemployment: Getting the Questions Right', *Economica*, Supplement.

—— (1988), 'Growth Theory and After', *American Economic Review*, June.

—— (1994), 'Perspectives on Growth Theory', *Journal of Economic Perspectives*, Winter.

Song, B. (1990), *The Rise of the Korean Economy*, Oxford University Press, New York.

Sorrentino, C. (1984), 'Japan's Low Unemployment: An In-Depth Analysis', *Monthly Labor Review*, March.

Steigum, E. (1983), 'A Financial Theory of Investment Behavior', *Econometrica*, May.

Stiglitz, J. and Weiss, A. (1981), 'Credit Rationing in Markets with Imperfect Information', *American Economic Review*, June.

Stock, J. and Watson, M. (1986), 'Does GNP Have a Unit Root?' *Economics Letters*, no. 2/3.

—— —— (1989), 'Interpreting the Evidence on Money–Income Causality', *Journal of Econometrics*, January.

Stockman, A. (1980), 'A Theory of Exchange Rate Determination', *Journal of Political Economy*, August.

Summers, L. (1981), 'Taxation and Corporate Investment: A *q*-Theory Approach', *Brookings Papers on Economic Activity*, no. 1.

—— (1986), 'Some Skeptical Observations on Real Business Cycle Theory', Federal Reserve Bank of Minneapolis Quarterly Review, Fall.

—— (1988*a*), 'Relative Wages, Efficiency Wages and Keynesian Unemployment', *American Economic Review*, May.

—— (1988*b*), 'Tax Policy and International Competitiveness', in J. Frenkel (ed.), *International Aspects of Fiscal Policies*, University of Chicago Press.

—— and Wadhwani, S. (1987), 'Some International Evidence on Labor Cost Flexibility and Output Variability', Harvard University Discussion Paper no. 1353, November.

Suzuki, Y. (ed.) (1987), *The Japanese Financial System*, Clarendon Press, Oxford.

—— (1988), 'The Macroeconomic Performance of Five Major Countries: An Introductory Presentation', in Y. Suzuki and M. Okabe (eds.), *Toward a World of Economic Stability*, University of Tokyo Press.

—— Kuroda, A. and Shirakawa, H. (1988), 'The Monetary Control Mechanism in Japan', Bank of Japan *Monetary and Economic Studies*, November.

Tachibanaki, T. (1987), 'Labour Market Flexibility in Japan in Comparison with Europe and the US', *European Economic Review*, April.

Taira, K. (1983), 'Japan's Low Unemployment: Economic Miracle or Statistical Artifact?' *Monthly Labor Review*, July.

Takeuchi, Y. (1991), 'Trends and Structural Changes in Macroeconomic Time Series', *Journal of Japan Statistical Society*, June.

Tarshis, L. (1939), 'Changes in Real and Money Wages', *Economic Journal*, March.

Taylor J. B. (1979), 'Estimation and Control of a Macroeconomic Model with Rational Expectations', *Econometrica*, September.

—— (1980), 'Aggregate Dynamics and Staggered Contracts', *Journal of Political Economy*, February.

—— (1986), 'Improvements in Macroeconomic Stability: The Role of Wages and Prices', in R. J. Gordon (ed.), *The American Business Cycle*, Chicago University Press.

—— (1989), 'Differences in Economic Fluctuations in Japan and the US: The Role of Nominal Rigidities', *Journal of Japanese and International Economies*, June.

Tesar, L. (1991), 'Savings, Investment, and International Capital Flows', *Journal of International Economics*, August.

Thirlwall, A. (1979), 'The Balance of Payments Constraint as an Explanation of International Growth Rate Differences', *Banca Nazionale del Lavoro Quarterly Review*, March.

Tirole, J. (1982), 'On the Possibility of Speculation under Rational Expectations', *Econometrica*, September.

Tobin, J. (1951), 'Relative Income, Absolute Income and Saving', in J. Williams (ed.), *Money, Trade and Economic Growth: Essays in Honor of John Henry Williams*, Macmillan, London.

—— (1952), 'Asset Holdings and Spending Decisions', *American Economic Review*, March.

—— (1955), 'A Dynamic Aggregative Model', *Journal of Political Economy*, April.

—— (1969), 'A General Equilibrium Approach to Monetary Theory', *Journal of Money, Credit, and Banking*, February.

—— (1970), 'Money and Income: Post Hoc Ergo Propter Hoc?' *Quarterly Journal of Economics*, May.

—— (1972), 'Inflation and Unemployment', *American Economic Review*, March.

—— (1975), 'Keynesian Models of Recession and Depression', *American Economic Review*, May.

—— (1978), 'A Proposal for International Monetary Reform', *Eastern Economic Journal*, July/October.

—— (1980), *Asset Accumulation and Economic Activity*, University of Chicago Press.

—— (1993), 'Price Flexibility and Output Stability: An Old Keynesian View', *Journal of Economic Perspectives*, Winter.

—— and Brainard, W. (1977), 'Asset Markets and the Cost of Capital', in R. Nelson *et al.* (eds.), *Economic Progress, Private Values and Public Policy: Essays in Honor of William Fellner*, North-Holland, Amsterdam.

Toyoda, T. (1972), 'Wage Adjustment and the Expectations Hypothesis: Some Empirical Evidence for Japan', *Kobe University Economic Review*.

Ueda, K. (1988*a*), 'Financial Deregulation and the Demand for Money in Japan', Osaka University Discussion Paper no. 66, July.

—— (1988*b*), 'Perspectives on the Japanese Current Account Surplus', in S. Fischer (ed.), *NBER Macroeconomics Annual*, iii, MIT Press, Cambridge, Mass.

—— (1988*c*), 'The Japanese Current Account Surplus and Fiscal Policy in Japan and the US', in J. Shoven (ed.), *Government Policy towards Industry*, Cambridge University Press.

—— and Yoshikawa, H. (1986), 'Financial Volatility and the *q* Theory of Investment', *Economica*, February.

Uzawa, H. (1961), 'Neutral Inventions and the Stability of Growth Equilibrium', *Review of Economic Studies*, February.

—— (1965), 'Optimum Technical Change in an Aggregative Model of Economic Growth', *International Economic Review*, January.

—— (1969), 'Time Preference and the Penrose Effect in a Two-Class Model of Economic Growth', *Journal of Political Economy*, July/August.

—— (1974), 'On the Dynamic Stability of Economic Growth: The Neoclassical versus the Keynesian Approach', in G. Horwich and P. Samuelson (eds.), *Trade, Stability, and Macroeconomics: Essays in Honor of Lloyd A. Metzler*, Academic Press, New York.

Verdoorn, P. (1949), 'Fattori che Regolano lo Sviluppo della Produttività del Lavoro', *L'Industria*.

Vernon, R. (1966), 'International Investment and International Trade in the Product Cycle', *Quarterly Journal of Economics*, May.

Volcker, P. and Gyohten, T. (1992), *Changing Fortunes*, Times Books, New York.

Weitzman, M. (1982), 'Increasing Returns and the Foundations of Unemployment Theory', *Economic Journal*, December.

—— (1986), 'Macroeconomic Implications of Profit Sharing', in S. Fischer (ed.), *NBER Macroeconomics Annual 1986*, MIT Press, Cambridge, Mass.

Wells, L. (1972), *Product Life Cycle and International Trade*, Harvard University, Cambridge, Mass.

West, K. (1992), 'Source of Cycles in Japan, 1975–1987', *Journal of Japanese and International Economies*, March.

World Bank (1993), *East Asian Miracle*, Oxford University Press, New York.

Wright, G. (1990), 'The Origin of American Industrial Success, 1879–1940', *American Economic Review*, September.

Yonekura, S. (1993), 'Postwar Reform in Management and Labour: The Case of the Steel Industry', in J. Teranishi and Y. Kosai (eds.), *The Japanese Experience of Economic Reforms*, Macmillan, London.

Yoshikawa, H. (1980), 'On the *q* Theory of Investment', *American Economic Review*, September.

—— (1981), 'Alternative Monetary Policies and Stability in a Stochastic Keynesian Model', *International Economic Review*, October.

—— (1982), 'On the Firm's Short-run Quantity Adjustment: The *q* Theory of Goods in Process', *Economica*, February.

—— (1984), 'Demand–Supply Constraints and Inventory Stock in Macroeconomic Analysis', *Economic Studies Quarterly*, December.

—— (1988), 'Fixed Investment in Japan', in M. Fünke (ed.), *Factors in Business Investment*, Springer Verlag, Berlin.

—— (1990), 'On Equilibrium Yen–Dollar Rate', *American Economic Review*, June.

—— (1993), 'Monetary Policy and the Real Economy in Japan', in Kenneth Singleton (ed.), *Japanese Monetary Policy*, University of Chicago Press.

—— and Ohtake, F. (1987), 'Postwar Business Cycles in Japan: A Quest for the Right Explanation', *Journal of the Japanese and International Economies*, December.

—— —— (1989), 'An Analysis of Female Labor Supply, Housing Demand and the Saving Rate in Japan', *European Economic Review*, May.

—— and Okazaki, T. (1993), 'Postwar Hyper-Inflation and the Dodge Plan, 1945–50: An Overview', in Juro Teranishi and Yutaka Kosai (eds.), *The Japanese Experience of Economic Reform,* Macmillan, London.

Young, A. (1928), 'Increasing Returns and Economic Progress', *Economic Journal*, December.

Works published in Japanese (titles translated into English)

Akamatsu, K. (1956), 'The Product Life-Cycle Approach to Japanese Industrial Development', *Hitotsubashi Ronso*, November.

Ando, A. (1986), 'The Savings of Japanese Households: A Micro Study Based on Data from the National Survey of Family Income and Expenditure, 1974 and 1979', *Keizai Bunseki*, no. 101, Economic Planning Agency (Government of Japan), January.

Asako, K. and Kuninori, M. (1989), 'Theory of Investment and Empirical Analyses for Japan', in H. Uzawa (ed.), *Ninonkeizai* (The Japanese Economy), University of Tokyo Press.

Asakura, K. and Nishiyama, C. (1974), *Nihonkeizai no Kaheiteki Bunseki* (A Monetary History of the Japanese Economy), Sobun Sha, Tokyo.

Bank of Japan (1977), 'On the Steady Rise in Marshallian *k*', *BOJ Monthly*, November.

—— (1985*a*), *Nihon Ginko Hyakunenshi* (Centennial History of Bank of Japan), v, Bank of Japan, Tokyo.

—— (1985*b*), 'Characteristics of Business Cycles in Recent Years', *BOJ Monthly*, November.

—— (1988), 'Finance and the Economy in 1987', *BOJ Monthly*, May.

Echigo, K. (1969), *Kibo no Keizai* (Economies of Scale), Shin-Hyoron, Tokyo.

Economic Counsel Board (1953), *Sengo no Kokumin Shotoku* (The National Income of Post-War Japan), Gakuyo Shobo, Tokyo.

Fujino, S. (1968), *Nihon no Keiki Junkan* (Business Cycles in Japan), Keiso Shobo, Tokyo.

—— (1986), 'The Loan Market and the Behaviour of Banks', *Keizai Kenkyu*, April.

—— (1988), 'Balance of Payment of Postwar Japan: The 360 Yen was Overvalued', *Keizai Kenkyu*, April.

Fukao, M. (1983), *Kawase Reito to Kinyu Shijo* (Exchange Rates and the Financial Market), Toyokeizai, Tokyo.

Furukawa, A. (1981), 'The Effectiveness of Window Guidance', *Keizai Kenkyu*, January.

Hamada, K. (1967), *Keizai Seicho to Kokusai Shihon-ido* (Economic Growth and International Capital Flows), Toyokeizai, Tokyo.

Higuchi, Y. (1980), 'Female Labour Supply and Asset Holding', *Mita Economic Studies*, August.

Homma, M., Atoda, N., Takabayashi, K., Fukuma, K., Nagamine, J., and Uekusa, K. (1986), 'Fiscal Deficits and Household Consumption: A Test of the Neutrality Hypothesis', Ministry of Finance, *Financial Review*, no. 3.

Horioka, C. (1987), 'On the Relationship between Housing Purchases and Household Saving in Japan', *Jutaku Mondai Kenkyu*, December.

Horiuchi, A. (1977), 'The Effectiveness of Window Guidance', *Keizai Kenkyu*, July.

—— (1980), *Nihon no Kinyu Seisaku* (Japanese Monetary Policy), Toyokeizai, Tokyo.

Hyodo, T. (1965), 'Labour–Management Relations after the First World War', *Journal of Economics*, University of Tokyo, January and April.

Ihara, T. (1976), *Kojin Chochiku no Kettei Riron* (The Theory of Personal Saving), Toyokeizai, Tokyo.

Ishikawa, T. (1978), 'Personal and Corporate Savings in Japan', *Chochiku Jiho*, December.

Koike, K. (1991), *Shigoto no Keizaigaku* (The Economics of the Job), Toyokeizai, Tokyo.

Kurosaka, K. and Goto, M. (1987), 'An International Comparison of Aggregate Supply Curves', *Keizai Kenkyu*, April.

Kurosaka, Y. (1988), *Makuro Keizaigaku to Nihon no Rodoshijo* (Macroeconomics and the Japanese Labour Market), Toyokeizai, Tokyo.

Minami, R. (1970), *Nihon Keizai no Tenkanten* (The Turning Point for the Japanese Economy), Sobunsha, Tokyo.

—— and Ono, A. (1987), 'Income Distribution in Pre-War Japan', *Keizai Kenkyu*, October.

Ministry of Finance (1975), *Showa Zaiseishi* (The History of Fiscal and Monetary Policies in Japan), 3, 10, 12, and 19, Toyo Keizai Shinpo Sha, Tokyo.

Miyazaki, M. and Ito, O. (1989), 'Industries and Firms, 1940–1950', in T. Nakamura (ed.), *Nihon Keizaishi* (The Economic History of Japan), vii, Iwanami Shoten, Tokyo.

Mizoguchi, T. (1964), *Shohi Kansu no Tokeiteki Kenkyu* (A Statistical Analysis of Consumption Function), Iwanami, Tokyo.

—— (1986), 'Long-Term Changes in the Size Distribution of Income in Japan', *Keizai Kenkyu*, April.

—— (1988), 'The Consumption Function in Japan: A Survey', *Keizai Kenkyu*, July.

Mizuno, A. (1983), 'An Analysis of the Dynamics of the Japanese Labour Market', *Journal of Economics* (Chuo University), March.

—— (1992), *Nihon no Shitsugyō Kōdō* (Unemployment in Japan), Chūo University Press, Tokyo.

Nakamura, T. (1970), 'The Behaviour of Firms in a High Growth Era', *Keizai Kenkyu*, April.

Nomura, M. (1992), 'A Survey of Labour Economics in 1980s Japan: A Critique of Kazuo Koike's Works', *Nihon Rodo Kenkyu Zashi*, December.

Odaka, K. (1993), 'The "Japanese" Labour–Management Relations', in M. Okuno and T. Okazaki (eds.), *Gendai Nihon Keizai Shisutemu no Genryu* (The Origin of the Japanese Economic System), Nihon Keizai Shimbun Sha, Tokyo.

Ohkawa, K., Noda, T., Takamatsu, N., Yamada, S., Kumazaki, M., Shionoya Y., and Minami, R. (1967), *Choki Keizai Tokei, viii Bukka* (Long-term Economic Statistics of Japan, viii Prices), Toyokeizai, Tokyo.

—— Takamatsu, N., and Yamamoto, Y. (1974), *Choki Keizai Tokei, i Kokumin Shotoku* (Long-term Economic Statistics of Japan, i, National Income), Toyokeizai, Tokyo.

Ohtake, F. (1986), 'On the Flexibility of Real Wages,' in K. Koike (ed.), *Unemployment and Employment*, Kansaikeizai Kenkyu Centre, Osaka.

—— (1987), 'Unemployment and Unemployment Benefits', *Economic Studies Quarterly*, September.

Okada, K. (1969), 'Scale Economies in the Japanese Car Industry', in K. Echigo (ed.) *Kibo no Keizaisei* (Scale Economies), Shinhyoron, Tokyo.

Okura-sho (Ministry of Finance) (1978), *Showa Zaisei-shi* (A Fiscal History of the Showa Era), xix, Toyokeizai, Tokyo.

Ono, A. (1972), 'Labour Mobility in Prewar and Postwar Japan', *Gendai Keizai*, November.

—— (1981), *Nihon no Rodoshijo* (The Japanese Labour Market), Toyokeizai, Tokyo.

Sano, Y. (1981), *Chingin to Koyō no Keizaigaku* (The Economics of Wages and Employment), Chūou Keizai Sha, Tokyo.

Shimada, H. (1981), *Rodoshijo Kiko no Kenkyu* (A Study of the Labour Market), Economic Planning Agency, Kenkyu Series no. 37.

—— Hosokawa, T., and Seike, A. (1982), 'An Analysis of Wage and Employment Adjustment in Japan', *Keizai Bunseki*, no. 84, Economic Planning Agency.

Shinohara, M. (1958), *Shouhi Kansu* (The Consumption Function), Keiso Shobo, Tokyo.

—— (1961), *Nihon Keizai no Seicho to Junkan* (Growth and Cycles in the Japanese Economy), Sobunsha, Tokyo.

—— (1964), *Keizaiseichō no Kouzou* (Economic Growth), Kunimoto Shobou, Tokyo.

—— (1972), *Choki Keizai Tokei, x, Kokogyo* (Long-term Economic Statistics, x, Mining and Manufacturing), Toyokeizai, Tokyo.

—— (1974), 'On the 360 Yen per Dollar Exchange Rate', *Economic Studies Quarterly*, April.

—— (1981), 'The Puzzle of the High Saving Rate', *Chochikujihou*, March.

—— (1989), 'Export-Led Growth and the Exchange Rate', *Keizai Kenkyu*, July.

—— and Asakawa, K. (1974), 'Estimations of Technological Progress for the Japanese Manufacturing Industries', *Keizai Bunseki*, no. 48, Economic Planning Agency, July.

Soejima, Y. (1994), 'Unit Root Tests of Macroeconomic Time Series in Japan', Bank of Japan Institute for Monetary and Economic Studies, *Kinyu Kenkyu*, December.

Somu-cho (Management and Co-ordination Agency) (1987), *Nihon Choki Tokei Soran* (Historical Statistics of Japan), iii, Japan Statistical Association, Tokyo.

Suda, M. (1987), 'Business Cycles and Flexible Exchange Rates', *Keizai Kenkyu*, July.

Suzuki, Y. (1985), 'The Macroeconomic Performance of the Japanese Economy and Monetary Policy', Bank of Japan, Institute for Monetary and Economic Studies, *Kinyu Kenkyu*, August.

Takayama, N., Funaoka, F., Ohtake, F., Sekiguchi, M., and Shibuya, T. (1989), 'Household Assets and Saving', Economic Planning Agency, *Keizai Bunseki*, no. 116, September.

Tsuda, M. (1983), 'Postwar Management and Industrial Relations', *Business Review* (Hitotsubashi University), October.

Ueda, K. (1983), *Kokusai Makurokeizaigaku to Nihon Keizai* (Open-Economy Macroeconomics and the Japanese Economy), Toyokeizai Shimpo Sha, Tokyo.

—— (1985), 'The Loan Market and Monetary Policy', *Osaka Daigaku Keizaigaku*, March.

Umemura, M. (1961), *Chingin Koyo Nogyo* (Wages, Employment and Agruculture), Taimeido, Tokyo.

Wago, H. (1983), 'Energy Price, Substitution Elasticities and Technical Change: Econometric Analysis by Translog Cost Function,' *Journal of Japan Statistical Society*, June.

Watanabe, T. and Adachi, H. (1992), *Zusetsu Asia Keizai* (The Asian Economy), Nihon Hyoron Sha, Tokyo.

—— and Saeki, Y. (1984), *Tenki ni Tatsu Sekiyukagaku Kougyou* (The Turning Point for the Japanese Petrochemical Industry), Iwanami, Tokyo.

Yamamoto, K. (1990), 'Labour Disputes in Post-War Japan', in Rodo Sogi Shi Kenkyukai (ed.), *Nihon no Rodosogi* (Labour Disputes in Japan), University of Tokyo Press.

Yoshikawa, H. (1989), 'Money Supply and the Real Economy', *Keizaigaku Ronshu* (University of Tokyo), October.

—— and Shioji, E. (1990), 'Macroeconomic Analysis of the Prewar Japanese Economy', in H. Yoshikawa and T. Okazaki (eds.), *Keizai Riron eno Rekishiteki Pasupekutibu* (Economic Theory in Historical Perspective), University of Tokyo Press.

Yoshioka, K. (1989), *Nihon no Seizougyo-Kinyugyo no Seisansei Bunseki* (Productivity of the Japanese Manufacturing and Financial Industries), Toyo Keizai, Tokyo.

INDEX